AF757538

JĪMŪTAVĀHANA'S *DĀYABHĀGA*

SOUTH ASIA RESEARCH

SERIES EDITOR
Janice Leoshko

A Publication Series of
The University of Texas Center for Asian Studies
and
Oxford University Press

THE EARLY UPANIṢADS
Annotated Text and Translation
Patrick Olivelle

INDIAN EPIGRAPHY
A Guide to the Study of Inscriptions in Sanskrit, Prakrit, and the Other Indo-Aryan Languages
Richard Salomon

A DICTIONARY OF OLD MARATHI
S. G. Tulpule and Anne Feldhaus

DONORS, DEVOTEES, AND DAUGHTERS OF GOD
Temple Women in Medieval Tamilnadu
Leslie C. Orr

JĪMŪTAVĀHANA'S *DĀYABHĀGA*
The Hindu Law of Inheritance in Bengal
Edited and Translated with an Introduction and Notes by Ludo Rocher

Jīmūtavāhana's *Dāyabhāga*

THE HINDU LAW OF INHERITANCE IN BENGAL

Edited and Translated with an
Introduction and Notes by
LUDO ROCHER

OXFORD
UNIVERSITY PRESS

2002

OXFORD
UNIVERSITY PRESS

Oxford New York
Athens Auckland Bangkok Bogotá Buenos Aires Cape Town
Chennai Dar es Salaam Delhi Florence Hong Kong Istanbul Karachi
Kolkata Kuala Lumpur Madrid Melbourne Mexico City Mumbai Nairobi
Paris São Paulo Shanghai Singapore Taipei Tokyo Toronto Warsaw

and associated companies in
Berlin Ibadan

Copyright © 2002 by the Center for Asian Studies at
the University of Texas, Austin

Published by Oxford University Press, Inc.
198 Madison Avenue, New York, New York 10016

Oxford is a registered trademark of Oxford University Press

All rights reserved. No part of this publication may be reproduced,
stored in a retrieval system, or transmitted, in any form or by any means,
electronic, mechanical, photocopying, recording, or otherwise,
without the prior permission of Oxford University Press.

Library of Congress Cataloging-in-Publication Data
Jimutavahana, 12th cent. Dayabhaga. English.
Jimutavahana's dayabhaga : the Hindu law of inheritance in Bengal
/ edited and translated with an introduction and notes by Ludo Rocher.
p. cm. — (South Asia research)
Includes bibliographical references and index.
ISBN 0-19-513817-1
1. Inheritance and succession (Hindu law). 2. Partition of decendents' estates (Hindu law).
I. Rocher, Ludo. II. Title. III. South Asia research (New York, N.Y.)
KNS770 .J5613 2001
346.5405'2—dc21 2001021133

1 3 5 7 9 8 6 4 2

Printed in the United States of America
on acid-free paper

For Rosane

PREFACE

Jīmūtavāhana's *Dāyabhāga* is one of the Sanskrit texts in India that "have ceased to be the fundamental source of Hindu law, and it is only in marginal contexts that for practical purposes reference to them will ever again be made in that country."[1] Indeed, according to Section 4 of *The Hindu Succession Act, 1956*:

> (1) Save as otherwise expressly provided in this Act,
> (a) any text, rule or interpretation of Hindu law or any custom or usage as part of that law in force immediately before the commencement of this Act shall cease to have effect with respect to any matter for which provision is made in this Act;
> (b) any other law in force immediately before the commencement of this Act shall cease to apply to Hindus in so far as it is inconsistent with any of the provisions contained in this Act.

As a result, differently from the several earlier editions and the single earlier translation of the *Dāyabhāga*, the present translation and edition are no longer primarily aimed at those who prepare for or are engaged in the practice of Hindu law, in the courts of law in India and, until 1947, in the Privy Council in London. Its goal is academic: to present, not only to Sanskritists and Indologists but also to legal historians, a translation and a text of a Sanskrit book that, for about one century and a half, has regulated all questions of partition and inheritance for Hindus living in Bengal.

Research on this volume was supported by a translation grant of the National Endowment for the Humanities and by two short-term research grants of the American Institute of Indian Studies. I am grateful to the officers of both institutions. I am also grateful to all the friends who facilitated my work in various libraries and research institutions. In Calcutta I worked in the library of the Asiatic Society, at the National Library, and, especially in the early stages of this project, in the library of Calcutta Sanskrit College. At Sanskrit College I could not have done as much as I did, without the support and friendship of Heramba Chatterjee.[2] For a brief period I returned to my first ever (1953–55) research base in India, the Deccan College in Pune. The Director, V. N. Mishra, and every member of staff, contributed much to making my visit to the Scriptorium of the Dictionary Department and to the Deccan College library pleasurable and fruitful. For this project, as for any earlier one, I had recourse to the unique resources in London. I

[1] Derrett 1958b: 17 (= *Essays* 1.217).

[2] Heramba Chatterjee died in Calcutta on August 11, 1999.

read law reports in the library of the School of Oriental and African Studies, worked in the—now old—reading room and Oriental Students' Room of the British Library, and, most of all, in the—now also old—reading room of the India Office Library and Records on Blackfriars Road.

I am grateful to Richard Lariviere and Patrick Olivelle for having agreed to include this volume in their series. Patrick especially was helpful in initiating me in the intricacies of preparing camera-ready copy, and in discussing several passages of the text with me. I regret that his two valuable volumes on the *Dharma-sūtras* reached me too late fully to incorporate his materials in this study. I greatly appreciate the support I received from Madhav Deshpande, who developed the Manjushree font for Roman and the Madhushree font for *devanāgarī* scripts used in this volume.

The staff of Oxford University Press has been supportive throughout. I thank Cynthia Read, Theodore Calderara, and others with whom I did not come in direct contact. Joy Matkowski proved to be a meticulous proofreader and editor. I am especially grateful to Nancy Hoagland who graciously and patiently guided me through the final stages.

I dedicate this volume to the one person without whose loving care I would not have lived to complete it.

CONTENTS

ABBREVIATIONS

ABORI	*Annals of the Bhandarkar Oriental Research Institute*
AIOC	*All-India Oriental Conference*
A.I.R.	All-India Reporter
AKM	*Abhandlungen für die Kunde des Morgenlandes*
ALB	*Brahmavidyā, Adyar Library Bulletin*
All.	Indian Law Reports, Allahabad Series
ĀnSS	*Ānandāśrama Sanskrit Series*
Āp	Āpastamba
AsRes	*Asiatic(k) Researches*
B	Bṛhaspati
Bau	Baudhāyana
Beng.	Bengal Law Reports
BenSS	*Benares Sanskrit Series*
BhV	*Bhāratīya Vidyā*
BI	*Bibliotheca Indica*
bM	Bṛhan-Manu
Bom.	Indian Law Reports, Bombay Series
BS	*Bibliotheca Sanskrita = Mysore Government Oriental Library Series*
BSOAS	*Bulletin of the School of Oriental and African Studies*
BSS	*Bombay Sanskrit Series*
Cal.	Indian Law Reports, Calcutta Series
ChSS	*Chowkhamba Sanskrit Series*
C.L.J	Calcutta Law Journal
C.W.N.	Calcutta Weekly Notes
D	Devala
Dhko	*Dharmakośa*
ERE	Hastings's *Encyclopaedia of Religion and Ethics*
G	Gautama
GOS	*Gaekwad's Oriental Series*
H	Hārīta
HOS	*Harvard Oriental Series*
I.A.	Indian Appeals
IHQ	*Indian Historical Quarterly*
JAOS	*Journal of the American Oriental Society*
JASB	*Journal of the Asiatic Society of Bengal*
JBBRAS	*Journal of the Bombay Branch of the Royal Asiatic Society*
JIH	*Journal of Indian History*
JOIB	Journal of the Oriental Institute, Baroda
JRAS	*Journal of the Royal Asiatic Society of Great Britain and Ireland*

K	Kātyāyana
KSS	*Kashi Sanskrit Series*
LQR	*Law Quarterly Review*
M	Manu
Mad.	Indian Law Reports, Madras Series
Mbh	*Mahābhārata*
M.I.A.	Moore's Indian Appeals
M.L.J.	Madras Law Journal
Mpu	*Mārkaṇḍeya-purāṇa*
MW	Monier-Williams's *Sanskrit-English Dictionary*
N	Nārada
NIA	*New Indian Antiquary*
OH	*Our Heritage*
Pai	Paiṭhīnasi
Pi	Pitāmaha
PW	Böhtlingk and Roth's *Sanskrit Wörterbuch*
SBE	*Sacred Books of the East*
S.C.J.	Supreme Court Journal
ŚL	Śaṅkha and Likhita
TLL	*Tagore Law Lectures*
TSS	*Trivandrum Sanskrit Series*
Va	Vasiṣṭha
Vi	Viṣṇu
vM	Vṛddha-Manu
Vy	Vyāsa
WZKM	*Wiener Zeitschrift für die Kunde des Morgenlandes*
Y	Yājñavalkya
ZVR	*Zeitschrift für vergleichende Rechtswissenschaft*

INTRODUCTION

THE PLACE OF JĪMŪTAVĀHANA'S *DĀYABHĀGA* IN HINDU LEGAL LITERATURE

Jīmūtavāhana's *Dāyabhāga* is part of a long tradition of Sanskrit texts concerned with legal matters.[1] The oldest legal prescriptions in India are contained in the *dharma-sūtras*. *Sūtras* are brief, aphoristic statements in prose. *Dharma-sūtras* are *sūtras* dealing with *dharma*, a Sanskrit term for which there is no Western equivalent, since it encompasses any kind of injunctions, legal and other, that govern the life of a Hindu. The *dharma-sūtras*, together with the more ritually oriented *gr̥hya-sūtras* (on domestic ritual) and *śrauta-sūtras* (on major ritual), belong to the latest phase of Vedic literature, called the *kalpa-sūtras*. Each Vedic school (*śākhā*, "branch") includes, in addition to the older *saṃhitā* (collection of hymns), a *brāhmaṇa* and an *āraṇyaka* (speculative treatises on a variety of topics), and metaphysical *upaniṣads*, its own *kalpa-sūtras*, and, hence, its own *dharma-sūtras*. Whereas the older strata of Vedic literature are labeled *śruti* (revelation; literally, "hearing"), the *sūtras* are considered to be *smr̥ti* (traditional lore; literally, "memory") and slightly less authoritative. All *sūtras* are attributed to ancient Sages or Seers (*r̥ṣis*). The Sages whose *dharma-sūtras* are referred to in the *Dāyabhāga* are Āpastamba, Baudhāyana, Gautama (or Gotama), and Vasiṣṭha (or Vaśiṣṭha).[2]

The period of the *dharma-sūtras* (600–300 B.C.E., Kane 1946: xvii) was followed by that of the *dharma-śāstras*. These texts deal with the same topics as the *sūtras* and, like the *sūtras*, are attributed to Sages, but they are in verse (*śloka*) and they are no longer considered to belong to specific Vedic schools. In addition to Manu, probably the oldest and definitely the most important, the Sages whose *dharma-śāstras* are mentioned in the *Dāyabhāga* are, in a generally accepted chronological order, Yājñavalkya, Viṣṇu, Nārada, Br̥haspati, Kātyāyana, and Vyāsa. More recent than the principal *dharma-śāstras* are a number of minor *smr̥ti* texts, some of which are both in verse and in prose, and which are attributed to

[1] Jolly (1896; English tr. 1928) provides a dated but still valuable general survey of Sanskrit legal literature and of Hindu law. The most encyclopedic treatment is to be found in Kane 1930–, especially in volume one (now in two parts, 1968, 1975), for a historical survey of authors and texts dealing with *dharma* generally, and in volume 3 (1946) for a study of the legal aspects of *dharma* in particular. A recent, highly original and provocative study on the history of Hindu law was produced by Lingat (1967; English tr., with additions, by Derrett, 1973). See also Derrett 1973a and 1973b. For a general bibliography on classical Hindu law, see Rocher 1965 and Sternbach 1973; for colonial and postcolonial Hindu law, see Alexandrowicz 1958, Derrett 1969, and H. C. Jain 1970.

[2] For two recent volumes on the *dharma-sūtras*, see Olivelle 1999, 2000.

Devala, Hārīta, Paiṭhīnasi, Parāśara, Pitāmaha, Śaṅkha and Likhita,[3] Uśanas, Vṛddha- or Bṛhan-Manu,[4] and Vṛddha-Śātātapa. If we accept that Manu's text as we have it was composed between 200 B.C.E. and 100 C.E., the period of the *dharma-śāstras* may well have extended over nearly ten centuries (Kane 1946: xvii–xviii). Compared to the *dharma-sūtras*, the *dharma-śāstras* treat the legal aspects of *dharma* more independently and more systematically. As far as the fully preserved *dharma-śāstras* are concerned, books eight and nine, out of twelve, of the *Manu-smṛti* (or *Mānava-dharma-śāstra*) are devoted uniquely to law, and so is the second book, out of three, of the *Yājñavalkya-smṛti*. Nārada's is the only *dharma-śāstra* entirely devoted to law and the administration of justice. The lost *dharma-śāstras*, Bṛhaspati's, Kātyāyana's, etc., probably displayed the same features, as is clear from the quotations preserved in later texts, some of which have been collected and translated by modern scholars.

What is understood as "law" in the West is expressed in Sanskrit by the terms *vivāda* and *vyavahāra*, the former corresponding to substantive law, the latter to legal procedure. Of the three preserved *dharma-śāstras*, Manu and Yājñavalkya deal with procedure in the context of the first chapter of substantive law, Nārada in a separate introductory section. Verses relevant to procedure describe the organization of the various levels of law courts, and the different types of judges—the king (*rājā*) is always the supreme justice—and their qualifications. They go on to determine who can sue whom and in what form, and lay down the rules on how persons who are sued ought to present their defense. Large sections of the texts are devoted to the different kinds of evidence and the criteria to which they should answer. "Human" forms of evidence include witnesses, written documents, and limitation; oaths and various forms of ordeals constitute the "divine" means of proof. The sections devoted to procedure end with rules on how to decide the case and on how to enforce the decision.

More important in the context of this volume is the treatment of substantive law. From Manu onward, substantive law (*vivāda*) is uniformly divided into eighteen—a traditionally significant number in ancient India—sections: there are eighteen *vivāda-padas*, "heads of litigation." The *Manu-smṛti* lists them at the beginning of its eighth chapter (8.4–7):

1. failure to pay debts (*ṛṇādāna*); 2. deposit and pledge (*nikṣepa*); 3. sale without ownership (*asvāmivikraya*); 4. partnerships (*sambhūyasamutthāna*); 5. resumption of gifts (*dattānapakarma*); 6. failure to pay wages (*vetanādāna*); 7. breach of contract (*saṃvidvyatikrama*); 8. rescission of sale or purchase (*krayavikrayānuśaya*); 9. disputes between owner and keeper of cattle (*svāmi-*

[3]According to the Hindu tradition, Śaṅkha and Likhita were brothers to whom a single *dharma* text is attributed. Some quotations from it are attributed to Śaṅkha and Likhita, others to Śaṅkha only.

[4] The names Vṛddha-Manu and Bṛhan-Manu are often used interchangeably (Vṛddha-Manu, p. 4). Cf. note at **11.1.7**.

pālavivāda); 10. boundary disputes (*sīmāvivāda*); 11. physical assault (*daṇḍa-pāruṣya*); 12. verbal assault (*vākpāruṣya*); 13. theft (*steya*); 14. violent crimes (*sāhasa*); 15. sex crimes (*strīsaṃgrahaṇa*); 16. rules for husband and wife (*strīpuṃdharma*); 17. partition and inheritance (*vibhāga*); 18. gambling and betting (*dyūtāhvaya*).

Other *dharma-śāstras*, while always maintaining the number eighteen, display slight variations on Manu's list, the principal effect of which is to make room at the end for "miscellaneous topics" (*prakīrṇaka*) in which are lumped together all kinds of materials that are not adequately covered in the eighteen *vivāda-padas* of the *Manu-smṛti*. Most important, in the context of this volume, is the fact that, from an early period onward, inheritance is one of the eighteen *vivāda-padas* in the Hindu literature on *dharma*.

Even though *dharma-śāstras* may have been composed at a later time, from a certain point (seventh century C.E. ?) onward the principal *smṛti* texts became the object of extensive commentaries. Among the several commentators on the *Manu-smṛti*. I will refer to Bhāruci, Medhātithi, Govindarāja, and Kullūka(bhaṭṭa). Commentaries on the *Yājñavalkya-smṛti* were composed by Viśvarūpa, Vijñāneśvara, Aparārka, Śūlapāṇi, and Mitramiśra. There are two commentaries on the *Nārada-smṛti*, one by Bhavasvāmin on the shorter version (*Manu-nāradīya-saṃhitā*), and one by Asahāya (only partly preserved) on a longer text.

Some of these often voluminous works, such as Vijñāneśvara's *Mitākṣarā*, which plays a major role in this introduction, are, in fact, more than straight commentaries. While commenting on the text of a particular *smṛti*, verse by verse, they draw into the discussion numerous quotations from other *smṛtis*, and, as a result, they become true encyclopedias of *smṛti* literature generally. In that respect such commentaries are not fundamentally different from a second type of commentarial literature called *nibandhas*. The *nibandhas* are digests or compendia, which do not take one single *smṛti* as their basic guideline, but which bring together and discuss indiscriminately passages from all *smṛtis* that are relevant to a particular topic. Many *nibandhas* comprise several more or less independent book-length sections, each of which is devoted to the study of a different aspect of Hindu *dharma*. One of these sections, most often, is devoted to *vyavahāra* "law" generally; a typical example is Mitramiśra's *Vyavahāra-prakāśa*, which is part of a vast digest called *Vīramitrodaya*. Or there are two separate sections, one dealing with *vyvavahāra* "procedure," the other with *vivāda* "substantive law;" typical examples are Caṇḍeśvara's *Vivāda-ratnākara* and *Vyavahāra-ratnākara* and Vācaspatimiśra's *Vivāda-cintāmaṇi* and *Vyavahāra-cintāmaṇi*. Finally, there are authors of *nibandhas* who devote separate parts of their works to even sections of substantive law. One such topic, on which many authors chose to write, is adoption (Kane 1975: 1039–40). If the date of Jīmūtavāhana which I propose later in this introduction is correct, he may have been one of the earlier authors of a *nibandha* who composed a separate treatise on inheritance, the *Dāyabhāga*.

JĪMŪTAVĀHANA

Life

Very little is known of the life of Jīmūtavāhana. Colebrooke originally (1798: 1.xvi) identified the author of the *Dāyabhāga* with Jīmūtavāhana, the son of the mythic king Jīmūtaketu, and the founder of the Śilāhāra (or Śilāra) dynasty of Tagara and the Konkan.[1] Colebrooke still referred to this mythic origin as "an obvious conjecture" twelve years later, but he added: "That, however, is not the opinion of the learned in *Bengal*; who are more inclined to suppose, that the real author may have borne the name which is affixed to his work, and may have been a professed lawyer who performed the functions of judge and legal adviser to one of the most celebrated of the *Hindu* sovereigns of *Bengal*" (1810: xii). There is no longer any doubt that the author of the *Dāyabhāga* indeed belonged to Bengal.[2] Early in the 17th century Kamalākara's *Vivādatāṇḍava* clearly identified Jīmūtavāhana as the first in a series of writers on *dharma* in Bengal.[3]

Golap Chandra Sarkar maintained that one of the traditional genealogies of Bengal describes Jīmūtavāhana as a descendant in the seventh generation of Bhaṭṭanārāyaṇa, one of the five brahmans whom the Hindu king Ādiśūra is said to have brought to Bengal from Kanauj at the time when he himself did not have any brahmans to perform the required Vedic rituals. Sarkar quotes a passage from Eḍumiśra's *Kulakārikā* according to which Bhaṭṭanārāyaṇa belonged to the Śāṇḍilya *gotra*. His grandson, Bhadra or Maṇibhadra, became "teacher of the world" (*jagad-guru*) in Pāri village. Bhadra's great-great-grandson, Caturbhuja, had two sons, Bilvamaṅgala and Jīmūta.

[1] The name Jīmūtavāhana was known from a copper plate that was published in the first volume of the *Asiatick Researches* (see Carnac 1788). The plate had been found "in digging foundations for some new works at the Fort of *Tanna*, the Capital of *Salset*," and was sent to Sir William Jones by J. Carnac. On the Śilāhāras, see Bhandarkar 1983: 169; Majumdar 1966: 184.

[2] Even though some scholars continued to adhere to the earlier identification. E.g., S.C. Sarkar 1883: xvii n.

[3] The main triumvirate of authors on *dharma* in Bengal are Jīmūtavāhana, Śūlapāṇi, and Raghunandana (or Smārtagauḍa). These were clearly the three whom Kamalākara had in mind, notwithstanding the faulty readings in the *Vivādatāṇḍava* edition: *Jīmūtavāhana-Vivādacintāmaṇi-Śūlapāṇi-Smārtagauḍādayaḥ* (1901: 307, where *Vivādacintāmaṇi* is out of place), and *Jīmūtavāhana-Śūlapāṇi-Gautamādayaḥ* (p. 305, where *Gautama* should be read *Gauḍa* or *Smārtagauḍa*). The former list, including *Vivādacintāmaṇi*, reappears in Chatterjee's 1959 edition (p. 14); the latter correctly reads *Jīmūtavāhana-Śūlapāṇi-Smārtagauḍādayaḥ* (p. 14). See also S. C. Banerji 1943–44: 197.

> At that time Jīmūta, who excelled in all subjects, became the minister and chief justice of the king of Bengal. He was unusually versed in the Vedas and Vedāṅgas. The king of Bengal was named Viśvaksena, a man famous for his austerities. To establish the right conduct among the people and remove any uncertainties Jīmūta composed the digest *Dāyabhāga*. (*Dāyatattva* 1904: xlii.)

The authenticity of this passage has, however, been questioned by Pramathanātha Tarkabhūṣaṇa, the editor of Jīmūtavāhana's *Kālaviveka* (1905: x-xiii).[4]

In the colophons of two of his works, too, Jīmūtavāhana is described as *Pāribhadrīya*, and in the final verses of two works he calls himself "born of the clan of Pāribhadra" (*Pāribhadra-kula-udbhavaḥ*). This statement, and the fact that in the *Kālaviveka* (pp. 290, 291) he compares astronomical measurements in Ujjayinī and Rāḍhā, has led to the generally accepted view that Jīmūtavāhana was a brahman from Rāḍhā and belonged to the Pārigāñi (or Pārigrāmika) clan.[5]

Works

Only three works attributed to Jīmūtavāhana have been preserved: the *Kālaviveka*, the *Dāyabhāga*, and the *Vyavahāramātṛkā*. The colophons of the first two include the formula *Jīmūtavāhanakṛtau Dharmaratne*, "in the *Dharmaratna*, a work by Jīmūtavāhana."[6] This suggests that Jīmūtavāhana, like other writers on *dharma* in

[4] Sarkar (*Dāyatattva* 1904: xlii) reports that he received a copy of the Eḍumiśra passage from Lālmohan Vidyānidhi, the author of the *Sambandhanirṇaya* (1865; 4th ed. Calcutta: M. C. Bhaṭṭācārya, 1949). Majumdar (1971: 469–70), who includes Eḍumiśra's *Kārikā* in his list of genealogical texts, suggests that the only manuscript of the text was "carefully guarded" and "never produced for inspection" by Nāgendranāth Vasu, the author of *Vaṅger Jātīya Itihāsa* ("Social History of Bengal"), Calcutta: Viśvakoṣa Press, 1911–33). Bengali scholars are obviously divided, not only on the authenticity of these texts but also on the Ādiśūra story in general. When Chakravarti (1912: 341) dismissed "the rather silly stories that in the eleventh century the king Ādiśūra had to import Brāhmaṇs from Kanauj because he could not find learned men in Bengal," the editor of the journal in which the article was published, Haraprasād Shāstrī, considered it necessary to add an appendix to Chakravarti's article and to defend the thesis that Ādiśūra indeed brought brahmans to Bengal, not in the eleventh but in the eighth century. On Ādiśūra, see also Paul 1940: 33–38; Majumdar 1971: 471–79; and Inden 1976: 53–60.

[5] G. C. Sarkar (*Dāyatattva* 1904: xliii) situates Pāri-grāma "on the Southern bank of the river Ajay, at a distance of about five miles in the NE direction from Gooskara station in the Loop Line." Guskara station is on the Sahibganj Loop, 33 kilometers from Burdwan, 18 from Bolpur.

[6] The third one does not exhibit such a colophon, except in a poorly written colophon in a single manuscript; see later.

the medieval period,[7] may have written or, at least, intended to write a digest far larger than the three books that have been preserved. Indeed, in one passage of the *Dāyabhāga* (**1.48**), he seems to announce a chapter or a treatise on *ṛṇādāna*, "failure to pay debts," which, as indicated previously, is one of the eighteen *vivādapadas*, "titles of law, heads of litigation," into which Hindu substantive law is traditionally subdivided.[8]

The *Dāyabhāga* was commented on repeatedly; it was translated into English as early as 1810 and edited numerous times beginning in 1813. The *Kālaviveka* and the *Vyavahāramātṛkā* have not been commented on; they have never been translated, and have been edited only once, in 1905 and 1914, respectively.

Kālaviveka

The *Kālaviveka*[9] was edited by Pramathanātha Tarkabhūṣaṇa, in the *Bibliotheca Indica* series published by the Asiatic Society of Bengal.[10] The editor's statement (1905: vii) to the effect that the only title mentioned in the text is *Dharmaratna*, not *Kālaviveka*,[11] proved to be mistaken: the latter term appears not only in the final colophon (p. 544, which may be a later addition) but also in a verse in the text (p. 380).

As the title indicates, the main object of the *Kālaviveka* is to ascertain (*viveka*) at which time (*kāla*) various religious acts ought to be performed. Even though it deals with matters of *dharma*, it does not address issues either of judicial procedure or of substantive law.

The *Kālaviveka* is quoted in Śūlapāṇi's *Durgotsavaviveka*, in Vācaspatimiśra's *Śrāddhacintāmaṇi* and *Kṛtyamahārṇava*, in Govindānanda's *Śrāddhakriyākaumudī* and *Varṣakriyākaumudī*, and in several of Raghunandana's *Tattvas*.[12]

[7] For a survey of some of the voluminous digests in this period, covering all aspects of *dharma*, see Rocher 1954.

[8] No manuscript of a treatise on *ṛṇādāna* by Jīmūtavāhana has been preserved; even though he intended to write it, he may not have done so. Derrett ranks Jīmūtavāhana among "the authors [who] were not encyclopedists, though they may have nursed ambitions in that direction, if life sufficed" (1973a: 50–51).

[9] On the *Kālaviveka*, see Chakravarti 1915: 314–15; Kane 1975: 700–02.

[10] In addition to the 1905 edition, the *Durgotsavanirṇaya* section has been printed in a collection of texts dealing with the *Durgāpūjā* festival (Sanskrit Sāhitya Parishad Series, 1. Calcutta: Siddheśvara Press, 1924, pp. 31–39).

[11] Pramathanātha maintained the title *Kālaviveka* nevertheless, because Madhusūdana Smṛtiratna (who started the edition of the text) had proposed it on the basis of quotations in Raghunandana's *Smṛtitattva*: *Kālaviveke Jīmūtavāhana āha*, "in the *Kālaviveka* Jīmūtavāhana says." *Smṛtitattva* 1.144,774; 2.49.

[12] Chakravarti 1915: 315.

Vyavahāramātṛkā

The *Vyavahāramātṛkā*[13] was edited by Asutosh Mookerjee, in the *Memoirs of the Asiatic Society of Bengal*, in 1912.[14] The title *Vyavahāramātṛkā* (first verse, p. 277) alternates with *Nyāyamātṛkā* (last but one verse, p. 353) and *Nyāyaratnamālikā* (colophon of one manuscript).[15]

The *Vyavahāramātṛkā* is a classical treatise on Hindu legal procedure: an introductory chapter on law courts and judges is followed by a detailed discussion of the traditional four parts of jurisprudence: plaint, reply, evidence, and decision.

The text is quoted in Vācaspatimiśra's *Kṛtyacintāmaṇi* and in Raghunandana's *Dāya-*, *Vyavahāra-*, and *Divya-tattvas*.

Date and Place in the Commentarial Literature

As is often the case with Sanskrit authors, Jīmūtavāhana's date is difficult to determine or even to place within narrow limits. For all practical purposes the sole criteria are, on the one hand, a *terminus post quem* to be established on the basis of the dates of authors whom Jīmūtavāhana quotes in his own works, and, on the other hand, a *terminus ante quem* to be determined by the dates of authors who refer to his works. It will soon be evident that these criteria are far from satisfactory.

Jīmūtavāhana's Predecessors

In all three works that have been preserved, Jīmūtavāhana quotes extensively from his predecessors. He does not hesitate wholeheartedly to agree with some of them, nor does he hesitate vigorously and consistently to disagree with others. Unfortunately, most of the earlier works to which he refers are lost, and the dates of their authors are often as uncertain as the date of Jīmūtavāhana himself. I list them in the order in which they are generally held to have flourished.

[13] On the *Vyavahāramātṛkā*, see Kane 1975: 702–03; Chakravarti 1915: 315–20; Rocher 1953-54.

[14] A critical edition of the text is under preparation by Richard W. Lariviere.

[15] *iti ma[hāma?]hopādhyāya-śrī-jīmūtavāhana-kṛtau dharmaratn[e...]a-kaṇṭha-priyā nyāyaratnamālikā samāptā* (Ramakrishna G. Bhandarkar: *Report on the Search for Sanskrit Manuscripts in the Bombay Presidency for the Years 1887–91*, Bombay: Government Central Press, 1897, #278). The manuscript is now at the Bhandarkar Oriental Research Institute, Pune (new #30).

1. Viśvarūpa

Viśvarūpa[16] is, with Govindarāja, one of the two commentators quoted in the *Dāyabhāga* whose work has been preserved. He is the author of the *Bālakrīḍā*, a commentary on the *Yājñavalkya-smṛti*.

The *Dāyabhāga* quotes Viśvarūpa six times: **4.3.5**, **4.3.13**, **6.1.48**, **11.2.29**, **11.5.12**, and **13.11**, in each case expressing agreement with Viśvarūpa's views.[17] Except for the last item, for which there is no like statement in the *Bālakrīḍā*, the other references can be compared with passages in the printed text. Yet, nowhere are the references literal or even close. (See notes to the Translation.) Since the same is true not only when Jīmūtavāhana quotes Viśvarūpa in the *Kālaviveka* and in the *Vyavahāramātṛkā* but also when Viśvarūpa is quoted by other successors than Jīmūtavāhana, "there are grounds to hold that [the printed edition of the *Bālakrīḍā*] is corrupt and deficient" (Kane 1925: 204; cf. 1968: 560). This conclusion is also supported by a different argument. In the second introductory verse of the *Mitākṣarā*, Vijñāneśvara makes the following claim:

> The *dharmaśāstra* composed by the sage Yājñavalkya, which was expanded upon at great length by Viśvarūpa, is analyzed here in straightforward, concise language (*mita-akṣara*), to make it understandable to the less well educated.[18]

This statement seems to suggest that the *Mitākṣarā* was meant as an abridgment of Viśvarūpa's much larger work. Yet, ever since Viśvarūpa's *Bālakrīḍā* was discovered near the end of the 19th century, there has been general disappointment with what turned out to be a "meager gloss," especially on inheritance (Jolly 1924: 3; Kane 1968: 553). The printed text of the *Bālakrīḍā* may, therefore, not accurately reflect Viśvarūpa's original work.

There is no doubt that Viśvarūpa is one of the earliest commentators on the ancient *dharma* texts. Jolly (1924: 9) placed him in the first half of the 9th century, Kane (1968: 564) more specifically between 800 and 825.

[16] On Viśvarūpa, see Jolly 1924; Kane 1925: 196–209; 1968: 553–65.

[17] A verse from the *Vyavahāramātṛkā*, which unfortunately is corrupt in the edition (p. 352) and in the manuscripts made available to me by Richard W. Lariviere, refers to Viśvarūpa as follows: *mayā prācāṃ nibandhṝṇām iyaṃ vāpi puraskṛtā / dūṣaṇaṃ Viśvarūpāder nirākṛtya prapañcitam*. Chakravarti, following the editor's suggestion to read *vyākhyā* instead of *vāpi*, translated the verse: "By me has been put forward this explanation (*vyākhyā*) of the eastern treatises, having discussed (the subject) after clearing the imputations of Viśvarūpa and others" (1915: 317), and interpreted it as indicative of the fact that "one main object of writing the Vyavahāramātṛkā was to clear Viśvarūpa's work from certain faults charged against him by some writers" (p. 318).

[18] *Yājñavalkyamunibhāṣitaṃ muhur Viśvarūpavikaṭoktivistṛtam / dharmaśāstram ṛjubhir mitākṣarair bālabodhavidhaye vivicyate.*

2. Śrīkara(miśra)

Śrīkara's[19] work has not been preserved. It is not even clear whether he wrote a commentary or a digest.

The *Dāyabhāga* quotes Śrīkara seven times, more often and at greater length than any other of Jīmūtavāhana's predecessors. Except for two occasions on which Jīmūtavāhana agrees with him (**6.1.25** and **11.5.12**), Śrīkara is accused of errors (**6.2.13**), of "incongruous" interpretations" (**11.5.16–17**), and of arguments that are "beside the point" (**11.5.31**). A string of three quotations (**6.1.41–45**) is followed by comments that label them "absurd," "even more absurd," and "the most absurd of all." Another statement by Śrīkara (**6.2.18–19**) is dismissed as "worse than absurd" and as "rushing to a conclusion without giving full consideration to the issue." In the *Vyavahāramātṛkā* as well, Śrīkara's opinions are said to be "incongruous" (p. 302) and "to be rejected" (p. 346).

Kane (1968: 573) dates Śrīkara between 800 and 1050, most probably in the ninth century.

3. Jitendriya

Not only has no work by Jitendriya[20] survived, he has also not been quoted by any later writers other than Jīmūtavāhana and Raghunandana.

There are five references to Jitendriya in the *Dāyabhāga*: **6.1.51**, **11.1.46**, **11.2.29**, **11.5.14**, and **13.11** (a specific reference to the author's *Prāyaścitta-kāṇḍa*). Jīmūtavāhana also quotes him in the *Kālaviveka* and in the *Vyavahāramātṛkā.*

Based on **11.2.29** (see note there) Kane (1925: 223) placed Jitendriya between Viśvarūpa and Bhojadeva. More recently (1975: 595) he suggested that Jitendriya flourished between 1000 and 1050, probably in Bengal.

4. Dhāreśvara a.k.a. Bhojadeva

Whereas Dhāreśvara's [21]works on poetics have been preserved and have been given much scholarly attention, whatever he wrote on *dharma*, whether one work or two as he did on poetics, whether a commentary or a digest, is lost.

The *Dāyabhāga* quotes this author three times: **2.15** (Dhāreśvara), **11.2.22** and **11.2.29** (both Bhojadeva), one of Kane's arguments (1975: 585) to claim that both names refer to the same person. Jīmūtavāhana also quotes him in the *Kālaviveka* and in the *Vyavahāramātṛkā.*

King Bhojadeva is supposed to have reigned from 1005 to 1054 (Kane 1975: 590).

[19] On Śrīkara, see Kane 1925: 213–16; 1968: 571–73.

[20] On Jitendriya, see Kane 1975: 593–95.

[21] On Bhojadeva as a writer on *dharma*, see Kane 1925: 221–24; 1975: 585–91. On his works on poetics, see most recently Gerow 1977: 269–71 and *passim.*

5. Bāla, Bālaka, or Bāloka

The *Dāyabhāga* manuscripts vary between these forms on each of the five occasions on which this author is quoted.[22] Except for the citation at **6.1.52**, Jīmūtavāhana is highly critical of Bāla: once he accuses him of providing a confused reading of an Āpastamba text (**5.2**), and twice, in a play on his name, he labels Bāla's interpretations as "no more than a babe's babble" (**11.2.27** and **13.16**: *bāla[ka]vacanam eva*).[23] A variant on this theme to the effect that "he demonstrates that he is no wiser than a child" (**11.1.51**: *ātmano bālarūpatvaṃ prakaṭīkṛtam*) suggested to Kane (1975: 597) the idea that Bāla might be identical with Bālarūpa, an author frequently quoted in other texts but whose works are lost as well. Bāla is also quoted in the *Kālaviveka* and in the *Vyavahāramātṛkā.*

For reasons based more on the assumed date of Jīmūtavāhana than on anything related to Bāla himself, Kane (1975: 596) describes him as an eastern or Bengali (because of the form Bāloka), who flourished before 1100.

6. Govindarāja

The *Dāyabhāga* refers twice to Govindarāja[24] (**11.2.23** and **11.2.29**), the first time explicitly as the author of a *Manu-ṭīkā,* "commentary on Manu." If this reference is correct, Jīmūtavāhana knew Govindarāja's commentary on Manu 9.131–136, whereas Govindarāja's commentary as we have it today breaks off after Manu 9.72. Govindarāja is also quoted in the *Kālaviveka* and in the *Vyavahāramātṛkā,* once (p. 347) as *Mañjarī-kāra,* "the author of the *(Smṛti)-mañjarī,*" which is the title of another known but still unpublished work by Govindarāja.

Both Jolly (Manu ed. 1885: preface p. 1; 1896: 31) and Bühler (Manu tr. 1886: cxxvii) dated Govindarāja in the 12th or 13th century. Any arguments that might be derived from this to date Jīmūtavāhana later than the 13th century were countered by Chakravarti (1915: 323), who demonstrated that Govindarāja "should be placed considerably earlier than 1150 A.D." Most recently Kane (1975: 663) suggested a date between 1000 and 1100.

7. Dīkṣita

Dīkṣita, to whom Jīmūtavāhana refers quite often in the *Kālaviveka,* is quoted only once in the *Vyavahāramātṛkā* and once in the *Dāyabhāga* (**11.2.3**).

Kane's "index of authors" (1975: 1185) suggests a date of ca. 1050–1100, in any case earlier than 1100.

[22] On Bāla, see Kane 1975: 595–96.

[23] A *bāla* is a young male, a minor less than sixteen years old and incapable of entering into any transaction on his own (N 1.35), occasionally also a boy less than five years old. Cf. note at **3.18**.

[24] On Govindarāja, see Kane 1975: 656–63.

8. **Udyota** or **Vidyodyota** (?)

The *Dāyabhāga* refers twice (**2.9** and **11.6.32**), in nearly identical terms and with full approval, to an author who is not otherwise known: "the meaning of a *smṛti* text 'is made clear' (*dyotita*) by *niravadyavidyodyota*." The commentators on the *Dāyabhāga* offer different explanations. Maheśvara and Acyuta think of an author by the name of Udyota "whose wisdom is blameless" (*niravadya-vidya*). Śrīnātha and Rāmabhadra I suggest that it is either the name of another author or a reference to Jīmūtavāhana himself, whereas Raghunandana exhibits the latter opinion only. Śrīkṛṣṇa, finally, interprets *niravadya* as "the best"; the best *vidyā* is "the sun"; its *udyota* refers to "sunrise."[25] In other words, according to ŚrIkṛṣṇa in both *Dāyabhāga* passages "the meaning is made clear by the rising sun." Even though, when Mitramiśra's *Vyavahāraprakāśa* (ed. p. 446; tr. II.i.12) quotes **2.9**, it says no more than "Jīmūtavāhana says," the wording of both passages in the *Dāyabhāga* seems to indicate that Jīmūtavāhana is indeed quoting from someone, but without using his real name. I translate *niravadyavidyodyota* as "the unimpeachable Luminary of Knowledge."[26] The case is similar to that of another author of a digest to whom Jīmūtavāhana refers in the *Vyavahāramātṛkā* as Bahujñajīrṇa, "the very learned old man."[27]

9. **Udgrāhamalla** (?)

I translate this term (**4.2.6**) as "someone who still wishes to throw down the gauntlet," not unlike Colebrooke's "one who persists in the controversy," and, in a note, "an obstinate wrestler." Kane (1975: 705–06), on the other hand, was inclined to interpret Udgrāhamalla as the name of an author, by analogy with other names ending in in *malla*, "wrestler, gymnast," as in Ṭoḍaramalla, the minister of Akbar and author of the digest *Ṭoḍarānanda*. I am not convinced by Kane's reference to the *Dāyabhāga* commentator Maheśvara in support of his view: even though Maheśvara opposes the opinion of the *granthakṛt*, "the author," i.e., Jīmūtavāhana himself, to that of one *udgrāhamalla*, he does not say that this is the name of an author.[28]

[25] Niravadyā *utkṛṣṭā yā* vidyā *saiva divākaraḥ; tasya* udyotena *udayena [artho]* dyotitaḥ *prakāśitaḥ*.

[26] The term reminds one of the phrase *niravadyavidyāvidyotanāni gurukulāni*, "schools made illustrious by blameless lore" in Bāṇa's *Harṣacarita* (ed. Kane 1965, text p. 19, notes p. 91).

[27] P. 305: *Vṛddhaśātātapavacanaṃ tu Bahujñajīrṇa(?)kṛtanibandhe 'smābhir dṛṣṭaṃ na punar Bhojadeve*, "I found the Vṛddhaśātātapa text in the digest composed by Bahujña-jīrṇa, not in Bhojadeva's."

[28] *Gautamavacanāni yautakadhanaparāṇi granthakṛtā vyākhyāsyante; udgrāhamallena etāni vacanāni . . . duhitrādhikāraparāṇi vyākhyāya . . . Manvādivacanāny api vyākhyāyante.*

As I indicated, except for the questionable Vidyodyota and Udgrāhamalla, all predecessors to whom Jīmūtavāhana refers in the *Dāyabhāga* are also quoted in his other two works. Most authors quoted only in the *Kālaviveka* and/or the *Vyavahāramātṛkā* are totally unknown and do not help to determine a *terminus post quem* for Jīmūtavāhana. These include: Bahujñajīrṇa, to whom I referred earlier, Bhavadhana, Dhavala, Jikana, and Nandana. Of Andhuka we at least know that he made astronomical observations in C.E. 1032/33 (see later). Yogloka, whom Jīmūtavāhana criticizes more often and more mercilessly than any other predecessor, seems to have been later than Śrīkara but earlier than Dīkṣita (Kane 1975: 598–99). Finally, if it is correct to say that Bhāguri, who is quoted in the *Kālaviveka*, is a "ghost" name for Bhāruci (Derrett 1975: 1.13–14), Bhāguri/Bhāruci may be dated as early as C.E.. 600–650.[29]

Keeping in mind the various caveats mentioned earlier, the predecessors whom Jīmūtavāhana quotes span a period of about five centuries:

Bhāguri/Bhāruci (?)	600–650
Viśvarūpa	800–825
Śrīkara	800–1050
Yogloka	950–1050
Dhāreśvara	1005–1054
Jitendriya	1000–1050
Andhuka	1000–1050
Bāla(ka)	before 1100
Govindarāja	1000–1040
Dīkṣita	before 1100

Under no circumstances can Jīmūtavāhana be dated earlier than C.E. 1100.

Jīmūtavāhana's Successors

There are no commentaries on the *Kālaviveka* or on the *Vyavahāramātṛkā*, but there are several commentaries on the *Dāyabhāga*.[30] Seven of these were published by Bharata Candra Śiromaṇi, six in 1863 and one in 1866. More recently Heramba Chatterjee edited the extant section of an eighth commentary attributed to Rāmabhadra, but different from the Rāmabhadra in the 1863 edition. I discuss the commentaries in the order in which they appear to have been written.

[29] Kane (1968: 567), writing prior to Derrett's edition and translation of Bhāruci's commentary, suggested that he was "at least as old as Viśvarūpa."

[30] For a list of preserved and reputed commentaries on the *Dāyabhāga*, see Kane 1975: 1044-45; also *New Catalogus Catalogorum* 9, 1977, 27–28.

1. **Śrīnātha Ācaryacūḍāmaṇi**: *Dāyabhāga-ṭippaṇī*

Śrīnātha's[31] is the oldest extant commentary on the *Dāyabhāga*; it breaks off at **11.5.23** (1863 ed., p. 321). Śrīnātha was the son of Śrīkarācārya, whose works include a commentary on Śūlapāṇi's *Śrāddhaviveka*. He was the father of Rāmabhadra Nyāyālaṅkāra and the teacher of Raghunandana, two later commentators on the *Dāyabhāga*. He criticizes Medhātithi (1863 ed., p. 80), and is criticized in turn by Acyuta (see later). There is general agreement that Śrīnātha has to be placed at the end of the 15th and the beginning of the 16th centuries (1475–1525, Kane 1975: 1044).

2. **Acyutānanda Cakravartin**: *Dāyabhāga-siddhāntakumudacandrikā*

Acyuta,[32] son of Haridāsa Tarkācārya, quotes, most often critically, Śrīnātha's earlier commentary. Among other authors and works he refers to are Medhātithi, the *Mitākṣarā*, Miśra, the *Vivādaratnākara*, and Śūlapāṇi. He also refers to his own commentary on Vācaspati's *Śrāddhaviveka* (1863 ed., p. 44). Acyuta is quoted in turn by two later commentators on the *Dāyabhāga*, Maheśvara and Śrīkṛṣṇa. Kane most recently (1975: 711) dated Acyuta between *ca.* 1510 and 1570.

3. **Rāmabhadra Nyāyālaṅkāra Bhaṭṭācārya**: *Dāyabhāga-vivṛti*

As indicated previously, Rāmabhadra[33] (henceforth Rāmabhadra I) was the son of Śrīnātha, whom he invokes as his predecessor, and whom he defends against the criticism of Acyuta (1863 ed., p. 89, on **2.55**). Chakravarti (1915: 351) places Rāmabhadra in the second and probably the third quarter of the 16th century; Kane dates him ca. 1525 (1975: 1214) and between 1510 and 1570 (1975: 711).

4. **Rāmabhadra II**: *Dāyabhāga-ṭīkā*

A fragment of Rāmabhadra II's commentary on the *Dāyabhāga* (up to **1.11**) was edited for the first time by Heramba Chatterjee (1958) on the basis of a single manuscript preserved at Calcutta Sanskrit College. It is also included in Chatterjee's 1978 edition of the *Dāyabhāga*.[34] Rāmabhadra II is critical of his predecessors, including Rāmabhadra I and, even more so, of Śrīnātha and Acyuta.

[31] On Śrīnātha, see Chakravarti 1915: 344–49; Hazra 1950b, 1951; H. Chatterjee 1978: xix–xxi.

[32] On Acyutānanda, see Chakravarti 1915: 362; H. Chatterjee 1978: xxi–xxii.

[33] *Dāyabhāga-vivṛti*: 1863 ed., p. 1; or *Dāyabhāga-dīpikā*, p. 359. On Rāmabhadra, see Chakravarti 1915: 349–51; H. Chatterjee 1978: xx–xxi.

[34] See there, pp. xxi–xxiii. Kane (1975: 711) confused the two Rāmabhadras.

5. **Raghunandana Bhaṭṭācārya**: *Dāyabhāga-vyākhyā(na)*

Raghunandana[35] was the son of Harihara Bhaṭṭācārya and, as I mentioned before, a disciple of Śrīnātha. He is the author of a highly respected, independent treatise on inheritance, the *Dāya-tattva*, one of twenty-eight *Tattvas* on various aspects of Hindu *dharma*. The *Tattvas* by Raghunandana, "the *Comyns* of India," were known to Sir William Jones as early as 1786 (Cannon 1970: 722). In 1788, while referring to the *Dāyabhāga* as "a fine treatise on Inheritance by *Jímútaváhan*, to which our Pandits often refer," Jones added: "though, on that subject, the work of *Raghunandan* seems to be generally approved in this province" (ibid., p. 800).

In his *Dāyabhāga* commentary, Raghunandana quotes Medhātithi, Kullūkabhaṭṭa, the *Mitākṣarā*, the *Vivādaratnākara*, Vācaspatimiśra's *Vivādacintāmaṇi* (often critically: 1863 ed., pp. 119, 125, 130, 138, 278), Śūlapāṇi, and others.

Colebrooke (1810: vii; followed by Eggeling 1891: 461) suspected that the *Dāyabhāga-vyākhyā* was not the work of the author of the *Dāya-tattva*; Chakravarti (1915) believed that it was, and Hazra (1950a) mentioned it as one of Raghunandana's works, without further comment; Kane (1975: 711–12, 892) accepted Raghunandana's authorship but not without some hesitation. Notwithstanding these doubts, Raghunandana's commentary shared in the high reputation of the *Tattvas*: the law courts in Bengal did not hesitate to resort to it to interpret difficult passages in the *Dāyabhāga*.[36]

Raghunandana lived in the 16th century: 1520–1570 (Hazra 1950a: 182); probably born in 1490 or 1500, literary activity 1520–1575 (Chakravorty 1965: 182); 1510–1580 (Kane 1975: 897).

6. **Maheśvara Bhaṭṭācārya**: *Dāyabhāga-ṭīkā*

Maheśvara's[37] commentary is preserved up to **11.1.67** (1863 ed., p, 283).[38] He quotes Śrīnātha and Acyuta. Colebrooke (1810: vii n.) was told that a great-grandson of Maheśvara, and one of Śrīkṛṣṇa, were living in 1806. He therefore concluded that both commentators were almost contemporary, living in the first half of the 18th century, "but Maheśvara seemingly a little the elder of the two." Kane

[35] On Raghunandana, see Chakravarti 1915: 351-57; Hazra 1950a; Chakravorty 1965, 1970; Kane 1975: 890–902; H. Chatterjee 1978: xxii-xxiv. Raghunandana's commentary on the *Dāyabhāga* appears to have been edited separately by Jīvānanda Vidyāsāgara; I have not seen that edition.

[36] E.g., *Ramnath Tolapattro* v. *Durga Sundari Debi* (1879) 4 Cal. 550, 554: "The authority of Raghunandana is acknowledged and respected universally in the Bengal school" (on **11.2.30–31**); *Ramananda* v. *Raikishori Barmani* (1895) 22 Cal. 347, 351: "Raghunandana, a high authority in the Bengal School, in his commentary on this passage of the Dayabhaga" (on **11.1.56**).

[37] On Maheśvara, see H. Chatterjee 1978: xxiii–xxiv.

[38] The 1863 ed. adds a note: *anumīyate granthakāraḥ pratyūhavyūhopaśamanāsamartha evābhilaṣitasaṃdarbhasamāpanāvakāśaṃ na lebha iti*, "we assume that, for the simple reason that the author was unable to figure out the objections and refutations, he did not see it fit to complete his book as desired."

dates Maheśvara between ca. 1530 and 1600 (1975: 711), or later than 1550 (1975: 1204).

7. Śrīkṛṣṇa Tarkālaṅkāra: *Dāyabbhāga-probodhinī*

Śrīkṛṣṇa,[39] the author of a separate treatise on inheritance, the *Dāyādhikārakrama-saṃgraha*, is, without a doubt, the most popular of all *Dāyabhāga* commentators.[40] Most editions of the *Dāyabhāga* include his *Prabodhinī*. In addition, it has been the object of supercommentaries, two of which are included in Chatterjee's 1978 edition,[41] and of numerous *ṭippaṇīs* and other brief notices, many of which are preserved in the manuscript collection of Calcutta Sanskrit College.

Śrīkṛṣṇa flourished in the middle of the eighteenth century (Kane 1975: 711).

8. Kṛṣṇakānta Vidyāvāgīśa Bhaṭṭācārya: *Dāyabhāga-ṭīkā*

Kṛṣṇakānta,[42] a resident of Navadvīpa, states that he composed his commentary in *śaka* year 1747, i.e., C.E. 1824/25.[43] The commentary was deliberately left incomplete. After the end of **11.5** Kṛṣṇakānta adds: "The rest is too easy and not worthy of further discussion to need a commentary to explain its meaning; therefore I have not written it."[44]

The chronology of the commentators on the *Dāyabhāga* can be summarized as follows:

Śrīnātha	1475–1525
Acyutānanda	1510–1570

[39] On Śrīkṛṣṇa, see H. Chatterjee 1978: xxiv–xxv.

[40] After he initially described Śrīkṛṣṇa as "a modern writer of no great authority" (1798: 1.xvi), Colebrooke reversed his opinion after translating the *Dāyabhāga*: "This is the most celebrated of the glosses on the text. It is the work of a very acute logician, who interprets his author and reasons on his arguments, with great accuracy and precision; and who always illustrates the text, generally confirms its positions, but not infrequently modifies or amends them. Its authority has been long gaining ground in the schools of law throughout *Bengal*; and it has almost banished from them the other expositions of the *Dáya-bhága*; being ranked, in general estimation, next after the treatises of Jīmūtavāhana and of Raghunandana" (1810: vi).

[41] One by Kṛṣṇanātha Nyāyapañcānana (Calcutta: the author, 1890), and one attributed to Madhusūdana, possibly Mahāmahopādhyāya Madhusūdana Smṛtiratna of Navadvīpa (B.Y. 1239–1307 = C.E. 1832/33–1900/01). On both, see H. Chatterjee 1978: xvii–xviii.

[42] Ed. Bharata Candra Śiromaṇi, 1866 (see Bibliography: *Dāyabhāga* eds.); the text is included in H. Chatterjee's 1978 edition. On Kṛṣṇakānta, see there, pp. xvi–xvii.

[43] If he was identical with Kṛṣṇakānta Vidyālaṅkāra whom Sir William Jones lists among teachers at Navadvīpa in 1785, he must have been about eighty-five years old when he wrote his commentary (*Notebook of Sir William Jones*. Yale University, Beinecke Rare Book Library, Osborne Collection, OSB c 400).

[44] *Itaḥ śeṣasyātisugamatayā vicārāsambalitatayā ca tadarthāvagamo na ṭīkām apekṣata iti taṭṭīkā mayā na kṛteti.*

Rāmabhadra I	1510–1570
Rāmabhadra II	?
Raghunandana	1510–1580
Maheśvara	1530–1600
Śrīkṛṣṇa	ca. 1750
Kṛṣṇakānta	ca. 1825

Consequently, Jīmūtavāhana cannot have lived later than C.E. 1500.

The *terminus post quem*, C.E. 1100, and the *terminus ante quem*, C.E. 1500, provided by quotations in and of the *Dāyabhāga*, added to the erroneous belief that no other author referred to Jīmūtavāhana in the period between these dates, left scholars with the task of fixing the date of the author of the *Dāyabhāga* somewhere within a span of four hundred years.

In earlier years there was a tendency to assign Jīmūtavāhana a late date rather than an early one. According to Sarvadhikari (1882: 403; unchanged 1922: 307), "you may view Dāyabhāga from any point you please, you cannot avoid coming to the beginning of the fifteenth century as the age of Jīmūtavāhana." Eggeling (1891: 460), following Sarvadhikari, suggested "the 15th (or at the latest, the beginning of the 16th century)." Jolly (1896: 79), too, proposed the 15th century, even though one decade earlier he mentioned "not earlier than the thirteenth century" (1885: 22).[45]

The main argument in favor of these late dates was the fact that the commentarors on the *Dāyabhāga* occasionally interpret Jīmūtavāhana's statements as direct criticisms of the views held by authors who are known to belong to the 14th and 15th centuries, in particular Caṇḍeśvara (1300–1350, Chakravarti 1915: 378; literary activity 1314–ca. 1364, Kane 1975: 775) and Vācaspatimiśra (literary activity 1450–1480, Chakravarti 1915: 400, and Kane 1975: 853).[46] These statements by the *Dāyabhāga* commentators were taken at face value by a number of scholars, including Sarvadhikari[47] and J. C. Ghose (1917: 2.xvi); they were not by

[45] This date was based on the fact that Jīmūtavāhana quotes Govindarāja, whom Jolly assigned to the 12th century (see earlier). The argument found additional support in the fact that Jīmūtavāhana is mentioned neither in the *Vivādaratnākara* nor in the *Vivādacintāmaṇi*. In view of the important role Vijñāneśvara's *Mitākṣarā* came to play in dating the *Dāyabhāga* (see later), it may be worth noting that the *Mitākṣarā* is mentioned six times in the *Vivādaratnākara* (## 95, 116, 404 thrice, and 711) and once in the *Vivādacintāmaṇi* (ed. p. 108; tr. p. 106), yet never in connection with partition or inheritance.

[46] For examples from Acyutānanda and Śrīkṛṣṇa (**2.27**, **4.3.23**, **11.1.31**) and Raghunandana (**12.4**), see Chakravarti 1915: 324.

[47] "The freedom again with which Jimutavahana discusses the doctrines of the author of the Vivada Chintamani shows that Vachaspati Misra and Jimutavahana were contemporaries, and that the former composed his treatise only a few years before the founder of the Bengal School composed his immortal work" (1922: 306–7). Yet, by the time this was written, it was known that Vācaspatimiśra quotes Jīmūtavāhana's *Kālaviveka* and *Vyava-*

Colebrooke (1810: xiii), Chakravarti (1915: 324), and P. Ghose (1917: 21). Kane (1975: 709) rightly pointed out that "we should not take them seriously. The commentators had no idea of the exact chronological position of writers long anterior to them. All they mean is that Jīmūtavāhana criticises views that were shared also by Caṇḍeśvara and others."

For a long time the argument in favor of a late date for Jīmūtavāhana also found support in the fact that, even in Bengal, he did not seem to have been quoted before ca. C.E. 1500. It was only Śrīnātha, his son Rāmabhadra, and his disciple Raghunandana who, in their several commentaries, "established the reputation of Jīmūtavāhana for all time to come" (Chakravarti 1915: 351). The fact that another author from Bengal, Śūlapāṇi (1365–1445, Kane 1975: 839), does not refer to the *Dāyabhāga* in his commentary on the *Yājñavalkya-smṛti* seemed to indicate that Jīmūtavāhana must have been later than Śūlapāṇi (J. C. Ghose 1917: 2.xvi).[48] However, as I pointed out earlier, Śūlapāṇi's *Durgotsavaviveka* (which, in turn, is quoted several times in Vācaspatimisra's *Śrāddhacintāmaṇi*) does refer to Jīmūtavāhana's *Kālaviveka*, with the result that Jīmūtavāhana's date had to be lowered by at least one century (Banerji 1949: 46, between Bhojadeva and Śūlapāṇi).

The tendency gradually to assign Jīmūtavāhana earlier and earlier dates continued: the middle of the 12th century (G. C. Sarkar *Dāyatattva* 1904: xli, xlii); 1100–1150 (Kane 1946: xviii); the beginning of the 12th century (Chakravarti 1915: 326; Lingat 1973: 119); 1090–1130 (Kane 1930: 326; 1975: 709; Derrett 1973a: 51); the latter part of the 11th century, during the reign of Vijayasena (P. Ghose 1917: 31).[49]

The principal reasons for assigning Jīmūtavāhana an earlier date are twofold. First, Pandit Pramathanātha Tarkabhūṣaṇa, the editor of the *Kālaviveka*, drew attention to the astronomical observations contained in that text (p. ix). He argued that, when Jīmūtavāhana speaks of observations in *śaka* year 955 (C.E. 1032/33), he explicitly states that these were seen (*dṛṣṭa*) and described (*likhita*) by Andhuka (p. 119). On the other hand, when he deals, at some length (pp. 21, 41, 46–49), with observations in *śaka* years 1013–1014 (C.E. 1090/91–1091/92), he uses the neuter and impersonal expression *dṛṣṭam* "has/have been seen" (p. 41), without referring to any person as the observer. Hence, Pramathanātha concluded, "the probability is that these observations were made by himself. In that case he must have been alive in Śaka 1013 = 1091 A.D."[50]

---

hāramātṛkā in his *Śrāddhacintāmaṇi*, *Kṛtyacintāmaṇi*, and *Kṛtyamahārṇava* (Chakravarti 1915: 315, 316, 395, 397, 398).

[48] Ghose placed Jīmūtavāhana in the first quarter of the fifteenth century, at the court of Jalāl-ud-Dīn Muhammad Shāh (1415–31), the son of Rājā Ganesh of Dinājpur born as Jadu or Jatmall, who converted to Islam but continued, according to Ghose, to encourage Hindu scholars.

[49] On Vijayasena (*ca* 1095–1158), see Majumdar 1971: 223–28.

[50] Pramathanātha adds (pp. viii–ix) that, since in the reign of Ballālasena (1158–79) the Pāri brahmans were relegated to the lowest rank of brahmans, and since Jīmūtavāhana calls himself Pāribhadrīya, he must have lived before that time.

The conclusion which Pramathanātha drew from the astronomical observations in the *Kālaviveka* did not convince everyone. According to Mayne (1950: 51), it does not outweigh the fact that, even in Bengal, Jīmūtavāhana is not referred to prior to the 13th century: "It is safer . . . to assign the composition of the Dayabhaga of Jimutavahana to the 13th century which would agree with Dr. Jolly's earlier estimate in his Tagore Law Lectures." J. C. Ghose (1917: 2.xvi), on his part, continued to argue that those who believe in the early dating on the basis of the *Kālaviveka* "forget that he clearly attempted to refute the opinion of Chandeswara." Pramathamātha's argument was, however, strongly endorsed by P. Ghose (1917: 24–26), and, via him, by then Acting Chief Justice Asutosh Mookerjee[51]; both agreed that Jīmūtavāhana must have been alive in C.E. 1091/92.[52] Most recently Kane (1975: 708–9), too, argued that Jīmūtavāhana's measurements demonstrate that he composed the *Kālaviveka* "soon after *śaka* 1013 or 1014 (i.e., 1091 or 1092 A.D.)."

A second argument that has contributed to an early dating of Jīmūtavāhana is of a very different nature and, as far as the history of Hindu law is concerned, it is far more important.

One of the earliest references to the *Dāyabhāga* in English appeared in the first volume of the *Asiatick Researches*, in 1788: "the system of *Hindu* law . . . consists of many tracts in high estimation, among which those current in *Bengal* are an excellent treatise on *Inheritance* by Jímútaváhana, and a complete *Digest*, in *twenty-seven* volumes, compiled a few centuries ago by Raghunandan, the Tribonian of *India*, whose work is the grand repository of all that can be known on a subject so curious in itself, and so interesting to the *British* Government."[53]

Whether or not the *Dāyabhāga* was actually "current in Bengal,"[54] the fact is that, in 1810, Henry Thomas Colebrooke translated the text into English, together

[51] *Rajani Nath Das* v. *Nitai Chandra Dey* (1920) 32 C.L.J. 333, 355; 48 Cal. 643, 687.

[52] P. Ghose (pp. 27–28) adds that Jīmūtavāhana, who was strongly influenced by *nyāya*, must have lived before the advent of *navyanyāya*, since he largely drew on the old school and used definitions that Gaṅgeśa (13th century) and the new school were to reject.

[53] "On the Literature of the Hindus, from the *Sanscrit*, communicated by Goverdhan Caul, with a short Commentary," pp. 340–55 at 352. Govardhan Kaul was one of the two pandits attached to the Supreme Court in Calcutta. The only earlier reference to the *Dāyabhāga*, as far as I know, appeared in William Jones's letter of October 24, 1786: in the ideal Digest of Hindu law Jones wished to see included "*Jimut Bahun*, the best book on Inheritance" (Cannon 1970: 722).

[54] I have expressed my doubts on this subject elsewhere (Rocher 1972). Cf. Alexander Hamilton (who lived in Bengal from 1783 to 1795): "The act of Parliament which enjoined that the natives should be protected in their rights, 'according to the laws and constitution of India,' meant unquestionably such rights as existed when the India Company obtained possession. The obvious intention was to maintain the state of society which then existed; and it certainly never entered into the imagination of any person, at home or abroad, that it was necessary to revert to laws, institutions and rights, which a lap of six centuries had obliterated from the minds of the natives" ([Hamilton] 1811: 359).

with the section on inheritance in the *Mitākṣarā*, Vijñāneśvara's commentary on the *Yajñavalkya-smṛti*.[55] His selection of these two texts was motivated by the consideration that "they are the standard authorities of the Hindu law of inheritance in the schools of Benares and Bengal" (1810: iii). Colebrooke thus seems to have been first to speak of two principal schools of the Hindu law of inheritance. The *Mitākṣarā* school, which was not only the school of Banaras but of the whole of India except Bengal, was later further subdivided into the Benares, Mithila, Maharashtra, and Dravida schools. In the law courts of Bengal, Jīmūtavāhana's *Dāyabhāga* remained the prime authority throughout, occasionally, however, supplemented or overruled by Raghunandana's *Dāyatattva* and Śrīkṛṣṇa Tarkālaṅkāra's *Dāyādhikārakramasaṃgraha*.[56] Two decades after Colebrooke's translation of the *Dāyabhāga*, Rammohan Roy (1832: 8) quoted the following saying "current among the learned in Bengal:"

> Opinions are said to be of two kinds, one founded on the authority of the Dayubhagu, and the other opposed to it; but what is opposed to the Dayubhagu is not approved by the learned.[57]

The differences between the *Mitākṣarā* law of inheritance and *Dāyabhāga* law are basic and far-reaching. I return to them later in this introduction. Meanwhile, in the context of the second argument that contributed to assigning Jīmūtavāhana an early date, it is important to point to the fact that, in 1810, two Sanskrit texts, including the *Dāyabhāga*, were elevated above all others as the main representatives of two distinct systems of inheritance. Comparison between the two, not only for their contents but also for their dates, became inevitable. The question which has largely dominated research on the history of Hindu law in recent years is

[55] According to Colebrooke's son, his father interrupted work on a supplement to the *Digest* dealing with succession, to translate the *Two Treatises*: "the highest advantage, he conceived, would arise from the publication, in a complete form, of these two treatises, from which the student would be enabled to collect at one view the leading doctrines of each school, a task which could scarcely be effected through a compilation of a general, and necessarily complex, nature" (Colebrooke 1873: 1.45–46).

[56] On the one hand, one finds opinions to the effect that "we should follow the Dayabhaga and not Srikrishna and Raghunandana, when it is evident that the latter have not fol lowed their master" (*Prosunno Kumar Bose* v. *Sarat Sashi Bose* [1908] 36 Cal. 86, 114). On the other hand, a ruling by Asutosh Mookerjee: "we are of opinion that it is impossible to accept the argument . . . that the text of the Dayabhaga by Jimuta Vahana must be regarded as in itself an authority absolutely binding on us without regard to the fact whether the doctrine propounded in the text has been accepted as a true exposition of the law and has been sanctioned by usage" (*Purna Chandra Bysack* v. *Gopal Lal Sett* [1908] 8 C.L.J. 369, 428), has been called a first step toward recognizing development in Hindu law, the next step being "that *Srikrishna* and *Raghunandana* should be followed and not the *Dayabhaga* because the former writers noted and marked the changes made in *Dayabhaga* by custom when they flourished and did really state in their works what the rules of Hindu law were in their time" (Acharyya 1914: 365).

[57] *Vyavasthā dvividhā proktā dāyabhāgamatāmatā / dāyabhāgaviruddhā yā matā na budhasaṃmatā.*

this: which of the two texts criticizes the system of inheritance set forth by the other, and thereby proves to be the more recent one?

The notion that it was Jīmūtavāhana who criticized Vijñāneśvara, and not the other way around, was well established in the Indian tradition. The several commentators on the *Dāyabhāga* occasionally label notions or views which Jīmūtavāhana opposes as being those "of the author of the *Mitākṣarā*."[58] Mitramiśra's *Vyavahāraprakāśa* (C.E. 1610–1650, Kane 1975: 948), which is generally critical of Jīmūtavāhana,[59] says that Jīmūtavāhana first quotes Vijñāneśvara's definition of partition in an adversary way, then goes on to criticize it, finally to state his own opinion.[60] Elsewhere Mitramiśra states that Jīmūtavāhana's criticism of Vijñāneśvara "results from the fact that he failed to grasp the true intent of the author of the *Mitākṣarā*."[61] More pointedly, Kamalākarabhaṭṭa's *Vivādatāṇḍava* (C.E. 1610–1640, Kane 1975: 932) summarizes Jīmūtavāhana's interpretation of Yājñavalkya 2.121 (**2.9, 15, 18–20**) and concludes that it results from "his being blinded by hatred of the *Mitākṣarā*."[62]

In modern scholarly literature, too, it seems to be the generally accepted opinion that it was Jīmūtavāhana who criticized Vijñāneśvara, and, consequently, that the *Dāyabhāga* is more recent than the *Mitākṣarā*. This trend was inaugurated by Colebrooke. Although he was not fully convinced by the statements of the commentators to the effect that on several ocaasions Jīmūtavāhana criticized the *Mitākṣarā* in particular: "it is however possible, that he may be there refuting the doctrine of earlier authors, which may have subsequently been repeated from them in the later compilation of Vijnyáneśwara," Colebrooke concluded nevertheless: "Assuming, however, that the opinion of the commentators is correct; the age of Jímútaváhana must be placed between that of Vijnáneśvara, whose doctrine he opposes, and that of Raghunandana who followed his authority" (1810: xii).

While the argument put forth by the *Dāyabhāga* commentators and some of the digest writers has continued to find occasional support in more recent years,[63] modern scholarship also added to it a different argument that was to become even more pervasive, and which has continued to find near general support up to the

[58] See, e.g., notes at **1.7, 1.39, 1.42, 2.18,** and **4.2.27**.

[59] G. C. Sarkar (*Vyavahāraprakāśa* 1879: x) describes the *Vyavahāraprakāśa* as a vindication of the doctrines of the *Mitākṣarā*, against the attacks of the *Dāyabhāga*.

[60] *Na ca . . . vācyam ity āśaṅkya . . . iti dūṣayitvā . . . ity uktam* (ed. p. 430; tr. I.55).

[61] *Mitākṣarāyāṃ Jīmūtavāhanenoktaṃ dūṣaṇam . . . tan Mitākṣarākṛdāśayāparijñānāt* (ed. p. 434; tr. II.i.2).

[62] *Tan Mitākṣarāpradveṣajāndhyakṛtam* (1901 ed.: 318–19); *tan Miktākṣarāpraveṣajaṃ maurkhyam* (1959 ed.: 18). Cf. H. Cowell: "It is [the] control of the son over his father's property, or rather the co-existent rights of father and son in the joint estate, which *provoked the hostility* of Jimutavahana and the school of Bengal" (1870–71: 1.93; emphasis added).

[63] E.g., G. C. Sarkar *Vyavahāraprakāśa* 1879: x ("Some of the doctrines of the Mitákshará . . . were attacked by the Dáyabhága"), and 1897: 180 (on **2.27**, "Jímútaváhana controverts the Mitákshará"; cf. 1927: 501); and Bhabatosh Bhattacharya 1935: 32.

present day: "the Mitakshara school is the orthodox school, and the Dayabhaga school is the reformed school, of Hindu law" (Mulla 1970: 77).

There are two component parts to this argument. First, many scholars, even in Bengal, believe that there was indeed a time when "the doctrines of the Mitacshara . . . were current in Bengal" (Trailokyanath Mitra 1881: 77-78).[64] Some of them proudly claim that Bengal "has the unique distinction that while the rest of India accepted the paramount authority of Vijñāneśvara on matters of law she has been the only province to examine the views of Vijñāneśvara critically and to reject them wherever necessary" (Banerji 1943–44: 197).[65]

Second, and more important for the date of Jīmūtavāhana, was the belief that, of all Bengali writers on inheritance, it was the author of the *Dāyabhāga* who was "the founder of the Bengal school." Colebrooke undertook to translate the *Dāyabhāga* rather than any other text in Bengal "decidedly due to the treatise of Jímútaváhana himself; as well because he was the founder of this school, being the author of the doctrine which it has adopted" (1810: v). The idea that Jīmūtavāhana was the founder of the Bengal school appears again and again in modern scholarly literature.[66]

Notwithstanding all this, as early as 1885 Julius Jolly realized that the situation may have been far more complex. He referred to the commonly held opinion that "the author of the latter work [= *Dāyabhāga*] has been sometimes regarded in the light of a bold reformer, who set up the actual usage of his own time against the letter of an obsolete law" (p. 108). But then he went on to show that the ideas that seem to be characteristic of Jīmūtavāhana (whom, at that time he placed in the 13th century) not only must have been older than the author of the *Dāyabhāga*, but that they may also not have been "peculiar . . . to the Bengal School of Lawyers" (p. 109). I will return to these arguments while discussing the difference between *Mitākṣarā* and *Dāyabhāga* laws of inheritance.

Meanwhile, I must refer, again with Jolly, to the "significant fact that [Jīmūtavāhana] quotes Vijñāneśvara's predecessor Viśvarūpa, though he never quotes Vijñāneśvara himself" (1885: 25). Since Vijñāneśvara does not quote the *Dāyabhāga* either, it is likely that neither author knew the other. When Vijñāneśvara or Jīmūtavāhana criticizes views which have by now become identified with the

[64] Cf. T. P. Banerjea 1893: 6; Sarvadhikari 1922: 307. I can only briefly refer here to the impact of this belief on modern Hindu law. It meant that "of all the commentaries, that by Vijnaneswara known as the Mitakshara has the widest range of influence. . . . Its authority is denied in Bengal in so far that it yields to the Dayabhaga in points where they differ" (Mitter 1913: 43–44), and that "the Mitákshará law should be therefore followed in Bengal where the Dáyabhága is silent" (G. C. Sarkar 1897: 178; cf. 1927: 498). Similarly, Mulla 1970: 77.

[65] According to S. C. Mookerjee (*Pitambar Chandra Saha* v. *Nishi Kanta Saha* C.W.N. [1919] 24, 215, 218), *Dāyabhāga* law in Bengal replaced Mithila law which the Brahmans and Kāyasthas brought with them when they migrated from Kanauj.

[66] E.g., Morley 1858: 221; Mitter 1870: 35; Cochrane 1872: 4; S. C. Sarkar 1883: xvii; G. C. Sarkar *Dāyatattva* 1904: v; Mulla 1970: 56.

writings of the other, it is possible that either one criticizes views that existged long before they were incorporated in the other one's work.[67]

The date of the *Mitākṣarā* can be determined within narrow limits. Vijñāneśvara was an ascetic in the reign of King Vikramāditya VI of the Cālukya dynasty, whose capital was Kalyāṇa (Kalyānī, Bidar district, in present-day Maharashtra), and who reigned from ca. 1076 to 1127. Dedicatory verses at the end of the *Mitākṣarā* seem to indicate that it was written at the acme of or late in the king's reign. The *Mitākṣarā* must, therefore, have been composed early in the 12th century: 1120–1125 (Derrett 1952b: 36, following *Dānakāṇḍa* p. 38) or 1100–1120 (Kane 1975: 609).

Added to the other arguments in favor of an early dating for Jīmūtavāhana mentioned earlier, Vijñāneśvara's and Jīmūtavāhana's mutual silence about one another increases the likelihood that the authors of the *Mitākṣarā* and the *Dāyabhāga* were contemporaries or near-contemporaries working independently of one another in different regions of India, in the beginning of the 12th century.[68]

[67] Kane's (1930: 327; 1975: 710) claim that, even though Vijñāneśvara's name is not mentioned, and even though Jīmūtavāhana may, therefore, have had other predecessors in mind, in certain passages of the *Vyavahāramātṛkā* "it is quite within the bounds of possibility that Jīmūtavāhana criticizes the Mit," has been rejected by Derrett (1952a: 8 = *Essays* 1.205).

[68] Based on a detailed examination of comparable passages in the *Mitākṣarā* and the *Dāyabhāga*, Derrett states, more categorically: "There can be no doubt but that *Jīmūtavāhana* and *Vijñāneśvara* were contemporaries" (1952a: 1 = *Essays* 1.198).

THE *DĀYABHĀGA*

Dāyabhāga Law v. *Mitākṣarā* Law

Jīmūtavāhana and Vijñāneśvara commented on the same body of *smṛti* literature. Yet, they came to very different conclusions.[1] There are two main underlying reasons for their differences. First, the author of the *Mitākṣarā* holds that any member, at least any male member, of a joint family becomes an undivided co-owner of the joint family estate by the mere fact of being born into the family. Jīmūtavāhana, on the other hand, starts from the premise that no member of the joint family has any proprietary right whatever unless and until the prior owner of the estate dies or becomes incapacitated. Second, both "schools" establish different, though not fundamentally different, orders of succession, based on divergent interpretations of the term *piṇḍa* in the ancient texts on *dharma*. I will briefly comment on these differences.

The chapter on inheritance in the *Mitākṣarā* opens with a lengthy, theoretical discussion (Colebrooke 1810: I.i).[2] After defining the terms *dāya* and *bhāga* (or *vibhāga*) Vijñāneśvara enters into a discourse on the concept of ownership (*svatva*). The sources of ownership are enumerated in the *Gautama-dharmasūtra*:

> A person becomes the owner by inheritance, purchase, partition, garnering, or discovery. In addition, a brahman becomes the owner of what he receives, a *kṣatriya* of what he conquers, a *vaiśya* and a *śūdra* of what they earn. [G 10.39–42]

The question then arises whether ownership is, indeed, a *śāstric* concept and, hence, limited to the ways of acquisition listed in the Gautama text, or whether it is a "worldly" (*laukika*) concept that allows for additional, non-*śāstric* ways of acquiring property. The *Mitākṣarā* lists various arguments in favor of the former view and, subsequently, rejects all of them in favor of the latter: ownership and the ways to acquire it are not limited to those listed in the definition provided in the Gautama text.

This conclusion opens the way for a second discussion: in the case of partition or inheritance (*vibhāga*), does ownership result from and arise at the time of partition, or are the survivors dividing among themselves something in which their ownership had been previously established? Vijñāneśvara cites arguments in favor

[1] See, e.g., Gharpure 1931: 31–32; Mayne 1950: 55–56; most recently Lingat 1973: 172–74, and, in detail, Pawate 1975.

[2] Rocher and Rocher: forthcoming.

of the former view, once again to reject them in favor of the latter, and to conclude that those who participate in a partition acquired their proprietary rights by birth.

Differently from the *Mitākṣarā*, the *Dāyabhāga* does not open with a long, theoretical discussion. Yet, Jīmūtavāhana makes it clear from the start (**1.3**) that, for a son or anyone else to claim a proprietary right in any joint property whatever, his father or any other prior owner must be deceased or disabled. Only briefly (**1.13–20**) does he refer to and reject the idea that "coming into the world" is a sufficient condition for a person to acquire a right of ownership. Hence, one of the main characteristic features of the law of inheritance in Bengal, even in modern times, has been that

> it wholly denies the doctrine that property is by birth, which is the corner-stone of the joint family system under the Mitaksara. Hence, it treats the father as the absolute owner of the property, and authorises him to dispose of it at pleasure. It also refuses to recognize any right in the son to a partition during the father's lifetime.[3]

As I indicated earlier, the second difference between the two "schools" is the result of their interpretations of the term *piṇḍa*. Both Vijñāneśvara (on Y 2.135; Colebrooke II.iii.3) and Jīmūtavāhana (**11.6.17**) quote and use Manu 9.187ab, which ordains that in each instance the inheritance goes to the nearest *sapiṇḍa*, that is, the person who has most *piṇḍas* in common with the deceased. Not only in their comments on Manu 9.187ab but also throughout their works the two authors, however, interpret the term *piṇḍa* differently.[4]

When commenting on the rule that a man should not marry a bride who is his *sapiṇḍa* (Y 1.52), Vijñāneśvara enters into a long digression on the meaning of *piṇḍa* and, hence, on the nature of *sapiṇḍa* relationship. He makes it clear that, for him, *piṇḍa* means "part of the body," and that *sapiṇḍa* relationship is based on "sharing particles of the same body" (*eka-śarīra-avayava-anvaya*). In other words,

[3] Mayne 1950: 55. I may note here that the ill-fated *Hindu Code Bill* of 1947 favored the *Dāyabhāga* view rather than that of the *Mitākṣarā*, by rejecting ownership by birth (*The Gazette of India*, April 19, 1947, Part V, pp. 387–410. See especially Part III-A, Division I). Again, when drafting Section 6 of *The Hindu Succession Act, 1956*, "it was generally felt that radical reform was required in the Mitakshara law of coparcenary. . . . Probably the best solution would have been to abolish the ancient legal formulae of acquisition of right by birth and devolution by survivorship since the logical way was to assimilate the Mitakshara to the Dayabhaga in this respect. . . . But there was some strong sentiment in favour of the retention of the Mitakshara coparcenary even in an attenuated form and the rules laid down in this section are a compromise having some of the merits and all the demerits which attend such adjustive legislation" (Mulla 1970: 778). Gupte concluded: "The present section is clearly a half-hearted attempt to preserve the old rule of survivorship" (1963: 365). According to others, "it would be proper to bring the Dayabhaga law in accordance with the Mitakshara" (Pawate 1975: xii; similarly Deshpande 1943).

[4] On *sapiṇḍa* relationship and inheritance, see, e.g., Setlur 1911: II.54–70; Kane 1941: 452–55; Gharpure 1943: 44–77; Derrett 1963: 381–94; Rocher 1992.

in the *Mitākṣarā* inheritance and the order of succession are based on the degree of consanguinity.

Jīmūtavāhana was obviously aware of that point of view. He rejects it on the grounds that the verse immediately preceding Manu 9.187ab refers to the offering of *piṇḍas*. The *sapiṇḍa* relationship mentioned at Manu 9.187ab, therefore, must be connected with those *piṇḍas*. A *piṇḍa*, according to Jīmūtavāhana, is the "ball" or "cake," made mostly of rice, which the living offer to the deceased in their funeral rites (*śrāddha*), and *sapiṇḍas* are those individuals who are in some capacity or other connected with the rice balls that are offered at the *śrāddha* ceremony.[5]

On the day after the period of mourning, a first *śrāddha* is performed for the deceased alone (*eka-uddiṣṭa*; **11.6.3**). This first *śrāddha* is followed by fifteen similar ceremonies, the last of which is theoretically but not necessarily performed on the first anniversary of the deceased person's death. The sixteenth *ekoddiṣṭa śrāddha*, called *sapiṇḍana* or *sapiṇḍīkaraṇa* (**11.1.29, 38**), has the specific purpose of including the deceased among the ancestors. From that time onward, the deceased no longer receives *śrāddhas* individually; he is only one of several ancestors to whom his descendants offer *piṇḍas* at their *pārvaṇaśrāddhas*.

When an individual performs a *pārvaṇaśrāddha*, he offers complete, "undivided," *piṇḍas* to three generations of male ancestors on his father's side, and to three generations of male ancestors on his mother's side. Even as this individual offers undivided *piṇḍas* to three generations of male ancestors on his father's side, he himself will eventually be offered undivided *piṇḍas* by three generations of male descendants.[6] Strictly speaking, therefore, each individual is a *sapiṇḍa* with six other generations.

In addition, at *pārvaṇaśrāddhas* three generations of ancestors beyond the great-grandfather receive "divided" offerings, scraps or fragments of *piṇḍas* (*piṇḍa-lepas*). Three generations from the great-great-grandfather up and from the great-great-grandson down, therefore, form a different group of relatives, called *sakulyas*. Finally, to seven generations above the *sakulyas* one offers the water used to rinse his hands after handling the *piṇḍas*, and one is in turn offered this kind of water by seven generations below his *sakulyas*. These generations are a person's *samānodakas*, "those who have water in common."

All agree that *sakulyas* and *samānodakas* inherit only if no *sapiṇḍas* are living, hence the importance of defining exactly which relatives are comprised in the category of *sapiṇḍas*. What is peculiar to Jīmūtavāhana and, through him, to the Bengal school of law is the emphasis they put on the extent to which those who offer *piṇḍas* are "of service" (*upakāraka*) to the deceased. The three generations of his descendants, whose *piṇḍas* are offered directly to him, are, of course, "of the greatest service." But others, such as a daughter's son, whose *piṇḍas* reach him via an intermediary, are "of service" to him as well. Finally, there is a third category of survivors who are "of service," namely, all those who at their *pārvaṇaśrāddhas*

[5] On *piṇḍa* and *śrāddha*, see Colebrooke 1801; Donner 1870; Caland 1888, 1893, 1896; Winternitz 1890; Crooke 1908; Schrader 1909: 23-29; Macdonell 1921: 618; Sarvadhikari 1922: 660–64; Kane 1941: 472–73; Shastri 1963; Müller 1992; Prasad 1995; Saindon 1998: 45–71.

[6] And also by his daughter's son. This is important for the place which Jīmūtavāhana assigns to the daughter's son in the general order of heirs (section **11.2**).

offer *piṇḍas* to deceased persons to whom the deceased would have offered *piṇḍas*, had he been living. All these individuals are, according to Jīmūtavāhana, included among a deceased person's *sapiṇḍas*.

Justice Dwaraka Nath Mitter[7] was first to point out that, in the *Dāyabhāga*, "the whole theory of inheritance is founded upon the principle of spiritual benefit, and . . . it is by this principle, and this principle alone, that every question relating to it must be determined" (1870: 35). Mitter appealed to "spiritual benefit" as a principle to include among the *sapiṇḍas* even a relative—in that case, a paternal uncle's daughter's son—who is not explicitly mentioned as an heir in the *Dāyabhāga*.

Mitter's absolute trust in spiritual benefit as the overarching principle of interpretation of *Dāyabhāga* law of inheritance has been challenged.[8] Those who believed that Jīmūtavāhana's goal was only to reform certain aspects of preexisting *Mitākṣarā* law held that the text of the *Dāyabhāga* ought to be construed narrowly and that on any point on which the *Dāyabhāga* is silent *Mitākṣarā* law applies.[9] Yet, Jīmūtavāhana's view of inheritance has continued to be seen as closely related to the idea of the survivor being "of service" to the deceased and, hence, to *śrāddha* and the offering of *piṇḍas*. To quote a modern treatise on Hindu law:

> The Dayabhaga lays down the principle of religious efficacy as the ruling canon in determining the order of succession; consequently it rejects the preference of agnates to cognates, which distinguishes the other system, and arranges and limits the cognates upon principles peculiar to itself. (Mayne 1950: 55)

The Origin of the Bengal School

Since Jīmūtavāhana has often been considered as having been later than the author of the *Mitākṣarā*, and because of the general belief that he was the founder of the

[7] On D. N. Mitter, see Sanyal 1883.

[8] Jolly (1885: 168–75) went into great detail to show that offering *piṇḍas* and acceding to the inheritance were not coincidental, not only in India generally but also not in Bengal. Cf. J. N. Bhattacharya 1893: 477–87. According to Derrett, "As a theory in itself 'spiritual benefit' has been shown again and again to be hollow, since the actual *performance* of the duty is not required, for many may perform who do not succeed, and many that succeed do not perform it" (1968: 116). Yet, Sarvadhikari, whose *Tagore Law Lectures* are known as *The Principles of the Hindu Law of Inheritance*, and according to whom "the rule of propinquity is the governing principle in succession, not only in the Mitakshara School, but also, we are bold to affirm, in the Dayabhaga School" (1922: 750), nevertheless opened his first lecture as follows: "The subject of the present course of lectures is 'The Nature and Origin of the Śraddha Ceremonies, and the Gradual Development of the Principles of Inheritance in the different Schools of Hindu Law'" (1922: 1).

[9] E.g., G. C. Sarkar: *Vyavahāraprakāśa* 1879: xii, *Dāyatattva* 1904: viii, and 1927: 498. Also Sen 1918: 161–62.

Bengal school, much attention has been paid in recent scholarly literature to the question of how and why the Bengal school came into existence.

I mentioned earlier that, even though the *Mitākṣarā* and the *Dāyabhāga* comment on the same body of *smṛti* texts, they do present different solutions. One of the premises that have dominated scholarship on Hindu law on this subject is that the differences between the two texts—and, for that matter, between all commentaries and digests—reflect differences in local customs and usages. According to Setlur, for instance, "no Hindu writer could hope to impose his treatise on his community or province without taking good care to bring it into harmony with their legal consciousness as expressed in their customs" (1907: 204).[10] The resulting assumption has been that "closer investigation into the systems of law prevailing in the different provinces of India with the aid of the history of their peoples seems to me to lead to the discovery of the true causes of their uniformity and differences" (S. C. Mitra 1905: 383). In the case of the *Dāyabhāga* that meant that one had to look for elements that would explain why the law of inheritance in Bengal was "different" from that of other parts of India as represented primarily by the chapter on inheritance in the *Mitākṣarā*.

As far as Jīmūtavāhana's definition of *piṇḍa* and his application of the concept of "being of service" to the deceased to decide the order of succession are concerned, I might refer to the attempt by G. C. Sarkar (*Dāyatattva* 1904: xxxviii–xlii) to explain Jīmūtavāhana's preference for some "dear and near cognates" over agnates in the context of the move of five brahmans—Jīmūtavāhana's ancestors——and five kāyasthas from Kanauj to Bengal under king Ādiśūra (see earlier). The newcomers, who were considered superior in rank, were given in marriage several daughters of the earlier residents of the same castes. These wives continued to reside and raised their children in their own fathers' houses, with the result that their offspring developed close relations not only with their agnates, as was to be expected, but also with some of their cognates. That would explain "why in Bengal the law of succession was changed" in favor of cognates. S. C. Mitra, by contrast, emphasized the impact of Buddhism, which, in his opinion, was stronger and of longer duration in Bengal than elsewhere. Under the influence of Buddhism, "natural affection and not the technical bond of agnatic relationship became the basis of the law of inheritance" (1905: 389). He also referred to Tantrism and the role it accords to various forms of the Goddess, to account for "a violent inroad into the patriarchical system, which confined the devolution of property to the male agnatic relations" (p. 390).

[10] Cf. Sarvadhikari 1922: 258; Mayne 1950: 321. Occasionally one finds this cause-effect relation reversed: "The Commentator puts his own gloss on the ancient text; and his authority having been received in one and rejected in another part of *India*, Schools with conflicting doctrines arose" (*Collector of Madura* v. *Mootoo Ramalinga* [1868] 12 M.I.A. 397, 435). Or both views are combined: "Their doctrines may often have moulded usage but still more frequently the doctrines have themselves been moulded according to the prevailing usage of which they are only the recorded expression" (*Jogdamba Koer* v. *Secretary of State for India in Council* [1889] 16 Cal. 367, 375).

None of these arguments have been widely approved.[11] First, scholars recognized that, rather than being an effort to bring the ancient texts into conformity with a custom peculiar to Bengal, Jīmūtavāhana's views on *piṇḍa* and on the connection between inheritance and *śrāddha* were actually closer to the ancient *smṛti* texts than those of Vijñāneśvara. According to Kane,

> many of the passages from the Dharmasūtras are capable of being explained away on the theory of Vijñāneśvara, but one cannot help feeling on a careful study of the Dharmasūtras that the ancient sūtra writers saw an intimate connection between taking the inheritance and the offering of *Piṇḍas* and laid little emphasis on mere relationship by blood. (1921–23: 79)

Similarly, in Derrett's (1978) opinion, Jīmūtavāhana's principle of spiritual benefit "was more true to the Hindu tradition than the much more sophisticated and difficult conceptions developed for the Peninsula by Vijñāneśvara in his *Mitākṣarā*."[12] According to Mayne (1950: 56) too, it was not Jīmūtavāhana's but Vijñāneśvara's definition that represented "a distinct departure from the earlier theory of sapindaship as being 'community of funeral oblations.'"

Second, some scholars objected to the appropriateness of the principle of spiritual benefit, at least in modern days, when the *pārvaṇaśrāddha*, the very occasion on which the living can be "of service" to the deceased, "has become obsolete among the Hindus and is not generally celebrated at all" (G. C. Sarkar *Dāyatattva* 1904: xiv).[13] In addition, some objected to the principle based on the argument that the *pārvaṇaśrāddha* ceremony is not performed to be of service to the deceased, but for the performer's benefit alone (G. C. Sarkar 1910: 337).

Third, even though it has been widely held that "the doctrine of spiritual benefit [was] introduced for the first time, by the founder of the Bengal school" (G. C. Sarkar 1927: 498),[14] I have shown elsewhere (Rocher 1992), not only that the principle is earlier than Jīmūtavāhana since he explicitly attributes it to some of his predecessors but also, more important, that it is not typically Bengali, since one of these predecessors is the Śilāhāra king Aparārka who ruled on India's west coast in present-day Surat District or even farther south.

[11] Influence of Buddhism on *Dāyabhāga* law was rejected by Setlur (1907: 219) and Kane (1946: 559). Derrett (1965b) demonstrated that the *Mahānirvāṇatantra*, on which Mitra relied heavily, is, in fact, "a juridical fabrication of early British India."

[12] Cf. *Lallubhái Bhápubhái* v. *Mánkuvarbhái* (1878) 2 Bom. 338, 423–24. According to a dissenting opinion, however, "[the *smṛtis*] leave absolutely no room for doubt that the theory of spiritual benefit as understood by the Bengal lawyers, was absolutely unknown to the Hindu Lawgivers" (P. Ghose 1917: 31).

[13] More elaborately, G. C. Sarkar 1910: 335–36. Colebrooke noted, as early as 1801, that "in most provinces the periods for these sixteen ceremonies, and for the concluding obsequies entitled *Sapiṇḍana*, are anticipated, and the whole is concluded on the second or third day; after which they are again performed at the proper times, but in honour of the whole set of progenitors instead of the deceased singly" (1873: 2.180).

[14] The same idea appears as early as Mayne 1878: 7. According to Derrett (1978), "Jīmūtavāhana discovered a principle, the famous principle of 'spiritual benefit', which he could use, like a knife, to cut his way through the jungle of texts, and to discover harmony amongst authorities which had previously been discrepant."

There have also been attempts to use Bengali history and customs to account for the absence of ownership by birth and the absolute power of alienation by the head of the family. According to S. C. Mitra, the Aryans came only late to Bengal, and those who came were very enterprising and fully integrated with a population that was actively engaged in navigation by river and by sea. "In fact, in the earlier centuries of the Christian era, Bengal was one of the great centres of the old world" (1905: 385). Setlur, who, as indicated earlier, rejected Mitra's references to Buddhism and Tantrism to explain Jīmūtavāhana's preference for a number of cognates over agnates, on the contrary, considers that his "explanation of the individual ownership prevalent in Bengal is perfectly justified" (1907: 219).[15] It is, he says, a striking illustration of the fact that the legal theories of the commentators are rooted in local customs. "The peculiar geographical character of the province made it, from time immemorial, a leading centre of trade. To a trading community any clog on the free transfer of property is very inconvenient. Therefore, even in a joint family, its members always had the power of alienation. Jimutavahana, the author of the Dayabhaga, with his great dialectical skill, gave a textual sanction to this by spelling out from the ancient texts a new theory of vested interests. He made the family spoken of by the Rishis to be a tenancy-in-common" (pp. 218–19).

J. C. Ghose (1917: 1.xvii–xviii), according to whom the *Dāyabhāga* was written at the court of Jalāl-ud-dīn Muhammad Shāh in the fifteenth century (see earlier), offered an entirely different interpretation, namely, that Jīmūtavāhana's efforts at "overthrowing the old ideas" were "the direct result of the prevailing Muhammadan influence."[16]

In reality, Jīmūtavāhana's views, first, that proprietary rights do not take effect at the time of birth and, second, that one only inherits after the previous owner's death, undoubtedly antedate "the founder of the Bengal school." The fact that Vijñāneśvara, who is definitely not more recent than Jīmūtavāhana, rejects these views at great length, in and of itself constitutes adequate proof of that conclusion.

In addition, Pratāparudra's *Sarasvatīvilāsa* (C.E. 1500–1525, Kane 1975: 875) clearly opposes both views on the origin of proprietary rights, and attributes each of them to specific writers. Pratāparudra (ed. p. 347; tr. nos. 19–20) assigns the view that *dāya* means the kind of property in which one acquires a right of ownership merely by being related to the owner to "Asahāya, Vijñānayogin (= Vijñāneśvara), and others." Asahāya's commentary on the chapter on inheritance of the *Nārada-smṛti* has not been preserved, but the phrase which Pratāparudra uses is identical with the definition of *dāya* in the *Mitākṣarā*.[17] Elsewhere (ed. p. 344; tr. no. 8) Pratāparudra defines *dāya* as "paternal property that becomes fit for partition."[18] He attributes that definition to "Bhāruci, Aparārka, and others,"[19] and he, not a Bengali but a Southerner, adds that that is the only correct definition. The fact that, besides Bhāruci and Aparārka, two other authors, Saṃgrahakāra and Bho-

[15] Kane (1946: 559) objects to this part of Misra's argument, as he does to the influence of Buddhism and Tantrism, on the grounds that commerce and seafaring were more prominent on the west coast of India than in Bengal.

[16] Elsewhere, speaking of the Bengal school, Ghose reiterates that "it is clear that it is the old Hindu Law modified by Muhammadan ideas of individual property" (1917: 2.xv).

[17] *Yat svāmisambandhād eva nimittād anyasya svaṃ bhavati tad dāyaśabdenocyate.*

[18] *Vibhāgārhaṃ pitṛdravyaṃ dāyam.*

[19] Pratāparudra does not mention Jīmūtavāhana.

jadeva, also held the view that property can be acquired solely in the ways laid down in the *śāstras* (i.e., not by birth), has been recorded in various later Sanskrit texts.[20] Here again we are faced not only with authors, some of whom (Bhāruci, Saṃgrahakāra, and Bhojadeva) undeniably preceded Jīmūtavāhana, but also all of whom lived outside Bengal.

In conclusion, from a historical point of view Jīmūtavāhana cannot have been "the founder of the Bengal school." In fact, the legal principles that have become characteristic traits of the Bengal school of inheritance were not even typically Bengali before Colebrooke translated the *Dāyabhāga*, in 1810. As I have pointed out elsewhere (Rocher 1972), Colebrooke was first to speak of "schools of Hindu law." There may have been a number of circumstances that led him to do so, but he eventually became instrumental in steering Hindu law under British rule and even in independent India in a new direction. Speaking of the differences between *Mitākṣarā* law and *Dāyabhāga* law, Lord Hobhouse, for the Privy Council, stated: "it appears to [their Lordships] that . . . from the earliest times, there have been two conflicting principles of law: one favouring the perpetual integrity and the fixed succession of family property, and the other the free use of such property for the circumstances of the day."[21]

Like all commentators and writers of *nibandhas*, Jīmūtavāhana was faced with these conflicting—from an orthodox point of view only apparently conflicting—*smṛti* texts on the subject of inheritance. It was his task to interpret these texts as one consistent and harmonious whole. He did so to the best of his abilities, while all the time trying to improve on the interpretations offered by his predecessors:

> *Dāya-bhāga* has repeatedly been the object of disagreements among scholars, because they failed properly to understand the relevant texts of Manu and others. I therefore consider it my duty correctly to define *dāya-bhāga* for their instruction. Pay attention, learned men. [**1.1**]

[20] On these texts, see, e.g., Jolly 1885: 109; Kane 1968: 538.

[21] *Rao Balwant Singh* v. *Rani Kishori* (1898) 25 I.A. 54, 71; 20 All. 267, 412. Cf. Mayne 1950: 55.

THE TRANSLATION

As I indicated earlier, Jīmūtavāhana's *Dāyabhāga* has been translated only once, in 1810, by Henry Thomas Colebrooke, at that time a *puisne* judge in the Calcutta Supreme Court.[1] Colebrooke's translation, produced solely on the basis of manuscripts and with the help of pandits,[2] has been criticized both for being opaque and obscure and for not always rendering the Sanskrit text correctly:

> Unfortunately his own education in England before he left for India had stopped at the stage at which the statuesque and the verbose were considered good style during the decay of the classical English of the mid-eighteenth century. Thus, in places where he (or his pandits) was not actually mistaken (and they are not a mere handful), he has always been obscure, and many students of Sanskrit have found the original plainer than the translation. (Derrett 1978: n.p.)

There are indeed passages where Colebrooke misunderstood the Sanskrit text. No one has pointed this out more clearly, yet more understandingly, than Theodor Goldstücker. Speaking of the early translations of Sanskrit legal texts generally,[3] Goldstücker concluded that "on the whole" one can say that "the present English translations of the law books can be implicitly relied upon as an equivalent for the originals" (1871: 10). And he went on to single out for special praise the translations by Colebrooke:

> And of all translations from Sanskrit into a European language I know of none to which, in my opinion, greater admiration is due than to the translation of Jímútaváhana and Vijnáneśvara's law of inheritance by Colebrooke. So great, indeed, was the conscientiousness of that scholar, so thorough his understanding of the Hindu mind, and so vast and accurate his Sanskrit learning, that there is always the strongest reason for hesitation whenever one might feel disposed to question a rendering of his.

On the other hand, Goldstücker, who was concerned primarily with "ensuring to litigants a proper administration of the Hindu law" (p. 6), fully realized that, even if the mistakes in the early translations were due mainly to the imperfect condition of

[1] For a biography of Colebrooke, see Colebrooke 1873, vol. 1; on his remarkable contributions to Sanskrit scholarship, see Rocher 1984.

[2] Colebrooke's own, annotated manuscript of the *Dāyabhāga* is preserved at the India Office Library. See Description of Manuscripts (L1).

[3] Most early translations of Sanskrit legal texts are reprinted in Setlur 1911. The bibliography in this volume includes references to Setlur for each translation.

the manuscripts used by the translators, "it is clear that they may become a serious impediment to rightful claims, and obstruct the course of justice" (p. 15).[4]

Whereas one may hope that today errors in the translation can be avoided, or corrected,[5] the expectation to produce translations of commentaries and digests of Hindu law that will escape the labels "opaque" and "obscure" presents a far greater challenge. Some of the early translators themselves overtly vented their frustration in their prefaces. To quote J. C. C. Sutherland, the translator of Kubera's *Dattaka-candrikā* and Nandapaṇḍita's *Dattakamīmāṃsā*:

> The method in which *Hindu* lawyers, (and indeed *Hindu* writers in general,) treat every subject, is highly uncongenial to the *European* taste: and in fact, in order to acquire or retain a correct knowledge of the subject, treated on, and the author's peculiar opinions, indistinctly blended, as they often are, with those of others, it is necessary to devote much attentive application, — genarally more, than inclination and leisure will admit of being bestowed, by the officers entrusted with the administration of civil justice in *India*. (1834: iv)

Sutherland realized that his translation "in many places, unavoidably partakes of the obscurity of the original" (p. vi). The author of the first English treatise on Hindu law, F. W. Macnaghten, went even further, and put the blame for the fact that "translators have their merit, but it does not follow that translations have their use," squarely on the Sanskrit texts themselves:[6]

> If we find nothing but perplexity and confusion, disorder and deformity, the fault is not his [= the translator's]. He is not answerable for the defects of his originals, nor ought he be held responsible for the uselessnes of his own labours. He does not undertake to alter the nature of things; and that which is unavailing when known, might as well have remained in concealment. (1824: xvi–xvii)

[4] As far as the *Dāyabhāga* is concerned, Goldstücker (pp. 11–14) singled out three passages: **4.3.31**, **4.3.36**, and **11.6.3**. See the notes to the translation.

[5] Opinions on the accuracy, or the lack thereof, of translations by Colebrooke and others continued to be divided among scholars of Hindu law. Speaking of Colebrooke's translation of the *Mitākṣarā*, Morley said that "it is impossible to rate too highly the utility of this translation" (1858: 218), and the *Dāyabhāga* translation "is annotated, commented upon, and illustrated with equal ability and learning" (p. 221). According to S. C. Sarkar, Colebrooke translated both texts "with accuracy and fidelity" (1883: xxx), and J. N. Bhattacharya judged that "Mr. Colebrooke's translations are as nearly accurate as any English translation can possibly be" (1885: iii–iv). V. N. Mandlik, however, was of the opinion that Colebrooke's translation "requires revision and examination" (*Vyavahāramayūkha* 1880: II.lxix). While Colebrooke's translations were occasionally questioned in the law courts, they remained the last and only resort: "It is unfortunate that we have only one translation known to me and others, viz., Colebrooke's" (*Rajani Nath Das* v. *Nitai Chandra Dey* [1920] 32 C.L.J. 333, 353; 48 Cal. 643, 649).

[6] Only rarely was the blame put equally squarely on the translators. Yet, T. Kristnasawmy Iyer's qualifications as a translator of Devaṇṇa Bhaṭṭa's *Smṛticandrikā* (1867) were questioned immediately and at length by Grady (1868: xlix).

The principal reasons for this disappointment, both on the part of the translators of the Sanskrit texts and on the part of those who were called upon to use the translations in legal practice, are threefold: the peculiar format in which the translations were presented, the fact that the texts were embedded in an ancient and complex civilization with which the early translators and their clientele were not familiar, and the misconceived expectation that the authors of the commentaries and digests were lawyers writing for lawyers. I will address these three points separately in the following pages and indicate how they affect the new translation of the *Dāyabhāga*.

Formatting the New Translation

Jīmūtavāhana's *Dāyabhāga* has been heralded as "one of the most striking compositions in the whole department of Indian Jurisprudence" (Jolly 1885: 21); it has been said that "it is certainly remarkable for its logic, lucidity and power" (Mayne 1950: 50); and Jīmūtavāhana has been praised as "der grösste der indischen Juristen" (Kohler 1910: 237). Be that as it may, the *Dāyabhāga* has also been called the "most difficult of all Hindu law-books" (J. N. Bhattacharya 1885: 27). In fact, Bhattacharya echoes a view I have heard many times in Bengal with reference to the *Dāyabhāga*, to the effect that "the style is so peculiar, that even native scholars, well versed in Sanskrit, never attempt the study of their legal treatises without the help of a teacher." As I indicated earlier, in the case of the *Dāyabhāga* there are several potential "teachers," that is, commentators, and Jīmūtavāhana's text is rarely, if ever, studied without the help of one of them, most often with the help of Śrīkṛṣṇa Tarkālaṃkāra. Yet, as I also mentioned earlier, the several commentators repeatedly disagree in their interpretations of crucial *Dāyabhāga* passages. In such cases Colebrooke often added their differing explanations in footnotes. Although I, too, occasionally refer to the commentators, I attempt above all to understand and translate the *Dāyabhāga* as Jīmūtavāhana wrote it, and only secondarily as it was interpreted by the commentators.

The greatest challenge for any reader of the *Dāyabhaga* is to follow and understand the often tortuous flow of Jīmūtavāhana's reasoning and argumentation. In an effort to make the author's reasoning and argumentation clear to the reader of this translation, I deviate considerably from the way in which Colebrooke arranged his in 1810.

Colebrooke presented his translation of the *Dāyabhāga* in the form of a law book, a code. Expectations ran high in Calcutta, at the end of the eighteenth and the beginning of the nineteenth centuries, that codes "compiled agreeably to the laws and tenets of the Mahometans and Gentoos" would contribute considerably "to render more complete the Judicial Regulations, to preclude arbitrary and partial judgments, and to guide the decisions of the several Courts."[7] When Sir William Jones wrote in 1786 of hiring pandits and *maulvis* to prepare a digest "like that of Tribonian," he added:

> Could I afford to pay them, I would begin with giving them a plan divided into Books, Chapters, and Sections; and would order them to collect the most appropriate texts under each head, with the names of the Authors, and their Works, and with *the chapters and verses of them*. (Cannon 1970: 721; emphasis added)

It should not come as a surprise, then, that Colebrooke took the initiative to divide the *Dāyabhāga* into chapters (fifteen), the longer chapters into sections (from two to six), and all chapters and sections into articles. Even though, except for quotations from the *dharmaśāstras*, works such as the *Dāyabhāga* are entirely in prose, Colebrooke's articles were often, though inappropriately, referred to as "verses."

In reality, the subdivisions introduced by Colebrooke in the *Dāyabhāga*—and in the *Mitākṣarā*, as well as by others in their translations of similar texts—were foreign to the Sanskrit originals. In the manuscripts all these texts are written in *scriptura continua* without any reference to numbers for chapters and their subdivisions.

With few exceptions, though, Colebrooke's chapters and sections do reflect indications to that effect in the original *Dāyabhāga* text. As authors of *nibandhas* and other Sanskrit works are wont to do, Jīmūtavāhana consistently introduces new topics with sentences starting with words such as *atha*, *idānīm*, or *samprati*, all of which can be translated as "now, next." Most often, although not consistently, those sentences are preceded by other sentences beginning with the word *iti*, "thus far for," the usual way to indicate that a chapter or a section of a book has come to an end. There is no reason not to maintain Colebrooke's chapters and sections in the new translation.

Colebrooke's subdivision of the chapters and sections into articles, however, creates major problems for a correct understanding of the text. First, it totally obliterates the important separation between the quotations from the ancient *dharma-sūtras* and *dharma-śāstras* on the one hand, and Jīmūtavāhana's commentary on the other.[8] I clearly signal the former by indenting the translations. In addition, when Jīmūtavāhana quotes more than one ancient text in succession in order to illustrate one particular point, often separating these by his own commentary and, occasionally even inserting another text or texts to illustrate his own

[7] From a letter by Warren Hastings to the Court of Directors, March 1773 (*Proceedings of the Governor and Council at Fort William respecting the administration of justice among the natives in Bengal*, 1774, p. 33, quoted by Morley 1858: 191–92).

[8] The situation is even worse in Colebrooke's translation of the *Mitākṣarā*. Not only does the translation not signal other *smṛti* texts which Vijñāneśvara quotes in his commentary, but even the basic Yājñavalkya verses on which the *Mitākṣarā* comments are not easily traced.

commentary, I mark the basic sequence of the *smṛti* texts by means of "[A]," "[B]," "[C]," and so forth.[9]

Second, as far as Jīmūtavāhana's commentary is concerned, "the division into small paragraphs . . . is very misleading, since one might fancy them to be complete in themselves, whereas in the generality of instances they may be only isolated links in a long chain of argument" (G. C. Sarkar *Vyavahāraprakāśa* 1879: xv).[10] Indeed, like other commentators, Jīmūtavāhana is engaged in a continuous discourse, arguing again and again, often at great length, with named or anonymous opponents, and trying to prove that his understanding and interpretation of the ancient Texts is more correct and coherent than theirs.[11]

Quotations from named predecessors are mostly, though not always, clearly marked in the Sanskrit text. I insert them in quotation marks. Jīmūtavāhana's discussions of them are normally also clearly marked.

Quotations from unnamed authors, whether real or imaginary, are indicated in the Sanskrit text by means of markers which all commentators employ to present prima facie views (*pūrvapakṣa*): either *nanu* . . . or . . . *iti cet* or *na ca* . . . *iti vācyam*. I introduce such sections with "[Objection]" or "[Question]." These are invariably followed by Jīmūtavāhana's own views, which I label "[Refutation]" or "[Answer]."

Finally, rather than translating the introductory words to successive arguments in the prose discussions in the *Dāyabhāga* literally as "moreover," "besides," "in addition," etc.,[12] I number the arguments "[1]," "[2]," "[3]," and so on, and, wherever necessary, I further subdivide them into "[a]," "[b]," "[c]," and so forth.[13]

[9] See, e.g., the beginning of section **4.1**.The first (Vi 17.18) and the second (M 9.194 = K 894) definitions of female property are separated by K 899–900 which define one of the categories of female property listed at Vi 17.18, plus Jīmūtavāhana's commentary on both K and Vi. The passage that separates the third (N 13.8) and the fourth (Y 2.143) definitions is even more complex. Neither the Sanskrit text nor Colebrooke's translation separates the four definitions from the intervening discussions.

[10] See, e.g., section **6.2**. A first quotation from Śrīkara (**41**) is followed by a refutation (**42**). The second quotation and its refutation form one "article" (**43**). The third quotation (**44**) is again followed by a separate refutation (**45**). In fact, Colebrooke did not always divide the *Dāyabhāga* into "small paragraphs"; some of his "articles" are excessively long. See, e.g, **2.37**.

[11] Cf. J. N. Bhattacharya: "The Hindu law treatises in Sanskrit deal chiefly with the interpretation and reconciliation of Sanhita texts" (1885: iv), and G. C. Sarkar: "The Mitákṣará and the Dáyabhága purport to be the mere commentaries on the Smrtis, and bear no resemblance to Codes of law" (*Dāyatattva* 1904: ix).

[12] It is not always immediately clear with what these terms correlate.

[13] I might mention here two other conventions that bear on the formatting of the translation. First, I introduce titles and subtitles in bold type; none of these are part of the Sanskrit original. Second, when Jīmūtavāhana refers to a *vacana*, i.e., a text from a *smṛti*, rather than resorting to cumbersome phrases such as "canonical text" or "authoritative text," I use the term "Text," with capital T. When he specifically refers to a *śruti* text, i.e., a text from the Vedas, I use the phrase "Revealed Text."

As a result, the format of the new translation only occasionally corresponds to Colebrooke's subdivision of the *Dāyabhāga* into articles. Yet, since in all editions of the Sanskrit text since 1863, in all law reports, and in all treatises and other studies on Hindu law, the *Dāyabhāga* has been quoted according to Colebrooke's subdivisions, I insert them in the translation: "<1>," "<2>," "<3>," and so on, and continue to use them as references.

The *Dāyabhāga* and Indian Culture

A second problem facing the translator, not only of the *Dāyabhāga*, but of all similar Sanskrit texts, stems from the fact that the authors of these texts repeatedly have recourse to terms and concepts that are unique to Indian culture and civilization and, as a result, often defy translation into a Western language. Earlier in this introduction I already introduced the various terms connected with ancestor worship.

Similarly, Jīmūtavāhana refers to a number of *saṃskāras* (**3.38**), a term that is most often translated as "sacraments," but which more appropriately indicates the several "rites of passage" a Hindu goes through, even before conception (*garbhādhāna*, **7.4**), and, later, *puṃsavana* and *sīmantonnayana* (**9.28**), *upanayana* (**5.5**), and marriage. When a male is referred to as *saṃskṛta* "having undergone *the rite* of passage" it usually means that he underwent the *upanayana*; when the same term is used for a female, it means that she went through the wedding ceremony, which is the single *saṃskāra* for women. The investiture with the sacred thread (*upanayana*), which is conceived as a second birth, makes the boy of one of the three higher castes (*varṇa*)[14] into a *dvija*, "twice-born," and introduces him to the first *āśrama*, "stage of life," that of a *brahmacārin*. Marriage leads to the second stage, that of a householder (*gṛhastha*, **1.33**), which in turn is followed by two other stages, that of a forest-dweller (*vana-prastha*, "one who has left for the forest") and of a renouncer (*sannyāsin*).[15] The traditional eight forms of wedding (**4.3.4**) determine whether some of the female property of a woman who dies childless goes to her husband or to her parents.

Of the twelve different kinds of sons (**10.1, 7**), the ones most often mentioned in the *Dāyabhāga* are the full-fledged son (*aurasa*, **2.39, 59**), the son of an appointed daughter (*putrikā*, **2.39**), and the son of a levirate marriage (*kṣetraja*, **2.51**).

One Sanskrit term, which appears frequently in the *Dāyabhāga*, deserves special mention. I translate *pratigraha* (Colebrooke **1.24** "receipt," **9.17** "acceptance [of a pious donation]," **9.19** "acceptance of donation") as "a brahman's entitle-

[14] Not to complicate matters I use the term "caste" for each of the four *varṇas* (*brāhmaṇa*/brahman, *kṣatriya*, *vaiśya*, and *śūdra*), even though the term has acquired a different meaning today.

[15] On Jīmūtavāhana's use of the term *pravrajita*, which sometimes refers to the *vanaprastha* only, sometimes to both the *vanaprastha* and the *sannyāsin*, see note at **1.4**.

ment," that is, the reception of gifts that a brahman, and a brahman only, is entitled to as one of three ways of earning a livelihood (**1.24**). As far as inheritance is concerned, the principal question is whether the property a brahman acquires by way of *pratigraha* is subject to partition or not; according to Jīmūtavāhana, it is (**6.1.53**).

The *Dāyabhāga* as a Treatise on the Law of Inheritance

The *Dāyabhāga* is, first and foremost, a commentary on the ancient *smṛti* texts dealing with inheritance. Many of these Texts are, by their very nature, ambiguous, and often easily and naturally susceptible to different interpretations.[16] Like any commentator, Jīmūtavāhana did not hesitate to exploit the ambiguities in the Texts to his own advantage, and, "under the guise of interpretation, often moulded the ancient texts according to his own views of justice and expediency."[17] Since I am translating Jīmūtavāhana's *Dāyabhāga*, it is my task to translate the Texts as he interpreted them. Yet, if I do so, his own commentary, which accounts for his interpretations, often becomes redundant. When appropriate, I therefore maintain or draw attention to the ambiguities in the *smṛti* texts, so that the reader may appreciate Jīmūtavāhana's often peculiar interpretations.[18]

I use the term "appreciate" purposely. Indeed, to justify his interpretations, like, and perhaps more than, other commentators, Jīmūtavāhana appeals to a vast spectrum of traditional, panditic Hindu learning, most of which has little, if anything, to do with law and jurisprudence. The following remarks may serve to illustrate the kind of extralegal background Jīmūtavāhana brings to a treatise on the law of inheritance.

[16] On the problems judges in India faced when they were handed highly different English translations of the same *smṛti* texts, see Goldstücker 1871: 7–11.

[17] H. Chatterjee 1978: iv. In connection with **9.24, 26** Sir Asutosh Mookerjee referred to "texts . . . which they professed to interpret but which they often made subservient to their views" (*Rajani Nath Das* v. *Nitai Chandra Dey* [1920] 32 C.L.J. 333, 353; 48 Cal. 643, 649). Cf. Sarvadhikari on Medhātithi's commentary on the *Manusmṛti*: "Manu was certainly the basis of Medhātithi's law; but the great commentator knew how to read between the lines, and he gave such an explanation of Manu's texts, that the inspired lawgiver, had he risen again from the dead, would have had great difficulty in recognising them as his own" (1922: 247).

[18] Note that the Anglo-Indian law courts deliberately refused to be concerned with any potential different meaning(s) of the *smṛti* texts. In connection with K 921 (**11.1.56**), for instance, the Privy Council, while aware that "nothing is more certain than that, in dealing with the same ancient texts, the Hindu commentators have often drawn opposite conclusions," held that it was not their duty to investigate all possible implications of the ancient texts, but only to look at "the conclusions which the author of the Dayabhaga has himself drawn from them" (Sir Barnes Peacock in *Moniram Kolita* v. *Keri Kolitani* [1880] 5 Cal. 776, 785–86).

In the first place, Jīmūtavāhana was well trained in the field of grammar and allied areas of knowledge, and he postulates like learning from his readers. Without overtly quoting grammatical rules, he makes use of grammatical concepts and theories to establish a variety of legal points. For instance, he uses the term *pitrya* "paternal" to show that, in order for sons to inherit, their father must be deceased (**1.3**). The *kāraka* theory allows him to hold that a gift is valid prior to its acceptance (**1.22**) (Rocher 1976). He admits that the term *svīkāra* is a *cvi* compound but proves that one can be an owner prior to appropriation nevertheless (**1.23**). Analyzing a nominal compound as as *tatpuruṣa* is preferable to interpreting it as a *bahuvrīhi* (**2.59**). Jīmūtavāhana rejects (**3.2**) and accepts (**4.1.6**) the interpretation of a Text by means of the principle of ellipsis (*ekaśeṣa*). He maintains that, even when two items are not united in a *dvandva* compound, they can be related by *itaretarayoga* (**4.2.2**). He relies on a grammatical rule to prove that only the woman called *patnī* inherits (**11.1.49**).

On a number of occasions, Jīmūtavāhana alludes to the *Dhātupāṭha*, the list of verbal roots and their meanings attached to grammatical treatises such as Pāṇini's *Aṣṭādhyāyī*: compare his remarks on the roots *bhaj* (**1.6**), *yu* (**4.2.14**), *vid* (**6.2.17**), and others. And he engages in the kind of etymologies that are characteristic of the Indian tradition, as on *dāya* (**1.4**), *putra* (**1.36** and elsewhere), *ādhivedanika* (**4.1.14**), *saudāyika* (**4.1.22**), and *paṅgu* (**5.10**).

In addition to grammar and related fields, commentators like Jīmūtavāhana also rely on two of the six schools of Indian philosophy (*darśana*). In one of his attempts to account for the difference between the *Mitākṣarā* and the *Dāyabhāga* schools of Hindu law, Colebrooke wrote as follows:

> The written law, whether it be *sruti* or *smriti*, direct revelation or traditional, is subject to the same rules of interpretation. Those rules are collected in the *Mímánsá*, which is a disquisition on proof and authority of precepts. It is considered as a branch of philosophy; and is properly the logic of the law.
>
> In the eastern part of India, viz. Bengal and Bahar, where the Vedas are less read, and the *Mímánsá* less studied than in the south, the dialectic philosophy, or *Nyáya*, is more consulted, and is there relied on for rules of reasoning and interpretation upon questions of law, as well as upon metaphysical topics. Hence have arisen two principal sects or schools, which, construing the same text variously, deduce upon some important points of law different inferences from the same maxims of law. (1825: 1.314)[19]

Colebrooke knew that Bengal was renowned for its development of the school of *navya-nyāya*, "new logic," starting with Gaṅgeśa's *Tattvacintāmaṇi*, and including a vast literature, both of commentaries and supercommentaries of Gaṅgeśa's text and of independent treatises. He knew that in the *ṭols*, the schools of traditional learning in Bengal, the two main topics of instruction were *navya-nyāya* and

[19] Colebrooke's idea that the difference between the *Dāyabhāga* and the *Mitākṣarā* schools of Hindu law resulted from their relying primarily on *nyāya* and *mīmāṃsā*, respectively, has been adopted by other scholars. See, e.g., Elberling 1844: 15.

dharmaśāstra.[20] In fact, he could not help facing *navya-nyāya* firsthand while reading the commentaries on the *Dāyabhāga*; as I indicated earlier, he described Śrīkṛṣṇa as "a very acute logician" (1810: vi).

Colebrooke's statement to the effect that the Bengal school was greatly influenced by the *nyāya* system of philosophy has been quoted approvingly in later scholarly literature. According to Panchanan Ghose, for example, "from this overwhelming influence of the Nyaya system, Jimutavahana neither did nor could make himself free" (1917: 27). Yet, Ghose also demonstrated that Jīmūtavāhana antedated Gaṅgeśa and the *navya-nyāya* school (p. 28), and his arguments were drawn, not from the *Dāyabhāga*, but from the *Vyavahāramātṛkā*.

In reality, there is little *nyāya* in the *Dāyabhāga*. Only once (**11.3.5**) does Jīmūtavāhana refer to *anumāna*, "inference," one of the principal topics in Indian logic, and does he use the technical terms *vyāpaka* and *vyāpta*, for the *probandum* and the *probans*, respectively; the common term *vyāpti*, which indicates the correct concomitance between the *vyāpta* and the *vyāpaka*, does not appear in the *Dāyabhāga*. And, even though there was scope to introduce its derivatives *avyāpti* and *ativyāpti*, which indicate that the definition of a word is too narrow or too broad (**1.6**), Jīmūtavāhana does not use the terms; instead of *ativyāpti*, he does use *atiprasaṅga* (**1.12**) and *atiprasakti* (**6.1.47**). On only two occasions (**6.1.27** and **11.1.57**) does he refer to the *nyāya* concepts of prior nonexistence (*prāg-abhāva*) and subsequent nonexistence (*pradhvaṃsa-abhāva*), and twice (**6.1.43, 45**) to the logical flaw called *vyabhicāra*.

Differently from *nyāya* and contrary to the statement by Colebrooke which I quoted earlier, *mīmāṃsā* is as omnipresent in the *Dāyabhāga* as it is in most other commentaries and digests dealing with aspects of Hindu law.[21]

Jaimini's *Mīmāṃsā-sūtras* and the commentaries on it are concerned with the correct exegesis of the Vedic (*śruti*) texts,[22] but the principles they established also govern the interpretation of the *dharma-sūtra* and *dharma-śāstra* (*smṛti*) texts. *Mīmāṃsā* categorizes Vedic and assimilated rules according to a variety of criteria. A Text is called *vidhi*, "outright injunction," when it establishes something that, without the injunction, would not be *prāpta*, "established," that is, failing the in-

[20] On the nature of and the activities in the *ṭols*, see, e.g., E. B. Cowell 1867; Chunder 1869: 1.23–44; and Long 1868 (passim).

[21] Colebrooke was the first Western scholar to comment on the important role *mīmāṃsā* plays in Sanskrit commentaries dealing with legal matters. In a lecture to the Royal Asiatic Society in 1826, after his return to England, he stated that "the logic of the *Mímánsá* is the logic of the law; the rule of interpretation of civil and religious ordinances" (1827: 317 = 1873: 2.342). For the most detailed treatment of this subject, see K. L. Sarkar 1909. Cf. also Kohler 1910, Sankararama Sastri 1926, and Nataraja Aiyyar 1952. Several modern treatises on *mīmāṃsā* include chapters on its application to legal texts, e.g., Jha 1911 and 1942a, Keith 1921, and Verpoorten 1987. Conversely, modern treatises on Hindu law deal with *mīmāṃsā* rules of interpretation, e.g., J. N. Bhattacharya 1893, Ganapathi Iyer 1915, J. C. Ghose 1917, and Kane 1962: 1283–1351.

[22] Neither Jaimini nor any of the three principal commentators on the *Mīmāṃsā-sūtras*, Śabara, Prabhākara, and Kumārila, are mentioned by name in the *Dāyabhāga*.

junction one would not know that the act has to be performed. A Text is a *niṣedha* or *pratiṣedha*, "negative injunction," if it prohibits doing something that, in the absence of the injunction, one might be inclined to do. If a Text prescribes or prohibits some-thing that is already *prāpta*, "established," either by another Text or by common sense (*nyāya-prāpta*), it is called *anuvāda*, "elaboration, amplification"; the sole purpose of an *anuvāda* is to praise or to condemn the act it refers to. Other types of rules mentioned in the *Dāyabhāga* include *niyama*, "admonitory injunction" (**1.27**), *parisaṃkhyā*, "injunction of exclusion" (**1.29**), and *paryudāsa*, "exception, proviso" (**5.1**). According to a different criterion, Texts are either *dṛṣṭa-artha*, "having a visible, mundane purpose," or, if they cannot be assigned such a purpose, they are *adṛṣṭa-artha*, "having an invisible, transcendent purpose" (**1.27**). According to a third criterion, some Texts are *kratv-artha*, "meant for, or reflecting on, the validity of the act," whereas other Texts are *puruṣa-artha*, "meant for, or reflecting on, the man, the performer of the act" (**6.1.44**).

In addition to these general principles of *mīmāṃsā*, Jīmūtavāhana also relies on a large number of specific *mīmāṃsā* chapters (*adhikaraṇa*) and rules (*nyāya*): the *holākā* chapter (**2.40**; **6.1.22, 27**), the *grahaikatva* rule (**6.1.15**), the *dvayoḥ praṇayanti* chapter (**11.5.16**), the rule of disconnection (*apaccheda nyāya*, **11.5.18**), the *ṣoḍaśi nyāya* (**11.5.21**), the rule of the *māṣa* and *mudga* beans (**13.16**), and others.

Finally, the commentators on the *Mīmāṃsā-sūtras* are wont to illustrate and debate the *sūtras* with numerous and detailed references to the complex system of Vedic ritual. As a result, the general principles and the specific terminology of Vedic ritual are prominent in Jīmūtavāhana's *Dāyabhāga* as well. For instance, the reader is supposed to be familiar with the principle that the new and full moon sacrifices (*darśapūrṇamāsa*, **11.5.19**) constitute the prototype (*prakṛti*) of a number of ectypes (*vikṛti*) of the *iṣṭi* kind of ritual, whereas the *jyotiṣṭoma* (**6.1.41**) is the prototype of all rituals in which the *soma* plant is bought, pressed, and offered. In one single paragraph (**11.5.19**) Jīmūtavāhana introduces the following ritual terms, all of which are relevant to the new and full moon sacrifices: *cāturhotra mantra*, *pañcahotra mantra*, *aindradadhi*, *upāṃśuyāga*, *aindrapayas*, *agnīṣomīya*, and *āgneya*.

There is no doubt that, in the *Dāyabhāga* as elsewhere, "the allusions to *Mīmāṃsā* principles easily interfere with the flow of the argument" (Derrett 1978: n.p.). In a translation meant for the use of legal practitioners, the often elaborate *mīmāṃsā* arguments might as well be omitted. What counts in legal practice are the interpretations which the commentators and digest writers of the different schools of law have given of the ancient *smṛti* texts, not the *mīmāṃsā* rules they used to reach their interpretations; these rules "are of doubtful utility in the present day administration of Hindu law."[23] Colebrooke included the *mīmāṃsā* passages in his

[23] Mayne 1950: 39. Nevertheless, this eleventh edition of Mayne's *Treatise* devotes seven pages (pp. 32–39) to *mīmāṃsā* in the chapter on the sources of Hindu law.

translation nevertheless,[24] providing additional information in occasionally lengthy footnotes. In the *mīmāṃsā* passages, more than elsewhere, his translations are often obscure,[25] "and to stop long over Colebrooke's notes is equivalent to stumbling" (Derrett 1978: n.p.).[26] Yet, the *mīmāṃsā* passages in the *Dāyabhāga* are an integral part of Jīmūtavāhana's text, even as they are integral parts of any similar "legal" commentary or digest and, for that matter, of any commentary that claims to interpret texts of the *śruti* or *smṛti* tradition. They are, therefore, again included in the translation, and they are again accompanied by explanatory footnotes. While writing these notes, I have made an effort both to do justice to the learning of the author of the *Dāyabhāga* and to make *mīmāṃsā* concepts understandable to readers who are not familiar with this Indian form of scholasticism.

[24] He did so, even though the thought of omitting certain passages did occur to him. See his note in the preface to the *Digest*: "Should it appear to [the reader] that much of the commentary might have been omitted without injury to the context, . . . he will remember, that the translator could use no freedom with the text, but undertook a verbal translation of it." (1798 = 1874: 1.xxi).

[25] E.g., **1.34**: "Here also, to show, that the sons' property in their father's wealth arises from such causes as the extinction of his worldly affections, this one period of partition, known to be at his pleasure, is recited explanatorily: for the recital is conformable to the previous knowledge; and the right of ownership suggests that knowledge."

[26] Derrett's frustration is that of the Professor of Oriental Laws in the University of London, and an accomplished Sanskritist, who used Colebrooke's translation to teach Hindu law to students who did not know Sanskrit.

THE TEXT

The text of Jīmūtavāhana's *Dāyabhāga* published in this volume is based on the following manuscripts, many of which I collated in their entirety, but some of lesser importance only partly.

C1

Asiatic Society of Bengal.[1] #2374. Yellow country-made paper. 61 folios. 36.2 x 10.2 cm. 6 lines/ page. Bengali script. A second hand takes over from fol. 26b3. Complete. After **15.3**: *samāptaś cāyaṃ granthaḥ*. Adopts readings that are peculiar to Maheśvara. E.g., **2.83** *vyādhyādinā* for *vyādhinā.*

C2

Calcutta Sanskrit College (hence *CSC*).[2] *Smṛti* #188. Country-made paper. 54 + 1 folios 40 x 8.5 cm. 5–7 lines/page. Bengali script. Complete. Original readings often covered with paint and replaced by other readings. Omits **15.3**. After **15.2**: *iti śrījīmūtavāhanakṛtaṃ dāyabhāgaprakaraṇaṃ samāptam.*

C3

CSC. Smṛti #497. Country-made paper. 60 folios. 45 x 8 cm. Average 6 lines/page. Bengali script. Complete. Omits **15.3**. After **15.2**: *ity upādhyāyajīmūtavāhanakṛte dharmaratne dāyabhāgaḥ samāptaḥ // oṃ namo gurave namaḥ // śrī durgā.* The colophon, in two stanzas in *anuṣṭubh* meter, contains the name of the scribe:

śrīmadvandhipuraṃ cādhivasatā tv agrajanmanā /
likhitaṃ pustakaṃ yatnāt śrīmṛtyuñjayaśarmaṇā //
yena me hriyate pustī likhitā yatnato mayā /
jananī hriyate tena satataṃ nātra saṃśayaḥ //.

C4

CSC, Smṛti #913. Yellow country-made paper. 9 folios. 45 x 9 cm. 7 lines/page. Bengali script. Incomplete: **1.1–2.55**. Carelessly written. **2.9** *putram utpādye* for *putram utpādya*; leaves open spaces where the scribe was not able to read the original: **2.23** *na [.]kaṃ [. . .] cāsya* for *narakaṃ pīḍane cāsya.*

C5

CSC. Smṛti #1276. Red and white country-made paper. 55 folios. 48.5 x 9 cm. 6 lines/page. Bengali script. Complete. After **15.3**: *oṃ namo gurave namaḥ*. The colophon provides a date and the name of the scribe, in a stanza in *triṣṭubh* meter:

[. . .]jaivāhṛtayuktaśāke sūrye gate nautvarayā lilekha /

[1] Haraprasad Sastri: *A Descriptive Catalogue of Sanskrit Manuscripts in . . . the Asiatic Society of Bengal.* Vol. 3 Smṛti *Manuscripts.* Calcutta: Baptist Mission Press, 1925.

[2] Handwritten list of manuscripts. Hṛishikeśa Śāstrī and Śiva Chandra Gui #153 (p. 145) corresponds to C2, its #155 (p. 146) to C10.

pāṭhāya ramyaṃ ciradāyabhāgaṃ śrī indranārāyaṇadevaśarmā //.
This is followed by a stanza in *anuṣṭubh* meter:
yo saṃharati cauryeṇa pustakaṃ lobhamohitaḥ /
tasya pitur mukheśakṛt mātā tasya ca śukarī //.
and by: *śrīkṛṣṇaḥ śaraṇaṃ śrīrāmaḥ śaraṇaṃ oṃ namo lambodarāya / oṃ namo durgāyai namaḥ.*

C6

CSC. Smṛti #2795. Yellow country-made paper. 67 folios. 38 x 8 cm. 6 lines/page. Bengali script. Complete. Folios 56b–62a missing, but replaced by a more modern hand.

C7

CSC. Smṛti #2799. Yellow country-made paper. 75 folios. 47 x 8.5 cm. 4–5 lines/ page. Bengali script. Complete. Looks old; writing is fading. After **15.3**: *śrī durgā.*

C8

CSC. Smṛti #1291. Yellow country-made paper. 75 folios. 40.5 x 9 cm. 6 lines/ page. Bengali script. Complete. Many nonsensical scribal errors. Omits **15.3** After **15.2**: *ity upādhyāyajīmūtavāhanakṛte dharmaratne dāyabhāgaḥ samāptaḥ,* The colophon includes the name of the scribe and a date (C.E. 1817/18): *śrīraghunāthaśarmaṇaḥ svākṣaram idam / śakābdāḥ 1740 //.*

C9

CSC. Smṛti #1384. Red and yellow country-made paper. 59 folios. 46.5 x 8 cm. 6 lines/page. Bengali script. Complete. Looks old. The colophon includes the name of the scribe: *śrīkamalākāntaśarmaṇaḥ pustakam idaṃ svākṣaraṃ ca.*

C10

CSC. Smṛti #552. Colorless country-made paper. 7 folios. 48 x 9 cm. 6–7 lines/page. Bengali script. Incomplete: **1.1–2.42** *upārjakatvena.* Looks old; writing faded in places.

C11

CSC. Smṛti #816.[3] Red country-made paper. 39 x 9 cm. 7–8 lines/page. Bengali script. Incomplete: fol. 6b (**2.40** *jyeṣṭhapade cārjakaparam*)–fol.41a (**15.3**), but only 26 folios preserved. It ends with a stanza in *śārdūlavikrīḍita* meter, containing a date (*śaka* 1721 = C.E. 1799):

rādhānāthaüpendranāthacaraṇau natvā viṣṇūpāsitau
hantārau kaluṣaṃ vibhāvanakṣatradharmārthadau mokṣadau /
śāke viśvatturaṅgacandragaṇite jyaiṣṭhāṣṭaviṃśāṃśake
pustī sā vyalikhata budhasya divase jīmūtavānoditāṃ //.

C12

CSC. Smṛti #1385. Red country-made paper. 124 folios. 43 x 9 cm. 4 lines/page. Bengali script. Complete. It ends: *śrīśrīdurgā // śrīśrīkālī jayati // śriśrīgurave namaḥ // śrīśrīśivacaraṇe mama matir āstāṃ //.*

C13

CSC. Smṛti #1390. Red country-made paper. 1 folio + 2 lines on folio 2. 44 x 7 cm. 6 lines/page. Bengali script. Incomplete: **1.1–13** *tannidhanāt.* On folio 2b: *oṃ namo gaṇeśāya / atha dāyabhāganirṇayaḥ //.* The text of the *Dayabhāganirṇaya* ends abruptly on folio 14a1.

[3] Described in *A Descriptive Catalogue of the Sanskrit Manuscripts Preservedin the Library of Government Sanskrit College Calcutta, OH* 5.1, 1957, 15.

C14

CSC. Smṛti #1663. Yellow country-made paper. 63 folios. 47 x 8.5 cm. 4–5 lines/page. Bengali script. Incomplete: **1.1–11.5.9** *tad uktam.*

C15

CSC. Smṛti #1665. Yellow country-made paper. 18 folios. 45.5 x 8.5 cm. 5–6 lines/page. Bengali script. Incomplete: **1.1–3.35** *putrāṇā.*

C16

CSC. Smṛti #1666. Red country-made paper. 12 folios. 46 x 8.5 cm. 5–6 lines/page. Bengali script. Incomplete: **1.1–2.64** *kimca para.* Looks old; writing is fading.

C17

CSC. Smṛti #2062. Yellow country-made paper. 49 folios. 47 x 8.5 cm. 6 lines/page. Bengali script. Complete. It ends: *śrīśrīkālī kuladāyinī.*

C18

CSC. Smṛti #2180. Country-made paper. 64 folios. 40 x 9.5 cm. 6 lines/page. Bengali script. Complete. It ends with a poorly written stanza in *pṛthvī* meter, including the name of the scribe and a date:

bṛhaspati<sa>rit patikṣitidharasthirā saṃmite
śake śanidine śraṭau grahaniteścake (?) *sadmani* /
bhavābdhibhavadaḥ anudbhavavadhūpadaṃ bhāvayān
na dhītaya imaṃ dharātridaśakuñcanātho 'likhat //.

C19

CSC. Smṛti #2191. Red country-made paper. Folios 8b-60a. 41 x 7 cm. 5–6 lines/page. Bengali script, Incomplete: **2.37** *kṛtiḥ vaṇḍo* (after G 28.6)–**15.2**. Omits **15.3**. After **15.2**: *upādhyāyajīmūtavāhanakṛte dharmaratne dāyabhāgaḥ samāptaḥ.*

C20

CSC. Smṛti #2273. Red country-made paper. Folios 3b-25a. 43.5 x 7.5 cm. 5–6 lines/page. Bengali script. Incomplete: **1.30** *nānārthaṃ manvādivacanam*–**5.4** *tayā gavā kiṃ kri* (B 26.36).

C21

CSC. Smṛti #2390. Yellow country-made paper. 117 folios. 34 x 8 cm. 3–7 lines/page. Bengali script. Complete.

C22

CSC. Smṛti #2443. Red country-made paper. 68 folios. 46 x 8.3 cm. 6 lines/page. Bengali script. Complete. After **15.2**: *durgamāti* (?) *hi te namaḥ* // *haraye namaḥ* // *śrīśrī-hariḥ* //

C23

CSC. Smṛti #2628. Yellow country-made paper. 57 folios. 46 x 10 cm. 6 lines/page. Bengali script. Incomplete: **1.6** *'saṃyuktatvam*–**11.6.28** *mṛtadhanasya tadupa.* The manuscript is a bad state of preservation; parts of it have become illegible.

C24

CSC. Smṛti #2826. White paper. 77 folios. 45 x 9.5 cm. 5 lines/page. Bengali script. Incomplete: **1.1–14.9** *vibhāgānumānaṃ dhīma* (last folio missing). Looks recent.

C25

CSC. Smṛti #2852. Red country-made paper. 50 folios. 47.5 x 8.5 cm. 6–7 lines/page. Bengali script. Complete. Even though the manuscript does not look old, both paper and writing are badly damaged throughout. Folios stick together due to humidity, there are holes in the paper, and so on. It ends: *śrīraghunātho jayati.*

C26

CSC. Smṛti #2895. Yellow country-made paper. 76 folios. 44 x 9 cm. 5 lines/page. Bengali script. Complete. Looks recent, well preserved.

C27

CSC. Smṛti #2962. Yellow and white paper. 69 folios. 33.5 x 8.5 cm. 6–7 lines/page. Bengali script. Complete. Contains several peculiar readings.: **9.2** *savarṇā strī* for *savarṇāgre*; **9.10** *brāhmaṇabhāryaṃ* for *dvijātibhārtām*; **9.23** *śūdro* for *śūdryāṃ*. Looks recent.

C28

CSC. Smṛti #2422. Yellow country-made paper. 30 folios. 44 x 10 cm. 6 lines/page. Bengali script. Incomplete: **1.1–5.3**. Many scribal errors: **1.5** *upame* for *uparame*; **1.6** *vibhaktāvayatvaṃ* for *vibhaktāvayavatvaṃ*. Damaged by humidity; writing looks modern.

C29

CSC. Smṛti #3055. Yellow country-made paper. 82 folios + 2 pages of contents. 45 x 9 cm. 5-6 lines/page. Bengali script. Complete. The colophon contains the name of the scribe and a date (C.E. 1827): *iti śrīmahāmahopādhyāyajīmūtavāhanakṛte dharmaratne dāyabhāgaḥ samāptaḥ / śubham astu / śākābdā 1749 / 5 / 10 / śrīrāmasarvasvaśarmaṇaḥ svākṣaram idam /.*

C30

CSC. Smṛti #3227. Yellow and red country-made paper. 60 folios. 47.5 x 8.5 cm. 6 lines/page. Bengali script. Complete. Omits **15.3**. Clearly written, but the writing is fading.

C31

CSC. Smṛti #3274. Yellow and white country-made paper. 69 folios. 38 x 8 cm. 6–7 lines/page. Bengali script. Complete. Borders are worn, and parts of some folios are torn off. It ends: *oṃ namo gurave namaḥ // śrī durgā //.*

C32

CSC. Smṛti #2006. Yellow and red country-made paper. 69 folios. 47 x 8.5 cm. 5–6 lines/page. Bengali script. Complete. Omits **15.3**. The colophon contains the name of the owner and a date (C.E. 1820): *samāptaś cāyaṃ granthaḥ // 0 // pustako 'yaṃ śrīṭhākuradāsaśarmaṇaḥ / śakābdāḥ 1742 / oṃ namo bhagavate vāsudevāya / śrīkṛṣṇaḥ śaraṇaṃ/*

yatnena pustakaṃ lekhyaṃ yaś corayati mandadhīḥ /
śukarī tasya mātā ca pitā tasya ca gardabhaḥ //.

L1

India Office Library (hence *IOL*)[4] #1225. 53 folios. 28 x 20.5 cm. 16–22 lines/page. Complete. Bengali script. "This was evidently Colebrooke's hand-copy. It is corrected throughout, and references and other notes have been added by him in the margin" (Eggeling 1891, p. 460).

L2

IOL #1416. 69 folios. 33 x 12 cm. 9 lines/page. Complete. *Devanāgarī* script. Corrected throughout.

L3

IOL #76A. 94 folios. 44.5 x 28 cm. European paper. Also contains commentaries.

[4] Eggeling 1891: 460.

V1

Vārāṇasīya Saṃskṛta Viśvavidyālaya (hence *VSV*)[5] #13323. White paper. 60 folios. 33 x 12.5 cm. 9 lines/page. *Devanāgarī* script. Complete. It ends: *namo viśveśvarāya / annapūrṇāyai namaḥ // śrīrāmaḥ //*. Scribal errors demonstrate that V1 (and some of the other Vārāṇasī manuscripts) were copied from originals in Bengali script.

V2

VSV #13659. White paper. 71 folios. 23 x 13 cm. 10 lines/page. *Devanāgarī* script. Complete. The colophon contains a date (C.E. 1828): *saṃvat 1885 // varṣe māśottama-māśe āśvinamāśe śuklapakṣe caturthīdine ravivāre // śrīḥ //*. Contains several peculiar readings: **4.3.27** *kātyāyana-* for *kātyāyanavacana-*; **4.3.30** *iti ca* for *ity api*.

V3

VSV #13824. Red country-made paper. 58 folios. 33 x 13 cm. 8–9 lines/page. *Devanāgarī* script. Complete. It begins: *oṃ namaḥ paramātmane / lambodara tvayi mano 'stu sadā madīyaṃ /*. The colophon provides more information including a date (C.E. 1602): *samāptaś cāyaṃ granthaḥ // yathādṛṣṭetyādi // śubham astu / śakābdāḥ 1523 saṃvat 1660 samaye poṣasudi caturthī śukravāre likhitam idam /*. This is followed by an incomplete stanza in *śikhariṇī* meter:

dukūlaṃ vibhrāṇodvalitaharitāladyutiharaṃ
yavā puṣya śreṇīrucirucirapādāmbujatalam /
tamālaśyāsāṃgodarahasitanīrlācitamukhaḥ
parānaṃdālogaḥ sphurati hadimeke [. . . .] //.

V4

VSV #13521. White paper. 82 folios. 24.5 x 12.5 cm. 9 lines/page. *Devanāgarī* script. Incomplete: fol. 72 missing. It begins: *oṃ namaḥ kṛṣṇāya paramātmane lambodara tvayi mano 'stu sadā madīyaṃ*. The colophon contains a date (C.E. 1797): *samāptaś cāyaṃ granthaḥ yathādṛṣṭetyādi // śubham astu śakābdāḥ saṃvat 1855 sitārāma // rāma // rāma // kṛṣṇajīsāhāya bhairunāthajīsāhāya rāmāya rāmacandrāya nama //*. Direct or indirect copy of V3.

V5

VSV #13135. White paper. 12 folios. 23.5 x 12.5 cm. 9 lines/page. *Devanāgarī* script. Incomplete: **1.1–2.37** *viṃśatibhāgo jyeṣṭha* (G 28.5). It begins: *śrīgaṇeśāya namaḥ śrīgurucaraṇakamalebhyo namaḥ lambodara tvayi mano 'stu sadā madīyaṃ*.

V6

VSV #12913. Red country-made paper. 94 folios. 31.5 x 7 cm. 3–5 lines/page. Bengali script. Incomplete: **1.1–9.12** *śūdrāsuto* (M 9.151); **11.1–38** *tena vṛddhaprapitāmahāt-* **11.1.61** *bhavati*. Marginal notes from Śrīkṛṣṇa's commentary. Looks old.

V7

VSV #12372. White paper. 50 folios. 51 x 11 cm. 7–8 lines/page. Bengali script. Complete.

V8

VSV #13398. Yellow country-made paper. 52 folios. 47.5 x 8.5 cm. 4–8 lines/page. Bengali script. Complete. Omits **15.3**. After **15.2**: *iti dāyabhāgaḥ*.

[5] *A Descriptive Catalogue of the Sanskrit Manuscripts . . . in the Government Sanskrit College Banaras*. Vol. 3. Edited Kuberanath Shukla: *Dharmaśāstra Mss*. Banares: Gopaldas, 1956.

V9

VSV #14216. Yellow country-made paper. 75 folios. 47.5 x 8.5 cm. 5–6 lines/page. Bengali script. Complete. After **12.2**: *samāpto 'yaṃ dāyabhāganāmadheyo granthaḥ // śrīśrīsarasvatī jayati / śrīr vaḥ pāyād iti //.*

After I collated these manuscripts and compared them with the available editions, it became clear that preparing a truly critical edition of Jīmūtavāhana's *Dāyabhāga* is no longer possible.

First, the known manuscripts of the *Dāyabhāga* are numerous, and public institutions and libraries continue to acquire new ones, mainly in Bengal.[6] However, it may be worth noting that, except for other collections in Bengal,[7] and in Varanasi[8] and Mithila,[9] there are very few manuscripts of the *Dāyabhāga* in other parts of India,[10] in Europe,[11] and in America.[12]

[6] The printed manuscript catalogue of Calcutta Sanskrit College (Hṛshīkeśa Śāstrī and Śiva Chandra Gui: *A Descriptive Catalogue of Sanskrit Manuscripts in the Library of the Calcutta Sanskrit College*. vol. 2, pp. 145–46, 494. Calcutta: Banerjea, 1898) describes four *Dāyabhāga* manuscripts without commentary (three complete, one incomplete). When I visited Sanskrit College in 1969, repeated searches throughout Bengal had increased that number of *Dāyabhāga* manuscripts, without commentary, to thirty-one. The manuscripts of Śrīkṛṣṇa's commentary, of which three were listed in 1898, had grown to twenty-seven.

[7] Amarendramohan Tarkatīrtha: *A Brief Catalogue of Sanskrit Manuscripts in the Post-graduate Department of Sanskrit* (Calcutta: University, 1954) lists six manuscripts. Chintaharan Chakravarti: *A Descriptive Catalogue of the Sanskrit Manuscripts in the Vangiya Sahitya Parishat* (Calcutta: Vangiya Sahitya Parishat, 1935) describes five. A typewritten *Alphabetical List of the Sanskrit Manuscripts in the Collection of the Dacca University* lists sixteen. For the manuscript at the Asiatic Society, see earlier.

[8] For the nine manuscripts I consulted at Vārāṇasīya Saṃskṛta Viśvavidyālaya, see earlier.

[9] Kashiprasad Jayaswal and Anantaprasad Śāstrī: *A Descriptive Catalogue of Manuscripts in Mithila*, vol. 1 (Patna: Bihar and Orissa Research Society, 1927) lists five manuscripts, one in Bengali script (dated C.E. 1694), four in Maithili script.

[10] The *Descriptive Catalogue of the Sanskrit Manuscripts in the Ganganatha Jha Research Institute, Allahabad*, vol. 1, part 1, 1967, describes two incomplete manuscripts. There is one manuscript, in Telugu script, at Adyar (F. Otto Schrader: *A Preliminary List of Saṃskṛt and Prākṛt Manuscripts in the Adyar Library* [Madras: Oriental Publishing Co., 1910]; also in C. Kunhan Raja: *Alphabetical Index of Sanskrit Manuscripts in the Adyar Library* [Madras: Adyar Library, 1944]).

[11] There is one manuscript in Paris (Jean Filliozat: *Liste des manuscrits de la Collection Palmyr Cordier conservés à la Bibliothèque Nationale* [*JA* 244, 1934]), one in Copenhagen (Erasmus Nyerup: *Catalogus librorum sanskritanorum quos Bibliothecae Universitatis Havniensis vel dedit vel paravit Nathaniel Wallach* [Copenhagen: Gyldendal, 1821]), two in Oxford (Theodor Aufrecht: *Catalogus codicum manuscriptorum postvedicorum quotquot in Bibliotheca Bodleiana adservantur* [Oxford: Clarendon Press, 1859]). For the manuscripts at the India Office Library, see earlier.

[12] Horace I. Poleman: *A Census of Indic Manuscripts in the United States and Canada* (New Haven, Conn., 1938 [#2847]) lists one manuscript at Harvard (#2330).

Second, as the notes to the text show, with very few exceptions the variant readings in the several manuscripts are minor and rarely affect the meaning of the text. When they do, they are discussed in the notes to the translation.

Third, the manuscripts are highly conflated. Very few of them are old. Many of the more recent ones appear to have been copied by teachers or students for use in the *ṭols*: original readings are covered up and overwritten with different ones, marginal notes provide synonyms for terms in the text, and so on.

As a result, the present edition of Jīmūtavāhana's *Dāyabhāga* is purely eclectic. I have made an effort to include in the notes as many variants as the manuscripts offer (excluding scribal errors and nonsensical readings that cannot have been part of the *Dāyabhāga* as Jīmūtavāhana wrote it). Yet, in all cases the choice of the readings printed in the text is mine. I repeat them in the notes, followed by one or more variants; all readings are separated by *daṇḍas* (।).

To the extent *devanāgarī* script and Sanskrit syntax allow, the text is formatted, not in accordance with Colebrooke's subdivisions, but in accordance with the translation. Yet, here, too, Colebrooke's paragraph numbers are inserted for easy reference.

In the text I occasionally regularize alternate forms which frequently occur, not only in different manuscripts, but within the same manuscript as well. In proper names I consistently write, with the majority of occurrences, गोतम for alternating गोतम / गौतम (the manuscripts uniformly write बौधायन, never बोधायन), वशिष्ठ for वशिष्ठ / वसिष्ठ. Elsewhere, I write यौतक for यौतक / यौतुक, and, except where the meter of a verse requires otherwise, रिक्थ for रिक्थ / ऋक्थ.

TRANSLATION

CHAPTER ONE

PARTITION OF PATERNAL PROPERTY

Homage to Gaṇeśa!

<1> *Dāyabhāga* has repeatedly been the object of disagreement among scholars, because they failed properly to understand the relevant texts of Manu and others.[1] I therefore consider it my duty correctly to define *dāyabhāga* for their instruction.[2] Pay attention, learned men.

The Term *Dāyabhāga*

<2> Let me first define *dāyabhāga*. On this subject Nārada says:

> When sons proceed to a partition of their paterenal property, this constitutes the head of litigation which the experts call *dāya-bhāga*.[3] [N 13.1]

[1] In conformity with the traditional practice of beginning a text with an auspicious (*maṅgala*) word, Jīmūtavāhana starts his *Dāyabhāga* with the sequence *Manvādi*,- "Manu and others," and thereby pays special homage to the *dharma-śāstras* generally and to Manu in particular. I leave the term *dāyabhāga* untranslated at this point, since Jīmūtavāhana discusses different interpretations for both *dāya* and *bhāga* (or *vibhāga*, **6**).

[2] Though generally critical of Jīmūtavāhana, Mitramiśra introduces his chapter on *dāyabhāga (Vyavahāraprakāśa*, ed. p. 411; tr. I.1) with a verse that not only is reminiscent of Jīmūtavāhana's but also uses nearly identical vocabulary: *yatra manvādivacanavyākhyāsu bahudhā budhāḥ / vivadante dāyabhāgaḥ sa prabandhena varṇyate*, "In this treatise I will elucidate *dāyabhāga*, a topic on which scholars repeatedly disagree in their interpretations of the texts of Manu and others."

[3] The *Dāyabhāga* commentators go into great detail on various possible meanings of this verse, depending on different interpretations of the word *tatra* (here translated as "when") and on variant readings for it. Cf. Pawate 1975: 25ff. On *dāyabhāga* as one of the eighteen "heads of litigation" (*vivāda-pada* or *vyavahāra-pada*), i.e., sections of substantive law, see Introduction.

<3> "Paternal" means "what has come from the father."[4] It means that the sons' proprietary rights take effect after their father's death.

Both terms, "paternal" and "sons," are synecdochic for relatives generally, for the term *dāyabhāga* is used to refer to the partition of the property of any relative by any relative. Indeed,

[1] after introducing the head of litigation *dāyabhāga* as shown above, Nārada himself goes on to deal with the partition of the property of the mother and of other relatives as well.

[2} Manu discusses the partition of the property of any relative by any relative, after an introductory verse that does not include terms such as "father" at all:

> I have thus explained the duties of husband and wife based on their mutual affection, and also how to secure offspring in cases of emergency. Now listen to *dāyabhāga*. [M 9.103]

<4> The word *dāya* is derived from the verb *dā*, "give." It means "something that is given."[5] In this case, however, *dā* is used figuratively. The result of the act of giving, i.e., one person acquiring a proprietary right when another person's proprietary right lapses, also obtains when a person dies, when he becomes a wanderer,[6] and the like. The difference is that in the latter case the owners do not formally forfeit their rights. <5> In this case, therefore, the term *dāya* is used in a conventional rather than in an etymological sense. It indicates those items in which a person acquires a

[4] By interpreting the term *pitrya*, "paternal" as *pitṛta āgatam*, "having come from the father" Jīmūtavāhana silently refers to a grammatical rule. According to Pāṇini's *Aṣṭādhyāyī* the suffix *-ya-* is used after the nominal stem *pitṛ*, "father" (4.3.79) to indicate *tata āgataḥ*, "having come from him" (4.3.74). The *Kāśikā*, in commenting on 4.3.74, specifies that the derivatives discussed in that section indicate that the tie with the person or object has been totally severed. Hence, says Jīmūtavāhana, the fact that the estate is called *pitrya* implies that the father is deceased. He thus establishes right from the start his fundamental position that sons have no proprietary rights in their father's estate in his lifetime, against the opinion of other authors who give the sons proprietary rights in their father's estate from the moment of their birth. See **13–20** and Introduction.

[5] Even though this etymology is possible (cf. *Aṣṭādhyāyī* 3.1.139, 141), and even though *dāya* appears in the literature with the meaning "gift," in the sense of inheritance it is normally derived from a different verb *dā* (or *do*) "cut, divide" (Mayrhofer 1956ff.: 2.35). Jīmūtavāhana's interpretation is followed by the *Dāyatattva* (ed. pp. 161–62; tr. I.5-6; it is quoted and criticized as too narrow, i.e., as not including ownership by birth, in the *Vyavahāraprakāśa* (ed. pp. 411–12; tr. I.3). Derrett (1962: 53) strongly objects to Kane's (1946: 543–44, 546) acceptance of "Jīmūtavāhana's false derivation." For an attempt to give the term *dāya* a Dravidian etymology, see Pawate 1975: iii–iv.

[6] The term *pravrajita*, "wanderer," is ambiguous. Here and at **31** it indicates either a man in the third stage of life, i.e., a *vanaprastha*, "forest-dweller," or, possibly, a man in either one of the two stages of life that follow after that of a householder, including the *sannyāsin*, "renouncer." At **2.57-58**, on the contrary, Jīmūtavāhana identifies *pravrajyā*, "the state of a *pravrajita*," with the fourth and final stage of life, called *vṛddhāśrama* at H 4.5, only. Cf. also at **5.11**, where Jīmūtavāhana uses *pravrajita* as a synonym for *liṅgin*.

proprietary right when the prior owner's right lapses,[7] the acquisition of this right being contingent on the new owner being related to the prior owner.[8]

<6> As to *vibhāga*, is it to be understood as "division of" the *dāya*, i.e., does it mean that the *dāya* is divided into several parts, or is it to be understood as "severance from" the *dāya*, i.e., does it mean that an item or items is/are severed from the rest of the *dāya*?[9]

It is not the former, for that might lead to situations in which the *dāya* is destroyed.[10] Nor is it the latter, for even of an item that is not severed from the rest, common usage allows one to say: "this item does not belong to me; it has been the object of a partition, and it belongs to my brother."[11]

<7> It is also wrong to understand *vibhāga* as the act by which proprietary rights, which all had acquired in the entire estate because they were all linked to it in the same way,[12] are made specific to a particular item or particular items.[13] Indeed,

[1] any one relative's link to the property is limited by the very existence of any other relative or relatives. All that link does is to give him a proprietary right in part of the estate, a right that remains to be made overt by partition.

[2] To posit that initially one has a proprietary right in the entire estate and that this right is canceled later on would be needlessly cumbersome.

[3] Such a view would be inept in that the result of ownership, i.e., the right to use what one owns as one wishes, would not follow.

<8> What *vibhāga* really means is that a proprietary right that has been acquired in only part of items such as land or gold, but which is as yet unspecified insofar as it does not allow for separate transactions since there is no way to know what belongs to

[7] Variant reading: "when the prior owner disappears."

[8] The proviso is required in order to exclude transactions such as purchase from the definition of *dāya*.

[9] At issue here is the syntactic relation between the two elements of the compound *dāya-bhāga* (or -*vibhāga*, from N 13.1, which Jīmūtavāhana uses henceforth). The meaning "sever" (*pṛthakkaraṇa*), which *Dhātupāṭha* 10.340 gives for the causative form of the verb *bhaj*, allows for two different interpretations of the compound: if the first element stands for a genitive case, the compound means "severing *of* the *dāya*;" if it stands for an instrumental case, the compound means "severing *off* the *dāya*."

[10] This sentence refers to cases in which the estate consists of a single, indivisible item, or of items that cannot be divided into the required number of shares.

[11] In rejecting both definitions, Jīmūtavāhana applies techniques commonly used in Indian logic (*nyāya*): the first definition is too broad since it covers situations in which it is inapplicable; the second definition is too narrow since it does not account for situations in which it ought to apply. On the application of *nyāya* concepts in the *Dāyabhāga*, see Introduction.

[12] The Sanskrit term for "link" is *sambandha*, which encompasses both a link in the sense of "claim, possession" (the Sanskrit genitive case expresses the *sambandha* between the owner and the thing owned) and in the sense of family relationship. The term "relative" in the next paragraph translates Sanskrit *sambandhin*, "someone having a link."

[13] According to Raghunandana's commentary, Jīnūtavāhana alludes here to the definition of *vibhāga* in the *Mitākṣarā* (introduction to Y 2.114; Colebrooke I.i.4). See, however, Rocher 1971.

whom, is made overt by a variety of procedures such as casting lots.[14] <**9**> Or else, what a *vibhāga* does is to divide the property explicitly, i.e., it discloses the proprietary rights.[15]

<**10**> Note that proprietary rights can be made overt even when a single female servant or any single piece of cattle is held in common;[16] in that case all the owners are severally entitled to use the draft animal or to milk the cow for specific periods of time. Says Bṛhaspati:

> Each shall use the services of one single female in his own house in proportion to his share.[17] [B 26.2ab]
> They shall get water drawn from a well or cistern in due order. [B 26.3ab]
> It must be divided justly lest it be for naught. [B 26.4]

These three half verses appear in separate places; they do not constitute a continuous Text.[18]

[14] Jīmūtavāhana's definition is labeled "that of the Easterners," i.e., of Bengal, in a commentary on the *Mitākṣarā* (*Subodhinī*, p. 419). It is criticized, though, by Raghunandana, who claims that, when the prior owner's right lapses, all those who have an equal claim obtain a right of ownership in the entire property (*Dāyatattva* ed. p. 163; tr. I.18–21).

[15] As an alternative, Jīmūtavāhana resorts to an etymological explanation of the term *vibhāga*. The preverb *vi-* is commonly interpreted as *viśeṣeṇa* "fully, exceedingly, especially, even more." The verb *jñāpayati*, "disclose, make known," implies that the heirs' proprietary rights existed prior to partition, but were as yet "unknown, hidden." Cf. **24**: partition provides the "cognizance" (*jñāna*) that one owns a particular item.

[16] The compound *dāsīgavādikam* is ambiguous: it either means (1) a female servant, (2) a cow, and (3) any other single item; or it means (1) a female servant, and (2) any piece of cattle such as a cow. I prefer the latter interpretation, since *vahana*, "carrying loads," is more appropriate for a draft animal than for a female servant.

[17] This verse has been commented on at length. According to the *Dāyatattva* (ed. p. 165; tr. 1.32) the assumption here is either that, while one individual temporarily uses the services of a single female, the proprietary rights of all others lapse, or that the proprietary rights of all are permanently restricted. Śrīkṛṣṇa clearly favors the latter alternative: if one of the heirs sells the single item while he is entitled to use it, the purchaser does not become the permanent owner, for the seller cannot transfer more than his restricted right of ownership.

[18] The reason for this unusual commentary is not clear. We can only guess that Jīmūtavāhana knew a six-verse-long quotation from the lost *Bṛhaspati-smṛti* dealing with the partition of clothes, ornaments, and other items that are not easily divided. Such a quotation appears, with only minor variants, in a number of digests; cf. *Dhko* pp. 1222–23 and Jolly's Bṛhaspati tr. 25.79–84. The three half verses cited by Jīmūtavāhana do not follow one another in this longer quotation.

Sons Become Owners of Their Father's Property at the Time of His Death

[Objection] <**11**> Consider the following Nārada text:

> After their father's death the sons may partition their father's property. [N 13.2ab]

Since this Text has to be construed as "they may partition property that belongs to their father,"[19] it follows that the sons have no proprietary rights prior to partition. On the other hand, it cannot be partition in and of itself that brings about proprietary rights; if that were the case, the term "partition" would also, but improperly, extend to the property of persons to whom they are not related.[20]

[Refutation] <**12**> Not so. Indeed,

[1] it is common practice for people to speak of the property as "ours" as soon as their father or other relative dies.[21]

[2] When there is only one son, he acquires the proprietary right without any partition whatever.

Consequently, it is the death of a relative, in and of itself, that brings about the proprietary rights. There is, therefore, no danger that the term "partition" might extend to cases to which it should not.

[Objection][22] <**13**> "Acquiring" is an act performed by the acquirer, and once the acquirer acquires something, he becomes its owner. As a result, "coming into the world," which is an act performed by the son, constitutes in and of itself an apt way of acquiring. Hence sons already have proprietary rights in their father's lifetime; these rights do not come about upon his death. That is why it has been said:

> In some cases, such as paternal property, birth in and of itself.[23]

[19] The objection points out that in the Nārada text the word *pituḥ* "their father's" is a possessive genitive to be construed with the immediately preceding word *dhanam*, "property." The point of the first part of the objection is that, since the property is still described as "belonging to the father" after the father's death up to the time of partition, it follows that, contrary to Jīmūtavāhana's opinion, the sons have no proprietary rights, not even unspecified ones, as soon as their father dies.

[20] If the property still belongs to the father when the sons proceed to a partition, it follows that it is partition that brings about the change in ownership. The point of the second part of the objection is that, if all it took for a set of brothers to become owners of a piece of property was that they divide it among themselves, they could do so to the property of anyone they please.

[21] The argument of common usage (*prayoga*) is used here to counter a strictly grammatical interpretation of a text. Jīmūtavāhana might also have argued that the true purpose of the entire verse, of which the objection quotes only the first half, is to point out that sons divide paternal property, whereas daughters divide maternal property (cf. **4.2.13**).

[22] Jīmūtavāhana now introduces, and rejects, the theory of ownership by birth, of which Vijñāneśvara's *Mitākṣarā* is the most obvious proponent.

[23] The anonymous text quoted here expresses the same notion as another text: *tathotpattyaivārthasvāmitvaṃ labhetety ācāryāḥ*, "the teachers also say that one acquires a right of

[Refutation] <**14**> Not so. Indeed,

[1] ownership by birth would be incompatible with a number of Texts by Manu and others. For instance,

[A] Manu says:

> After their father and mother,[24] brothers together may partition their paternal property equally;[25] for they have no right to it as long as their parents live. [M 9.104]

<**15**> This Text provides the answer to the question why sons cannot also proceed to partition of the property while their parents live: they do not yet own it at that time.

<**16**> Note that it would be wrong to say that, like Manu 8.416,[26] all Manu 9.104 means to say is that the sons may not dispose of their property as they please. Indeed,

[a] there is a difference. In Manu 9.104 there are no grounds on which to base the notion that they might be owners at that time. Manu 8.416, on the contrary, says "whatever they obtain," i.e., whatever they acquire. Since such a phrase clearly establishes that wives and others do not have proprietary rights, it makes sense to interpret that Text as stating that they may not dispose of their possessions as they please.

[b] <**17**> If those referred to at Manu 8.416 did not actually own the property even though they acquired it on their own, that would be incompatible with the Veda, for it would bar them from performing the Vedic rites which they must perform at their own expense.[27]

[B] <**18**> A Devala text also makes it perfectly clear that sons have no proprietary rights in their father's property:

> After their father's death his sons may partition his property; for they do not own it as long as he is alive and competent.[28] [D 1563]

---

ownership in property simply by being born," which the *Mitākṣarā* (Colebrooke I.i.23) quotes in support of its contention that ownership is acquired by birth. This second text, which the *Mitākṣarā* attributes to Gautama, does not appear in the *Gautama-smṛti*, a fact that led Jolly (1885: 110) to suggest that Vijñāneśvara may have fabricated it.

[24] For the reason I refrain from translating "after the death of their father and mother," see **46**.

[25] On the impact of the word "equally" (*samam*), see **35**. "Equally" is the interpretation favored by most commentators. *Samam* could, however, also mean "equitably." The *Vivādaratnākara* (ed. #1305; tr. I.4) records a variant reading *saha* "together, among themselves." I translate "paternal property" rather than "parental property" in view of Jīmūtavāhana's later comment on M 9.104 (**3.2**).

[26] Manu 8.416: "According to tradition there are three kinds of people who do not have any property: a wife, a son, and a slave; whatever they obtain belongs to him whose wife, son, or slave they are."

[27] The duty to perform Vedic rites at their own expense, to which only a brief allusion is made here, is a major argument in the *Mitākṣarā* and elsewhere in favor of ownership by birth for all members of the joint family. Cf. *Mitākṣarā* (Colebrooke I.i.18 and 26).

[28] Differently from the passages in the *Manu-smṛti* quoted earlier, which use the potentially ambiguous terms *an-īśa* (9.104 "having no right") and *a-dhana* (8.416 "having no property"), Devala uses the explicit term *a-svāmya*, "having no ownership," i.e., the sons "do not own" their father's property in his lifetime.

[2] <**19**> If sons already had ownership in their father's property in his lifetime, they would be able to proceed to a partition even against his will.[29]

[3] There are no grounds to accept that birth in and of itself brings about proprietary rights,[30] for birth does not appear in any Text as a form of acquisition. <**20**> As for the Text: "In some cases birth in and of itself" [**13**], it describes the situation in stages: the son's birth first brings about the father-to-son relationship; the father's death later brings about the son's proprietary right.

<**21**> There is nothing wrong with the notion of one person acquiring a proprietary right by way of an act performed by someone else:[31] the practice has its roots in the Texts, and we see it happen in daily life as well. For instance, in the case of a gift the beneficiary becomes owner by the simple fact that the gift is ceded in favor of a specifically named sentient being, i.e., by an act performed by the donor.[32]

<**22**> Note that the donee's proprietary right is not the result of his appropriation. Indeed,

[1] if that were the case, the appropriator, not the donor, would be the agent of the act of giving. Something, then, would become a gift by its result, i.e., the fact that another person's proprietary right takes effect, and that result would be dependent on the beneficiary.[33] If so, the situation would resemble that of an oblation (*ho-ma*): even though the patron of the sacrifice cedes the matter with a specific deity in mind, he is not the agent of the oblation (*ho-tr̥*); the only person to have the title *ho-tr̥* is the priest who casts the ceded matter into the fire to make it into what is called a *ho-ma*.[34]

[29] The argument that there can be no partition without the father's consent will be developed further later.

[30] I translate the reading *janmanaiva svatvam iti*. Commentators who read *janmanaiva svatvam ity atra*, "in the text 'ownership by birth in and of itself,'" take this to refer to the passage attributed to Gautama in the *Mitākṣarā* (note 23).

[31] If, as the objection suggests (**13**), there has to be an act in order to acquire something, Jīmūtavāhana now argues that the act does not necessarily have to be performed by the acquirer.

[32] Jīmūtavāhana's view to the effect that a gift is valid before acceptance has provoked much controversy. See, e.g., Kane 1946: 474–75. It was relied on by V. Ramaswami, J., in favor of the right of a testator to bequeath property to an unborn person, in *Raman Nadar Visvanathan* v. *Snehappoo Rasalamma* (1970) 2 S.C.J. 738; A.I.R. 1970 S.C. 1759. See, however, Derrett 1971 (= *Essays* 4. 1–7). On gifts, see Nath 1987.

[33] This argument is based on linguistic theory. According to the Indian grammarians, an act involves several "factors" (*kāraka*). Of these factors (agent, object, beneficiary, instrument, etc.) only one, the "agent" (*kar-tr̥*, "do-er") is "independent" (*svatantra*). He alone performs the act. In the case of a gift the agent is the *dā-tr̥*, "giv-er;" all other factors including the person to whom the gift is made, i.e., the beneficiary, are dependent on him. To say that it is the appropriation of the gift that effects the change in ownership would be tantamount to making the *svīkar-tr̥*, "appropriator" the independent agent rather than a dependent beneficiary. See Rocher 1976.

[34] The patron of the sacrifice (*yajamāna*), i.e., the one who performs the act of *yaj* (*Dhātupāṭha* 1.1051: *yaj* means "give"), cedes (verb *tyaj*) the matter to a specific deity: *yāgaḥ = devatām uddiśya dravyatyāgaḥ*. In this case, however, to make the matter into an oblation

[2] In the Text:

> Mentally referring to a recipient he shall pour water on the earth; there is a limit to the ocean but there are no limits to gifts,[35] [*Agni-purāṇa* 209. 56]

one sees that something is called a "gift" prior to any reference to its appropriation.

[Objection] <**23**> Appropriating (*svī-kāra*) means taking possession. *Svī-kāra* is a *cvi* compound, i.e., a compound which indicates that something is made into something different from what it was prior to the act; it refers, therefore, to an act whereby one makes one's own an object that was not one's own prior to the act. So, how could any proprietary right exist before the object has been appropriated?[36]

[Refutation] <**24**> The meaning of the term *svī-kāra* is this: even though the proprietary right took effect earlier, *svī-kāra* makes it possible for the beneficiary to use the item as he pleases, since he takes cognizance of the fact that it is his, and that cognition is an act of the beneficiary.

Note that, even though a brahman's entitlement does not bring about the right of ownership, it may still be considered a form of acquisition, because it is associated with performing sacrifices for others and teaching the Veda.[37] The difference is that in the latter two cases the brahman's proprietary right takes effect only when he is given a fee.[38]

(*ho-ma*; verb *hu*), a *ho-tṛ* priest has to cast the ceded matter into the fire: *ho-maḥ* = *tyaktasya vahnau prakṣepaḥ*. Cf. *Mīmāṃsā-sūtras* 4.2.27–28.

[35] As Sanskrit authors are wont to do, Jīmūtavāhana refers to this verse by quoting its first quarter, even though the principal word, "gifts," appears in the fourth quarter. The commentators provide the full text: *manasā pātram uddiśya bhūmau toyaṃ vinikṣipet / vidyate sāgarasyānto dānasyānto na vidyate*. According to Āpastamba (2.4.9.8) "all gifts must be accompanied by pouring water" (*sarvāṇy udakapūrvāṇi dānāni*). The verse is attributed to the *Agni-purāṇa* in the *Dānakriyākaumudī* (p. 3). For variants on this text, see Derrett 1956: 493 (= *Essays* 1.351, 357).

[36] The preceding paragraph showed that ownership of a gift passes to the beneficiary when the donor makes the gift, not when the beneficiary appropriates it (*svī-kāra*). This, however, requires that Jīmūtavāhana refute an objection that might be raised on grammatical grounds: the *ī* in *svī-kāra*, which makes the word a *cvi* compound (*Aṣṭādhyāyī* 5.4.50), seems to indicate that it is the act of the beneficiary that makes him the owner of an object that was not his previously.

[37] The commentators quote a verse: "A brahman shall acquire (*arjayet*) property by performing sacrifices for others, by teaching theVeda, and by his entitlement." Cf. also Śabara on *Mīmāṃsā-sūtra* 4.1.2: a brahman shall "acquire (*arjayet*) property" by his entitlement and so forth, a *kṣatriya* by conquest and so forth, a *vaiśya* by agriculture and so forth. Performing sacrifices for others (*yājana*), teaching the Veda (*adhyāpana*), and brahmanical entitlement (*pratigraha*) are the three means of livelihood (*vṛtti*, *jīvikā*) the tradition prescribes for brahmans. Cf. Rocher 1975.

[38] The brahman's entitlement is different from the other two means of livelihood, which involve services in return for which the brahman receives a fee (*dakṣiṇā*). The entitlement results from a gift and, consequently, the brahman's right of ownership takes effect as soon as

<25> Alternatively,[39] the very fact that a son lives when his father dies may suffice for him to acquire a proprietary right.

Besides, when it comes to the property of brothers and so forth, it would be hard to deny the fact that the proprietary rights of other brothers and so forth take effect either as the result of the death of the prior owners or because they themselves are living at that time.

<26> At this point we can return to Manu 9.104 **[14]**. That Text merely elaborates on the sons' right to partition the property, a right that is established at the very moment of their father's death and which they can then exercise at their own discretion. And the purpose of the elaboration is to make it understood that the sons' proprietary rights do exist at that time.[40] Indeed,

[1] Manu 9.104 cannot be an outright injunction, for the sons' right to proceed to a partition at that time is established.

[2] **<27>** Nor can Manu 9.104 be an admonitory injunction.[41] Indeed,

[a] it would, then, be incompatible with another Manu text:

> They may either stay together, or live apart if they strive for *dharma*. [M 9.111ab; **37**]

[b] Since partition has a mundane purpose, there cannot be any restriction on whether it should occur or not, nor on its timing.[42]

---

the donor resolves to make a gift; the moment at which the entitlement is handed over constitutes appropriation (*svī-kāra*) as defined in the preceding paragraph.

[39] Jīmūtavāhana now offers an alternative to **21**: if someone still persists in finding it difficult to accept that an heir can acquire a proprietary right by an act of the prior owner, e.g., his dying, there is also an act on the part of the heir: his being alive when the prior owner dies.

[40] Jīmūtavāhana defends the thesis that M 9.104 must be interepreted as an *anuvāda*, i.e., a statement that merely "elaborates on" something—in this case, the right to partition—that is already established (*prāpta*), either by an "outright injunction" (*vidhi*) or, as in this case, by common sense (*nyāya*). To justify that the text is a mere *anuvāda*, he has to demonstrate not only that it is not an outright injunction (**26**), but also that it cannot be taken as an "admonitory injunction" (*niyama*) (**27–28**) or as an "injunction of exclusion" (*parisaṃkhyā*) (**29**). What Jīmūtavāhana really does is use M 9.104 for something it does not actually say, namely that sons own the property when their father dies.

[41] An "admonitory injunction" (*niyama*) is an injunction that serves to restrict to a fixed number the several ways or means in which a certain act might be performed, thereby excluding other ways or means which, without the admonitory injunction, could also be resorted to (*Arthasaṃgraha* par. 74). If M 8.104 was a *niyama*, it would mean that the sons must proceed to a partition after their father's death; it would exclude the alternative of staying together.

[42] The division of *smṛti* injunctions into rules that are *dṛṣṭa-artha*, "having a visible, mundane purpose," and rules that are *adṛṣṭa-artha*, "having an invisible, transcendent purpose," is often discussed, though not always agreed on in detail, in *mīmāṃsā* literature. In essence, when an outright or a negative *smṛti* injunction is *dṛṣṭa-artha*, it is considered to be nothing more than a recommendation; a breach of such injunction does not thereby make the act null and void. When the purpose of a *smṛti* injunction is not easily perceptible, i.e., when it is *adṛṣṭa-artha*, it is supposed to be based on a known, or unknown, Vedic injunction;

[c] <**28**> The phrase "after their father's death" [**18**] would then mean that partition must take place immediately after the father's death and not at any later time, even as the ritual that must be performed immediately for a newborn child.[43] This is not possible. First, in the case at hand there is not the same need to act without delay as there is in the other case, namely, because of the risk that the newborn child might die. Second, the sons' right to partition, at their own pleasure, any time after their father's death and as long as they live, is established.

[3] <**29**> One might, of course, argue that all Manu 9.104 means to say is that, even though the sons have proprietary rights while their father lives, they are not entitled to a partition.[44] That, however, goes against reason: it would be tantamount to saying that the intent of Manu 9.104 is at odds with its content.[45]

<**30**> The notion that Texts such as Manu 9.104 really intend to convey, therefore, is this: sons have no proprietary rights in their parents' property as long as their parents live, but they do at the time of their deaths. The former part is stated explicitly; the latter can be gathered by implication.[46]

<**31**> Note that the term "death" in these Texts is not meant to be taken literally. It subsumes other situations such as being expelled from one's caste or becoming a wanderer.[47] These situations are similar to death insofar as they, too, cause the individual's proprietary right to lapse. <**32**> Says Nārada:

---

transgressing that kind of *smṛti* rule makes the act nonexistent. Also, it is generally accepted that, whenever a mundane purpose exists, one should not look for a transcendent one. In a law case, in which Kane, acting as an attorney, referred to the distinction beteen *dṛṣṭa-artha* and *adṛṣṭa-artha* in connection with the qualifications required of a bride (quoting the *Mitākṣarā* on Y 1.53), Justice Gajendragadkar decided that "the rule is both artificial and irrational; and . . . I would certainly not be prepared to adopt it as a safe guide in interpreting Sanskrit texts for the purpose of administering Hindu law" (*Madhavrao Raghavendra* v. *Raghavendrarao*, A.I.R. [33] 1946 Bombay 377, 393). Cf. Kane 1941: 437–38; Derrett 1968: 98–100, 233 n. 1; Nataraja Aiyyar 1952: 11–14.

[43] Devala 1563 (**18**) states that partition should take place *pitary uparate*, a locative absolute which can mean either "when their father dies" or "after their father's death." Other texts use similar expressions for the birth ritual: *kumāraṃ jātam* (*Āśvalāyana-gṛhyasūtra* 1.15.1), *jātasya kumārasya* (*Pāraskara-gṛhyasūtra* 1.16.4), etc.; also *putre jāte* (*Taittirīya-saṃhitā* 2.2.5.3). Jīmūtavāhana insists that, notwithstanding the syntactical similarity of the expressions, they mean different things in different circumstances. On the birth ritual (*jāteṣṭi* or *jātakarman*), see R. B. Pandey 1969: 70–71.

[44] I.e., one might try to avoid interpreting M 9.104 as an admonitory injunction (*niyama*) by interpreting it as an injunction of exclusion (*parisaṃkhyā*:) (*Arthasaṃgraha* par. 75): M 9.104 excludes the possibility of proceeding to a partition while their father lives.

[45] In this case the content, "they may partition after," would be interpreted as intending to say "they may not partition before."

[46] I.e., the latter part can be inferred from the fact that the texts entitle the sons to divide the property at that time.

[47] On the ambiguity of the term *pravrajita*, "wanderer," see note 7. *Pravrajita* here anticipates Jīmūtavāhana's commentary on *aśaraṇa* at N 13.3 (**33**): "one who has abandoned the life stage of a householder."

> When their mother has reached menopause, when their sisters have been given away, or when their father is broken or without a home, or when he abandons all worldly desires.[48] [N 13.3]

<**33**> "Broken" here means expelled from his caste. "Without a home" means that the father has abandoned the life stage of a householder. Were one to adopt the reading *nivṛtte vāpi maraṇāḍ*, "or spared by death," the second half of the Text would mean "or when the father lives but abandons all worldly desires." This variant is, however, without foundation.[49]

<**34**> Nārada 13.3, too,[50] merely elaborates on one possible time for partition, a time which is established and at which the sons can exercise their right at their own discretion. The purpose of the elaboration is to make it understood that sons acquire proprietary rights in their father's property as a result of events such as his abandoning all worldly pleasures.[51] Indeed, an elaboration presupposes that something is established, and what is established here is that the sons own the property.

<**35**> Since any one individual has full right of ownership in his own property, it is established that partition must take place even when a single partner asks for it. Hence, the term "together" [Manu 9.104; **14**] elaborates on one established alternative only. If that were not the case, even though it would be obvious from the Text that three or more individuals can ask for a partition, two of them would not be able to do so together, for there would be no Text that provides for a partition by two individuals.[52]

[Objection] <**36**> After the father's death his eldest son alone is entitled to inherit the property, to the exclusion of the other sons.[53] Says Manu:

[48] This verse must be read in conjunction with N 13.2ab (**11**). Only the second half of the verse is relevant in this context. On the import of the phrase "when their mother has reached menopause," see **45**; on "when their sisters have been given away," see **47**.

[49] The discussion pertains to a variant reading in the third quarter of N 13.3: *nivṛtte vāpi maraṇād* instead of *vinaṣṭe vāpi maraṇād*. The reading adopted in the *Dāyabhāga*, Jīmūtavāhana's subsequent commentary on N 13.3, and his objection to the variant reading are quoted in the *Vyvavhāraprakāśa* (ed. p. 433; tr. I.1, p. 46). Mitramiśra, however, has, instead of *nivṛtte vāpi maraṇād*, the reading *nivṛtte vāpi ramaṇāḍ*, "or when he is no longer interested in sex," which he defends on the grounds that "it appears in many other works such as the *Mitākṣarā*."

[50] I.e., even as M 9.104 (**26**).

[51] In view of Jīmūtavāhana's parallel statement apropos of M 9.104 (**26**), and following Śrīkṛṣṇa's commentary, I translate the ablative *jñāpanāt* "because of . . ." as a dative, "to make it understood."

[52] On the one hand, any one brother can ask for a partition as the logical consequence of his being master of his own property and, as a result, being entitled to act with it as he pleases. On the other hand, the text of M 9.104 provides for the possibility of "the brothers" (in the plural which, in Sanskrit, means three or more) "together" to ask for partition. Unless Manu is interpreted as referring to only one alternative, two brothers could not "together" ask for partition.

[53] Jīmūtavāhana now briefly addresses those *smṛti* texts according to which, differently from M 9.104 (**14**), the eldest son alone inherits his father's property. Note that the text quoted in support of this view is M 9.105, i.e., the verse following immediately after M 9.104. On

The eldest son alone shall take the entire paternal property; the other brothers shall live as his dependents as they did with their father. [M 9.105]

"The eldest" here means the son who saves his father from the hell called *Put*.[54] It does not necessarily mean the oldest in age. Says Manu:

By the mere fact that he is born a first son makes a man the father of a son,[55] and frees him of the debt to his ancestors. That is why the son is entitled to inherit the property. [M 9.106; **11.1.31**]
That son alone to whom he passes on his debt and through whom he becomes immortal is born-of-duty; all other sons are born-of-lust. [M 9.107]

[Refutation] <**37**> Not so. Indeed,

[1] there are Texts to the effect that, for the eldest son to inherit the property, all brothers must agree to it. Says Nārada:

Or,[56] if they all agree, the eldest brother may provide for the others like a father, or else the youngest brother if he is most competent, for competence is what the family needs. [N 13.5; **3.15**]

Note that, if there is a general consensus to that effect, even the youngest brother may be in charge of the family; hence, being the eldest is not the sole criterion.[57]

[2] In the verse:

They may either stay together, or live separate if they strive for *dharma*. Their *dharma* increases when they live separate. Separating the family, therefore, is in accordance with the *dharma*, [M 9.111; **27**]

with the phrase "stay together or live separate" and with the words "if they strive for," Manu demonstrates that the sons can opt for either solution as they please.

---

this and other contradictions in the *Manu-smṛti*, see Rocher 1993: 264–67. On the law of primogeniture in India, see Pal 1929.

[54] This statement alludes to the traditional etymology of the word *putra*: he saves (*trā*) his father from the hell called *Put*. See M 9.138 = Vi 15.44 (**5.6**; **11.1.31**). Also **2.53**.

[55] The phrase "the father of a son" inadequately translates the Sanskrit term *putrin*. A *putrin* is a person "who has a *putra*," i.e., a person "who has a son," but, at the same time, a person "who has someone who saves him from the hell called *Put*."

[56] This rule is an alternative to N 13.4 (**2.81**), according to which an aging father can divide his property among his sons.

[57] I.e., the phrase "the eldest son alone" at M 9.105 (**36**) needs to be qualified: provided he is most competent.

Two Possible Times for Partition of Paternal Property

<**38**> What all this amounts to is that there are two possible times for partition: [1] when the father's ownership lapses, and [2] when it has not lapsed, but, in that case, at the father's discretion.

<**39**> One should not heed the opinion of those who say that there are three possible times for partition: [1] when the father dies; [2] when the father abandons all worldly desires and the mother reaches menopause; and [3] at the father's discretion, even before the mother reaches menopause and while the father has not yet abandoned all worldly desires.[58]

If the mother's menopause is added as a qualifier to the father's abandoning all worldly desires, his sons would not be able to proceed to a partition at that time, even if they wanted to. Indeed, Manu enjoins the times for marriage as follows:

> A man thirty years old shall marry an attractive girl aged twelve, or a man twenty-four years old a girl aged eight. They should marry earlier if their *dharma* would suffer by not doing so. [M 9.94]

On the other hand, the Text:

> He shall retreat to the forest at the age of fifty,[59]

enjoins the time at which a husband ought to enter a new stage of life. Hence, it would not be possible for the mother to have reached menopause by the time the father abandons all worldly desires and becomes a forest dweller.[60]

<**40**> If one were to claim, on the contrary, that the moment when the father abandons all worldly desires is the right time for partition of paternal property, without any qualification whatever, no partition could take place before the father abandons all worldly desires, even if he was expelled from his caste. <**41**> If the time when the father becomes an outcaste was to be taken as yet another possible time for partition, there would be four such times: [1] when the father dies, [2] when he is expelled from his caste, [3] when he abandons all worldly desires, and [4] when he wishes to proceed to a partition.

<**42**> As for those who claim that the sons are at liberty to divide their father's property when he becomes incapable of managing his affairs, they only show how ignorant they are of the Texts.[61] Indeed,

[58] This is one of the cases in which Acyuta, Raghunandana, Maheśvara, and Śrīkṛṣṇa state that Jīmūtavāhana refutes Vijñāneśvara (cf. Introduction). The *Mitākṣarā* (on Y 2. 115; Colebrooke I.ii.7) does mention the second item in this list of three (the one which Jīmūtavāhana is about to object to), but it also adds a fourth possible time for partition, namely, when the mother has not yet reached menopause and even against the father's will in case he behaves unrighteously or is afflicted with a chronic desease.

[59] The same quarter verse is quoted anonymously by Kullūkabhaṭṭa on M 3.50.

[60] Based on the ages given at M 9.94 and in the anonymous text, the mother could not be more than thirty-four, or thirty-two, years old, too early for menopause, by the time the father becomes a forest dweller.

[61] Raghunandana again claims that Jīmūtavāhana rejects the opinion of Vijñāneśvara.

[A] Hārīta says:

> As long as their father lives sons are not at liberty to take, expend, or pledge his property, although the eldest son may look after it if his father is distressed, absent, or ill. [H 4.1,3]

[B] Śaṅkha and Likhita say it most clearly:

> If a father is incapable of taking care of family affairs, the eldest son may do so in his stead; or, with his permission, even the next son if he is competent to do it. The property, however, shall not be partitioned against the father's will. If the father becomes old, loses his mind, or suffers from a chronic disease, the eldest son alone shall, like a father, safeguard the property on the others' behalf. Since hereditary property is the foundation of the family, sons are not independent as long as they have a father nor as long as their mother lives. [ŚL 270; **3.7**]

<**43**> These two Texts prohibit partition when the father is incapable of taking care of family affairs or when he is chronically ill. They state, on the contrary, that the eldest son shall single-handedly look after the household, or else a younger brother, provided he is competent to do so.[62] Hence, the correct reading is: "the property, however, shall not be partitioned against the father's will"; the reading "the property shall be partitioned when the father is incapable of taking care of family affairs" is in error.[63]

<**44**> In conclusion, there are only two possible times for partition: [1] when the father's proprietary right lapses because he becomes an outcaste, abandons all worldly desires, or dies, and [2] at the father's discretion while he still holds the proprietary right.

<**45**> As for the phrase "when their mother reaches menopause" [N 13.3a; **32**],[64] that pertains to the father's ancestral property. Since no other sons can be born after that time, the sons can proceed to the partition of that kind of property, although even then only if their father is willing. The reason why one has to wait for the mother's menopause is that, if ancestral property were partitioned prior to that time, sons born after the partition might be left unprovided for, which would not be proper, according to the Text:

[62] Jīmūtavāhana glosses the term *anantara* "the next (son)" in the ŚL text as *tad-anuja*, literally "(a son) born after him." He may thereby wish to indicate that, according to him, any younger brother may manage the household, provided he is competent to do so.

[63] Jīmūtavāhana seems to refer to a variant reading *kāryākṣame pitari* instead of *tv akāme pitari*. This variant does not, however, appear in any known commentary or digest in which ŚL 270 is quoted (*Dhko* p. 1147).

[64] Jīmūtavāhana here returns to the mother's menopause, which he did not comment on at **33–34**. He shows that this should not be taken as an additional criterion for the partition of paternal property. Cf. **2.1**.

> Those born, the unborn, and those yet in the womb, all of these are entitled to maintenance. Not to provide for them would be reprehensible. [Vy 253][65]

<**46**> It is clear, once again, that there are only two times at which paternal property may be partitioned. The first of these is the one mentioned by Manu [9.104; **14**], Gautama [28,1; **2.4**], and others: they avoid using the word "deceased," and rather say "after," meaning "after the father," to indicate any time at which the father's proprietary right lapses. The second time is the one pointed out by Manu 9.216 = Nārada 13.44/42n [**7.1**], i.e., partition at a time when the father still has worldly desires, but, then, at his discretion.[66]

<**47**> The phrase "when the sisters have been given away" [N 13.3b; **32**] is not intended to specify a time at which partition may take place. It merely emphasizes the fact that a partition may not take place before the sisters have been given away.[67]

The same is true for the following Nārada text:

> Brothers may divide among themselves whatever is left of the paternal property after paying their father's debts, so that he not remain a debtor. [N 13.32]

This Text is intended to stress the fact that it is imperative for sons to clear their father's debts; it is not meant to set a time at which they may divide his property.

<**48**> It also follows from this Nārada text that those who proceed to a partition can, with the approval of the creditors, either singly pay a share of the debt of their father, etc., or they can clear the debt jointly. The sole intent of the Text is to establish that only what is left of the property after the debts have been cleared can be partitioned.

That is why, of maternal property, too, only what is left after the mother's debts have been cleared can be partitioned. Says Yājñavalkya:

> After the death of their mother daughters divide what is left after paying her debts; failing daughters, her offspring. [Y 2.117cd; **3.4**; **4.2.13**]

All this will be fully explained in connection with failure to pay debts.[68]

[65] This verse has been attributed to various *dharma-śāstras* (most often Vyāsa), or just to an unidentified *smaraṇam*. The 1863 and other editions of the *Dāyabhāga* read *Manu-vacanāt* "according to the Manu text," but all manuscripts I consulted have *vacanāt* only. When the verse is quoted by authors outside Bengal, instead of *vṛttilopo vigarhitaḥ*, the end of the verse reads *na dānaṃ na ca vikrayaḥ*, "they should neither gift nor sell" (*Dhko* p. 1587).

[66] The reference to M 9.216 = N 13.44/42n to justify the second possible time for partition is unexpected. Jīmūtavāhana's reasoning must have been that that text indicates that a partition can be made while the father is still living the life of a householder, and, since at that time he is still the sole owner of the property, partition is at his discretion.

[67] Jīmūtavāhana now addresses another section of N 13.3 (**31**) which he did not comment on earlier, namely, that the sisters must have been given away.

[68] Śrīkṛṣṇa takes this statement to refer to **3.4** where Y 2.117 is quoted again. However, since *ṛṇādāna*, "failure to pay debts," is a *vivādapada*, "head of litigation," distinct from inheritance, Jīmūtavāhana, when saying *ṛṇādāne vakṣyate*, "it will be discussed in *ṛṇādāna*,"

<**49**> Alternatively, the phrase "when their sisters have been given away" [N 13.3b; **47**] means that, if their sisters have been married off, the sons alone divide their mother's property; if the sisters have not been married off, the sons divide the property together with them. That, too, will be discussed at the appropriate time [section **4.2**].[69]

<**50**> In this way I have demonstrated that there are only two possible times at which paternal property may be partitioned.

seems to indicate that he intended to elaborate on this point in a separate book (cf. Maheśvara: *granthāntare*) or chapter on debts, outside the *Dāyabhāga*. Cf. Introduction.

[69] Jīmūtavāhana shows later that this solution obtains only in the case of property that is not *yautaka*. In the case of *yautaka* property, sons inherit only in the absence of any kind of daughter, whether married off or not. Cf. **4.2.17–21**.

CHAPTER TWO

PARTITION OF ANCESTRAL PROPERTY

Time of Partition

<**1**> Let me now discuss the time at which ancestral property may be partitioned.
On this subject Br̥haspati says:

> Brothers may proceed to a partition when both parents are deceased. They may also do so while both live, provided their mother has reached menopause. [B 26.9; **3.10**]

<**2**> This Text does not pertain to paternal property; if it did, M 9.216 = N 13.44/42n [**7.1**] would never have occasion to apply, for no son can be born once the mother reaches menopause. Nor can one say that it pertains to maternal property, for, if it did, the mother herself might be left without anything. Hence, the phrase "has reached menopause" suggests that the Text pertains to ancestral property.[1]

<**3**> Note that the mother's menopause in and of itself is not a sufficient condition for partition to take place. A desire to do so is required as well, for partition can take place only if people want it. <**4**> If it be asked who must want it, the answer is: the father and he alone, on the basis of the following Gautama text:

> Sons may partition the property after their father,[2] or, while their father lives, once their mother reaches menopause, provided he wants it. [G 28.1–2]

[1] The conclusion that B 26.9 as a whole pertains to ancestral property is based entirely on the wording of its second half, and the beginning of Jīmūtavāhana's commentary (**2–4**) is devoted to that section of the text alone; only at **5** will he address the first half. The reference to partition after the mother's menopause has two implications. [1] The text cannot refer to the father's property, for if that could not take place before that time, M 9.216 = N 13.44/42n, which deals with the share of a son born after partition, could never apply and, therefore, would be useless, which is unthinkable. [2] The partition cannot refer to the mother's property either, since if that could be partitioned as soon as she reaches menopause, she might be left with very little for the rest of her life. Conclusion: since the text can pertain neither to paternal nor to maternal property, it must pertain to ancestral property. Cf. **3.10–11** and Rocher 1997.

[2] For the translation "after their father," see **1.46**.

<**5**> So, one possible time for partition is "when both parents are deceased." Because Bṛhaspati 26.9 [**1**] says "both parents," brothers german can partition even property that comes to them from their father only when their mother is deceased.[3] <**6**> The fact that the phrase "when both parents are deceased" alludes to the mother's decease does not mean that the first part of the Text pertains to the partition of maternal property. Indeed,

[1] since the phrase "while both live" precludes that the second half of the Text pertains to maternal property [**2**], that part necessarily pertains to the partition of a different kind of property.

[2] Because of the word "also" in "also while both live," the kind of property which may be partitioned on the grounds that both parents are deceased must be the same as that of which it is said that it can "also" be partitioned while they live. The mother's death should, therefore, not be interpreted as referring to maternal property. Partition of that kind of property will be discussed in detail later [chapter **4**].

<**7**> In conclusion, there are also two possible times for the partition of ancestral property:[4] [1] when both parents are deceased, and [2] when the mother reaches menopause, provided the father wants it. <**8**> Indeed, under no circumstances can ancestral property be partitioned if the father does not want it. There are a number of Texts to that effect by Manu, Nārada, Gautama, Baudhāyana, Śaṅkha and Likhita, and others, as follows:

> [A] They have no right to it as long as their parents live. [M 9. 104d; **1.14**]
>
> [B] They do not own it as long as their father is alive and competent. [D 1563cd; **1.18**]
>
> [C] While their father lives, provided he wants it. [G 28.2; **4**]
>
> [D] Partition of inheritance with the father's consent. [Bau 2.2.3.8]
>
> [E] Partition of inheritance during the father's lifetime, with his consent. [ŚL 274]

All these and other Texts to the same effect, first, establish in absolute terms that sons have no proprietary rights in any property whatever as long as their father lives, and that partition is at their father's discretion. Second, none of them mentions any time at which ancestral property in particular may be partitioned. Consequently, the fact that sons have no proprietary rights and that the father's wishes are paramount pertains to ancestral property as well.

[3] Since Jīmūtavāhana clearly wishes B 26.9 to pertain to ancestral property, I here translate the compound *pitṛ-dhana*, literally "paternal property," as "property that comes from their father." The reference to brothers german means that Jīmūtavāhana envisages a situation in which a man has more than one wife, so that when one of the wives dies her own sons can claim a partition of their share in their father's ancestral property.

[4] "Also" here means "even as for the partition of paternal property" (**1.44**).

<**9**> As for the Yājñavalkya text:[5]

> If land, a promissory note, or chattel was acquired by the grandfather, the father's and the son's proprietary rights in it are equal,[6] [Y 2.121]

its meaning has been luminously and truly explained by the unimpeachable Luminary of Knowledge:[7]

"If of two brothers whose father lives and who have not yet received their shares, one dies leaving a son and the other lives on, and if their father subsequently dies, the surviving brother alone might get his father's property, on the grounds that he is more closely related to the deceased than his nephew. It is to preclude this outcome that the Text says that their proprietary rights are equal.

"The purport of the Text is as follows: sons' sons have the same proprietary rights in their paternal grandfather's property as their deceased fathers would have had. In this case the fact of being more or less closely related makes no difference whatever, since both are of equal service to the deceased by offering him *piṇḍas* at their *pārvaṇaśrāddhas*.[8]

<**10**> "By the same token even a great-grandson whose grandfather and father are deceased has the same right as his great-grandfather's son or grandson, for they are in no way different when it comes to offering *piṇḍas*.

<**11**> "On the other hand, if grandsons had any proprietary rights in their grandfather's property while their fathers live, then, in a partition between brothers with sons and brothers without sons, the formers' sons would also receive shares, for their rights would in no way be different from those of the other participants in the partition."

<**12**> Note that this interpretation should not be rejected on the grounds that it takes the verse out of context. On the contrary, the very context [Y 2.120cd; **3.22**] is one of sons of different fathers.[9]

[5] The phrase "as for" (*yat tu*) most often introduces texts which, at first glance, seem incompatible with an earlier statement by Jīmūtavāhana; he then proves that, if correctly interpreted, they are not.

[6] For the definitions of a promissory note (*nibandha*) and chattel (*dravya*), see **13–14**. For a restriction of this rule to a particular kind of son (*kṣetraja*), see **59**.

[7] On Vidyodyota "Luminary of Knowledge," see Introduction. Jīmūtavāhana fails to make clear where the opinion attributed to Vidyodyota ends. Much depends on the interpretation of **12** (see note 9). If one accepts the reading on which my translation of **12** is based, Vidyodyota's text goes up to the end of **11**. If one accepts the variant reading, it goes up to the end of **12**, and possibly even includes **13** and **14**.

[8] On *piṇḍas* and being of service to the deceased at one's *pārvaṇaśrāddhas*, see Introduction.

[9] The beginning of this sentence exhibits two different readings. My translation is based on the reading *na ca*, literally "and it is not so that." This is the reading of nearly all *Dāyabhāga* manuscripts, including Colebrooke's, and of the quotation of this passage in the *Vyavahāraprakāśa* (ed. p.446; tr. II.i.13). With this reading the sentence appears to be a statement by Jīmūtavāhana in support of the Luminary's interpretation of Y 2.121. However, in some editions (e.g., 1829, 1863, 1893) and in Śrīkṛṣṇa's commentary (the only one

<**13**> A "promissory note" is a commitment such as "I will give you such and such in every month of Kārttika."[10] <**14**> "Chattel," when mentioned together with land, refers to slaves.[11]

<**15**> Alternatively, Dhāreśvara proffered the following interpretation of Yājñavalkya 2.121:

"If a father of his own accord proceeds to a partition of the property, then, as far as ancestral property is concerned, he and his sons have equal proprietary rights, i.e. differently from property he acquired on his own, the father cannot at his discretion give them larger or smaller shares."[12]

<**16**> Says Viṣṇu:

> If a father partitions property with his sons, he can do whatever he pleases with property he acquired on his own; in ancestral property, however, the proprietary rights of father and son are equal. [Vi 17.1–2; **55**, **76**]

<**17**> One thing is perfectly clear: if a father partitions property with his sons, he may, as he pleases, give them shares of different sizes of property he acquired on his own; the same is not true, however, of ancestral property, for there "their proprietary rights are equal," meaning that there the father cannot act as he pleases.

<**18**> At any rate, two notions must be rejected, namely, [1] that the phrase "their proprietary rights are equal" at Yājñavalkya 2.121 means that father and son receive equal shares in ancestral property; and [2] that it means that sons can initiate the partition.[13] <**19**> The other Text should be interpreted in the same way.[14]

---

that is explicit) the sentence starts with *tathā ca*, "besides." In that case the sentence belongs within the quotation and continues the argument begun at **11**: "Besides, Y 2.121 cannot be intended to say that sons and their fathers, if alive, have equal rights to ancestral property, for this would take the verse out of context, the context being exclusively one of sons of different fathers."

[10] Wilson (1855: 375) explains *nibandha* as "a *corrody*, a fixed allowance granted by the Rája or person in authority, to be received from the proceeds of a manufactory, mine, or estate"; Jolly (1885: 93) as "a hereditary right or income." See Derrett 1962: 74–75 (= *Essays* 2.67–68).

[11] On the close connection between land and slaves in Hindu law, see Strange 1825: 127. On the use of the term *dvipad*, "biped," for slaves to distinguish them from other, quadruped possessions, see J. N. Bhattacharya 1885: 5. The *Mitākṣarā* (Colebrooke I.v.4) gives *dravya*, which I translate "chattel," its ordinary meaning, "movable property such as gold and silver."

[12] Differently from the preceding quotation, in this case Jīmūtavāhana makes it clear where the citation ends. The interpretation of Y 2.121, which is here attributed to Dhāreśvara, is identical with that of the *Mitākṣarā* (Colebrooke I.v.5).

[13] Acyuta and Śrīkṛṣṇa again attribute these opinions to "the author of the *Mitākṣarā* and others."

[14] Maheśvara interprets the phrase "the other Text" as a reference to B 26.14 (**50**); it may also refer to Vi 17.2 (**16**), where *tulyaṃ svāmitvam* has the same meaning as *sadṛśaṃ svāmyam* at Y.121.

<**20**> Hence, it follows [1] that a father is entitled to two shares in ancestral property,[15] and [2] that the partition is at the sole discretion of the father, not of the sons.

<**21**> Now, as to Manu and Viṣṇu:[16]

> If a father retrieves ancestral property that had not been retrieved, he cannot be forced to partition it with his sons; it constitutes self-acquired property, [M 9.209 = Vi 18.43; **6.2.32**]

since they set the circumstance that the father retrieved ancestral property on his own as the necessary and sufficient condition for not having to partition it against his will, they thereby seem to imply that, for ancestral property which he did not retrieve on his own, his sons can indeed force him to proceed to a partition.

What the verse really means is that, when a father proceeds to allot shares, he does not have to partition against his will ancestral property he retrieved on his own, but that he must partition other ancestral property even if he would prefer not to, i.e., that partitioning it is not at his own discretion. Even here, though, the two Sages do not wish to convey the notion that the partition can be at the discretion of the sons.

<**22**> On the other hand, in the case of ancestral gems, pearls, and the like, which the father did not retrieve on his own, he is their sole owner nevertheless, as if he had recovered them on his own, and he may divide them into shares of different sizes as he pleases. Says Yājñavalkya:

> The father is master of gems, pearls, and corals, all of it; neither the father nor the grandfather is master of immovable property, all of it. [17]

<**23**> This Text contains the word "grandfather," so it must pertain to ancestral property. Since, after first mentioning gems, pearls, and the like, the Text then adds "all of it," it authorizes the father to dispose by gift or otherwise of everything, except land and the like; he is not master of immovable property, promissory notes, or chattel.[18] Since, with regard to the latter the Text likewise says "all of it," it forbids the father to dispose by gift or otherwise of anything that is needed to provide for the family, for the family must be provided for at all costs. Says Manu:

[15] The *Dāyabhāga* commentators refer to texts such as B 26.16 and N 13.12ab (**35**, **46**).

[16] This sentence is introduced with the formula *yac ca* (cf. **9** *yat tu*), which indicates that, in addition to Y 2.121, there is yet another text that needs to be interpreted differently from what it appears to say at first glance.

[17] This often quoted verse is not part of the *Yājñavalkya-smṛti*. It has been attributed to a variety of Sages, most often to Nārada (*Dhko* p. 1219), yet it does not appear in the *Nārada-smṛti* either. It is quoted anonymously in the *Mitākṣarā* (introduction to Y 2.114; Colebrooke I.i.21); Colebrooke's conclusion (in a note on **22**) that Jīmūtavāhana evidently took it from the *Mitākṣarā* has been questioned by Jolly (1885: 113 n.). The somewhat forced repetition, in English, of the phrase "all of it" (twice *sarvasya* in Sanskrit) anticipates Jīmūtavāhana's interpretation of the verse.

[18] On "promissory note" and "chattel," which are mentioned together with land at Y 2.121 (**9**), see **13–14**.

> Providing for those who need to be provided for is a sure means to gain heaven; he who hurts them goes to hell. Hence one should provide for them by any means.[19]

<**24**> That does not mean, however, that the father cannot dispose by gift or otherwise of some of it, as long as it does not interfere with the maintenance of the family. Otherwise, the phrase "all of it" would be redundant.[20]

<**25**> Since the Yājñavalkya verse uses the phrase "immovable property," it follows as a matter of course that the prohibition to dispose of it by gift or otherwise also applies to promissory notes and chattel.[21]

<**26**> On the other hand, it is self-evident that, if there is not other way properly to provide for the family than by selling all property including immovables, under these circumstances the father may dispose by sale or otherwise of everything, in accordance with the rule:

> One shall protect oneself by all possible means.[22] [G 9.34]

[Objection] <**27**> There are two Vyāsa verses that deny any single individual the right to dispose by sale or otherwise of immovable property:[23]

> No single individual shall,[24] without the consent of the others, trade or gift any immovables that are common to his *gotra*.[25] [Vy 254]

[19] This verse is not part of the *Manu-smṛti*. A few *Dāyabhāga* manuscripts attribute it to Bṛhan-Manu. Böhtlingk 1870–73 no. 4537 (2018) quotes it from "Manu in the *Dāyabhāga*." The phrase "those who need to be provided for" translates Sanskrit *poṣya-varga*, "group of people to be provided for." According to a verse quoted by Śrīkṛṣṇa, *poṣya-varga* includes father, mother, teacher, wife, offspring, persons in distress, servants, and guests.

[20] I.e., if he could not dispose of some of it, it would have been useless to say that what he cannot dispose of is all of it.

[21] Jīmūtavāhana here appeals to the popular *daṇḍāpūpanyāya* "the rule of the staff and the cake." Although there are minor variants in the ways in which this rule is illustrated, it basically comes down to this: if a cake that was kept on a wooden pole has disappeared and the wood has been gnawed by a rat, since eating the cake is easier than gnawing wood, "it follows as a matter of course" that the rat has eaten the cake. See Kane 1962: 1344. Cf. **4.3.14**, **4.3.30**, **11.1.66**, and **11.2.30**.

[22] This rule is taken out of context. In the *Gautama-dharmasūtra* it refers to one of several duties of a *snātaka*, i.e., a person who has taken the ritual bath that signals the end of his first stage of life (*brahmacarya* "studentship"), and who is about to marry and enter the stage of a householder (*gṛhastha*). The commentator Haradatta illustrates the rule by saying that a *snātaka* should not go out on the road unaccompanied.

[23] This is one of the passages of the *Dāyabhāga* which the commentators interpret as a refutation of Caṇḍeśvara's *Vivādaratnākara*. See Introduction.

[24] Within the objection I translate the Sanskrit optative as "shall." Jīmūtavāhana's refutation will be based on a different interpretation of the same verbal form as "ought."

[25] "The Brahmanical *gotra*, which persists with little modification to the present day, may be defined as an exogamous patrilineal sibship, whose members trace their descent back to a common ancestor" (Brough 1953: 3). Cf. **60**, **5.14–15**, **11.1.4**, and **11.6.10**. On *gotra*, see also Kane 1941: 479–82, and Brough 1946–47.

> Whether separated or not, *sapiṇḍas* are equal with regard to immovable property; each of them individually is powerless to gift, pledge, or sell any of it.[26] [Vy 255]

[Refutation] Not so. The definition of what constitutes a proprietary right in any other kind of property, i.e., the right to dispose of it as one pleases, applies in this case as well. <**28**> The notion, which Vyāsa 254 worded in the form of a negative injunction, is meant to convey is that, since the family suffers when a wicked individual, acting in his capacity of owner, disposes of immovable property by sale, gift, or otherwise, that person incurs a loss of *dharma*. The verse does not mean to say that such sales and the like are null and void.

<**29**> Other similar Texts, such as the following, should be interpreted in the same light:

> No gift or sale of immovables or slaves without calling all his sons together, even if he acquired them on his own.[27] [Vy 252]

Indeed, such Texts must necessarily be supplemented with the phrase "ought to be made."[28] <**30**> The result of prescribing that a gift or sale "ought not to be made" is that he who makes it defies an injunction, not that the sale and the like are null and void. No deed once done can be changed even by a hundred Texts.[29]

<**31**> By the same token Nārada says:[30]

[26] On *sapiṇḍa*, see Introduction.

[27] Differently from the two Vyāsa verses at **27**, this verse has been quoted repeatedly, most often anonymously (*Dhko* p. 1587). On "slaves," literally "bipeds," see note 11.

[28] Śrīkṛṣṇa raises the question why texts such as Vy 252 must "necessarily" (*avaśyam*) be supplemented with the gerundive *kartavya*, "ought to be made" (with the result that the transaction, though *na dharmya*, "improper," stands), rather than with a verb such as *sidhyati*, "is valid" (with the result that the transaction is null and void). Śrikṛṣṇa's defense of Jīmūtavāhana's point of view is linguistic. In a Sanskrit sentence the agent (*kartṛ*) of a subordinate clause, here "calling . . . together," must of necessity be identical with the agent of the main clause, here the father. In this case that result can be achieved only by supplementing "ought to be made (namely, by him)," not by supplementing "is valid," the agent of which would be "no gift or sale."

[29] This passage of the *Dāyabhāga* has become famous for its formulation of the principle of *factum valet*. Cf. Jolly 1885: 113; Derrett 1958a (= *Essays* 3.1–24); Rocher 1995.

[30] The commentators on the *Dāyabhāga* and Mitramiśra, who provides a free rendering of this entire passage (*Vyvahāraprakāśa* ed. p. 460; tr. II.i.22), adduce various reasons why, at this point, Jīmūtavāhana quotes two Nārada verses which appear to indicate that after partition anyone can act with his share, including immovable property, as he pleases. All failed to note, however, that the Vyāsa verses (**27**) deal with the disposal of immovables that are common to the *gotra*, "whether the members are separated or not." According to Jīmūtavāhana, Vyāsa's negative injunctions about members who are not separated reflect badly on the transgressor but the act stands by the principle of *factum valet*. He now turns to the case of family members who are not separated: Nārada's outright injunction to the effect that they may dispose of immovables has to be interpreted with restrictions, so as to bring it in accordance with Vyāsa's negative injunctions.

> When several individuals who are descended from the same father perform their religious duties separately, do their work separately, earn the benefit of their work separately, and do not consult one another about their affairs, if they gift or sell their own shares, they may do all that as they please. They are indeed masters of their own property. [N 13.42–43/41–42]

<**32**> Let us now return to our subject. The conclusion of our earlier discussion [**18**] was that Yājñavalkya 2.121 [**9**] cannot possibly enjoin that father and son should get equal shares in ancestral property, and that it cannot be intended to establish that the sons can initiate a partition. Its purpose, therefore, is either to prohibit that the father give shares of different sizes as he pleases [**15**], or to establish that a brother's son who lost his father has the same right as his paternal uncle [**9**].

<**33**> So, even as with paternal property, in the case of ancestral property as well, partition can take place only at the father's discretion. The difference is that in this case it can take place only when the mother reaches menopause, except for property the father acquired on his own, for which it is not necessary that the mother has reached menopause. As far as partition after the father's death is concerned, paternal and ancestral properties are in no way different.

<**34**> In conclusion, in the case of ancestral property as well, there are two possible times at which it may be partitioned.

A Double Share for the Father

<**35**> At one of these times, namely, when the father takes the initiative to partition property with his sons, he may take two shares of the ancestral property for himself. Indeed,

[1] there are two Texts in which the father's right to two shares is set forth unconditionally:[31]

[A] Bṛhaspati says

> When a father proceeds to a partition in his lifetime, he may take two shares for himself. [B 26.16; **46**]

[B] Nārada says:

> When a father partitions property, he may take two shares for himself. [N 13.12ab; **46**]

[31] As a result, these texts also apply to ancestral property even though the term does not appear in them. The *Mitākṣarā* (on Y 2.122; Colebrooke I.v.7), on the contrary, interprets the texts as applying solely to property which the father acquired on his own.

[2] <**36**> There is yet another reason why the father is entitled to take two shares of ancestral property.[32] Indeed,

[A] <**37**> the following two Manu texts first provide for preemptions of five percent together with what is best in the entire property, of one half of that, and of one quarter of it. After that they provide for a full additional share, for one-half additional share, and for one-quarter additional share:

> The eldest son gets a preempted share of five percent and whatever constitutes the best part of the entire property; the middle one gets one half of that; each of the younger ones one quarter of it. [M 9.112]

And then:

> Once special shares have thus been preempted, the rest is divided into equal shares. If no special shares were preempted, shares shall be apportioned as follows: the eldest gets one additional share, the next one gets one share and a half, and all the younger ones get one share each. That is the law. [M 9.116–117]

[B] Gautama has similar rules:

> The eldest son gets a preempted share of five percent, a pair, a carriage yoked to an animal with incisor teeth in both jaws, and a bull with a cow. [G 28.5]

"A pair" here means a male and a female sheep or other such animals. "An animal with incisor teeth in both jaws" means a horse and the like;[33] the eldest gets a carriage yoked to such an animal. He gets not just a bull, but a bull along with one or more cows.[34] So far for the several items that go to the eldest. And then:

[32] Śrīkṛṣṇa points out that, following the textual argument (*vacana*) [**5**], Jīnūtavāhana now proceeds to show that giving the father a double share in ancestral property is also the right thing to do (*yukti*). Indeed, Jīmūtavāhana enters into a lengthy excursus dealing with the fact that there are situations in which sons get double shares, to conclude [**46**] that, if this is true for sons, a fortiori, it is also true for the father.

[33] As early as the *Śatapatha-brāhmaṇa* (ed 1.6.3.30; tr. vol. 1, p. 171) a distinction is made between creatures that have incisor teeth in both jaws (*ubhayato-dat*; the term *ubhayā-dat* is found at *Ṛgveda* 10.90.10) and creatures that have incisors in the lower jaw only (*anyataro-dat*). The former include humans and horses (cf. *Taittirīya-saṃhitā* 5.1.2.6: "by its incisors the horse is stronger than those with incisors in one jaw only"); the latter include animals such as cows and sheep.

[34] Jīmūtavāhana explains the anomalous compound *go-vṛṣaḥ* "cow-bull" (masculine singular) as a bull together with a cow or cows (*go-yukta-vṛṣaḥ*). Śrīkṛṣṇa defends this interpretation and explains the term as a *madhyapadalopisamāsa*, i.e., a compound in which the middle term (here -*yukta*-, "along with") has been dropped. According to the *Kāśikā* (6.2.144), however, *go-vṛṣa* means " one who impregnates cows," i.e., a bull. Cf. M 9.150, where the commentators agree with the *Kāśikā*.

> If there are several animals, the middle one gets an animal blind in one eye,[35] a limping one, one without horns, and a crippled one. [G 28.6]

"A limping one" means an old one. "One without horns" means one that is undersized. "A crippled one" means one whose penis has been cut.[36] The animals mentioned here go to the middle one, provided several animals are available.[37] And, then, each of the younger brothers gets a sheep and so forth:

> For the younger ones a sheep, grain, iron, a house,[38] an animal yoked to a carriage, and one of each of the quadrupeds. All the rest is divided equally. [G 28.7–8]

After laying down that a sheep and other items go to the younger ones, and that they must divide all the rest equally, Gautama goes on to enjoin that the eldest may get two shares:

> Or else, the eldest gets two shares, the others one share each. [G 28.9–10]

[Objection] <**38**> When the eldest son is said to get two shares, it is because he acquired the property.[39]

[Refutation] Not so. Indeed,

[1] Manu 9.116–117 [**37**] enjoins a double share "if no special shares were preempted," and it is inconceivable that the preemption of special shares would have anything to do with the fact that those to whom they are allotted acquired the property.

[2] In their capacity of acquirers the middle and youngest brothers are in no way different from the eldest. They could not, therefore, be allotted an additional half share and a quarter share, respectively, and the words "eldest," "middle," and "younger" at Manu 9.117 would be redundant.

[3] <**39**> By the same token, when Manu discusses the partition of paternal property between an appointed daughter and a full-fledged son,[40] he says this:

[35] The tern *kāṇa* is often translated as "one-eyed." The *Kāśikā* (2.1.30; 2.3.20), however, cites the expression *akṣṇā kāṇaḥ*, "blind in one eye."

[36] The term *lāṅgūla*, in Jīmūtavahana's comment on *vaṇḍa* at G 28.6 as *vikṛta-lāṅgūla*, "whose *lāṅgūla* has been mutilated," is often translated as "tail." Hence Colebrooke's translation of *vaṇḍa* as "having a distorted tail," and Bühler's and Olivelle's (Gautama tr.) "tailless." Yet, *vaṇḍa* most often means "emasculated," and *lāṅgūla* indicates both the tail and the male organ. Cf. PW 6: 428.

[37] If there are several animals of a given kind, the middle one gets those that are less desirable; the eldest brother gets the best of each.

[38] Based on ŚL 268, Śrīkṛṣṇa interprets "a house" as a home different from the father's residence.

[39] I.e., the double share is not allotted to the eldest son on the grounds of primogeniture. It represents a special case of a broader rule by which anyone who acquired property on his own receives a double share in it at the time of partition.

[40] On the appointed daughter (*putrikā*) and the full-fledged son (*aurasa*), see note at **10.1,** Introduction, and Rocher 1999.

> If a daughter has been appointed and a son was born later, their shares shall be equal; there is no seniority right for women. [M 9.134; **10.1**]

By making their shares equal on the grounds that the daughter is not senior because she is a woman, Manu at the same time establishes that, if the older sibling is a male, he does get a double share.[41]

<**40**> Some people have said this:[42] "To account for the fact that Easterners observe the *holākā* festival, the *holākā* chapter posits the existence of a Revealed Text in the form: '*Holākā* must be observed.'[43] This much suffices to account for the observance of *holākā*. The Revealed Text need not include phrases such as 'by Easterners,'[44] for that would make it needlessly cumbersome. In the same way, in the case at hand a Revealed Text should be posited as follows: 'The acquirer shall get two shares'; it need not include phrases such as 'the father.'"

That is beside the point.

True, the observance of *holākā* among Easterners is accounted for by a general Revealed Text that must necessarily be posited.[45] It would be wrong to say that the Revealed Text must include the phrase "by Easterners" to account for the fact that other people than Easterners do not observe *holākā*. Indeed, the fact that other people do not observe it, i.e., that the custom does not exist among them, cannot be a sufficient ground to posit a Revealed Text that includes such a phrase.[46]

Yet, the case at hand is different. Indeed,

[41] By denying primogeniture to women, M 9.134 demonstrates that additional shares based on primogeniture do exist for men.

[42] These are people who support the view that anyone who receives a double share does so on the grounds that he is the acquirer.

[43] The *holākā-adhikaraṇa*, "*holākā* chapter," also called *sāmānyaśrutikalpanā-adhikaraṇa* "the chapter on positing a general Revealed Text," corresponds to *Mīmāṃsāsūtras* 1.3.15–23. *Holākā* is a festival observed in the spring, mainly by Easterners. In principle, every such custom (*ācāra*), and every *smṛti* text, is supposed to be based on a revealed, Vedic text (*śruti*). The question raised in the *holākā* chapter is whether, in cases in which the application of the custom or the *smṛti* text involves a restriction, the presumed *śruti* text should include a reference to that restriction. The final answer is negative: the posited Text should be as brief and general as possible. For other references to *holākā*, see **6.1.22**, **27**. On the use of the *holākā* chapter in legal contexts, see Kane 1946: 851–52; 1962: 1281–82; K. L. Sarkar 1909: 83–85; Sankararama Sastri 1926: 145–47.

[44] "Phrases such as," in the plural, refers to the fact that, even as it is unnecessary to include the phrase "by Easterners" in the Revealed Text on *holākā*, it is also unnecessary to include "by Southerners" for the *āhnīnaibuka* rite which is observed in the South, or "by Northerners" for the *udvṛṣabhayajña* which is observed in the North (Śabara on *Mīmāṃsāsūtra* 1.3.15).

[45] I.e., by the minimal Vedic text: "*holākā* must be performed," without the addition "by Easterners."

[46] Custom (*ācāra*) is recognized as one of the sources of *dharma* (cf. note 59). Hence, the fact that it is customary in other areas than the East not to observe *holākā* means that the injunction applies only to those among whom the celebration is accepted by custom.

[1] Manu and others do use the phrase "the eldest." To account for this it is necessary to posit a Revealed Text that includes the phrase "the eldest."

[2] There is no reason why we should posit a Revealed Text that includes the phrase "the acquirer."[47]

[3] Nothing authorizes us to posit a Revealed Text that would include both "the eldest" and "the acquirer."[48]

[Objection] To make it possible for the acquirer to get two shares in situations other than this,[49] a Revealed Text to that effect does have to be posited. Hence, in compliance with the principle of conciseness, let the same Revealed Text serve both purposes, and let the phrase "the elder" refer to the acquirer.[50]

[Refutation] Not so. Indeed,

[1] this proposition could be reversed. If we were to posit a Revealed Text including a phrase "the eldest" that applies to the acquirer, we might as well posit a Revealed Text including the phrase "the acquirer" that refers to the eldest. There is no reason why one of these alternatives should be preferable to the other.

[2] If you apply principles such as conciseness in this fashion, you might as well infer that there is one single Revealed Text consisting of one, three, four, or more words, and say that all phrases in the *smṛtis* somehow are based on it either metaphorically or by suggestive power.[51] That would surely demonstrate your exceptional knowledge of the *smṛti* texts!

In conclusion, the purport of the *holākā* chapter is as follows: if a Revealed Text has to be posited because of a custom or a *smṛti* text, it must be posited in such a way that it accounts for the existence of the custom to which it refers among certain people or for the wording of the *smṛti* text, but for nothing more than that.

<**41**> That is also why[52] Vasiṣṭha first mentions a double share for the eldest, and then, elsewhere, again for the individual who acquired property. First he says:

> Now, partition of inheritance among brothers. The eldest gets two shares. [Va 17.40,42]

Then, a little later, he says:

> And, if one of them produced something on his own, he too gets two shares. [Va 17.51]

[47] Indeed, the texts that give the eldest a double share (e.g., M 9.117 and G 28.9; **37**) do not include the phrase "the acquirer."

[48] Śrīkṛṣṇa comments that the two terms do not appear together in any single *smṛti* text.

[49] I.e., when someone else than the eldest, namely, a younger brother, acquired the property.

[50] The principle of *lāghava*, "conciseness," subsumes the axiom that "where one rule or proposition would suffice, more must not be assumed" (K. L. Sarkar 1909: 78).

[51] On the use of *lakṣaṇā*, "suggestive power," in legal texts, see, e.g., K. L. Sarkar 1909: 133; Keith 1921: 99. As a rule, one should not resort to an interpretation based on the sug-gestive of a word as long as a literal interpretation is possible. Cf. **4.2.18**.

[52] I.e., again to show that the reason why the eldest gets a double share is not because he acquired the property (cf. the objection at **38**); in fact, getting a double share as the eldest and getting a double share as the acquirer are mutually independent.

If the latter rule was meant to show that the eldest must have acquired the property in order to get two shares, the former explicit reference to the fact that the eldest gets two shares would be redundant.

<**42**> Besides, the right to get two shares is not determined by primogeniture alone. Says Bṛhaspati:

> The one who is senior in years, knowledge, or competence gets two shares of the inheritance; the others get equal shares. Such a man is like a father to them. [B 26.21]

If the man in question got two shares because he acquired the property, there would be no point in stipulating age, knowledge, and so forth.

<**43**> Note that the allocation of two shares pertains to partitions in which all brothers are brothers german, whereas the preemption of five percent for the eldest pertains to partitions involving both brothers german and half brothers. Says Bṛhaspati:

> If all sons of a twice-born man were born of wives of the same caste, a special share shall be preempted for the eldest; the others get equal shares. [B 26.11 = M 9.156]

<**44**> Since Bṛhaspati here specifically provides for preempted shares in partitions between sons born of different wives of the same caste, it follows that his allocation of two shares at **42** pertains only to partitions in which all brothers are brothers german. This distinction also makes sense, for, when the eldest brother is a brother german to boot, he commands even greater respect.

<**45**> When there are only ten cows or other animals, even the preempted share need not always be allotted.[53] Thus Manu:

> There is no preempted share out of ten when the brothers are equally accomplished in their activities. The eldest shall then only be given something or other, as a token of respect. [M 9.115]

<**46**> One thing stands out clearly as a result of the foregoing discussion. If there are situations in which someone who is only an eldest brother receives two shares in the paternal property, how could it be that the father—the one to whom his sons owe their existence, the one who is entitled to gift, sell, or forfeit the property, the one from whom stems the link which the others have with ancestral property, the one who commands more respect than anyone—would not get two shares of his father's property?

Also, when Bṛhaspati [26.21; **42**] assigns two shares to the eldest by analogy, namely, because "he is like a father," he thereby indirectly conveys the notion that the father is entitled to two shares.

[53] In the *Manu-smṛti* this verse constitutes an exception to the immediately preceding one (not quoted in the *Dāyabhāga*) which contains an outright injunction to the effect that the eldest brother gets the best out of every kind of property, including the best out of ten animals.

Elsewhere Bṛhaspati enjoins two shares outright by referring to them in absolute terms:

> When a father proceeds to a partition in his lifetime, he may take two shares for himself.[54] [B 26.16; **35**]

And so does Nārada:

> When a father partitions property, he may take two shares for himself. After her husband's death the mother gets a share equal to that of her sons. [N 13.12; **35**]

<**47**> The way in which this sentence is to be construed is that, when a father proceeds to a partition, he may take two shares "for himself." It does not mean that he may do so when he partitions property "of himself," for, if that were the case, the Text would be incompatible with what we said earlier.[55]

<**48**> Moreover,[56] when father and son are said to have "equal shares" in ancestral property, that would have to be interpreted as the son having "as much" property as his father, not that he has "as much in the same items" as his father.[57] Indeed, these items would then have two owners, and there could be no partition, even as there is no partition between husband and wife.[58] <**49**> Yet, even then, in a partition between brothers in which the eldest, *qua* eldest, gets a double share, and in which a double share would also be allotted to his son, the eldest and his son would get four shares, the other brothers a single share each. And, if the eldest brother happened to have several sons all of whom are allotted a share equal to their father's, the younger brothers would get very little indeed. This approach would be incompatible with the practice of the couth.[59]

[54] As far as the allotment of two shares to the father is concerned, B 26.21 is a *jñāpana*, "indirect indication," whereas B 26.16 is, in Jīmūtavāhana's words, an *upadeśa*, a term that is synonymous with *vidhi*, "outright injunction." Cf. Kane 1962: 1183–84 n. 1930.

[55] The genitive *ātmanaḥ* at N 13.12 is to be construed with the verb *pratipadyeta*, "take for himself," not with *vibhajan* and an understood noun *dravyam*, "when he partitions property of his own." With his own property the father can do as he pleases (Vi 17.1; **16**, **55**, **76**); cf. H 4.5 (**57**).

[56] Jīmūtavāhana introduces more arguments to show that the shares of father and son in ancestral property cannot be equal.

[57] Jīmūtavāhana must be thinking of texts (e.g., Vy 255; **27**) in which the ambiguous term *sama* appears. A *sama-bhāga* can mean an equal but separate share, but it can also mean a single share held in common.

[58] This is a reference to texts such as Āp 2.6.14.16–17: "There is no partition between husband and wife, for ever since their wedding they are united in their ritual activities." Cf. H 4.8.

[59] This is one of few cases (cf. **3.22**) in the *Dāyabhāga* in which Jīmūtavāhana rejects an argument on the grounds that it would be incompatible with *śiṣṭa-ācāra*, "the practice of the cooth," which is recognized as one of the sources of *dharma*. Cf. Va 1.4–6: "*Dharma* is enjoined by the *śruti* and *smṛti*. Failing these, *dharma* is based on *śiṣṭa-ācāra*. A *śiṣṭa* is one who is free of passion." Instead of *śiṣṭa-ācāra*, M 2.6 reads *ācāraḥ sādhūnām*, Y 1.7 *sad-ācāra*.

<50> Now, as to the Bṛhaspati text:[60]

> In both immovable and movable property acquired by the grandfather, father and son have equal shares,[61] [B 26.14]

the phrase "have equal shares" here means that they both have shares. What the Text means is that, differently from property which the father acquired on his own, in this case he cannot give shares of different sizes as he pleases. It does not mean that their shares are equal. <51> Alternatively, the Text does prescribe equal shares, and pertains to a situation in which the father is the son of two fathers.[62]

<52> The correct interpretation of the Text to the effect that "father's and son's proprietary rights in it are equal" [Y 2.121; **9**] has been given earlier.

<53> Also, some say the following: "If the father in question happens to be an eldest son, i.e., a son who saved his own father from the hell called *Put*,[63] he gets a share twice as large as that of his brothers on the grounds that he is like a father to them. In that case it is even more appropriate that he should get a share twice as large as that of his sons, whose sole link to the ancestral property is through him. But, if the father is not his own father's eldest son, then he shall divide the ancestral property equally with his sons."

<54> That is wrong. Indeed,

[1] since there are outright injunctions of one and a half share and so on for the middle and other sons, it is even more appropriate that a father get a full double share, because he is the father.

[2] It would not be proper for you or the Sages to present the reference to equal shares for father and son as the general rule.[64]

<55> Also, it is out of the question to say that references to two shares for the father pertain to property he acquired on his own. Indeed,

[1] as outright injunctions they would be pointless, since it is established,[65] first, that in that case partition is at his pleasure and, second, that he can take two shares, three shares, or less or more, as he pleases.

[2] Nor could they be intended as admonitory injunctions.[66] Indeed,

[60] "Now, as to . . ." Cf. note 16.

[61] Jīmūtavāhana does not comment on the presence of the phrase "movable property" in this verse. Yet, the first of the two interpretations he is about to propose is incompatible with his statement at **22**, to the effect that, as far as ancestral movable property is concerned, the father can divide it into shares of different sizes. The commentators on the *Dāyabhāga* did note the problem and proposed a variety of solutions (cf. Colebrooke, note).

[62] The phrase "the son of two fathers" refers to a *kṣetraja* son, i.e., the son of a levirate marriage (**10.7**), who is held to be the son both of the husband of his mother and of the man who begot him, and who therefore inherits from both. Cf. **59–62**.

[63] On the etymology of the term *putra*, see **1.36**.

[64] Śrīkṛṣṇa refers to the phrase "equal shares" (B 26.14; **50**). Positing equal shares as the general rule would mean that any deviation, such as for the eldest son who saves his father from hell, would be an exception that needs to be justified.

[65] On the technical meaning of the term "established" (*prāpta*), see note at **1.27**.

[66] On admonitory injunction, see **1.27**. In this case an admonitory injunction would restrict the various ways in which a father can divide self-acquired property to a single one:

[a] this kind of interpretation would be incompatible with the following Viṣṇu text:

> If a father partitions property with his sons, he can do whatever he pleases with property he acquired on his own; in ancestral property, however, the proprietary rights of father and son are equal. [Vi 17.1–2; **16, 76**]

<**56**> This means that, as far as property he acquired on his own is concerned, the Texts allow him to take anything he pleases, one half share, two shares, or three shares, but that he cannot do the same when it comes to ancestral property.

[b] <**57**> It would be incompatible with Hārīta:

> While he lives, he either becomes a hermit or enters the final stage of life after partitioning the property among his sons; or he stays on after partitioning some of the property and keeping most of it for himself, and, if he becomes destitute, he claims it back from them. [H 4.5]

<**58**> This Text explicitly allows a father to partition just a small portion of the property and keep most of it for himself. "The final stage of life" here means the life of a wanderer.[67]

<**59**> Now, as to the text of Śaṅkha and Likhita:[68]

> If he is the son of one father (*eka-putra*) he may take two shares for himself, [ŚL 263]

its meaning is as follows.[69] The compound *eka-putra* means "the son of one father"; it is not a *bahuvrīhi* compound meaning "a father who has one son." Indeed, a *ṣaṣṭhī-tatpuruṣa* is preferable to a *bahuvrīhi*, because in the latter a word that does not appear in the compound is determinant.[70]

---

a double share. Jīmūtavāhana will quote two texts which explicitly allow various ways of dividing this kind of property.

[67] On Jīmūtavāhana's identification of *pravrajyā*, "the life of a wanderer," with the fourth stage of life, see note at **1.4**.

[68] "Now, as to . . ." cf. note 16.

[69] Jīmūtavāhana's commentary on ŚL 263 continues through **64**.

[70] By saying that a *bahuvrīhi* compound is *anya-padārtha-pradhāna* Jīmūtavāhana borrows terminology from the Sanskrit grammarians. Pāṇini (2.2.24) describes a *bahuvrīhi* as *anya-padārthe* "meaning something else (that is, than what its component parts express)." The phrase Jīmūtavāhana uses appears in the *Mahābhāṣya* (2.1.6,20,49) to refer to the type of compound the meaning of which is not determined by any of its component parts but by a word outside the compound. *Eka-putra* as a *bahuvrīhi* refers neither to "one" nor to the "son," but to the father. As a *ṣaṣṭhī-tatpuruṣa*,, i.e., a determinative compound the first member of which stands for a noun in the genitive, by contrast, *eka-putra* does refer to "son" with the additional qualifier "of one." As a result, the interpretation as a *ṣaṣṭhī-tatpuruṣa* is preferable to the interpretation as a *bahuvrīhi*. On this principle see J. N. Bhattacharya 1893: 66. A similar discussion appears at *Mīmāṃsā-sūtra* 6.1.51, where it is argued that an interpretation as a *ṣaṣṭhī-tatpuruṣa* is less desirable than as a *karmadhāraya*, "descriptive compound," i.e., in the case of *eka-putra*, "one son."

Note that "the son of one father" here means a full-fledged son.[71] If the father is that kind of son, he gets two shares, whereas the same is not true for a father who is a *kṣetraja* son. The phrase "the father's and the son's proprietary rights in it are equal" [Y 2.121cd; **9**] must be interpreted as applicable only to a father who is a *kṣetraja* son.[72] <**60**> A *kṣetraja* son has two fathers. Indeed,

[A] Baudhāyana says:

> If a man fathers a son in the "field" (*kṣetra*) of a man who is deceased, or one who gives his permission because he is impotent or seriously ill, the son is called *kṣetraja*.[73] [Bau 2.2.3.17]
> That one person has two fathers and two *gotras*;[74] he offers funeral rites to and shares in the inheritance of both. [Bau 2.2.3.18]

<**61**> This means that, if a man fathers a son in the "field" of a eunuch and the like, with their permission, that son is a *kṣetraja*.

[B] <**62**> Nārada says:

> If someone sows his seed in another man's field, with the permission of the owner of the field, the offspring is considered to belong both to the possessor of the seed and to the owner of the field. [N 12.58]

<**63**> The interpretation of the Śaṅkha and Likhita text proposed above [**59**] also allows for the term *eka-putra* as a qualifier in the outright injunction "a father who is *eka-putra* may take two shares for himself," to be taken literally. As such this interpretation rules out the other interpretation according to which *eka-putra* is an illustrative qualifier and, therefore, does not mean to say what it says.[75] <**64**> Be-

[71] On the full-fledged son (*aurasa*), see note at **10.1** and Introduction.

[72] This restriction was not mentioned at **9**. On the *kṣetraja* son, see note 62.

[73] Only the *Dāyabhāga* and the 18th-century *Vivādacandrikā* by Anantarāma quote this part of the Bau text in a versified form (*Dhko* p. 1269). The texts repeatedly refer to the female as the "field" (*kṣetra*) and to the male as the "possessor of the seed" (*bījin*), which leads to lengthy discussions on who owns the "crop" in case the "possessor of the seed" is not the legal owner/husband of the "field."

[74] On *gotra*, see note 25.

[75] Jīmūtavāhana here alludes to the distinction between *vidheya* words, i.e., words that mean exactly what they say and can be interpreted literally, and *uddeśya* words, which do not mean exactly what they say and should not be taken literally. In the case at hand, in Jīmūtavāhana's interpretation of ŚL 263 the term *eka-putra*, "the son of one father," cannot mean anything else than that. It is a *vidheya* qualifier of the agent of the act ("he may take"). If *eka-putra* means "who has one son," it is an *uddeśya* word; it refers to only one possible situation out of many, for we know that the father takes two shares whatever the number of his sons. In this case *eka-putra* is not a strict qualifier of the agent; according to a *mīmāṃsā* maxim (*uddiśyamānasya viśeṣaṇam avivakṣitam*), such a qualifier does not have to be taken literally. As is clear from the next sentence, in injunctions (*vidhi*) laid down by the Sages the former interpretation is superior to the latter. Cf. J. N. Bhattacharya 1893: 66; Kane 1962: 1286, 1341.

sides, those who contend time and again that words used by Manu, Gautama, Dakṣa, and other most highly judicious Sages are not intended to say what they say, thereby proclaim loud and clear that they themselves ought not to be taken literally.

<**65**> Next,[76] a father gets two shares even in property acquired by his sons: the Texts prescribe "two shares" [N 13.12; **35, 46**] and "he may take two shares" [B 26.16; **35, 46**] unconditionally. Kātyāyana says it most clearly:

> A father takes two shares or one half out of property acquired by his sons. If the father is deceased, the mother gets a share equal to that of her sons. [K 851]

<**66**> What this Text means is that a father takes either two shares or one half out of property acquired by his sons.[77]

[Objection][78] <**67**> In the compound *putra-vitta-arjanāt*, "from son-property-acquisition," the words "son" and "property" form a *dvandva* compound, meaning "son(s) and property." Hence, if a father acquires both property and a son or sons, he gets two shares; if he does not acquire any son he gets it all.[79]

[Refutation] Not so. Indeed,

[1] when a man proceeds to a partition with his brothers, he may take two shares as the acquirer of the property even if he has not acquired a son; he definitely cannot take it all. Hence, what Kātyāyana 851 would have to mean is this: whenever there is a relative who is entitled to participate in the partition, the person who acquired property gets two shares of it; he gets it all if there is no other relative. In that case, however, the words "father" and "son" in the Text would be no more than a drunkard's prattle.[80]

[76] Jīmūtavāhana now shows that it is proper for the father to get a double share even in property he did not acquire himself: he gets a double share in property acquired by his sons.

[77] On Jīmūtavāhana's interpretation of K 851, which was upheld in *Dharma Das Kundu* v. *Amulyadhan Kundu* (1906) 33 Cal. 1119, 1126, 10 C.W.N. 765, but has since then become "a forgotten chapter of Dāyabhāga law," see Derrett 1965a.

[78] To follow the ensuing discussion, which continues up to **72**, it is important to keep in mind the wording of K 851, which says that the father is *dvy-aṃśa-hara*, "two-share-taking," *ardha-haro vā*, "or one-half-taking," *putra-vitta-arjanāt*, "from (ablative) son-property-acquisition," which Jīmūtavāhana (**66**) interpreted as "from acquisition of property by the son."

[79] According to this interpretation, K 851 pertains to property acquired by the father, not by the son(s): if a father acquires property and he has a son or sons, he gets two shares of it; if he has no son, he takes all the property he acquired. The view that *putra-vitta* is a *dvandva* compound appears in an extensive criticism of **66–68** in the *Vyavahāraprakāśa* (ed. pp. 444–45; tr. II.i.12).

[80] *Pramatta-gīta*, "a drunkard's prattle," is a favorite term with the Indian grammarians. The *Kāśikā* quotes it as an example for Pāṇini 6.2.149: *itthambhūtena kṛtam*, "something done by one in such a condition." Cf. also *Mahābhāṣya* vol. 1, p. 3.

[2] Acquisition is an act that engenders ownership, according to the saying "acquisition that does not result in ownership is a contradiction in terms."[81] On the other hand, it has been demonstrated in connection with a gift of everything one owns that a father has no proprietary right over his sons.[82] Consequently, in the Kātyāyana verse the term "acquisition" would be used metaphorically with regard to sons, and literally with regard to property. That, however, is not possible when a word is used only once.[83]

[Objection][84] <**68**> Since it is established that a son takes two shares in what he acquired, and since it is also established, even without this Text, that the father takes two shares in it, both would then get equal shares in what the son acquired, and the injunction would be redundant.[85]

[Refutation] Not so. Indeed,

[1] the rule is perfectly meaningful, since, were it not for this Text, it would not be established that the father takes two shares in property acquired by his son.

[2} <**69**> If the expression *putra-vitta-arjanāt* referred to property acquired by the father, it would be out of the question to stipulate that he can take two shares or one half, as he pleases. Since he can take at his discretion, and since there are no restrictions on his discretion, it would be equally possible for him to take one share and a half, one share and a quarter, or three quarters of a share. Why, then, would the Text stipulate only two alternatives? The fact that the allotment of two shares cannot be an admonitory rule pertaining to the father's property has been shown above [**55–58**]. What makes sense in this case is that, even as he can take two shares of property acquired by his son, he can take one half of that property as well.

[81] This saying is quoted in the *Mitākṣarā* (introduction to Y 2.114; Colebrooke I.i.10) from Prabhākara's *Bṛhatī*. See Rocher and Rocher forthcoming.

[82] The *locus classicus* where sons, or rather relatives including sons, are excluded from a gift of everything one owns is at *Mīmāṃsā-sūtras* 6.7.1–20, especially at 1–2: at the *viśvajit* sacrifice *sarvaṃ dadāti*, "one gifts everything," except *pitrādayaḥ*, "his father and so on," because one has no real *prabhutva*, "ownership," over them. The *smṛti* texts are not unanimous: the older ones grant the father the right to sell or gift his son, the later ones do not (cf. Kane 1941: 849–50; 1946: 563–64; 1962: 1312–13). On *patria potestas* in classical India, see N. C. Chatterjee 1923.

[83] On the often quoted principle that a word that is used once in a sentence cannot have its primary meaning for one part of the sentence and a secondary meaning for another part, see K. L. Sarkar 1909: 85; Kane 1962: 1292–93, 1350. Cf. **3.30** and **11.1.6**; for an exception, see **11.5.9**.

[84] Another objection to Jīmūtavāhana's interpretation (**66**) to the effect that K 851 pertains to property acquired by the son(s).

[85] Once something is *prāpta*, "established," either by another text or by common sense, an injunction is useless. Cf. note at **1.27**. In this case the son's right is established by the general rule that the acquirer gets a double share in what he acquired; the father's right to a double share in what his son acquired is established by the general rule that, when a father partitions property in his lifetime, he gets a double share in everything (B 26.16; **35**, **46**).

[Objection] <**70**> One half of two shares is one share; that is what the Kātyāyana text wants the father to get.[86]

[Refutation] Not so. Indeed,

[1] "one half" and "two shares" are relative terms, both of which require correlatives.

[2] Since they are similar both as qualifiers of the agent and as objects of the act of taking, they cannot possibly correlate with one another.[87]

[3] No one denies that it makes sense to construe the relative term "two shares" with the ablative case ending in the word *vitta-arjanāt*, "out of property acquired"; it is, therefore, also proper to construe that ablative with the term "one half."

[4] Since the words "one half" and "out of property acquired" are contiguous in the Kātyāyana text, they clearly denote "one half of the property"; there is no reason for them to denote "one half of two shares," i.e., one share.

[5] Since it goes against reason to use vague terminology when the precise term "one share" could have been used, it is only proper that one should think of "one half" as "one half of the property."

<**71**> The difference between the circumstances in which the father gets one half and those in which he gets two shares is as follows. If the son acquired property by drawing on his father's property, the father gets one half of it; the son who acquired it gets two shares, the others get one share each. If the father's property was not drawn on, the father gets two shares, and so does the son who acquired the property; the others get no shares.

<**72**> Or else,[88] the father gets one half if he excels in knowledge or some other quality. It is, indeed, on account of his greater knowledge and the like that the senior son is given a share as well [**42**]. If the father does not excel in knowledge or some other quality, he gets two shares for the simple reason that the son owes his existence to him.

<**73**> As a result, the meaning of the Texts [from **35** onward] is this: a father may take for himself two shares of property, whether ancestral or acquired by his son; even if he should wish to take more, he may not do so. Herein lies the difference with property he acquired on his own; of that he may take as much as he wants.

<**74**> When a father partitions ancestral property with his sons, the only latitude he has is either to preempt or not to preempt for them a share of five percent. Of the property he acquired on his own, on the other hand, it is perfectly legitimate for him to give unequal shares, should he wish to allot larger shares to

[86] According to the objection the father gets either two shares or "one half of that," i.e., a single share.

[87] Śrīkṛṣṇa quotes a rule to the effect that qualities (*guṇa*) relate to something else, and, since they are equal in that respect, they cannot relate to each other (*Mīmāṃsā-sūtra* 3.1.22: *guṇānāṃ ca parārthatvād asambandhaḥ samatvāt syāt*).

[88] Śrīkṛṣṇa suggests that Jīmūtavāhana proposes this alternative solution to obviate a possible objection against the first: it makes sense that the father get one half when his property was drawn on, but there is no obvious reason why he should get two shares when it was not.

recognize a son as especially deserving, support one who has to provide for a large family, out of compassion for a son's disabilities, or because he is pleased with a son's singular filial devotion. Indeed,

[A] <**75**> Yājñavalkya says:

> It is legitimate for a father to give his sons smaller or larger shares. [Y 2.116cd]

[B] Bṛhaspati says:

> If a father allots to some of his sons equal, smaller, or larger shares, they must be upheld; if the sons do not uphold them, they shall be punished. [B 26.15]

[C] Nārada says:

> Whether a father allots his sons equal, smaller, or larger shares, they must accept the partition as legitimate. A father, indeed, is master of everything. [N 13.15]

<**76**> Since what is required for the father to be able to divide property into smaller or larger shares is that he be master of the entire property, and since that condition does not obtain in the case of ancestral property, partition in unequal shares by a father is proper only with regard to his own property. Says Viṣṇu:

> If a father partitions property with his sons, he can do whatever he pleases with property he acquired on his own; in ancestral property, however, the proprietary rights of father and son are equal. [Vi 17.1–2; **16, 55**]

[Question][89] <**77**> It is understood, from a Yājñavalkya text, that a father can give his eldest son "the best share," i.e., a preempted share:

> When a father partitions property with his sons, he may give shares as he pleases; he may give the eldest son the best share or give all sons equal shares.[90] [Y 2.114]

How, then, can Yājñavalkya 2.116cd [**75**] speak of shares that are smaller or larger than that?

[Answer] Yājñavalkya 2.116cd does not refer to the same thing.[91] Indeed,

[89] This section (**77–82**) is meant to reject the view that Y 2.116cd (**75**) might pertain to partitions of ancestral property with or without preempted shares.

[90] The Sanskrit text of Y 2.114 is ambiguous. The translation follows Jīmūtavāhana's interpretation, according to which the two halves of the verse refer to two different situations (cf. the end of **79**). According to a different interpretation, adopted by the *Mitākṣarā*, the first half of the verse establishes the father's free choice between the two alternatives mentioned in the second half: either he gives his eldest son the best share, or he gives equal shares to all.

[91] I.e., "smaller or larger" at Y 2.116cd does not pertain to partitions of ancestral property with or without preempted shares, but to a different kind of partition in which the father is free to give unequal shares, namely, when he divides property he acquired on his own.

[1] if it did, it would be redundant, since the best share, i.e., the preempted share of five percent, is known to apply even when brothers proceed to a partition after their father's death **[3.24–27]**.[92]

[2] <**78**> Some say that the purport of Yājñavalkya 2.116cd is to allow a father legitimately to partition the property in equal shares, even without preempting a special share. This does not help, for the only thing a father could then legitimately do would be to make some shares smaller, with the result that the phrase "or larger" would be redundant.

[3] <**79**> If one interprets the phrase "smaller or larger" at Yājñavalkya 2.116cd as allowing the father to partition ancestral property with or without a preempted share, the quarter-verse "he may give shares as he pleases" at Yājñavalkya 2.114 would be redundant. Anything the verse would be supposed to say is said in the other three quarter-verses.[93]

According to my interpretation, however, the phrase "he may give shares as he pleases" [Y 2.114; **77**] pertains to property the father acquired on his own, whereas the alternative of the best share or equal shares pertains to ancestral property. Indeed,

[1] in this way nothing is redundant.

[2] <**80**> After the father's death, too, there are two kinds of partition. Says Bṛhaspati:

> There are two kinds of partition among heirs: one is by order of seniority, the other by giving equal shares. [B 26.17]

With the phrase "by order of seniority" he provides for preempted shares; the other kind of partition is by equal shares. Since there are, thus, two kinds of partition even when brothers divide the property among themselves, it should not be different when the partition is made by the father. <**81**> Says Nārada:

> When a father is getting old, he himself should partition the property with his sons. Either he assigns the best share to his eldest son, or he acts as he sees fit. [N 13.4]

<**82**> This Text first enjoins that the eldest son gets the best share, and then, with the phrase "or he acts as he sees fit," it separately mentions the kind of partition in smaller or larger shares which a father may decide to make as he sees fit, for reasons mentioned earlier [**74**]. It is clear, therefore, that partition in smaller or larger shares is different from partition with the best share.

<**83**> As to the Nārada text:

> A father may not preside over a partition if he is ill, angered, swayed by his senses, or if he fails to act in accordance with the Texts, [N 13.16/15n]

[92] Jīmūtavāhana's argument is that, if brothers can give the older ones preempted shares, a fortiori their father can do so.

[93] I.e., the verse might as well read: "If a father partitions property, he may give the eldest son the best share, or give all sons equal shares." Cf. note 90.

it pertains to situations in which a father might be led to proceed to a partition that does not conform to the rules laid down in the Texts, either because his mind is disturbed by an illness and the like, or because he is at odds with one of his sons, or because he is biased in favor of the son of a favorite wife.

On the other hand, if an unequal partition results from one of the causes mentioned earlier [**74**], it is not against the Texts at all. <**84**> Says Kātyāyana:

> If a father proceeds to a partition in his lifetime, he shall not favor one son, nor shall he exclude one from the partition, on the spur of the moment, without just cause. [K 843]

<**85**> "He shall not favor one son" by giving him more, nor "shall he exclude one" by giving him no share at all, "without just cause." Differences resulting from preempted shares and so forth invariably affect several sons, not one. Since it is understood from this Text that one son should not be singled out without just cause, but at the same time that the father is fully justified in singling out even one son if there is just cause, this kind of distinction does not refer to preempted shares but to a distinction made solely at the father's discretion, as explained earlier.

<**86**> If, on the other hand, it is the sons who request a partition during their father's lifetime, then the father cannot give them unequal shares. Says Manu:

> If undivided brothers together wish to leave the joint estate,[94] their father shall, under no circumstances, give them unequal shares. [M 9.215]

<**87**> He may, of course, give them preempted shares, for these do not qualify as unequal shares. The only thing he may not do is to give them smaller or larger shares.

<**88**> Thus far for partition made by the father.[95]

[94] The translation reflects Jīmūtavāhana's unusual interpretation of Manu 9.215: the phrase *bhrātṝṇām avibhaktānāṃ yady utthānaṃ bhavet saha* is normally understood as "if undivided brothers together acquire something by their joint effort." Cf. Y 2.120ab: *sāmānyārthasamutthāne vibhāgas tu samaḥ smṛtaḥ.* Śrīkṛṣṇa defends Jīmūtavāhana's interpretation of M 9.215 against that proposed by Kullūkabhaṭṭa: since in this case division into equal shares is established (*prāpta*) by common sense, the text would be redundant.

[95] This sentence concludes chapters one and two.

CHAPTER THREE

PARTITION BY BROTHERS AFTER THEIR FATHER'S DEATH

Introductory Remarks

<**1**> Let me now deal with partition by brothers after their father's death.

The rule is that it is not proper for brothers german to proceed to this kind of partition either as long as their mother lives,[1] notwithstanding the fact that because of their father's death they actually own the property.[2] The phrase "after their father and mother" (M 9.104; **1.14**], indeed, conveys the notion that brothers german divide paternal property after the death of both parents.

<**2**> Note that the phrase "after their mother" does not mean that Manu 9.104 pertains to maternal property. Indeed,

[1] from the word "paternal" in the same verse it is understood that the Text pertains only to the father's property, there being no valid reason to interpret "paternal" as an elliptical expression for "paternal (and maternal)."[3]

[1] "not . . . either," i.e., not any more than in the case of maternal property (**2.1**).

[2] As he did at **2.30**, Śrīkṛṣṇa takes it upon himself to defend Jīmūtavāhana's view that partition by sons during their mother's lifetime stands, even though it is not proper (*na dharmya*). He first introduces a possible objection: why needlessly complicate matters by introducing here the concept of impropriety, which requires that there be a transcendent purpose for it, when it is possible to interpret the relevant texts as declaring partition during their mother's lifetime null and void, even as other texts declare partition by sons null and void during their father's lifetime? Śrīkṛṣṇa counters that, if the texts meant to say that partition during the mother's lifetime is null and void, a transcendent purpose would have to be assumed, and one would have to account for the fact that in this case sons are not allowed to divide property of which they are the owners. The difference is that partition during the father's lifetime is null and void because the sons do not own the property; while the mother still lives after the father's death, each son owns a part of the property, and nothing can pre-vent them from proceeding to a partition

[3] M 9.104 uses the term *paitṛka*, which means either "paternal" or "parental," the latter by applying the principle of *ekaśeṣa*, "ellipsis"; *paitṛka* = "paternal (+ maternal)." Jīmūtavāhana rejects the latter interpretation for M 9.104, whereas he accepts it for K 896 (**4.1.6**) See also **11.3.4**.

[2] <**3**> Partition of maternal property after the mother's death will be dealt with in another Manu verse below [M 9.192; **4.2.1**]. Hence, if "after their mother" at Manu 9.104 also pertained to maternal property, it would be redundant.

<**4**> [A][4] Yājñavalkya says:

> After the death of their parents sons shall divide assets and debts equally. After the death of their mother daughters divide what is left after paying her debts; failing daughters, her offspring. [Y2.117; ab **3.25**, cd **1.48**, **4.2.13**]

<**5**> The second half of this verse lays down what happens with the partition of the mother's property: if there are daughters, her sons, here referred to as "her offspring," have no right to it; failing daughters, her sons get it. The phrase "of their parents" in the first half of the verse must, therefore, pertain to property of the father; otherwise the verse would be redundant. <**6**> Since the Text that allows brothers to partition the property after the death of their "father and mother" thereby enjoins that the partition be made at a time subsequent to the death of both parents,[5] the Sanskrit dual form for "parents" here really means to say "both parents."[6]

[B] <**7**> Śaṅkha and Likhita say:

> Since hereditary property is the foundation of the family, sons are not independent as long as they have a father, nor as long as their mother lives. [ŚL 270 end; **1.42**]

What these Sages say is that sons "are not independent," i.e., are not entitled to a partition as long as their mother lives either.

[C] <**8**> Vyāsa says very clearly:

> The rule is that brothers stay together as long as their parents live; once their parents are no longer, their *dharma* increases if they separate. [Vy 247]

<**9**> In the guise of an outright injunction to the effect that the sons must stay together,[7] the Text is actually intended to forbid that they live separately and to

[4] From **4** to **9** Jīmūtavāhana introduces texts marked [A] to [D] to the effect that partition ought not to take place; from **12** onward he discusses what happens when it takes place nevertheless.

[5] Some *Dāyabhāga* manuscripts and editions read: "Since the Yājñavalkya text," instead of "Since the Text." Y 2.117, however, contains the word "parents," not "father and mother." The phrase "father and mother" appears at M 9.104 (**1**).

[6] A single noun with a dual ending, even as a two-member *dvandva* compound, usually means "both A and B," but it might also mean "either A or B." The first is true at Y 2.117, the second at Vy 247 (**9**).

[7] The Vyāsa text states that the sons' living together *vidhīyate*, i.e., that it is the object of a *vidhi*, an outright injunction. Yet, the fact that sons originally live together is established (*prāpta*) and hence cannot technically be the object of a *vidhi*. That is why Jīmūtavāhana says that Vy 247 is not a true *vidhi*, but a negative injunction (*niṣedha*) in the guise of a *vidhi*: sons should not stop living together as long as one of their parents lives.

prohibit partition as long as either their father or their mother lives. In this Text, therefore, the dual number in the phrase "their parents live" does not mean both together.[8] Partition is not proper as long as one of the parents lives; it is proper only after both parents are deceased.

[D] <**10**> Bṛhaspati says:

> Brothers may proceed to a partition when both parents are deceased. They may also do so while both live, provided their mother has reached menopause. [B 26.9; **2.1**]

<**11**> The partition allowed here in the mother's lifetime, when she has reached menopause, cannot pertain to maternal property. The term "also," in the phrase "also . . . while both live," shows that the partition that is deemed acceptable in the second half of the verse is of the same type as that allowed after the death of both parents in the first half. It follows from these two premises that the partition by brothers after the death of both parents mentioned in this Text can pertain only to property that comes to them from their father.[9]

<**12**> All this explains why, if partition takes place in the mother's lifetime,[10] she plays a pivotal role in it. Indeed,

[A] Vyāsa says:

> If there are several sons equal in caste and number, born of the same father by different mothers, it is commended that they receive their shares via their mothers. [Vy 249]

[B] Bṛhaspati says:

> If a father has several sons equal in caste and number by different mothers, the law requires that these sons partition via their mothers' shares. [B 26.24]

<**13**> Since these sons, being equal in caste and number, are in no way different from each other as far as the partition is concerned, the partition shall be made on the principle that it takes place between the mothers, not the sons.[11]

[8] On the ambiguity of a noun in the dual number, see note 6.

[9] I translate *pitṛ-dhana* as "property that comes to them from their father" rather than as "paternal property," because at **2.1** Jīmūtavāhana explicitly states that B 26.9 does not apply to paternal property.

[10] Note that partition in the mother's lifetime is not null and void, but that it is not *dharmya* either. Cf. note 2.

[11] The *Vyavahāraprakāśa* (ed. p. 451; tr. II.i.18) provides the following free rendering of this paragraph: "Even though they are sons of different wives, there is no reason for their shares being different, since they are equal in caste and number. If these texts nevertheless enjoin that the shares are the mothers', their sole purpose is to enjoin that the mothers are the pivotal persons. Hence, the partition should be made, not between the sons, but between their mothers." Some commentators add another verse (B 26.25ab) to the effect that, if the sons are of the same caste but different in number, the share allotted to each mother shall be determined by the number of her sons.

As a result, even as with other property of the mother, in this case, too, the sons should not take the initiative to partition the property among themselves as long as their mother lives; partition during the mother's lifetime is proper only if she consents to it. <**14**> Texts such as that of Gautama:[12]

> If they partition, their *dharma* increases, [G 28.4]

should, therefore, be taken to apply after the mother's death.

<**15**> If, even at that time, they wish to stay together, then the eldest son gets everything, provided he is capable of safeguarding the property; the others shall live as his dependents even as they did with their father. Indeed,

[A] Manu says:

> The eldest son alone takes all paternal property; the others shall be his dependents as they were with their father. [M 9.105]

[B] Gautama says:

> Alternatively, all property shall belong to the eldest son; he shall sustain the others like a father. [G 28.3]

The word "alternatively" shows that they can either separate or stay together.[13]

Note that in order to stay together it is necessary that they all agree to do so. Says Nārada:

> Or[14] if they all agree, the eldest brother may provide for the others like a father, or else the youngest brother if he is most competent, for competence is what the family needs. [N 13.5; **1.37**]

Even the youngest brother may provide for all his brothers if he is competent to do so. It follows as a matter of course that a middle brother may do so as well.[15]

<**16**> On the other hand, as indicated earlier, a partition has to take place as soon as any one member wants it.[16] Indeed,

[A] <**17**> that is why Kātyāyana says, in connection with partition:

> After the necessary deductions have been made. the property of minors and absentees should be deposited with their kinsmen or friends.[17] [K 845]

[12] Cf. M 9.111 (**1.37**).

[13] For the first alternative, partition, see G 28.1–2 (**2.4**). Note that G 28.4 (**14**) follows immediately after this rule.

[14] This rule provides an alternative to N 13.4 (**2.81**), according to which an aging father may partition the property.

[15] Application of the *daṇḍāpūpanyāya* (**2.25**).

[16] Cf. **1.35.** On the question whether, when one coparcener partitions, the others are still joint, separated, or reunited, see Mulla 1959: 504-07. The fact that Jīmūtavāhana quotes K 845 and G 10.48 in support of his statement seems to indicate that he considers all members to be separated under these circumstances.

[17] "Minors" (*aprāpta-vyvahāra*), literally "those who have not yet reached the age to transact business." The counterpart of *aprāpta-vyvahāra* is "superannuated" (*atīta-vyavahāra*), literally "those whose time to transact business is past" (**5.12**).

[B] There is this Text:

> The property of minors shall be guarded until they reach majority.[18] [G 10.48]

<**18**> Note that what has been said here for partition among sons applies equally to sons, sons' sons, and sons' sons' sons. It is not because they are further removed by birth that their right to inherit diminishes. Indeed, at the *pārvaṇa-śrāddhas* all three—sons, sons' sons, and sons' sons' sons—offer both kinds of *piṇḍas*, those that the deceased would have had to offer and those that he is to enjoy. Indeed,

[A] that is why Devala says:[19]

> A father, a paternal grandfather, and a paternal great-grandfather revere the birth of a son even as birds revere the *pippal* tree:[20] "During the rainy season when the moon is in Maghā[21] he will offer us funeral oblations of honey, meat, vegetables, milk, and boiled rice."[22] [D 1308–1309]

[B] Śaṅkha, Likhita, and Yama say:

> A father, a paternal grandfather, and a paternal great-grandfather praise the birth of a son even as birds praise the *pippal* tree: "During the rainy season when the moon is in Maghā he will nurture us with honey, rhinoceros meat, milk, and boiled rice." [ŚL 281]

Because of the term "paternal great-grandfather" the word "son" in these Texts must be understood to subsume descendants down to the great-grandson.

In other words, since descendants down to the great-grandson offer funeral rites and, as such, are of service to their ascendants up to their paternal great-grandfather, their right to inherit is equal. <**19**> Conversely, grandsons and great-grandsons do not inherit as long as their respective fathers live, since they are not then qualified to perform *pārvaṇaśrāddhas* and, hence, do not offer *piṇḍas*.

[18] Śrīkṛṣṇa sets at sixteen the age at which boys (*bāla*) reach majority, literally "the age at which they become capable of transacting business" (*vyavahāra-prāpti*).

[19] The two verses which are here attributed to the lost *Devala-smṛti* correspond to Va 11.39–40.

[20] The theme of birds revering the *pippal* tree, i.e., the Indian fig tree, goes back as far as the *Ṛg-veda* (1.164.20). It is part of "a parable dealing with the attainment of immortality, which is represented by the sweet fruit of a tree, presumably the tree of knowledge" (Brown 1968: 214; cf. 208).

[21] I.e., on the lunar day (*tithi*) on which, during the two months of the rainy season (*Śrāvaṇa* and *Bhādrapada*), the moon is in the lunar mansion (*nakṣatra*) Maghā. According to similar verses in other texts (M 3.273; Vi 78.52) the day referred to here corresponds to the thirteenth *tithi* in the dark half (*kṛṣṇa-pakṣa*) of the month *Bhādrapada*.

[22] On various kinds of meat to be offered at *śrāddhas*, see Kane 1953: 422–25.

<**20**> Note that, when brothers proceed to a partition after the death of their parents, any special distinctions their father might have made between them become totally null and void, but anything else than these must be upheld.[23]

<**21**> If there are one son and several sons of another son, then one share goes to the son, the other to the several grandsons. Since the latters' link to the property is through their birth,[24] which they owe to their father, they cannot claim more than the property to which he himself would have been entitled.

<**22**> Note that the Text:

> Sons of different fathers shall be allotted shares from their fathers,[25] [Y 2.120cd = Vi 17.23ab]

does not pertain to the situation at hand.[26] Since all the property belonged exclusively to the father of the paternal uncle, according to this Text everything would then go to the paternal uncle, nothing to his brother's sons. If "shall be allotted from their fathers" meant "shall be allotted shares as in a partition between a father and his sons," the paternal uncle would get a double share because a father is entitled to a double share, and his nephews would get one share each. That, however, would be incompatible with the practice of the couth.[27] <**23**> Rather, this Text pertains to a situation in which one predeceased brother has fewer or more sons than another predeceased brother. It means that, in that case, the shares shall be allotted "through the sons' fathers," i.e., *per stirpes*.

Partition among Brothers of Equal Caste

<**24**>[28] As far as partition among brothers of equal caste is concerned, there are two options: either with preempted shares of five percent and so forth, or simply in equal shares. Indeed,

[A] <**25**> Hārīta prescribes equal partition without preemptions as well.[29] With the word "father" carried over from a preceding rule, he says:

> After his death his inheritance shall be divided equally. [H 4.4]

[23] On special distinctions the father cannot make without just cause, see **2.83–85.** On decisions that must be upheld, see **2.74–76**.

[24] On the term "link" in the phrase "link to the property," see note at **1.7**.

[25] I translate *pitṛ-tas*, "from their fathers," in as open-ended a manner as possible, since Jīmūtavāhana discusses several possible interpretations.

[26] I.e., to a partition between paternal uncles on the one hand, and the sons of their predeceased brothers on the other.

[27] On "the practice of the couth" (*śiṣṭa-ācāra*), see note at **2.49**.

[28] Since **24** begins with the word *idānīm* "now," as do several chapters of the *Dāyabhāga*, Colebrooke and most editions at this point open a "Section II" (*dvitīyaḥ paricchedaḥ*). Differently from what they do in other similar situations, however, here they continue the paragraph numbering.

[29] The phrase "as well" here means in addition to partition with preempted shares, mentioned earlier. Śrīkṛṣṇa refers to M 9.112 (**2.37**) and other texts like it.

[B] Uśanas says:

> We have, thus, indicated the rule for a partition among brothers born of mothers of a lower caste than their fathers. If the brothers belong to the same caste as their fathers, they shall divide his property equally. [*Dhlo* p1238]

[C] Paiṭhīnasi says:

> When a father's inheritance is divided, it shall be divided equally. [Pai 118]

[D] Yājñavalkya says:

> After the death of their parents sons shall divide assets and debts equally. [Y 2.117ab; **4**]

Hence, there are two options: partition with preempted shares, or partition without preempted shares.

[Objection] <**26**> Since there also Texts that speak of equal partition as the sole form of partition, that is the form one should observe in all cases.

[Refutation] Not so. Indeed,

[1] it can also happen that younger brothers agree to a preemption for their elder siblings because they are specially devoted to them; the brothers do, therefore, have a choice between the two options, even as they have the choice to partition or not to partition. <**27**> The reason why, in practice, one sees nothing but equal partition is that special devotion is hard to find among people these days,[30] and that there are no elder brothers who deserve to receive preempted shares.

[2] <**28**> On the other hand,[31] if one of the brothers does not wish to participate in the partition of paternal or ancestral property, on the grounds that he can manage on his own, he shall be forced to participate to the extent that he be given at least something, be it just a measure of rice,[32] so as to avoid future unpleasantness on the part of his sons and so forth. Indeed,

[A] Manu says:

> If one of the brothers does not want any property because he can provide for himself by his own occupation, he may be divested of the share to which he was entitled, but he shall be given some maintenance. [M 9.207]

[B] Yājñavalkya says:

[30] Śrīkṛṣṇa specifies: "among today's younger brothers."

[31] After pointing out that partition among brothers is usually equal but that there are cases in which some of them get larger shares, Jīmūtavāhana now turns to a situation in which one of the brothers gets less than a full share.

[32] The phrase "a measure of rice" translates Sanskrit *taṇḍula-prastha*. The term *prastha* indicates a particular, though not easily definable, quantity or measure. Jha (*Vivāda-cintāmaṇi* tr., p191) translates *taṇḍula-prastha* as "a seer of rice."

> If one of the brothers is capable of providing for himself and does not wish to participate in a partition, he may be severed, but he must be given something. [Y 2.116ab]

Mothers' and Unmarried Sisters' Shares

<**29**> When brothers german proceed to a partition after the death of their father, their mother shall be given a share equal to that of her sons, according to the Text:

> The mother gets an equal share. [N 13.12c; **2.46**]

<**30**> Note, first, that, since the term "mother" primarily refers to the natural mother, it does not also refer to any other wife of the father.[33] In a single occurrence a word cannot have both its primary and secondary meanings.[34]

<**31**> Note also that the mother's right to an equal share applies when neither her husband nor anyone else gave her any female property;[35] if she was given female property, she gets half a share.

The criteria to be applied here are the same as those one applies when the father gives his sons equal shares and is supposed to give all his wives shares equal to those of the sons.[36] On the latter situation, compare Yājñavalkya:

> If he makes his sons' shares equal, his wives are also entitled to equal shares, provided they were not given female property by their husband or their father-in-law. [Y 2.115]
> A wife who is superseded by another woman shall be given as compensation an amount equal to what he spends on his new wife, provided she was not already given female property;[37] if she did receive female property, she shall be given half that amount. [Y 2.148]

<**32**> Note that equal shares go to those wives who have no sons, not to those who have sons.[38] Says Vyāsa:

[33] Each mother gets a share equal to the share her own sons receive, and these shares are different if the sons are of different castes. Cf. **9.12**.

[34] For this often applied principle, see **2.67**.

[35] Female property (*strī-dhana*) is the subject of chapter **4**.

[36] This paragraph is intended to show that it is indeed proper for sons to decrease their mother's share if she received female property, since under these circumstances her share is reduced by her husband as well.

[37] The compensation given to a wife who is superseded (*ādhivedanika*, **4.1.14**) is a form of female property.

[38] It is not clear whether this sentence and Vy 250 quoted in support of it continue the comparison with a partition made by the father (as in Y 2.115 and Y 2.148), or whether from here on Jīmūtavāhana addresses directly partitions made by the sons. Śrīkṛṣṇa, whom I follow, quotes an anonymous predecessor who is in favor of the latter alternative, only to reject that view and establish at length that Jīmūtavāhana is still dealing with partitions

> Those of the father's wives who have no sons get equal shares, and so do all paternal grandmothers, for they are held to be equal to mothers.[39] [Vy 250]

Viṣṇu says:[40]

> Mothers get shares proportionate to those of sons, and so do unmarried daughters. [Vi 18.34-35]

<**33**> "Proportionate to those of sons" means that, even as sons get four shares, three shares, two shares, or one share in the descending order of their castes [**9.12**], so do the father's wives. <**34**> Unmarried daughters get one quarter share proportionate to the shares of the sons. Says Bṛhaspati:

> Mothers are entitled to shares equal to theirs, unmarried girls to one quarter thereof. [B 26.22cd]

<**35**> The son gets three parts, the daughter one. Says Kātyāyana:

> Daughters not yet given away get one quarter, sons get three quarters; sons are the sole owners if the property is small.[41] [K 858]

<**36**> If the property is small,[42] each son takes his own share and, out of it, gifts one quarter to his unmarried sisters. Indeed,

[A] Manu says:

> The brothers shall each gift one quarter of their respective shares to the girls. They shall be expelled from their castes if they are reluctant to do so. [M 9.118]

<**37**> By using the phrase "they shall gift" and by saying that the brothers will be expelled from their caste if they refuse to make the gift, this Text makes it clear that unmarried girls must not be led to believe that they should get the property on the grounds that they are entitled to it; the brother, who is entitled to inherit, is not "gifted" anything by another brother from his share.

---

made by the father. Since the *Vyāsa-smṛti* has not been preserved, it is not possible to ascertain in which context the verse appeared there.

39 The word "all" caused problems for the commentators on this verse. Some took it to include not only the father's natural mother but also the father's father's other wives. This can hardly have been Jīmūtavāhana's interpretation, since he explicitly restricted the term "mother" to the natural mother (**30**).

40 I presume that from here onward Jīmūtavāhana addresses the shares brothers ought to give to their unmarried sisters.

41 I translate K 858cd in light of Jīmūtavāhana's reading of the text and his interpretation (**36–37**). Kane (Kātyāyana ed. tr.), who reads *sāmyam* instead of *svāmyam* (the only reading attested in the *Dāyabhāga* manuscripts), translates: "but if the (family) property be small they (sons and daughters) share equally."

42 Śrīkṛṣṇa considers the paternal property that is to be divided "small" if one quarter of it is not sufficient to pay for an appropriate wedding of the unmarried girls. In that case the brothers should divide the property among themselves and, subsequently, out of their own property, arrange for the weddings of their sisters

[B] <**38**> Yājñavalkya says:

> Those brothers who have undergone their rites of passage shall arrange for the rites of passage of those who have not; they shall arrange for the weddings of their unmarried sisters, giving them one quarter out of their own shares.[43] [Y 2.124]

What this Text means is that sisters shall be married off, not that they are entitled to any shares.[44] <**39**> That being the case, it follows that, when there is ample property available the gift shall be such that it is fitting for the sister's wedding; the rule of gifting one quarter is not restrictive.

<**40**> Note that this rule should be applied only when there are as many sons as there are daughters. If it were to apply when their numbers are unequal, it might happen either that a single daughter gets an unduly large amount of property, or that a single son ends up having nothing, which would not be proper, since a son is superior to a daughter.

<**41**> Some people oppose this view,[45] on the basis of the following Text:

> On the other hand,[46] if there is no paternal property left, they shall take it out of their own shares; under any circumstances brothers who have undergone the rites of passage must arrange for the rites of passage of those who have not. [N 13.34]

This Nārada text, they say, demonstrates that the sisters' wedding ceremonies have to be conducted "under any circumstances." Even the possibility that the brothers might be left without a share is no excuse.

<**42**> That is beside the point, for Nārada 13.34 pertains to the rites of passage for brothers. Indeed,

[1] the variant reading: "whatever the case may be, those who have undergone the rites of passage must arrange for the rites of passage of their brothers and sisters," is without foundation.[47]

[43] On "rites of passage" (*saṃskāra*), see Pandey 1969 and Introduction.

[44] The immediately following sentence makes it clear that, according to Jīmūtavāhana, Y 2.124 does not mean that brothers ought to marry their sisters off *and* give them one quarter of their own shares, but rather that they should use one quarter of their shares to defray the cost of their sisters' weddings.

[45] I.e., the view that marrying off his sisters should not leave a brother penniless.

[46] This verse should be read in conjunction with the immediately preceding one in the *Nārada-smṛti* (N 13.33; **42**). Because of the different meaning of *saṃskāra* for males and females (women have only one *saṃskāra*, their wedding), it is possible for the opponent to interpret N13.34 as referring to sisters' weddings, and for Jīmūtavāhana to have it refer to the brothers' rites of passage generally.

[47] Jīmūtavāhana objects to a variant reading *bhrātṝṇām* (genitive) instead of his own reading *bhrātṛbhiḥ* (instrumental); both readings are well attested in quotations from the *Nārada-smṛti* (*Dhko* p1584). The difference is that, if one reads *bhrātṛbhiḥ*, the term *bhrātṛ* indicates the persons who arrange the rites of passage; these can only be the brothers. If one adopts the reading *bhrātṝṇām*, however, the word *bhrātṛ* indicates the persons who undergo

[2] The context in which the verse appears in the *Nārada-smṛti* is that of rites of passage to be arranged for brothers. The verse that immediately precedes the one quoted above is as follows:

> If the father did not arrange in due time for the rites of passage of some of them, their brothers shall make these arrangements for them out of the paternal property. [N 13.33]

The phrases "of some of them" and "for them" are in the masculine gender. Immediately after that Nārada 13.34 goes on: "On the other hand, if there is no paternal property left." This verse, too, therefore, pertains to rites of passage to be arranged for brothers.

<**43**> Thus far for the partition of paternal and ancestral property.[48]

---

the rites of passage; it could, then, be an elliptical expression (see note 3) for brothers and sisters.

[48] This sentence serves as a conclusion for chapters one to three.

CHAPTER FOUR

FEMALE PROPERTY

SECTION ONE

Definition of Female Property

<**1**> Before dealing with partition of female property (*strī-dhana*), let me first define the term.

[A][1] On this subject Viṣṇu says:

> The following items constitute female property: [1] what a woman is given by her father, mother, sons, or brothers; [2] what she acquires at the fire [**5**], and [3] when she is superseded [**14**]; [4] what she is given by her kin; [5] gratuities [**4.3.19–24**]; and [6] later settlements [**4.3.16–18**]. [Vi 17.18]

<**2**> Kātyāyana defines later settlements (*anvādheya(ka)*) as follows:

> What a woman receives after her wedding from her husband's family and from the family of her kin is called later settlements. [K 899; **4.3.16**]
>
> Bhṛgu defines later settlements as anything a woman receives after her wedding, as a token of affection, either from her husband or from her parents. [K 900; **4.3.18**][2]

[1] The six definitions of *strīdhana* that follow are interspersed with commentary and texts in support of the commentary. The six definitions are marked [A] to [F].

[2] Whereas several commentaries and digests quote K 899, K 900 apears only in the *Dāyabhāga* and the *Vivādaratnākara* (ed. #1483; tr. XI.10). Jīmūtavāhana not only uses it in his commentary (**3**) but also quotes it again at **4.3.18**.

<3> The word "kin" at Kātyāyana 899 refers to the woman's father and mother.[3] The meaning of the two Kātyāyana texts, therefore, is as follows: later settlements are the kinds of property a woman receives after her wedding [1] from relatives on her father's and mother's side; and [2] from her husband's and her husband's relatives, i.e., from her father-in-law and the like.[4] In the Viṣṇu text, on the other hand, the word "kin" refers to maternal uncles and the like, since the father and so forth are mentioned there in their own right.

The reason why Kātyāyana defines later settlements as he does is that the property which a woman receives at her wedding goes to her husband if the wedding was of a higher type, to her parents if it was of a lower type [**4.3.1–9**].[5]

[B] <4> Manu and Kātyāyana define female property as follows:

> There are six kinds of female property: [1] property acquired at the fire [**5**], and [2] when she is taken away [**5**]; [3] what a woman is given as a token of affection;[6] and [4–6] what she receives from her brothers, her mother, or her father. [M 9.194 = K 894]

[C] Nārada says:

> There are six kinds of female property: [1] property acquired at the fire, and [2] when she is taken away; [3] property given by her husband; [4] gifts from her brothers, and [5–6] from her parents [N 13.8]

<5> Kātyāyana defines "property acquired at the fire" (*adhyagni*) and "when she is taken away" (*adhyāvāhanika*) as follows:

[3] This commentary confirms Jīmūtavāhana's reading *bandhu-kulāt*, "from the family of her kin." Elsewhere the reading is either *sva-kulāt*, "from her own family," or, as in the *Mitākṣarā* (on Y 2.144), *pitṛ-kulāt*. Hence Colebrooke's translation there (II.xi.7): "from the family of her father."

[4] Śrīkṛṣṇa notes that Jīmūtavāhana's definition excludes from the *anvādheyaka* type of female property gifts which a mother receives from her son. Indeed, being directly (*sākṣād eva*) related to his mother, a son is not included among "relatives on her father's and mother's side," literally "relatives through (*dvāreṇa*) her father and mother."

[5] What Jīmūtavāhana means is that the repetition of the phrase "after her wedding" in Kātyāyana's definition is intended to emphasize the difference between later settlements and the gifts she receives at her wedding. As will be seen at **4.3.10**, if a woman dies childless, later settlements go to her brothers, not to her husband or parents.

[6] The reading *prītitaḥ striyai*, "as a token of affection for the woman" appears in the *Dāyabhāga* and the *Vivādaratnākara* (ed. #1475; tr. XI.2) only. Caṇḍeśvara comments: "what she is given by her father-in-law and the like, who felt affection for her because of her good nature, her good behavior (*dharma*; variant reading *karma*), her expertise, etc." Except for two digests that display a similarly general reading, *prīti-pūrvakam*, "as a result of affection.," in all other commentaries and digests M 9.194 reads more specifically *prīti-karmaṇi*, literally "on the occasion of an act of affection."

> The wise call what a woman is given in front of the fire at the time of her wedding female property acquired at the fire. [K 895] What a woman receives from her father's side when she is taken away is called female property acquired when she is taken away. [K 896]

<**6**> Since "from her father's side" is an elliptical expression,[7] property acquired when she is taken away is the kind of property a woman receives from her father's side and from her mother's side at the time when she is taken to her husband's home.[8]

<**7**> The phrase "property given by her husband" (*bhartṛ-dāya*) at Nārada 13.8 means property which is actually given to her by her husband (*bhartṛ-datta*).[9] Indeed,

[1] Manu and others do not use the term *bhartṛ-dāya*, but *bhatṛ-datta*, whereas Nārada uses the term *bhartṛ-dāya*, not *bhartṛ-datta*.

[2] <**8**> There are other Texts that use the term *bhartṛ-dāya* instead of *bhartṛ-datta*:

[a] Such is the case, for instance, in the following Kātyāyana text:

> After her husband's death a woman may do as she pleases with *bhartṛ-dāya*; as long as he lives she shall save it or else spend it on his family.[10] [K 907]

[7] On the commentators' use of ellipsis, see note at **3.2**.

[8] The text of K 896 is ambiguous: *yat . . . labhate nīyamānā paitṛkāt* literally means "what . . . she receives, being led, from her father's." Jīmūtavāhana, followed by Śrīkṛṣṇa (*Dāyādhikārakramasaṃgraha* ed. p. 15; tr. II.ii.8–9), clearly construes "from her father's" with "what she receives." Others construe "from her father's" with "being led"; the *Mitākṣarā* even glosses *paitṛkāt* by *pitur gṛhāt*, "from her father's house." This accounts for Colebrooke's translation, in the verse: "that which a woman receives while she is conducted from the parental [abode]," which is incompatible with his translation of the commentary at **6**. The difference is important: according to the latter interpretation K 896 pertains to property the woman received from anyone (explicitly so in the *Vivādacintāmani*, ed. p. 212; tr. p. 223), according to Jīmūtavāhana only to property the woman received from her father's and mother's sides. On Jīmūtavāhana's tendency to exclude anything received from outsiders, see note 18.

[9] According to Jīmūtavāhana the verb *dā* in (*bhartṛ-*)*dāya* is used here in its primary sense of "give," not in the figurative sense it has in *dāya*, "inheritance" (**1.4**).

[10] Even though K 907 has been used in the courts with reference to gifts made by the husband (e.g., *Venkata Ráma Rau* v. *Venkata Suriya Rau*, [1877] 1 Mad., 281, 286), a number of digests interpret *bhartṛ-dāya* in this verse as pertaining to property which a childless widow inherits from her husband after his death (e.g., *Vivādaratnākara* ed. #1446, tr. VIII.8; *Vivādacintāmaṇi* ed p. 215, tr. p. 227). On the phrase "or else spend it on his family" (*kṣapayet tatkule 'nyathā*), Śrīkṛṣṇa comments: "or else, i.e., if she is not able to guard it herself, she shall place it with his family." He also mentions a different interpretation: "if she cannot maintain herself with it, she shall continue to live with his family."

<**9**> This means that after her huaband's death she may use the property he gave her as she pleases, but while he lives she must "save" it, i.e., she must be thrifty with it.

[b] <**10**> The term *dāya* also appears in the following Vyāsa text, which is meant to indicate the extent to which a husband can make gifts to his wife:

> The *dāya* a woman may be given (*deya*) is limited to two thousand;[11] and she may use the property her husband gave her as she pleases. [Vy 265]

The maximum a woman may be given is two thousand, nothing more. As to the question "by whom," the logical way to construe the first half of the sentence is with the words "her husband," which appear later in the Text; there is no reason to posit words that do not appear in it.[12] In this way the verb *dā* in *deya*, "may be given," can be taken in its literal meaning, whereas if it referred to the amount of property of which the wife becomes the owner after her husband's death, the verb would be used in a figurative sense, which goes against reason. <**11**> And she may put to any use she pleases such property given to her by her husband.

Hence, the interpretation which some have suggested, namely, that, if a husband dies without leaving a son, his wife inherits his property up to a maximum of two thousand, but not the whole of it, is unacceptable to the learned. <**12**> The widow's right to inherit her husband's property will be dealt with at length below [section **11.1**].

[D] <**13**> Says Yājñavalkya:

> Female property consists of gifts a woman receives from her father, mother, husband, or brother, what she acquires at the fire, and when she is superseded.[13] [Y 2.143]

[11] As Sanskrit texts are wont to do, Vy 265 says "two thousand" without specifying the monetary unit. Intended in such cases is a copper coin of uncertain value, variously called *paṇa* or *kārṣāpaṇa*. For a detailed discussion of the various interpretations of the figure two thousand (or, according to a variant reading, three thousand) at Vy 265 and texts to the same effect, see Derrett 1958b. Contrary to Derrett's expectation, the critical edition of a nearly identical verse in the *Mahābhārata* (13.47.23) shows evidence for *tri-sahasra*, "three thousand," only.

[12] I.e., according to Jīmūtavāhana there is no reason to interpret Vy 265 as consisting of two independent clauses referring to two different situations, the former dealing with the amount which a woman may be given indirectly, as maintenance, out of her deceased husband's estate by a third party such as his father or brothers who inherit his property, and the latter dealing with property a wife receives directly from her husband.

[13] "and when she is superseded" (*ādhivedanikaṃ caiva*) is the reading adopted in all *Dāyabhāga* manuscripts, and also in a number of other commentaries and digests in which the verse is quoted (*Dhko* p. 1443). Other compendia, including the *Mitākṣarā*, exhibit a different reading: "when she is superseded, etc." (*ādhivedanikādyaṃ ca*). This accounts for Colebrooke's translation of Y 2.143, even in the *Dāyabhāga*: "or presented to her on her husband's marriage to another wife, [as also any other separate acquisition]." Cf. note 18.

<**14**> "Property acquired when she is superseded" (*ādhivedanika*) is the property a husband gives a prior wife as compensation when he wishes to marry another wife. It is so called because it is given with the intent of "taking" an "additional" wife.[14]

[E] <**15**> Devala says:

> A woman's maintenance allowance,[15] jewelry, gratuities [**4.3.19–22**], and profits[16] constitute female property. A wife may put them to use as she pleases; her husband has no claim to them except in an emergency. [D 1604]

[F] <**16**> Vyāsa says:

> Whatever dedicated property a bridegroom is given at the time of the wedding belongs entirely to the bride; it is excluded from partition with his relatives. [Vy 266]

<**17**> The word "dedicated" means that the text pertains to property that is given to the bridegroom with the dedication "this shall belong to your bride," and that it does not pertain to property given without that intent. That is why the phrase "at the time of the wedding" is merely illustrative and not the determining factor, for ownership depends primarily on the intent of the donor. Besides, the authoritative Text:[17]

> Whatever is given to a daughter's husband goes to his wife, whether her husband is alive or dead; it goes to her offspring when she is no longer, [*Dhko* p. 1463]

does not specify "at the time of the wedding." To be sure, the donor's intent is not mentioned here either; yet, it is understood, for the Text explicitly says that the property goes to her daughters.

<**18**> It should be clear from all this that the number of types of female property exhibited in the Texts is not fixed, with the result that the number six which appears in some of them is not to be taken literally. The main purpose of the Texts of the Sages is to provide an overall description of female property: female property is anything a woman is entitled to gift, sell, or put to use independently of her husband.[18] <**19**> Kātyāyana says quite clearly:

[14] Etymological explanation of the term *ādhivedanika*, from *adhika* "additional" and *vid* "take" (*Dhātupāṭha* 6.138: *vid-ḷ lābhe*). On supersession and polygamy generally, see, e.g., Jolly 1928: 140–47; Kane 1941: 540–54; Banerjee repr. 1984: 137–39 and 191–92.

[15] On "maintenance allowance" (*vṛtti*) Śrīkṛṣṇa and other commentators specify that it refers to an allowance in excess of food and clothing.

[16] According to Śrīnātha and Śrīkṛṣṇa "profits" (*lābha*) are interests on loans, etc.; according to Acyuta, revenue from usury.

[17] This is the only case in which Jīnūtavāhana refers to a *prāmāṇika*, "authoritative," text. Yet, besides the *Dāyabhāga*, this verse is quoted only in the *Vivādatāṇḍava* (1901 ed., p. 442) and in the *Vivādārṇavasetu*. The edition (1888, p. 52) of the latter wrongly attributes it to a ghost author, "Sūta." See R. Rocher 1983–84.

[18] This means that, according to Jīmūtavāhana, the term "female property" has a technical meaning: it is that property, and only that property, in which the woman acquires

> Anything she acquires through arts and crafts and anything she receives as a token of affection from an outsider becomes the property of her husband. The rest is called female property. [K 904]

<**20**> Anything she receives "from an outsider," i.e., from anyone other than the relatives of her father, mother, or husband, and anything she acquires through an art or craft, "becomes the property" of her husband, which means that he can use it on his own. The husband can take it even when there is no emergency.[19] As a result, even though the property is hers, it is not female property, since she cannot do anything with it on her own.

<**21**> Except for property of the said two types, however, all the rest is the exclusive property of the woman, for she is entitled to dispose of it by gift, sale, or otherwise. Says Kātyāyana:

> Whatever a married woman or a young girl receives from her husband or from her parents, in her husband's or in her father's house, is called a loving gift. [K 901]
> When women receive loving gifts, they become their independent owners, for these are given to them for their well-being, in a kindhearted spirit.[20] [K 905]
> Women can forever act on their own with what they received as loving gifts; they can sell or gift them as they please, even if it involves immovable property. [K 906]

<**22**> "A loving gift" (*saudāyika*) is what one receives from loving (*sudāya*) relatives.[21]

<**23**> As far as immovable property is concerned, however, a wife is not entitled to dispose of it by gift or otherwise, if it was given to her by her husband. Says Nārada:

> Whatever a husband gives to his wife out of affection, she may put to use or gift as she pleases, even after his death, except for immovable property. [N 1.28/24]

Since the qualifier "her husband" is used here, she is, however, free to gift immovables other than those given by her husband. Otherwise N 1.28/24 would be in-

---

an absolute right of ownership. In this he differs from others (cf. note 13), including the *Mitākṣarā*, which makes it clear that the term *strīdhana* has to be interpreted etymologically, not technically (on Y 2.143; Colebrooke II.xi.3).

[19] The situation is different with regard to female property, which the husband can use only in an emergency (**24**).

[20] "In a kindhearted spirit" (*ānṛśaṃsyārtham*): Śrīkṛṣṇa: "out of sympathy"; Colebrooke: "to sooth them;" Kane (Kātyāyana tr.): "in order that they may not be reduced to a terrible (or wretched) way." Cf. M 9.163 (**10.13**). The *Mahābhārata* repeatedly refers to *ānṛśaṃsya* as "the supreme *dharma*."

[21] For a nearly identical definition of *saudāyika*, see **6.1.11**. On *saudāyika* as a general term for different kinds of female property, see Kane 1946: 778.

compatible with the phrase "as they please, even if it involves immovable property" [K 906; **21**].

<**24**> If, in times of famine and the like, a husband is unable to provide for his family without seizing his wife's female property, he may do so, but under no other circumstances. Says Yājñavalkya:

> If a husband seizes his wife's female property during a famine, in order to perform a religious duty, in case of a serious illness, or when he is under restraint,[22] he need not reimburse her for it. [Y 2.147]

Yet, he is not entitled to do so under any other circumstances. Says Kātyāyana:

> When it comes to female property, neither the woman's husband, nor her sons, father, or brothers have any right to take it as their own or give it away. [K 911]
> If any of them forcibly draws on female property, he shall be made to reimburse it with interest, and he shall be punished. [K 912]
> If he draws on it after cajoling her into giving her consent, he shall be forced to reimburse the principal only, provided he has the means to do so. [K 913]
> If a husband takes a second wife and disregards his first wife, he shall be forced to reimburse her female property, even what she ceded to him out of affection. [K 908]
> If a wife is no longer provided with food, shelter, and clothing, she may take what is hers and a share of the heirs as well.[23] [K 909]

<**25**> If, after seizing his wife's property, a husband goes to live with another wife, and spurns his first wife, the king shall force him to return the property he seized.

If a husband fails to provide his wife with food, shelter, and so on, she may take this for herself as well.

<**26**> Thus far for the definition of female property.

[22] According to most *Dāyabhāga* commentators, "when he is under restraint" (*sampratirodhake*) refers to a situation in which a creditor prevents his debtor from bathing, eating, and so forth, to force him to pay his debt. Cf. the *Mitākṣarā* on Y 2.147 (Colebrooke II.xi.33: "during confinement in prison or under corporal penalties").

[23] Śrīkṛṣṇa understands "what is hers and a share of the heirs as well" (*svam . . . vibhāgaṃ riktināṃ tathā*) as "her own food and shelter, and from her brothers-in-law and the like, who hold joint property with her husband, the share that would normally go to him"; he quotes, but rejects, the interpretation "she should take her own share, in the form of food, shelter, etc., from the relatives of her husband." Kane (Kātyāyana tr.): "she may exact her own *strīdhana* and also the share (that would have fallen to her husband on partition) from the coparceners (of her husband)." Jīmūtavāhana (**25**) comments solely on the wife's right to claim food, shelter, etc.

CHAPTER FOUR
SECTION TWO

Partition of Female Property

<**1**> Let me now deal with the partition of female property.[1]

[A] Manu says:

> When their mother dies, all brothers german and sisters german divide the maternal inheritance equally.[2] [M 9.192]

<**2**> Even though this Text does not use a *dvandva* compound, the word "and" serves the same purpose, and establishes that brothers and sisters partition equally.[3] The only thing the Text can, therefore, mean is that both brothers and sisters german shall divide the property.

[B] <**3**> Bṛhaspati, too, uses the word "and" in the sense of "together:"

> Female property goes to a woman's offspring, and a daughter gets a share if she has not yet been given away; a married daughter should not be given any maternal property. [B 26. 31cdef]

<**4**> "Offspring" here means sons; they divide their mother's property together with daughters who have not yet been given away.[4]

[1] Section **4.2** deals solely with partition of female property when there are descendants. The order Jīmūtavāhana establishes, except for property received at the wedding (*yautaka*; **13**), is as follows: [1] sons and unmarried daughters (either one of these in the absence of the other); [2] married daughters; [3] grandsons (sons' sons and daughters' sons); and [4] barren and widowed daughters.

[2] For the translation of *samam* as "equally," see **8**. Cf. **1.14**.

[3] According to Bhaṭṭojī Dīkṣita's *Siddhāntakaumudī* (#901, on Pāṇini 2.2.29) there are four circumstances in which words with case endings stand in a relation that can be expressed by *ca* "and." In two of these, of which *itaretayoga*, "mutual conjunction," is one, the construction with *ca* is normally replaced by a *dvandva* compound. Hence the need for Jīmūtavāhana to justify the fact that, although M 9.192 uses *ca*, he nevertheless interprets the relation between brothers german and sisters german in this case as "mutual conjunction." See also **11.5.33**. Others, including the *Mitākṣarā* (on Y 2.145; Colebrooke II.xi.19–20), argue that, because M 9.192 uses *ca* rather than a *dvandva* compound, this is not a case of *itaretarayoga*, and sons and daughters do not inherit equally; rather "sons divide equally and daughters divide equally." Cf. Banerjee repr. 1984: 375–77.

[4] Jīmūtavāhana's point is that sons and unmarried daughters inherit "together." Married daughters inherit only in their absence (**26**), not together with them. It should be noted that the reading "a married daughter should not get any maternal property" (*samūḍhā tu na*

[C] Śaṅkha and Likhita say:

> All sons and unmarried daughters of the same mother have equal rights in her property. [ŚL 297]

<**5**> The fact that in all these Texts sons are mentioned first indicates that they are entitled to inherit their mother's property, irrespective of their status in life.[5] The word "and," which follows in each Text, indicates others who inherit together with them.

<**6**> If, notwithstanding all this, someone still wishes to throw down the gauntlet,[6]

[1] the following Devala text will suffice to throttle him:

> When a woman dies, her female property is common to her sons and unmarried daughters. If she has no offspring, it goes to her husband, mother, brother, or father. [D 1611]

<**7**> This Text states most clearly that maternal property is common to sons and unmarried daughters.[7]

[2] If unmarried daughters alone were entitled to inherit all maternal property, Texts such as Manu 9.131ab [**14**], which pertain specifically to property received at the wedding (*yautaka*), would be redundant, for the daughters would be entitled to inherit anything, irrespective of the kind of property involved.[8]

<**8**> There are some who try to justify the word "equally" [M 9.192; **1**] as follows. If both brothers and sisters have like claims to their mother's property, it makes sense to enjoin outright that their shares must be equal. If only sisters and, failing them, only brothers had a claim to the property, the word "equally" would be redundant, for in that case it would be a foregone conclusion that their shares

---

labhen mātṛkaṃ dhanam) is peculiar to the *Dāyabhāga*. The common reading of the end of the verse is "a married daughter should get only some token of respect, i.e., some trifle" (*samūḍhā tu labheta mānamātrakam*).

[5] The phrase "irrespective of their status in life" means, according to Śrīkṛṣṇa, irrespective of whether they are *saṃskṛta* or not, i.e., irrespective of whether they underwent the initiation ceremony (*upanayana*) or not. On the other hand, he uses the terms *sahodara* (M 9.192; **1**) and *sodarya* (ŚL 297; **4**) to restrict "sons" to the daughters' brothers german and to exclude all other types of sons, whom he refers to as "adopted sons and so forth." On the importance of this expression used by an 18th-century author, see note at **10.7**. Cf. also note at **4.3.32**.

[6] On Kane's suggestion that this sentence may refer to an author called Udgrāhamalla, see Introduction.

[7] Devala uses the unequivocal term *sāmānya*, "the fact of being common." In addition, differently from the texts quoted so far, which use the copulative particle "and," Devala has a *dvandva* compound

[8] Jīmūtavāhana refers to a number of texts which do state that female property first goes to unmarried daughters alone (**13**).

must be equal, by virtue of the maxim that, unless there is a Text to the contrary, shares are equal.[9]

They might be told the following:

[1] Even when both brothers and sisters are entitled to inherit the property, it is a foregone conclusion that their shares must be equal, by virtue of the same maxim. Since there is nothing that makes this case special, the word "equally" would be redundant in that case as well.

[2] The word "equally" is perfectly meaningful even when only brothers are entitled to inherit the property. It then prevents the preemption of five percent and the like, which obtain in the case of paternal property, from being applied to maternal property as well.

So, how could it be redundant? Any knowledgeable person should have nothing but contempt for the man of slight knowledge who knows neither the Texts nor the principles of common sense.[10]

<**9**> Anyhow, the reasons I have proffered above suffice to show that a son and an unmarried daughter have equal claims. Failing either one, the other gets his or her mother's property.

Failing both, a married daughter who has a son and one who may be expected to have one have equal claims, for through their sons they offer *piṇḍas* at *pārvaṇaśrāddhas*. <**10**> That is why, failing the said daughters, their sons are entitled to inherit the property, in accordance with the following Manu text:

> Even as a son's son, a daughter's son, too, saves his grandfather in the other world. [M 9.139cd; **11.6.9**]

Daughters who are either barren or widowed do not inherit, for neither personally nor through their offspring can they offer *piṇḍas* at *pārvaṇaśrāddhas*. That is why Nārada says:

> Failing sons, daughters inherit, provided they can have offspring just as they can.[11] [N 13.50ab/47ab]

<**11**> When there are both a son's son and a daughter's son, the son's son alone inherits. Since a son bars a married daughter, it stands to reason that the son of the barring son bars the son of the barred daughter.

[9] Jīmūtavāhana refers to the principle that partition is presumed to be equal, failing any rule to the contrary, as a *nyāya*, "a rule of logic, common sense." J. N. Bhattacharya (1893: 77) lists it among the legal maxims relating to property. Cf. note at **11.6.13**. See also Kane 1962: 1350.

[10] The phrase "principles of common sense" again translates Sanskrit *nyāya*. The translation cannot possibly reflect the special effect, which the Sanskrit text achieves by using several derivatives of the verb *jñā*, "know": *ato vacananyāyānabhijñaḥ sarvaiḥ prājñair avajñeya eva kiṃcijjñaḥ*. Cf. note at **4.3.41**.

[11] I translate "provided" since Jīmūtavāhana uses this text to exclude widowed or barren daughters from inheriting. In the context of the *Nārada-smṛti*, however, the verse means that, if a man has no sons, his daughters inherit, "for they are as much part of his lineage as they are."

<**12**> Failing all those mentioned so far, including a daughter's son, even a barren daughter or a widowed daughter is entitled to inherit her mother's property. They, too, are their mother's offspring, and only when there is no offspring do any others have a claim.[12]

<**13**> To be sure, there are Texts that entitle daughters alone to inherit their mother's female property first. Indeed,

[A] Gautama says:

> Female property goes to daughters not yet given away, to daughters not yet fully settled,[13] and to married daughters. [G 28.24; **22**]

[B] Nārada says:

> The mother's property goes to her daughters; failing daughters, to her offspring. [N 13.2cd]

[C] Kātyāyana says:

> Failing daughters, the inheritance goes to her sons. [K 918ab]

[D] Yājñavalkya says:

> After the death of their mother daughters divide what is left after paying her debts; failing daughters, her offspring.[14] [Y 2.117cd; **1.48**; **3.4**]

Since these Texts are incompatible with the Devala text quoted earlier [**6**], they pertain to *yautaka* property. Indeed,

[A] that is why Manu says:

> Whatever constitutes a mother's *yautaka* becomes the share of her unmarried daughters alone. [M 9.131ab]

[12] Banerjee (repr. 1984: 433) notes that, by placing barren and widowed daughters immediately after daughters' sons, Jīmūtavāhana "allows the doctrine of spiritual benefit to be subordinated to other considerations." Invoking the doctrine of spiritual benefit, Raghunandana (*Dāyatattva* ed. p. 185; tr. 10.8) interposes the son's son's son; Śrīkṛṣṇa (*Dāyādhikārakramasaṃgraha* ed. p. 25; tr. II.4.9) interposes not only the son's son's son of the deceased, but also the son, son's son, and son's son's son of other wives of the husband.

[13] Daughters "not yet fully settled" (*apratiṣṭhitā*) are daughters in the period between their engagement and their wedding. I adopt this translation (cf. Colebrooke: "those not actually married") in view of **23**, where Jīmūtavāhana clearly interprets the term *apratiṣṭhitā* as *prattā* "promised in marriage, engaged," and opposes it to *samūḍhā*, "married." Other commentators, including the *Mitākṣarā* (on Y 2.145; Colebrooke II.xi.13) take *apratiṣṭhitā* to refer to a married woman, but "one not fully settled in her husband's home," i.e., one who is childless, poor, or ill-fated. In that case the order in which daughters inherit is as follows: [1] unmarried daughters; [2] married daughters who are not yet fully settled; and [3] married daughters who are fully settled (*pratiṣṭhitā*).

[14] *Tad-anvaya* (N 13.2cd), *anvaya* (Y 2.117cd), and *putra* (K 918 ab) are ambiguous: they can refer either to the mother's offspring/sons or to the daughters' offspring/sons. Both interpretations appear in the commentaries and digests. For Jīmūtavāhana's opinion, which is reflected in the translation of the three texts, see **17–21**.

<**14**> *Yautaka* is property received at the wedding. Since the verb *yu* means "mix,"[15] its passive past participle *yuta* means "having been mixed." In the case of a man and a woman, "having been mixed" means "having become one," and that is achieved by their wedding, in accordance with the Text:

> Her bones with his bones, her flesh with his flesh, her skin with his skin. [*Pāraskara-gṛhyasūtra* 1.11.5]

The derivative *yautaka*, therefore, means something that is received at the wedding.[16]

[B] <**15**> For the same reason Vasiṣṭha says:

> The women shall divide their mother's *pāriṇāyya*. [Va 17.46]

Pāriṇāyya is property received at a *pariṇayana*, i.e., at a wedding.

<**16**> As for the Manu text:

> Any property a woman was somehow given by her father goes to a maiden brahman daughter, or it goes to her offspring,[17] [M 9.198]

since the property referred to here is qualified as "given by her father," the intention is that anything given by the father, not only at the time of the wedding, but at any other time as well, goes to her unmarried daughters alone.[18]

[15] Jīmūtavāhana quotes *Dhātupāṭha* 2.23: *yu miśraṇe*. In fact, the *Dhātupāṭha* reads *yu miśraṇe 'miśraṇe 'pi*, " mixing and also non-mixing." Many commentators prefer the latter etymology; they identify *yautaka* with *strīdhana* and, as a result, have all the mother's separate property pass on to her unmarried daughters. Hence also Bühler's translation of M 9.131ab: "But whatever may be the separate property of the mother, that is the share of the unmarried daughter alone." *Yautaka* or *yautuka* (both forms are acceptable according to the *Dāyatattva* ed. p. 186; tr. 10.14) survives in some areas of Bengal: "*Jautuk* is the property with which a woman is endowed, and which she brings to her husband in marriage. It is the same as the English dower" (Hunter 1875–77: 5.379; cf. Kohler 1888: 326–27).

[16] According to the *Dāyatattva* (ed. p. 186; tr. 10.15), quoting the *Vivāhatattva*, and the *Dāyādhikārakramasaṃgraha* (ed. p. 14; tr. II.ii.3), the phrase "at the wedding" encompasses a period before and a period after the actual wedding ceremony. It begins with the *śrāddha* for prosperity (*vṛddhi-śrāddha*), which precedes the wedding proper and ends with the wife's prostration (*abhivāda*) before her husband. Cf. Bose 1880: 9–10; Sarvadhikari 1922: 69; Banerjee repr. 1984: 95, 435.

[17] The phrase "her offspring" (*tad-apatya*) is again ambiguous (cf. note 14). The *Mitākṣarā* (on Y 2.145; Colebrooke II.xi.24) clearly says: "Failing sons, the grandsons inherit the property of their paternal grandfather's wife." Following the opinion of a number of commentators on the *Manu-smṛti*, Bühler (Manu tr.) renders *tad-apatya* as "that daughter's issue."

[18] On the meaning of the introductory phrase "as for," see note at **2.9**. At first glance M 9.198 seems to be incompatible with M 9.131ab (**13**), according to which only a woman's *yautaka* goes exclusively to her daughters. Śrīkṛṣṇa, more explicitly than Jīmūtavāhana, explains that M 9.131ab pertains to any *yautaka*, i.e., any property anyone gave the woman at the time of her wedding; M 9.198 pertains to property the woman was given by her father at any time, at the wedding or not.

Note that the word "brahman" is a mere amplification. Or else, lest the word "brahman" be redundant, the Text means that, if wives of the *kṣatriya* or other lower castes die without offspring, property given to them by their fathers goes to the unmarried brahman daughter of another wife of their husband.[19] It does not mean, however, that the Text pertains to the kind of situation covered by Yājñavalkya 2.145 **[24]**.[20] Otherwise the several Texts would not be consistent with one another.[21]

[Objection][22] <**17**> Nārada 13.2cd and Yājñavalkya 2.117cd **[13]** clearly show that, failing daughters, it is the daughters' sons who are entitled to inherit the property, for the word "offspring" can be construed only with the word "daughters" which is nearest to it.[23]

[Refutation] Not so. Indeed,

[1][24] since in the phrase "failing daughters" the word "daughters" refers to a specific kind of descendants and, hence, requires their ascendant as its correlative, it cannot be construed with a different kind of descendants referred to by the word "offspring," namely, the daughter's sons. Daughters and sons are parallel in this Text.[25]

[19] According to the *Mitākṣarā* (on Y 2.145; Colebrooke II.xi.23) the word "brahman" stands for "of higher caste" generally. E.g., if a *vaiśya* wife dies without offspring, her property goes to the daughter of a *kṣatriya* wife.

[20] Jīmūtavāhana's justification of the term "brahman" (*brāhmaṇī*) at M 9.198 is not clear. I take it to proceed in three stages. [1] The term can be a mere amplification (*anuvāda*), i.e., its sole purpose is to praise the mother's unmarried daughter who inherits, whatever her caste. [2] If someone insists on giving "brahman" its full meaning, Jīmūtavāhana is willing to have the verse refer more specifically to the inheritance of a woman of lower caste who has no offspring of her own; in that case the inheritance goes to the unmarried daughter of another wife of the husband who belongs to the brahman caste. [3] Under no circumstances is he willing to accept that the term "brahman" at M 9.198 pertains to the daughter of parents married in a *brāhma* form of wedding; in that case the inheritance goes to the wife's husband (Y 2.145; **24**).

[21] Jīmūtavāhana uses the technical term *asāmañjasya*, "inconsistency." According to a rule of interpretation, one must avoid inconsistency between words or phrases whenever it is possible to reconcile them. Cf. Sarkar 1909: 91–92.

[22] At **17–21** Jīmūtavāhana argues that, if there are no daughters, the mother's *yautaka* property goes to her own sons, not to her daughter's sons. The discussion concentrates on the terms "her offspring" and "her sons" in three of the texts quoted at **13**. Other commentaries, including the opponent whom Jīmūtavāhana introduces at **17** and the *Mitākṣarā* (on Y 2.145; Colebrooke II.xi.18), use the same texts to claim that the property goes to the daughter's sons.

[23] This is obvious in the Sanskrit texts but not in the translations, at least not at Y 2.117. The Sanskrit texts are as follows: N 13.2cd *mātur duhitaro 'bhāve duhitṝṇāṃ tadanvayaḥ*; Y 2.17cd *mātur duhitaraḥ śeṣam ṛṇāt tābhya ṛte 'nvayaḥ*.

[24] The first section of Jīmūtavāhana's refutation deals with the interpretation of N 13.2cd.

[25] According to Jīmūtavāhana the second half of N 13.2cd actually says: "failing daughters *of the mother*, it goes to the offspring of that (same mother)."

<**18**> The counterargument to the effect that the suggestive power of the word "offspring" here correlates it with a different point of reference,[26] is wrong. Indeed, all these terms—"daughters," "offspring," and "sons"—can have their primary meanings only if one correlates them with "mother." And everyone will agree that here the word "daughter" in correlation with the word "mother" has its primary meaning.

<**19**> Nor should one argue that the reason why it is proper to construe "offspring" with the daughters is that they are the ones the pronoun *tad* brings to mind. Indeed, since *tad* is a pronoun that refers to a noun mentioned earlier, this argument would require that, in the case at hand, daughters be the only noun that *tad* can bring to mind.[27]

[2][28] <**20**> The word for "daughters" in the Yājñavalkya text is expressed in the nominative case, the word for "them" in the ablative. Neither one can be construed with the word for "offspring," which, being in the nominative, would require a complement in the genitive. The only word with which "offspring" can be construed is "of the mother," even though the two are not contiguous in the sentence.

Since, therefore, there is no doubt that at Yājñavalkya 2.117cd "offspring" must be construed with "the mother," it stands to reason that at Nārada 13.2cd and at Kātyāyana 918ab "her offspring" and "the sons" must be construed with "the mother" as well. In that way the Texts are not incompatible with one another.

[3] <**21**> In accordance with the Baudhāyana text:

> When there are persons born-of-the-body, the property goes to them,[29] [Bau 1.5.11.11; **11.1.37**]

it stands to reason that in the case at hand it is the son born-of-the-body who is entitled to inherit by dint of immediacy, not the daughter's son who, not being born-of-the-body, is further removed.

<**22**> So,[30] the female property which a woman received at her wedding first goes to her daughters alone, not to her sons. A number of Texts subsequently establish the order of succession among different kinds of daughters. Indeed,

[A] Gautama says:

[26] This paragraph is difficult and has been variously interpreted. Jīmūtavāhana uses the technical term *adhiṣṭhāna-lakṣaṇā*, i.e., the power of a word by way of *lakṣaṇā* (cf. note at **2.40**), to suggest a different *adhiṣṭhāna*, "basis, point of reference." According to the opponent, in the case at hand this kind of interpretation allows the word "offspring" at N 13.2d to refer to the offspring of the daughters.

[27] This argument is different from the one used at the beginning of **17**, namely, that in the Sanskrit text the word for "daughters" is nearer to *tad* than the word for "mother." In this case the opponent argues that, when one hears/reads *tad*, it is "daughters" that comes to mind (*buddhi-stha*, Śrīkṛṣṇa). Jīmūtavāhana counters that, at N 13.2cd, the word for "mother" also precedes *tad*, and that it may be brought to mind by *tad* as well.

[28] Jīmūtavāhana now addresses Y 2.117cd (**13**).

[29] Cf. **11.1.37**, where this text is used for a different purpose and with a different meaning.

[30] Jīmūtavāhana returns to the daughters' right to inherit their mother's *yautaka* property, which was interrupted at **17**.

> Female property goes to daughters not yet given away, to daughters not yet fully settled, and to married daughters. [G 28.24; **13**]

<**23**> Female property first goes to daughters not yet engaged; failing these, to daughters who are engaged; and, failing these, to daughters who are married. The phrase "female property goes to daughters" establishes the general rule; the rest of the Text is intended to list the daughters in the order in which they inherit.[31]

[B] <**24**> Yājñavalkya says:

> In the four higher forms of wedding beginning with the *brāhma* form,[32] the female property of a woman who dies without offspring goes to her husband; if she has children, it goes to her daughters. In the other forms of wedding it goes to her father. [Y 2.145; ab **4.3.2**].

<**25**> Whatever a woman receives in front of the fire at one of the higher forms of wedding goes to her daughters when she dies and, here again, first to a daughter who is not yet engaged; failing her, to one who is; and, failing her, to one who is married.[33] If she has no daughters, it goes to her sons, for her husband is entitled to inherit "the female property of a woman who dies without offspring."

[C] <**26**> Bṛhaspati [26.31cdef; **3**], on the other hand, by using the phrase "a daughter who has not yet been given away," indicates that, failing daughters not yet engaged and daughters not yet married, a married daughter, too, is entitled to inherit.[34]

[Objection] <**27**> Yājñavalkya 2.145 does not pertain solely to property received at the wedding, but to any kind and any amount of property received, at the

[31] The reason for this commentary is that, if one reads G 28.24 literally, it merely says that the property goes "to daughters not yet given away and (*ca*) to those not yet fully settled," without establishing any priority among them (cf. the translation at **13**). In addition to establishing an order of priority among daughters not yet engaged and those not yet married, both of whom are mentioned in the text, Jīmūtavāhana employs a device often resorted to by Sanskrit commentators also to include, in third place, married daughters who are not mentioned explicitly: these are supposed to be referred to by the particle *ca* at the end of the Sanskrit sentence: [1] *aprattānām*, [2] *apratiṣṭhitānām*, and [3] *ca*.

[32] The Sanskrit term *vivāha*, alone or with the names of the eight forms it may assume (cf. **4.3.1–9**), designates both the marriage ceremony (nuptials) and the married state (wedlock). I translate it as either "wedding" or "marriage" as fits the context and Jīmūtavāhana's interpretations. His interpretation of the text here, and even more so at **27–28** and **4.3.4-9**, makes it clear that he considers the locative plural *vivāheṣu* to mean "at the weddings," not "in case of such marriages."

[33] The reasoning here is that Y 2.145 refers to "her daughters" without any restriction, i.e., to all her daughters, not yet engaged, engaged, and married.

[34] See, however, note 4: the reading of the end of B 26.31cdef is peculiar to the *Dāyabhāga*.

wedding or not, by a woman married according to the *brāhma* or other higher forms of wedding.[35]

[Refutation] Not so. Indeed,

[1] Yājñavalkya 2.144 [**4.3.10**] would become inoperative.[36]

[2] Yājñavalkya 2.145 would be incompatible with Manu:

> In *brāhma*, *daiva*, *ārṣa*, *gāndharva*, or *prājāpatya* weddings, the property of a woman who dies without offspring goes to her husband alone. [M 9.196; cf. **4.3.4**]
> But what was given to a woman at *āsura* or other lower forms of wedding goes to her mother and to her father, if she dies without offspring. [M 9.197; cf. **4.3.4**]

The phrase "what was given to a woman" in the second verse also applies in the first. As a result, the combination "what was given at any kind of wedding" makes it clear that Manu 9.196 pertains to property given at weddings only, not to any kind of property whatever.[37]

[3] <**28**> Yama's verse:

> Whatever property is given at an *āsura* or other lower forms of wedding,[38] [*Dhko* p. 1462]

pertains to property that is given while the successive rites of the wedding ceremony are in progress. It is clear, therefore, that this applies only to property received at the wedding.

[Objection] <**29**> Lest there be no Texts that regulate the devolution of female property received before or after the wedding when a woman dies without offspring, the words *brāhma* and so forth must be taken to pertain not to the weddings themselves but to women married by these forms of wedding.

[Refutation] Not so. The devolution of property received before or after the wedding will be explained in detail hereafter.

[35] The opponent (the *Mitākṣarā*, according to Acyuta and Śrīkṛṣṇa; cf. note at **4.3.4**) asserts that the locative at Y 2.145 does not mean "at such weddings" but "in the case of such marriages." On the ambiguity of the locative *vivāheṣu*, see note 32.

[36] If Y 2.145 did not specifically deal with property received at the wedding, in the absence of sons or daughters all female property, including property received before and after the wedding, would go either to the husband or the father; property received before or after the wedding could not go to the brothers as enjoined by the immediately preceding verse (Y 2.144).

[37] At first sight, M 9.196 uses the same ambiguous expression as Y 2.145, which might mean: "in the case of *brāhma* and other marriages." Yet, Jīmūtavāhana uses the phrase "what was given to her" at M 9.197 as an argument to make M 9.196 mean "at *brāhma* and other weddings." Hence, Y 2.145 would be incompatible with M 9.196, if it referred to gifts other than those made at the wedding. Jīmūtavāhana provides a more cogent argument why the locatives mean "at the weddings" at **4.3.4**.

[38] That is, "goes to her father alone, if she dies without offspring" (*Dhko* p. 1462).

CHAPTER FOUR
SECTION THREE

Inheritance of Female Property When a Woman Dies without Offspring

<1> Let me now point out who is entitled to inherit a woman's female property when she dies without offspring.[1]

<2> On this subject Yājñavalkya says:

> In the four higher forms of wedding beginning with the *brāhma* form the female property of a woman who dies without offspring goes to her husband.[2] [Y 2.145ab; **4.2.24**]

<3> The four forms of wedding beginning with the *brāhma* form actually amount to five, namely: *daiva*, *ārṣa*, *prājāpatya*, and *gāndharva*, in addition to *brāhma*. Indeed, Manu 9.196 [**4.2.27**] states that there are five higher forms of wedding. What the Yājñavalkya text says is that, if a woman dies without offspring, the property she received while any of these five forms of wedding was being performed goes to her husband. The term "offspring" here means descendants.[3]

<4> It would not be appropriate to interpret Yājñavalkya 2.145ab as saying that any kind and any amount of property a woman acquires before and/or after her wedding goes to her husband, provided he married her by a *brāhma* or other higher

[1] In the first part of this section (**1–30**) Jīmūtavāhana proposes the following order of succession:

for unmarried women: 1. brothers german; 2. mother; 3. father.

for married women:

A. gifts received at the wedding:

a. higher wedding: husband;

b. lower wedding: 1. mother; 2. father.

B. gifts received before or after a wedding of any form:

1. brothers; 2. mother; 3. father; 4. husband.

[2] On the classical eight forms of wedding, see Banerjee repr. 1984: 79–87; Kane 1941: 516–26; H. Chatterjee 1972–74; Rocher 1979.

[3] The purport of the synonym "descendants" (*saṃtati*) for "offspring" (*prajā*) is not clear. According to **4.2.25** being "without offspring" means only not having daughters and/or sons. The *Dāyādhikārakramasaṃgraha* (ed. pp. 22–23; tr. II.3.9–13) adds, in this order, daughters' sons, sons' sons, sons' sons' sons, stepsons, stepsons' sons, and stepsons' sons' sons. According to the *Mitākṣarā* (on Y 2.144; Colebrooke II.xi.9) "offspring" here includes daughters, daughters' daughters, daughters' sons, sons, and sons' sons.

form of wedding.[4] Rather, the phrase "in the four higher forms of wedding beginning with the *brāhma* form," which is expressed in the locative case, refers to the time at which the weddings took place. Indeed,

[1] if the compound "in *brāhma*, *daiva*, *ārṣa*, *gāndharva*, or *prājāpatya* weddings," in the locative plural, at Manu 9.196 [**4.2.27**] referred to a woman who was married by one of these weddings, it ought to have been expressed in the singular number and in the genitive case, because the word indicating the woman is expressed in the genitive singular in the next verse [M 9.197; **4.2.27**].[5]

[2] If the words with locative endings suggest the actual time of the wedding, the suggestion relates to something that is immediate.[6] If they referred to the woman who had such a wedding, the suggestion would be in relation to the wedding ceremony which occurred at an earlier time. The latter type of suggestion is of a lower order, and, therefore, less appropriate.

[3] The terms *brāhma* and so forth do not designate women thus wedded, for Manu and others use them to indicate different forms of wedding with their own distinctive features. Indeed,

[a] following the introductory statement:

> Listen to a brief description of the following eight ways to wed a woman, [M 3.20cd]

Manu goes on to enumerate them in the next verse:

> *Brāhma*, *daiva*, *ārṣa*, *prājāpatya*, *āsura*, *gāndharva*, *rākṣasa*, and, the eighth and lowest, *paiśāca*. [M 3–21]

[b] Nārada says:

> There are eight ways by which to consecrate the weddings of caste members. The first is the *brāhma* form, etc. [N 12.38-39]

[c] Viṣṇu says:

[4] On the ambiguity of the locative plural forms indicating either "at such weddings" or "in the case of such marriages," see note at **4.2.24**. The *Mitākṣarā* (Colebrooke II.xi.11) says that Y 2.145 pertains to property of "women who have become wives by such weddings."

[5] This argument is not obvious from the translation at **4.2.27**. In the Sanskrit text the word for "woman" appears neither in M 9.196 nor in M 9.197. The former literally says: "When one-without-offspring dies (*aprajāyām atītāyām*, locative singular: locative absolute), property in the five forms of wedding goes to her husband." The latter starts with the words: "But what was given to her (*yat tv asyāḥ syād dhanaṃ dattam*, genitive singular) in the other forms of wedding." Jīmūtavāhana wishes "given to her" also to apply to "property" in the previous verse. If the compound listing the five forms of wedding meant "having had one of these," it would be a *bahuvrīhi* (adjectival, exocentric compound; cf. note at **2.59**), and it would have to correspond in number, gender, and case endings with the pronoun it qualifies (*asyāḥ*), and it would have been expressed in the genitive singular female. It might have been less cumbersome to say that, if the compound was a *bahuvrīhi*, it would have had to correspond with "when one-without-offspring" in the same verse.

[6] On *lakṣaṇā*, "suggestive power," see note at **2.40**.

> There are eight forms of wedding: *brāhma*, *daiva*, etc. [Vi 24.17–18][7]

<**5**> For all these reasons one should heed Viśvarūpa's opinion: "The Text about *brāhma* and other forms of wedding pertains to female property received at the time of these weddings."[8]

<**6**> On the other hand, female property received at *āsura* and other lower forms of wedding first goes to the woman's mother and, failing her, to the woman's father, even if her husband is living. Indeed,

[1] the phrase "to her mother and to her father" [Manu 9.197d; **4.2.27**] clearly sets forth an order of succession. If they were supposed to inherit jointly, this Text would simply have said "to their parents."

[2] Since in the case of the property of an unmarried woman there are Texts which explicitly state that her father inherits her property only if her mother is deceased, it is fitting that the same order be observed in this case. <**7**> Says Baudhāyana:

> The inheritance of a woman who dies unmarried goes to her brothers german; failing them, to her mother; failing her, to her father.[9]

<**8**> Note that this Text suffices to explain what happens to the property of unmarried women.[10]

<**9**> It would be wrong, though, to say that, even as with the property of unmarried women, in the case at hand the brothers should inherit first as well. There are no Texts to that effect; the only rights of succession the Texts mention are those of the mother and the father.

<**10**> On the other hand, property which a woman received before or after her wedding from her father's, mother's, or husband's side does go to her brothers. Says Yājñavalkya:

> If a woman dies without offspring, the following go to her *bāndhavas*: [1] what was given to her by her kin [**11–15**], [2] later settlements [**16–18**], and gratuities [**19–25**]. [Y 2.144]

[7] The lists of eight forms of wedding at N 12.38-39 and Vi 24.17-18 are identical with M 3.21, except that they place *gāndharva* before *āsura*.

[8] The printed *Bālakrīḍā* commentary (on Y 2.149 which corresponds to Y 2.145 at **4.2.24**) uses the same ambiguous locative form as the Yājñavalkya text itself: *brahmādivivāhacatuṣṭaye yat strīdhanaṃ tad aprasūtāyāṃ bhartuḥ*. As Kane (1925: 200) points out, these words "appear to convey the same view (scil., as Jīmūtavāhana's), though not quite clearly." On the transmission of Viśvarūpa's commentary, see Introduction.

[9] Although this text is often attributed to Baudhāyana (*Dhko* p. 1427), it does not appear in the *Baudhāyana-dharmasūtra*.

[10] I.e., the inheritance of unmarried women's property need not be discussed again anywhere else.

[1] Gifts from Her Kin

<**11**> "What was given to her by her kin (*bandhu-datta*)" means what was given to her by her mother and/or father. The latters' sons are her *bāndhavas*, i.e., her brothers.[11] <**12**> Says Vṛddha-Kātyāyana:

> If a daughter dies without offspring, all immovable property given to her by her parents invariably goes to her brothers. [vK = K 919]

<**13**> Since it is clear that her dying without issue in and of itself is the necessary and sufficient condition for her brothers to inherit, the point of the word "invariably" is that brothers get the property of a sister who dies without offspring, regardless of the form of her wedding, from the *brāhma* form down to the *paiśāca* form. Viśvarūpa's statement to that effect should be heeded.[12] <**14**> In view of the phrase "immovable property" in the Text, it follows as a matter of course that the same is true for all other property as well.[13]

<**15**> "What was given to her by her kin" refers to property she was given by her parents while she was yet unmarried. First, property she received after her wedding is referred to by the term *anvādheya* [**16–18**]. Second, what she received at the time of the wedding goes to her parents [**2–9**].

[2] Later Settlements

<**16**> Kātyāyana defines later settlements (*anvādheya*) as follows:

> What a woman receives after her wedding from her husband's family and from the family of her kin, is called later settlements. [K 899; **4.1.2**]

<**17**> "From her husband's family" means from her father-in-law and so forth. "From the family of her kin" means from the families of her father and mother.[14]

<**18**> He also provides a second definition:

> Bhṛgu defines later settlements as anything a woman receives after her wedding, as a token of affection, either from her husband or from her parents. [K 900; **4.1.2**]

[3] Gratuities

<**19**> He defines gratuities (*śulka*) as follows:

[11] A *bāndhava* is so called because he is the descendant of a *bandhu*, in accordance with *Aṣṭādhyāyī* 4.1.92: *tasyāpatyam*. The *Mitākṣarā*, which does not restrict Y 2.144 to gifts made before and/or after the wedding (cf. note 4), takes Y 2.144 as a general rule introducing Y 2.145 (**2**; **4.2.24**) and, hence, interprets *bāndhavas* as "her husband, etc."

[12] The printed *Bālakrīḍā* (2.148) merely states, without any reference to the form of the wedding: "If she dies without offspring, her *bāndhavas*, i.e., her brothers german, get it" (*etac cānapatyāyāṃ mṛtāyāṃ bāndhavāḥ sodaryabhrātaro gṛhṇīyuḥ*). On the transmission of Viśvarūpa's commentary, see Introduction.

[13] On the phrase "as a matter of course" (*daṇḍāpūpanyāya*), see note at **2.25**.

[14] Cf. note at **4.1.3**.

> Whatever compensation she gets from workmen on houses or dealers in utensils, draft animals, milch animals, or jewelry is called a gratuity. [K 898]

<**20**> Whatever a woman is given by builders or other craftsmen as an inducement for her to prompt her husband and others to use their services, is a gratuity.[15] It is a compensation, because it is a payment for her intervention.

<**21**> Vyāsa gives a different definition:[16]

> What is given to her to make her come to her husband's house is called a gratuity, [Vy 268]

i.e., what is given to her as a kind of inducement to make her go to her husband's house.

<**22**> Note that this kind of *śulka* is common to the *brāhma* and all other forms of wedding;[17] even as other female property received after the wedding it goes to the woman's brothers if she dies without offspring. <**23**> This kind of *śulka* is different, however, from the *śulka* that is given for girls in the lower forms of wedding from the *āsura* onward, for that kind of *śulka* occurs in *āsura* weddings only.[18] That is why Manu says:

> An *āsura* wedding follows upon the receipt of money, a *gāndharva* wedding upon mutual consent, a *rākṣasa* wedding upon forcible abduction, a *paiśāca* wedding upon a ruse on the girl. [Y 1.63]

[15] K 898 is interpreted differently by various commentators (for a survey, see Jolly 1885: 232–33). Colebrooke, followed by Banerjee (repr. 1984: 310), translates Jīmūtavāhana's commentary: "as a bribe to send her husband or other person [of her family] to labour on such particular work." In the *Digest* Colebrooke (1798: V.9.468) translates K 898 as follows, in accordance with Jagannātha's commentary, which, in turn, is based on Vācaspatimiśra's interpretation (*Vivādacintāmaṇi*, ed. p. 213; tr. p. 224): "The trifle which is received by a woman as the price (or reward) of household (labour), of (using household) utensils, of (keeping) beasts of burden, of (watching) milch-cattle, of (preserving) ornaments of dress, or of (superintending) servants, is called her 'perquisite.'"

[16] I translate "different" because the Sanskrit text reads *Vyāsoktaṃ vā*. Śrīkṛṣṇa takes Kātyāyana's and Vyāsa's definitions cumulatively.

[17] The Sanskrit expression *brāhmādi*, "*brāhma*, etc.," is ambiguous: it can be intended to mean either the five higher forms of wedding, or all eight forms of wedding. In view of Jīmūtavāhana's conclusion (**26**) I prefer the latter interpretation. According to Jīmūtavāhana's comments on K 898 and Vy 268 (**20**, **21**), the common denominator of the two definitions is the price paid as an inducement, literally as a bribe (*utkoca*), to a wife after her wedding, to make her do certain things. That inducement may occur in any kind of wedding. Jīmūtavāhana is about to argue, first, that the *śulka* discussed here is different from the *śulka*, "bride price," that is characteristic of the *āsura* wedding, i.e., of the first of the lower kinds of wedding, and, hence, that the *śulka* as defined at K 898 and Vy 278 is not limited to the lower forms of wedding.

[18] I translate "for" girls rather than "to" girls. Although something may be given to the girl as well (e.g., M 3.31), the main recipient is her father or whoever gives the girl away. Cf. **24**.

<**24**> Hence, one should take exception with the statement that the *śulka* goes to the brothers if the wedding was one of the three lower forms, since only those forms are supposed to be associated with *śulka*. Indeed,

[1] there is no such *śulka* at a *rākṣasa* or a *paiśāca* wedding.

[2] This kind of *śulka* is not female property. What is called *śulka* here is property taken by the father or others. Says Manu:

> The father of an unmarried girl, if he is wise, shall not take the slightest *śulka*. If he is greedy and takes it, he is a man who sells his offspring. [M 3.51]

The term "father" here is synecdochic. Hence, brothers or any other persons who take such property also share in the characterization of one who takes a *śulka*. On the other hand, only what the father and the like take qualifies as this kind of *śulka*.

<**25**> By the same token I have also refuted the view that, since female property of the *śulka* type is supposed to exist only in the *āsura* and other lower types of wedding, only if the wedding is one of these forms do the brothers also inherit what was given to her by her kin and her later settlements, which are mentioned together with *śulka* in the same Text [Y 2.144; **10**]. <**26**> In fact, the *śulka* form of female property as defined above [**18–22**] can occur in any form of wedding, and the brothers inherit it in all cases, since there are no Texts upon which to base any distinction.

<**27**> There is a Gautama text that has the same tenor as that of Kātyāyana [**12**]:

> A sister's gratuities go to her brothers german, next to her mother; some say before.[19] [G 28.25–26]

<**28**> That means that they go first to her brothers german, and, failing them, to her mother. "Some say before" represents the opinion of other Sages.

<**29**> Hence, the woman's property first goes to her brothers german; failing them, to her mother; failing the mother, to her father; failing all of these, to her husband. Says Kātyāyana:

> Failing her kin, whatever they gave her goes to her husband. [K 918cd]

[19] I translate G 28.25–26 according to Jīmūtavāhana's interpretation (**28**). The usual interpretation is that the brothers get their sister's gratuities "after their mother's death; according to some, even before." A few manuscripts of the *Dāyabhāga*, followed by the 1863 and other editions, as well as Colebrooke's translation, insert *pituś ca*, "and to her father," after *mātuś ca*, "to her mother," in the Gautama text. Those words do not, however, appear in the *Gautama-dharmasūtra* or in the many quotations of this *sūtra* in other commentaries and digests, nor are they referred to in Jīmūtavāhana's immediate gloss on the text (**28**). Jīmūtavāhana's mention of the father (**29**) is clearly based on the fact that K 918cd, which he proceeds to quote, has "her kin" (*bandhūnām*) before her husband in the order of succession.

<**30**> "Failing her kin" subsumes "failing a brother." This follows as a matter of course,[20] for parents inherit only in the absence of brothers.

<**31**> Failing all the above, up to and including the husband, the following rules apply, as stated by Bṛhaspati:

> A mother's sister, a maternal uncle's wife, a paternal uncle's wife,
> a father's sister, a mother-in-law, and the wife of an elder brother
> are said to be like a mother.[21] [B 26.32]
> If these women have no *aurasa*, no son, no daughter's son, or a
> son of these, their property goes to their sister' sons and so forth.[22]
> [B 26.33]

<**32**> The term *aurasa* here refers to both a son and a daughter, for both of these bar everyone else.[23]

The term "son" refers to the son of another wife of her husband, according to the Text:

> When, of all of a man's wives, one has a son, through that son
> they all have a son. So says Manu. [M 9.183]

It is not a qualifier of the term *aurasa*.[24] First, it would be redundant, and, second, the sister's son and so forth would then be entitled to inherit even if there is a son.[25]

<**33**> Failing an *aurasa* son or daughter and a son of another wife, the daughter's son inherits.[26]

<**34**> The word "these" in "a son of these" refers to the son of the woman herself and the son of another wife. Hence, the sons of these two inherit, not,

[20] On the phrase "as a matter of course" (*daṇḍāpūpanyāya*), see note at **2.25**.

[21] Colebrooke's "maternal uncle" for "a maternal uncle's wife, a paternal uncle's wife" obviously results from the accidental loss of a few words in the translation. A male is patently out of place in this enumeration of women. Cf. Goldstücker 1871: 11–12.

[22] For the list of "their sisters's sons and so forth," see note 28.

[23] According to Śrīkṛṣṇa the term *aurasa* here includes the substitute sons whom he again refers to as "adopted sons and so forth" (cf. note ar **4.2.5**). Raghunandana includes *atideśika-putras*, "sons by assimilation," under "the son of another wife." On the background of these inclusions, see Derrett 1977a: 87–88.

[24] Jīmūtavāhana argues in favor of his own interpretation, "no *aurasa*, no son," against the more common interpretation "no *aurasa* son."

[25] I.e., the son of another wife of her husband, who is also a "son" of the deceased (M 9.183), would not appear in the list of heirs. He could inherit only in the absence of all those who appear in the list, including the deceased's sister's son.

[26] Colebrooke rightly pointed out that this sentence was suspect in the eyes of the *Dāyabhāga* commentators. Śrīkṛṣṇa goes into great detail to show that a daughter's son inherits prior to a son of another wife. Both the *Dāyatattva* (ed. p. 187; tr. 9.24) and the *Dāyādhikārakramasaṃgraha* (ed. p. 27; tr. II.6.2), which quote Jīmūtavāhana's commentary nearly verbatim, omit this sentence. In modern Hindu law, too, the passage has been considered interpolated and, hence, not applicable in the law courts. See, e.g., *Purna Chandra Bysack* v. *Gopal Lal Sett* (1908) 8 C.L.J. 269, 428; cf. Acharyya 1914: 365.

however, the son of a daughter's son, for he is beyond the pale of those who offer *piṇḍas*.[27]

<**35**> Next, failing these, i.e., starting from the sons and so forth, down to brothers, mother, father, and husband, the property goes to the sisters' sons and so forth, even if there are *sapiṇḍas* such as a father-in-law or an elder brother of the husband. Indeed,

[1] it is the only kind of devolution the Text [**31**] provides for.

[2] By saying of a number of women that they are like a man's mother, and thereby conveying the notion that he is like a son to them, the Text indicates that he offers *piṇḍas* for them. To say that in the chapter of inheritance is tantamount to saying that he inherits their property.

<**36**> The phrase "sister's sons and so forth" [B 26.63; **31**] might lead one to believe that, among the woman's sisters' sons, her husband's sisters' sons, her husband's younger brothers' sons, her husband's elder brothers' sons, her brothers' sons, her sons-in-law, and her younger brothers-in-law, each of these inherits failing the preceding ones, with the result that the younger brothers-in-law would inherit only in the absence of all of these.[28] This, however, would run counter to the practice of the couth. I will, therefore, interpret the Text according to its intrinsic merit.[29]

[1] The following statement by Manu appears in the chapter on inheritance:

> Three generations shall be given water, three generations shall be offered *piṇḍas*. It is the fourth generation that offers these. The fifth generation plays no role in this. [M 9.186; **11.1.40, 11.6.7, 11.6.17**]

[2] Yājñavalkya points out that the right to inherit is based on the offering of *piṇḍas*:

> The one among them who offers *piṇḍas* gets a share. [Y 2.132c]

[27] On *piṇḍa* and *sapiṇḍa*, see Introduction.

[28] This sentence enumerates all those who might consider the deceased to be like their mother and therefore claim to inherit from her, according to and in the order established at B 26.32 (**31**). The deceased is

1. a mother's sister to her sisters' sons, (3)
2. a maternal uncle's wife to her husband's sisters' sons, (4)
3. a paternal uncle's wife to her husband's younger and elder brothers' sons, (2)
4. a father's sister to her brothers' sons, (5)
5. a mother-in-law to her sons-in-law, (6)
6. the wife of an elder brother to her husband's younger brothers. (1)

The figures in parentheses indicate the order of succession which Jīmūtavāhana proposes at **37**.

[29] Most commentators make it clear that the phrase "according to its intrinsic merit" (*vastubala*) here means "according to the degree to which the heirs are of service to the deceased"; Maheśvara equates it with *nyāya*, "rule of logic, common sense" (cf. note at **4.2.8**).

[3] In the case of a son it is obvious that his right to inherit prevails over anyone else's, because he is the one who saves his father from hell by offering more *piṇḍas*.[30]

[4] There is the following Vṛddha-Śātātapa text:

> Those who know the Veda hold that funeral offerings should be made by a maternal uncle for his sister's son, by a sister's son for his maternal uncle, for one's father-in-law, one's teacher, one's friend, one's maternal grandfather, as well as for the wives of these persons, and for the sisters of one's mother and father.[31]

<37> Since it is thus established that those who inherit are those who offer *piṇḍas*, the order in which they inherit must be based on the differing degrees to which they offer these, as follows.

[1] First, the younger brother of a woman's husband inherits her property: he offers *piṇḍas* to her, to her husband, and to three ancestors to whom her husband would have had to offer them; he is also a *sapiṇḍa*.

[2] Failing him, the son of the husband's elder or younger brother inherits the property of his paternal uncle's wife: he offers *piṇḍas* to her, to her husband, and to two ancestors to whom her husband would have had to offer them; he is also a *sapiṇḍa*.

[3] Failing him, the sister's son inherits the property of his mother's sister: even though he is not a *sapiṇḍa*, he offers *piṇḍas* to her, and he offers the *piṇḍas* which her son would have had to offer to her father, grandfather, and great-grandfather.

[4] Failing him, the son of the husband's sister inherits the property of his maternal uncle's wife: since a husband's claim is weaker than a son's, it stands to reason that the claims of those who appear in their stead have the same relative strengths.[32] He offers *piṇḍas* to three ancestors to whom her husband would have had to offer them, and he offers *piṇḍas* to her and her husband.

[5] Failing him, the brother's son inherits the property of his father's sister: he offers *piṇḍas* to her father and paternal grandfather, and to her.

[6] Failing him, the son-in-law inherits the property of his mother-in-law: he offers *piṇḍas* to his father-in-law and to his mother-in-law.

[30] The son offers one *piṇḍa* for his father to enjoy, and he offers two *piṇḍas*, to his paternal grandfather and great-grandfather, which his father would have had to offer.

[31] Goldstücker (1871: 12–13) deals at length with this passage. He points out an error in Colebrooke's translation, quotes the correct interpretation of the Śātātapa text as given in the *Dāyanirṇaya* (quoted in the *Dāyakaumudī*, p. 156), and refers to *Giridhari Lall Roy* v. *The Bengal Government* (1869) 12 M.I.A. 448, in which "the judgment of the High Court must have been different, had it been able to avail itself of the correct translation of the passage quoted, proving as it does, the maternal uncle's duty to perform the Śrāddha for a sister's son."

[32] The sister's son offers three *piṇḍas* which her son would have had to offer; the husband's sister's son offers three *piṇḍas* which her husband would have had to offer. A son's claim is stronger than a husband's. Therefore, the sister's son inherits prior to the husband's sister's son.

<**38**> Such is the order to be followed. The phrase "their sisters' son and so forth" [**31**] does not bear on the order of succession.[33] Its sole purpose is to indicate that those individuals are entitled to inherit.

<**39**> It should be understood that, if none of the six mentioned above are extant, the right to inherit is vested in the nearest *sapiṇḍa*: the father-in-law, the husband's elder brother, and so on. <**40**> To say that the Bṛhaspati text takes effect only in cases where there are no *sapiṇḍas* left is wrong. Indeed, its series of heirs subsumes the husband's younger brother and his son and the husband's elder brother's son, whereas nearer relatives such as the father-in-law and the husband's elder brother are not mentioned. <**41**> Hence, those who are guided by the right standards must object to any practice that rests on insufficient knowledge of the true intent of the Text.[34]

<**42**> Thus far for the extremely opaque subject of female property when a woman dies without offspring.[35]

[33] I.e., the phrase "their sisters' sons and so forth" (B 26.33d) does not mean that the sisters' sons come first, followed by the husband's sisters' sons, etc., in the order suggested at B 26.31 (**31**).

[34] This sentence has been interpreted differently by the several *Dāyabhāga* commentators. I take it to mean that "those who are guided by the right standards" are those who realize, with Jīmūtavāhana, that the main criterion to determine the order of succession established by the Bṛhaspati text is the offering of *piṇḍas*. They should treat any other interpretation, such as the one based on propinquity, as having no foundation. It is not possible to maintain in English the special effect which Jīmūtavāhana creates with the phrase *pramāṇa-para-tantrair a-tantrī-kartavyaḥ*. Cf. note at **4.2.8**.

[35] Cf. the *Vivādatāṇḍava* (1901 ed., p. 437), which introduces the chapter on female property by saying that it is a subject *yuddhaṃ yatra kacākaci*, "on which opponents fight tooth and nail, a donnybrook."

CHAPTER FIVE

PERSONS BARRED FROM PARTITION

<1> Let me now deal with those who are said to be barred from partition and, by elimination,[1] point out those who are entitled to a share.[2]

[A] Āpastamba says:

> In fact,[3] all those who behave righteously are entitled to a share and ought to receive property.[4] But he who manages property unrighteously shall be deprived of his share, even if he is an eldest son.[5] [Āp 2.6.14.14–15]

<2> Bāla offers a confused reading of the latter half of this Text: "But if the eldest son manages property righteously, he shall be given a share equal to his father's."[6] Such a reading is without foundation.

[1] Jīmūtavāhana uses the technical term *paryudāsa* (cf. **6.1.31**, **36–37**). A *paryudāsa* is a negative rule, but different from a *pratiṣedha/niṣedha*, which may create a real conflict with an outright injunction (*vidhi*). The *paryudāsa* is merely an exception or proviso to a *vidhi* (*Arthasaṃgraha* par. 84–85). Śrīkṛṣṇa justifies Jīmūtavāhana's statement by the fact that he announced (**1.1**) that he would define partition, not the absence of it.

[2] Jīmūtavāhana is about to quote seven texts that describe individuals who are barred from partition. These texts are marked [A] to [G].

[3] These two *sūtras* conclude a brief discussion of whether the eldest son should receive the entire property, or at least a preferred share. Āpastamba's final view is that receiving shares is not a question of age or primogeniture, but of righteous behavior.

[4] Only in the *Dāyabhāga* and in Anantarāma's *Vivādacandrikā* (*Dhko* p. 1387) is the phrase "ought to receive property" (*dravyam arhanti*) quoted as part of Āp 2.6.14.14. It may well have been a gloss on *bhāginaḥ*, "are entitled to a share," which was later incorporated into the original reading of the text.

[5] *Pratipādayati*, which I translate "manages," is ambiguous. Colebrooke: "dissipates"; Bühler (Āpastamba tr.): "expends" (with a question on its correctness in a footnote).

[6] Instead of *yas tv adharmeṇa dravyāṇi pratipādayati jyeṣṭho 'pi tam abhāgaṃ kurvīta*, Bāla reads *yas tu dharmeṇa dravyāṇi pratipādayati jyeṣṭhas taṃ pitṛsamabhāgaṃ kurvīta*.

[B] <**3**>[7]

> An *apapātrita* is excluded from partition, and from offering *piṇḍas* or water.[8] [ŚL 299]

An *apapātrita* is a person with whom one no longer shares water.[9]

[C] <**4**> Bṛhaspati says:

> Even a son born of a mother of the same caste as her husband's has no claim to his father's property if he is worthless.[10] It goes to sons who are learned and who offer *piṇḍas* for him. [B 26.34]
> The point of having a son is that he releases his father from his higher and lower debts.[11] Hence, a son who fails to do so is of no use whatever to his father. [B 26.35]
> What is the use of having a cow that has neither milk nor calves? What is the use of having a son who is neither learned nor righteous? [B 26.36]
> A son who lacks learning, courage, and purpose, who has neither moral nor intellectual strength, and whose behavior is not what it ought to be, is worth no more than human waste. [B 26.37]

<**5**> What this means[12] is that a son who did not undergo the rite of passage but who dutifully performs the funeral rites for his father and other ancestors is preferable by far to one who is well versed in the Vedas but who fails to perform the funeral rites.[13] <**6**> Texts such as the following:

[7] This text, which is most often quoted anonymously, is sometimes attributed to Śaṅkha or to Śaṅkha and Likhita (and, hence, is included in Kane's collection of ŚL fragments), occasionally to Āpastamba, as Jīmūtavāhana seems to do here.

[8] On offering water and *piṇḍas*, see the often quoted verse M 9.186 (**4.3.36, 11.1.40, 11.6. 7, 11.6.17**).

[9] *Apapātrita* literally means a person with whom one does not share the same vessels (*pātra*) to drink from; M 10.51, for example, says that members of the *cāṇḍāla* and *śvapaca* mixed castes "must be made *apapātras*."

[10] A son is considered "worthless" (*aguṇavat*) if he does not possess the necessary qualities (*guṇa*) to take care of his father's material and transcendental welfare (*Smṛticandrikā* ed. p. 630; tr. V.16).

[11] "Higher debts" are the debts a person owes to the gods, the sages, and his ancestors, i.e., sacrifices, study of the Veda, and a son, respectively (Va 11.48; cf. M 6.36). "Lower debts" are those he owes to his creditors.

[12] The 1863 and other editions, as well as Colebrooke's translation, introduce this sentence with the phrase "The meaning of the Āpastamba text is this" (*Āpastambasyāyam arthaḥ*), rather than with "What this means is" (*ayam arthaḥ*). That reading is not supported by the manuscripts of the *Dāyabhāga*.

[13] The specific rite of passage alluded to here is the investiture with the sacred thread (*upanayana*), which is a prelude to studying the Vedas with a *guru*. A son who failed to undergo this rite cannot be "well versed in the Vedas." On rites of passage (*saṃskāra*), see note at **3.38**.

> The Self-existent himself called a son *putra* because he saves (*trā*) his father from the hell called *Put*,[14] [M 9.138 = Vi 15.44; **11.1.31**]

reveal the considerable benefits which a man derives from acts performed by his son. The son's accession to the father's property is, therefore, a form of compensation for his performing those acts. Conversely, there is no reason to give any compensation to a son who fails to perform them. That is why Manu says:

> If any of the brothers fails to perform the acts expected of him,[15] he shall have no right to inherit the property. [M 9.214ab]

[D] <**7**>

> The following are barred from receiving shares: the impotent, outcastes, the congenitally blind or deaf, the insane, the retarded, the mute, and the handicapped. [M 9.201]

<**8**> Kātyāyana defines "impotent" as follows:

> If a man's urine does not foam, if his stool sinks in water, if his penis has no erection or sperm, he is called impotent. [K 861]

<**9**> The word "congenitally" is to be construed with both "blind" and "deaf." "Mute" means unable to produce articulate sounds. "Retarded" means incapable of acquiring a knowledge of the Vedas.[16]

[E] <**10**> Says Yājñavalkya:

> Outcastes, their sons,[17] the impotent, the lame, the insane, the retarded, the blind, and those suffering from incurable diseases[18] are barred from receiving shares.[19] They shall, however, be provided for. [Y 2.140]

[14] For other references to this etymology, see **1.36**, **2.53**, and **11.1.31**.

[15] According to some commentators the term *vikarmastha*, "failing to perform acts expected of him," at the same time implies the notion of "performing acts that are not expected of him" (Śrīkṛṣṇa's example: having intercourse with women with whom one should not have intercourse).

[16] Jīmūtavāhana does not comment on "handicapped" (*nirindriya*). It literally means "missing an organ." For other interpretations, see Jolly 1885: 272–74.

[17] According to Vi 15.35–36 this rule only applies to sons born after their father becomes an outcaste. Śrīkṛṣṇa refers to this restriction, yet finds it necessary to add a further justification for the presence of "their sons" in the text: it means that only sons of outcastes are excluded, not the sons of any of the others.

[18] Śrīkṛṣṇa claims that, if the illness happens to be cured subsequent to the partition, the individual gets a share in his own right.

[19] The reading adopted by Jīmūtavāhana and others, "those suffering from incurable diseases" (*acikitsyarogārtāḥ*). makes the enumeration at Y 2.140 restrictive. The more common reading, "the incurably diseased, etc." (*acikitsyarogādyāḥ*), allows commentaries such as the *Mitākṣarā* (Colebrooke II.x.3–4) to subsume under Y 2.140 all those who are barred from partition in other texts.

"Lame" (*pa-ṅ-gu*) means not (*na*) able to walk (*gam*) on one's feet (*pad*).[20] <**11**> Even though they "are barred from receiving a share," all of these, except outcastes and their sons, must be provided for. Says Devala:

> The following are barred from receiving shares of the inheritance after the death of their father: the impotent, lepers, the insane, the retarded, the blind, outcastes, the offspring of outcastes, and those who wear emblems. [D 1573]
> All of these, except outcastes, must be provided with food and clothing. Their shares in the estate go to their sons, provided these do not suffer from the same disabilities. [D 1574]

"Those who wear emblems" (*liṅgin*) means wanderers and the like.[21] <**12**> The word "outcastes" in the second verse subsumes their sons, for being born to an outcaste makes one an outcaste. Says Baudhāyana:

> One must provide food and clothing to the superannuated,[22] and to all those who are unable to live a normal life,[23] i.e., the blind, the retarded, the impotent, the disabled, the sick, and so on, not however to outcastes and sons of outcastes. [Bau 2.2.3.37–40]

[F] <**13**> Nārada says:

> Sons who ill-treat their father,[24] outcastes, the impotent, and the delinquent[25] are barred from receiving shares, even if they are

[20] In fact, the etymology of *paṅgu* is uncertain. The word may well be of Dravidian or Munda origin (Mayrhofer 1956–: 2.185).

[21] On "wanderers" (*pravrajita*), see note at **1.14**.

[22] On the term "superannuated" (*atītavyavahāra*), literally "those whose time to transact business has passed," see note at **3.17**.

[23] The term *akarmin*, which I translate "unable to live a normal life," is uncommon, if not unique, in texts dealing with inheritance. The examples Baudhāyana provides show, however, what kind of incapacities, in addition to old age, are meant here. The commentator Govindasvāmin interprets *akarminaḥ* as an independent item in the list: "those who are able but without energy (*samarthā api nirutsāhāḥ*); hence Bühler's translation: "those who neglect their duties and occupations." Cf. Olivelle: "those who neglect their duties."

[24] According to the *Dāyatattva* (ed. p. 172; tr. 4.9) and other commentaries on this verse, ill-treating one's father includes harming him physically while he lives and neglecting his funeral rites after his death.

[25] The term "delinquent" renders the Sanskrit term *aupapātika*, which is attested in all the *Dāyabhāga* manuscripts I have consulted. It is also supported by the *Dāyatattva* (ed. p. 172; tr. 4–9), and by the manuscripts of the *Nārada-smṛti* (no variants are listed in Lariviere's edition). Yet, it has been replaced by a variety of readings in other digests (*Dhko* p. 1401). This is due to the fact that, if taken literally, as in the *Dāyatattva* and in the *Dāyādhikārakramasaṃgraha* (ed. p. 30; tr. III.4), the reading *aupapātika* excludes from partition individuals who are guilty of *upapātakas*, "minor offenses."

full-fledged sons; a fortiori, if they are *kṣetraja* sons.[26] [N 13.21/20]

[G] <**14**> Says Kātyāyana:

> Sons born to wives wedded in the wrong order by a man of the same *gotra*,[27] and those who renounce the life of a wanderer,[28] should be barred from inheriting. [K 862]

<**15**> If a man first weds a woman of a lower caste and later a woman of a higher caste, both women are "wedded in the wrong order." If a *kṣetraja* son is born to either one of them as the result of a levirate with a man of the same *gotra*, he should be barred from inheriting.[29]

Even if a woman was wedded in the wrong order, and a son was born to her by a husband of the same caste, he does inherit.[30] And so does the son of a mother wedded in the right order, even if her husband is of a different caste.[31] <**16**> Says Kātyāyana:

> The son of a woman wedded in the wrong order inherits, provided he is of the same caste as his father; and so does a son who is of a different caste, provided his mother was wedded in the right order. [K 863]
> The son of a woman wedded to a man of a lower caste does not receive a share of the inheritance. He receives only food and clothing, as his kin see fit. [K 864]
> Failing kin, however, he gains control of his father's property. Kinsmen cannot be forced to give him anything they inherited from their own fathers.[32] [K 865]

[26] On *aurasa* sons and *kṣetraja* sons, see note at **2.59**.

[27] I translate the first half of the verse in accordance with Jīmūtavāhana's unusual commentary (**15**). Even though Colebrooke and the *Dharmakośa* state that the *Vyavahāraprakāśa* follows the *Dāyabhāga*, its edition (p. 560) reads *tayoḥ sagotrād aniyogotpannaḥ kṣetrajaḥ putro* instead of Jīmūtavāhana's *tayoḥ sagotrān niyuktād utpannaḥ kṣetrajah putro*, and Sarkar (VIII.9) translates accordingly: "A *ksetraja* or son of the wife, procreated by a kinsman of the same family without being authorized to raise up issue, is unworthy of inheritance." According to the more common interpretation, this part of the verse bars from inheriting, first, the sons of women wedded in the wrong order, and second, sons born of parents who belong to the same *gotra*. On *gotra*, see note at **1.4**.

[28] On "the life of a wanderer," see note at **1.4**.

[29] I.e., from inheriting the property of his mother's deceased husband.

[30] I.e., if a man first weds a woman of a lower caste and then a woman of his own caste, the sons of the latter inherit, not the sons of the former.

[31] I.e., if a man first weds a woman of his own caste and then a woman of a lower caste, the latter inherit as well as the former. Their shares will, however, be different. Cf. **9.12**.

[32] That is, if they did not get anything from the father of the person born against the order of the castes. I translate *svapitryam* "inherited from their own fathers," which is the only reading attested in the *Dāyabhāga* manuscripts. Colebrooke translates *apitryam* ("not

<**17**> Note that it may happen that the impotent and the like marry:

> If the impotent and the like ever wish to have mates, and if they have issue, their offspring are entitled to a share. [M 9.203]

"Issue" here equals "offspring."[33]

<**18**> [Question] The impotent lack virility and, hence, are incapable of having children. The others, such as the mute, are incapable of reciting the Veda; as a result, they do not undergo the initiation ceremony, and they become outcastes. So, how can they marry?[34]

[Answer] As far as the impotent are concerned, it is possible for other men to beget sons by their wives. And someone who is not initiated because he is unfit for the initiation ceremony is like a *śūdra*; he does not become an outcaste. <**19**> Consequently, their sons, full-fledged or *kṣetraja* as the case may be, receive shares to the same extent that their fathers would have received them, provided they themselves are not impotent and the like. Their daughters shall be provided for until they are wedded, and their wives who have no sons for as long as they live. Says Yājñavalkya:[35]

> Their full-fledged sons and *kṣetraja* sons receive shares, provided they do not suffer from the same disabilities. Their daughters shall be provided for until they have husbands to provide for them. [Y 2.141]
> If their wives have no sons, they shall be provided for as long as they are of good conduct; if they misbehave or become contrary, they shall be forced to leave. [Y 2.142]

---

being his patrimony"), which is adopted in other digests and discussed as a variant reading in some *Dāyabhāga* commentaries. Kane (Kātyāyana ed. tr.), who also reads *apitryam*, translates: "when the kinsmen have taken no wealth of his father."

[33] Jīmūtavāhana merely wants to say that the vague term *tantu* and the precise term *apatya* at M 9.203 mean the same thing.

[34] For a Hindu to get married and thereby enter the stage of a householder (*gṛhastha*), he should have passed through the previous stage, that of a *brahmacārin*, and have learned to recite, i.e., recite aloud, the Vedas.

[35] The following text should be read in conjunction with the immediately preceding one (Y 2.140; **10**).

CHAPTER SIX

SECTION ONE

PROPERTY THAT IS SUBJECT TO PARTITION AND PROPERTY THAT IS NOT

General Remarks

<1> Let me now deal with property that is subject to partition and with property that is exempt from partition.

On this subject Kātyāyana says:

> Ancestral property, paternal property, and other, self-acquired property, all these are divided when heirs proceed to a partition. [K 840]

<2> The copulative particle "and" in the phrase "and other" must be construed with the word "self," i.e., "and self-acquired property."[1] This means that, because of the word "and," for the "other," i.e., self-acquired property, too, to be subject to partition, it must have been acquired with the help of common property.[2] <3> The following Texts,[3] indeed, ordain that, if property was acquired without drawing on joint property, it is exempt from partition.

[1] At first glance K 840: *paitāmahaṃ ca, pitryaṃ ca, yac ca anyat svayam arjitam,* appears to declare three kinds of property subject to partition: (1) ancestral property, (2) paternal property, and (3) other property which the participants acquired on their own. The last enclitic particle *ca* immediately after the first word, *yac*, of the third kind of property makes this into a category independent of the other two; it pertains to any property the participants acquired on their own. By placing the last *ca* after *svayam* instead, and thereby reading *yad anyat svayaṃ ca arjitam,* "and other (such) self-acquired," Jīmūtavāhana gives the third category of property an element that is common with the earlier two, namely, that, even as in the case of ancestral and paternal property, here, too, joint property is involved. Hence his conclusion that the third category listed by Kātyāyana is limited to self-acquired property for which common property was used to acquire it.

[2] Since, later in this chapter, Jīmūtavāhana most often refers to property that is exempt from partition as property acquired "by expending one's own property and/or one's own labor." Śrīkṛṣṇa here adds "and/or common labor" to "with the help of common property."

[3] The following three texts, marked [A] to [C], explicitly say that property acquired without drawing on joint property is exempt from partition.

[A] Manu and Viṣṇu say:

> If a family member acquired something by his own labor, without drawing on the paternal property, it was earned by his own effort. He cannot be forced to give it away. [M 9.208 = Vi 18.42; **31**]

<**4**> Since the paternal property was not drawn on, the other family members did not contribute financially; since the property was acquired through the individual's own labor, they did not participate physically either. Hence it belongs exclusively to the person who acquired it, the necessary and sufficient condition being stated in the phrase "it was earned by his own efforts."

[B] <**5**> Vyāsa says:

> If a family member acquired property thanks to his own talents, without having recourse to the paternal property, he shall not give it to his co-heirs. This also applies to property earned by knowledge. [Vy 256; **35**]

<**6**> This Text states unconditionally: "if someone acquired property thanks to his own talents"; it follows that any kind of property acquired in this way is not joint.[4] Even though rewards of knowledge are also acquired thanks to one's own talents,[5] the fact that they are mentioned separately serves a purpose: since this kind of property is joint with those who have as much knowledge as or more knowledge than the person who acquired it, the phrase "earned by knowledge" is meant to bar those who have less knowledge or none.

[C] <**7**> Yājñavalkya says:

> Any other property,[6] which someone acquired on his own without drawing on the paternal property, a present from a friend, or a wedding gift,[7] shall not go to the other heirs. [Y 2.118; **33**).

[4] Instead of "not joint" (*asādhāraṇam*) the *Dāyabhāga* manuscripts and editions offer a variety of readings, none of which, however, alters the meaning of the text. E.g., immediately after *asādhāraṇam* the 1863 ed. adds *svakīyam*, the 1893 ed. *svīyam*, both meaning "personal." A number of manuscripts have *svakīyam* only, without *asādhāraṇam*. The 1893 ed. adds, as part of the *Dāyabhāga* text, glosses both on *svīyam* and on *asādhāraṇam*: *svīyaṃ svadhanaśramamātrārjitam* ("acquired with his own property and/or labor") *asādhāraṇaṃ bhrātrantarair avibhājyam* ("not to be shared with the other brothers").

[5] I prefer to translate the term *vidyā-dhana* as "rewards of knowledge" rather than by the traditional phrase "gains of learning." In this context *vidyā* is used is a broader sense than that of "learning." Cf. **6.2.1–9**, 17.

[6] I.e., other than paternal or maternal property, which are discussed in the preceding verse (Y 2.117; **3.4**).

[7] The wedding gift (*audvāhika*) is defined at **13**.

<**8**> The phrases "a present from a friend" and "a wedding gift" in this Text are illustrative only, for there are other circumstances like these, in which joint property is not normally drawn on either.[8] Indeed,

[A] <**9**> Manu says:

> Rewards of knowledge, a present from a friend, a wedding gift, a welcoming present,[9] all these belong exclusively to those who acquired them. [M 206; **31**]

[B] <**10**> Vyāsa says:

> Property earned by knowledge or prowess and loving gifts belong exclusively to those who acquired them; their co-heirs shall not seek these at the time of partition. [Vy 257; **33**]

<**11**> "A loving gift" (*saudāyika*) is the kind of property one acquires as a special favor and the like from loving (*sudāya*) relatives such as one's father or paternal uncle.[10]

[C] <**12**> Nārada says:

> Save for property gained by prowess or through one's wife, and save for rewards of knowledge. These three types of property are exempt from partition, and so is a special favor received from one's father. [N 13.6; **33**]

<**13**> "Property gained through one's wife" (*bhāryā-dhana*) here means a wedding gift (*audvāhika*; **7**, **9**) which a man acquires when he takes his wife away. Save for these, anything else "he should divide"; this verbal phrase carries over into this verse from a preceding one. [N 13.4; **2.81**]

<**14**> None of the above,[11] nor any other Texts to the same effect, mean to say that the fact that property is acquired by a person's prowess and the like is, in and of itself, a sufficient condition for it to be exempt from partition. There are, indeed, Texts to the effect that even property acquired by prowess and the like is included in the partition. The following Texts state that such property shall be divided if it was acquired with the help of joint property.[12]

[A] Vyāsa says:

[8] The following three texts, marked [A] to [C], list a number of items that are exempt from partition. Note that none of these mention the condition that the property should be acquired without drawing on joint property. Jīmūtavāhana adds that condition at **14**.

[9] "A welcoming present" (*mādhuparkika*), which has often been interpreted as a fee which a priest receives for performing a sacrifice (Bühler's note to his translation; also Śrīkṛṣṇa), is the present which some guests receive along with a welcoming *madhuparka*, "honey-based mixture." For persons who must be honored with *madhuparka*, see, e.g., M 3.119-120.

[10] On *saudāyika* in the context of *strīdhana*, see **4.1.22**.

[11] I.e., the last three texts: M 9.206, Vy 257, and N 13.6.

[12] The texts marked [A] provide the general rule, those marked [B] the special rules to be applied to rewards of knowledge.

> Whatever property one of the brothers acquired by his prowess and the like, be it a carriage or a weapon, his brothers share in it if he had recourse to joint property to acquire it. [Vy 259; **28**]
> The one who acquired it shall be given two shares, the others one share each. [Vy 260; **28**]

[B] Nārada says:

> If a brother provides for the family of another brother while the latter acquires knowledge, he shall get a share in his brother's rewards of knowledge, even if he himself has no education whatever. [N 13.10]

<**15**> The phrase "if he provides for" is expressed in the singular. Hence, if any other brother expends his own property and/or his labor to raise the family of one of his brothers while the latter acquires knowledge, he, too, is entitled to a share in the property acquired as a result of the other's knowledge.[13]

> <**16**> A person endowed with knowledge cannot be forced to give a share of his property to one who has no knowledge, unless he had recourse to paternal property to acquire it. [N 13.11]

<**17**> "Paternal" here stands for any joint property.[14] Unless a knowledgeable person acquired property by drawing on this, he cannot be forced to give anything of the property he acquired to one who has no knowledge.

On the other hand, he must give of it to one who is knowledgeable, i.e., learned, even if he acquired the property without using joint property. Says Gautama:

> A person endowed with knowledge cannot be forced to give anything he acquired on his own to persons who have no knowledge. [G 28.30]

<**18**> "Acquired on his own" means acquired with his own property and/or by his own labor. He cannot be forced against his will to give any of this to persons who are not knowledgeable, but he must give of it to those who are.

<**19**> Note that this distinction applies solely to rewards of knowledge. Says Kātyāyana:

> A person endowed with knowledge shall never give any of his rewards to persons who have no knowledge. But a person endowed with knowledge must give of this kind of property to those who are equally knowledgeable or more. [K 875]

[13] Jīmūtavāhana points out that the singular form used in this verse ought not to be taken literally. In doing so he applies a well-known principle of textual exegesis (*Mīmāṃsā-sūtras* 3.1.13–15), the *grahaikatva-nyāya*, according to which a word that appears in the singular in a text can also stand for more than one. Cf. K. L. Sarkar 1909: 278–79; Kane 1962: 1285–86, 1343.

[14] Śrīkṛṣṇa observes that, if one were to interpret "paternal" strictly, a grandson could draw on his ancestral property and not be forced to enter it in the partition.

<**20**> The word "knowledgeable," which appears only once in the compound *sama-vidyā-adhika*, must nonetheless be construed both with "equally" (*sama*) and with "more" (*adhika*).[15] He must, therefore, give of it both to those who are as knowledgeable as he is and to those who are more knowledgeable than he is, whereas those who have less knowledge or no knowledge whatever are not entitled to anything.

<**21**> These and other Texts to the same effect make it clear that, even in the case of property acquired by knowledge, prowess, and the like, the question whether it is subject to partition or not depends on whether the property was acquired with or without drawing on joint property. Indeed,

[1][16] since drawing on joint property is the sole determining factor, one should posit a Revealed Text that contains only the words "property acquired by drawing on joint property is subject to partition."[17] This Text should not include additional terms such as prowess and the like, for these can be subsumed by the general Revealed Text that must necessarily be posited. <**22**> This is again a case in which the *holākā* chapter applies.

<**23**> To be sure,[18] it is a matter of common sense[19] that, if someone acquires something, it belongs to him as long as he lives, provided there is no specific Text

[15] This gloss is intended to rule out other possible interpretations of the compound *sama-vidyā-adhika*, "equal-knowledge-more," such as "superior in similar knowledge" or "of equal knowledge and superior (in other ways)." The use of the term *tantra* in the sense of "only once" is based on the *Mīmāṃsā-sūtras*; Śabara (11.1.1) defines *tantra* as something that, although done only once, is beneficial to many, such as a single lamp lit in the midst of many brahmans. The *Dāyādhikārakramasaṃgraha* (ed. p. 32; tr. IV.1.8) interprets the single occurrence of *vidyā* by means of the *kākākṣi-nyāya*, "the rule of the crow's eye"; crows are believed to have only one eye, which can move from one cavity to the other.

[16] From here onward Jīmūtavāhana presents a number of arguments leading to the conclusion (**30**) that property acquired without drawing on joint property belongs to the acquirer alone.

[17] On the concept of positing a Revealed Text (*śruti*), see **2.40**. See also there for "the *holākā* chapter," to which reference is made later in this paragraph. The application of the *holākā* chapter to this passage has been discussed by K. L Sarkar (1909: 84–85).

[18] My translation differs from Colebrooke's who translated the introductory word *yadvā* of this paragraph literally as "or," and interpreted it as an alternative to the need to posit a Revealed Text. I see it as a specification of how to apply the Revealed Text and how to fix the shares at the time of partition if one or more of the participants had engaged in operations using joint property. The first half of the paragraph deals with a situation in which the operation was successful and led to the acquisition of new assets; the second half shows how to share losses if the operation in which joint property was used was unsuccessful.

[19] "A matter of common sense" translates Jīmūtavāhana's technical expression *nyāya-prāptam eva*. If something is already (*eva*) established (*prāpta*) by common sense (*nyāya*), it does not require an outright injunction. Cf. note at **1.26**.

to the contrary.[20] Yet, if one person operated exclusively with joint property and another with his own financial and/or physical means, common sense requires that the former receive a single share, the latter a double share. At the same time, it also follows that, if joint property was drawn on, the share of each participant shall be fixed in such a way that it is diminished in direct proportion with the larger or lesser amounts they are entitled to receive.[21]

[2][22] <**24**> There is the following Kātyāyana text:

> If sons proceed to a partition to separate themselves from their father's property, then go and live together again, and later proceed to a second partition, the one through whom the property increased gets a double share.[23] [K 892]

<**25**> Śrīkara comments on this Text as follows: "If a reunited brother acquired property by drawing on joint property, he receives two shares, the others get one share each." <**26**> As a result, what both the Sage and the commentator indirectly suggest is that, even when a family reunites, property acquired without drawing on joint property belongs to the person who acquired it and to him alone; such property does not become joint. Indeed, nowhere is there any explicit reference to a specific share if the property was acquired without drawing on joint property.

<**27**> This being the case, it is only proper that what applies to a reunited brother also applies to one who never separated. Since the necessary and sufficient condition, living together in one and the same place, equally obtains when there has not been a partition yet and when a partition is no longer in effect,[24] even Kātyāyana 892 can be taken to convey the notion that, in both cases, the person who acquired property gets a double share if he acquired it by drawing on joint property. It would not be proper to make the Text bear on reunited brothers only, for this is a perfect case in which to invoke the *holākā* chapter.[25]

[20] As an example of "a specific Text to the contrary," Śrīkṛṣṇa refers to K 875cd (**19**): one shall share one's rewards of knowledge with those who are equally or more knowledgeable.

[21] These proportionate deductions obviously refer to cases in which the common property that was drawn on has to be divided among sons by wives of different castes who, in principle, receive unequal shares. Cf. **9.12**.

[22] Jīmūtavāhana now argues that K 829, without saying so explicitly, "conveys the notion" (*jñāpana*) that in all cases, i.e., before partition and after reunion, the individual who acquires property without drawing on joint property does not have to share it with others at the time of partition.

[23] The phrase "go and live together again" implies that they reunite their assets.

[24] Jīmūtavāhana uses technical vocabulary borrowed from *nyāya*, "logic." He speaks of *prāg-abhāva*, "prior nonexistence" and *pradhvaṃsa-abhāva*, "subsequent nonexistence," of partition. The classical example is that of a pot, which does not exist prior to being molded on the potter's wheel, and which does not exist subsequent to being broken into pieces. Cf. **11.1.57** and Introduction.

[25] I.e., the minimal Revealed Text to be posited in this case is as follows: "he who acquires property by drawing on joint property gets a double share," without specifying the acquirer as being reunited.

[3] <**28**> One thing at least is beyond dispute, namely, that the person who acquired property gets a double share if he acquired it by drawing on joint property:

> Whatever property one of the brothers acquired by his prowess and the like, be it a carriage or a weapon, his brothers share in it if he had recourse to joint property to acquire it. [Vy 259; **14**]
> The one who acquired it shall be given two shares, the others one share each. [Vy 260; **14**]

Since this Text restricts the double share to cases in which joint property was used, it stands to reason that, if the property was acquired exclusively with personal property and/or personal labor, the acquirer does not get just a double share, but more, i.e., either everything or slightly less than that. Since neither the Sages nor the commentators ever mention this "slightly less," and since it is clear that, when the other brothers get a share, it is because the acquirer used joint property, it makes sense that, if he did not use joint property, they do not get any share whatever.

<**29**> It is also pertinent to say that the fact that a person who acquired property gets twice as much is based on common sense. Otherwise, either the Texts ought to include wording to the effect that the person who gets a double share is the one who acquired the property,[26] or this right ought to be stated separately in absolute terms.

<**30**> In conclusion, it is well established that anything that was acquired without drawing on joint property belongs to the acquirer alone, to the exclusion of all others.

<**31**> It would definitely not be advisable to posit a Text saying, in general terms, that "all are entitled to a share in property acquired by an undivided partner,"[27] for there are exceptions which involve property earned by prowess and the like.[28] Indeed,

[26] Śrīkṛṣṇa cites the example of B 26.16 (**2.35**, **46**), in which the father is said to take two shares for himself, without the explicit addition that he is the person who acquired the property. If that had to be added in this text and in all other texts that prescribe a double share, the texts would be "unnecessarily cumbersome" (*gaurava*), a flaw that must be avoided at all cost.

[27] Śrīkṛṣṇa sees this argument as an answer to a statement by Śrīkara (who will be quoted and refuted later in this chapter): "If the shares that go to those who acquired property (namely, by drawing on joint property) were based on common sense, they should be strictly proportionate to the amount of effort the acquirers put in; it would not be reasonable to prescribe two shares in absolute terms. The only reasonable basis for the fact that he who acquired the property gets a double share must be a general Revealed Text to the effect that 'of property acquired by undivided brothers a double share goes to the one who acquired it, single shares to evereyone else.' That is why, in practice, one sees that everyone participates in a partition of a brahman's entitlement, even though this was acquired without drawing on joint property, for the sole reason that it was acquired by an undivided partner." The conclusion of this discussion appears in the last sentence of this section (**56**).

[28] That is, if acquired by drawing on joint property. On the technical term *paryudāsa*, "exception, proviso," see note at **5.1**. The term is used again at **36–37**.

[A] Manu says:

> Rewards of knowledge, a present from a friend, a wedding gift, or a welcoming present, all these belong exclusively to those who acquired them. [M 9.206; **9**]

[B] Manu and Viṣṇu say:

> If a family member acquired something by his own labor, without drawing on the paternal property, it was earned by his own effort. He cannot be forced to give it away. [M 9.208 = Vi 18.42; **3**]

<**32**> The phrase "without drawing on" also applies to the types of property mentioned at Manu 9.206, for there are Texts that enjoin that these, too, shall be included in the partition if joint property was drawn on.

[C] <**33**> Yājñavalkya says:[29]

> Any other property,[30] which someone acquired on his own without drawing on the paternal property, a present from a friend, or a wedding gift, shall not go to the other heirs. [Y 2.118; **7**]
> He who recovered ancestral property that had been stolen shall not share it with the other heirs; the same applies to property earned by knowledge. [Y 2.119; **40**]

[D] Nārada says:

> Save for property gained by prowess or through one's wife, and save for rewards of knowledge. These three types of property are not subject to partition, nor is a special favor received from one's father. [N 13.6; **12**]

[E] Vyāsa says:

> Property earned by knowledge or prowess and loving gifts belong exclusively to those who acquired it; their co-heirs shall not seek this at the time of partition. [Vy 257; **10**]

<**34**> "A loving gift" (*saudāyika*) is the kind of property one acquires from loving (*sudāya*) relatives.

> <**35**> Nothing that was given as a token of affection either by a paternal grandfather or a father, nor anything given by a mother,

[29] The *Mitākṣarā* uses these two verses to establish that only the kinds of self-acquired property explicitly listed here are exempt from partition if they were acquired without drawing on joint property. That means not only that these kinds of self-acquired property are subject to partition if their acquisition did involve joint property but also that any other self-acquired property is subject to partition irrespective of whether joint property was used or not. The *Mitākṣarā* (Colebrooke I.iv.7) specifically adds that, as a result, even a brahman's entitlement, acquired without spending joint property, is subject to partition. See Jīmūtavāhana's conclusion on the brahman's entitlement (**53**).

[30] I.e., other than property described in the preceding verse (Y 2.117; **3.4**).

can be taken away from the person to whom it was given. [Vy 261]
If a family member acquired property thanks to his own talents, without having recourse to paternal property, he shall not give it to his co-heirs. This also applies to property earned by knowledge. [Vy 256; **5**]

<**36**> These and other Texts to the same effect provide exceptions to what can be divided among people born of parents of the same caste, of parents of different castes, and of parents of mixed castes:[31] [1] anything acquired by knowledge, [2] loving gifts received from relatives, [3] things received as gifts from friends, wedding gifts, and welcoming presents, [4] property obtained by prowess in battle and the like, [5] property acquired by labor in agriculture, service, trade, and the like, and [6] property acquired solely on one's own without drawing on joint property.

This means that everything that was acquired without drawing on joint property has been made the object of exceptions to the outright injunction posited at **31**; and, since there is nothing else left,[32] the injunction would have no occasion to apply.

<**37**> Let us even assume that somehow one or two situations could be found in which the outright injunction would have occasion to apply.[33] If so, it would have been fitting for the Sages to mention these situations by name: "let them divide such and such property that was acquired by an undivided partner."[34] That would be the least cumbersome way, and it would have the advantage that something mentioned by name is more readily understood. Describing these situations as

[31] This is the sole passage in the *Dāyabhāga* where Jīmūtavāhana seems to wish to state explicitly that rules in *smṛti* texts pertain to all sections of society, not only to caste members, but to members of mixed castes as well. The two terms he uses for mixed castes, *varṇāntarāla* and *saṃkīrṇajāta*, are ambiguous. I take them to refer to members of mixed castes in the first degree (*anulomas* and *pratilomas*) and to members of mixed castes in the second degree (descendants of *anulomas* and/or *pratilomas*), respectively. A similar but different reference to mixed castes appears in the *Mitākṣarā* in its commentary on the term *sarvavarṇeṣu*, "in all castes," at Y 2.135–136 (Colebrooke II.i.4; **11.1.4**).

[32] The only thing that would be left is property acquired by drawing on joint property. Partition of that kind of property, however, is *nyāya-prāpta*, "established by common sense," and, therefore, does not need an outright injunction (*vidhi*). Cf. note at **1.26**, and note 19.

[33] I.e., situations in which an undivided partner acquired property without drawing on joint property, but which are not listed among the exceptions. Śrīkṛṣṇa illustrates this with the examples of a treasure found by an undivided partner, or something an outsider gave him out of compassion. These obviously are cases in which no knowledge and/or labor was required on the part of the acquirer.

[34] Again, that is, without drawing on joint property.

"other than property acquired by prowess, etc.,"[35] on the other hand, would be verbose and, hence, unnecessarily cumbersome.

Note that, if these were exceptions, each single Sage would have had to list every individual case by name, for without a complete list it would not be possible to indicate what "other than them" are. Such Texts containing all the exceptions would look like child's babble on the part of the Sages. On the other hand, if they are meant only as illustrations, it is perfectly proper not to list them all: one Sage can, without undue concern, list just a few, another Sage another few.

<**38**> In conclusion, the outright injunction should be that "one shall partition any property acquired by drawing on joint property"; the words "prowess" and the like used in the Texts are meant only as illustrations.[36] <**39**> Hence there is no validity to the statement that property is joint as soon as it was acquired by undivided partners.

<**40**> Even you will admit that, based on the Yājñavalkya text:

> He who recovers ancestral property that had been stolen shall not share it with the other heirs; the same applies to property earned by knowledge, [Y 2.119; **33**]

he who recovers property even of his father, grandfather, and so on, after someone had stolen it, becomes its sole owner, to the exclusion of the others. Consequently, by denying brothers, even when they are undivided,[37] any right to this kind of property with which at least a trace of an earlier link exists, and this on the grounds that the acquirer recovered it, Yājñavalkya a fortiori rejects the idea that the others have any right to something one of them acquired on his own and to which they had no prior link whatever.[38]

<**41**> Śrīkara made the following statement: "If a person who acquires something without drawing on paternal property became its sole owner, then the other brothers could never have a share in the property which one of them acquired as a brahman's entitlement, for a brahman's entitlement cannot entail drawing on paternal property.[39]

[35] The text the opponent posited at **31** would, then, have to be modified as follows: "all undivided partners are entitled to a share in property one of them acquired by drawing on joint property, other than property acquired by prowess, etc."

[36] If one posits a rule, as the opponent did: "All are entitled to a share in property which an undivided partner acquired by drawing on joint property" (**31**), or even in its revised form: "All undivided partners are entitled to a share in property one of them acquired by drawing on joint property, other than property acquired by prowess, etc." (note 35), "property acquired by prowess, etc." are exceptions (*paryudāsa*; note at **5.1**) and ought to be listed in full. On the contrary, if one formulates the rule as Jīmūtavāhana does: "One shall divide any property acquired by drawing on joint property," property acquired by prowess, etc,. are mere illustrations the list of which does not have to be exhaustive.

[37] Since Y 2.119 does not specify that it pertains to divided brothers only, it follows that it applies to undivided brothers as well.

[38] On the term "link" (*sambandha*), see note at **1.17**. Cf. also **3.21** and **51** below.

[39] Śrīkṛṣṇa (cf. note 27) observes that Śrīkara is of the opinion that, in real life, brothers share everything, including a brahman's entitlement (*pratigraha*). Jīmūtavāhana him-

[Objection][40] "In a brahman's entitlement, property is being used as a means to gratify the donor. The situation is similar to that in which things like a one-year-old heifer are used while buying *soma*, or to the milk observance and the like for the physical sustenance of the performer of a *jyotiṣṭoma*.[41]

[Refutation] "The situation is different in the case at hand.[42] Indeed,

[1] no property is being used to gratify the donor, for in a gift of a transcendent nature the donor need not be gratified by receiving other property in return.[43]

[2] Since a brahman's entitlement is an act of short duration, the brahman who receives the entitlement does not require food in the process,[44] whereas one who secures heaven for himself by performing a sacrifice of long duration such as the *jyotiṣṭoma* does."

<**42**> That is absurd. One sees it happen all the time in real life that property is being drawn on in order to gratify the person from whom one expects to receive a donation, by giving him complimentary presents and the like.[45] Besides, in the Kali age property received as a brahman's entitlement is tantamount to paying for service. That is why a Text says: "In the Kali age gifts are made as a *quid pro quo*."[46]

<**43**> He also said the following:[47] "Since a brahman's entitlement can be the result of his offering prolonged residence to a person, it is not necessarily grat-

---

self admits to this practice later in this chapter (**53**), but he finds a way to include the brahman's entitlement among rewards of knowledge. On *pratigraha*, see note at **1.24**.

[40] This is an objection, followed by a refutation, within the quotation from Śrīkara.

[41] Performing a *soma* sacrifice requires that *soma* be bought. To do so the patron of the sacrifice has to offer in exchange "a ruddy cow one year old" (*Taittirīya-saṃhitā* 7.1.6.2; cf. *Mīmāṃsā-sūtra* 3.1.12). Similarly, at the beginning of a five-day-long *jyotiṣṭoma* ritual, the patron has to acquire one cow for himself and one for his wife to enable both of them to observe the "milk observance" (*payo-vrata*) and subsist exclusively on cow's milk (*Taittirīya-saṃhitā* 6.2. 5.2–3; cf. *Mīmāṃsā-sūtras* 4.3.8–9). In both cases joint property is drawn on.

[42] The two arguments that follow demonstrate how a brahman's entitlement is different from buying *soma* and performing a *jyotiṣṭoma*, respectively.

[43] That is, whereas, to buy *soma*, one has to offer a cow in return.

[44] I.e., the recipient of an entitlement does not need to spend property to buy food for his sustenance.

[45] In addition to *upahāra*, "complimentary present," Śrīkṛṣṇa records a variant reading *upadā*, "bribe."

[46] Śrīkṛṣṇa quotes the following verse: *kṛte tu dīyate gatvā tretāyām āhutāya vai / dvāpare yācamānāya kalau tv anugamānvite*, "in the Kṛta age folks go out of their way to make gifts, in the Tretā age they ask people to come and get them, in the Dvāpara age they make gifts if people ask for them, in the Kali age gifts are made as a *quid pro quo*." This verse alludes to the four Hindu world ages (*yugas*), from the perfect Kṛta age down to the wretched Kali age in which we now live.

[47] Jīmūtavāhana uses the common impersonal passive construction: "it has also been said," without specifying the name of the person who said so. Yet, this introductory statement is so parallel to that at **41** that it is safe to assume that here, and at **44**, Jīmūtavāhana again refers to Śrīkara.

ification that causes the entitlement.[48] Hence, what the brahman expends toward his entitlement may be expended in other ways than by gratification."

That is even more absurd. It is precisely as means of gratification that prolonged residence and the like are causes of brahmans' entitlements. Because different individuals have different dispositions of mind, some choose to gratify by giving things, others by offering prolonged residence and the like, others again by just acknowledging some of the donor's virtues.[49] The fact that the effect does not appear because a particular expedient is not present does not prevent the latter from being a true cause of the former.[50] That is why one says: "since gratification results from a variety of means."[51]

<**44**> Finally, he said this:[52] "It has been said that, since a brahman's entitlement cannot occur without the donor being present, and since it would not be proper not to feed him, it is the property expended under these circumstances that indirectly brings about the brahman's entitlement. If that was true, the food someone consumes to sustain his body prior to rituals such as the *jyotiṣṭoma* would, indirectly, be meant for the *jyotiṣṭoma*, for one cannot perform the *jyotiṣṭoma* if he does not maintain a sound body. All food would, then, be for the sake of ritual acts, not for man's sake.[53] Property used to acquire it would be for the sake of the ritual as well, and so would the means to acquire that property. This would defeat the notion that acquiring property, property itself, and food are for man's sake."

<**45**> That is the most absurd of all. Even though, indirectly, food is useful for the *jyotiṣṭoma*, it is obviously and primarily meant for personal nourishment. It is in its capacity of being for man's sake that it is useful for the ritual; nothing proves that it is for the sake of the latter. The fact that something is useful for something

[48] Śrīkara's argument is based on a concept of Indian logic, *vyabhicāra*. *Vyabhicāra*, "indecision," is one of the flaws that make the *probans* in a syllogistic reasoning fallacious (*Nyāya-sūtras* 1.2.4–5). Instead of proving only the presence or only the absence of the *probandum*, it cannot be used to prove either one. According to the standard example, smoke on a mountain is a valid *probans* for the presence of fire, whereas the absence of smoke proves neither the presence nor the absence of fire, since there may be fire without smoke. Similarly, in the case at hand Śrīkara argues that gratification does not prove the absence of expenditure, nor does it prove its presence, for expenditure may have other causes such as prolonged residence.

[49] Or, "the virtues of one or the other."

[50] In *nyāya* the example would be: the fact that there is no smoke when there is no fire does not prevent fire from being a true cause of smoke.

[51] I have not been able to trace the source of the phrase *ānater aniyatopāyapariṇāmatvāt*.

[52] Cf. note 47.

[53] This is an allusion to a well-known distinction elaborated in the *Mīmāṃsā-sūtras* (4.1) between acts that are *kratv-artha*, "meant for the ritual act," and acts that are *puruṣa-artha*, "meant for the performer of the act." The distinction is important because, if a *kratv-artha* act is faulty, the ritual suffers, not the performer; if a *puruṣa-artha* act is imperfect, the act stands but the performer incurs guilt. See Kane 1962: 1232–35. Cf. **11.5.24**.

does not necessarily mean that it is for the sake of it.[54] So, how could acquiring property, property itself, and food be taken to be for the sake of ritual acts?

<**46**> That is why the following chicanery is uncalled for as well:[55] if it was true that property is useful for the entitlement through the food obtained with it prior to the entitlement, it would follow that, since the body cannot be sustained without food right from the time of birth, it is not possible to acquire anything without drawing on joint property. Indeed,

[1] in that case every means of acquiring property would involve drawing on paternal property, so that the phrase "without drawing on paternal property" [M 9.208 = Vi 18.42; **3**] would be meaningless as a qualifier of "acquiring property." What that phrase refers to are forms of drawing on property and the like, other than drawing on property one uses for the consumption of food and so on, for the very reason that, if it referred to the latter, the qualifier would be meaningless indeed.

[2] <**47**> Even someone who stays at home cannot help drawing on the property by consuming food and the like. In that case, however, the drawing is not for the sake of acquiring property, and the determining factor is precisely that it must be made for that specific purpose. Taken in this way the phrase "drawing on" is not stretched too broadly.

<**48**> That is why Viśvarūpa said: "If someone acquires property without giving away any paternal wealth in the process, that property is said to belong to him alone, exactly like something received as a wedding gift. The restriction does not, however, apply to paternal wealth given away solely for the consumption of food and things like that, for these are tantamount to sucking one's mother's milk and the like."[56]

<**49**> That is also why, even if a vain and prodigal father spends an excessive amount of property on his son's initiation ceremony or wedding, anything the son acquires while begging as a student and the like[57] or as wedding gifts does not

[54] Jīmūtavāhana again makes use of the concept of *vyabhicāra* (cf. note 48): food may be useful for a brahman's entitlement, but that does not prove that it is or is not meant for it. Śrīkṛṣṇa cites the example of a lamp that is lit for the sake of one person but that also happens to be helpful to others.

[55] The *Dāyabhāga* commentators disagree on the meaning of this sentence and of the paragraph it introduces. I take it to mean that, if one pursues the reasoning adopted in the preceding paragraph, any form of acquisition would ultimately involve drawing on joint property. Jīmūtavāhana then adduces two reasons why that is not so. First, the qualifier "without drawing on joint property" would be meaningless. Second, the joint property must have been drawn on in order to acquire something.

[56] Even though Jīmūtavāhana presents this paragraph as a quotation and even clearly marks the beginning and the end of it, the corresponding passage in the *Bālakrīḍā* (2.122) is worded differently and does not contain the last sentence. On Jīmūtavāhana's quotations from Viśvarūpa, see Introduction.

[57] Śrīkṛṣṇa uses the phrase "and the like" to include gifts which the king is supposed to offer the student when he returns home after the *samāvartana*, i.e., the rite that concludes the period of studentship (even as the *upanayana* starts it). He quotes M 7.82: "Let him

constitute joint property, for the expenditures were not made with the intent of acquiring property.

<**50**> In conclusion, it is clear that only what is acquired by drawing on joint property with the specific intent of making acquisitions becomes joint property, nothing else.

<**51**> Jitendriya on his part, after considering this matter in great detail, concluded with the following statement: "So, to sum up, what the foregoing detailed discussion comes down to is that any property that was acquired by using personal property is personal, and that any property acquired by means of joint property is joint. To make this clear a number of examples have been spelled out in Texts such as Manu 9.206 [**9**, **31**]. Such property is excluded from partition only if it is personal, but the same kind of property is joint if it was produced under joint conditions. To make clear what these conditions are, the Texts provide illustrations: sometimes the property used for the acquisition was joint, sometimes the acquisition was the result of a joint effort, or the partners have a joint link with it."[58]

<**52**> Even Bālaka said: "When one brother earns something by his knowledge and the like, the other brothers cannot claim any share in it, for there is no authority for this."[59]

<**53**> As to the practice to divide brahmans' entitlements that were acquired without drawing on joint property, a practice that is observed among the couth, there is nothing wrong with it. It can be done either because of the brothers' affection for one another or in a spirit of solidarity.[60]

Or else, there is nothing improper in the fact that people have acted differently in this matter, for the following reasons. A brahman's entitlement is a reward of knowledge, and in the case of rewards of knowledge there are Texts that uphold partition with persons equally or more knowledgeable, even though these rewards were earned without drawing on joint property; as a result people noticed that these are subject to partition. They did not realize that partition of rewards of knowledge results from special rules that are applicable to knowledge only. In the mistaken belief that these partitions were based on the fact that the property was acquired by an undivided family member, they themselves acted likewise.

<**54**> As to the Manu text:

---

honor the brahmans when they return from their teachers' homes; for this gift to brahmans is an imperishable treasure for kings."

[58] On the term "link" (*sambandha*), see note at **1.17**; cf. **3.21**, and **40** above. To illustrate "a joint link," Śrīkṛṣṇa cites the example of a gift made to one brother with the specification that it is made to him as the son of his father; in that case all the father's sons have a claim on the property.

[59] In view of Jīmūtavāhana's general contempt for Bālaka elsewhere (see Introduction), I translate "even Bālaka said," rather than "Bālaka on his part said," as I did for Jitendriya (**51**).

[60] On Vijñāneśvara's argument why a brahman's entitlement is subject to partition, see note 29.

> Any property that the eldest son acquires after his father's death he shall share with his younger brothers, provided they cherish knowledge,[61] [M 9.204]

it means that, in accordance with the Text:

> The eldest son shall provide for his younger brothers like a father for his sons; they, in turn, shall respect their elder brother as if they were his sons. Such is the law, [M 9.108]

in this situation the eldest son and his brothers live in a father-to-son relationship. The younger brothers are therefore entitled to a share in their elder brother's property, even if he acquired it without drawing on joint property, even as they would have been entitled to a share in what their father acquired. The only difference is that they share in their father's acquisitions whether they are educated or not, whereas only those who are educated share in the acquisitions of their elder brother.

<**55**> This interpretation also follows from the fact that, otherwise, the phrases "the eldest son," "after their father's death," "his younger brothers," and "provided they cherish knowledge" would be meaningless.[62]

<**56**> In conclusion, it would be inappropriate to say that, for the simple reason that property is acquired by an undivided brother, it necessarily also belongs to the other undivided brothers [**31**].

[61] This verse obviously applies to a situation in which brothers continue to live together after their father's death.

[62] The four phrases mentioned here refer to sections of M 9.204. "After their father's death" implies that younger brothers do not share in what the eldest acquires on his own prior to their father's death. "The eldest son" and "his younger brothers" require that they live together in the relationship described at M 9.108. "Provided they cherish knowledge" is an obvious condition explained at **54**.

CHAPTER SIX
SECTION TWO

Rewards of Knowledge

<**1**> Of the various kinds of property that are exempt from partition, let me first deal with rewards of knowledge.

On this subject Kātyāyana says:[1]

> [1] What someone earns by his knowledge when he is challenged to solve a conundrum following a wager is a reward of knowledge; he does not have to enter it in a partition. [K 868]
> [2] What he earns from a disciple, [3] for officiating as a priest, [4] as a result of a question, [5] by deciding a doubtful point, [6] by displaying his learning, [7] in a disputation, or [8] by excelling in reciting the Veda, all these are called rewards of knowledge: they are exempt from partition. [K 869]
> [9] The same rule applies to artists and craftsmen; and anything above the regular price is theirs. [K 870]
> [10] What someone earns by his knowledge when he defeats an opponent in a game of dice is a reward of knowledge; it is not subject to partition. [K 871]

[1] <**2**> The wager referred to here is as follows: "I will give you that much if you solve this conundrum successfully." Whatever the other person then receives by solving the conundrum is exempt from partition.[2]

[2] <**3**> "From a disciple" means: from someone who receives instruction from him.[3]

[3] <**4**> "For officiating as a priest" means: what someone receives from the patron of a sacrifice by way of sacrificial fee and the like. <**5**> Note that a sacri-

[1] K 868–871 lists ten sources of rewards of knowledge, which I mark [1] to [10]. They are again so marked in the translation of Jīmūtavāhana's commentary (**2–12**).

[2] Kātyāyana's first form of *vidyādhana* has been interpreted differently, and not always clearly, by the commentators. Jha (*Vivādacintāmaṇi* tr. p. 218) translates Jīmūtavāhana's comment as follows: "'If you are able to put forward a *Bhadraka* I pay you so much,'– on being thus challenged, if one answers it successfully and thus wins the wager."

[3] Instruction (*adhyāpana*) is one of the three means of livelihood for a brahman. Cf. note at **1.24**.

ficial fee is different from a brahman's entitlement, since it is a form of remuneration.[4]

[4] <6> What someone gives him as a token of appreciation when he provides the correct answer to a question that requires knowledge, no wager having been set previously.

[5] <7> What someone earns by clearing the doubts of one who consults him and says: "I will give this gold coin to anyone who clears my doubts as to what this Text means." Or, whatever commission, one sixth or the like, one earns when two parties seek him out as an arbitrator in a disputed case, and he provides them with the right solution.

[6] <8> What someone earns by way of a brahman's entitlement and the like for displaying his superior knowledge of the *śāstras* and so forth.[5]

[7] <9> What someone earns by being victorious in a disputation between two people on their knowledge of the *śāstras*, or in a disputation on their knowledge of any other branch of learning.

[8] <10> What someone earns by giving the best recitation of the Veda, when there are many competitors but only one prize to be given away.

[9] <11> What painters, goldsmiths, and the like earn by their knowledge of their respective crafts.[6]

[10] <12> What someone earns by defeating an opponent in a game of dice.[7]

<13> All of these are exempt from partition with others. What this means is that, if someone earns something by any kind of knowledge, it belongs to the acquirer alone, not to anyone else. Kātyāyana's detailed enumeration is meant to be illustrative, in order to forestall the kind of errors committed by Śrīkara and others.[8]

[4] "Sacrificial fee" (*dakṣiṇā*) is the remuneration a brahman receives for acting as a priest for other people (*yājana*), another means of livelihood for a brahman. It is different from what is received as a brahman's entitlement (*pratigraha*), to which Jīmūtavāhana refers under [6].

[5] Jīmūtavāhana's peculiar way of including the brahman's entitlement among rewards of knowledge is followed by the *Dāyatattva* (ed. p. 173; tr. 5.3) and the *Dāyādhikārakramasaṃgraha* (ed. p. 34; tr. IV.1.20). Other commentators interpret *svajñāna-praśaṃsanāt* at K 869 literally: "by a public display of one's knowledge."

[6] Jīmūtavāhana does not comment on the ambiguous phrase "and anything above the regular price" (*mūlyād yac cādhikaṃ bhavet*). I take it to mean that, if any one craftsman acquires a skill above that of his ordinary fellow-craftsmen, the earnings of that special skill are his. Śrīkṛṣṇa interprets it as referring to a skilled craftsman who uses common precious metal to make an ornament and thereby increases its value. The particle "and" (*ca*) that connects the two halves of K 870 may imply that the second half of the verse no longer bears on craftsmen. Kane (Kātyāyana ed. tr.) suggests that it refers to a family member selling joint property for a higher price than was expected.

[7] Not only were the game of dice, and gambling generally, popular in India but also they constituted one of the eighteen heads of litigation. Cf. Introduction.

[8] Śrīkṛṣṇa again sees in this statement a reference to Śrīkara's view that, if an undivided partner acquires something, all are entitled to a share of it (cf. note at **6.1.31**). It may well be a more specific reference to Śrīkara's and Jīmūtavāhana's difference of opinion on

<**14**> Hence, what one earns by way of a brahman's entitlement for displaying his knowledge and the like, that, too, resorts under the general category of rewards of knowledge, for only on account of his knowledge is a wise man given a brahman's entitlement.[9] <**15**> Says Yama:

> If a brahman is knowledgeable, righteous, composed, patient, mild, honest, appreciative, destitute, good to cows, a protector of cows, generous, and a good priest, he is said to be a worthy recipient of gifts.
> Brahmans shall not be given entitlements if they fail to fulfill their vows, if they are ignorant of the Vedic mantras, or if their lifestyle is that of their caste in name only. A stone does not drive a stone across.

<**16**> Indeed, their knowledge is the only thing that makes them worthy recipients; without knowledge they are not.[10]

<**17**> Hence, if someone says: "one calls something a reward of knowledge if it derives from the teaching of knowledge," his opinion must be rejected as not being countenanced by the Texts quoted above.[11] The word "knowledge" (*vidyā*) derives from the verb *vid*, which means "know";[12] it therefore indicates any kind of knowledge whatever.

<**18**> Śrīkara, on his part, contends that, if proceeds from brahmans' entitlements, too, are included among rewards of knowledge, the result would be that performing sacrifices, teaching the Veda, and brahmans' entitlements would be indistinguishable.[13]

That is worse than absurd. Even though several discrete acts including performing sacrifices, teaching, and brahmans' entitlements are linked together by the common characteristic "rewards of knowledge," it does not follow that these discrete acts are indistinguishable, since even then performing sacrifices and teaching are not subsumed under brahmans' entitlements. No one would dispute the fact that, even though individual cows, black, tawny, or gray, share the common inherent quality "cow," they are therefore indistinguishable. <**19**> For the same reason, when Kātyāyana [869; **1**] mentions property received from a disciple and

---

brahmans' entitlements (cf. **6.1.41–42** "absurd," **6.1.43** "more absurd," **6.1.44–45** "most absurd"), and the discussion that now follows, leading up to **18** "worse than absurd."

[9] Śrīkṛṣṇa draws the conclusion that a brahman's entitlement must be shared with those who are as learned as or more learned than the acquirer.

[10] If this sentence is intended as a half *śloka* ending the Yama quotation (as it is presented in some editions), the meter is flawed. It is not included in the Yama text as cited in the *Dānasāgara* (pp. 16, 26).

[11] Teaching (*adhyāpana*) is only one of the ten sources of knowledge listed at K 868 (**3**).

[12] Jīmūtavāhana refers to *Dhātupāṭha* 2.55: *vid-a jñāne*.

[13] I.e., because teaching the Veda and performing sacrifices for others are also listed among rewards of knowledge at K 869: "what he earns from a disciple, for officiating as a priest" (**1**).

for officiating as a priest among rewards of knowledge, he is not concerned in the least that performing sacrifices and teaching the Veda might be indistinguishable.

Hence, since Śrīkara's statement stems from his rushing to a conclusion without giving full consideration to the issue,[14] one ought to take exception with it.

Other Kinds of Property That Are Exempt from Partition

[A][15] <**20**> Kātyāyana defines rewards of prowess and the like as follows:

> When someone performs an act of courage at great risk to himself, and his chief is pleased with his performance, whatever he receives on that occasion as a special favor is called a reward of prowess. [K 876]
> Spoils of war are said to be exempt from partition. Spoils of war are items brought back from combat, after defeating the forces of the enemy and putting one's life at risk for his chief. [K 878]
> <**21**> A wedding gift is what comes along with a bride. [K 880 ab]

<**22**> "Wedding gift" here means anything a man receives when he takes a bride.[16]

[B][17] <**23**> Manu and Viṣṇu list further items as being exempt from partition:

> Clothes, conveyances, jewelry, cooked food, water, women, and household items are pronounced to be exempt from partition.[18] [M 9.219 = Vi 18.44]

<**24**> "Clothes" includes worn and new clothes.[19] "Conveyances" means mounts such as horses. "Jewelry" means rings and the like. "Water" means water in wells

[14] A good argument must look first at the prima facie view (*pūrva-pakṣa*) and then refute it with the final view (*siddhānta-pakṣa*). According to Śrīkṣṇa Jīmūtavāhana dismisses Śrīkara's statement as nothing more than a *pūrva-pakṣa*.

[15] The six basic texts in this section are marked [A] to [F].

[16] On wedding gifts, here called *vaivāhika*, being exempt from partition, see M 9.206 (**6.1.9, 31**) and Y 2.118 (**6.1.7, 33**), both of which use the term *audvāhika* instead. Śrīkṛṣṇa adds that the term "wedding gifts" subsumes anything a man received as a son-in-law.

[17] Jolly (1895: 91) notes about the lists contained in [B], [C], [D], and [E]: "The variety of reading and of interpretation in the texts on indivisible property is extremely great. . . . The uncertainty prevailing on this head is partly due to the ambiguity of some of the terms used in the old texts."

[18] Instead of the verb "are pronounced to be" (*pracakṣate*, literally "they pronounce") Vi 18.44 reads *ca pustakam*, "and also a book." Cf. **28**.

[19] The terms used by Jīmūtavāhana for both kinds of clothing are unclear, even to the *Dāyabhāga* commentators. According to the *Mitākṣarā* (on M 9.219 at Y 2.119; Colebrooke I.iv.17) only worn clothes are exempt from partition, new clothes are not; at a partition after the father's death his worn clothes must be given to the brahmans who are fed at

or pools used for irrigation.[20] "Women," except female slaves.[21] "Household items"[22] include one's bed, vessels for food or drink, and so forth.

[C] <**25**> Vyāsa says:

> A sacrificial place, a field, a conveyance, cooked food, water, and women are exempt from partition among *sagotras* even up to one thousand generations. [Vy 262]

<**26**> "A sacrificial place" (*yājya*) here means either a place to sacrifice or the image of a deity, not property received for performing sacrifices for others, since it is understood that that is subsumed under the general category of rewards of knowledge [**1, 4**].[23]

[D] <**27**> Kātyāyana says:

> A cow pasture, a road, worn clothes,[24] anything that has a specific use, and a tool for one's craft shall be exempt from partition. So says Bṛhaspati. [K 884]

<**28**> "Anything that has a specific use" means anything that serves someone's specific needs, such as books and the like for a man of learning; these shall not be partitioned with rubes.[25] Similarly, anything needed to practice a particular craft is the exclusive property of men who are skilled in that craft, not of those who are not.

[E] <**29**> Śaṅkha and Likhita say:

---

the funeral rites. The term I translate as "worn clothes" (*aṅgayojita*) appears again at K 884 (**27**).

[20] Colebrooke, following Śrīkṛṣṇa, translates "as suited to use." Yet, if Jīmūtavāhana specifies "water" as water that is useful for *pracāra*, he must have had in mind the text of ŚL 278, which he quotes later (**29**), and in which the more commonly attested reading is *apāṃ pracārarathyānām* or *apāṃ pracāravartmanām* (Vra *jalapracaraṇamārgāṇām*).

[21] Elsewhere, including in the *Mitākṣarā*, "women" at M 9.219 are identified with female slaves. Śrīkṛṣṇa defends Jīmūtavāhana's interpretation on the grounds that even a single female slave shall be shared by the heirs (B 26.2; **1.10**).

[22] I translate the Sanskrit compound *yoga-kṣema-pracāra* in accordance with Jīmūtavāhana's commentary. The *Mitākṣarā* has a long commentary on this term, which led Colebrooke (I.iv.16) to translate it as "sacrifices and pious acts, as well as the common way." He was followed by Bühler (Manu tr.) and Jolly (Vi tr.).

[23] The interpretation of *yājya* that is rejected here appears in the *Mitākṣarā* (on Y 2.119; Colebrooke I.iv.27), which attributes the verse to Uśanas.

[24] See note 19.

[25] Jīmūtavāhana's interpretation of things that are of use to a particular person such as books which are not to be shared with rubes (*mūrkha*, also appears in the lost digest *Pārijāta* (quoted *Vivādaratnākara* ed. #1431; tr. VII.19). Śrīkṛṣṇa introduces a restriction: books are exempt from partition on the condition that there is other property of equal value; otherwise, if there were only books, the rubes would be left without anything.

> Are exempt from partition: a homestead, water vessels, jewelry, things that would be useless,[26] women, clothes, and canals for irrigation.[27] So says Prajāpati. [ŚL 278]

<**30**> If someone builds a house, a garden, and the like, on a homestead while his father lives, that belongs exclusively to him and is exempt from partition. Since his father did not prevent it, he may be presumed to have approved of it.

[F] <**31**> If a father recovers long-lost property, even if it is ancestral, and he does so at his own expense and by his own labor, while others did not recover it because they were either not capable of, or not interested in, doing so, the property belongs to the father alone; it does not become joint. Indeed,

[a] <**32**> Manu says:

> If a father retrieves property of his own father that had not been retrieved, he cannot be forced to partition it with his sons; it constitutes self-acquired property. [M 9.209 = Vi 18.43; **2.21**]

<**33**> "Property of his own father that had not been retrieved," i.e., not recovered by his sons.[28] The readings "that could not be retrieved" (*anavāpyam*) and "without retrieving it earlier" (*anavāpya*) are without foundation.[29]

[b] <**34**> Says Bṛhaspati:

> Ancestral property that had been stolen and which a father retrieves on his own, and property acquired by his knowledge, prowess, and the like, belong to the father. [B 26.58]
> He may give away as much of this property as he wishes, or use it as he pleases. After his death, however, his sons receive equal shares of it. [B 26.59]

<**35**> The phrase "on his own" means that he does so at his own expense and by his own labor.

<**36**> At both Manu 9.209 and Bṛhaspati 26.58 the word "father" is synecdochic: the necessary and sufficient condition mentioned in the Texts is that he who acquires the property do so on his own. <**37**> This being the case, the conclusion has to be that what is true for self-acquired property that is not ancestral also applies to such property when it is ancestral, with the exception of landed property. <**38**> Indeed, for landed property Śaṅkha has the following special rule:

[26] Śrīkṛṣṇa again refers to things such as books, which would be useless for rubes.

[27] See note 20. For other meanings of the term *pracāra*, see Scharfe 1993: 194-200.

[28] I translate literally "property of his own father" (*paitṛkam*), although the term may refer here to ancestral property generally. "By his sons" (*putraiḥ*, Colebrooke "by the sons") is ambiguous. It may refer to the sons of "his own father," i.e., the brothers of the individual who recovered the property. Or it may refer to the sons of "a father," i.e., the sons of the father who retrieved it.

[29] The two readings Jīmūtavāhana rejects are attested in quotations of this verse in other digests: *anavāpya* less often (e.g., *Kṛtyakalpataru*, *Vyavahārakāṇḍa* p. 140), *anavāpyam* repeatedly (e.g., *Vivādaratnākara* ed. #1317; tr. II.2: "that could not be retrieved by his own father").

> If an individual all on his own takes pain to recover land that had been lost, the others shall give him one quarter of it prior to dividing the rest into equal shares. [Ś 273]

<**39**> Even though the word "all" in "all on his own" underscores that he recovers it at his own expense and by his own labor, land does not become the exclusive property of the person who recovered it. He shall, however, receive one quarter of the recovered land in addition to his regular share.[30] By dint of the word "land," there is no reason not to take the term literally.[31]

<**40**> Thus far for the description of property that is subject to partition and property that is exempt from partition.

[30] Śaṅkha's text is ambiguous. It might also be taken to mean that the individual who recovered the land must be given one quarter of it, no more (thus the *Mitākṣarā* on Y 2.119; Colebrooke I.iv.3). Śrīkṛṣṇa justifies Jīmūtavāhana's interpretation by saying that, if the one who recovered the land received one quarter only, his share would be smaller than that of one person or two persons who did not participate in the recovery.

[31] Differently from Śrīkṛṣṇa, who interprets this sentence as an argument in favor of the acquirer getting one quarter of the land, I take it to mean that, because of the presence (*sāmarthya*, "power") of the word "land" in Śaṅkha's text, this rule must be interpreted as applying to land and to land only. It reconfirms the fact that landed property presents a special case (**38**).

CHAPTER SEVEN

THE SHARE OF A SON BORN AFTER PARTITION

<**1**> Let me now deal with the share of a son born after partition.

[A] On this subject Manu and Nārada say:

> A son born after partition takes his father's property, no more, no less; if, however, some of his brothers were reunited with their father, he divides the property with them. [M 9.216 = N 13. 44/ 42n; cf. **1.46**]

<**2**> If a father partitions his property with his sons, taking for himself the share to which the Texts entitle him, and if he dies without being reunited with any of his sons, a son born to him after partition is the sole heir to his property, this also being the only share he can claim.[1] On the other hand, if the father dies after being reunited with some of his sons, a son born to him after partition takes his share from the reunited brothers.

[B] <**3**> Gautama says:

> A son born after partition is entitled to his father's property, no more, no less. [G 28.29]

<**4**> "A son born after partition" (*vibhakta-ja*) is a son for whom the *garbhādhāna* ceremony is performed after partition, i.e., a son who is begotten (*janita*) by a father who is separated (*vibhakta*), for a begetter does not engage in begetting unless the *garbhādhāna* ceremony has been performed.[2] Hence, if sons partition property at a time when they are unaware that their mother is pregnant, and a brother is born soon after the partition, he shall take a share from his brothers, not from his father.[3]

[1] Note that Jīmūtavāhana construes the restrictive particle *eva*, "only," which in the verse appears only once, after "his father's property," with "a son born after partition" as well. Hence the translation "no more, no less."

[2] *Garbhādhāna*, "impregnation rite," is the first of the several rites of passage (*saṃskāra*; cf. **3.38** and Introduction). It is performed at a wife's first menstruation or, accord-ing to some, at each menstruation, to ensure conception. See R. B. Pandey 1969: 48–59.

[3] Śrīkṛṣṇa restricts the rule that a share should be taken "from his brothers, not from his father" (literally "from his brothers only") to situations in which the father is still living, after having taken his lawful share and having given the rest to his sons. If the father died, however, all assets must be reunited and divided in accordance with the *śāstras* in a new

<**5**> The provision that a son born after partition takes his father's property, no more, no less, is not restricted to cases in which there is only one such son; it also applies when there are several. Says Bṛhaspati:[4]

> Once brothers, whether born of the same mother or of different mothers, have been separated from their father, any brothers of theirs born thereafter receive their shares from their father. [B 26.54]
> A son born before partition no longer has any right to his father's property, nor does a son born thereafter have any right to his brothers' shares. [B 26.55]

<**6**> A son who was born before partition no longer has any claim to his father's property, and a son born after partition no longer has any claim to his brothers' property.

He also says this:

> If a father who was separated from his sons acquires property on his own, it goes entirely to the son born after partition; those born earlier have no right to it. [B 26.56]
> What is true for assets also applies to debts, gifts, pledges, and purchases. [B 26.57ab]

<**7**> The word "entirely" shows that all property acquired by the father, even if it is considerable, goes exclusively to the son born after partition.

> <**8**> They have no hold on each other, except for ritual impurity and water offerings.[5] [B 26.57cd]

<**9**> By citing such things as ritual impurity and water offerings as examples of what they continue to have in common, Bṛhaspati effectively eliminates any mutual claim on property.

<**10**> Note, however, that all this applies solely to property acquired by the father. If, on the other hand, ancestral property such as land was included in the partition, the son born after partition shall receive a share of it from his brothers, for the rule is that partition of that kind of property should take place after the mother has reached menopause [**2.1**].[6] Indeed,

---

partition. Śrīkṛṣṇa quotes Śrūnātha, according to whom the latter procedure must be followed even when the father is still living, since the share which the father took for himself is no longer valid after the birth of another son.

[4] Whereas M 9.216 = N 13.44/42n and G 28.29 quoted earlier refer to the son born after partition in the singular, Bṛhaspati uses the plural. The plural, not the singular, must be taken literally. Cf. **6.1.15**.

[5] B 26.57cd forms a syntactical unit with B 26.57ab: "even as they have no hold on each other as far as assets are concerned, they have no hold on each other with regard to debts, etc. . . ." I translate them as independent units, because a comment on B 26.56 is inserted between the two half verses.

[6] The restriction to ancestral property is not mentioned at Vi 17.3 or Y 2.122, which will now be quoted, but the Viṣṇu and Yājñavalkya texts are in conflict with those quoted

[A] <**11**> Viṣṇu says:

> Sons who have been separated from their father shall give a share to one who is born after partition. [Vi 17.3]

[B] <**12**> Yājñavalkya says:

> If, after brothers have been separated, a son is born to a mother of the same caste as theirs, he is entitled to a share. His share shall be taken out of the property as then found, corrected for income and expenditure.[7] [Y 2.122]

<**13**> Since these two Texts are incompatible with the rule "he takes his father's property, no more, no less" (**1–3**), and on the basis of the rationale mentioned earlier,[8] they pertain to ancestral property.

---

earlier in this chapter. One way of reconciling conflicting texts, in addition to interpreting them as options—a solution that should be avoided if at all possible (cf. **11.5.21**)—is to assign them different fields of application. This is the solution Jīmūtavāhana resorts to in this case: the earlier texts pertain to property the father acquired on his own, Viṣṇu and Yājñavalkya pertain to ancestral property.

[7] Jīmūtavāhana does not comment on this verse. I follow the majority of *Dāyabhāga* commentators who interpret the connecting particle *vā* in the second half as underscoring what was said in the first half. *Vā* in its ordinary meaning "or" may, however, indicate that the two half verses pertain to different situations. That is how the commentator Maheśvara understands it: the second half of the verse applies if the income and expenditures can be adequately measured, the first half if they cannot. According to the *Mitākṣarā* the first half applies if the father is still living when the new son is born, the second half applies if the father is dead at that time. Colebrooke, quoting the *Subodhinī*, and probably influenced by translating *vā* as "positively" in the *Dāyabhāga*, renders *vā* in the *Mitākṣarā* as "absolutely" (I.vi.9). For various interpretations of Y 2.122 see Jha (*Vivādacintāmaṇi* tr. pp. 249–53).

[8] This phrase refers to the fact that ancestral property should not have been included in the partition as long as the mother did not reach menopause (**10**); if it was included, the partition was, to that extent, invalid, and the son born after partition is entitled to a share in it.

CHAPTER EIGHT

THE SHARE OF AN HEIR WHO COMES FORWARD AFTER PARTITION

<1> Let me now deal with the share of an heir who comes forward after partition. On this subject Bṛhaspati says:

> Whether a partition took place or not,[1] as soon as an heir comes forward, he is entitled to a share in any joint property there was or is. [B 26.63]
> Even if he has been absent for a long time, on his return he is entitled to a share in anything ancestral, be it a documented debt,[2] a house, or a field. [B 26.64]
> <2> If a man leaves the community of his *gotra* to settle in a different location, and a descendant of his returns, he must by all means be given a share. [B 26.65]
> Whether he be of the third, fifth, or seventh generation,[3] he shall receive his share, provided his birth and his name are properly ascertained. [B 26.66]
> <3> If neighbors who have been local residents for generations know that someone owned a piece of land, and a descendant of his comes forward, his relatives shall give the land to him. [B 26.67]

[1] I.e., in the heir's absence.

[2] I follow the interpretation proposed by Śrīkṛṣṇa, who points out that the returnee not only shares in the assets but also shares in the debts. Colebrooke and Jolly (Bṛhaspati tr.) interpret differently: "a debt, or a writing/document."

[3] The *Dāyabhāga* commentators disagree on the meaning of this clause. According to some, the particle *vā*, "or," which connects the seventh generation with the third and the fifth, means that the returnee may be removed by even more than seven generations, e.g., if the absentee himself was the great-grandson of the deceased owner. I am inclined to follow others who make *vā* include all descendants up to the seventh generation, but no further ones. In support of this interpretation Śrīkṛṣṇa refers to a text quoted anonymously in Harinātha's *Smṛtisāra* (*Dhko* p. 1529): *ā saptamād rikthivicchitiḥ*, "inheritance ceases with the seventh generation." Cf. M 5.60ab (**11.1.42, 11.6.17**): "*sapiṇḍa* relationship ceases with the seventh generation."

<**4**> In other words, the descendant of a person who has been absent for a long time shall take his share, provided he has his identity established by neighbors whose families have lived on the spot for a long time.

<**5**> Thus far for the share of an heir who comes forward after partition.

CHAPTER NINE

THE SHARES OF SONS OF ONE FATHER BY WIVES OF EQUAL AND OF LOWER CASTES

<**1**> Let me now deal with the shares of sons of one father by wives of equal and of lower castes.

<**2**> It is indeed possible for a man to wed women of his own caste and women of lower castes.[1] Says Manu:

> For men of the twice-born castes a woman of their own caste constitutes a proper first wife, but, if lust impels them, they may have further wives in descending order of caste.[2] [M 3.12]
> A *śūdra* may wed no one but a *śūdra* woman; a *vaiśya* may wed women of that caste and of his own caste; a *kṣatriya* may wed women of those two castes and of his own caste; a brahman may wed women of those three castes and of his own caste. [M 3.13]

<**3**> The phrase "no one but," in "no one but a *śūdra* woman," applies throughout the sentence, for each subsequent "that," "those two," and "those three" refers to that or those mentioned immediately before. What this means is that under no circumstances may a man wed a woman of a higher caste than his own.[3]

<**4**> The phrase "but, if lust impels them, they may have further wives" is there to indicate that the flaw is a minor one, not that there is no flaw at all. <**5**> That is why Śaṅkha and Likhita say:

[1] The chapter opens with a brief introduction on mixed marriages (**2–11**). On the caste status of descendants of mixed marriages in the ancient texts, see Rocher 1980–81; on mixed castes generally, see Brinkhaus 1978.

[2] I translate the reading *kramaśo 'varāḥ* (= *avarāḥ*), "gradually lower," which is attested in most *Dāyabhāga* manuscripts. There is, however, a variant reading: *kramaśo varāḥ* "the higher (her caste), the better (the wife)," which anticipates the statement in the next verse. Hence Colebrooke: "but for such, as are impelled by desire, those following are preferable in the order of the classes."

[3] Even though the *smṛti* texts deal with the offspring of marriages that are *pratiloma*, "against the grain," even as they deal with the offspring of marriages that are *anuloma*, "with the grain," according to a number of them, e.g., G 28.45 and Vi 15.37–39, *pratiloma* marriages are forbidden. On the application of these rules in modern times, see Mayne 1950: 164–72; Mulla 1959: 609–11.

> The primary rule is that men should wed women of their own castes; these are best for all. The secondary rule is as follows: a brahman may wed four in descending order; a *kṣatriya* three, a *vaiśya* two, and a *śūdra* one. [ŚL 64]

<6> The numbers "four" and so on only restrict the castes to which the women belong.[4]

<7> Note that the women discussed here are the husband's duly wedded wives. Says Paiṭhīnasi:

> A brahman may have four duly wedded wives; the others three, two, and one.[5]

<8> The reference to "the others" here means that *kṣatriyas*, *vaiśyas*, and *śūdras* may have three, two, and one, respectively.

<9> Even though the marriage of a twice-born male to a *śūdra* woman qualifies as a marriage with a woman of a lower caste,[6] Manu and Viṣṇu consider it a major flaw:

> Twice-born men who are foolish enough to wed women of the lowest caste soon reduce their entire families, including their offspring, to the rank of *śūdras*. [M 3.15 = Vi 26.6]
> According to Atri and the son of Utathya,[7] a twice-born man is expelled from his caste if he weds a *śūdra* woman; according to Śaunaka he is expelled if a son is born; according to Bhṛgu if a grandson is born.[8] [M 3.16]
> If a brahman weds a *śūdra* woman, he loses of his prestige; if he has a son by her, he ceases to be a brahman. [M 3.17]

<10> In other words,[9] these Texts pertain to wives wedded in the right order. The following Hārīta text, being consonant with the texts of Manu and Viṣṇu, also pertains to duly wedded wives:

[4] In other words, it does not preclude a man from having more than one wife of any of these castes.

[5] The Paiṭhīnasi text as quoted in the *Dāyabhāga*—it is not included in Chintamani's collection of fragments—exhibits the explicit term *vivāhitās* or *pariṇītās*, "wedded." Cf. *Mahābhārata* 13.47.4: *catasro vihitā bhāryā brāhmaṇasya*.

[6] And, as such, it would be expected to be no worse than a minor flaw (cf. **4**).

[7] I.e., Gautama.

[8] Śrīkṛṣṇa and Kullūkabhaṭṭa suggest that these three alternatives pertain to brahmans, *kṣatriyas*, and *vaiśyas*, respectively. For different interpretations by other Manu commentators, see Bühler's note to his translation.

[9] I.e., since these texts use phrases such as "wed women of the lowest caste" and "he weds a *śūdra* woman," the "major flaw" obtains when both parties are actually married, not, as one predecessor of Jīmūtavāhana must have said, when they are not married (cf. **11**).

> The husband of a woman of low caste is a brahman murderer just like any other brahman murderer; when he creates a fetus in her, he thereby kills a brahman.[10]

That is why Śaṅkha does not include *śūdra* women among the wives of twice-born men:[11]

> A brahman may wed a brahman woman, a *kṣatriya* woman, and a *vaiśya* woman; a *kṣatriya*, a *kṣatriya* and a *vaiśya* woman; a *vaiśya* may only wed a *vaiśya* woman; a *śūdra* a *śūdra* woman only. [ŚL 65]

<**11**> Hence, the flaws mentioned earlier do not obtain when a twice-born man has offspring by a *śūdra* woman who is not his own wedded wife.[12] He will explain later that this is a minor flaw, which requires a minor penance.[13]

<**12**> When a man has sons by wives of all four castes, Manu determines their shares as follows:

> The brahman gets three shares of the inheritance, the son of a *kṣatriya* wife two, the son of a *vaiśya* wife one share and a half, the son of a *śūdra* wife one share. [M 9.151]
> Alternatively, a man who knows the *dharma* shall divide the entire estate into ten parts, and perform a legitimate partition according to the following rule: [M 9.152]
> The brahman gets four shares, the son of a *kṣatriya* wife three, the son of a *vaiśya* wife two, the son of a *śūdra* wife one. [M 9.153]

<**13**> One can resort to either one of these two modes of partition, depending on whether any of the heirs are somewhat more deserving than others.[14]

[10] Killing a brahman is one of the five *mahāpātakas*, "major offenses." The text here attributed to Hārīta appears neither in Jolly's collection of Hārīta fragments nor in the *Dharmakośa*. Colebrooke understands it differently: "No other is so sacrilegious, as the husband of a woman of the servile tribe; for that Bráhmana is slain by the child, which he himself begets on her."

[11] Namely, in view of the major offense that results from wedding *śūdra* women and having offspring by them.

[12] I follow Śrīkṛṣṇa, and Colebrooke, in translating the ambiguous expression *svayam anūḍhāyām* as "who is not his own wedded wife," rather than "who is not married herself." The phrase "not his own wedded wife" implies that the woman is married to someone else. In this way there is no contradiction with Jīmūtavāhana's interpretation of M 9.178 (**28**) as referring to the offspring of a brahman and a *śūdra* woman who is not married to anyone.

[13] The active future form *vakṣyati*, which is attested in most editions and in all the manuscrpts I have consulted, is strange. It looks as if a marginal gloss had found its way into the text of the *Dāyabhāga*, "he" referring to Jīmūtavāhana. Cf. **25**.

[14] The *Dāyabhāga* commentators differ on which sons ought to benefit from being "somewhat more deserving." Some say that it pertains to the twice-born sons; others maintain that it applies when the son of a *śūdra* wife is the more deserving one. Maheśvara suggests that, if the more deserving son is twice-born, he should take his share according to

<**14**> Viṣṇu devotes an entire chapter to this subject, beginning with the statement: "If a brahman has sons by wives of all four castes" [Vi 18.1] down to the rule: "Shares shall also be allotted in this order in other cases." [Vi 18.40]

<**15**> If, of all the sons of a brahman, the son by a *kṣatriya* wife is the eldest in years and if he is deserving as well, he gets a share equal to that of a brahman son. If a *vaiśya* son of a brahman or of a *kṣatriya* answers this description, he gets a share equal to that of a *kṣatriya* son. Indeed,

[A] Bṛhaspati says:

> If a son by a *kṣatriya* wife is the eldest in years and if he is deserving, he gets a share equal to that of a brahman son; under the same circumstances the share of a son by a *vaiśya* wife is equal to that of a *kṣatriya* son. [B 26.120]

[B] Baudhāyana says:

> If, between a son by a woman of the husband's own caste and a son by a woman of the next lower caste, the latter is more deserving, he gets the share due to the eldest, for a son who is more deserving is better able to provide for the others. [Bau 2.2.3.12–13]

<**16**> By the same token these Texts show that, if a *śūdra* son answers this description, he, in turn, gets a share equal to that of a *vaiśya* son.

<**17**> When, however, it comes to land the father acquired as a brahman's entitlement,[15] that goes entirely to his sons by a brahman wife, to the exclusion of sons by a *kṣatriya* or any other wife. A house and an ancestral field go to his sons of the twice-born castes, to the exclusion of *śūdra* sons. Says Bṛhan-Manu:

> Sons by a brahman wife get the land that their father received as a brahman's gift (*brahma-dāya*);[16] all twice-born are entitled to inherit a house or an ancestral field.[17] [*Dhko* p. 1252]

<**18**> Any descendant belonging to a twice-born caste can accede to ancestral land,[18] i.e., land acquired by a paternal grandfather, a paternal great-grandfather,

---

the division into ten parts; the others should then resort to the division into seven and one half parts. Maheśvara also rightly observes that, if the more deserving one is the son of a *śūdra* wife, the division into seven and one half parts must apply. It is, indeed, true that the son of a *śūdra* wife is the only one who benefits from this kind of division. No commentator notes, however, that it is also true that the only one who benefits from a division into ten parts is the son of a *kṣatriya* wife, and that the shares of the sons of a brahman wife and a *vaiśya* wife are the same in both kinds of division.

[15] On *pratigraha*, "a brahman's entitlement," see **1.24**.

[16] The term *brahma-dāya* will be discussed at **19–23**.

[17] Although this verse is also quoted in the *Vivādaratnākara* and the *Vivādacintāmaṇi*, it is missing in Herberich's collection of Bṛhad-/Vṛddha-Manu fragments.

[18] Or, according to a variant reading, in the dual number, "if both are ancestral," i.e., land and a house. It is, indeed, not clear whether in the Bṛhan-Manu verse the adjective "ancestral" qualifies field only or both house and field. Although Jīmūtavāhana's introductory sentence, too, is slightly ambiguous, he seems to prefer the former interpretation. The

and so forth, for the word "ancestral" is unconditional. When it comes to land acquired as a brahman's entitlement, however, the fact that sons by *kṣatriya* wives and wives of other lower castes are denied any right to it implies that like grandsons and other descendants have no right to it either. <**19**> Says Bṛhaspati:

> Land received as a brahman's entitlement shall never be given to a son of a *kṣatriya* wife or a wife of any other lower caste; even if a father should gift it to him, it will still go to the son by a brahman wife when the father dies. [B 26.121]

What all this means is that what Bṛhan-Manu calls land received as a "brahman's gift" (*brahma-dāya*) is the same as land received as a brahman's entitlement (*pratigraha*) in the Bṛhaspati text.[19] Indeed, *brahma* means Veda, and receiving *pratigraha* is ordained on the grounds that someone has memorized the Veda and studied its meaning. <**20**> *Brahma-dāya* does not refer to land which a brahman receives as a token of respect as described by Manu:

> He shall pay homage to brahmans when they return from the houses of their teachers;[20] this is an eternal injunction to be observed by kings toward brahmans.[21] [M 7.82]

Indeed, whatever the king gives them on that occasion is given as a token of respect.[22]

<**21**> Or else, Bṛhan-Manu excludes the sons of *kṣatriya* wives and wives of other lower castes from getting land of one type, and the Bṛhaspati text prevents them from getting land of the other type.[23]

---

main difference is that, if "ancestral" qualifies "field" only, a house that is ancestral, and even one acquired as a brahman's entitlement, goes to sons of all three twice-born castes.

[19] Both the *Vivādaratnākara* (ed. #1504; tr. XIII.20) and the *Vivādacintāmaṇi* (ed. pp. 222–23; tr. p. 243) define *brahma-dāya* as property a brahman acquires by any of his three lawful means of livelihood: teaching, performing sacrifices, and *pratigraha*. The *Vivādaratnākara* quotes the lost *Pārijāta*, which agrees with Jīmūtavāhana in equating *brahma-dāya* with *pratigraha*.

[20] When the subject of sentences such as this is not specified, it refers to the king.

[21] The translation reflects the reading of the *Dāyabhāga* manuscripts, which is supported by its commentators: *vidhiḥ*, "outright injunction." A different reading, which is supported by the commentators of the *Manu-smṛti*: *nidhiḥ*, "treasure," is reflected in Bühler's translation: "for that (money which is given) to Brāhmaṇas is declared to be an imperishable treasure for kings."

[22] "Homage" (*pūjā*) or "a token of respect" (*arcana*) is different from a brahman's entitlement. The former is a gift made on a specific occasion and for a "mundane purpose" (*dṛṣṭa-artha*). The purpose of the latter is not evident; it is "transcendent" (*adṛṣṭa-artha*).

[23] If one argues that "brahman's gift" is different from "brahman's entitlement," then Bṛhan-Manu's *brahma-dāya* refers to the gift received as a token of respect. In that case not only land received as a brahman's entitlement but also the other type of land goes exclusively to the sons by a brahman wife.

<**22**> Whatever the case may be, *brahma-dāya* does not refer to "land that belongs to a brahman."[24] The fact that all twice-born sons accede to ancestral land is attested in the above mentioned Text [**17**]. Here only *śūdra* sons are barred. Says Bṛhaspati:

> The son of a twice-born man by a *śūdra* wife is not entitled to a share of land. The son by a wife of his own caste inherits everything;[25] that is the law. [B 26.122]

<**23**> Since this Text mentions "land" in general, it follows that a *śūdra* son has no right to any kind of land that belonged to his twice-born father, irrespective of the way in which the latter acquired it, whether by purchase, as a special favor, or in any other way.

<**24**> If a *śūdra* is a brahman's only son, he is entitled to a share equal to one third of the total. The other two thirds go to his father's *sapiṇḍas*; failing them, to his *sakulyas*; and, failing them, to any other person who performs his funeral rites. Says Devala:

> If a brahman's only son is a *niṣāda*, he gets one third; a *sapiṇḍa*, a *sakulya*, or whoever performs the funeral rites for the deceased gets two thirds.[26] [D 1594]

<**25**> A *niṣāda* is the son of a brahman by a *śūdra* wife.[27] He will explain the difference between a *sapiṇḍa* and a *sakulya* later.[28]

[24] Jīmūtavāhana was prepared to accept one alternative interpretation of *brahma-dāya*, in the sense of property acquired as "a token of respect" (*arcana*, *pūjā*), in which case this kind of property, too, devolves on his brahman sons only (**21**). He now rejects a third interpretation of the term, as something that came to the brahman father as "property that belongs to a brahman." That would, indeed, include ancestral land for which there is textual evidence that it can go to any twice-born descendant.

[25] I translate the second half of B 26.122 in accordance with Jīmūtavāhana's statement at **17** (and Jolly's Bṛhaspati tr.). Cf. also Colebrooke (*Digest* 5.3.164): "he who is born in an equal class, shall take the whole," and the commentary: "begotten on a woman of equal class, or born in the same class with his father." Here, however, following Śrīnātha and Śrīkṛṣṇa, Colebrooke interprets differently: the son of a *śūdra* by a wife of his own caste inherits everything.

[26] In the *Vivādaratnākara* (ed. #1505) this verse appears immediately after B 26.122 (**22**). Hence it became B 26.123 in Rangaswami Aiyangar's collection of Bṛhaspati texts.

[27] In all but one listing of mixed castes the *niṣāda*, or *pāraśava* (**28**), is indeed the son of a brahman by a *śūdra* woman (Rocher 1980–81: 137). Note that Jīmūtavāhana uses D 1594 to restrict Vi 18.32 (**26**), which enjoins a half share for sons of all twice-born men by *śūdra* wives, to sons of *kṣatriyas* and *vaiśyas*. Cf. note 29.

[28] This is again (cf. **11**) a statement that reads as if a marginal gloss had been inserted into the text of the *Dāyabhāga*. Yet, both Acyuta and Śrīkṛṣṇa comment on it as an integral part of the *Dāyabhāga* text. The difference between *sapiṇḍas* and *sakulyas* will be explained in section **11.6**.

<**26**> On the other hand,[29] if a *śūdra* is the only son of a *kṣatriya* or a *vaiśya*, he gets one half of his father's property. Those who will be listed below [chapter **11**] as heirs to the property of a man who dies without male offspring get the other half, and in that order. Thus Viṣṇu:

> If a *śūdra* is the only son of a man of a twice-born caste, he gets one half. The other half shall be treated as if it were the inheritance of a man who dies without male offspring. [Vi 18, 32–33]

<**27**> Note that for a *śūdra* to inherit one third or one half he must excel in knowledge, good behavior, and righteousness. Indeed,

[A][30] Manu says:

> Whether or not he has sons of a higher caste, the law requires that he give a son by a *śūdra* wife no more than one tenth. [M 9.154]

Since this Text prevents the father from giving a son by a *śūdra* wife more than one tenth even if he has no twice-born sons, it is understood that the earlier Texts apply solely if the son by a *śūdra* wife is the only son and if he is of exceptional character.

[B] As to the Manu text which bars a son by a *śūdra* wife from receiving any share whatever of the inheritance:

> The son of a brahman, a *kṣatriya*, or a *vaiśya* by a *śūdra* wife does not share in the inheritance. The only property he can own is what his father gave him, [M 9.155]

that must be understood to pertain to a situation in which the son has already received property equivalent to one tenth as a special favor from his father.

[C] <**28**> As to the Bṛhaspati text:

> When a father has no other descendants, a son by a *śūdra* wife shall be provided maintenance if he is obedient and deserving; the rest goes to the father's *sapiṇḍas*, [B 26.125]

it means that the son should be given at least something so that he may engage in agriculture or some other activity by which he can earn a living. If he is not com-

[29] This passage has been referred to in a far-reaching opinion by Acting Chief Justice Asutosh Mookerjee: "If we were called upon to investigate, whether in each instance, rules enunciated, for example, by Vijnaneswara in his Mitaksara or by Jimutavahana in his Dayabhaga, could really be supported to the fullest extent by the texts of the institutional writers quoted, which they professed to interpret but which they often make subservient to their views (see, for instance, the attempt by Jimutavahana to reconcile the texts of Devala and Vishnu, in the Dayabhaga, Chapter IX, paragraphs 24 and 26), we would have to undertake afresh the duties discharged by authoritative expounders of Hindu Law centuries ago in the different Provinces" (*Rajani Nath Das* v. *Nitai Chandra Dey* [1920] 32 C.L.J. 333, 353-54; 48 Cal. 648, 685).

[30] Jīmūtavāhana is about to quote four texts, marked [A] to [D], according to which the son of a brahman or other twice-born gets less than a third (Devala) or one half (Viṣṇu). He will assign all these texts different fields of application.

petent, yet willing to do service, he shall be given food and other necessities of life, even as one does with an apprentice.[31]

[D] As to the Manu text:

> If, out of lust, a brahman begets a son by a *śūdra* woman, this son is no more than a corpse (*śava*), even if he is able-bodied (*pārayan*); that is why he is called *pāraśava*,[32] [M 9.178]

that pertains to the son of a brahman by an unmarried *śūdra* woman.[33] If she was married to him, it would be mandatory for him to have intercourse with her once in every reproductive cycle, and it is during this intercourse that she would conceive, not during any subsequent ones.[34] Indeed,

[A] Yājñavalkya says:

> The brother of a man who died without leaving a son shall have intercourse with his brother's widow once during her reproductive cycle.[35]

[B] Manu says:

> He shall approach her according to the rules, she being dressed in white and being of pure intent, and have intercourse with her discreetly, in every reproductive cycle, until she is pregnant. [M 9.70]

[31] According to N 5.3 the *antevāsin*, "apprentice," together with the *śiṣya*, "disciple," the *bhṛtaka*, "hired servant," and the *adhikarmakṛt*, "supervisor of hired servants," are the four types of *karmakaras*, "performers of labor." These four, together with the fifteen kinds of slaves (N 5.26–28/24–26), constitute the five types of *śuśrūṣakas* "attendants" (N 5.2). Since both the *śiṣya* and the *antevāsin* live in their respective *guru*'s house, the former to acquire knowledge, the latter to learn a craft, the term *antevāsin* is often used in the sense of *śiṣya*. Cf. **11.1.37** (Bau) and **11.6.13** (Āp). On the status of an apprentice, see Kane 1946: 482–83.

[32] This is again one of Manu's several etymologies. *Pāraśava* is the name of a member of a mixed caste, the son of a brahman by a *śūdra* woman, often synonymous with *niṣāda* (**24–25**). Cf. Rocher 1980–81: 136–37.

[33] For the translation of *apariṇītaśūdrā* as "an unmarried *śūdra* woman" rather than "a *śūdra* woman who is not his wedded wife," see note 12. Colebrooke, following Śrīkṛṣṇa, considers both B 26.125 and M 9.178 to pertain to this situation: "These [two] passages imply . . ." This seems to contradict the word "this," in the singular, i.e., M 9.178 only, in this sentence, as well as the concluding sentence of **28**.

[34] A husband cannot "beget a son out of lust" with his wife. If she becomes pregnant, it is the result of the first intercourse after the beginning of the woman's reproductive cycle, and that intercourse is enjoined by the *smṛti* texts. Any subsequent intercourse would be "out of lust," but on none of these occasions would the husband "beget a son." Jīmūtavāhana goes on to compare the situation with that of a levirate marriage, in which one intercourse per cycle is mandated.

[35] This half verse does not appear in the *Yājṇavalkya-smṛti*, nor is it assigned to any other *smṛti* in the *Dharmakośa*. On the practice of *niyoga*, "levirate," see Kane 1941: 599–607.

If only the first intercourse brings about conception, the word "once" in these Texts has a mundane purpose. If not, one would have to posit a transcendent purpose for it.[36] That is why, in daily life, too, for such rites as the *puṃsavana* and the *sīmantonnayana*, which have to be performed in certain fixed months to be effective, one takes the day of the first intercourse as the starting point in calculating the months.[37]

So, to come back to Manu 9.178, the phrase "if, out of lust, he begets a son," can only pertain to an unmarried *śūdra* woman.

<**29**> On the other hand,[38] the son of a *śūdra* by an unmarried *śūdra* woman such as a female slave,[39] gets a share equal to that of other sons of his father,[40] provided the father agrees to it. Thus Manu:

> If a *śūdra* has a son by a female slave or by the female slave of a slave,[41] this son gets a share, subject to his father's consent.[42] That is the law. [M 9.179]

<**30**> Failing his consent, however, the son gets half a share. Says Yājñavalkya:

[36] For the opposition "transcendent purpose"/"mundane purpose," see note at **1.27**. The rule is that one should not posit a transcendent purpose as long as a mundane purpose can be found.

[37] *Puṃsavana*, "bringing forth a male," and *sīmantonnayana*, "parting of the hair," are two *saṃskāras*, "rites of passage," to be performed during the woman's pregnancy, the former in the third, the latter in the fourth, sixth, or eighth month. Cf. R. B. Pandey 1969: 60–63 and 64–69.

[38] I.e., as opposed to the son of a twice-born by an unmarried *śūdra* woman.

[39] Referring to the Manu and Yājñavalkya texts that follow, Jolly (1885: 186) points out that "these texts contain everything that is to be found in the Smṛitis on the subject, but the various constructions put on, and the important rules derived from, them in the modern works have given rise to several interesting controversies." Indeed, in an effort to limit the range of a *śūdra*'s illegitimate sons who can inherit his property, Colebrooke's translation, which corresponds to mine, was rejected in court, and replaced by: "But the son of a sudra by an unmarried female slave &c, may share . . .," with the result that an illegitimate son whose mother was not a slave could not inherit (*Narain Dhara* v. *Rakhal Gain* [1873] 1 Cal. 1, 5). This translation, in turn, was challenged but upheld in *Kirpal Narain Tewari* v. *Sukurmoni* (1892) 19 Cal. 91 and in *Ram Saran* v. *Tek Chand* (1901) 28 Cal. 194, but eventually overruled, in Bengal, by a Full Bench in *Rajani Nath Das* v. *Nitai Chandra Dey* (1920) 32 C.L.J. 333; 48 Cal. 643. Cf. Mayne 1950: 631–32; Mulla 1952: 36.

[40] "Other" here refers to the father's legitimate sons.

[41] *Dāsadāsī*, "the female slave of a slave," has been variously interpreted by the commentators on this verse, as an unmarried woman guarded by a slave, as a female attendant of a slave, as a woman who became a slave by marrying a slave, etc. Nārada lists fifteen kinds of slaves (cf. note 31), Manu (8.415) seven. On *dāsadāsī*, see Rocher: forthcoming.

[42] The Sanskrit text merely says "subject to consent." I supplement "his father's" in accordance with the way in which Jīmūtavāhana introduces the text and in agreement with all commentators on Manu as well. See, however, Mayne (1950: 633): "if permitted (by the other sons)," based on Sir William Jones's translation of the *Manu-smṛti*.

> Even the son of a *śūdra* by a female slave gets a share, if his father is willing; after the father's death his brothers shall provide him with half a share. [Y 2.133cd–134ab]

<**31**> Finally, if such a son has no brothers born to a woman who was wedded to his father,[43] he gets the entire property, provided there is no daughter's son either. Says Yājñavalkya:

> If he has no brothers he gets everything, unless there is a daughter's son. [Y 2.134cd]

If there is a daughter's son, he shall share equally with him. Indeed,

[1] there is no Text to say that it should not be so in this case.[44]

[2] Equal shares are the only reasonable solution, for the one, although born to a woman who was not his father's wedded wife, is his own son, whereas the other, although his offspring by a woman who was his wedded wife, is only the son of their daughter.

[43] Instead of *pariṇītastrījātabhrātṛśūnyas tu*, "if he has no brothers born to a woman who was wedded to his father," several *Dāyabhāga* manuscripts and editions adopt the variant reading *apariṇītastrījāto bhrātṛśūnyas tu*, "if the son born to a woman who was not wedded to his father has no brothers." What follows makes it clear that, in either case, Jīmūtavāhana refers to brothers who are the father's legitimate sons.

[44] On equal partition by default, see also **4.2.8**.

CHAPTER TEN

PARTITION BETWEEN A FULL-FLEDGED SON AND AN APPOINTED DAUGHTER OR OTHER KINDS OF SONS

A Full-Fledged Son and an Appointed Daughter

<1> Let me now deal with partition in case a full-fledged son was born after a daughter was made an appointed daughter.[1]

<2> In that case the appointed daughter and the full-fledged son get equal shares. The fact that the appointed daughter is older does not qualify her for a pre-empted share of five percent. Says Manu:

> If a daughter had been appointed and a son was born later, their shares shall be equal; there is no seniority right for women. [M 9.134; **2.39**]

The reason is that an appointed daughter does not herself perform the duties of an eldest son. She only offers *piṇḍas* through the intermediary of her own son. Again Manu says:

> A person who has no son shall make his daughter an appointed daughter, with the understanding that her offspring will perform his funeral rites. [M 9.127]

<3> It would be wrong to say that, if an appointed daughter has a son first and a full-fledged son is born to her father later, the son of the appointed daughter gets the special share due to an eldest son. Indeed, he is still no more than a son's son. Says Manu:

[1] The texts recognize twelve different kinds of sons (cf. **7**) of whom the *aurasa*, "full-fledged son" (cf. **2.59**), is the first. He is the son whom a man begets on a duly wedded wife, according to some texts though not all, of the same caste as her husband (Rocher 1999). A *putrikā*, "appointed daughter," is a daughter whom a father gives away in marriage on the condition that her son shall also be held to be an agnate of his and that this son will therefore perform funeral rites for him. As Jīmūtavāhana will make clear later (**6**), the appointed daughter inherits only if she has a son. The treatment of partition between a full-fledged son and an appointed daughter concludes at **6**; from **7** onward Jīmūtavāhana deals with partition between a full-fledged son and other kinds of sons.

> When a daughter, whether appointed or not, has a son by a man of the same caste, her father has a son's son who offers *piṇḍas* for him and inherits his property. [M 9.136; **11.2.20**]

Since an appointed daughter is equivalent to a son, her son is a son's son, and, through him, her father is a paternal grandfather. And there is no Text that provides for a larger share for a son's son on the grounds that he is the eldest.

<**4**> To be sure, there is a Vasiṣṭha text to the effect that the son of an appointed daughter is a son in his own right:

> I will give you in marriage a daughter covered with jewels who has no brothers; the son she will bear will be my own son. [Va 17.17]

The appointed daughter and her son would, then, both qualify as sons.

Not so, for that would be incompatible with Manu 9.136 above. The son of an appointed daughter is her father's son only to the extent that he offers *piṇḍas* for him; he is, therefore, a son in a figurative sense only, for he is no more than the intermediary through whom the appointed daughter offers *piṇḍas*. Being a father's son in one's own right and being his son by reason of offering *piṇḍas* for him are two different things.[2]

<**5**> Note that the aforesaid [**2**] equal partition between a full-fledged son and an appointed daughter applies when they are of the same caste. If they are not of the same caste, they divide the property in the same way in which full-fledged sons of different castes do it [**9.12**], for an appointed daughter is equal to a full-fledged son.

<**6**> Note also that, if a properly appointed daughter is widowed without bearing a son or if she proves to be barren, she is no longer entitled to inherit any of her father's property. Indeed, the reason why a daughter is made an appointed daughter is that her son is to perform her father's funeral rites; if she has no son, she is just like any other daughter.

[2] This sentence, which is extremely terse in the Sanskrit text (*ekasya svato 'nyasya tadyogāt*), has been variously interpreted by the commentators. Most of them take it as a comparison between the appointed daughter and her son, overlooking the fact that both individuals being compared here are referred to in the masculine gender. My interpretation is supported by the commentator Maheśvara.

A Full-Fledged Son and Other Kinds of Sons

<7> Now, if any other kinds of sons—the son of an appointed daughter, the son of a levirate marriage, the son of an unmarried woman, a clandestine son, an abandoned son, a stepson, the son of a remarried woman, an adopted son,[3] a son who offered himself, one whom one treats as a son, or one who was bought[4]—partition property together with a full-fledged son, they are entitled to one third of the share of the full-fledged son, provided their caste is the same as that of their father and higher than that of the full-fledged son.[5] Says Devala, after enumerating the twelve kinds of sons:

> The reason why there are these twelve kinds of sons—some begotten by the father himself, some born of another man, some formally accepted, and some taken in informally—is to ensure that the lineage not be discontinued. [D 1582]
> The first six are also heirs to their father's kin, the other six to their father only; there are also differences depending on these sons' relative rankings.[6] [D 1583]
> All these sons inherit their father's property if he has no full-fledged son, but, if a full-fledged son is born to him later, they have no seniority right over him. [D 1584]
> Those among them whose caste is the same get a share of one third; those whose caste is lower shall live as dependents of the full-fledged son who shall provide them with food and shelter.[7] [D 1585]

[3] Note that the adopted son is not given any special treatment in the *Dāyabhāga*: he is mentioned only as one of the eleven sons who are not full-fledged. For an investigation on why "the treatises dedicated especially to Adoption seem to have been written for the most part during the 17th and subsequent centuries," see Derrett 1957c (= *Essays* 3.25–83). Cf. also note at **4.2.5**.

[4] The corresponding Sanskrit terms are *putrikāputra*, *kṣetraja*, *kānīna*, *gūḍhaja*, *apaviddha*, *sahoḍha(ja)*, *paunarbhava*, *dattaka*, *svayam āgata*, *kṛtaka*, and *krīta*.

[5] Instead of "higher than," some *Dāyabhāga* editions but none of the manuscripts I have consulted, nor Colebrooke's translation, read "higher than or equal to." The insertion of "or equal to" may result from an attempt at covering not dealt with in the *Dāyabhāga*. For Śrīkṛṣṇa's solution of this problem, see note 9.

[6] The term *ānupūrvyā*, "one after the other, in due order," is ambiguous. I translate it in light of the distinctions that are made in the last Devala verse and in Jīmūtavāhana's commentary, based on the caste rankings vis-à-vis the father and the full-fledged son. Colebrooke translates: "the rank of sons is distinguished in order as enumerated."

[7] D 1585 is ambiguous. Jīmūtavāhana (**9**, **13**) applies the first half of it to brothers whose caste is the same as their father's (and higher than that of the full-fledged son), the second half to brothers whose caste is lower than the castes of their father and the full-fledged son. In between he adds (**11**) a situation not covered by Devala: brothers whose caste is lower than their father's but higher than that of the full-fledged son. I mark the three situations [1] to [3].

<**8**> The six kinds of sons headed by the full-fledged son not only inherit from their father but also from his kin, i.e., *sapiṇḍas* and so on. The others, i.e., the latter group of six, inherit fully from their father, but not from *sapiṇḍas* and so on.

[1] <**9**> They get everything if their father has no full-fledged son, but if there is a full-fledged son, they get a share equal to one third of his.[8] <**10** > The same allocation of shares applies when they inherit together with an appointed daughter, for she is exactly like a full-fledged son.

[2] <**11**> Those, however, whose caste is lower than their father's, yet higher than that of the full-fledged son, get a share that is equal to either one fifth or one sixth of that of the full-fledged son, depending on whether they are more of less deserving.[9] Says Manu:

> When a full-fledged son divides his paternal property, he shall give the son of a levirate marriage a share of either one sixth or one fifth out of their father's property. [M 9.164]

<**12**> Since the Devala text says that all sons other than the full-fledged son are like the son of a levirate marriage,[10] the term "son of a levirate marriage" in this Manu text is synecdochic for all.

[3] <**13**> If their caste is lower than their father's and the full-fledged son's, they are entitled only to food and shelter. Indeed,

[A] Manu says:

> The full-fledged son is the sole master of the paternal property; yet, out of a sense of solidarity he should provide the others with maintenance.[11] [M 9.163]

[B] Kātyāyana says:

[8] Colebrooke's translation (based on a comment by Śrīkṛṣṇa) and the editions, beginning with that of 1829, add the specification that this rule pertains to sons who are of the same caste as their father's. This phrase does not appear in any of the *Dāyabhāga* manuscripts I have consulted. In a handwritten note in Colebrooke's own manuscript (India Office Library #1225, fol. 64a), where the proviso was added by a second hand in the margin, Colebrooke observed that "this is an insertion in all other copies as well as in this," and he added in pencil "& perhaps not genuine."

[9] Śrīkṛṣṇa records that the criterion "depending on whether they are more or less deserving" is well established in the tradition, but he adds that, since the case in which the other sons are of the same caste as the full-fledged son is not covered, it would be logical to give the other sons one fifth if their caste is higher than that of the full-fledged son, and one sixth if their caste is the same as his. Cf. notes 7 and 12.

[10] This statement refers to D 1584 (**7**), according to which, failing a full-fledged son, all other sons receive (that is, equal) shares.

[11] For other possible translations of the phrase "out of solidarity," see **4.1.21**. According to Śrīkṛṣṇa, since the full-fledged son's sense of solidarity is the determining factor, his providing maintenance to the others is totally at his discretion.

> If a full-fledged son was born to him, the others get one third of a share if they are of the same caste;[12] if they are not of the same caste, they can claim only food and shelter. [K 857]

<**14**> The phrases "the others" in the Manu text and "not of the same caste" in the Kātyāyana text actually mean that they are of a lower caste, for these Texts are consonant with the Devala text above [**7**].

<**15**> With regard to a partition involving a full-fledged son and a son begotten in an unauthorized levirate marriage, Manu says this:

> If two sons, one of them a full-fledged son, the other a son born of a levirate marriage, claim the inheritance of one and the same man, they each get the inheritance of their own father; the other has no right to that.[13] [M 9.162]

<**16**> This means that each son gets the property of the man from whose sperm he sprang; the son who sprang from another man's sperm does not get a share in that. That is why Nārada says:

> If two sons born of different fathers contend for the property held by one and the same woman, each of them gets what came from his own father; the other has no right to that. [N ? = M 9.191]

<**17**> Any property the woman was given by each of the two fathers goes to the son of that father, i.e., to the son who sprang from the man's sperm, not to the son of the other man.

What more is there to say?

[12] All *Dāyabhāga* manuscripts read "one third." Other commentaries, including the *Mitākṣarā* (on Y 2.132; Colebrooke I.xi.25), have a variant reading: "one fourth." One fourth fits in well for brothers who are of the same caste as the full-fledged son, in between one third when their caste is higher and one fifth or one sixth if their caste is lower. On K 857 see Derrett 1957c: 82–83 (= *Essays* 3.73–74).

[13] This verse has been interpreted differently by the several commentators on the *Manu-smṛti* (see Bühler's note to his translation). Jīmūtavāhana interprets it so as to avoid a conflict with statements earlier in this chapter, according to which a son born of a levirate marriage does get a share of the property of his mother's wedded husband. Although M 9.162 does not say so, Jīmūtavāhana limits its application to cases in which the levirate was not authorized and, hence, irregular. According to Śrīkṛṣṇa the verse applies to a situation in which a husband dies after having sired a full-fledged son, and his wife, at a later time, accepts a reward (*śulka*) from another man to bear him a son; if no reward was given, the son born of a levirate is considered to be the son of the woman's husband.

CHAPTER ELEVEN

THE INHERITANCE OF A MAN WHO DIES WITHOUT MALE OFFSPRING

SECTION ONE

THE WIDOW[1]

<1> The Texts that deal with the property of a man who dies without male offspring[2] appear to be incompatible with one another, with the result that their interpreters disagree on what happens to such property.

Texts That Make the Widow Her Husband's Heir

[A][3] <**2**> Bṛhaspati says:

> The experts on the Vedas, on the Tradition, and on valid custom hold the wife to be one half of her husband's body, sharing as an equal partner the results of his acts, be they meritorious or not. [B 26.92]
>
> Till a man's wife dies one half of his body lives. How could anyone else gain control of his property as long as one half of his body lives? [B 26.93]

[1] The *smṛti* texts quoted in this section and Jīmūtavāhana himself use the term *patnī* and other Sanskrit words which actually mean "wife." Except when these terms indicate wives whose husbands are living, I translate them as "widow."

[2] I translate the Sanskrit term *aputra*, literally "without leaving a son," as "without male offspring." A more accurate translation would require "without leaving a son, a son's son, and a son's son's son."

[3] From here up to **14** Jīmūtavāhana quotes and comments on four basic texts, marked [A] to [D], according to which the widow inherits in the absence of male offspring.

> If a man dies without male offspring, his widow inherits his property, even if relatives such as his father, mother, or brothers german are extant. [B 26.94; **54**]
> If a good and faithful wife dies before her husband, she gets his *agnihotra*;[4] if he dies first, she gets his property. That is the eternal law. [B 26.95]
> She gets his property, movable and immovable, gold and base metals, grains, liquids, and clothes; in return she shall see to it that his funeral rites be performed every month, every six months, and so forth. [B 26.96]
> She shall honor with gifts to the dead and to the living[5] her husband's paternal uncles, parents,[6] daughters' sons, sisters' sons, and maternal uncles, as well as the aged, the poor, guests, and women. [B 26.98; **63**]
> If some of his *sapiṇḍas* or kinsmen challenge her and do harm to the property, the king shall inflict on them the punishment mandated for thieves. [B 26.105]

<**3**> These seven verses suffice to show that any kind and any amount of property, immovable, movable, gold, and so forth, that belonged to a husband becomes the exclusive property of his widow, even if he has brothers german, paternal uncles, daughters' sons, and so on. By adding that, should any of them try to prevent her from taking possession of the property or to appropriate it to themselves, they shall receive the punishment mandated for thieves, Bṛhaspati forcefully rejects the notion that a father, brothers, and the like are entitled to inherit the deceased man's property while his widow is alive and well.

[B] <**4**> Yājñavalkya says:

> The widow, daughters, parents, then brothers, their sons, those born in the same *gotra*,[7] kin,[8] disciples, and fellow students: each in order inherits the property failing the prior one. This rule ap-

[4] The *agnihotra* is a ritual to be performed at the beginning and the end of the day (M 4.25). If a man's wife has been faithful to him and she dies first, he shall cremate her with the fire used for his *agnihotra* (M 5.167). The idea is that, by doing so, the faithful wife earns a place near her husband after death (M 5.166).

[5] The Sanskrit term is *kavya-pūrta*, *kavya* meaning oblations to the manes, *pūrta* food and drink offered to the living.

[6] The word "parents," perhaps "parents and brothers german" (cf. **3**), translates the ambiguous Sanskrit term *guru*. For Jīmūtavāhana's interpretation of the other terms in this enumeration, see **63**.

[7] For Jīmūtavāhana's interpretation of the term *gotraja*, see **11.6.10**.

[8] For his interpretation of *bandhu*, "kin," see **11.6.12**.

> plies to all castes when a man passes away without male offspring.[9] [Y 2.135–136]

By saying here that each in order is entitled to inherit the property failing the immediately preceding one, Yājñavalkya most explicitly states that, prior to anyone else, the widow alone is entitled to inherit.[10]

[C] <**5**> Viṣṇu says:

> The property of a man who dies without male offspring goes to his widow; failing her, to his daughters; failing them, to his father; failing him, to his mother; failing her, to his brothers; failing them, to his brothers' sons; failing them, to his kin; failing them, to his relatives;[11] failing them, to his disciples; failing them, to his fellow students; failing them, it goes to the king, except for the property of a brahman.[12] [Vi 17.3–14]

<**6**> In this Text, too, it is clearly said that the widow alone ranks first in being entitled to inherit the property.

{Objection] The only thing the term "widow" in these Texts means is that widows are entitled to as much property as is required for their maintenance.

[Refutation] Not so. It goes against reason that the term "property," which is mentioned only once,[13] should refer to two different things, namely, to part of the property as far as the widow is concerned and to the entire property in the case of brothers and so on.[14] Hence, the correct interpretation of the Texts is that the widow is entitled to inherit her husband's property in its entirety.

[D] <**7**> Vṛddha-Manu says:[15]

[9] Y 2.135–136 and Viṣṇu 17.3–14 (**5**) are the two basic texts governing the inheritance of a man who dies without male offspring. Jīmūtavāhana returns to them throughout this chapter. On the phrase "all castes," see note at **6.1.36**.

[10] In a lengthy commentary on these two verses, Vijñāneśvara (Colebrooke II.i.30, 39) restricts the right of the widow to inherit to widows whose husbands were separated from their joint families (cf. the objection introduced at **19**). For a critical discussion of this restriction, see Jolly 1885: 197–98.

[11] On the term *sakulya*, "relatives," see **11.6.21**.

[12] Jīmūtavāhana will quote this Viṣṇu text piecemeal as he progresses in the discussion of the various classes of heirs.

[13] I.e., right at the beginning of the entire lists of successive classes of heirs, from the widow to the king.

[14] For the principle that a word that is used only once in a sentence cannot have different meanings for different parts of the sentence, see **2.67** and **3.30**; for an exception, see **11.5.9**.

[15] I prefer the reading "Vṛddha-Manu" to "Bṛhan-Manu," even though this reading appears in a number of *Dāyabhāga* manuscripts and editions, on the grounds that the verse is consistently attributed to Vṛddha-Manu at the end of Jīmūtavāhana's commentary (**14**). As noted by Herberich (Vṛddha-Manu, p. 4), the two names are often interchanged.

> If a widow who has no male offspring remains chaste and faithful to her husband, she alone shall offer his *piṇḍa* and take the entire share for herself. [vM 92]

<**8**> The word "his" in "his *piṇḍa*" remains valid throughout the rest of the sentence. Since "his" refers back to the husband, it follows that what the widow shall take for herself is her husband's entire share, not her own entire share.[16] Indeed, an outright injunction to the effect that "she shall take for herself" is out of the question with regard to her own share. The notion this Text is meant to convey is that she becomes the owner of something. And it is not worth establishing that she becomes the owner of her own share, since just by conveying the notion that the share is hers, it is understood that she owns it.

<**9**> It would also be wrong to say that this Text is meant as an outright injunction for the widow to take possession of her own share. Indeed, taking possession of one's own property need not be enjoined; it is the natural thing to do.[17] <**10**> Nor would it be right to say that the Vṛddha-Manu text is intended as an admonitory injunction.[18] If so, the rule would have a transcendent purpose,[19] and one would have to posit a motivation, etc., for the restriction.

<**11**> Some have argued the following: "When a Text says that a son, provided he is not disqualified by being blind and the like, 'shall get the entire share,' that does not mean that he gets his father's entire share but that he gets his own entire share. In the Text at hand, therefore, the word 'entire' refers to the widow's own share as well."

That, too, is wrong. Indeed,

[1] there are no Texts to the effect that a son, provided he is not disqualified by being blind or the like, shall get the entire share; they cannot, therefore, be used as paradigms in this case.

[16] I.e., not just what she is entitled to in her own right for her maintenance, etc. The interpretation to which Jīmūtavāhana objects: "The widow shall offer his *piṇḍa* and take her own share," is, in fact, the more obvious one, and one that avoids a number of grammatical difficulties which Śrīkṛṣṇa discusses in his commentary. Even though a variant reading *artham* instead of *aṃśam* in the Vṛddha-Manu text is well attested in the commentaries and digests (*Dhko* p. 1537): "she shall take the entire property for herself," Jīmūtavāhana—and Vijñāneśvara (on Y 2.135; Colebrooke II.i.6)—does not seem to have known it. Colebrooke observes that, "if it (= *artham*) be the genuine text, the whole of Jímútaváhana's argument in the subsequent paragraphs (up to **13**) falls to the ground."

[17] Taking possession of one's own property is an example of a situation in which no outright injunction is needed, since the right to do so is "established" (*prāpta*) by natural instinct (*rāgād eva*). Cf. note at **1.26**.

[18] I.e., she may or may not take possession of her share, but she ought to do so unless there are good reasons to do otherwise. Having shown, in two ways (**8–9**), that, if the phrase "the entire share" were to mean "her entire share," the Vṛddha-Manu text does not qualify as an outright injunction (*vidhi*), Jīmūtavāhana now demonstrates that, if that was the meaning, the verse would not qualify as an admonitory injunction (*niyama*) either. On "admonitory injunction," see note at **1.27**.

[19] On "transcendent purpose," see note at **9.20**.

[2] Even if there were such Texts, the word "the" in "the entire share" could only be interpreted with reference to the father, because, for the reason mentioned earlier, "one shall get one's own share" cannot be a valid outright injunction. <**12**> That is why the ancient Sages invariably convey the notion that one person accedes to the property of a different person, e.g., sons to their father's property, the widow and so forth to a man who dies without male offspring, and so on. They never enjoin anyone to take possession of his or her own share.

<**13**> Some also argued as follows: "When a word indicates something that needs a correlative, it evokes something that is correlated to itself.[20] For example, when someone mentions the word 'mother,' no one would imagine that he is speaking of the mother of someone else."

That, too, is beside the point. It only applies to cases in which the correlative is not made explicit. On the other hand, when someone says: "Bring Ḍiṭṭha's mother here," this refers neither to the mother of the one who receives the order nor to the mother of the one who gives the order. In the same way, in the case at hand the correlative of "share" is made explicit by the word "his" in "his *piṇḍa*." So, how could "the share" refer to the widow? That such an outright injunction is out of the question anyhow has been stated earlier [**8**].

<**14**> In conclusion, what Vṛddha-Manu means is that the widow shall take possession of her husband's entire share.

Texts That Do Not Make the Widow Her Husband's Heir

<**15**> There are also Texts that seem to say the opposite,[21] namely, that a widow is not entitled to inherit her husband's property. Indeed,

[A] Śaṅkha and Likhita, Paiṭhīnasi, and Yama say:

> When a man passes away without male offspring, his property goes to his brothers; failing them, his parents get it, or else his senior widow, his *sagotras*, disciples, or fellow students. [ŚL 293; Pai 119; cf. **11.2.27**]

<**16**> This Text appears to be incompatible with the preceding ones, because here parents inherit if there are no brothers, and the widow inherits if there are no parents.[22]

[B] <**17**> Devala says:

[20] The argument of Jīmūtavāhana's interlocutor is that in the phrase "she shall take the entire share for herself," the correlative of "the share" is "she," i.e., the widow: "she shall take her share."

[21] I translate *viparīta-bodhaka* as "seem to say the opposite," rather than as "declare the contrary" (Colebrooke). In the Indian tradition *smṛti* texts cannot be contradictory; as Jīmūtavāhana demonstrates later (**19–55**), apparently incompatible texts can, and indeed must, be harmonized.

[22] For Jīmūtavāhana's own interpretation of the text of Śaṅkha and others, see **45**.

> Next, when a man dies without male offspring, his brothers german inherit his property, or else his daughters of equal standing, or else his father if he survives him, his brothers of the same caste, his mother, and his widow, in that order. Failing these, his property goes to those relatives who lived with him. [D 1570–1571; **50, 11.5.6**]

<**18**> The apparent incompatibility in this Text is the fact that here the brothers occupy the very first place, the widow the very last.[23]

Refutation of a Prior Attempt to Harmonize the Texts

<**19**> Some people have tried to harmonize the two sets of Texts as follows: brothers are entitled to inherit first if they were never separated from or if they were reunited with the deceased; the widow comes first if the brothers were separated from and not reunited with him.[24]

<**20**>[25] That view is incompatible with the following Bṛhaspati text:

> If brothers who were separated resume life in common out of affection for each other, there is no seniority right if they proceed to a new partition. [B 26.106cdef; **12.2**]
>
> If one of them dies or somehow becomes a wanderer,[26] his share does not vanish. It goes to his brothers german. If he has sisters, they ought to get a share of it. This rule applies when a man dies without offspring[27] and leaves neither a widow nor parents. [B 26. 107–108]
>
> If one of the reunited brothers acquired property by his knowledge, prowess, and the like, he is entitled to two shares, the others to one share each. [B 26.112]

[1] <**21**> Both the beginning and the end of this Text specifically mention reunion. The intervening passage: "his share does not vanish. It goes to his brothers german," must, therefore, be interpreted as pertaining to reunited brothers. If so, the next passage: "This rule applies when a man dies without offspring and leaves neither a widow nor parents," means to say that reunited brothers german

[23] For Jīmūtavāhana's own interpretation of the Devala text, see **50**.

[24] Cf. note 10.

[25] The first argument against the solution presented at **19**: there is a Bṛhaspati text to the effect that, even if brothers are reunited, the property goes to the widow of the deceased before it goes to his brothers.

[26] On "becoming a wanderer" (here *pravrajet*), see note at **1.4**.

[27] I translate "without offspring" rather than "without male offspring," because the Sanskrit text here uses the term *an-apatya*, not *a-putra*.

are entitled to inherit, provided there are no sons, daughters, a widow, or parents. So, how could it bar the widow?

[2] <**22**> The Text says: "does not vanish."[28] The phrase "does not vanish" is relevant only if there is a danger that the property might vanish, i.e., that it might not be easily recognizable, which happens either when a brother was never separated, or when he was reunited so that his property again became blended with that of the other brothers. When it comes to the property of a brother who was separated and not reunited, there is no danger that his property might vanish, because, having been the object of a partition, it is easily recognizable.

In conclusion, the Bṛhaspati passage pertains to brothers who were not separated from or who were reunited with the deceased.[29]

<**23**>[30] The claim that the text of Śaṅkha and others [**15**], which conveys the notion that a man's brothers inherit prior to his widow and so on, pertains to situations in which the brothers were reunited ought to be supported either by Texts or by common sense.

[1] It is definitely not supported by Texts, for there are no Texts that call for any such restriction. Indeed,

[a] Yājñavalkya 2.138 [**11.5.10**] and other similar Texts are intended to lay down special rules to be observed in situations in which different kinds of brothers might be entitled to inherit;[31] these Texts cannot, therefore, pertain to the brothers' right to inherit generally.

[b] <**24**> Since the Bṛhaspati verses quoted earlier [**20**], which convey the notion that brothers german inherit, failing sons, daughters, the widow, and parents, pertain to reunited brothers, the logical conclusion must be that Texts that are incompatible with Bṛhaspati's pertain exclusively to brothers who were not reunited, not to reunited brothers.[32]

[2] <**25**> Some resort to the argument of common sense,[33] as follows: "If brothers are reunited,[34] anything that belongs to one brother also belongs to the

[28] Śrīkṛṣṇa notes that, whereas argument [1] relied solely on the verses that surround B 26.107–108, on the basis of the "rule of being caught between tongs" (*saṃdaṃśa-patita-nyāya*), argument [2] draws on the text of B 26.107–108 itself.

[29] That is, the passage thereby says that even in this case the widow inherits prior to the brothers of the deceased. Note that here and occasionally also elsewhere Jīmūtavāhana uses the term *saṃsṛṣṭa* to indicate not only individuals who were reunited but also those who never separated.

[30] The second argument against the solution presented at **19**: there is no indication whatever that the text of Śaṅkha and others (**15**) pertains exclusively to brothers who were not separated or who were reunited.

[31] Jīmūtavāhana more specifically alludes to the fact that, according to Y 2.138, only brothers who were reunited with the deceased inherit; brothers who were not reunited do not.

[32] I.e., texts that put the brothers first (**15**, **17**) would then pertain to brothers who are not reunited, which is exactly the opposite of what Jīmūtavāhana's interlocutor argued at **19**.

[33] Namely, to claim that, if a reunited brother dies, his property goes to his brothers, not to his widow.

other. Even though when one of them dies his proprietary right lapses, the ownership in that property on the part of a brother who lives does not cease. Hence the property belongs to him alone, not to the deceased brother's widow, for with her husband's death the wife's proprietary right lapses as well, even as a wife ceases to have any claim to her husband's property as soon as there are sons and the like."

<**26**> That is absurd. Even when two brothers are reunited it is not so that anything that belongs to one of them also belongs to the other. It is true, as I said right at the beginning [**1.8–9**], that they do not know which particular part of the property belongs to each, but that does not mean that the entire property belongs to both of them, for nothing authorizes the assumption that the proprietary rights extend over the entire property. Nor is there anything that authorizes the statement that a wife's proprietary right in her husband's property, a right that stems from their marriage, lapses when the husband dies. It is different when there is a son; in that case it is understood that the wife's proprietary right lapses, since a son's right to inherit from his father derives directly from Texts.

[Objection] <**27**> In the case at hand, too, it is understood that the widow's proprietary right lapses, because there are Texts [**15**, **17**] that entitle reunited brothers to inherit.

[Refutation] Not so. It is not as yet established that these Texts do pertain to reunited brothers. If you were to use the Texts to establish that they do, that would result in pure circular reasoning: [a] if the proprietary right of the widow lapses when her husband was reunited with his brothers at the time of his death, the Texts that establish his brothers' right to inherit pertain to reunited brothers; [b] if the Texts pertain to reunited brothers, the widow's proprietary right lapses.

<**28**>[35] If the text of Śaṅkha and others [**15**] pertained to brothers who never separated or who were reunited, it would have to be construed as follows: the property of a brother who was not separated or who was reunited goes to like brothers; "failing these," i.e., failing like brothers, "his parents take the property." In that case there would be two possibilities, and the question arises: do parents who were separated and not reunited take it, or do parents who were not separated or who were reunited take it?

The first alternative is impossible. Parents who were separated from and not reunited with their son would be barred by his widow, on the grounds of Texts such as Yājñavalkya 2.135 [**4**]. So, how could they be entitled to inherit prior to her?[36]

[34] Or, if they never separated (cf. note 29).

[35] The third argument against the solution proposed at **19**: if the text of Śaṅkha and others pertained to brothers who did not separate or who were reunited, the fact that the parents of the deceased are listed in between the brothers and the widow would create a problem.

[36] If the Śaṅkha text is supposed to pertain to situations in which the deceased was either not separated or reunited, situations in which he was separated would resort under Y 2.135 and similar texts in which the widow—and the daughters—bar the parents.

Nor is the second alternative possible. Indeed,

[a] no one will dispute the fact that, even if there are brothers who did not separate from or who were reunited with the deceased, his property nevertheless goes to his parents if they were not separated from or were reunited with him.

[b] <**29**> If both the father and the brothers were separated from and not reunited with the deceased, there are good reasons why the father should take the property prior to the brothers. First, since the father gave his son life, the Revealed Text: "He himself is reborn again in his son"[37] establishes that both are one. Consequently, the father is master over his son's property and his body. Second, after his *sapiṇḍana*[38] the deceased shares in the two *piṇḍas* which his father offers to his grandfather and great-grandfather, whereas sons do not offer *pārvaṇaśrāddhas* as long as their father lives.[39] The same reasons why the father takes the property prior to the brothers when both were separated from and not reunited with the deceased also hold in the opposite case.

Or else,[40] since there is no difference between the father and the brothers as far as their not being separated from or being reunited with the deceased is concerned, it might make sense that they are entitled to inherit simultaneously. Under no circumstances would it be proper, however, for the father to inherit only when there are no brothers.

[c] <**30**> It would not be possible to say, as the Śaṅkha text [**15**] does, in the dual number, that "parents" who were not separated from or reunited with their son take his property, for one neither divides nor abstains from dividing property with one's mother, and, for the same reason, one does not reunite with her either. Says Bṛhaspati:

> If a man who was a party to a partition resumes life together with his father, brother, or paternal uncle, out of affection for them, he is said to be reunited. [B 26.113; **12.3**]

What Bṛhaspati points out in this verse is this: when and only when individuals such as a father, a brother, a paternal uncle, and so forth,[41] who on account of their descent have an undivided interest in the property acquired by their ancestors,[42] proceed to a partition, they can, out of affection for one another, reunite, if they annul the earlier partition, and if they again live under one roof, as members of a

[37] The idea that a father is born again in the form of his son is a common one in Vedic and post-Vedic literature. E.g., *Aitareya-brāhmaṇa* 7.13.1 (= 33.1): *ātmā hi jajña ātmanaḥ*, "(the father) himself is born from himself." Cf. the etymology of the term *jāyā*, "wife": "a wife is called *jāyā* because her husband is born (*jāyate*) again in her" (M 9.8cd).

[38] *Sapiṇḍana* or *sapiṇḍīkaraṇa* is the particular *śrāddha* ceremony at which the deceased is included among the performer's ancestors. See Knipe 1977 and Introduction.

[39] The "sons" referred to here are the deceased man's brothers.

[40] Jīmūtavāhana is willing to concede that the father and the brothers might take the property together, but that is as far as he will go.

[41] On the phrase "and so forth," see note at **12.4**.

[42] Śrīkṛṣṇa notes that the phrase "on account of their descent" (*utpattitaḥ*) excludes the mother whose link to the common property is through marriage.

single household, with the understanding "what is yours is mine and what is mine is yours."

Reunion is out of the question, however, for people who do not answer these criteria. Merchants, for instance, cannot reunite, for they act jointly only to the extent that they pool their assets. Nor are separated family members reunited if they pool their assets without the aforementioned intent caused by mutual affection.

Hence, since, as far as the mother is concerned, being separate from her and being reunited with her is out of the question, how could one harmonize the apparently conflicting views about whether, when there are brothers, she takes her son's property before or after them?

How Best to Harmonize the Texts

<**31**> Let me now explain how truly discerning people harmonize the two sets of Texts.

The Texts of Viṣṇu and others [**5**, **7**, etc.] make it perfectly clear that the widow is entitled to inherit only if there are no sons or other male offspring. It also makes sense that the property of the deceased first and exclusively goes to his sons, their sons, and the sons of his sons' sons.[43] Indeed,

[A] Manu and Viṣṇu say:

> The Self-existent himself called a son *putra* because he saves (*trā*) his father from the hell called *Put*. [M 9.138 = Vi 15.44; **5.6**][44]

[B] Hārīta says:

> There is a hell called *Put*. If a man's lineage is cut off, he goes to that hell. A son is called *putra* because he saves his father from it. [H 4.10]

[C] Śaṅkha and Likhita say:

> As soon as a father beholds the face of a son, he is freed of his debt to his ancestors;[45] as soon as a son is born, his father passes his debt on to him and is bound for heaven. [ŚL 285]

[43] Before returning to the widow's right to inherit (**43**), Jīmūtavāhana enters into a lengthy digression to demonstrate the basic criterion which, in his opinion, determines the right to inherit generally and the order of succession in particular, namely, the fact that and the extent to which an heir is of service to the deceased. Cf. Introduction.

[44] For other references to this etymology of the word *putra*, see **1.36** and **2.53**.

[45] Cf. Va 11.48: "The Vedas stipulate that, when a brahman is born, he is indebted to three creditors: he owes sacrifices to the gods, offspring to his ancestors, and the study of the Vedas to the Sages. Hence, he pays off his debts if he offers sacrifices, if he has a son,

> An *agnihotra*,[46] the three Vedas, and sacrifices with fees of a hundred cows, none of these are worth even a fraction[47] of the birth of a first son. [ŚL 284]

[D] Manu, Śaṅkha, Viṣṇu, Vasiṣṭha, and Hārīta say:

> Through a son a man conquers the worlds, through a son's son he attains immortality, through a son of a son's son he reaches the world of the sun. [M 9.137 = Ś 283 = Vi 15.46 = Va 17.5 = H 4.14]

[E] Yājñavalkya says:

> Through a son, a son's son, and the son of a son's son a man conquers the world, attains immortality, and reaches the world of the sun, respectively. [Y 1.78ab]

<**32**> In other words, right from the time of their birth sons and other male descendants provide their father with something that will be of great service to him in reaching the other world; and, when the father dies, they offer him *piṇḍas* at their *pārvaṇaśrāddhas*. Hence, Texts to the effect that sons and other male descendants become the owners of the property of their father and so forth are based on a principle of common sense,[48] namely, that in the hands of sons and other male descendants the property of the deceased is of service to him.

Manu, too, says that the single reason why someone accedes to the property of a deceased person is that he is of service to him:[49]

> By the mere fact that he is born a first son makes a man the father of a son,[50] and frees him of the debt to his ancestors. That is why the son is entitled to inherit his property. [M 9.106; **1.36**]

<**33**> Since the phrase "that is why" indicates a necessary and sufficient condition, and since references, in the chapter on inheritance, to various ways in which sons and other male descendants are of service to their father and other male ancestors cannot serve any other purpose, it follows that Manu concurs with the notion that the sole reason for acceding to someone's property is that one is of service to him. <**34**> That is why the word "son" in this Text must be taken to indicate all descendants in the male line down to the great-grandson, because all of these including the great-grandson are equally of service through the *piṇḍas* they offer at their *pārvaṇaśrāddhas*. <**35**> If that was not the case because the word "son" is not sup-

---

and if he studies the Veda." Cf. also *Taittirīya-saṃhitā* 6.3.10.5; *Śatapatha-brāhmaṇa* 1.7.2.1–5.

[46] On *agnihotra*, see note 4.

[47] Literally, "one sixteenth part."

[48] Literally, the ownership of sons and other male descendants, as "verbalized in Texts" (*śruta*), is something that is "established by common sense" (*nyāya-prāpta*; cf. note at **1.26**).

[49] "accedes to the property"; literally, "obtains a link (*sambandha*) to the property." Cf. note at **1.17**.

[50] On the phrase "the father of a son," see note at **1.26**.

posed to convey anything more than its original meaning, then, even if it might somehow be possible to find a Text that conveys the notion that a son's son should inherit,[51] there definitely would be no Text that specifically mentions the son of a son's son.[52] **<36>** In conclusion, since the son of a son's son is entitled to inherit for the very reason that he, too, is of service, the word "son" at Manu 9.106 is synecdochic and includes him as well.

<37> That is also why Baudhāyana says:

> The paternal great-grandfather, the paternal grandfather, the father, oneself, brothers german, a son, a son's son, and a son's son's son, provided the latter three were born of women of the same caste,[53] all these partake of undivided shares and are called *sapiṇḍas*. Those who partake of divided shares are called *sakulyas*. When there are persons born-of-the-body, the property goes to them. Failing *sapiṇḍas*, *sakulyas* get it; failing them, a teacher, an apprentice,[54] or a priest; failing them, the king.[55] [Bau 1.5.11. 9–14; cf. **4.2.21**]

<38>[56] What this Text means is the following. Since, as a result of his *sapiṇḍana*,[57] a deceased person shares in the three *piṇḍas* that are offered to his father, his paternal grandfather, and his paternal great-grandfather, and since three generations from his son down offer *piṇḍas* to them and/or to him,[58] it follows that after

[51] Śrīkṛṣṇa cites as examples M 9.136 (**10.3**; **11.2.20**) and the text attributed to Vi (**11.2.23**). Both texts qualify daughters' sons as heirs and, thereby, by implication, also sons' sons.

[52] I.e., on the sole basis of the texts the great-grandson would not be able to inherit his great-grandfather's property.

[53] It is not clear from the Sanskrit text whether the proviso "born of women of the same caste" pertains to a son, a son's son, and a son's son's son, or whether it pertains solely to "a son" born of a woman of the same caste (Colebrooke, Bühler, Olivelle, etc.). I prefer the former interpretation on the grounds that what is required of a son must, a fortiori, also be required of his descendants.

[54] On the use of the term *antevāsin*, "apprentice," in the sense of *śiṣya*, "disciple," see note at **9.28**. Cf. also **11.6.13**.

[55] The *Dāyabhāga* manuscripts are almost uniform in their readings of this text. There are, however, major differences between Jīmūtavāhana's readings and those found in the Baudhāyana manuscripts. Hence the translation deviates from Bühler's (Bau tr.) at various points.

[56] This entire paragraph is quoted, anonymously and approvingly, and with only minor variant readings, in the *Vyavahāraprakāśa* (ed. pp. 504–05; tr. III.i.11). According to Mitter (1870: 39–40), "the entire doctrine of sapinda is contained in [this] passage of the Dayabhaga."

[57] On the consequences of *sapiṇḍana*, see note 38 and Introduction.

[58] The Sanskrit term *tat-piṇḍa* is ambiguous, since the pronominal stem *tat* in the compound does not specify gender or number. The son of the deceased offers *piṇḍas* to his own father and also to the father and the paternal grandfather of the deceased; the son's son of the deceased offers *piṇḍas* to his own father (the son of the deceased), to the deceased,

his death, from the time of his *sapiṇḍana* on, he shares in the *piṇḍas* offered to those to whom he had to offer *piṇḍas* in his lifetime.

That being the case, a propositus[59] who offered *piṇḍas* to his ancestors in his lifetime and who shares in the *piṇḍas* offered to them after his death, became a beneficiary of *piṇḍas* offered to them by later generations as long as they were living, and, when they, too, are dead, he shares with them in the *piṇḍas* to be offered to them by his daughter's son and so forth.[60]

Hence, since those to whom he offered *piṇḍas*, or else those who offer *piṇḍas* to him, consume gifts in the form of undivided *piṇḍas*, they are *sapiṇḍas*, i.e., persons who share in undivided gifts.[61]

On the other hand, when the propositus is fifth in line, he does not offer a *piṇḍa* to his ancestor in the fifth generation, nor does he share in *piṇḍas* offered to him. In the same way the descendant in the fifth generation does not offer a *piṇḍa* to the propositus, nor does he share in the *piṇḍas* offered to him. Therefore, the three earlier generations from the great-great-grandfather up and the three later generations from the great-great-grandson down do not share in any single whole *piṇḍa*.[62] They share in divided gifts and are called *sakulyas*.

<39> Note that the definitions of *sapiṇḍa* and *sakulya* given above pertain specifically to inheritance. **<40>** That is why Manu, too, first says:

> Not his brothers, not his father, but his sons inherit from their father, [M 9.185ab]

and then, to answer the question why this is so, he adds:

> Three generations shall be given water, three generations must be offered *piṇḍas*. It is the fourth generation that offers these. The

---

and to the father of the deceased. In both cases *tat* stands for "them." The son's son's son offers no *piṇḍas* to any ancestor of the deceased, but only to "him."

[59] Jīmūtavāhana uses the term *madhyastha*, "a person in the middle," in between his ancestors and his descendants.

[60] According to M 9.136 quoted by Śrīkṛṣṇa (see note 51), failing sons and sons' sons—and according to Jīmūtavāhana also sons' sons' sons—the daughter's son offers *piṇḍas*. The phrase "and so forth" must refer to the son's daughter's son who offers *piṇḍas* to the deceased, his father, and his son, and to the son's son's daughter's son who offers *piṇḍas* to the deceased, his son, and his son's son.

[61] In this complex paragraph Jīmūtavāhana accounts for the fact that a group of males belonging to seven generations—a propositus plus three generations of ancestors and three generations of descendants—are called *sa-piṇḍas*, "having *piṇḍas* in common." They are so called because they are *avibhakta-dāya-ādal-ada*, "undivided-gift-taker" ("-taker" with the reading *-āda*; "-consumer, -eater" with the reading *-ada*, which Jīmūtavāhana prefers). Jīmūtavāhana plays on the double meaning of *dāya*, which indicates both the "gift" the living *sapiṇḍa* offers to the deceased, and the "share" the deceased leaves behind for the living. Kane (1941: 473) objects to the fact that Jīmūtavāhana "assigns the meaning of piṇḍa to the word dāya in Baudhāyana's passage for which there is no warrant."

[62] *Sakulyas* partake of only the "fragments of *piṇḍas*" (*piṇḍa-lepa*) that are wiped off the hands of the person who first prepared whole *piṇḍas* for his nearest ancestors. Cf. Introduction.

> fifth generation plays no role in it. [M 9.186; **4.3.36, 11.6.7, 11.6.17**]

<**41**> On the other hand, as the *Mārkaṇḍeya-purāṇa* points out, in matters of ritual pollution and the like,[63] even those who share only in fragments of *piṇḍas* are considered to be *sapiṇḍas*, on the grounds that they do share in the fragments of *piṇḍas* that are offered to them:[64]

> Another three generations share in fragments of *piṇḍas*, from the paternal grandfather's paternal grandfather up; the one who offers them is the seventh. That is what the Sages call the seven-generation bond. [Mpu 31.4–5ab]

This means that this is the bond that causes ritual pollution among them. <**42**> That is also why, in the chapter on pollution, Manu says:

> *Sapiṇḍa* relationship ceases with the seventh generation, *samānodaka* relationship when people no longer know their ancestors' names or their exact filiation. [M 5.60; ab **11.6.17**]

Otherwise,[65] this Text would be incompatible with Manu 9.186 [**40**].

<**43**> Now,[66] since, failing descendants in the male line down to the great-grandson, a wife, as soon as she becomes a widow, contributes to her husband's well-being in the other world by remaining faithful to him and so forth, she is next in line after the sons, the sons' sons, and the sons' sons' sons. Therefore, failing these, the widow is entitled to inherit her deceased husband's property. Says Vyāsa:

> After her husband's death a dutiful widow shall observe a vow of chastity and, every day, after bathing, offer her husband a *salilāñjali*.[67] [Vy 241]
> Every day she shall devoutly worship the gods; she shall fast regularly and propitiate Viṣṇu. [Vy 242]

[63] In fact, the chapter of the *Mārkaṇḍeya-purāṇa* from which Jīmūtavāhana is about to quote deals with *śrāddha*, not ritual pollution.

[64] The fact that Jīmūtavāhana accepts different definitions for the term *sapiṇḍa* in the context of impurity (*aśauca*) and in the context of inheritance, constitutes a second ground (cf. note 61) on which Kane (1941: 473) criticizes Jīmūtavāhana's view. According to Jolly (1885: 174, 209), that distinction did not exist before the *Dāyabhāga*.

[65] I.e., if M 5.60 pertained to inheritance, not to ritual pollution.

[66] After the preceding digression (**31–42**) Jīmūtavāhana now returns to the widow's right to inherit, by pointing out first (**43–44**) that the widow, too, in her own way, can be of service to her deceased husband.

[67] *Salilāñjali* is an offering of water from one's cupped hands. Some *Dāyabhāga* manuscripts and editions offer a variant reading: *satilāñjali*, "an offering with sesame seeds from one's cupped hands." The *Dāyabhāga* commentators quote a verse from the *Kāśīkhaṇḍa* of the *Skanda-purāṇa*: "Every day she must satiate, with offerings of *kuśa* grass, sesame seeds, and water, her husband, his father, and his paternal grandfather, addressing them by name, with the name of their *gotra*, and so forth."

> To increase her merit she shall offer gifts to eminent brahmans, and she shall observe the various fasts prescribed in the *śāstras*, oh dear lady.[68] [Vy 243]
> A widow who is forever devoted to her duties, oh fair-faced one, provides safe passage for her departed husband and for herself. [Vy 244]

<**44**> These and other Texts to the same effect say in so many words that a man's widow, too, can save him from hell. Vice versa, since her former husband shares equally with her the consequences of her acts, whether meritorious or not, it follows that, if for lack of adequate resources she does anything contrary to her duties, she can also cause him to go to hell. Therefore, since the prior owner's property is used here for his own benefit, it is only proper that the widow becomes the owner of it.[69]

<**45**> To come back now to the text of Śaṅkha and others [**15**], here the two ends of the sentence must be construed together, and the phrase "failing . . ." which appears once in the middle must be construed both with the preceding phrase "it goes to his brothers" and with the following "his parents get it," as follows:

> When a man passes away without male offspring, his property goes to his senior wife; failing her, his parents get it; failing them, it goes to his brothers.[70]

In this way it is not incompatible with the other Texts. That it is also the reasonable thing to do has been shown earlier [**44**].

<**46**> In any case, there is no reason to posit that this Text pertains to brothers who were not separated or who were reunited, an assumption which is not supported by the wording of the Text. One should, therefore, heed Jitendriya's statement to the effect that the widow's right to inherit the entire property of her hus-

[68] Although these verses are presumed to belong to the lost *Vyāsa-smṛti*, they probably originally were part of the epic and puranic texts which are most often in the form of dialogues. Only the first half verse appears in the *Mahābhārata* (1.App.69.11a).

[69] Mitter (1870: 37) used this sentence to show that, even though women cannot be of service to the deceased by offering *piṇḍas*, the ability to be of service in one way or the other invariably constitutes Jīmūtavāhana's basic criterion to determine someone's right to inherit.

[70] The Sanskrit text is as follows: *aputrasya svaryātasya bhrātṛgāmi dravyaṃ tadabhāve pitarau haretāṃ patnī vā jyeṣṭhā*. Jīmūtavāhana takes together *aputrasya*, "(the property) of a man who dies without male offspring," and *patnī jyeṣṭhā*, "(goes to) his senior wife" (the particle *vā*, "or," is left out of consideration). The word *tadabhāve*, which means "failing him/her/them"—*tad-* being unmarked for gender and number—is then construed, in reverse order, with *pitarau haretāṃ*, "his parents get it," and with *bhrātṛgāmi*, "it goes to his brothers." Some commentaries (e.g., *Vivādaratnākara* #1676; tr. XXXIV.12) read *patnī vājyeṣṭhā* and interpret this as *patnī vā ajyeṣṭhā*, "a wife who is not senior," because, they say, it is established (*prāpta*) that the senior wife inherits prior to the brothers. Other commentaries, including the *Mitākṣarā* (on Y 2.135; Colebrooke II.i.7), unequivocally read *jyeṣṭhā vā patnī*, and make the senior wife inherit after the brothers, the father, and the mother.

band who leaves no male offspring applies unconditionally, irrespective of whether he was separated from his brothers or not.

<**47**>[71] Note that the status of being a man's "wife" belongs, first, to the spouse of the highest caste. The text of Śaṅkha and others [**15**], indeed, explicitly mentions the "senior wife," i.e., senior in the order of castes. Says Manu:

> If twice-born men wed women of their own caste and of other castes, the women's seniority, prestige, and accommodation are commensurate with their respective castes. [M 9.85]

Hence, the spouse of the same caste is the senior one, even if she was wedded later than the others; she is "the wife," for she alone is entitled to participate in her husband's sacrifices and the like. Again Manu:

> Only a spouse of the same caste as that of her husband shall attend to his physical welfare and participate in his everyday ritual duties, not ever a spouse of a different caste. [M 9.86]
> If the husband is foolish enough to have another wife perform these duties when he has a wife of the same caste, the ancients consider him to be as bad as a *brāhmaṇa-cāṇḍāla*.[72] [M 9.87]

Only if a man does not have a spouse of the same caste as his own is a spouse of the immediately lower caste considered to be his wife. Says Viṣṇu:

> Failing a spouse of the same caste, in an emergency, with one of the immediately lower caste; under no circumstances, however, a twice-born man with a *śūdra* spouse. [Vi 26.3–4]

The phrase "he shall perform his ritual duties" carries over into this sentence from an earlier one [Vi 26.1].

Consequently, "the wife" of a brahman is a spouse of the brahman caste; failing her, in an emergency, one of the *kṣatriya* caste; never, however, one of the *vaiśya* or *śūdra* castes, even if she was duly wedded. "The wife" of a *kṣatriya* is a spouse of the *kṣatriya* caste, or, failing her, a *vaiśya* spouse, since her caste is the immediately lower one, but not a *śūdra* spouse. The only "wife" of a *vaiśya* is a spouse of the *vaiśya* caste, for the phrase "under no circumstances, however, with a *śūdra* spouse" rules out a *śūdra* wife for any man of the twice-born castes.

<**48**> The same rank ordering that governs the status of spouses as wives also determines their right to inherit as widows. Hence, the following Nārada text pertains exclusively to spouses who, though duly wedded, do not have the status of widows:

[71] Before giving his own interpretation (**50**) of the Devala text (**17**), which also seems to place the brothers of the deceased ahead of the widow, Jīmūtavāhana discusses the restrictions to be placed on the term "widow" and on the kind of widows who are entitled to inherit (**47–49**).

[72] A *brāhmaṇa-cāṇḍāla* is a man who is a brahman in name only, but who behaves like an outcaste. Strictly speaking, a *cāṇḍāla* is the son of a *śūdra* father and a brahman mother. Cf. Rocher 1980–81.

> If one of several brothers dies without male offspring or becomes a wanderer, the others shall divide his property among themselves, with the exception of female property. [N 13.25/24]
> They shall provide lifelong maintenance to the deceased man's spouses, provided they remain faithful to their husband, but they shall discontinue it if they do not. [N 13.26/25]

Again, the same Sage says:

> Except for the property of brahmans.[73] A king who is intent on fulfilling his duties shall provide maintenance to the spouses of the deceased. Such is the law of inheritance. [N 13.52/49]

Providing maintenance to their spouses who are not "widows" is not incompatible with their "widows" being entitled to inherit the entire property. <**49**> That is why Bṛhaspati points out that the king takes the entire property in case there are no widows:

> If *kṣatriyas*, *vaiśyas*, or *śūdras* die without male offspring, and if they have no wives or brothers, the king shall take their property, for he is the master of everything. [B 26.119]

The apparent incompatibility with Nārada's "he shall provide maintenance to the spouses of the deceased" [N 13.52/49; **48**], according to which the king accedes to the entire property except for what he gives as maintenance, must be reconciled by the distinction between wives and spouses.

That is why Texts which deal with the widow's right to inherit use the term *patnī*, whereas those concerned with maintenance use words such as *strī*, *nārī*, *bhāryā*, and the like.[74]

<**50**> Now, to return to the Devala text [**17**]:

> Next, when a man dies without male offspring, his brothers german inherit his property, or else his daughters of equal standing, or else his father if he survives him, his brothers of the same caste, his mother, and his widow, in that order. Failing these, his property goes to those relatives who lived with him. [D 1570–1571; **11.5.6**]

"Daughters of the same standing" here means daughters of the same caste as their father's. "Brothers of the same caste" refers to sons of other wives of the father of the deceased; since brothers german have been mentioned in their own right earlier in the Text, the qualifier "of the same caste" cannot apply to them.

[73] This phrase concludes a sentence started in the preceding verse (N 13.51/48): "In the absence of all others, the property goes to the king" (on this, see **11.6.27**, **34**). The phrase is irrelevant in the present context: it is not Jīmūtavāhana's intention to restrict the application of N 13.52/49 to brahmans.

[74] Jīmūtavāhana alludes to a grammatical rule according to which the term *patnī* is derived from *pati*, "husband," to single out the wife who joins her husband in the performance of his ritual duties (*Aṣṭādhyāyī* 4.1.33: *patyur no yajñasaṃyoge*).

There is no problem here either.[75] The sequence beginning with brothers german and ending with the widow, as it appears in the Text, is not intended to establish the order in which these individuals inherit, for that would be incompatible with the texts of Viṣṇu [5] and others. It means that they shall get the property in the order prescribed by Viṣṇu and others.[76] To make it clear that the order in which he lists the heirs is of no importance, Devala twice uses the words "or else": "or else his daughters," and "or else his father," and this phrase applies elsewhere in the list as well. The Devala text itself thus makes the point that the order in which it lists the heirs—either brothers german, or daughters, or the father—is inconsequential.

<**51**> Bālaka proposed the following interpretation: "The text of Śaṅkha and others either pertains to widows of a different caste than that of their husband, or it is intended to apply to young widows,[77] or it pertains to brothers who were not separated or who were reunited." By thus professing that the scope of the *śāstras* is unsettled, he demonstrates that he is no wiser than a child. Indeed, when it is questionable to which of several situations a Text pertains, it cannot be invoked in any one of them.

<**52**> The interpretation of the Text about maintenance as pertaining to women whom a man kept in his house out of wedlock, must be rejected as well, out of regard for his duly wedded wives.[78] Indeed, the kinds of women to whom the rules about maintenance apply have already been mentioned earlier [**48–49**].

<**53**> Next, even if we were to grant that the widow's right to inherit before or after the brothers depends on whether or not her caste is the same as that of her husband, how does one reconcile the apparently incompatible rules on the order in

[75] At **45** Jīmūtavāhana returned to the text of Śaṅkha and others (**15**, to demonstrate that it does not cause any problem if interpreted correctly. He now returns to the Devala text quoted immediately after Śaṅkha's (**17**) to show that this verse does not cause any problems either.

[76] Jīmūtavāhana interprets *yathākramam*, "in that order," to refer not to the order in which the heirs are listed in the Devala text itself, but to the order established in other texts, i.e., "in the right order."

[77] The commentators attribute a rule to that effect to Hārīta (4.9): "Lest a youthful (*yauvanastha*) widow become a debauched woman, one should provide her with maintenance, to save her life." A "young widow" (*yuvati*) refers to a widow during the time of her life when she would normally have a husband to guard her. Cf. M 9.3: "Her father guards her in her childhood, her husband in her youth (*yauvana*), her son when she gets old: at no time should a woman be left on her own."

[78] Śrīkṛṣṇa and others attribute this intepretation to Bālaka as well. Yet, the point made here is different from what is attributed to Bālaka at **51**. With the phrase "the Text about maintenance" Jīmūtavāhana seems to refer to N 13.52/49 (**48**). The phrase "out of regard for his duly wedded wives" (*dharmapatnīnām anugrahārtham*) has been variously interpreted. Colebrooke's "as intending a favour to the matrons" reflects Śrīkṛṣṇa's commentary: "the term duly wedded wives here refers ironically to women a man kept in his house out of wedlock; the point is that, since they are not his wives, there is no reason that they should receive maintenance." Śrīkṛṣṇa, however, also adds the literal interpretation which I adopt in the translation.

which the parents and the brothers inherit? If this depends on whether or not they were reunited with the deceased, that should be the criterion throughout. What is the use of contriving other criteria such as being of the same caste when it comes to the widow? Besides, I have already rejected the distinction based on reunion or the absence thereof earlier in the discussion **[19–30]**.

<**54**> Finally, the distinction based on whether the brothers are brothers german or half brothers[79] is ruled out by Bṛhasapati:

> If a man dies without male offspring, his widow inherits his property, even when relatives such as his father, mother, or brothers german are extant. [B 26.94; **2**]

This Text shows that the widow accedes to the property even when brothers german—here called *sanābhi*—are extant. The phrase "his property" makes it clear that she gets the entire share of her husband, not just part of it.

<**55**> In conclusion, the true scope of the *śāstras* is well settled,[80] in the way I have shown.

The Widow's Limited Estate

<**56**> Note that the only right the widow has is the usufruct of her husband's property; she may not gift, mortgage, or sell it. Indeed,

[A] Kātyāyana says:

> If a widow who has no male offspring remains faithful to her husband[81] and continues to live with one of the elders, she may, within reason,[82] enjoy the usufruct of his property till she dies; after that it goes to her husband's heirs. [K 921; cf. **11.2.30**]

[79] I.e., brothers german would take the property prior to the widow, the widow prior to half brothers.

[80] As opposed to the unsettled state advocated by Bālaka (**51**).

[81] Based on the principle that "what (their Lordships) have to consider is not so much what inference can be drawn from the words of Catyayana's text taken by itself, as what are the conclusions which the author of the Dayabhaga has himself drawn from them" (Sir James Colville, in *Collector of Madura* v. *Moottoo Ramalinga Sathupathy* [1868] 12 M.I.A. 397, 436), the Privy Council, *per* Sir Barnes Peacock, used Jīmūtavāhana's silence on the phrase "remains faithful to her husband" throughout the following paragraphs (**57–64**) to rule that it would be wrong to infer "that, in his opinion, the text implied continuous chastity as a condition for the duration of her estate, or that a breach of chastity subsequent to the death of her husband would operate as a forfeiture of her right" (*Moniram Kolita* v. *Keri Kolitani* [1880] 5 Cal. 776, 785–86).

[82] The Sanskrit term *kṣāntā*, which I translate "within reason," is ambiguous. Rather than putting a restriction on the extent to which the widow can use the property, *kṣāntā* may also refer to a moral requirement: "if she remains quiet, patient."

<**57**> "If she continues to live with one of the elders," i.e., in her husband's family together with her father-in-law and the like, "she may enjoy the usufruct" of her husband's property for as long as she lives. Differently from her female property, however, she may not also gift, mortgage, or sell it as she pleases.

When the widow dies, the property goes to those who would have been entitled to inherit it if she had not been there; i.e., it goes to daughters and so forth. Indeed,

[1] it does not go to her relatives. These cannot bar daughters and so forth because they rank lower than them. In fact, it is not a question of barring at all, for, the widow being the one who barred the daughters and so forth, her relatives are as unable to bar them after the widow's right lapses as they were before she exercised her right.[83]

[2] <**58**> Nor does the property go to those who are entitled to inherit the widow's female property. First, these people's claim is only to her female property. Second, since Kātyāyana himself deals with those who are entitled to female property in other verses, this would amount to a useless tautology.

<**59**> Hence, even as all those listed at Yājñavalkya 2.135 [**4**]—each latter one failing each former one—would have taken the property had there been no widow to begin with, in the same way they acquire whatever is left after the widow's right to the usufruct of the property lapses.

Since at that time the daughters and so on are of greater service to the deceased than anyone else, it is only proper that they inherit the property.

[B] <**60**> In the *Dānadharma* it is said:[84]

> Widows may enjoy the usufruct of their husbands' inheritance, but under no circumstances may they detract from it.[85] [Mbh 13.47.24]

<**61**> Even though they may enjoy the usufruct of the property, they may not use it to dress themselves with fancy clothes and the like. On the other hand, since they are of service to their husbands by taking good care of their own physical needs, they can legitimately use the usufruct for anything suitable for that purpose. In the same way they are allowed to dispose of whatever is required to perform their husbands' funeral rites and the like. That is why the Text says "may not detract from"; detract here means use it for a purpose that is not useful for the prior owner of the property. <**62**> That is also why even a mortgage is allowable if it is the only way for her to support herself. And if even that is not enough, she may go as far as to sell the property, for the rationale is the same in all these cases.

[83] On the concepts of prior nonexistence and subsequent nonexistence, see note at **6.1.27**.

[84] A number of *Dāyabhāga* manuscripts add "in the *Mahābhārata*" after "in the *Dānadharma*." Jīmūtavāhana's reading of the verse is different from that in the critical edition of the *Mahābhārata*, and it does not appear in its critical apparatus.

[85] The Sanskrit text says that the widow should not cause *apahāra* of her husband's inheritance. On the negative connotation of this term, see note at **13.2**.

<**63**> For the sake of her husband's funeral rites she should make to his paternal uncles and so forth gifts that are commensurate with the property at hand. Says Bṛhaspati:

> She shall honor with gifts to the dead and to the living her husband's paternal uncles, parents, daughters' sons, sisters' sons, and maternal uncles, as well as the aged, the poor, guests, and women.[86] [B 26.98; **2**]

The term "paternal uncles" here means all her husband's *sapiṇḍas*. The term "daughters' sons" means any descendants of her husband's daughters. The term "sisters' sons" means any descendants of her husband's sisters. The term "maternal uncles" means the family of her husband's mother. In other words, she should make gifts to these and other like persons, but, as long as such people are extant, not to members of her own father's family, for that would render the words "paternal uncles" and so forth redundant. <**64**> With their permission, however, she may also make gifts to the families of her own father and mother.[87] Says Nārada:

> After her husband's death his family is master of his widow if she has no male offspring. They oversee her expenditures, her savings,[88] and her maintenance. [N 13.28/27]
> If her husband's family is extinct, without males, or without resources, and if none of his *sapiṇḍas* are left, her own father's family is master of the widow. [N 13.29/28]

"Expenditures" means gifts and the like.[89] If her husband leaves no male offspring, she is a ward of his family.

<**65**> What has been said so far about the widow also holds true for daughters:[90] even though the daughter's right to inherit took effect, those who get her father's property after she dies are those who would have inherited that property had there been no daughter, not those who are entitled to inherit the daughter's own property.

<**66**> Note that a widow may gift one quarter of her husband's property to marry off a daughter. Since the right to make such a gift is explicitly given to

[86] For the translation of this verse, see notes 5 and 6.

[87] At first sight it is not clear how N 13.28/27 supports this statement. According to Śrīkṛṣṇa, if the widow's expenditures are under the control of her in-laws, it is obvious that she may make gifts to her own family with their permission.

[88] The reading *artharakṣā*, which I translate as "savings," is unique to the *Dāyabhāga* and the *Vivādārṇavasetu* (*Dhko* p. 1555). Elsewhere the reading is *ātmarakṣā*, "to regulate her mode of life" (Jolly: N tr.), "to protect her" (Lariviere: N tr.). Possibly under the influence of *ātmarakṣā* in the *Digest* (4.1.13: "the government of herself") Colebrooke here translates "care of herself."

[89] According to Bhavasvāmin, the commentator on the *Manunāradīyasaṃhitā* (13. 27), the term *viniyoga*, translated here as "expenditures," is synonymous with *niyoga*, "levirate." In that case the in-laws decide whether the widow should have a *kṣetraja* son.

[90] In fact, Śrīkṛṣṇa notes, it holds true a fortiori (*sutarām*) for the daughters of the deceased, because they are less "venerable, honorable" (*abhyarhita*) than his widow.

sons,[91] it follows as a matter of course[92] that a widow and others have that right as well.

<**67**> Thus far for the widow's right to inherit her husband's property.

[91] "Sons" here means the brothers of the bride. Cf. **3.34–35**.
[92] On the application of the *daṇḍāpūpa-nyāya*, see note at **2.25**.

CHAPTER ELEVEN
SECTION TWO

DAUGHTERS AND DAUGHTERS' SONS

<1> Failing the deceased man's widow, his daughters are entitled to inherit his property.[1]

On this subject Manu and Nārada say:

> A man's son is just like himself, and a daughter is equal to a son. How can anyone else get the father's property while she, who is like himself, lives? [M 9.130][2]

Nārada further specifies the term "daughter":

> Failing sons,[3] the daughter, for sons and daughters equally provide their father with descendants. Both a son and a daughter perpetuate their father's lineage. [N 13.50/47]

The necessary and sufficient condition set here for the daughter to inherit is that she provide her father with a descendant, and the term "descendant" more specifically means someone who offers *piṇḍas*. Indeed, if a person does not offer *piṇḍas* to the deceased, he is of no service to him; he is then in no way different from a person who is someone else's descendant or from something that is no one's descendant.[4]

<2> Note that a deceased man's daughter's son offers *piṇḍas* to him, whereas his daughter's son's son does not, nor does his daughter's daughter. With them the offering of *piṇḍas* comes to an end. <3> One should, therefore, heed Dīkṣita's opinion: "A daughter is entitled to inherit if she has a son or if she is capable of having one; she does not inherit if she cannot have sons, either because she is a widow, or because she is barren, or because she has only daughters."

[1] Jīmūtavāhana is silent on the interpretation of the general term *duhitṛ*, "daughter," in the narrow sense of "appointed daughter" (*putrikā*), which was proposed by two of the predecessors whom he quotes elsewhere in the *Dāyabhāga*. We know that this was the case with Viśvarūpa (on Y 2.139) and, according to the *Smṛticandrikā* (ed. p. 684), with Dhāreśvara (as well as Devasvāmin and Devarāta). Vijñāneśvara (on Y 2.135; Colebrooke II.ii.5) explicitly rejects that interpretation.

[2] Even though this verse is attributed to Manu and Nārada, or even to Nārada alone, in other commentaries and digests (*Dhko* pp. 1294, 1512), it is absent from the *Nārada-smṛti*.

[3] I translate "sons," in the plural, in view of Jīmūtavāhana's comment (**27**).

[4] On the phrase "something that is no one's descendant" Śrīkṛṣṇa comments: a pot and similar things.

<**4**> If there are different kinds of daughters, the unmarried daughter inherits her father's property first. Indeed,

[A] Parāśara says:

> When a man dies without male offspring, his unmarried daughter gets the inheritance; failing her, a married daughter. [*Dhko* p. 1527]

The phrase "married daughter" here refers to a married daughter as specified above.[5]

[B] <**5**> Devala says:

> Unmarried daughters should be given what is required for their weddings out of their father's property; if the father has no appointed daughter, his own, legitimately born unmarried daughter gets his inheritance, like a son. [D 1598]

The "appointed daughter" here subsumes the son. "His own" means that she must belong to the same caste as her father's. "Legitimately born" means that she must be of the *aurasa* type.[6]

<**6**> It also makes sense that the unmarried daughter should inherit first, for there are Texts to the effect that, should a daughter remain unmarried for lack of resources, she causes her father and others to go to hell when she starts menstruating. Indeed,

[A] Vasiṣṭha says:[7]

> Each time an unmarried girl menstruates after she was asked in marriage by a man of equal caste, and she herself is willing to be wedded, her father and mother kill a living being.[8] Such is the rule of the law. [Va 17.71]

[B] Paiṭhīnasi says:

> A girl should be given in marriage before she develops breasts. If she is unmarried when she begins to menstruate, both he who ought to have given her away and he who should have taken her go to hell. Her father, his father, and the latter's father are reborn as worms in feces. Hence she must be given in marriage before she reaches puberty. [Pai 11]

[5] I.e., a daughter who has a son or is capable of having one (**3**). By saying that Jīmūtavāhana's phrase "the unmarried daughter alone" (*kanyā eva*) excludes the daughter who has been promised in marriage (*dattā*), Śrīnātha and Śrīkṛṣṇa subsume the latter under the title "married daughter." However, "this doctrine is not concurred in by any other authority" (Elberling 1844: 75).

[6] On *aurasa*, "full-fledged," mostly used for sons rather than for daughters, see note at **10.1** and Introduction.

[7] A number of *Dāyabhāga* editions and some manuscripts attribute this passage to Viṣṇu; it does not, however, appear in the *Viṣṇu-smṛti*.

[8] Instead of *bhūta*, "living being," the *Vasiṣṭha-dharmasūtra* reads *bhrūṇa*, "embryo."

<7>In conclusion, by being fit to be given in marriage a daughter saves her father and others from hell;[9] and, once married, she is also of service to them through her son. For these two reasons, property going to her directly benefits its prior owner. It stands to reason, then, that, failing his widow, a man's property goes to his unmarried daughter.

<**8**> Failing unmarried daughters, the right to inherit belongs to the married daughter who is capable of having a son and to the married daughter who has a son.[10] Says Bṛhaspati:

> If she is like him, married to a husband like her, and submissive to her husband, she gets her father's property if he dies without male offspring, whether he appointed her or not. [B 26.132; **18**]

<**9**> A daughter "like him" means a daughter who belongs to the same caste as her father. "Married to a husband like her" means that her husband should not be of a higher or lower caste than hers, because the son of a daughter married above or below her caste is barred from performing funeral rites for his maternal grandfather and so forth who belong to a lower or higher caste, respectively.[11] A daughter who is married to a man of the same caste, on the other hand, is of service to her father through her son.

<**10**> Since an appointed daughter is equal to a son on the grounds that her son is of the highest service to her father, exactly like a real son, an appointed daughter and a full-fledged son have equal rights to inherit their father's property [**10.1–6**]. The difference with a daughter who was married without being appointed is that she is of service through the intermediary of her son, who is of less service than a son and so forth. It, therefore, makes sense that her right to inherit her father's property takes effect only when there are no other potential heirs up to and including an unmarried daughter.

[Objection] <**11**> Judging by this criterion,[12] a daughter who has a son should inherit first and alone and, only failing her, a daughter who is capable of having a son.

[Refutation] Not so. Indeed,

[9] Or "because the property she inherits from her father can be used for her wedding, it saves her father and others from hell." Cf. Colebrooke: "Since then the father and the rest are saved from hell by sufficient property becoming applicable to the charges of the marriage."

[10] Jīmūtavāhana's refutation of the objection introduced at **11** makes it clear that, in his opinion, both kinds of married daughters inherit jointly.

[11] Contrary to what he said earlier (**9.3**), Jīmūtavāhana clearly refers here to a situation in which the wife is of a higher caste than her husband. This statement was criticized as "unacceptable" by Mitramiśra: "The word 'married' excludes the possibility of a husband of a lower caste, for a woman of a higher caste cannot marry a man of a lower caste. Therefore, the only purpose of the phrase 'like her' is to exclude a husband of a higher caste" (*Vyahāraprakāśa* ed. p. 519; tr. III.ii.3).

[12] I.e., if being of service to the deceased is the sole criterion to establish the order of succession.

[1] if a son was to be born to the latter at some later time, he would then not be entitled to inherit at all. That, however, would not make sense, for in their capacity of daughters' sons the one born prior to partition and the one born after it are of equal service to their maternal grandfather.

[2] <**12**> By saying that his Text pertains to a woman who is "submissive to her husband" and thereby showing that it applies to any married daughter who is not a widow, Bṛhaspati points out that the Text does bear on a married daughter who is capable of having a son.[13]

<**13**> Note that the word "she" in this Text refers back to "a daughter" mentioned in an earlier verse [B 26.127; **14**]. In other words, by means of the qualifiers that she ought to be "like him," "married to a husband like her," and so forth, Bṛhaspati shows that the daughter's right to inherit does not result from the mere fact that she is a daughter. <**14**> Otherwise, if the earlier verse:

> Even as a son a daughter is born of a man's every limb. How could anyone other than she get her father's property, [B 26.127]

had established that the right to inherit belongs to "the daughter," mentioning that right again with the phrases "like him," "married to a husband like her," and so on, would be redundant. But, if Bṛhaspati 26.132 further specifies what the earlier verse established in general terms, there is no redundancy whatever.

<**15**> The same condition under which a daughter is entitled to inherit her father's property, namely, that through her son she offers *piṇḍas* to him, also obtains in the case of an appointed daughter. If an appointed daughter accedes to her father's property at the time of his death, and if she later dies without leaving a son, either because she was barren or because her husband was impotent, her property does not go to her husband. Indeed,

[A] Śaṅkha and Likhita say:

> If an appointed daughter dies without leaving a son,[14] her husband does not get her property. [ŚL 295]

[B] Paiṭhīnasi says:

> If an appointed daughter dies without leaving a son, her husband does not get her property. It goes to her unmarried sister, or else to another sister. [Pai 120]

[13] I.e., the criterion that allows a daughter to inherit at B 26.132 is not that she have a son, in which case the widowed daughter who has a son would have been included. The sole criterion mentioned in this text is that the daughter be married, irrespective of whether she has a son or is capable of having one.

[14] The term *aputrāyāḥ*, "without leaving a son," appended to a half verse *pretāyāḥ putrikāyās tu na bhartā dravyam arhati*, appears in all *Dāyabhāga* manuscripts. Kane omitted the half verse in his edition of the Śaṅkha-Likhita fragments; the editor of the *Dharmakośa* (p. 1429) wondered whether it should be taken as part of the quotation or as Jīmūtavāhana's commentary. The only other commentary in which the fragment appears, including *aputrāyāḥ*, is Aparārka's (on Y 2.145).

As a result, the property of an appointed daughter goes either to an unmarried sister, or to another sister who has a son or is capable of having one,[15] so that as long as there is a female who is entitled to inherit, her right prevails over the right of anyone else.

<**16**> As for the Manu text:[16]

> Should an appointed daughter die without leaving a son, her husband gets the property without fail, [M 9.135]

that must be taken to pertain to the death not of an appointed daughter who did not have a son, but to the death of one who had a son who did not survive her.

<**17**> Bṛhaspati further elaborates on the offering of *piṇḍas* as the one and only condition to inherit both for a daughter and for her son:

> Even as she becomes the owner of her father's property even if he has kin, in the same way her son, too, becomes the owner of his maternal grandfather's property.[17] [B 26.133]

"Even as," i.e., because of the *piṇḍa* that will be offered to him by her son, a daughter is entitled to inherit her father's property, "in the same way," i.e., on account of the same *piṇḍa* offering the daughter's son, too, becomes the owner of his maternal grandfather's property, even if the latter's father or other kin are extant.

<**18**> Note that Bṛhaspati 26.133 is not meant exclusively for the son of an appointed daughter.[18] Indeed,

[1] the pronoun "she" and the pronoun "her" in "her son" refer to the appointed daughter and to the nonappointed daughter, both of whom are mentioned in the preceding half verse:

> Whether appointed or not appointed, she gets her father's property if he dies without male offspring. [B 26.132cd; **8**]

The only reasonable alternative would be that the pronouns at Bṛhaspati 26.133 refer exclusively to a nonappointed daughter, for they are closer to "not appointed" than to "appointed" at Bṛhaspati 26.132cd. Under no circumstances, however, would it be reasonable to assume that they exclude the nonappointed daughter.[19]

[2] <**19**> That is also why Manu says:

[15] The phrase "who has a son" is omitted in several *Dāyabhāga* manuscripts.

[16] On the meaning of the introductory phrase "as for" (*yat tu*), see note at **2.9**.

[17] The term *mātṛmātāmaha*, which I translate "his maternal grandfather's property," is ambiguous: it can also mean "his mother's and his maternal grandfather's property" (thus Jha: *Vivādacintāmaṇi* tr. 272, even though, in a footnote, he refers to the maternal grandfather's property only; also Sarkar: *Vivādaratnākara* tr. XIX.9).

[18] Such is the view of the *Vivādaratnākara* (ed. #1582; tr. XIX.9). The *Vyavahāraprakāśa* (ed. p. 521; tr. III.iii.2), on the other hand, agrees with the *Dāyabhāga*.

[19] In the phrase "appointed or not appointed" (*kṛtā akṛtā vā*) in the preceding verse (B 26.132cd), the nonappointed daughter is mentioned last. The pronouns "she" and "her" in the next verse (B 26.133), therefore, refer either to both kinds of daughter or to the one mentioned last, definitely not to the one mentioned first only.

> A daughter's son gets the entire inheritance of his mother's father if his grandfather dies without male offspring; he shall offer *piṇḍas* both to his own father and to his maternal grandfather. [M 9.132]
>
> By law there is no difference in this world between a son's son and a daughter's son, for their respective father and mother are the issue of the body of the same man. [M 9.133]

The necessary and sufficient condition for a daughter's son to inherit mentioned in this Text is that his mother be born of the body of his maternal grandfather. It is not also necessary for her to have been made an appointed daughter; if it was, the Text would have said so.

[3] <**20**> Elsewhere the same Sage clearly says:

> When a daughter, whether appointed or not appointed, has a son by a husband of the same caste, her father has a son's son who offers *piṇḍas* for him and inherits his property. [M 9.136; **10.3**]

This Text explicitly affirms the daughter's son's right to inherit, even if he is the son of a daughter who was not appointed.

[4] <**21**> Some Texts use the term "daughter's son" in the restricted sense of a son of a nonappointed daughter.[20] E.g., Baudhāyana, with the phrase "one should know that" carried over from a preceding rule, says:

> A son born of a daughter after a covenant has been made is "the son of an appointed daughter"; any other is "a daughter's son." [Bau 2.2.3.15]

[5] <**22**> That is also why, when Bhojadeva quotes Bṛhaspati 26.133 [**17**], he introduces it with the words: "On the right to inherit of appointed and nonappointed daughters, Bṛhaspati says."

<**23**> In his commentary on the *Manu-smṛti* Govindarāja on his part asserts that a daughter's son is entitled to inherit prior to a married daughter, on the basis of the following Viṣṇu text:

> When a man dies without leaving a son or a son's son, his daughter's son gets his property, for sons' sons and daughters' sons are equal with regard to the performance of funeral rites for their ancestors.[21]

<**24**> I cannot agree with him on this point, for it would be incompatible with Bṛhaspati 26.132 [**8**]. <**25**> In fact, it is only when there is no married daughter as

[20] The idea is that the term *dauhitra*, "daughter's son," is occasionally, as at Bau 2.2.3.15, used to indicate the son of a daughter who was not appointed, to distinguish him from the son of an appointed daughter who is then referred to as *putrikā-putra*. Hence the *dauhitra* who is said to be entitled to inherit his maternal grandfather's property at M 9.132 and M 9.133 (**19**), cannot exclude the son of a nonappointed daughter.

[21] This text is often quoted and attributed to Viṣṇu (*Dhko* p. 1471); yet it does not appear in the *Viṣṇu-smṛti*. I translate *pūrveṣām*, "ancestors," literally, even though the person meant here more specifically is the paternal/maternal grandfather.

qualified there that the daughter's son inherits, even if the deceased man's father or other kin are still extant. First, the phrase "in the same way" at Bṛhaspati 26.133 [**17**] enjoins that a daughter's son is only "similar to" daughters. Second, the phrase "her son too" in the same Text is intended to indicate that a daughter's son inherits "as well."[22] It follows that daughters' sons inherit immediately after, but only after, all daughters.

<**26**> What the phrase "even if he has kin" at Bṛhaspati 26.133 [**17**] indicates is [1] that, although it might seem logical that, failing a deceased man's widow, his parents should inherit his property, they are barred by his daughters and daughters' sons; and [2] that, as a result, if these are not there to bar them, the parents are entitled to inherit. That is why, in the next verse, Bṛhaspati goes on to say:

> Failing these, his brothers german, brothers' sons, *sakulyas*, *bāndhavas*, disciples, and learned brahmans get his property. [B 26. 134]

The word "these" here refers not only to daughters' sons but also to the parents who were hinted at in the earlier verse.[23] Hence, failing all these, the property goes to the deceased man's brothers and so forth.

<**27**> Bālaka's statement to the effect that "since Yājñavalkya 2.135 [**11.1.4**] establishes a strict order of succession: the widow, daughters, parents, and brothers, the daughter's son is only entitled to inherit after them" is no more than a babe's babble.[24] Indeed,

[1] it is incompatible with Bṛhaspati 26.133 [**17**].

[2] The mere fact that, at Yājñavalkya 2.135, the word "daughters" is expressed in the plural means that it indicates the unmarried daughter, the married daughter, and the daughter's son.[25] The latter's right to inherit prior to the father and so forth, therefore, is not incompatible with Yājñavalkya's order of succession.

One might compare the case at hand with Śaṅkha and Likhita: "when a man passes away 'without male offspring' (*a-putra*)" [**11.1.15**], where the word *putra*, "son," subsumes the male descendants down to the great-grandson because they all equally offer *piṇḍas* to the deceased. In the same way the word "daughters" in the Yājñavalkya text subsumes the daughter's son, for he, too, offers *piṇḍas* to his maternal grandfather. Or, one might compare it with Nārada: "failing sons, the daughter, for sons and daughters equally provide their father with descendants" [**1**], where the word "sons" means all heirs down to and including the widow.

[22] Jīmūtavāhana asserts that the particle *api* in *tatsuto 'pi*, "her son too," must be taken literally: a daughter's son "as well," but only if there are no daughters.

[23] The parents were not mentioned specifically but "hinted at" with the word "kin" (*bandhu*), at B 26.132.

[24] On Jīmūtavāhana's reference to Bāla(ka)'s statement as *bāla-vacana*, "a babe's babble," see Introduction. The three arguments that follow can be summarized thus: [1] Bālaka's statement is incompatible with B 26.133; [2] "daughters" at Y 2.135 subsumes daughters' sons; [3] if it did not, the daughters' sons would never inherit.

[25] In Sanskrit, which has a dual form to indicate two items, the plural inevitably refers to a minimum of three.

Otherwise there would have been no point using the plural form "daughters," and Yājñavalkya would have used the singular, as he does for "widow" and "son." I will explain later why the plural form "brothers" is meaningful as well [**11.5.37**].

[3] <**28**> Since there is a strict order of succession from the parents to the king [Vi 17.3–14; **11.1.5**], one would have to conclude that the daughter's son inherits only failing the king. Since, however, there never is a time when there is no king, that would mean that the Yājñavalkya text denies the daughter's son any right to inherit whatever.

<**29**> In conclusion, one must heed the view of Viśvarūpa,[26] Jitendriya, Bhojadeva, and Govindarāja to the effect that, failing daughters, daughters' sons inherit.

<**30**> Note that, if an unmarried daughter inherited and dies after she was married at a later time,[27] then, even though she dies after her right to inherit took effect, the property goes exclusively to the married daughters and so forth, i.e., to those to whom it would have gone had the unmarried daughter died before the right was invested in her. The property does not go to her husband and so forth, because their right to inherit from her pertains to her female property [**4.3.**].

Kātyāyana 921 [**11.1.56**] demonstrates with regard to the widow that, if she dies after her right to inherit from her husband took effect, the property goes to her daughters and so on, i.e., to those who would have qualified as heirs to the previous owner had the widow died before the right was invested in her. It follows, as a matter of course,[28] that the same is true for daughters and daughters' sons, since their right to inherit is of a lower order than that of the widow. <**31**> Or else, the term "widow" at Kātyāyana 921 is to be taken synecdochically, in which case the idea is that the same is true for a woman's right to inherit generally.[29]

[26] In the printed text Viśvarūpa uses Y 2.134 (= *Bālakrīḍā* 2.138) (**9.31**), according to which the illegitimate son of a *śūdra* inherits everything if the *śūdra* has no legitimate sons *and no daughters' sons*, to conclude that among the twice-born castes, too, failing sons, the inheritance goes to daughters' sons. Kane (1925: 223) may make too much of the order in which the four commentators are listed in this *Dāyabhāga* paragraph, when he suggests that Viśvarūpa was "probably the first jurist to expressly recognize the daughter's son as an heir after the daughter."

[27] And, according to Śrīkṛṣṇa (in his *Dāyabhāga* commentary and at *Dāyādhikārakramasaṃgraha* I.3), if she leaves no son. This implies that, if there is a son, the inheritance goes to him. Śrīkṛṣṇa's proviso was accepted in some early British treatises on Hindu law, e.g., W. H. Macnaghten (1829: 24–25) and Elberling (1844: 76), but it was rejected by a Full Bench in *Tinumoni Dasi* v. *Nibarun Chunder Gupta* (1882) 9 Cal. 154, 161–62.

[28] Another application of the *daṇḍāpūpa-nyāya*. Cf. **2.25**.

[29] J. N. Bhattacharya (1893: 477–78) uses this passage to show that, if several reasons separated by such particles as "or else" (*yadvā*) are given to justify a statement, only the last reason represents the author's opinion: "The reason here given for the doctrine that the estate taken by daughters is similar to that taken by widows, can by no means be accepted as correct. For if the fact of the daughter's pretensions being inferior to those of the widow's be the cause of the similarity, then the estate taken by the daughter's son and other remoter heirs must be equally limited. The reason first adduced being thus untenable, a second reason is given in para. 31, which is unexceptionable." I do not read Jīmūtavāhana's first rea-

<**32**> Thus far for the right to inherit of daughters and daughters' sons.

sons—here and elsewhere in the *Dāyabhāga*—as being intentionally unconvincing and incorrect; I understand them as true first reasons to which, lest they appear unconvincing to some, Jīmūtavāhana subjoins additional arguments.

CHAPTER ELEVEN
SECTION THREE

THE FATHER

<**1**> Failing daughters' sons, the father is entitled to inherit, not the mother,[1] nor both parents together,[2] for that would be incompatible with the Viṣṇu text:

> Failing these,[3] the deceased man's property goes to his father; failing him, to his mother.[4] [Vi 17.6–7; **11.1.5**]

<**2**> As for the Manu text:[5]

> If a son dies without offspring, his mother gets his inheritance; if his mother and others are deceased, his father's mother also gets it,[6] [M 9.217]

and the Bṛhaspati text:

> If a son dies without leaving a widow or a son, his mother gets his inheritance, or, if she consents, his brother, [B 26.135cdef]

these Texts must be taken to refer to cases in which there are no heirs up to and including the father.

<**3**> It also stands to reason that the father inherits after the daughter's son, but prior to the mother. Indeed,

[1] the father, who offers two *piṇḍas* to others in which the deceased shares, ranks lower than the daughter's son, who, in addition to offering two *piṇḍas* to others in which the deceased shares, also offers a *piṇḍa* to the deceased himself.[7]

[1] According to the *Mitākṣarā* (on Y 2.135; Colebrooke II.iii.1–5) and a number of other commentaries (Jolly 1885: 203-04), the mother inherits prior to the father. Cf. Derrett 1952a: 5 (= *Essays* 1.202). Jīmūtavāhana addresses two texts that appear to support this view at **2**.

[2] That conclusion might be drawn from the term *pitarau*, "both parents," at Y 2.135 (**11.1.4**). Jīmūtavāhana rejects this interpretation at **4–5**.

[3] In fact, at Vi 17.6 "these" does not refer to daughters' sons, but to daughters.

[4] Some *Dāyabhāga* manuscripts and editions quote Vi 17.7 only.

[5] For the meaning of "as for," see note at **2.9**.

[6] Even though the second half of the verse is irrelevant in the present context, I abstain from a literal translation: "if his mother is deceased as well, his father's mother gets it," to conform to Jīmūtavāhana's tortuous interpretation of the text at **11.4.4–6**.

[7] The father offers *piṇḍas* to his F, FF, and FFF, i.e. to the deceased man's FF, FFF, and FFFF. The deceased shares in those to his FF and FFF. The daughter's son, in addition

[2] On the other hand, the father ranks higher than the mother and so on, first, because he offers *piṇḍas* to two others in which the deceased share, and, second, because the following Manu text clearly spells out that he is superior to her:

> Of the sperm and the womb, the sperm is held to be superior. [M 9.35ab]

<**4**> In the term "parents" (*pitarau* Y 2.135; **11.1.4**), too, it is clear that the father comes first, the mother later. Since the word for "father" (*pitṛ*) is the nominal base of the word *pitarau*, it is clear that the father is primary; the dual ending *-au* added to that base secondarily includes the mother, by ellipsis.[8]

<**5**> Hence, it is not right to make the following inference: "one may conclude that parents inherit one after the other only when there is an explicit statement to that effect in a Text; since the term *pitarau* at Yājñavalkya 2.135 does not provide that explicit statement, it is not possible to conclude from it that parents inherit one after the other."[9] First, it is not an established fact that *pitarau* does not say so explicitly.[10] Second, the parents inheriting jointly would be incompatible with the Viṣṇu text above [**1**].

<**6**> Thus far for the father's right to inherit.

---

to the *piṇḍas* offered to his paternal ancestors, offers *piṇḍas* to his MF, MFF, and MFFF, i.e., not only to the deceased man's FF and FFF, but also to the deceased himself.

[8] Jīmūtavāhana alludes to a form of interpretation that is current among Indian grammarians: the word *pitarau* actually means *pitṛ(mātar)au* (cf. *Aṣṭādhyāyī* 1.2.70). On "ellipsis" (*ekaśeṣa*), see note at **3.2**.

[9] In this paragraph Jīmūtavāhana uses technical vocabulary of Indian "logic" (*nyāya*). According to the standard example of a valid inference, to be able to infer that there is fire when one sees smoke, fire (the *probandum*) has to be invariably present (*vyāpya*) when there is smoke (the *probans*); i.e., there is fire wherever there is smoke, and, conversely, there is no smoke when there is no fire. In the case at hand the opponent holds that the dual form *pitarau*, "both parents," does not always and invariably mean "the parents in succession," i.e., the father first, the mother second, and, therefore, that it is not a valid *probans* (*vyāpaka*) from which to derive that conclusion in the specific case of *pitarau* at Y 2.135.

[10] I.e., as Jīmūtavāhana demonstrated at **4**.

CHAPTER ELEVEN
SECTION FOUR

THE MOTHER

<1> Failing the father, the mother is entitled to inherit. Immediately after dealing with the father's right to inherit, the Viṣṇu text continues:

> Failing him, it goes to the mother. [Vi 17.7; **11.1.5**]

<2> This also makes sense, for it stands to reason that the mother is entitled to inherit prior to the brothers of the deceased. Indeed,

[1] she must of necessity be compensated for having been of service to her son by everything she did for him while carrying him in her womb and while nurturing him.[1]

[2] She is of service to her deceased son by being the person who gave birth to other sons who offer *piṇḍas* in which the deceased shares.

<3> To come back to Vi 17.7, that Text means that one must reject the notion that the mother should be entitled to inherit prior to the father because there are Texts that describe her as more deserving of respect than the father.[2] Indeed, if being more deserving of respect was the necessary and sufficient condition for a person to accede to property,

[1] the teacher would be entitled to inherit prior to the father, in accordance with Manu:

> Of his two fathers, the one who begets him and the one who gives him the Veda, it is the one who gives him the Veda who is more deserving of respect; [M 2.146ab]

[2] a paternal uncle and so forth would be entitled to inherit even when a younger brother or a brother's son is living.

Hence it is said that the mother inherits only after the father.

<4> Note that, by saying that the mother is entitled to inherit after the father of the deceased but prior to the father's offspring, one thereby also indicates that the father's mother is entitled to inherit the property of her son after the paternal

[1] Or "by nurturing him while carrying him in her womb."

[2] According to M 2.145, for example, the mother is one thousand times more deserving of respect (*gaurava*) than the father. Such texts, the sole purpose of which is to extol persons or objects, are not supposed to be taken at face value. The same verse, indeed, also says that the father is one thousand times more deserving of respect than the teacher, which contradicts M 2.146ab quoted immediately hereafter.

grandfather but prior to the paternal grandfather's offspring. To do otherwise would be incompatible with the sequence "parents, then brothers" [Y 2.135; **11.1.4**].

That is why Manu:

> If his mother and others are deceased, his father's mother also gets it, [M 9.217cd; **11.3.2**]

means: if his mother and her offspring are deceased. <**5**> The words "and others" and "also" must be construed each with a different half of the sentence.[3] As a result, when the mother and others are deceased, not only does the father's mother inherit but also, a fortiori, the brothers and so forth up to and including the paternal grandfather. The brothers and so forth are subsumed by the word "also." <**6**> The meaning of Manu 9.217cd, therefore, is as follows. Parents are entitled to inherit, in the order established earlier, after the offspring of the deceased down to and including his daughter's son, but prior to their own offspring. By the same token the Text shows that, subsequently, the paternal grandfather and the paternal grandmother likewise inherit prior to their offspring.

That is also why Yajñavalkya [2.135; **11.1.4**] does not mention the grandparents separately, on the grounds that, merely by citing the example of the mother's right to inherit, he also indicates that the paternal grandfather and the paternal grandmother inherit prior to the paternal uncles and so forth.

<**7**> Thus far for the mother's right to inherit.

[3] This interpretation obviously stretches the Manu text: *mātary api ca vṛttāyāṃ pitur mātā hared dhanam*, literally "if his mother is deceased as well, his father's mother inherits the property." In Sanskrit *api ca*—rather *apica*, *ca* being enclitic—normally go together and mean "also, as well." Yet, here Jīmūtavāhana separates them. He construes *ca* with *mātari* and resorts to a device often used by the commentators: *mātari ca* means "his mother and others," in this case, her offspring. He then lifts *api* out of the first half of the sentence and construes it with the second half: *pitur mātā api*, "his father's mother also," i.e., the paternal grandmother inherits after "others," from the deceased man's brothers (who inherit after the mother) up to the paternal grandfather.

CHAPTER ELEVEN
SECTION FIVE

BROTHERS

Brothers Inherit after the Mother

<1> Failing the deceased man's mother, his property goes to his brothers. Indeed,

[A] after the words "it goes to his mother" [**11.4.1**], the Viṣṇu text continues:

Failing her, it goes to his brothers. [Vi 17.8; **11.1.5**]

"Her" here refers to the mother.

[B] "Parents, then brothers" [Y 2.135; **11.1.4**], too, makes it clear that, failing parents, brothers are entitled to inherit.

Brothers Inherit prior to Brothers' Sons

<2> It would be wrong to claim that, based on Yājñavalkya 2.135, immediately after the mother a brother's son has the same right to inherit as his father.[1] Indeed,

[1] if so, Yājñavalkya 2.135 would be incompatible with the Viṣṇu text which, after the words "it goes to his brothers," continues: "failing them, to his brothers' sons" [Vi 17.9; **11.1.5**. **11.6.1**]. "Them" there refers to the brothers.

[2] **<3>** It also stands to reason that the brothers inherit first, for a brother is of service to the deceased by offering to three ascendants *piṇḍas* in which the deceased shares.[2] In addition, he substitutes for his deceased brother by offering the three *piṇḍas* which the latter would have had to offer to their maternal grandfather

[1]Jīmūtavāhana's first concern (**2–8**) is to prove that brothers inherit prior to brothers' sons. The relevant and potentially ambiguous section of Y 2.135 reads: *pitarau bhrātaras tathā tatsutāḥ*. Jīmūtavāhana insists that the conjunction *tathā* be construed with *tatsutāḥ*: "parents, brothers, then their sons," not with the preceding *bhrātaras*: "parents, then brothers and their sons," nor (cf. **4**) as linking *bhrātaras* with *pitarau*: "parents and brothers, then brothers' sons."

[2] I.e., to their common father, father's father, and father's father's father.

and so on. For these reasons a brother ranks higher than a brother's son, who is not in a position to do as much.

On the other hand, it makes sense that a brother is entitled to inherit only after the mother: even though he can do the said things, he ranks lower than her, because he owes his existence to her.

[3] <**4**> One might as well construe the conjunction at Yājñavalkya 2.135 with "brothers."[3] In that case the Text would say: "parents and brothers," and it would be the parents and the brothers who would have equal rights to inherit.

<**5**> The conclusion is that this chicanery must be shunned, for the simple reason that it makes the Yājñavalkya text incompatible with Viṣṇu's. The same is true for the chicanery resorted to in the other case.[4]

Manu likewise says that brothers alone get the property,[5] while brothers' sons are not entitled to anything:

> The inheritance of a man who dies without male offspring goes to his father, or to his brothers alone. [M 9.185cd]

[4] <**6**> As to the question why a brother's son is not entitled to inherit while his father lives, the one and only reason for it is that a person whose father lives is not of service to the deceased, since he does not offer *piṇḍas*. This being the deciding factor,[6] how could a nephew whose father is deceased have the same right to inherit as a brother, since he is not of the same service as a brother? That is why Devala says:

> Next, when a man dies without male offspring, his brothers german inherit his property, or else his daughters of equal standing, or else his father if he survives him, brothers of the same caste, his mother, and his widow, in that order. [D 1570-1571ab; **11.1. 17, 50**]

The brother's son does not appear in this list of heirs, which includes the widow, daughters of equal standing, the father, the mother, brothers german, and half brothers.[7] In this way Devala indicates that brothers' sons inherit only in the absence of half brothers [cf. **12**].

<**7**> As to the Text to the effect that a brother's son is also one's own son:

> All brothers are considered to have a son when one of them has one, [M 9.182c]

its purpose is to make it possible for a brother's son to offer *piṇḍas* to his uncle and to inherit his uncle's property if he has no brothers. Otherwise this Text would be

[3] Cf. note 1.

[4] I.e., lumping together brothers and brothers' sons.

[5] Jīmūtavāhana wishes to give the particle *eva*, "only, alone," in *bhrātara eva* at M 9.185cd its full meaning, rather than take it as nothing more than a verse filler.

[6] I.e., since being of service and, more specifically, the degree to which one is of service determine who inherits.

[7] Note that, according to Jīmūtavāhana (**11.1.50**), the order in which the heirs are listed in the Devala text is inconsequential.

incompatible with those cited earlier [**11.1.4–5**]. Also, there would be no reason why the nephew should not inherit even prior to a brother.[8]

<**8**> In conclusion, brothers alone are entitled to inherit first.

Inheritance among Different Kinds of Brothers

<**9**> When there are different kinds of brothers, brothers german inherit first. This is stated in the Text: "a brother german of a brother german" [Y 2.138b; **10**]. What it means is that, when "brothers" become heirs under Yājñavalkya 2.135b [**11.1.4**], brothers german get the inheritance first. Failing them, it goes to half brṛothers, for they, too, were born of the same father, and the word "brother" applies to them as well. <**10**> The Yājñavalkya text:

> A reunited brother gives to and gets the share of a reunited brother when the latter is born and when he dies, respectively. Similarly, a brother german gives to and gets the share of a brother german,[9] [Y 2.138]

likewise shows that the term "brother" can be used both for a brother german and for a half brother. Otherwise, i.e., if "brother" meant only brother german, there would have been no need to specify "a brother german gives to and gets the share of a brother german." It would have been enough to say "brother" to refer to a brother german.

<**11**> In conclusion, the word "brothers" at Yājñavalkya 2.135b points to the fact that, after the parents, both brothers german and half brothers inherit, whereas the words "brothers german" at Yājñavalkya 2.138b point out that brothers german inherit first.[10]

<**12**> One should heed the opinion of Śrīkara and Viśvarūpa, to the effect that a half brother inherits after a brother german but prior to the son of a brother german.[11]

[8] If a nephew was also a son to his deceased uncle, he would accede to his property even prior to his own father and the other brothers of the deceased.

[9] I translate "share" as the object of "gets" only, not of both "gives to" and "gets," even though the latter translation might more accurately reflect the intent of the Yājñavalkya text. From Jīmūtavāhana's point of view, however, a person does not take a share at the time of his birth. See Introduction.

[10] Jīmūtavāhana thus uses the textual authority of Y 2.138 to overrule the general principle (cf. **2.67**, **3.30**, **11.1.6**) according to which the single word "brothers" at Y 2.135 should not have both its primary and secondary meanings.

[11] While commenting on the term "brothers" at Y 2.135 (= *Bālakrīḍā* 2.139), Viśvarūpa states that it includes any kind of brother, and so does the phrase "their sons" (*tathāśabdaḥ prakārārthaḥ sāpatnādisarvabhrātṛsaṃgrāhakas tatsutās tadanusāreṇaiva*). On Jīmūtavāhana's quotations from Viśvarūpa, see Introduction.

On the one hand, a half brother ranks lower than a brother german: the latter offers to six ancestors *piṇḍas* that ought to have been offered by the deceased, whereas the former offers, to their father and so on, only three *piṇḍas* in which the deceased shares.[12]

On the other hand, a half brother ranks higher than a brother's son, since he is of greater service: the brother's son offers two *piṇḍas* in which the deceased shares, whereas the half brother offers three *piṇḍas* in which the deceased shares.[13]

<**13**> One might raise the question whether a half brother still ranks lower than a brother german in case he was reunited with the deceased.[14] In answer to that Yājñavalkya says:

> A half brother gets the property if he was reunited, not any half brother; he who was not reunited gets it as well, not the half brother who was reunited.[15] [Y 2.139]

<**14**> This means that a half brother gets the property first, provided he was reunited, not just any half brother. The second half of the verse addresses the question whether the fact that he gets it first means that he actually bars the brother german, or that he takes it jointly with him. The answer is this: "even if he was not reunited," "he," i.e., the brother german—the words "brother german" carry over from the preceding verse [Y 2.138; **10**]—gets it; the reunited half brother does not get it alone.

Alternatively, the word "reunited" in the second half of the verse itself indicates the brother german. That is why Jitendriya substitutes "brother german" for "reunited" near the end of the Bṛhad-Yājñavalkya text.[16] In this case the adjective "reunited," going with "the half brother," carries over from the first half of the verse.[17]

[12] This phrase is highly elliptic. What it means is that a brother german offers *piṇḍas* to six ancestors to whom the deceased would have had to offer them, three ancestors on their father's side (F, FF, and FFF) and three ancestors on their common mother's side (MF, MFF, and MFFF). Three of these *piṇḍas*, those offered to their F, FF, and FFF, are also of service to the deceased, since he shares in them. The half brother, on the other hand, offers *piṇḍas* to his—and the deceased's—F, FF, and FFF, and to three ancestors on his own mother's side, his MF, MFF, and MFFF. The latter three are of no service to the deceased. The only *piṇḍas* offered by a half brother that are of service to him are those in which he shares, namely, those offered to their F, FF, and FFF.

[13] A half brother offers *piṇḍas* to the deceased's F, FF, and FFF, the son of a brother to the deceased's brother (in which the deceased does not share), F and FF.

[14] It is assumed in this discussion that the brother german was not reunited.

[15] The Sanskrit text of this verse reads: *anyodaryas tu saṃsṛṣṭī nānyodaryo hared dhanam; asaṃsṛṣṭy api cādadyāt saṃsṛṣṭo nānyamātṛjaḥ*. In view of the various interpretations that will be discussed later, at this point I intentionally keep the translation vague.

[16] Jitendriya reads the last quarter of the verse as *sodaro nānyamātṛjaḥ*, rather than *saṃsṛṣṭo nānyamātṛjaḥ*. All *Dāyabhāga* manuscripts here attribute Y 2.139 either to Bṛhad-Yājñavalkya or to Vṛddha-Yājñavalkya.

[17] The second half of the verse then reads: "even though the brother german was not reunited, he gets it; the reunited half brother does not get everything."

<**15**> In any case, the meaning of the verse is as follows: the property does not go to the half brother who was reunited alone but also to the brother german even though he was not reunited. As a result, both kinds of brothers share it together, the brother german who was not reunited and the half brother who was. That is why the Text [**13**] uses the phrase "as well."

<**16**> Śrīkaramiśra made the following statement:

"When the rule 'a reunited brother gets the share of a reunited brother' [**10**] applies solely to half brothers who were reunited, it operates independently of the other rule. Likewise, when the rule 'a brother german gets the share of a brother german' applies solely to brothers german, it operates independently as well. But, when both phrases become operative simultaneously when there are both reunited half brothers and non-reunited brothers german, the two outright injunctions become dependent on each other. It is, however, not proper for the same rule to be an outright injunction that operates dependent on and independent of another one, for that would constitute 'rule asymmetry.'

"As has been shown in the *dvayoḥ praṇayanti* chapter,[18] it is not possible to prohibit an altar in two segments of a sacrifice after enjoining it outright in all four segments. If the outright injunction was dependent on an alternative for two segments of the sacrifice, and independent for the other two segments, that would result in 'asymmetry' in the injunction about the northern altar.

"The same is true in the case at hand. The phrase 'a reunited brother gets the share of a reunited brother' and 'a brother german gets the share of a brother german' can be operative only in cases in which they act as independent injunctions. Since neither one can be operative if there are both reunited half brothers and non-reunited brothers german, the result would be that neither one would get the deceased man's property.

"In conclusion, the correct interpretation is this. The phrase 'a reunited brother gets the share of a reunited brother' establishes the general principle that a reunited brother gets a share in reunited property. The phrase 'a brother german gets the share of a brother german' is meant as an exception to the general rule. In other

[18] The phrase *dvayoḥ praṇayanti*, "they bring (fire) to two (altars)," refers to a complex discussion at *Mīmāṃsā-sūtras* 7.3.19–25. In connection with the *cāturmāsya*, "the four-month sacrifice," a first rule lays down that a northern altar (*uttaravedi*) must be built on this occasion (*upātra vapanti*), whereas the following rule states that it should not be done in the first and fourth parts (*na vaiśvadeve uttaravedim upakiranti na śunāsīrīye*) (*Kāṭhaka-saṃhitā* 36.5–6). If both rules are taken as injunctions, it follows that the first rule is absolute for the second and third parts of the *cāturmāsya*, whereas it is optional for the other two, because in case two injunctions are in conflict they establish an option. The first rule would then suffer from "rule asymmetry" (*vidhi-vaiṣamya*). Commentators such as Śabara avoid the difficulty by interpreting only the first rule as an outright injunction and the second as an exception to it. Śrīkara proposes a similar solution in the case at hand. He is about to argue that, on principle, the property goes to reunited brothers, except when there are brothers german; whether they are reunited or not, they and they alone accede to the property. On the *dvayoḥ praṇayanti* chapter, see K. L. Sarkar 1909: 317–28; Kane 1946: 704–05 and 1962: 1344.

words, when there are brothers german, the half brother, even if he was reunited, has no right whatever. The only one who counts is the brother german, irrespective of whether he was reunited after a partition or not."

<17> This explanation is incongruous, for the fact that two rules which operate separately in two different situations become operative simultaneously in one and the same situation does not automatically create rule asymmetry. Indeed,

[1][19] <**18**> there are two rules, one to the effect that the patron of the sacrifice shall gift his entire property as a sacrificial fee, the other that he shall pay no sacrificial fee whatever. Both rules operate independently of each other if it is the *pratihartṛ* priest or the *udgātṛ* priest who disconnects, respectively. If both disconnect simultaneously, neither rule would be operative, because there would be rule asymmetry.[20]

[2] <**19**> There are also the following two rules: "at the full moon sacrifice he should touch the substance while reciting the *cāturhotra mantra*, at the new moon sacrifice while reciting the *pañcahotra mantra*." These rules operate separately with regard to the *aindradadhi* at the *upāṃśuyāga* and the *aindrapayas* at the *agnīṣomīya*. But when both rules become operative at the *āgneya*, neither one could do so because there would be rule asymmetry.[21]

<**20**> In conclusion, the correct definition of asymmetry is that one and the same rule, in one set of circumstances, is an injunction in absolute terms, not dependent on anything that might bar it and, in a different set of circumstances, an injunction that depends on another injunction that bars it.

[19] Jīmūtavāhana now introduces two examples to show that, if Śrīkara's view of rule asymmetry was correct, there would be problems in other situations as well. Both examples pertain to Vedic ritual, as discussed in the *mīmāṃsā* texts.

[20] Jīmūtavāhana refers to a particular moment in the ritual at which several priests, including the *pratihartṛ* and the *udgātṛ*, are supposed to move in one line, each following one holding on to the garment of the one who precedes him. The *Āpastamba-śrautasūtra* (14. 26.4–5) explains what has to be done when either the *udgātṛ* or the *pratihartṛ* happens to stumble and let go of his predecessor's loincloth. The Mīmāṃsakas (*Mīmāṃsā-sūtras* 6.5. 49–54) raise the question of which rule, if any, is to apply if both let go simultaneously, a situation that is not provided for in the ritual texts. Śabara concludes that, in this case, one should be free to adopt either course of action mentioned by Āpastamba.

[21] For one part of the full moon sacrifice, the *upāṃśuyāga*, there is a rule to the effect that the substance of the oblation (in this case the *aindradadhi*) should be touched while reciting the *cāturhotra mantra*, "the *hotṛ* priest is the earth" (*pṛthivī hotā*). For one part of the new moon sacrifice, the *agnīṣomīya*, there is a rule to the effect that the substance of the oblation (in that case the *aindrapayas*) should be touched while reciting the *pañcahotra mantra*, "the *hotṛ* priest is Agni" (*agnir hotā*). A problem arises with regard to another part of the new and full moon sacrifices, the *āgneya* ritual, during which both substances must be touched: which of the two *mantras* mentioned earlier ought to be recited? The problem, although not in exactly the same terms as in the *Dāyabhāga*, is discussed in the *Mīmāṃsā-sūtras* (3.7. 8, 8.1.26, 9.1.11): to avoid a situation in which neither rule would apply in the *āgneya* ritual, it is decided that the use of either *mantra* is optional.

Thus,[22] the negative injunction, "not at the *vaiśvadeva* and the *śunāsīrīya*," depends on the outright injunction regarding the altar, "they place fire on it."[23] Since the negative injunction could not be an injunction in its own right unless it suspended something ordained in the positive rule, the negative injunction has to be an injunction that depends on the outright injunction regarding the altar. Note, however, that it does not suspend the outright injunction in absolute terms. If that were the case, the negative injunction would be useless, for even without it it would be established that one does not prepare the altar.[24] Therefore, even though the rule concerning the altar is an injunction, it is in the nature of an injunction that depends on a suspension provided by another injunction for two sections of the four-month sacrifice, whereas it does not depend on any other rule as far as the other two sections are concerned. This, then, would be rule asymmetry, and there would be an option.[25] The case at hand is different from one in which people might do something by natural inclination; in that case a negative injunction suspends the act in absolute terms,[26] even though it is established that, without the negative rule, there are times when they would not be engaged in the act.

<**21**> That is also why there is option between the rule that prescribes to take up the *ṣoḍaśin* vessel and the other rule that prescribes not to take it up.[27]

<**22**> As for those who say that this option is based on the principle that, since a negative injunction presupposes that something is previously established, it does not annul the object at whch it is aiming, they are wrong. Indeed,

[22] Jīmūtavāhana now returns to the *dvayoḥ praṇayanti* chapter, referred to earlier in the quotation from Śrīkaramiśra (**16**).

[23] The fact that something is prohibited in a negative injunction presupposes that, without the negative rule, one would do it for one of two reasons, either because there is an outright injunction to that effect or because one would do it by natural inclination, instinctively. The case of the northern altar belongs to the former category. Later in the paragraph Jīmūtavāhana will point out the difference between this and the latter category, the standard example of which is *na kalañjaṃ bhakṣayet* "one should not eat the flesh of the animal called *kalañja*."

[24] If the negative rule laid down in absolute terms that the altar should not be prepared in two out of four cases, the outright injunction preceding it would have to be interpreted as pertaining to something different than enjoining that they should. If so, there would be no outright injunction to the effect that these two altars should be prepared, and it would be useless to prohibit them.

[25] I.e., the outright injunction would mean that it is optional to prepare the altar in two segments of the *cāturmāsya* sacrifice and not optional in the other two.

[26] In other words, in cases such as *na kalañjaṃ bhakṣayet*, "one should not eat the flesh of the animal called *kalañja*," there is no option between the natural inclination to do certain things and the negative injunction that prohibits them.

[27] *Mīmāṃsā-sūtra* 10.8.6 quotes two injunctions: *atirātre ṣoḍaśinaṃ gṛhṇāti* and *na atirātre ṣoḍaśinaṃ gṛhṇāti*. This is the standard example of two injunctions that are in direct opposition to each other, not as a general rule *versus* a specific rule, but as two rules bearing on the same specific act. In such cases, and only in such cases, can option be allowed. Cf. Kane 1962: 1249, 1350.

[1] if so, there would also be option in cases such as "one does not make the two portions of clarified butter at the animal sacrifice," as well as in negative injunctions on things one would do by natural inclination.[28]

[2] <23> If, as they say, a negative injunction that aims at a certain object is incapable of annulling the object it aims at, how could it annul it even partly,[29] since the two are not of equal strength? In fact, since the very nature of a negative injunction is that it uproots the particular object at which it aims, it should uproot it at all times, for something that was established is less strong than the negative injunction.

<24> Then, there are those who say that the negative injunction about taking up the *ṣoḍaśi* cup prohibits this kind of act when it was established accidentally,[30] not when it was established as a result of an outright injunction. That is the talk of ignoramuses. Indeed,

[1] taking up the cup as ordained in the outright injunction on the one hand, and a negative injunction concerning a cup not taken up as the result of an outright injunction on the other, are two things that cannot be in conflict with each other at the same time.[31] Hence, there could not be option between the two either.

[2] Since the act of taking up a cup accidentally could not possibly refer to taking up a cup as part of a ritual, the negative injunction would not refer to a cup in a ritual context either.[32]

[28] The "object at which a negative injunction is aiming" (its *nimitta*) is either an outright injunction or something that people would do by natural inclination. An outright injunction in the new and full moon sacrifices says that one should make two *ājyabhāgas*, "two portions of clarified butter" (*Mīmāṃsā-sūtra* 4.4.30). The new and full moon sacrifices are considered to be the prototype (*prakṛti*) of a number of other sacrifices called *vikṛti* "variants, ectypes," one of which is the animal sacrifice (*paśubandhu*). The ritual texts describe the prototype in detail. The ectypes are described only insofar as they differ from the prototype; all common elements are to be introduced into the ectypes by *atideśa*, "transfer." Hence, when it is said that "one does not make these two at the animal sacrifice (*na tau paśau karoti*), the object at which the negative injunction aims is the transfer of the two *ājyabhāgas* to the animal sacrifice. In this case there is no transfer, and an option is ruled out. Cf. *Mīmāṃsā-sūtra* 10.8.5. Similarly, in the case of *na kalañjaṃ bhakṣayet*, "one should not eat the flesh of the *kalañja*," the object at which the negative injunction aims is *rāga*, "people's natural inclination." Even though the injunction cannot eliminate this kind of eating, it is not meant to establish an option.

[29] And, as a result, create an option.

[30] "Accidentally" (*yādṛcchika*) is more or less synonymous with the more common "by natural inclination, instinctively" (*rāga*).

[31] Śrīkṛṣṇa quotes a variant reading in which "cannot be" (*-asambhavāt*) is replaced by "can be" (*-sambhavāt*), which requires a different meaning for *upasaṃhāra*: "can exist in one place at the same time."

[32] Differently from its use in a more technical sense (cf. **6.1.44**), the term *kratv-artha* here refers to "a part of a ritual." Cf. Śrīkṛṣṇa: *kratv-artha* = *kratv-aṅga*.

<**25**> In conclusion, the only sound principle upon which to base the option is the one I proposed earlier.[33] So, let the matter rest here. What else is there to say?

<**26**> Now, to come back to Śrīkaramiśra,[34]

[1] the way in which he interprets Yājñavalkya 2.138 [**10**], namely, that, when there are both half brothers who were reunited and brothers german who were not, the phrase "a reunited brother gets the share of a reunited brother" first establishes that the half brothers accede to the property,[35] but the phrase "a brother german gets the share of a brother german" is intended as an exception to that,[36] is inappropriate as well. Were we to accept this reasoning, it would be equally possible to say that the brothers german accede to the property on the basis of "a brother german gets the share of a brother german," and that it is the phrase concerning the reunited brothers that is intended as an exception to it. There is no good reason to consider either one of these alternatives preferable to the other.

[2] <**27**> As for his interpretation to the effect that Yājñavalkya 2.139 [**13**] serves as a mere clarification of Yājñavalkya 2.138, that, too, is most inappropriate. Indeed, it would mean that the sense both verses are intended to convey could be gathered from Yājñavalkya 2.139 alone, and that Yājñavalkya 2.138 would be redundant.

[3] <**28**> He says: "Yājñavalkya 2.139 means that a half brother who was reunited does not get the property of his half brother; it is the brother german—the term 'brother german' is carried over from the preceding verse—who gets it all for himself, even if he was not reunited. The half brother, even though he was reunited, does not get it." That, too, is wrong. First, one of the two terms "half brother" in the first half of the verse would be redundant. Second, the phrase "not a half brother" in the second half would be redundant as well. Third, the word "even" in "even if he was not reunited" cannot be interpreted to mean that he gets it "all."[37]

[4] <**29**> If one interprets the phrase that deals with brothers german to mean that, when there is a brother german who was not reunited, even a reunited half brother is barred from the inheritance, the rule is not operative when neither the brother german nor the half brother was reunited. As a result, in that situation either

[33] The option to which Jīmūtavāhana refers in this concluding sentence is the one he proposed for the *dvayoḥ praṇayanti* chapter (**20**).

[34] After the extended discussion of parallel injunctions in the field of ritual, Jīmūtavāhana now returns, with the words *yac ca svayam eva varṇitam,* "as to the interpretation which he himself proposes," to Śrīkaramiśra whose name appears at the beginning of **16** only, and he continues to refute Śrīkara's views with four new arguments marked [1] to [4], up to the end of **30**. Not until **31** does he return to his own view on the subject.

[35] I.e., when there are only half brothers, some of whom were reunited whereas others were not.

[36] With the result that, when there are half brothers who were reunited and brothers german who were not reunited, the latter alone inherit. Cf. **16**.

[37] Jīmūtavāhana's argument is that the second half of Y 2.139 says: "even if he was not reunited (*asaṃsṛṣṭy api*) he gets," without saying what he gets. It does not say that, when he was not reunited, he gets it "all," for that would require the particle *eva* instead of *api*: *asaṃsṛṣṭy eva ādadyāt,* "(the brother german) who was not reunited alone gets it."

both of these would have equal rights to inherit[38] or neither one would have any right whatever. <**30**> If he says that the same phrase that deals with brothers german operates in this case as well, then in one situation it needs to suspend the phrase that deals with reunited brothers, while it operates independently in the other situation.[39] By doing so he would be the one who is guilty of rule asymmetry. One might compare this case with that in which it is said that the rule according to which an altar shall be built for *soma* rituals must be interpreted as intended for those *soma* sacrifices which would not otherwise have an altar. There would, indeed, be asymmetry if, in the case of the *dīkṣaṇīya* and the like, it suspended the outright injunction to build an altar which, in these rituals, is established by transfer, whereas elsewhere it operates without suspending anything.[40]

<**31**> In my interpretation, on the contrary, there is no rule asymmetry; even Śrīkara would have to admit that. First, the two phrases at Yājñavalkya 2.138, one concerning reunited brothers, the other concerning brothers german, have their separate fields of application. Second, Yājñavalkya 2.139 conveys the notion that a brother german who was not reunited and a half brother who was have the same right to inherit. Indeed, the first half of Yājñavalkya 2.139 means that a half brother who was reunited gets the property even if there is a brother german who was not; it does not also go to a half brother who was not reunited. The second half of the verse answers the question whether, in that case, a brother german does not get anything: "even if he was not reunited, he—the brother german, carried over here—gets it." That means that the half brother who was reunited does not get it all for himself; rather, the two divide the property among themselves. In this way rule asymmetry is avoided as well.

<**32**> Manu stipulates the very same thing:

> Brothers german and brothers who were reunited, as well as sisters german, shall get the property together and divide it equally among themselves.[41] [M 9.212]

[38] On the principle that shares are equal by default, see note at **4.2.8**.

[39] In the second situation, in which both brothers were not reunited, it is obvious that the brother german inherits first.

[40] The *dīkṣaṇīya* rite is a *vikṛti*, "variant, ectype" (cf. note 28), of the full moon sacrifice; as a result, unless otherwise specified, it shares all characteristics of its *prakṛti*, "prototype," including the building of an altar. The *dīkṣaṇīya* is, however, also a ritual in which *soma* is used, and, as such, it is subject to the general rules for *soma* sacrifices, which also include the building of an altar. In the case of the *dīkṣaṇīya*, therefore, the *soma* rule would be suspended by the transfer rule from the full moon sacrifice, whereas it is not suspended by anything in other *soma* rituals which, but for it, would not have an altar at all.

[41] I translate M 9.212 in accordance with the interpretation Jīmūtavāhana is about to propose for it. In fact, the verse is ambiguous and it has been the object of a number of differing interpretations. Cf. the note to Bühler's Manu tr. and *Vivādacintāmaṇi* (tr., pp. 291-93). One of the commentators on the *Manu-smṛti*, Medhātithi, according to whom the property goes to the brothers german only, whether they were reunited or not, explicitly rejects the opinion that half brothers should inherit together with brothers german.

<**33**> The fact that "brothers german" and brothers "who were reunited" are each separately referred to in the plural makes it clear that brothers german generally, whether reunited or not, and reunited half brothers are to be treated in mutual conjunction. Indeed,

[1] the only sensible explanation of the phrase "together . . . among themselves" is that it is intended to join the two kinds of brothers together.[42] Otherwise the phrase would be redundant. Hence, to say that this is not so because the Text itself does not use the phrase "in mutual conjunction" amounts to speaking out of ignorance.

[2] When the Text uses the conjunction "and" in the phrase "and those who," this is equivalent to using a *dvandva* compound in the sense of "A plus B." Therefore, to say that the wording of the Text does not join the two together would be tantamount to saying that a *dvandva* compound would not do so either.

<**34**> In conclusion,

[1] in principle,[43] if there are brothers german and half brothers, only brothers german inherit. That is why Bṛhan-Manu says:

> As long as a brother german lives, a half brother does not get the property. This is true even for immovable property. Failing a brother german, the half brother inherits. [bM 93]

<**35**> The phrase "this is true even for immovable property" pertains to immovables that were already divided, for Yama adds immediately:[44]

> Whatever immovable property was not divided goes to all of them; under no circumstances shall half brothers get divided immovable property. [*Dhko* p. 1561]

<**36**> The phrase "all of them" here means both brothers german and half brothers.

[2] If there are only brothers german, the property of the deceased goes solely to those who were reunited.

[3] If there are brothers german who were not reunited and half brothers who were, it goes to both.

[4] If there are only half brothers, the property of the deceased half brother goes first to those who were reunited with him; failing these, to half brothers who were not reunited.

<**37**> That is why Yājñavalkya 2.135 [**11.1.4**] uses the plural "brothers," to establish that different kinds of brothers are entitled to inherit, in the order given above. Otherwise the plural would be useless.[45] <**38**> The phrase "a reunited brother . . . of a reunited brother" at Yājñavalkya 2.138 [**10**] in turn establishes that,

[42] On the concept of *itaretarayoga*, see **4.2.2**.

[43] I.e., if all brothers, both brothers german and half brothers, were either reunited or not reunited.

[44] Although one might expect that this verse again be attributed to Bṛhan-Manu, the *Dāyabhāga* manuscripts unanimously read "Yama."

[45] This explanation was announced at **11.2.27**. The singular does not necessarily indicate a single item (cf. **6.1.15**); the plural invariably indicates three items or more.

when relatives of the same rank are in competition, it makes a difference whether they are reunited or not. <**39**> As a result, among any relatives of the same rank, be they brothers german, half brothers, brother's sons, father's brothers, and so on,[46] those who were reunited with the deceased inherit his property, for Yājñavalkya 2.138 is worded in general terms.[47] At Yājñavalkya 2.135 all of these appear in the same context, and the same question arises with regard to all.[48] One should, therefore, not heed the opinion that Yājñavalkya 2.138 pertains exclusively to brothers.

<**40**> Thus far for the brothers' right to inherit.

[46] Jīmūtavāhana refers to all the male relatives of the deceased, beginning with the brothers, who are listed at Y 2.135.

[47] Although, given the context in which it occurs, Y 2.138 clearly intends to speak of "a reunited brother . . . of a reunited brother," as I translated, it is indeed the case that the word "brother" is not expressed. The text says *saṃsṛṣṭinas tu saṃsṛṣṭī*, "a reunited of a re-united," so that any male member who is reunited may come under its purview.

[48] I.e., the question of who among them should inherit first.

CHAPTER ELEVEN
SECTION SIX

BROTHERS' SONS

<**1**> Failing brothers, brothers' sons inherit. After the words: "It goes to his brothers" [Vi 17.8; **11.5.1, 11.1.5**], the Viṣṇu text continues:

> Failing them, it goes to his brothers' sons. [Vi 17.9]

<**2**> When there are sons of different kinds of brothers, in that case, too,[1] sons of brothers german inherit first; failing them, sons of half brothers, based on the Text: "a brother german gets the share of a brother german" [Y 2.138; **11.5.10**]. Sons of half brothers, indeed, rank lower than sons of brothers german, for, when sons of half brothers offer *piṇḍas* to the father of the deceased, they offer them to him as the husband of their own paternal grandmother, without any concern for the mother of the deceased. They therefore inherit after the sons of a brother german.[2]

<**3**> Note that, when someone performs funeral rites, it is not the case that his stepmother, his father's stepmother, and his paternal grandfather's stepmother share in these rites with their husbands on the grounds that they, too, were paternal ancestors' wives.[3] Indeed,

[1] the words "mother," "grandmother," and "great-grandmother" primarily mean one's own natural mother, one's father's natural mother, and one's father's father's natural mother, and it is these words that are used for the women who share in the funeral rites with their husbands:

> The mother shares with her husband in the oblations at the funeral rites, the father's mother with her husband, the father's father's mother with hers. [B *Śrāddha* 75]

[2] On the other hand, a stepmother, a father's stepmother, and a paternal grandfather's stepmother are barred from sharing with their husbands in the offerings at the *pārvaṇaśrāddhas* of their stepson and so forth. Indeed,

[1] I.e., even as, when there are different kinds of brothers, brothers german inherit first.

[2] When the son of a brother german offers *piṇḍas* to his paternal grandfather, he dedicates them not only to the father but also to the mother of the deceased. When a half brother's son offers *piṇḍas* to the same paternal grandfather, he dedicates them to him and to a woman who is only the deceased brother's stepmother; as Jīmūtavāhana is about to prove, the mother of the deceased does not share in them.

[3] This sentence was misunderstood by Colebrooke, who translated: "the stepmother, grandmother and great grandmother." Cf. Goldstücker 1871: 13–14.

[a] there is the following Text:

> If certain women or men die without male offspring, they may be given an *ekoddiṣṭa* but no *pārvaṇaśrāddha*.[4]

[b] <**4**> The injunction to the effect that one must offer funeral rites to his ancestors together with their wives is universally applicable, since every individual faces that situation; stepmothers and so forth, on the other hand, are incidental. Since universals and incidentals cannot be combined,[5] it is only proper that the rules about funeral rites for ancestors and their wives pertain exclusively to natural mothers and so forth.

[Objection] <**5**> A brother german of the deceased man's father has the same right to inherit as a son of his brother german, for even as the son of a brother german the father's brother german offers *piṇḍas* which the deceased would have had to offer to two generations of ancestors and their wives.[6]

[Refutation] Not so. A paternal uncle indeed offers *piṇḍas* to the deceased man's paternal grandparents and great-grandparents, but the two generations to whom a brother's son offers *piṇḍas* include the person who is most important to the deceased, namely, his father. A brother's son, therefore, ranks higher than a father's brother and inherits prior to him.

<**6**> That is why even a brother's grandson bars a paternal uncle, for he, too, offers *piṇḍas* to the person who is most important to the deceased, namely, his father.[7]

[4] This verse, most often attributed to Āpastamba (but not part of the *Āpastambadharmasūtra*), appears in a number of commentaries (e.g., Aparārka on Y 1.255) and in digests on *śrāddka* (e.g., *Śrāddhakriyākaumudī* p. 476, *Śrāddhasāgara* p. 267). The latter two add a second verse which lists a number of individuals, including the stepmother, to whom monthly and yearly *śrāddhas* may be offered. The commentators interpret the first verse as an exception to the second: monthly and yearly *śrāddhas* for these individuals are allowed except when they die without male offspring, in which case they can receive only *ekoddiṣṭas*. The only individual in the list who is relevant in the present context is the stepmother.

[5] This sentence refers to *Mīmāṃsā-sūtra* 6.7.5: *nityatvāc ca anityair na asti sambandhaḥ*. The commentators illustrate this maxim with a rule concerning the *viśvajit* sacrifice (cf. **2.67**): "on the occasion of a *viśvajit* one should gift 'everything one owns' (*sarvasva*)." The question arises as to whether the term *sarvasva* applies to the property as it exists at the time of the sacrifice, or whether it also includes property one might acquire at a later time. The answer is that the term applies only to property one owns at the time of the ritual, because that property is *nitya*, "certain, universal; it is always there," whereas property to be acquired later is *anitya* "uncertain, incidental; it may or may not be there." *Mīmāṃsāsūra* 6.7.5 prohibits joining *nitya* elements and *anitya* elements together.

[6] The deceased would have had to offer *piṇḍas* to his F, FF, and FFF; the brother's son does so to the B, F, and FF of the deceased; the father's brother to the FF, FFF, and FFFF of the deceased. In the first case the F and FF are in common; in the second case the FF and FFF.

[7] The brother's grandson offers *piṇḍas* to the BS, B, and F of the deceased.

<**7**> Even though a brother's great-grandson is a descendant of the deceased man's father, he is barred by the paternal uncle. He represents the fifth generation and, hence, does not offer *piṇḍas* to the father of the deceased.[8] Thus the following Manu text, which bars the fifth generation:

> Three generations shall be given water, three generations must be offered *piṇḍas*. It is the fourth generation that offers these. The fifth generation plays no role in it. [M 9.186; **4.3.36**, **11.1.40**, **11.6.17**]

<**8**> What happens is that, failing male offspring of the deceased man's father down to his great-grandsons, the father's daughter's son inherits.[9] The situation is similar to that in which the property of the deceased goes to his daughter's son if he has no male offspring down to a great-grandson. <**9**> And the right to inherit devolves likewise among the descendants of the paternal grandfather and great-grandfather, each time down to their daughters' sons, and in decreasing order of the number of *piṇḍas*. The Text:

> Even as a son's son, a daughter's son, too, saves his grandfather in the other world, [M 9.139cd; **4.2.10**]

lays down the necessary and sufficient condition for daughters' sons to inherit, without any specification. Hence, since sons of daughters of the father, grandfather, and so forth offer *piṇḍas* in which the deceased shares, they, too, help him reach the other world, as much as his own daughters' sons.

<**10**> That is why Manu does not mention the rights to inherit of all these individuals separately, for they are subsumed in the two verses 9.186–187ab [**17**]. And when Yājñavalkya 2.135 [**11.1.4**] uses the term *gotraja*, it is to establish that all those born of (*-ja*) the same *gotra* as the deceased, including the sons of daughters of his father and so forth,[10] inherit in the order in which they are close to him when they offer *piṇḍas*. At the same time the term *gotraja* is intended to exclude the wives of *sapiṇḍas*,[11] since these were not born of the same *gotra*. <**11**> That is why

[8] The BSSS offers *piṇḍas* to the BSS, BS, and B, not to the F, of the deceased.

[9] I.e., failing a BSS, the inheritance does not go to the BSSS, but rather to the SiS.

[10] This statement is important. According to G. C. Sarkar (1897: 187–88), "The term *gotraja* in Y's text is, according to the Mitáksará, equivalent to *sagotra* or a member of the same *gotra* with the *propositus*. But the Dáyabhága explains the word to include also cognates descended from a member of the *gotra*, such as the daughter's son, the sister's son, the father's sister's son, and so forth. And the word *bandhu* which, according to the Mtá, signifies all cognates, is restricted by the Dbhá to cognate relations connected through the mother, the father's mother, and so forth. Thus Jímútaváhana controverts the interpretation put on the texts of Y by the Mtá, which postpones all cognates save and except the daughter's son, to agnates comprised by the terms *sapinda* and *samanodaka*."

[11] In Jīmūtavāhana's reading of Y 2.135 the term *gotraja* appears in the masculine singular (*gotrajo*). The *Mitākṣarā*, on the other hand, reads *gotrajā* (for *gotrajāḥ*), which is both masculine and female plural, and it includes among the *gotrajas* the father's mother, who, according to the *Dāyabhāga* (**11.4.6**), inherits after the father's father.

Baudhāyana says, with the phrase "a wife is entitled to" carried over from a preceding rule:

> no inheritance, because of the Revealed Text: "wives are without strength and without inheritance."[12] [Bau 2.2.3.46]

The construction here is: "wives are not entitled to inherit." This, of course, is not incompatible with the fact that widows and so forth are entitled to inherit, for these rights are based on specific Texts.

KIN

<**12**> Failing descendants of the paternal great-grandfather down to his daughter's son, all of whom offer *piṇḍas* in which the deceased shares, the property goes to the maternal uncle and so forth. At this stage they are closest to the deceased *sapiṇḍa*,[13] for they offer *piṇḍas* to his maternal grandfather and so on, which the deceased would have had to offer. To encompass this class of heirs Yājñavalkya 2.135 [**11.1.4**] uses the term *bandhu*, whereas Manu 9.187ab [**17**] achieves the same result by means of a general statement on being closest in offering *piṇḍas*.

<**13**> Since the maternal uncle and so forth offer to the maternal grandfather and so on of the deceased three *piṇḍas* which he would have had to offer, his property goes to the maternal uncle and so on, for through the medium of this property they, too, offer *piṇḍas* to them.

There are, indeed, two incentives to acquire property: to use it for one's own enjoyment, or to reserve it for transcendent purposes such as gifts.[14] Since in the present case the person who acquired the property can no longer enjoy it himself because he is deceased, it makes sense that it be reserved for transcendent purposes only. Indeed,

[12] In view of the use which Jīmūtavāhana makes of this text, I consistently translate Sanskrit *strī* as "wife," notwithstanding the fact that Baudhāyana uses the term in the sense of "woman" generally. The first two words, *na dāyam*, "no inheritance," in the accusative, appear in only a few Baudhāyana manuscripts. Jīmūtavāhana makes *dāyam* the object of the phrase *strī arhati*, "a wife is entitled to," in the preceding *sūtra*, where it, however, has its own object *na svātantryam*, "no independence." Note that, without *na dāyam*, Bau 2.2.3.46 is a perfect half stanza. On the confused transmission of this passage, see Hulztsch's critical apparatus and Bühler's (Baudhāyana tr., pp. 231–32) and Olivelle's (2000: 596) notes. The *śruti* text quoted by Baudhāyana appears in the *Taittirīya-saṃhitā* (6.5.8.2) in the context of the *soma* sacrifice and actually means that women are without strength and hence do not take a portion of the *soma*. Cf. Kane 1946: 606, 712.

[13] I translate *piṇḍānantarya*, literally "closest with regard to *piṇḍas*," as "being closest to the deceased *sapiṇḍa*," in accordance with *anantaraḥ sapiṇḍāt* at M 9.187ab (**17**).

[14] J. N. Bhattacharya (1893: 76) lists this sentence as one of the legal maxims relating to property. Cf. note at **4.2.8**.

[1] that is why Bṛhaspati says:

> One half of the property he left them they shall set aside for him, especially for monthly, half-yearly, and yearly funeral rites, [B 26.137]

[2] and why Āpastamba says:

> Or an apprentice[15] shall use the property for rituals that benefit the deceased, or a daughter.[16] [Āp 2.6.14.3–4]

The necessary and sufficient condition for someone to inherit property is that he or she uses it for transcendent purposes, here called "rituals," so that the deceased may enjoy it through monthly and other funeral rites. That is why people say: "property serves two purposes, to be gifted and to be enjoyed."[17]

In conclusion, it simply stands to reason that, if there is no one to offer *piṇḍas* in which the deceased shares, the right to inherit his property goes to his maternal uncle and so on, i.e., to persons who offer *piṇḍas* which he would have had to offer.[18]

<**14**> That is why[19] Manu, considering this issue to have been settled with the two verses 9.186–187ab [**7, 17**], immediately goes on to say:

> Failing these, let it be a *sakulya*, a teacher, or a disciple. [M 9.187cd; **21**]

<**15**> A *sakulya* is a descendant of the paternal great-great-grandfather and so forth. The term here subsumes the *samānodakas*. They inherit in order, *sakulyas* first, *samānodakas* later [**21–23**]. Failing them, the property goes to the deceased man's teacher, his disciple, and so on.

<**16**> If Manu had been opposed to including the maternal uncle and the like at this stage, where else could they be inserted? In conclusion, there is nothing that prevents us from saying that Manu settled this issue with the two verses in question.

<**17**> That is why, in the chapter on inheritance, Manu, after the statement:

[15] On the use of the term *antevāsin*, "apprentice," in the sense of *śiṣya*, "disciple," see note at **9.28**. Cf. also **11.1.37**.

[16] The *Dāyabhāga* and the *Dāyatattva* (ed. p. 196; tr. 11.79) present a truncated version, including a variant reading, of the text of Āp 2.6.14.3: "Failing *sapiṇḍas*, his teacher inherits. Failing him, his apprentice, who either must use the property for rituals that benefit the deceased, or (scil. use it for himself)." The point Jīmūtavāhana wishes to stress by quoting this text is that an inheritance or part of it shall always be used for rituals that benefit the deceased. The fact that this appears in a text that involves an apprentice or a daughter is coincidental.

[17] The quarter verse *datta-bhukta-phalaṃ dhanam* appears more than once in the *Mahābhārata*, e.g., 2.5.10b, 3.243.24d, 5.39.51d.

[18] The maternal uncle, for example, offers *piṇḍas* to three generations of his own paternal ancestors, i.e., to three generations of maternal ancestors of the deceased.

[19] I.e., because the maternal uncle and others also are entitled to inherit, in the order in which they offer *piṇḍas* the deceased would have had to offer.

> Three generations shall be given water, three generations shall be offered *piṇḍas*. It is the fourth generation that offers these. The fifth generation plays no role in it, [M 9.186; **4.3.36**, **11.1.40**, **11.6.7**]

continues:

> Property always goes to the one who is closest to the deceased *sapiṇḍa*.[20] [M 9.187ab]

What this means is that, as long as there is someone, either on the father's or on the mother's side, who is linked to the deceased even by a single *piṇḍa*, "the fifth," i.e., one who is not linked to him by a single *piṇḍa*, does not inherit. Otherwise,[21] since *sapiṇḍa* relationship has been defined as follows:

> *Sapiṇḍa* relationship ceases with the seventh generation, [M 5. 60ab; cf. **11.1.42**]

and since "the one who is closest to the deceased *sapiṇḍa*" [M 9.187ab] mentions closeness as the reason why a particular person gets the property, Manu 9.186 would be redundant.

[Objection] The real purpose of Manu 9.186 is to enjoin that funeral rites must be offered to three earlier generations.[22]

[Refutation] Not so. First, the verse appears in the midst of the chapter on inheritance. Second, funeral rites are enjoined in other verses. Says Manu:

> One should honor in the prescribed way the Sages by studying the Veda, the gods with oblations, the ancestors with funeral rites, men with food, and the evil spirits with *bali* offerings. [M 3.81]

[Objection] <**18**> The term "closeness" at Manu 9.187ab is meant to be understood in terms of birth rather than in terms of offering *piṇḍas*.

[Refutation] Not so. Nothing in the wording of that verse hints at the order of birth. On the contrary, Manu introduces the term "closeness" after having said that, even as water, *piṇḍas* shall be offered to three generations, that the fourth at the lower end offers the *piṇḍas*, and that neither the fifth at the top receives *piṇḍas* nor does the fifth at the lower end offer them. In doing so he makes it known that the decision on who is closer to the deceased depends on his superiority as far as the offering of *piṇḍas* is concerned.

<**19**> In conclusion, Manu 9.186 is intended to establish the right to inherit for any individual, either one born in the family of the deceased but not necessarily of the same *gotra*, e.g., a daughter's son or a father's daughter's son, or one not born in his family, e.g., a maternal uncle, provided this individual offers *piṇḍas* within three generations of ancestors in the deceased owner's father's or mother's family,

[20] For the various interpretations of this verse by the commentators, see Bühler (Manu tr. pp. 366–68). Cf. note 13.

[21] I.e., if M 9.186 did not specifically pertain to maternal uncles and the like.

[22] The objection claims that M 9.186 pertains to *śrāddha*, "funeral rites," not to *dāyabhāga*, "inheritance."

and, as such is a *sapiṇḍa* of the deceased by being linked to him by at least one *piṇḍa*. Manu 9.187ab must be interpreted as establishing distinctions between these individuals based on their relative closeness to the deceased.

<**20**> The right to inherit in order of closeness must, therefore, be understood as follows: failing persons who offer to three generations from the father upward *piṇḍas* in which the deceased shares or which he would have had to offer, i.e., the father's daughter's son and so forth, the inheritance goes to the maternal uncle and so on, i.e., to those who offer *piṇḍas* which the deceased would have had to offer to his maternal grandfather and so on.[23]

RELATIVES AND OTHERS

<**21**> Failing all those mentioned so far, relatives (*sakulya*) inherit. Says Manu:

> Failing these, let it be a *sakulya*, a teacher, or a disciple. [M 9. 187cd; **14**]

Sakulyas are those who offer divided *piṇḍas*, i.e., the three generations beginning with one's great-great-grandson, as well as the descendants of one's great-great-grandfather and so forth.[24]

<**22**> Here again, the great-great-grandson and so forth are closer, for they are of service to the deceased on the grounds that they offer him fragments of *piṇḍas*.[25] Failing them, the descendants of the great-great-grandfather, for they offer *piṇḍas* to the great-great-grandfather and so forth who would have shared in fragments of *piṇḍas* which the deceased would have had to offer.

<**23**> Failing this kind of *sakulyas*, the *samānodakas* of the deceased inherit his property.[26] One must consider them to have been subsumed under the term *sakulya* at Manu 9.187cd [**21**].

<**24**> Failing them, the teacher of the deceased inherits; failing him, his disciples, in accordance with the Manu text: "a teacher, or a disciple" [M 9.187d; **21**].

Failing them, fellow students inherit, in accordance with the rule: "disciples, and fellow students" [Y 2.135d; **11.1.4**].

[23] The fact that Jīmūtavāhana makes maternal relations inherit prior to *sakulyas* has been criticized by G. C. Sarkar as "opposed to well-known principles universally acknowledged by learned Pandits, and also opposed to the actual usages and practices of the people" (1910: 334–35).

[24] On *sakulyas*, see Introduction.

[25] On "fragments of *piṇḍas*," see note at **11.1.38**.

[26] The *samānodakas*, literally "persons connected by libations of water," include: (1) male descendants from the eighth to the fourteenth generation (including the deceased); (2) male ascendants from the eighth to the fourteenth generation; (3) male descendants of these ancestors. Cf. Introduction.

<**25**> Failing these, men of the same *gotra* inherit; failing them, men of the same *pravara*, in accordance with the Gautama text:

> The inheritance goes to those who were connected with the deceased through *piṇḍas*, through their *gotra*, or through their Seer.[27] [G 28.21]

<**26**> Failing all those mentioned so far, the deceased man's property goes to brahmans. Says Manu:

> Failing all others, the inheritance goes to brahmans who are learned in the three Vedas, ritually pure, and disciplined. In this way his *dharma* is not lost.[28] [M 9.188]

Even if his *dharma* was diminished by being used, it is not lost, for, when his property goes to a brahman, his *dharma* is replenished by the acquisition of other *dharma*. This Text, therefore, once again underscores the principle that property shall always be of service to its owner.[29]

<**27**> Failing these, the inheritance goes to the king, except for property that belonged to a brahman.

The absence of members of the deceased man's *gotra* or *pravara* and of brahmans must be taken to be restricted to their absence within the village of the deceased. Otherwise the rule to the effect that the king inherits would never have occasion to apply.

<**28** > If Manu 9.186 [**17**] did not point to the right to inherit of the father's daughter's son, the maternal uncle, and so on, they would have no right to inherit whatever. It is, indeed, impossible to insert them anywhere within the *sakulyas* and the rest, for these follow one another in strict sequence.

It would be wrong to say that these people should not inherit anyway. Indeed, Yājñavalkya [2.135d; **11.1.4**] refers to them with the words *gotraja* and *bandhu*. Manu 9.186 must, therefore, also be interpreted as referring to them.

In conclusion, in each case those entitled to inherit must be ranked in such a way as to make the property of the deceased of the greatest service to him.

<**29**> That is why the sons', grandsons', and great-grandsons' rights to inherit are considered to be equal. Indeed, Texts such as Manu 9.137 [**11.1.31**] lay down that they are of equal service since they offer *piṇḍas* to the deceased in the same way.

This, in turn, explains why a grandson or a great-grandson does not inherit as long as his father lives: a grandson or a great-grandson is of no service to the de-

[27] Whereas members of the same *gotra* are descended in the male line from the same patriarch (**11.1.4**), members of the same *pravara* adhere to the same ancient Seer.

[28] I translate the phrase *evaṃ dharmo na hīyate* at the end of the verse in accordance with Jīmūtavāhana's interpretation. Cf. Colebrooke: "Thus virtue is not lost." Kullūkabhaṭṭa comments: " They offer *piṇḍas* to him and, in this way, his *dharma*, such as his funeral rites, are not lost." Bühler (Manu tr.): "thus the law is not violated."

[29] D. N. Mitter (1870: 38–39) refers to inheritance by a brahman of the same village as "an instance of the extreme solicitude evinced by the author of the Dayabhaga to provide for the spiritual welfare of a deceased proprietor."

ceased, since the Text: "one should not make offerings that bypass a living father"[30] prohibits both descendants to perform their own *pārvaṇaśrāddhas* while bypassing their living fathers. Otherwise, either they would have the same right to inherit as a grandson or great-grandson whose father is deceased, or the son would inherit alone, to the exclusion of a grandson or a great-grandson, on the grounds that he is closer to the deceased *sapiṇḍa* in order of birth.

Nor is there a Text that establishes that all three, sons, grandsons, and great-grandsons, inherit simultaneously. Consequently, the son's, grandson's, and great-grandson's right to inherit the property equally must be taken to result solely from the fact that they are of equal service to the deceased. <**30**> Similarly, in all other cases, too, one must bear in mind that the property of the deceased is to be of service to him, in the way and in the order described above.

<**31**> The notion, grounded on common sense, that the right to inherit the property of the deceased is determined by the degree to which the heir is of service to him may also be considered to have been countenanced by Manu and other Sages. Indeed,

[1] the fact that in their chapters on inheritance they state that sons and so forth are of greater service than anyone else can have no other purpose.

[2] In the Text:

> And he frees him of the debt to his ancestors. That is why he ought to inherit his property,[31] [M 9.106cd]

it is clearly stated that the fact that a son frees his father of his debt is the necessary and sufficient condition for him to get the property.

[3] The Text:

> Even as a son's son, a daughter's son, too, saves his grandfather in the other world, [M 9.139cd; **9**, **4.2.10**]

also mentions saving as the necessary and sufficient condition for him to acquire the property.

[4] There is no other reason for the three generations from the son down to have equal rights to inherit than the fact that all three save the deceased. Otherwise, Manu 8.186 [**17**] would be redundant.

[5] The sole reason that makes it possible for the Texts to say that eunuchs, outcastes, those congenitally blind, and so on, receive no share [**5.7**, **10**, **11**, **13**] is that such people are of no service.

[6] To formulate Texts that establish the right to inherit for each and every relative individually would be needlessly cumbersome.

[7] It stands to reason that one ensures that property acquired by a man be of service to him by giving it to those who, under the circumstances, are of the greatest service to him.

[30] *Kātyāyana-śrautasūtra* 4.1.27.

[31] The first half of this verse reads: "By the mere fact that he is born, a first son makes of a man the father of a son." Cf. **1.36** and **11.1.32**.

<**32**> Such is the luminous explanation expounded by the unimpeachable Luminary of Knowledge.[32] The learned should heed it.

<**33**> If this interpretation does not satisfy the learned, and should they require one purely founded on Texts, so be it. But even then the interpretation of the two Manu verses as given above is the only acceptable one. What more is there to say?[33]

<**34**>[34] The king shall get the property, except if it belonged to brahmans. Says Manu:

> The rule is that the king shall never take the property of a brahman. Failing all other heirs, he takes the property of members of any other caste. [M 9.189]

The phrase "all other heirs" means everyone up to and including brahmans.

<**35**> The property of a wanderer, an ascetic, and a Vedic student goes to a brother-in-the-*dharma*, a worthy disciple, and his teacher, respectively.[35] Failing these, it goes to one who lives at the same sacred spot, i.e., in the same hermitage. Says Yāyñavalkya:

> The property of a wanderer, an ascetic, and a Vedic student goes, respectively, to his teacher, to a worthy disciple, to a brother-in-the-*dharma*, and to one who lives in the same sacred spot.[36] [Y 2.137]

[32] On Vidyodyota, see **2.9** and Introduction.

[33] Śrīkṛṣṇa sees this paragraph as the answer to an objection to the effect that, if the texts were based on common sense, then even when there is a person who can offer *piṇḍas* in which the deceased shares, any outsider who happens to throw the bones of the deceased in the holy Ganges or who happens to offer *piṇḍas* to him in the sacred city of Gayā would be entitled to inherit. "The interpretation . . . as given above," i.e., the criterion of closeness based on the capacity of certain relatives to offer fragments of *piṇḍas* in which the deceased shares and which he would have had to offer, prevents the outsider from claiming the inheritance. While raising objections to Jīmūtavāhana's view of spiritual benefit, Kane (1941: 473) refers to this passage: "Besides he himself is not sure of his ground, since he says that although learned men may not approve of his theory that spiritual benefit is the guiding principle in taking property by inheritance they must admit that the order of heirs as stated by him relying on Manu IX.186–187 is the proper one." Cf. J. N. Bhattacharya 1893: 480.

[34] Jīmūtavāhana returns to the discussion that was interrupted after **27**.

[35] The terms "wanderer," "ascetic," and "Vedic student" translate *vānaprastha*, *yati*, and *brahmacārin*, respectively.

[36] I translate Y 2.137 in accordance with Jīmūtavāhana's interpretation: after enumerating the brother-in-the-*dharma*, a worthy disciple, and the teacher, he goes on: "failing these," and adds "one who lives at the same sacred spot" to the list. Śrīkṛṣṇa notes that this interpretation poses a problem: it creates four classes of recipients for three kinds of inheritance. He suggests that the term *dharma-bhrātṛ*, "brother-in-the-*dharma*," at Y 2.137 should be taken as an adjective qualifying *eka-tīrthin*, "one who lives at the same sacred spot." The *Mitākṣarā*, too, describes the third recipient as one who is both a *dharma-bhrātṛ* and an *ekatīrthin* (Colebrooke II.viii.2). For other interpretations, see Jolly 1885: 223.

<**36**> Note that, as far as possible, each of these properties goes to each of these heirs "respectively," i.e., in this case, in reverse order.[37] "Vedic student" here means one who made a vow of permanent celibacy, i.e., one who made the commitment to leave his father and so forth, and to live and serve in his teacher's family for the rest of his life. The property of a student who undergoes only the regular course of study, however, goes to his father and so forth.

<**37**> Thus far for the inheritance of a man who dies without male offspring.

[37] Y 2.137 says that these kinds of property go to the heirs listed in the text *krameṇa* "in order." Jīmūtavāhana and other commentators, including Vijñāneśvara (Colebrooke II. viii.2), in this case rightly interpret *krameṇa* as *pratiloma-krameṇa* "in reverse order." More problematic is the fact that, immediately after *pratilomakrameṇa*, Jīmūtavāhana adds *yathāsambhavam* or *yathāsambhavaṃ ca*. Śrīkṛṣṇa, who adopts the latter reading, illustrates the phrase by giving examples of specific kinds of property that may belong to a wanderer, an ascetic, and a Vedic student. This interpretation probably accounts for Colebrooke's translation: "goods, such as they may happen to possess, should be delivered in the reverse order of this enumeration." Since the particle *ca* is missing in most *Dāyabhāga* manuscripts, with the result that *yathāsambhavam* does not necessarily specify *pratiloma-krameṇa*, I prefer to give it the more common meaning "as far as possible."

CHAPTER TWELVE

PARTITION BY PERSONS WHO WERE REUNITED

<1> Let me now deal with the partition of property of persons who were reunited.[1]
On this subject Manu and Viṣṇu say:

> If persons who were parties to a partition reunite, and if they subsequently proceed to a new partition, their shares shall then be equal. In that case there is no seniority right. [M 9.210 = Vi 18.4]

<2> The phrase "their shares shall then be equal" pertains to a reunion by brothers of the same caste. If, however, a brahman and a *kṣatriya* were reunited, their shares shall again be determined according to the rules discussed earlier [**9.12–23**]. Indeed, the sole purpose of the word "equal" here is to rule out preempted shares for older brothers as determined earlier. That is why Bṛhaspati says:

> If brothers who were separated resume life in common out of affection for each other, there is no seniority if they proceed to a new partition. [B 26.106cdef; **11.1.20**]

The only thing the latter Text does is to prevent that special shares be preempted for older brothers; it does not, however, say that the shares shall be equal.

<3> Note that Bṛhaspati defines reunited persons as follows:

> If a man who was a party to a partition resumes life together with his father, brother, or paternal uncle, out of affection for them, he is said to be reunited. [B 26.113; **11.1.30**]

<4> The special rule about reunion [**1**] shall, therefore, not be heeded for persons not included in this enumeration. Otherwise the enumeration would be redundant.[2]

[1] In 1824 F. W. Macnaghten, who was then a judge in the Supreme Court of Bengal, noted: "After separation, and a partition actually made, families may again be reunited. This, however, is an event which seldom happens. I do not know an instance of it, and the Supreme Court *Pandits* inform me that none has ever fallen within their knowledge" (1824: 107). Sixty years later Jolly confirmed Macnaghten's statement on reunion, "though I am informed that they are not quite uncommon in Benares" (1885: 224).

[2] Even though at **11.1.30** Jīmūtavāhana speaks of reunions by "a father, brother, paternal uncle, and so forth," and at that point seems to accept reunion between any individuals

<5> On the other hand, all other special rules, as set forth in the section on brothers inheriting from brothers [**11.5**], shall be taken into consideration for them.[3]

<6> Thus far for partition by persons who were reunited.

who were first united, then separated, and eventually out of affection reunited, nevertheless, on the basis of the present passage, it has generally been accepted that, with regard to reunion, Jīmūtavāhana agrees with the *Mitākṣarā,* which quotes B 26.113 unequivocally to interpret the concept of reunion in a restricted way: "one cannot reunite just with anyone, but only with one's father, brother, and paternal uncle" (on Y 2.138; Colebrooke II.ix.3). Other commentators hold a different view. Even the author of the *Vyavahāraprakāśa*, who generally agrees with the views of Vijñāneśvara, objects to the restrictive interpretation of B 26.113, and says that its list of persons who can reunite is merely illustrative (ed. p. 533; tr. IV. 3): one can reunite with any relative with whom one previously proceeded to a partition, including nephews and even one's mother; the sole purpose of B 26.113 is to prevent the term "reunion" from being applied to merchants and the like who again join their business assets together (ed. p. 512; tr. III.i.13). Cf. Jolly 1885: 224–25; Sarvadhikari 1922: 830–36; Kane 1946: 766 and 1962: 1302–03. On the application of both the restricted and the broad definitions of reunion—and the exclusion of females from it—in modern law, see, e.g., Mayne 1950: 568–69; Mulla 1959: 516–17.

[3] Śrīkṛṣṇa identifies the "other special rules" as the rules to the effect that property acquired without drawing on joint property belongs to the acquirer alone, except for rewards of knowledge which have to be shared with brothers who are equally or more knowledgeable than the acquirer, and the rule that everyone shares in property acquired by drawing on joint property. Jīmūtavāhana obviously also refers to section **11.5**; cf. his conclusions at **11.5.34-36**.

CHAPTER THIRTEEN

PARTITION OF PROPERTY THAT WAS WITHHELD AT THE TIME OF PARTITION

<**1**> Let me now deal with the partition of property that was withheld at the time of partition and that comes to light at a later time.[1]

[A] Manu says:

> If anything comes to light subsequent to the time when all debts and assets were divided according to the rules, it shall be divided equally. [M 9.218]

<**2**> The phrase "it shall be divided equally" here means that each person shall be allotted exactly the same kind of share he was given earlier. On the one hand, it does not mean that the one who removed a certain item shall be given a smaller share of it or no share whatever on the grounds that he removed it.[2] On the other hand, the Text is not intended to say that everyone should be given an equal share in that property. First, there is no reason to bar such things as the preempted share of five percent. Second, brahmans, *kṣatriyas*, and so forth, would then get equal shares.

[B] <**3**> Yājñavalkya says:

> If any item they removed from one another comes to light after partition, the rule is that they shall divide it into equal shares. [Y 2.126]

[C] <**4**> Kātyāyana says:

> If an item which someone concealed again comes to light, even if he died in the meanwhile, his sons shall divide it equally with his

[1] Jīmūtavāhana is about to quote four *smṛti* texts that deal with this topic. They are marked [A] to [D].

[2] Of the various Sanskrit verbs used in this chapter to indicate that property had been "concealed"/"withheld" at the time of partition, the one I translate "remove" (*apa-hṛ*), used here by Jīmūtavāhana, and appearing again at Y 2.126 (**3**), K 886 (**4**), and K 888 (**7**), is particularly important. The Sanskrit verb *apa-hṛ*, literally "take away," comes close to suggesting the idea of "stealing" the property that was withheld, a topic that will be discussed from **8** onward. Jīmūtavāhana will argue later (**9**) that *apa-hṛ* is different from stealing. Yet, in the quotation from Jitendriya (**12**) *apa-hṛ* is obviously synonymous with theft.

> brothers.[3] [K 885]
> If they removed an item from one another, or if an item had been improperly divided, and the item later comes to light again, it shall be divided equally. So says Bhr̥gu. [K 886]

<**5**> The latter Text also provides for a new partition of an item that had been incorrectly divided. Manu 9.47a, which says that "shares shall be allotted only once,"[4] pertains to cases in which the partition was done correctly. <**6**> The phrase "later comes to light again" means that anything that has already been the object of an earlier partition shall not also be divided again.

[D] <**7**> Kātyāyana says:

> If kin removed any property, one shall not use force to have it restituted. Nor shall one force undivided kin to refund benefits they derived from the use of any property. [K 888]

One shall not use force but rather reconciliation and other such means to have it restored.[5] Nor must an individual kinsman who has taken unfair advantage of an item be forced to refund the benefits.

<**8**> Some are of the opinion that, since joint property also includes the property of others, the individual who deprives his co-owners of joint property is nothing but a thief and a sinner.[6]

My answer to them is as follows.

Only when someone has the distinct knowledge that something belongs to someone else, yet without just cause arrogates to himself ownership of the other's property, is he commonly understood to be a thief. In the case at hand, however, it is not possible to distinguish between what belongs to oneself and what belongs to others, since the property is undivided.

The situation here resembles in some ways that of a gift.[7] It is only when an owner, having the distinct knowledge that something belongs to him, cedes it to

[3] The sons of the deceased shall divide the property which their father withheld from partition, with his brothers, not with their brothers, as Colebrooke, Kane, and others translate.

[4] M 9.47, an often quoted verse, says that there are three acts that can be done only once: partition, promising a girl in marriage, and a gift.

[5] This sentence alludes to the traditional four means to achieve one's goal: *sāman* "reconciliation," *dāna*, "gift, bribery," *bheda*, "sowing dissension," and *daṇḍa* or *bala*, "force." The latter includes lawsuits before the courts and enforcement by the king (**9**).

[6] Criminal behavior in Hindu law invariably involves both accountability to the worldly authority resulting in punishment (*daṇḍa*) in a court of law, and sin (*pāpa*, *kilbiṣa*) to be accounted for to a superhuman authority. The *Mitākṣarā* (on Y 2.126; Colebrooke I.ix) does not mention the word "theft" but says that he who withholds property from a partition incurs *doṣa*, "fault"/"guilt." Others, including the *Vyavahāraprakāśa* (ed. p. 555; tr. VI.2), more specifically argue that withholding property at a partition constitutes theft indeed. Cf. Mayne 1950: 542–43.

[7] Jīmūtavāhana is about to demonstrate that one cannot steal joint property, any more than one can gift it. One cannot gift joint property, because one can gift only something one

bring about the ownership of another person, and when the other person distinctly realizes that he has become the owner by saying "this is mine," that one can speak of a gift. Since it is not possible to do so in the case of joint property, it is said that joint property cannot be made the object of a gift. In the same way, since theft requires that someone actually knows that something is not his but someone else's, one cannot speak of theft when someone removes joint property.

<**9**> To be sure, the word "remove" implies the intent to conceal the act.[8] The term "theft," however, is not equivalent with concealing. Indeed,

[1] the term "theft" is used as well for seizing things without concealment. Says Kātyāyana:

> Taking someone else's property, whether stealthily or openly,
> whether by day or by night is called theft. [K 810]

[2] I said earlier [**7**] that force, in the person of the king, should not be used to have the person who withheld joint property make restitution. It would be quite different if he was a thief. Based on the Text:

> The king shall make a thief restitute the stolen goods and make
> him suffer various forms of corporal punishment, [Y 2.270 ab]

not only would one not use reconciliation and other such means to have him make restitution, but he would also have to undergo corporal punishment.

<**10**> The same conclusion imposes itself in view of the fact that the Sages prescribe that even he who has removed joint property shall be given a share in it when it is partitioned. <**11**> Viśvarūpa, too, says: "Hence he is not guilty of theft." What he intends to say is that by dint of the wording of Yājñavalkya 2.126 [**3**][9] the meaning of the verb *sten*, "steal," does not apply here.[10]

<**12**> That is also why Jitendriya says the following in the *Prāyaścittakāṇḍa*: "If someone seizes someone else's gold thinking that it is iron or some other metal, or something that is not gold thinking that it is gold, or something that belongs to someone else thinking that it is his because it looks like something he owns, in none of these cases does the term 'theft' apply,[11] for in each case the one who seizes

---

owns, and one does not know what one owns in joint property. One cannot steal joint property, because one can only steal something that belongs to others, and one does not know what belongs to others in joint property.

[8] Cf. note 2.

[9] The quotation from Viśvarūpa does not appear in the printed *Bālakrīḍā*. One can only guess that, when Jīmūtavāhana quotes Viśvarūpa as saying *vacanārambhasāmarthyāt*, "by dint of the wording of the text," he refers to Viśvarūpa's commentary on Y 2.126. On Jīmūtavāhana's quotations from Viśvarūpa, see Introduction.

[10] This is a reference to *Dhātupāṭtha* 10.349: *sten-a caurye*.

[11] On the term *apa-hāra*, which Jitendriya uses here and which I translate "theft," see note 2.

the object does not realize that he is taking something that, in fact, belongs to someone else."[12]

The same is true in the case at hand, for prior to partition one cannot recognize the individual proprietary rights; only partition will make these rights overt with regard to specific segments of the joint property. Hence, the word "theft" does not apply in this case either.

<**13**> Or else,[13] assuming that his act constitutes theft, the one who removes joint property still is not burdened with the guilt connected with theft, since the Texts explicitly allot him a share in the partition. Otherwise, if someone withholds gold and the like, he would become an outcaste and he would not receive a share.[14]

[Objection] < **14**> Since there are Texts stating specifically that the thief gets a share even if he removes gold, which is a necessary and sufficient condition to expel him from his caste, the injunctions that allot the thief a share must be interpreted as pertaining to theft of things other than gold. Also, if you were right, why does the general rule that forbids stealing things such as gold not specify that they must belong exclusively to someone else and not be held jointly? In any case, there is no reason to doubt which of the two alternatives is the right one.[15]

[Refutation] Because of the phrase "someone else" in the definition "theft is taking someone else's property" [K 810; **9**], it is clear that for something to be stolen it must belong to someone else, thereby excluding any ownership in it on the part of the thief. Hence, as far as joint property and separate property are concerned, when one speaks of theft, it is the latter alone that comes to mind first. The situation at hand is similar to the one one faces with the expression "an *iṣṭi* ritual involving an oblation characteristic of the full moon sacrifice." The only kind of

[12] I.e., in none of the three examples provided by Jitendriya does the one who seizes the object have the intention to take the thing as it actually, "in fact" (*yathāvastu*), belongs to someone else.

[13] On the meaning of the phrase "or else" see note at **11.2.31**. Jīmūtavāhana is willing to grant that some people label the removal of joint property theft; yet, he continues to maintain that, technically, it is not.

[14] Stealing gold is one of the four or five major sins (*mahā-pātaka*). Unless the perpetrator of such acts performs penance, he shall not only be punished, but also be treated as an outcaste (e.g. M 9.236-239). On the exclusion of outcastes from inheritance, see **5.7**, **10**, **11**, **13**, etc. Jīmūtavāhana's point here is that, since the *smṛti* texts that allot shares to individuals who withhold property are couched in general terms and, thereby, include the one who withholds gold, withholding joint property cannot be considered to be theft.

[15] The text of this paragraph is difficult; it has been differently interpreted by the *Dāyabhāga* commentators. I take the entire paragraph as an objection by the opponent who persists in identifying the removal of joint property with theft. His arguments are twofold. First, he who steals gold becomes an outcaste and, as such, cannot inherit. As a result, the texts that allot a share to one who removes joint property apply to joint property other than gold. For the remover of gold to be entitled to a share there ought to be special rules to that effect, but there are no such rules. Second, the rules that forbid stealing gold do so in general terms; they do not say that the gold must belong exclusively to someone else. The two alternatives mentioned in the last sentence refer to the question whether withholding gold from joint property constitutes theft; according to Jīmūtavāhana's interlocutor it does.

oblation that stands out here is the sacrificial cake offered to Agni and Soma, not the clarified butter offered at the *upāṃśuyāga*, because the latter is common to oblations to Agni and Soma and to oblations that are not for Agni and Soma.[16] <**15**> That is why in daily life one does not notice any hesitation between the alternative solutions in this kind of matter either.[17]

<**16**> Consequently, the following statement by Bālaka is no more than a babe's babble: "Even if the removal involves property that belongs both to oneself and not to oneself, removing property that does not belong to oneself is prohibited. The situation is similar to that in which, in the absence of enough *mudga* beans one uses *māṣa* beans as a substitute, and thereby links both *mudga* beans and *māṣa* beans to the sacrifice; because of the rule: '*māṣa* beans are unfit for the sacrifice,' *māṣa* beans are prohibited."[18]

In fact, the two situations are different. When one co-owner seizes joint property, the term "theft" as defined earlier [K 810; **9**] does not apply at all. On the other hand, even when fragments of *māṣas* are added to the *mudgas*, one cannot say that the sacrifice is performed without *māṣas*, and it is clear that only *mudgas* that are not mixed with *māṣas* are fit for a sacrifice.

<**17**> Thus far for the partition of property that, at the time of an earlier partition, was removed by one of the participants from the others.[19]

[16] The full moon and the new moon sacrifices (*darśapūrṇamāsa*) are the prototypes of all rituals of the *iṣṭi* type. Cf. Hillebrandt 1879. When the performance of a particular *iṣṭi* requires an oblation that is characteristic of the full moon sacrifice, there are two possibilities: either an oblation of clarified butter (*ājya*) which, in the full moon sacrifice, is offered to Agni and Soma and at the time of the *upāṃśuyāga* or an oblation in the form of a sacrificial cake (*puroḍāśa*) which is offered exclusively to Agni and Soma. The latter form of oblation is, therefore, more characteristic of the full moon sacrifice than the former

[17] The two alternatives referred to here are the same as those mentioned in the final sentence of the objection; according to Jīmūtavāhana withholding gold from joint property does not constitute theft.

[18] The *Mīmāṃsā-sūtras* (6.3.20) make it clear that, if there are not enough *mudgas*, "green kidney beans," to prepare the sacrificial pap, they should never be complemented, even unintentionally, with *māṣas*, "black kidney beans." Indeed, the *Taittirīya-saṃhitā* (5.1.8.1) says that *māṣa* beans are unfit for a sacrifice (*amedhyā vai māṣāḥ*). Both Bālaka (and the *Mitākṣarā* on Y 2.126; Colebrooke I.ix.11) and Jīmūtavāhana agree on this rule, but they draw opposite conclusions from it when it comes to seizing property. Cf. Kane 1946: 637 and 1962: 1320, 1347. According to Bālaka the person who withheld joint property improperly mixed together property of his own and property of his co-owners, which he, in fact, stole. As a result he is guilty of theft, even though property of his own was involved as well. Jīmūtavāhana's view follows in the next paragraph.

[19] In this final sentence Jīmūtavāhana again uses the verb *apa-hṛ*, "remove." Cf. note 2.

CHAPTER FOURTEEN

EVIDENCE TO PROVE THAT A VALID PARTITION TOOK PLACE

<1> Let me now discuss what to do when questions arise about the validity of a partition.[1]

On this subject Nārada says:

> If heirs raise questions about the legality of a partition, a decision shall be made by relying on relatives (*jñāti*), the deed of partition, or the fact that the parties transact business separately. [N 13.36]

Witnesses

<2> The fact that Nārada 13.36 says "relatives" means that one should not resort to any other witnesses if relatives are available. That is why Yājñavalkya says:

> If some deny that a partition took place, one shall prove that it did with the help of *jñātis* and *bandhus* as witnesses, documents, or separately held houses or land. [Y 2.149]

<3> First *jñātis*, i.e., *sapiṇḍas*, serve as witnesses; failing them, those relatives who are subsumed under the term *bandhu*; failing them, outsiders. If any one of these three could be called on first, the Text would have used the single word "witnesses," and the terms *jñāti* and *bandhu* would be redundant.

<4> That is also why Śaṅkha says:

> If questions arise with regard to the allotment of shares within a *gotra*, and members of the *gotra* do not know about it, members of the *kula* may serve as witnesses. [Ś 280]

[1] Jolly (1885: 104-06) rightly wonders why no ritual attended the partition of property. There were even few documents to attest it. Even in modern Hindu law "a partition may be effected without any instrument in writing" (Mayne 1950: 544). For the precaution taken when someone declines the share to which he is entitled, see **3.28**.

"Members of the *gotra*" here means *jñātis*. If they do not know about the matter, "members of the *kula*," i.e., *bandhus*, may serve as witnesses, but not people who are not relatives. Others may serve as witnesses only if the *bandhus* do not know about it either.

<5> That is why Nārada [13.36; **1**] mentions only *jñātis*, for they are the primary witnesses. The variant reading "people who know" instead of "relatives" is without foundation.[2]

Documents

<**6**> Alternatively, the decision may be based on a written document. In fact, it has been said that a written document is superior to witnesses.[3]

Transacting Business Separately

<**7**> The decision may also be based on a demonstration that the parties transact their businesses separately. Indeed,

[A] Nārada says:

> When brothers are separated, they manage separately their giving, receiving, cattle, food, houses, land, servants, cooking, ritual, income, and expenditure. [N 13.38]
> Separated brothers may act for each other as witnesses or sureties, and they may give to and receive from one another. Brothers who are not separated may not. [N 13.39]
> Anyone who performs these activities publicly with property of his own should be considered separated, even if there is no written document to that effect. [N 13.40]

[B] <**8**> Bṛhaspati says:

> If there are neither documents nor witnesses, then the facts relating to an act of violence, to immovable property, to a deposit, or to a prior partition by co-heirs may be ascertained by means of circumstantial evidence. [B 26.143]

[2] The reading *jñātṛbhir* instead of *jñātibhir*, which Jīmūtavāhana rejects, appears neither in any of the several quotations of N 13.36 in later texts (*Dhko* p. 1579) nor in Lariviere's Nārada ed.

[3] Jīmūtavāhana here refers to texts such as K 315b: *sākṣibhyo likhitaṃ guru*, "a written document is weightier than witnesses."

> A propensity to resort to violence, a wound, or a weapon points to an act of violence; usufruct points to ownership of immovable property; separate property points to a partition. [B 26.146]
> If people manage their income, expenditure, and property separately, or if they engage in money lending or trade with one another, there can be no doubt that they are separated. [B 26.147]

<**9**>[4] One brother makes a gift, and the other accepts it. Their houses and the like and the management of their income and expenditure are all separate. When one of them incurs debts and the like, the other acts as a witness or a surety for them. They borrow money and have other like dealings with each other. One buys some item from a third party and sells it commercially to his brother. Each and every one of these activities and others like them is possible only between individuals who are separated. Such activities are sufficient for reasonable people to infer that the parties are separated.

<**10**> Note that it would be wrong to say that, since "these activities" is expressed in the plural, Nārada 13.40 requires that all these activities take place cumulatively. The Texts are founded on common sense, and the inference that a partition took place is valid when any one of these activities occurs.

<**11**> The phrase "if there are neither documents nor witnesses" [B 26.143; **8**] explicitly states that one may resort to circumstantial evidence only when neither documents nor witnesses are available.

[4] **9** and **10** constitute Jīmūtavāhana's commentary on N 13.38–40 (**7**).

CHAPTER FIFTEEN

EPILOGUE

<1> There can be no pleasure in this book for those whose understanding of the true nature of inheritance has been removed by heeding the opinions of certain teachers.[1] Yet, the author has striven to show that the Sages, whose wisdom derives from the true authorities, are in complete agreement with one another.

<2> Please consider this work, composed by Jīmūtavāhana, as intended to dispel the uncertainties created by the earlier commentators' varying interpretations.[2]

<3> Thus ends the *Dāyabhāga*, a section of the *Dharmaratna*, a work composed by the Pāribhadrīya Mahāmahopādhyāya Jīmūtavāhana.[3]

[1] According to Śrīkṛṣṇa, Jīmūtavāhana here refers to the wrong kind of teachers, Śrīkaramiśra and others.

[2] After these two stanzas, in *vasantatilaka* and *āryā* meter, respectively, some *Dāyabhāga* editions (1863, etc.) add another stanza in *anuṣṭubh* meter: "The eminent Jīmūtavāhana, born of the Pāribhadra family, composed this *Dāyabhāga* to clear the uncertainties that are prevalent among the learned." This verse, however, is absent from the earlier editions, from Colebrooke's translation, and from all the *Dāyabhāga* manuscripts I have collated.

[3] This colophon, in prose, appears in most editions, in Colebrooke's translation, and in a large majority of the manuscripts. As copyists are wont to do, a number of them add various additional statements. Cf. Introduction.

TEXT

<**1.1**> ।। नमो गणेशाय[1] ।।

मन्वादिवाक्यान्यविमृष्य येषां
यस्मिन् विवादो बहुधा बुधानाम् ।
तेषां प्रबोधाय स दायभागो
निरूपणीयः सुधियः शृणुध्वम् ।।

<**2**> अथ दायभागो निरूप्यते । तत्र **नारदः** —
विभागोऽर्थस्य पित्र्यस्य पुत्रैर्यत्र[2] प्रकल्प्यते ।
दायभाग इति प्रोक्तं तद्विवादपदं बुधैः ।। [N 13.1]

<**3**> पितृत आगतं पित्र्यम् । तच्च पितृमरणोपजातस्वत्वमुच्यते । पित्र्यस्येति पुत्रैरिति च द्वयमपि[3] संबन्धिमात्रोपलक्षणं[4] संबन्धिमात्रेण[5] संबन्धिमात्रधनविभागेऽपि[6] दायभागपदप्रयोगात् । अत एव दायभागं[7] विवादपदमुपक्रम्य **नारदो**ऽपि[8] मात्रादिधनविभागमप्युपदर्शितवान् । तथा **मनुर**पि पित्रादिपदमदत्त्वैव[9] —
एष स्त्रीपुंसयोरुक्तो धर्मो वो रतिसंहितः[10] ।
आपद्यपत्यप्राप्तिश्च दायभागं निबोधत ।। [M 9.103]
इत्युपक्रम्य यावत्संबन्धिधनविभागमुक्तवान् ।

[1] नमो गणेशाय । ॐ गणेशाय नमः । ॐ शिवाय । ॐ दुर्गायै नमः । ॐ नमः कालिकायै । श्रीराधाकृष्णाभ्यां नमः
[2] यत्र । यस्तु
[3] द्वयमपि । द्वयं । *om*
[4] संबन्धि- । संबन्ध-
[5] संबन्धि- । संबन्ध-
[6] संबन्धिमात्र- । संबन्धि-
[7] दायभागं । दायभाग-
[8] ऽपि । *om*
[9] -दत्त्वैव । -कृत्वैव । अनुक्त्वैव
[10] -संहितः । -संज्ञितः । -संस्थितः

<4> दीयत इति व्युपत्त्या दायशब्दः । ददातिप्रयोगश्च[11] गौणः मृतप्रव्रजितादिस्वत्वनिवृत्तिपूर्वकपरस्वत्वोत्पत्तिफलसाम्यात्[12] । न तु मृतादीनां तत्र त्यागोऽस्ति[13] । **<5>** ततश्च पूर्वस्वामिसंबन्धाधीनं[14] तत्स्वाम्योपरमे[15] यत्र द्रव्ये तत्र निरूढो दायशब्दः ।

<6> ननु किं दायस्य विभागो विभक्तावयवत्वं यद्वा दायेन सह विभागोऽसंयुक्तत्वम् । न तावत्पूर्वो दायविनाशापत्तेः[16] । नापि द्वितीयः संयुक्तेऽपि न ममेदं विभक्तं स्वं भ्रातुरिति[17] प्रयोगात् ।

<7> न च संबन्धाविशेषात्सर्वेषां सर्वधनोत्पन्नस्य स्वत्वस्य द्रव्यविशेषे व्यवस्थापनं विभाग इति वाच्यम् । संबन्ध्यन्तरसद्भावप्रतिपक्षस्य संबन्धस्यावयवेष्वेव विभागव्यङ्ग्यस्वत्वापादकत्वात् । कृत्स्नपितृधनगतस्वत्वोत्पादविनाशकल्पनागौरवात् । यथेष्टविनियोगफलाभावेनानुपयोगाच्च ।

<8> उच्यते — एकदेशगतस्यैव[18] भूहिरण्यादावुत्पन्नस्य स्वत्वस्य विनिगमनाप्रमाणाभावेन वैशेषिकव्यवहारानर्हतया अव्यवस्थितस्य गुटिकापातादिना व्यञ्जनं[19] विभागः । **<9>** विशेषेण भजनं स्वत्वज्ञापनं वा विभागः।

<10> यत्रापि चैकं दासीगवादिकं बहुसाधारणं तत्रापि तत्तत्कालविशेषवहनदोहनादिफलेन स्वत्वं व्यज्यते । तदाह **बृहस्पतिः** —

एकां स्त्रीं कारयेत्कर्म यथांशेन गृहे गृहे । [B 26.2ab]
उद्धृत्य कूपवाप्यम्भस्त्वनुसारेण गृह्यते । [B 26.3ab]
युक्त्या विभजनीयं तदन्यथानर्थकं भवेत् ।। [B 26.4]

इदं श्लोकार्धत्रयं नानास्थानस्थं न तु क्रमिकम्[20] ।

[11] ददाति- । ददातिपद-
[12] -स्वत्वोत्पत्ति- । -स्वत्वापत्ति-
[13] तत्र त्यागोऽस्ति । त्यागस्तत्रास्ति । तत्र त्यागोऽस्तीति
[14] पूर्वस्वामि- । पूर्वद्रव्यस्वामि-
[15] तत्स्वाम्योपरमे । तत्स्वाम्युपरमे
[16] दाय- । दायस्य
[17] भ्रातुरिति । भ्रातुरिदमिति
[18] एकदेशगतस्यैव । एकदेशोपात्तस्यैव
[19] व्यञ्जनं । स्वत्वव्यञ्जनं
[20] क्रमिकम् । सक्रमकम्

<**11**> ननु —

पितर्यूर्ध्वं गते[21] पुत्रा विभजेयुर्धनं पितुः । [N 13.2ab]

इति **नारद**वचनात्[22] पितुर्धनं विभजेयुरित्यन्वयाद्विभागात्पूर्वं न पुत्राणां तत्र[23] स्वत्वम् । न च विभागस्य स्वत्वकारणता असंबन्धिधनेऽप्यतिप्रसङ्गात् ।

<**12**> उच्यते — पित्रादिनिधनानन्तरमेवास्मदीयमिति[24] प्रयोगात् एकपुत्रे च विभागं विनैव स्वत्वस्वीकारात्[25] संबन्धिनिधनमेव स्वत्वकारणमतो नातिप्रसङ्गः ।

<**13**> नन्वर्जयितृव्यापारोऽर्जनम् । अर्जनाधीनस्वामिभावश्चार्जयिता । तेन पुत्रव्यापारो[26] जन्मैवार्जनं युक्तम् । अतो जीवत्येव पितरि पुत्राणां तत्र[27] स्वत्वं न तु तन्निधनात् । अत एवोक्तम् — क्वचिज्जन्मैव यथा पित्र्ये धने।

<**14**> नैतन्**मन्वादि**विरोधात् । यथा **मनुः** —

ऊर्ध्वं पितुश्च मातुश्च समेत्य भ्रातरः समम् ।
भजेरन् पैतृकं रिक्थमनीशास्ते हि जीवतोः ।। [M 9.104]

<**15**> जीवतोरपि पित्रोः पुत्राणां कुतो[28] न विभाग इत्याशङ्कायामिदमुत्तरं तदानीमस्वामित्वादिति ।

<**16**> न च भार्या पुत्रश्चेत्यादिवदस्वातन्त्र्याभिप्रायमिदमिति वाच्यं तदानीं स्वत्वे[29] प्रमाणाभावात् । भार्यादिषु तु यत्ते समधिगच्छन्त्यर्जयन्तीति स्वत्वे सिद्धे युक्तमस्वातन्त्र्यवर्णनम् ।

[21] पितर्यूर्ध्वं गते । पितर्युपरते
[22] **नारद**वचनात् । वचनात्
[23] पुत्राणां तत्र । तत्र पुत्राणां
[24] -स्मदीयमिति । -स्मदीयधनमिति
[25] स्वत्वस्वीकारात् । स्वत्वस्वीकाराच्च
[26] पुत्र- । पुत्रस्य
[27] तत्र । तत्- । *om*
[28] पुत्राणां कुतो । कुतो पत्राणां
[29] स्वत्वे । स्वामित्वे

<**17**> किंच स्वोपात्तेऽपि[30] तेषामस्वामित्वे स्वधनसाध्यवैदिककर्मोच्छेदात् श्रुतिविरोधः स्यात् ।

<**18**> **देवलश्च** पितृधनेऽस्वाम्यमेव स्पष्टयति । यथा —

पितर्युपरते पुत्रा विभजेयुर्धनं पितुः ।
अस्वाम्यं हि भवेदेषां निर्दोषे पितरि स्थिते ।। [D 1563]

<**19**> किंच जीवत्यपि पितरि पितृधने पुत्राणां स्वामित्वे पितुरनिच्छयापि[31] विभागः स्यात् ।

जन्मनैव स्वत्वमिति[32] प्रमाणाभावाच्च अर्जनरूपतया जन्मनः स्मृतावनधिगमात् । <**20**> क्वचिज्जन्मैवेति च[33] जन्मनिबन्धनत्वात् पितापुत्रसंबन्धस्य पतिमरणस्य च स्वत्वकारणत्वात् परम्परया वर्णनम् ।

<**21**> अन्यव्यापारेणान्यस्य[34] स्वत्वमविरुद्धं शास्त्रमूलत्वादस्य । दृष्टं च लोकेऽपि । दाने हि चेतनोद्देशविशिष्टत्यागादेव दातृव्यपारात् संप्रदानस्य द्रव्ये[35] स्वामित्वम् ।

<**22**> न च स्वीकरणात्स्वत्वं स्वीकर्तुरेव दातृत्वापत्तेः । परस्वत्वापत्तिफलेन हि दानरूपता । तच्च फलं संप्रदानाधीनम् । यथाहि[36] देवतोद्देशेन द्रव्यत्यागं कुर्वन्नपि यजमानो न होता । किंतु तस्यैव त्यागस्य होमाभिधाननिमित्तं प्रक्षेपं कुर्वन्नृत्विगेव होतेत्युच्यते । तद्वदत्रापि स्यात् ।

किंच मनसा पात्रमुद्दिश्येत्यादिशास्त्रे स्वीकारात्प्रागेव दानपदं दृष्टम् ।

<**23**> ननु ग्रहणं स्वीकारः । अभूततद्भावे च्विप्रयोगात् । अस्वं स्वं कुर्वन् व्यापारः स्वीकारो भवति । कथं ततः प्रागेव[37] स्वत्वम् ।

30 स्वोपात्तेऽपि । स्वोपार्जितऽपि
31 पितुरनिच्छयापि । पितुरनिच्छया
32 स्वत्वमिति । स्वत्वमित्यत्र
33 च । *om*
34 अन्यव्यापारेणान्यस्य । अन्यव्यापारेणाप्यन्यस्य
35 द्रव्ये । द्रव्य-
36 यथाहि । यथा
37 ततः प्रागेव । तत्प्रागेव

<**24**> उच्यते — उत्पन्नमपि स्वत्वं संप्रदानव्यापारेण ममेदमिति ज्ञानेन यथेष्टव्यवहारार्हं[38] क्रियत इति स्वीकारशब्दार्थः ।

याजनाध्यापनसाहचर्याच्च प्रतिग्रहस्य स्वत्वमजनयतोऽप्यर्जनरूपता न विरुद्धा याजनादौ दक्षिणादानादेव स्वत्वात् ।

<**25**> पितृनिधनकालीनं वा जीवनमेव पुत्रस्यार्जनं भविष्यति ।

किंच भ्रात्रादिधने[39] तन्मरणात्तन्मरणकालीनजीवनाद्वा भ्रात्रन्तरादेः स्वत्वमकामेनापि वाच्यम् ।

<**26**> अत ऊर्ध्वं पितुश्चेत्यादि तत्कालीनस्वत्वज्ञापनार्थं तदानीमेव चेच्छाप्राप्तं[40] विभागमनुवदति प्राप्तत्वाद्विधानानुपपत्तेः ।

<**27**> न च नियमः संभवति —

एवं सह वसेयुर्वा पृथग्वा धर्मकाम्यया । [M 9.111ab]

इति **मनु**विरोधात्[41] । दृष्टार्थत्वाच्च विभागस्य न तन्नियमः कालनियमो वा संभवति । <**28**> किंच पितर्युपरत इत्यनन्तरकाल एव निभागः स्यान्न तु परस्तादपि जातेष्टिवज्जातप्राणवियोगापत्तिसमानस्यात्र विरोधस्याभावात् पित्रुपरमानन्तरस्य[42] च यावज्जीवपर्यन्तस्य स्वेच्छात एव प्राप्तत्वात् ।

<**29**> अतो जीवति पितरि सत्यपि पुत्राणां स्वाम्ये विभागनिषेधार्थं **मनु**वचनम्[43] वाच्यम् । तच्चान्याय्यमस्वार्थपरत्वापत्तेः ।

<**30**> अतो जीवतोः पित्रोस्तद्धने[44] पुत्राणां स्वाम्यं नास्ति किंतूपरतयोरिति[45] ज्ञापनार्थं **मन्वादि**वचनम् । एकः शाब्दोऽपरश्चार्थः ।

[38] यथेष्टव्यवहारार्हं । व्यवहारार्हं

[39] -धने । -धने च

[40] चेच्छा- । स्वेच्छा-

[41] **मनु**विरोधात् । **मनु**वचनविरोधात्

[42] पित्रुपरमानन्तरस्य । पित्रुपरमानन्तर्यस्य

[43] **मनु**वचनम् । वचनम्

[44] पित्रोस्तद्धने । पित्रोर्धने

[45] किंतूपरतयोरिति । किंतूपरतयोस्तयोरिति

<**31**> न चोपरममात्रमेव[46] विवक्षितं किंतु पतितप्रव्रजितत्वाद्युपलक्षयति[47] स्वत्वविनाशहेतुतासाम्यात् । <**32**> तदाह **नारदः** —

मातुर्निवृत्ते रजसि दत्तासु भगिनीषु च ।
विनष्टे वाप्यशरणे पितर्युपरतस्पृहे ।। [N 13.3]

<**33**> विनष्टे पतिते । अशरण इति[48] गृहस्थाश्रमरहिते । यदा[49] निवृत्ते वापि मरणादिति पाठस्तदा मरणान्निवृत्ते जीवति निस्पृह इति पाठान्तरमनाकरम् ।

<**34**> अत्राप्युपरतस्पृहत्वादिना पुत्राणां स्वत्वं पितृधने[50] भवतीति ज्ञापनादयमेकः कालो विभागस्येच्छाप्राप्तोऽनूद्यते प्राप्त्यनुसारित्वाच्चानुवादस्य स्वामित्वाच्च प्राप्तेः ।

<**35**> एकस्यापि स्वधने स्वाम्यादेकेच्छयापि विभागप्राप्तेः समेत्येति सहितत्वं पक्षप्राप्तमनूद्यते । अन्यथा साहित्यवद्बहुत्वस्याप्यवगतेर्द्वयोर्विभागो न स्यादेव द्वयोर्विभागप्रतिपादकशास्त्राभावात् ।

<**36**> ननूपरते पितरि ज्येष्ठ एव धनाधिकारी नेतरः । यथा **मनुः** —

ज्येष्ठ एव तु गृह्णीयात्पित्र्यं धनमशेषतः ।
शेषास्तमुपजीवेयुर्यथैव पितरं तथा ।। [M 9.105]

ज्येष्ठोऽत्र पुन्नामनरकव्यावर्तकोऽभिप्रेतो[51] न तु जीवदपेक्षः । यथा[52] **मनुः**—

ज्येष्ठेन जातमात्रेण पुत्री भवति मानवः ।
पितृणामनृणश्चैव स तस्माल्लब्धुमर्हति ।। [M 9.106]
यस्मिन्नृणं संनयति येन चानन्त्यमश्नुते ।
स एव धर्मजः पुत्रः कामजानितरान्विदुः ।। [M 9.107]

<**37**> नैतत् सर्वेच्छाधीनज्येष्ठाधिकारश्रुतेः । यथा **नारदः** —

बिभृयाद्वेच्छतः सर्वान् ज्येष्ठो भ्राता यथा पिता ।

[46] -मात्रमेव । -मात्रं
[47] -त्वाद्युपलक्षयति । -त्वाद्यप्युपलक्षयति
[48] अशरण इति । अशरणे
[49] यदा । *om*
[50] स्वत्वं पितृधने । पितृधने स्वत्वं
[51] -नरकव्यावर्तको । -नरकाद्व्यावर्तको
[52] यथा । तथ

भ्राता शक्तः कनिष्ठो वा शक्त्यपेक्षा कुले स्थितिः[53] ॥ [N 13.5]

सर्वेच्छया कनिष्ठोऽपि शक्तः सन् बिभृयादिति ज्येष्ठता चातन्त्रम् । यथा **मनुः**[54] —

एवं सह वसेयुर्वा पृथग्वा धर्मकाम्यया ।
पृथग्विवर्धते धर्मस्तस्माद्धर्म्या पृथक्क्रिया ॥ [M 9.111]

सह पृथग्वेति पदाभ्यां काम्ययेति चेच्छातो[55] वैकल्पकत्वं[56] दर्शयति ।

<38> तदेवं पितृस्वत्वापगम एकः कालोऽपरश्चानपगत एव पितृस्वाम्ये पितुरिच्छयेति कालद्वयम् ।

<39> न पुनः पितर्युपरत इत्येकः[57] पितर्युपरतस्पृहे मातुश्च निवृत्ते रजसीत्यपरोऽनिवृत्तेऽपि[58] मातृरजसि[59] पितरि सस्पृहे तदिच्छयेति कालत्रयमादरणीयम् ।

मातृरजोनिवृत्तेः पित्रुपरतस्पृहत्वविशेषणत्वे

त्रिंशद्वर्षो वहेत्कन्यां[60] हृद्यां द्वादशवार्षिकीम् ।
त्र्यष्टवर्षोऽष्टवर्षां वा धर्मे सीदति सत्वर[61] ॥ [M 9.94]

इति **मनुना** विवाहकालविधानात्[62] । वनं पञ्चाशतो व्रजेदित्याश्रमान्तरगमनकालविधानात्[63] । तदा च रजोनिवृत्तेर्मातुरसंभवे पतिरि चोपरतस्पृहे वानप्रस्थ्ये तत्पुत्राणामिच्छतामप्यविभागप्रसङ्गात् ।

[53] कुले स्थितिः । कुलस्थितिः
[54] यथा **मनुः** । **मनुः** । *om*
[55] चेच्छातो । चेच्छाया । चेच्छा-
[56] वैकल्पकत्वं । वैकल्पिकत्वं । विकल्पकत्वं
[57] इत्येकः । इत्येकः कालः
[58] ऽपि । *om*
[59] मातृरजसि । रजसि
[60] कन्यां । भार्यां
[61] सत्वर । सत्वरे
[62] विवाहकाल- । काल-
[63] **-गमन-** । *om*

<**40**> निर्विशेषणमुपरतस्पृहत्वमेव पितृधनविभागकाल[64] इति चेन्न अनुपरतस्पृहे पितरि पतितेऽप्यविभागप्रसङ्गात् । <**41**> अयमप्यपरः काल इत्यभिधाने कालचतुष्टयापत्तिः पितुरुपरमः[65] पतितत्वं निस्पृहत्वमिच्छा चेति ।

<**42**> यच्च कार्याक्षमे पितरि पुत्राणां निभागे स्वातन्त्र्यमुक्तं तद्वचनानभिज्ञत्वेन । तथा च **हारीतः** —

> जीवति पितरि पुत्राणामर्थादानविसर्गाक्षेपेषु न स्वातन्त्र्यम् ।
> कामं दीने प्रोषिते आर्तिं गते वा ज्येष्ठोऽर्थांश्चिन्तयेत् ॥
> [H 4.1,3]

सुव्यक्तमाहतुः **शङ्खलिखितौ** —

> पितर्यशक्ते कुटुम्बव्यवहारान्[66] ज्येष्ठः प्रतिकुर्यादनन्तरो वा कार्यज्ञस्तदनुमतो न त्वकामे पितरि रिक्थविभागः । वृद्धे विपरीतचेतसि दीर्घरोगिणि[67] वा ज्येष्ठ एव पितृवदर्थान् पालयेदितरेषाम् । रिक्थमूलं हि कुटुम्बमस्वतन्त्राः पितृमन्तो मातुरप्येवमवस्थितायाः ॥ [ŚL 270]

<**43**> एतद्वचनद्वयं कार्याक्षमे दीर्घरोगिणि वा[68] पितरि विभागं निषिध्य ज्येष्ठ एव गृहं चिन्तयेत्तदनुजो वा कार्यज्ञ इत्याह । अतो न त्वकामे पितरीत्येतदेव । कार्याक्षमे पितरि रिक्थविभाग इति भ्रान्तलिखितम्[69] ।

<**44**> तस्मात्पतितत्वनिस्पृहत्वोपरमैः स्वत्वापगम[70] एकः[71] कालोऽपरश्च[72] सति स्वत्वे तदिच्छात इति कालद्वयमेव युक्तम् ।

[64] पितृधनविभाग- । पितुर्धनविभाग- । पितुर्धन-
[65] पितुरुपरमः । पित्रुपरमः
[66] कुटुम्बव्यवहारान् । व्यवहारान्
[67] दीर्घरोगिणि । रोगिणि
[68] वा । च
[69] भ्रान्तलिखितम् । भ्रान्तिलिखितम्
[70] स्वत्वापगम । स्वत्वोपगम
[71] एकः । इत्येकः
[72] कालोऽपरश्च । काल अपरश्च

<**45**> मातुर्निवृत्ते रजसीति तु[73] पितामहादिधनाभिप्रायं निवृत्ते रजसि पुत्रान्तरसंभावनाभावात्[74] । तदानीमपि पितुरिच्छयैव पुत्राणां विभागः अ-निवृत्ते रजसि क्रमागतधनविभागे पश्चाज्जातानां वृत्तिलोपापत्तेः । न चासौ युक्तः —

ये जाता येऽप्यजाताश्च[75] ये च गर्भे व्यवस्थिताः ।
वृत्तिं तेऽपि हि काङ्क्षन्ति वृत्तिलोपो विगर्हितः[76] ॥ [Vy 253]

इति वचनात्[77] ।

<**46**> यत एव पितृधने कालद्वयमत एव **मनु-गोतमादि**भिर्मृतपदं परि-त्यज्य ऊर्ध्वमित्युक्तमूर्ध्वं पितुरिति पितुस्तदा स्वत्वापगमात् । तदर्थमे-वोर्ध्वमित्युक्तम्[78] । अतोऽयमेको विभागकालः । ऊर्ध्वं विभागाज्जात-स्त्वित्यनेन[79] च[80] सस्पृहे पितरि तदिच्छया विभागकालोऽपरो दर्शितः[81] ।

<**47**> दत्तासु भगिनीषु चेति न कालार्थं किंतु तासामवश्यंदानार्थम् ।

तथा —

यच्छिष्टं पितृदायेभ्यो दत्त्वर्णं पैतृकं ततः ।
भ्रातृभिस्तद्विभक्तव्यमृणी न स्याद्यथा पिता ॥ [N 13.32]

इदं[82] **नारद**वचनं पित्रर्णशोधनावश्यंभावार्थं न विभागकालार्थम् ।

<**48**> अस्माच्च **नारद**वचनादयमर्थः सिध्यति यद्विभागकर्तृभिरुत्तमर्णा-नुमत्यैव पित्राद्यृणं[83] विभजनीयं परिशोध्यं वा शोधनावशिष्टधनविभाग-प्रतिपादनस्यैव तत्प्रयोजनत्वात् ।

[73] तु । *om*
[74] -संभावनाभावात् । -संभवाभावात्
[75] ऽप्यजाताश्च । ऽप्यजाता वा
[76] विगर्हितः । न विद्यते
[77] वचनात् । **मनु**वचनात्
[78] -मित्युक्तम् । -मित्यभिधानम्
[79] विभागाज्जातस्त्वित्यनेन । विभागाज्जातस्तु पित्र्यमेव हरेद्धनमित्यनेन
[80] च । *om*
[81] ऽपरो दर्शितः । ऽपरः प्रदर्शितः
[82] इदं । इति
[83] पित्राद्यृणं । पित्रादिधनं

अत एव मातृधनस्याप्यृणावशिष्टस्यैव विभागमाह **याज्ञवल्क्यः** —

मातृर्दुहितरः शेषमृणात्ताभ्य ऋतेऽन्वयः ।। [Y 2.117cd]

एतच्च विस्तरेणर्णादाने वक्ष्यते ।

<**49**> यद्वा दत्तासु भगिनीषु मातृधनं पुत्रैरेव विभजनीयम् । अदत्तासु ताभिः सह साधारणम्। एतच्चावसरे वाच्यम् ।

<**50**> एवं तावत्पितृधनविभागस्य कालद्वयमुक्तम्[84] ।

[84] कालद्वयमुक्तम् । कालद्वयमप्युक्तम्

<**2.1**> संप्रति पितामहादिधनविभागकालोऽभिधीयते[1] ।

तत्र **बृहस्पतिः** —

पित्रोरभावे भ्रातृणां विभागः संप्रदर्शितः ।
मातुर्निवृत्ते रजसि जीवतोरपि शस्यते ।। [B 26.9]

<**2**> नास्य[2] वचनस्य पितृधनगोचरत्वम् ऊर्ध्वं विभागाज्जातस्त्वित्यस्य निर्विषयत्वापत्तेः । निवृत्ते रजसि पुत्रोत्पत्त्यभावात्[3] । मातृधनविषयत्वं च नाशङ्कनीयं[4] एवं मातुरेव निर्धनत्वापत्तेः । अतो निवृत्ते रजसीति पितामहादिधनविषयम्[5] ।

<**3**> न चेच्छामनपेक्ष्य रजोनिवृत्तेर्विभागनिमित्तत्वं संभवतीति[6] अनिच्छया विभागाभावात् । <**4**> सत्यामिच्छायां कस्येच्छयेत्यपेक्षायाम् —

ऊर्ध्वं पितुः पुत्रा रिक्थं विभजेयुः[7] । निवृत्ते रजसि मातु-
र्जीवति चेच्छति ।। [G 28.1-2]

इति **गोतम**वचनात् पितुरेवेच्छात इति निर्णीयते ।

<**5**> अतः पित्रोरभाव एकः कालः । पित्रोरिति द्विवचननिर्देशात् सोदरभ्रातृणां पितृधनविभागोऽपि मातुरभाव एव कार्यः[8] । <**6**> न तु मातृधनविभागार्थं मातुरभावस्योपादानं जीवतोरपीत्यस्य मातृधनगोचरत्वानुपपत्तेरन्यधनगोचरत्वमवश्यं वाच्यम् । तेन यत्रैव पित्रोरभावो निमित्तं तत्रैव जीवतोरपीत्यपिशब्देन जीवनस्यापि शस्तत्वकीर्तनान्न मातुरभावो मातृधने व्याख्येयः । एतच्च विस्तरेण वक्तव्यम्[9] ।

[1] पितामहादि- । पितामह- ।। कालोऽभिधीयते । काल उच्यते

[2] नास्य । न चास्य

[3] पुत्रोत्पत्त्यभावात् । पुत्रोत्पत्तेरभावात्

[4] च नाशङ्कनीयं । चास्य नाशङ्कनीयं

[5] पितामहादि- । पैतामहादि-

[6] संभवतीति । संभवति

[7] विभजेयुः । विभजेरन्

[8] कार्यः । धर्म्यः

[9] वक्तव्यम् । वाच्यम्

<**7**> तस्मात्पितामहादिधनस्यापि[10] पित्रोरभाव इत्येको विभागकालः । तथा मातुर्निवृत्ते रजसि पितुरिच्छात इत्यपरः[11] । <**8**> न तु पितुरिच्छाम-न्तरेणैव[12] तस्य विभागः । अनीशास्ते हि जीवतोः [M 9.104d] । तथा — अस्वाम्यं हि भवेदेषां निर्दोषे पितरि स्थिते [D 1563cd] । तथा — जीवति चेच्छति[13] [G 28.2] । तथा — पितुरनुमत्या दायविभागः [Bau 2.2.3.8] । तथा — जीवति पितरि रिक्थविभागोऽनुमतः [ŚL 274] । तदेवमादि**मनु**-**नारद**-**गोतम**-**बौधायन**-**शङ्खलिखितादि**भिरविशेषेण जीवति पितरि पुत्राणां याव-द्धनगोचरास्वामित्वस्य पितुरिच्छाधीनविभागस्य च प्रतिपादनात् पैतामह-धनविभागकालस्य च[14] पृथगेभिरनभिधानात् पैतामहधनगोचरत्वमप्यनीश-त्वपित्रनुमतिवचनानाम्[15] ।

<**9**> यत्तु **याज्ञवल्क्य**वचनम् —

भूर्या पितामहोपात्ता निबन्धो द्रव्यमेव वा ।
तत्र स्यात्सदृशं स्वाम्यं पितुः पुत्रस्य चोभयोः ।। [Y 2.121]

तस्य **निरवद्यविद्योद्योतेन** द्योतितस्तत्त्वतोऽयमर्थः — यत्र द्वयोर्भ्रात्रोर्जीव-त्पितृकयोरप्राप्तभागयोरेकः पुत्रमुत्पाद्य विनष्टोऽन्यो जीवति अनन्तरं पिता मृतस्तत्र पुत्र एव तद्धनं प्राप्नोत्यतिसंनिकर्षात्[16] । तदर्थं सदृशं स्वाम्य-मिति वचनम् । यथा पैतामहधने पितुः स्वाम्यं तथैव तस्मिन्मृते तत्पुत्रा-णामपि । न तत्र संनिकर्षविप्रकर्षाभ्यां कोऽपि विशेषः । पार्वणविधिना पिण्डदानेन[17] द्वयोरपि तदुपकारकत्वाविशेषादित्यभिप्रायः ।

[10] पितामहादि- । पितामह-

[11] इत्यपरः । इत्यपरः कालः

[12] पितुरिच्छामन्तरेणैव । पितुरिच्छामन्तरेण

[13] चेच्छति । चेच्छतीति

[14] च । *om*

[15] -वचनानाम् । -बोधकवचनानाम् । -प्रतिपादकवचनानाम्

[16] प्राप्नोत्य- । प्राप्नोत्व- ।। मृतस्तत्र पुत्र एव तद्धनं प्राप्नोत्य- । मृतस्तदा तत्पुत्र-स्यैव तद्धनं भवत्य-

[17] पिण्डदानेन । पिण्डदाने

<10> अत एव मृतपितृकः प्रपौत्रोऽपि पुत्रपौत्राभ्यां सह तुल्याधिकारी[18] भवति पिण्डदत्वाविशेषात्[19] ।

<11> जीवति तु पितरि पुत्राणां पैतामहधनस्वामित्वे[20] सपुत्रापुत्रभ्रातृद्वयविभागे तत्पुत्राणामपि भागः[21] स्यात् स्वामित्वाविशेषात् ।

<12> न[22] चाप्रक्रान्तत्वेनातदर्थत्वं वचनस्यानेकपितृकानामेव प्रक्रमात् ।

<13> निबन्धः कार्त्तिक्यां कार्त्तिक्यामिदं दास्यामीति यन्निबद्धम् । **<14>** द्रव्यं[23] भूसाहचर्याद् द्विपदमभिहितम्[24] ।

<15> अयं वा **धारेश्वर**पुरस्कृतो वचनार्थः — इच्छया विभागदानप्रवृत्तस्य पितुः पैतामहधने[25] सदृशं स्वाम्यं पुत्रैः सह । न तत्र स्वोपार्जितधन इव[26] न्यूनाधिकविभागमिच्छातः[27] कर्तुमर्हतीति ।

<16> यथा **विष्णुः** —

> पिता चेत्पुत्रान् विभजेत्तस्य स्वेच्छा स्वयमुपात्तेऽर्थे । पैता-
> महे तु पितापुत्रयोस्तुल्यं स्वामित्वम् ।। [Vi 17.1–2]

<17> इदं सुव्यक्तम् — यदि पिता पुत्रान् विभजति तदा स्वोपात्ते[28] न्यूनाधिकविभागं[29] स्वेच्छया पुत्रेभ्यो दद्यात् । पैतामहे तु नैतद्यस्मात्तत्र तुल्यं स्वामित्वम् । न पुनः स्वच्छन्दवृत्तिता ।

[18] तुल्याधिकारी । तुल्यवदेवाधिकारी । तुल्यवदेकाधिकारी
[19] पिण्डदत्वाविशेषात् । पिण्डदानाविशेषात्
[20] पैतामह- । पितामह-
[21] भागः । विभागः
[22] न । तथा
[23] द्रव्यं । द्रव्यं च
[24] -भिहितम् । -भिमतम्
[25] पैतामह- । पैतामहादि-
[26] इव । -वन्
[27] -विभागमिच्छातः । -विभागं
[28] स्वोपात्ते । स्वोपात्तेऽर्थे
[29] -विभागं । -भागं

<**18**> अतः पितापुत्रयोः पैतामहधने समविभागार्थं सदृशं स्वाम्यमिति वचनं पुत्राणां वा विभागस्वान्त्र्यार्थमिति[30] मतद्वयमपि हेयम् । <**19**> एवमेवापरमपि वचन[31] व्याख्येयम् ।

<**20**> अतः पैतामहादिधने[32] पितुर्भागद्वयं पितुरिच्छात एव विभागो न[33] पुत्रेच्छयेति सिद्धम् ।

<**21**> यच्च **मनु-विष्णू** —

पैतृकं तु पिता द्रव्यमनवाप्तं यदाप्नुयात् ।
न तत्पुत्रैर्भजेत्सार्धमकामः स्वयमर्जितम् ।। [M 9.209 = Vi 18.43]

स्वार्जितत्वेन[34] हेतुना नाकामो विभजेदिति वदन्तौ स्वयमनर्जिते पैतामहधने पितुरनिच्छयापि पुत्राणां[35] विभागं दर्शयतस्तत्रापि विभागदानप्रवृत्तेः पिता पितामहधनं स्वार्जितं नाकामो विभजेत् । अन्यत्पुनरकामोऽपि[36] विभजेदित्यस्वेच्छात एवेत्यर्थः । न पुनः पुत्रेच्छया[37] विभागं ज्ञापयतः ।

<**22**> मणिमुक्तादौ पुनः[38] पैतामहे पित्रनर्जिते[39] स्वार्जित इव पितुरेव स्वाम्यं न्यूनाधिकविभागदानार्हत्वं च[40] । यथा[41] **याज्ञवल्क्यः** —

मणिमुक्ताप्रवालानां सर्वस्यैच पिता प्रभुः ।
स्थावरस्य तु सर्वस्य न पिता न पितामहः ।। [Y ?]

<**23**> पितामहश्रुतेस्तद्धनविषयम्[42] । मणिमुक्ताद्युपादाय पुनः सर्वस्येत्युपादानात्सर्वेषां भूम्यादिव्यतिरिक्तानां दानादिषु पितुः प्रभुत्वं न स्थावरनि-

[30] विभाग- । विभागे
[31] एवमेवापरमपि वचनं । एवमेवापरं वचनमपि
[32] पैतामहादि- । पैतामह-
[33] न । न तु । न पुनः :
[34] स्वार्जितत्वेन । इति स्वार्जितत्वेन
[35] पुत्राणां । *om*
[36] ऽपि । *om*
[37] पुत्रेच्छया । पुत्रेच्छयापि
[38] पुनः । *om*
[39] पित्रनर्जिते । पित्रनर्जितेऽपि
[40] च । *om*
[41] यथा । तथा
[42] -विषयम् । -विषयकम् । -विषयकवचनम्

बन्धद्रव्याणाम् । तत्रापि सर्वस्येत्युपादानात्सर्वस्य कुटुम्बवर्तनहेतोर्दानादिनिषेधः कुटुम्बस्यावश्यं[43] भरणीयत्वात् । यथा **मनुः**[44] —

भरणं पोष्यवर्गस्य प्रशस्तं स्वर्गसाधनम् ।
नरकं पीडने चास्य तस्माद्यत्नेन तं भरेत् ।। [M ?]

<**24**> अल्पस्य तु[45] वर्तनाविरोधिनो[46] न दानादिनिषेधः सर्वस्येत्यानर्थक्यापत्तेः ।

<**25**> स्थावरग्रहणान्निबन्धद्विपदयोर्दण्डापूपन्यायाद्दानादिनिषेधसिद्धिः ।

<**26**> यदि पुनः सर्वस्थावरादिविक्रयमन्तरेण कुटुम्बवर्तनमेव न भवति तदा सर्वस्यापि विक्रयादिकमित्यर्थात्सिध्यति[47] —

सर्वत एवात्मानं गोपायीत । [G 9.34]

इति वचनात्[48] ।

<**27**> न च —

स्थावरस्य समस्तस्य गोत्रसाधारणस्य च ।
नैकः कुर्यात्क्रयं दानं परस्परमतं विना ।। [Vy 254]
विभक्ता अविभक्ता[49] वा सपिण्डाः स्थावरे समाः ।
एको ह्यनीशः सर्वत्र दानाधमनविक्रये ।। [Vy 255]

एतद्**व्यास**वचनद्वयेनैकस्य विक्रयाद्यनधिकार इति वाच्यं यथेष्टविनियोगार्हत्वलक्षणस्य[50] स्वत्वस्य द्रव्यान्तर इवात्राप्यविशेषात् । <**28**> **व्यास**वचनं तु स्वामित्वेन दुर्वृत्तपुरुषगोचरविक्रयदानादिना[51] कुटुम्बविरोधादधर्मभागिताज्ञापनार्थं न तु विक्रयाद्यनिष्पत्त्यर्थम् ।

<**29**> एवं च —

43 कुटुम्बस्यावश्यम् । कुटुम्बस्याप्यवश्यम् । कुटुम्बस्यावश्य-
44 **मनुः** । **बृहन्मनुः**
45 तु । *om*
46 वर्तनाविरोधिनो । कुटुम्बवर्तनाविरोधिनो
47 विक्रयादि- । विक्रयणादि-
48 वचनात् । वचनाच्च
49 अविभक्ता । वाविभक्ता
50 -लक्षणस्य । -लक्षण-
51 -गोचर- । -गोचरतया ।। -विक्रयदानादिना । -विक्रयादिना

स्थावरं द्विपदं चैव यद्यपि स्वयमर्जितम् ।
असंभूय सुतान् सर्वान्न दानं न च विक्रयः ।। [Vy 252]

इत्येवमादिकं तदप्येवमेव[52] वर्णनीयम् । तथाहि कर्तव्यपदमवश्यमत्राध्याहार्यम्[53] । **<30>** तेन दानविक्रयकर्तव्यतानषेधात् तत्करणाद्विध्यतिक्रमो भवति न तु दानाद्यनिष्पत्तिः वचनशतेनापि वस्तुनोऽन्यथाकरणाशक्तेः ।

<31> अत एव **नारदः** —

यद्येकजाता बहवः पृथग्धर्माः पृथक्क्रियाः ।
पृथक्कर्मगुणोपेता न चेत्कार्येषु संमताः ।। [N 13.42/41]
स्वभागान् यदि दद्युस्ते विक्रीणीयुरथापि वा ।
कुर्युर्यथेष्टं तत्सर्वमीशास्ते स्वधनस्य वै ।। [N 13.43/42]

<32> प्रकृतमनुसरामः । तदेवमुक्तप्रबन्धेन पितामहादिधने[54] पितापुत्रयोः समविभागविधानानुपपत्तेः[55] । पुत्राणां च[56] विभागे[57] स्वातन्त्र्यप्रतिपत्तिपरत्वाभावाच्च जनकेच्छाधीनन्यूनाधिकविभागनिराकरणार्थं[58] मृतपितृकस्य भ्रातृपुत्रस्य पितृव्येण सह तुल्याधिकारार्थं वा वचनम् ।

<33> एवं च पितामहधनस्यापि[59] पितुरिच्छयैव विभागः कार्यः । किंतु निवृत्ते[60] रजसीति विशेषः । स्वोपात्ते तु[61] रजोनिवृत्तिमन्तरेणापि पितुरूर्ध्वमित्युभयत्राप्यविशिष्टम्[62] ।

<34> तेन पैतामहेऽपि[63] कालद्वयम् ।

[52] इत्येवमादिकं तदप्येवमेव । इत्येवमादिकमेवमेव
[53] -पदमवश्यमत्राध्याहार्यम् । -पदमत्रावश्यमध्याहार्यम्
[54] पितामहादि- । पैतामहादि-
[55] समविभागविधानाननुपपत्तेः । समभागानुपपत्तेः
[56] च । *om*
[57] विभागे । विभाग-
[58] -निराकरणार्थं । -निराकरणार्थं वा
[59] पितामह- । पैतामह-
[60] निवृत्ते । मातुर्निवृत्ते
[61] तु । *om*
[62] पितुरूर्ध्वमित्युभयत्राप्यविशिष्टम् । पितुरूर्ध्वमिति तूभयत्राप्यविशिष्टम्
[63] पैतामहे । पैतामहधने । पैतामहे धने

<35> तत्र यदा पितैवेच्छातः पुत्रान् विभजति तदा[64] पैतामहादिधना-द्भागद्वयं[65] स्वयं गृह्णीयात् —

जीवद्विभागे तु पिता गृह्णीतांशद्वयं स्वयम् । [B 26.16]

इति **बृहस्पतिना** । तथा[66] —

द्वावंशौ प्रतिपद्येत विभजन्नात्मनः पिता । [N 13.12ab]

इति **नारदेन** चाविशेषेण प्रतिपादनात् ।

<36> किंच इतोऽपि पितामहधनात्पितुर्भागद्वयम् —

<37> ज्येष्ठस्य विंश उद्धारः सर्वद्रव्याच्च यद्वरम् ।
ततोऽर्धं मध्यमस्य स्यात्तुरीयं तु यवीयसः ।। [B 9.112]

तथा —

एवं समुद्धृतोद्धारे समानंशान् प्रकल्पयेत् ।
उद्धारेऽनुद्धृते त्वेषामियं स्यादंशकल्पना ।। [M 9.116]
एकाधिकं हरेज्ज्येष्ठः पुत्रोऽध्यर्धं ततोऽनुजः ।
अंशमंशं यवीयांस इति धर्मो व्यवस्थितः ।। [M 9.117]

एतै**र्मनु**वचनैः सर्वद्रव्यवरसहितविंशतदर्धतत्तुरीयोद्धारा दर्शिताः । तथैकांशाधिकार्धांशाधिकचतुर्थभागाधिकभागाः प्रतिपादिताः ।

गोतमेनापि —

विंशतिभागो ज्येष्ठस्य मिथुनमुभयतोदद्युक्तो रथो गोवृषः ।
[G 28.5]

मिथुनमजादीनाम् । उभयतोदत्[67] अश्वादि । तद्युक्तो[68] रथः। गोयुक्तो वृषः। एतत्सर्वं ज्येष्ठस्य । तथा —

काणखोरकूटवण्डा[69] मध्यमस्यानेकाश्चेत्[70] । [G 28.6]

[64] बिभजति तदा । विभजेत्तदा
[65] पैतामहादि- । पैतामह-
[66] तथा । *om*
[67] उभयतोदत् । *om*
[68] अश्वादि तद्युक्तो । अश्वादियुक्तो
[69] -खोर- । -खोड-
[70] मध्यमस्यानेकाश्चेत् । मध्यमस्यानेकश्चेत्

खोरो[71] वृद्धः । कूटो वामनाकृतिः । वण्डो विकृतलाङ्गूलः । एते मध्यमस्य यदि बहवः पशवो भवन्ति[72] । तथा —

अविर्धान्यायसी गृहमनोयुक्तं चतुष्पदां चैकैकं यवीयसः ।
सममितरत्सर्वम् । [G 28.7-8]

अविप्रभृतयः कनीयसः[73] । अवशिष्टं सर्वं समं विभजेरन्निति प्रतिपाद्य —

द्व्यंशी वा पूर्वजः । स्यादेकैकमितरेषाम् । [G 28.9-10]

इति सूत्रेणांशद्वयं ज्येष्ठस्योक्तम् ।

<38> न चोपार्जकत्वेन ज्येष्ठस्यांशद्वयमिति वाच्यम् । उद्धारेऽनुद्धृते भागद्वयस्य विधानात् । अर्जकत्वे[74] चोद्धारस्यासंभवात् । मध्यमकनीयसोश्चोपार्जकतया ज्येष्ठेनाप्यविशेषात्तयोरध्यर्धादिविधानानुपपत्तेः । ज्येष्ठादिपदानर्थक्याच्च ।

<39> अत एव पुत्रिकौरसयोः पितृधनविभागे **मनु**राह —

पुत्रिकायां कृतायां तु[75] यदि पुत्रोऽनुजायते ।
समस्तत्र विभागः स्याज्ज्येष्ठता नास्ति हि स्त्रियाः ।। [M 9.134]

इति स्त्रीत्वेन ज्येष्ठत्वाभावात् समभागतां[76] प्रतिपादयन् पुरुषस्य भागद्वयं ज्ञापयति[77] ।

<40> यदुक्तं — होलाकाधिकरणे प्राच्यकर्तृकहोलाकानुष्ठानोपपत्तये होलाका कर्तव्येति श्रुतिः कल्पिता तावतैव तदुपपत्तेः । न तु प्राच्यादिवती कल्पनागौरवात् । तद्वदत्राप्यर्जकोंऽशद्वयं गृह्णीयादिति श्रुतिः कल्पनीया न पुनः पित्रादिपदवतीति ।

[71] खोरो । खोडो

[72] बहवः पशवो भवन्ति । बहवो भवन्ति पशवः

[73] अविप्रभृतयः कनीयसः । अविप्रभृतयो यवीयसः

[74] अर्जकत्वे । अर्जकत्वेन

[75] तु । च

[76] समभागतां । समभागं

[77] ज्ञापयति । प्रतिपादयति

तदयुक्तम् । तत्र प्राच्यकर्तृकस्यानुष्ठानस्यावश्यकल्पनीयसामान्यश्रुत्यैवोपपत्तेः[78] । न चाप्राच्यानामननुष्ठानार्थं प्राच्यपदवती कल्प्यतामिति वाच्यम् । तेषामननुष्ठानस्यानाचाररूपस्य[79] श्रुतिकल्पनानिमित्तत्वानुपपत्तेः ।

इह तु **मन्वादीनां** ज्येष्ठपदप्रयोगात्तदुपपत्तये ज्येष्ठपदवत्या एव श्रुतेः कल्पनार्हत्वात् । अर्जकपदवत्या अवश्यकल्पनीयत्वाभावात् । ज्येष्ठपदवत्या अर्जकपदवत्याश्च कल्पनायां विशेषप्रमाणाभावात्[80] ।

न चान्यत्रार्जकस्य भागद्वयार्थं श्रुतेरवश्यकल्पनीयत्वादत्रापि[81] सैव मूलमस्तु लाघवात् ज्येष्ठपदं चार्जकपरमस्त्विति वाच्यम् । वैपरीत्यस्यापि संभवात् । अत्रैव ज्येष्ठपदयुक्तश्रुतिकल्पनायामर्जकपदस्यापि ज्येष्ठपरत्वकल्पनासंभवात् । विनिगमनाप्रमाणाभावात् । किंचैवं[82] लाघवादिना यत्किंचित् त्रिचतुरादिपदवतीमेकां श्रुतिमनुमाय सकलस्मृतिपदानां गौण्या लक्षणया वा वृत्त्या तत्परत्वमपि[83] वाच्यमित्यतीवात्मनः स्मृतिनिपुणता[84] निरूपिता ।

तस्माद्यस्मादेवाचारात्स्मृतिवाक्याद्वा या श्रुतिरवश्यकल्पनीया[85] तयैव तद्गतस्याचारांशस्य स्मृतिपदस्य चोपपत्तेर्न तत्राधिककल्पनेति होलाकाधिकरणस्यार्थः ।

<**41**> अत एव **वशिष्ठेन** ज्येष्ठस्यांशद्वयमभिधाय[86] उपार्जकस्यांशद्वयं पृथगभिहितम् । यथा[87] —

अथ भ्रातृणां दायविभागः[88] । द्व्यंशं ज्येष्ठो हरेत् ।। [Va 17.40, 42]

78 -कर्तृकस्यानुष्ठान- । -कर्तृकस्य होलाकानुष्ठान-
79 तेषामननुष्ठान- । अननुष्ठान-
80 विशेषप्रमाणाभावात् । विशेषाभावात्
81 -वश्य- । -वश्यं-
82 किंचैवं । किंच
83 तत्परत्वमपि । तत्परत्वं
84 स्मृति- । श्रुतिस्मृति-
85 -वश्य- । -वश्यं-
86 ज्येष्ठस्यांश- । ज्येष्ठांश-
87 यथा । *om*
88 दायविभागः । दायभागः

ततोऽनतिदूरे[89] पुनराह —

येन चैषां समुत्पादितं स्यात्सोऽपि[90] द्व्यंशमेव हरेत् ॥ [Va 17.51]

अनेनार्जकतया भागद्वये दर्शिते ज्येष्ठस्यांशद्वयाभिधानमनर्थकं[91] स्यात् ।

<**42**> द्व्यंशहरत्वमपि न ज्येष्ठतामात्रेण । यदाह **बृहस्पतिः** —

जन्मविद्यागुणज्येष्ठो द्व्यंशं दायादवाप्नुयात्[92] ।
समांशभागिनस्त्वन्ये तेषां पितृसमस्तु सः ॥ [B 26.21]

उपार्जकत्वेन भागद्वये जन्मविद्यादिकीर्तनमनुपयोगि[93] ।

<**43**> एतच्च भागद्वयं सोदरमात्रभ्रातृविभागविषयम्[94] । सोदरासोदर-विभागगोचरश्च ज्येष्ठस्य विंशोद्धारः । यदाह **बृहस्पतिः** —

समवर्णासु ये जाताः सर्वे पुत्रा द्विजन्मनाम् ।
उद्धारं ज्यायसे दत्त्वा भजेरन्नितरे समम् ॥ [B 26.11]

44> समवर्णासु[95] बह्वीषु स्त्रीषु जातानामुद्धारपूर्वकविभागश्रुतेर्भागद्वयं[96] सोदरमात्रगोचरमेव[97] सिध्यति । युक्तं चैतत् सोदरतयाधिकगौरवात् ।

<**45**> उद्धारोऽपि[98] दशसु गवादिषु न कार्यः । तथा[99] **मनुः** —

उद्धारो न दशस्वस्ति संपन्नानां स्वकर्मसु ।
यत्किंचिदेव देयं स्याज्ज्यायसे मानवर्धनम् ॥ [M 9.115]

<**46**> तदेवमुक्तप्रबन्धेन यत्र ज्येष्ठभ्रातुरेव पितृधने भागद्वयं कथं तत्र जनकस्य दानविक्रयपरित्यागक्षमस्य पितामहधनसंबन्धमूलस्यातिगुरोः पितु-रेव स्वपितृधने भागद्वयं न भवति[100] ।

[89] ततोऽनतिदूरे । ततोऽनतिदूरणे । अतो नातिदूरेण
[90] ऽपि । *om*
[91] ज्येष्ठस्यांशद्वयाभिधानमनर्थकं । ज्येष्ठस्य भागद्वयाभिधानमननुपपन्नं
[92] दायादवाप्नुयात् । दायाद आप्नुयात्
[93] -विद्यादि- । -विद्या-
[94] सोदरमात्रभ्रातृ- । सादरभ्रातृमात्र-
[95] समवर्णासु । सवर्णासु
[96] -पूर्वक- । पूर्वं
[97] -गोचरमेव । गोचरमिति । -विषयमेव । -परमेव
[98] ऽपि । *om*
[99] तथा । यथा
[100] भवति । संभवति

जन्मविद्यागुणज्येष्ठ इति वाक्येन च पितृसमत्वेन भागद्वयं ज्येष्ठस्यातिदिशन् पितुर्भागद्वयोपदेशं[101] ज्ञापयति **बृहस्पतिः** —

जीवद्विभागे तु पिता गृह्णीतांशद्वयं स्वयम् । [B 26.16]

इति सामान्येनांशद्वयाभिधानादुपदेशो[102] **बृहस्पतिना** दर्शितः ।

तथा **नारदः** —

द्वावंशौ प्रतिपद्येत विभजन्नात्मनः पिता ।
समांशहारिणी माता पुत्राणां स्यान्मृते पतौ ।। [N 13.12]

<**47**> द्रव्यं विभजन् पिता द्वावंशावात्मनो गृह्णीयान्न पुनरात्मनो द्रव्यं विभजन्निति संबन्धः पूर्वोक्तविरोधात् ।

<**48**> किंच पैतामहधने पितापुत्रयोः समभागत्वे[103] यावद्धनं पितुस्तावदेव पुत्रस्यापीति वाच्यम् । न तु यदेव यावदेव[104] धनं पितुस्तदेव तावदेव[105] पुत्रस्य मध्यगत्वापत्तेः । जायापत्योरिव विभागाभावप्रसङ्गात् ।
<**49**> एवं च सति भ्रातृणां विभागे यदा ज्येष्ठस्य ज्येष्ठतया भागद्वयकल्पनं तदा तत्पुत्रस्यापि भागद्वयकल्पने पुत्रेण सह ज्येष्ठस्य चत्वारोंऽशाः[106] भ्रात्रन्तरस्यैकोंऽशः[107] स्यात् । बहुपुत्रत्वे च ज्येष्ठस्य तत्पुत्राणां पितृसमभागकल्पने[108] कनिष्ठभ्रातुर्यत्किंचिदेव स्यादिति महाजनविरोधः ।

<**50**> यच्च[109] **बृहस्पति**वचनम् —

द्रव्ये पितामहोपात्ते स्थावरे जङ्गमे तथा ।
सममंशित्वमाख्यातं पितुः पुत्रस्य चैव हि ।। [B 26.14]

[101] पितुर्भागद्वयोपदेशं । पितुर्भागद्वयं
[102] सामान्येनांशद्वया- । सामान्येना-
[103] समभागत्वे । समभागित्वे
[104] यदेव यावदेव । यावदेव यदेव
[105] पितुस्तदेव तावदेव । तावदेव तदेव
[106] चत्वारोंऽशाः । चत्वारो भागाः
[107] भ्रात्रन्तरस्यैकोंऽशः । भ्रात्रन्तरस्यैको भागः
[108] -भाग- । -विभाग-
[109] यच्च । यत्तु

अंशित्वं समं समानम् । न[110] स्वेच्छया स्वोपात्तद्रव्यवन्न्यूनाधिकविभागं[111] दातुमर्हति । न पुनरंशः सम इति तस्यार्थः । <**51**> द्विपितृकपित्रभिप्रायं वा समभागवचनम् ।

<**52**> तत्र स्यात्सदृशं स्वाम्यमिति वचनं तु प्रागेव व्याख्यातम् ।

<**53**> किंच यद्यसौ पिता स्वपितुः पुन्नामनरकनिवर्तको[112] ज्येष्ठस्तदा तस्य स्वभ्रातृनेवापेक्षया[113] यत्र पितृसमत्वेन भागद्वयं सुतरां तस्य पुत्रापेक्षया भागद्वयं युक्तं पुत्राणां क्रमागतधनसंबन्धस्य पित्रधीनत्वात् । अथ यः स्वपितुर्न[114] ज्येष्ठः पुत्रस्तस्य स्वपुत्रैः सह समांशितोच्यते ।

<**54**> तन्न मध्यमादिपुत्राणामप्यध्यर्धादिविधानात् पितृतया भागद्वयस्यैव सुतरां युक्तत्वात् । सामान्येन च पितापुत्रयोः समानांशाभिधानस्य[115] भवतो मुनीनां चानुचितत्वात् ।

<**55**> किंच पितुरंशद्वयाभिधानं[116] स्वोपात्तद्रव्यगोचरमित्यप्यनुपपन्नम्। तदिच्छानुरोधित्वाद्विभागस्य इच्छातश्च भागद्वयत्रयन्यूनाधिकानामपि[117] प्राप्तेर्विफलो विधिः । नियमार्थत्वं च[118] वचनस्य न वर्णनीयं[119] **विष्णु**विरोधात् । तदाह —

पिता चेत्पुत्रान् विभजेत्तस्य स्वेच्छा स्वयमुपात्तेऽर्थे ।
पैतामहे तु पितापुत्रयोस्तुल्यं स्वाम्यम्[120] ।। [Vi 17.1-2]

<**56**> अस्यार्थः — स्वोपात्ते यावदेव ग्रहीतुमिच्छत्यर्धं भागद्वयं त्रयं वा तत्सर्वं तस्य शास्त्रानुमतं न तु पैतमहेऽपि ।

<**57**> तथा **हारीतः** —

[110] न । न च । न तु
[111] -द्रव्य- । -धन-
[112] -निवर्तको । -व्यावर्तको
[113] स्वभ्रातृनेवापेक्षया । स्वभ्रातृनपेक्षया
[114] स्वपितुर्न । पितुर्न
[115] समानांशाभिधानस्य । समांशाभिधानस्य
[116] -भिधानं । -विधानं
[117] -न्यूनाधिकानामपि । -न्यूनाधिकानां
[118] च । तु
[119] वर्णनीयं । वचनीयं
[120] स्वाम्यम् । स्वामित्वम्

जीवन्नेव वा[121] प्रविभज्य वनमाश्रयेद् वृद्धाश्रमं वा गच्छेत्
स्वल्पेन वा प्रविभज्य[122] भूयिष्ठमादाय वसेत् । यद्यपदस्येत्
पुनस्तेभ्यो गृह्णीयात् ॥ [H 4.5]

<58> अनेन स्वल्पस्य विभागो भूयिष्ठद्रव्यग्रहणं[123] च पितुरभिहितम् । वृद्धाश्रमः प्रव्रज्या ।

<59> यच्च **शङ्खलिखित**वचनम् —

स यद्येकपुत्रः स्याद् द्वौ भागावात्मनः कुर्यात् । [ŚL 268]

अस्यायमर्थः — एकस्य पुत्र एकपुत्रः । न पुनरेक एव पुत्रो यस्येति बहुव्रीहिः तस्यान्यपदार्थप्रधानत्वेन षष्ठीतत्पुरुषाद्दुर्बलत्वात् ।

एकपुत्रश्चौरसः । तथाविधस्य पितुर्भागद्वयम् । न तु[124] क्षेत्रजस्य पितृत्वेऽपि तत्र स्यात्सदृशं स्वाम्यमिति वचनं क्षेत्रजपित्रभिप्रायमेव वर्णनीयम् ।

<60> क्षेत्रजो हि द्विपितृकः । तदाह **बौधायनः** —

मृतस्य च प्रसूतो यः क्लीबस्य व्याधितस्य वा ।
अन्येनानुमतो[125] वा स्यात् स्वक्षेत्रे[126] क्षेत्रजः स्मृतः ॥ [Bau 2.2.3.17]
स एव द्विपिता[127] द्विगोत्रश्च । द्वयोरपि स्वधाकारो रिक्थभाग्भवति ॥ [Bau 2.2.3.18]

<61> अस्यार्थः — क्लीबादेः स्वे[128] क्षेत्रे तदनुमतोऽन्येन प्रसूतः क्षेत्रजः ।

<62> तथा **नारदः** —

क्षेत्रिकानुमते क्षेत्रे बीजं यस्य प्रकीर्यते ।
तदपत्यं द्वयोरेव बीजिक्षेत्रिकयोर्मतम् ॥ [N 12.58]

<63> अतश्चैकपुत्र आत्मनो भागद्वयं कुर्यादिति विधावेकपुत्रत्वस्य कर्तृविशेषणताया विवक्षार्हत्वादुद्देश्यविशेषणत्वेनाविवक्षितत्वमित्यपि परास्तं

[121] वा । वा पुत्रान्
[122] प्रविभज्य । विभज्य
[123] भूयिष्ठद्रव्य- । भूयिष्ठद्रव्यस्य
[124] तु । *om*
[125] अन्येनानुमतो । अन्येनानुमते
[126] स्वक्षेत्रे । स्वे क्षेत्रे
[127] द्विपिता । द्विपितृको
[128] स्वे । स्व-

भवति । <**64**> किंच परमप्रेक्षावन्**मनु-गोतम-दक्षादि**प्रयुक्तपदानां प्रतिक्षणमविवक्षामाचक्षाणः स्वस्यैव साक्षादविवक्षितत्वं ख्यापयति ।

<**65**> तथा पुत्रार्जितेऽपि[129] धने पितुरंशद्वयं द्वावंशाविति गृह्णीतांशद्वयमिति चाविशेषश्रुतेः । सुव्यक्तमाह **कात्यायनः** —

द्व्यंशहरोऽर्धहरो वा पुत्रवित्तार्जनात्पिता ।
मातापि पितरि प्रेते पुत्रतुल्यांशभागिनी[130] ॥ [K 851]

<**66**> पुत्रस्य वित्तार्जनात्पितुर्द्व्यंशहरत्वमर्धहरत्वं वेत्यस्यार्थः[131] ।

<**67**> न च पुत्रश्च वित्तं च[132] पुत्रवित्ते । तयोरर्जनात्पिता द्व्यंशहरः पुत्रानर्जनात्सर्वहर इति चाच्यम् । अनर्जितपुत्रस्यापि भ्रातृभिर्विभागे वित्तार्जकतया अंशद्वयस्येष्टत्वात् कथं सर्वहरत्वम् । अतो बिभागार्हसंबन्धिनि विद्यमानेऽर्जकस्य द्व्यंशित्वमसति तु सर्वहरत्वमिति[133] वाच्यम् । तथाच[134] पितापुत्रपदयोः प्रमत्तगीतता स्यात् । किंचार्जनं स्वत्वहेतुभूतो[135] व्यापारः अर्जनं स्वत्वं नापादयतीति विप्रतिषिधमित्यभिधानात् । न च पुत्रेषु स्वत्वमस्तीति सर्वस्वदाने प्रदर्शितम्[136] । अतस्तत्र गौणमर्जकपदं वित्ते च मुख्यम् न चैतत्सकृच्छ्रुतस्य संभवति ।

<**68**> न च पुत्रेणार्जितत्वात्पुत्रस्य[137] द्व्यंशप्राप्तेः पितुश्च भागद्वयस्यास्माद्वचनादृतेऽपि प्राप्तेः समभागत्वापाताद्विधानमनर्थकमिति वाच्यम् । एतद्वचनमन्तरेणापि[138] पुत्रधने पितुर्भागद्वयस्याप्राप्तेर्वचनस्यर्थवत्त्वात् । <**69**> किंच पुत्रवित्तार्जनादित्यस्य पितृधनविषयत्वे पितुरिच्छातो द्व्यंशहरत्वमर्धहरत्वं वेत्यनुपपन्नम् । इच्छानुरोधित्वाद्ग्रहणस्येच्छायाश्चानियतत्वात्सार्ध-

[129] ऽपि । *om*
[130] -भागिनी । -हारिणी
[131] वेत्यस्यार्थ : । वेति तस्यार्थः
[132] च । चेति
[133] सर्वहरत्वमिति । सर्वहरत्वं
[134] तथाच । तथात्र
[135] -भूतो । -भूत-
[136] प्रदर्शितम् । दर्शितम्
[137] पुत्रेणार्जितत्वात्पुत्रस्य । पुत्रेणार्जितात्पुत्रस्य
[138] एतद्वचनमन्तरेणापि । एतद्वचनमन्तरेण

सपादपादोनांशग्रहणस्यापि संभवात् कथं पक्षद्वयमात्रकीर्तनम् । नियमार्थत्वं च पितृधनगोचरं[139] न संभवतीत्युक्तं प्राक् । अत्र च पुत्रार्जितवित्तस्य यथा द्व्यंशहरत्वं तथा तस्यैव वित्तस्यार्धहरत्वमिति[140] युक्तम् ।

<70> न पुनर्द्व्यंशस्यार्धमेकोंऽशस्तद्ग्रहणार्थं वचनम् । अर्धस्य द्व्यंशस्य चैकदेशत्वेनैकदेशस्याकाङ्क्षितत्वात्[141] । पुरुषविशेषणतया हरणकर्मत्वेन च द्वयोः समत्वात् परस्परसंबन्धानुपपत्तेश्च[142] । वित्तार्जनादिति पञ्चम्यन्तेन[143] द्व्यंशरूपैकदेशान्वयार्थोपादानस्याविवादर्धपदेनापि तस्यान्वयो युक्तः । वित्तार्जनार्धपदयोश्चाव्यवधानाद्वित्तस्यैवार्धं प्रतीयते । न पुनर्द्व्यंशस्यार्धमेकोंऽशः प्रतीयते । स्वायत्ते चैकांशपदे प्रयोक्तव्येऽवाचकपदप्रयोगस्यान्याय्यत्वाद्वित्तस्यैवार्धं युक्तम् ।

<71> तत्र पितृद्रव्योपघातेन पुत्रार्जितवित्तस्यार्धं पितुरर्जकस्य पुत्रस्यांशद्वयमितरेषामेकैकांशिता[144] । अनुपघाते तु[145] पितुरंशद्वयमर्जकस्यापि तावदेवेतरेषामनंशित्वम् ।

<72> यद्वा विद्यादिगुणसंपन्नस्य पितुरर्धहरत्वं विद्यादिना ज्येष्ठस्यैवाधिकांशदर्शनात्[146] । विद्यादिशून्यस्य जनकतामात्रेण द्व्यंशित्वम् ।

<73> तेन क्रमागतधनाद्वा पुत्रार्जितधनाद्वा भागद्वयं पिता स्वयं गृह्णीयात् । अतोऽधिकमिच्छन्नपि नार्हतीति वचनार्थः । स्वार्जितधनात्तु यावदेव ग्रहीतुमिच्छति तावदेव गृह्णीयात् ।

<74> पुत्राणां तु पैतामहधनाद्विंशोद्धारं[147] दत्त्वादत्त्वैव वा विभजेत् । स्वोपार्जितधनात्पुनर्गुणवत्त्वेन संमानार्थं बहुकुटुम्बत्वेन वा भरणार्थमयोग्य-

139 -गोचरं । -गोचरत्वं

140 वित्त- । पुत्रवित्त-

141 -देशस्याकाङ्क्षित्वात् । -देश्याकाङ्क्षित्वात् । -देशिन आकाङ्क्षित्वात्

142 -संबन्धानुपपत्तेश्च । संबन्धानुपपत्तेः

143 पञ्चम्यन्तेन । पञ्चम्यन्तत्वेन

144 -कांशिता । -कांशः

145 तु । *om*

146 ज्येष्ठस्यैवा- । ज्येष्ठस्या-

147 पैतामह- । पितामह- ।। -शोद्धारं । -शोद्धारादिकं

त्वेन वा कृपया भक्तत्वेन वा प्रसन्नतयाधिकदानेच्छुर्न्यूनाधिकविभागं कुर्वन् धर्मकारी पिता । <**75**> तदाह **याज्ञवल्क्यः** —

न्यूनाधिकविभक्तानां धर्म्यः[148] पितृकृतः स्मृतः ।। [Y 2.116cd]

तथा **बृहस्पतिः** —

समन्यूनाधिका भागाः पित्रा येषां प्रकल्पिताः ।
तथैव ते पालनीया विनेयास्ते स्युरन्यथा ।। [B 26.15]

तथा **नारदः**[149] —

पित्रैव तु विभक्ता ये समन्यूनाधिकैर्धनैः ।
तेषां स एव धर्म्यः[150] स्यात्सर्वस्य हि पिता प्रभुः ।। [N 13.15]

<**76**> सर्वधनप्रभुत्वस्य हेतुत्वात्पैतामहे च तस्यासंभवात्[151] न्यूनाधिकभागः पितृकृतः पितृधनविषय एवायं[152] धर्म्यः । तथाच **विष्णुः** —

पिता चेत्पुत्रान् विभजेत्तस्य स्वेच्छा स्वयमुपात्तेऽर्थे ।
पैतामहे तु पितापुत्रयोस्तुल्यं स्वामित्वम्[153] ।। [Vi 17.1–2]

<**77**> ननु —

विभागं चेत्पिता कुर्यादिच्छया विभजेत्सुतान् ।
ज्येष्ठं वा श्रेष्ठभागेन सर्वे वा स्युः समांशिनः ।। [Y 2.114]

इति **याज्ञवल्क्य**वचनादुद्धाररूपश्रेष्ठभागावगतेः कथं ततो[154] न्यूनाधिकत्वमभिधीयते ।

उच्यते — उपरते पितरि भ्रातृभिरपि विभागे क्रियमाणे विंशोद्धाररूपश्रेष्ठांशस्य सिद्धत्वाद्वचनानर्थक्यान्न तदर्थत्वम् । <**78**> अथ विनाप्युद्धारं समांशतायाः पितृकृताया धर्म्यत्वार्थं वचनमुच्यते । तन्न न्यूनत्वमेव तर्हि पितृकृतं धर्म्यं स्यादित्यधिकपदमनर्थकं स्यात् । <**79**> किंचोद्धाराभिप्रायेण

[148] धर्म्यः । धर्मः

[149] तथा **नारदः** । **नारदश्च**

[150] धर्म्यः । धर्मः

[151] तस्यासंभवात् । तदसंभवात्

[152] एवायं । एव

[153] स्वामित्वम् । स्वाम्यम्

[154] ततो । ततोऽन्य-

न्यूनाधिकत्ववर्णने[155] इच्छया विभजेदित्यनर्थकं पदं एतदितरपदत्रयेणैव[156] वक्तव्यस्याभिहितत्वात् ।

अस्मन्मते त्विच्छया विभजेदिति स्वोपात्तधनविषयम्[157] । श्रेष्ठांशतासमानांशतयोस्तु पैतामहधनगोचरत्वमिति न किमप्यनर्थकम् । **<80>** किंच पितर्यपरतेऽपि द्विप्रकारो विभागो **बृहस्पति**नोक्तः । यथा —

द्विप्रकारो विभागस्तु दायादानां प्रदर्शितः[158] ।
वयोज्येष्ठक्रमेणैकः समा परांशकल्पना ॥ [B 26.17]

ज्येष्ठक्रमेणोद्धारं दर्शयति । तथा समांशता परेति । भ्रातॄणामपि परस्परविभागस्य द्विप्रकारत्वात्पितृकृतस्य विशेषो न स्यात् ।**<81>** तथा **नारदः** —

पितैव वा स्वयं पुत्रान् विभाजेद्वयसि स्थितः ।
ज्येष्ठं वा श्रेष्ठभागेन यथा वास्य मतिर्भवेत् ॥ [N 13.4]

<82> ज्येष्ठस्य श्रेष्ठभागमभिधाय पुनर्यथा वास्य मतिर्भवेदित्यनेन[159] यादृशे न्यूनाधिकविभागे पितुः पूर्वोक्तकारणात्कर्तव्यमतिर्भवेदिति[160] पृथगभिधानात् श्रेष्ठभागादन्य एवायं न्यूनाधिकविभागः प्रतीयते ।

<83> यत्पुन**र्नारद**वचनम् —

व्याधितः कुपितश्चैव विषयासक्तचेतनः ।
अयथाशास्त्रकारी च न विभागे पिता प्रभुः ॥ [N 13.16]

इति तद्व्याध्यादिना[161] आकुलचित्ततया[162] कस्मिंश्चित्पुत्रे क्रोधाद्वा सुभगापुत्रस्नेहाद्वा अयथाशास्त्रं विभजति तद्विषयम् ।

पूर्वोक्तकारणात्तु शास्त्रीय एव विषमविभागः।**<84>** यथा **कात्यायनः** —

जीवद्विभागे तु पिता नैकं पुत्रं विशेषयेत् ।
निर्भाजयेन्न चैवैकमकस्मात्कारणं विना ॥ [K 843]

[155] न्यूाधिकत्व- । समन्यूनाधिकत्व-
[156] -पद- । -पाद-
[157] -धन- । *om*
[158] प्रदर्शितः । प्रकीर्तितः
[159] मतिर्भवेदित्यनेन । मतिरित्यनेन
[160] कर्तव्यमतिर्भवेदिति । कर्तव्यतामतिर्भवेदिति
[161] तद्व्याध्यादिना । तद्व्याधिना
[162] आकुल- । आकुलित-

<**85**> नैकमधिकदानेन विशेषयेत् । न च निर्भाजयेद्विभागशून्यं कुर्यात्[163] कारणं विना । उद्धारादिविशेषो हि बहूनामेव नैकस्य । एकस्यापि च पुत्रस्य कारणं विना विशेषो न कार्यः । कारणवशात्तु कार्य एव । एकस्यापीत्यवगतेर्नोद्धारापेक्षो विशेषः किंतु पितुरिच्छाकृत एवेति यथोक्त एवार्थः ।

<**86**> यदि पुनः पितरि जीवति पुत्रा एव विभागमर्थयन्ते तदा बिषम-विभागः[164] पित्रा न दातव्यः । तदाह **मनुः** —

भ्रातॄणामविभक्तानां यद्युत्थानं भवेत्सह ।
न तत्र भागं विषमं[165] पिता दद्यात्कथंचन ॥ [M 9.215]

<**87**> उद्धारस्तु तदा[166] पित्रा दातव्य एव तस्य विषमविभागरूपत्वाभावात् न्यूनाधिकविभागस्यैव निषेधात् ।

<**88**> इति पितृकृतो विभागः ।

[163] कुर्यात् । न कुर्यात्
[164] -विभागः । -भागः
[165] भागं विषमं । विषमं भागं
[166] तदा । तदापि । *om*

<**3.1**> इदानीमुपरते पितरि भ्रातॄणां विभागः कथ्यते ।

सोऽपि च मातरि जीवन्त्यां पुत्राणां[1] सत्यपि पित्रुपरमाद्धनस्वामित्वे[2] धर्म्यो विभागः सोदराणां न[3] भवतीति कथ्यते[4] ऊर्ध्वं पितुश्च मातुश्चेत्युभयोरुपरमे सोदराणां पैतृकधनविभागस्य ज्ञापनात् ।

<**2**> न पुनर्मातुरूर्ध्वं मातृधनविभागार्थं पैतृकपदात्पितृधनमात्रस्यैव विभागावगतेः पैतृकपदस्यैकशेषकल्पनायां[5] प्रमाणाभावात् । <**3**> किंच जनन्यां संस्थितायामित्यनेनैव[6] मातरि मृतायां तदीयधनविभागस्य[7] वक्ष्यमाणत्वादूर्ध्वं मातुरिति पुनरुक्तं स्यात्[8] ।

<**4**> तथा[9] **याज्ञवल्क्यः** —

विभजेरन् सुताः पित्रोरूर्ध्वं रिक्थमृणं समम् ।
मातुर्दुहितरः शेषमृणात्ताभ्य ऋतेऽन्वयः ॥ [Y 2.117]

<**5**> मातृधनविभागस्य दुहितॄणां सद्भावेऽनधिकारः असद्भावे चान्वयपदेन पुत्राणामधिकार इत्युत्तरार्धेनैव प्रतिपादनात् । पूर्वार्धे पित्रोरिति पितृधनविषयमेव अन्यथा पुनरुक्तत्वापत्तेः । <**6**> मातापित्रोरुपरमे भ्रातरो विभजेरन्निति वदता[10] उभयोरुपरमानन्तरकालस्य विभागार्थतया[11] विधानात् साहित्यं विवक्षितम् ।

<7> तथाच **शङ्खलिखितौ** —

रिक्थमूलं हि कुटुम्बम् । अस्वतन्त्राः पितृमन्तो मातुरप्येवमवस्थितायाः ॥ [ŚL 270]

[1] प्रत्राणां । *om*

[2] पिुरुपरमाद्धनस्वामित्वे । पितुरुपरमेण स्वामित्वे

[3] विभागः सोदराणां न । न बिभागः सोदराणां

[4] कथ्यते । कल्प्यते

[5] -कल्पनायां । -कल्पना-

[6] जनन्यां संस्थितायामित्यनेनैव । जनन्यां संस्थितायां त्वित्यनेनैव

[7] -विभागस्य । -विभागस्य **मनुना**

[8] स्यात् । भवेत्

[9] तथा । यथा

[10] वदता । वदता **याज्ञवल्क्यः**

[11] विभागार्थतया । विभागार्हतया

मातुरपि सकाशादस्वतन्त्रा विभागानधिकारिण इत्याहतुः ।

<**8**> सुव्यक्तमाह **व्यासः** —

भ्रातॄणां जीवतोः पित्रोः सहवासो विधीयते ।
तदभावे विभक्तानां धर्मस्तेषां विवर्धते ॥ [Vy 247]

<**9**> सहवासविधानमुखेन पृथग्भावनिषधात् पितृमातृजीवनवतश्च विभाग-निषेधात् जीवतोरिति साहित्यमविवक्षितम् । अत[12] एकस्मिन्नपि जीवति विभागो न धर्म्यः किंतु द्वयोरभावे[13] ।

<**10**> तथा[14] **बृहस्पतिः** —

पित्रोरभावे भ्रातॄणां विभागः संप्रदर्शितः ।
मातुर्निवृत्ते रजसि जीवतोरपि शस्यते ॥ [B 26.9]

<**11**> निवृत्तरजस्कायां मातरि जीवन्त्यां विभागस्य मातृधनगोचरत्वानुप-पत्तेः । उभयाभावोक्तविभागस्यैव जीवतोरपीत्यपिकारनिर्दिष्टस्य[15] शस्तत्व-कीर्तनात् उभयाभावे[16] भ्रातृविभागः पितृधनगोचर एवावधार्यते[17] ।

<**12**> अत एव जीवन्त्यां मातरि मृतप्रधानकं विभागं निर्दिशति[18] **व्यासः** —

समानजातिसंख्या ये जातास्त्वेकेन सूनवः ।
विभिन्नमातृकास्तेषां मातृभागः प्रशस्यते ॥ [Vy 249]

तथा[19] **बृहस्पतिः** —

यद्येकजाता बहवः समाना जातिसंख्यया ।
सापत्नास्तैर्विभक्तव्यं मातृभागेन धर्मतः ॥ [B 26.24]

[12] अत । अत एव
[13] द्वयोरभावे । उभयोरभावे
[14] तथा । यथाह । तथाच
[15] -कार- । -कारेण
[16] उभयाभावे । उभयोरभावे
[17] एवावधार्यते । एवावधार्यः । एव प्रशस्यते
[18] निर्दिशति । दर्शयति
[19] तथा । तथाह

<**13**> पुत्राणां जातिसंख्यासाम्येन विभागे विशेषाभावान्मातुरेवायं विभागो न पुत्राणामित्युद्दिश्य विभागः कर्तव्यः[20] ।

तेनेतरमातृधन इवात्रापि पुत्राणां मातरि जीवन्त्यां न परस्परविभागे स्वातन्त्र्यम्[21] । किंतु मातुरनुमत्यैव परं विभागो धर्म्यः । <**14**> अतो य**द्गौतमादि**भिरुक्तम् —

विभागे तु धर्मवृद्धिरित्यादि ।। [G 28.4]

तन्मातुरुपरमे वेदितव्यम् ।

<**15**> तत्र यद्यविभक्ता एव स्थातुमिच्छन्ति तदा ज्येष्ठ एव योगक्षेमशक्तः सर्वं गृह्णीयात् । इतरे पितरमिव तमुपजीवेयुः । यथा **मनुः** —

ज्येष्ठ एव तु गृह्णीयात् पित्र्यं धनमशेषतः ।
शेषास्तमुपजीवेयुर्यथैव पितरं तथा ।। [M 9.105]

तथा **गोतमः** —

सर्वस्वं[22] वा पूर्वजस्य[23] । स इतरान् बिभृयात्पितृवत् ।। [G 28.3]

वाशब्दात्पृथग्वा भवेयुः सह वा वसेयुः ।

सहवासश्च[24] सर्वेषामिच्छात एव । यथा **नारदः** —

बिभृयाद्वेच्छतः सर्वान् ज्येष्ठो भ्राता यथा पिता ।
भ्राता शक्तः कनिष्ठो वा शक्त्यपेक्षा कुले स्थितः ।। [N 13.5]

शक्तः सन् कनिष्ठोऽपि[25] सर्वान् बिभृयात्। मध्यमोऽत्र दण्डापूपन्यात्सिद्धिः ।

<**16**> विभागस्त्वेकस्यापीच्छया भवतीत्युक्तं प्राक् । <**17**> अत एव विभागमुपक्रम्याह **कात्यायनः** —

अप्राप्तव्यवहाराणां धनं व्ययविवर्जितम् ।
न्यसेयुर्बन्धुमित्रेषु प्रोषितानां तथैव च ।। [K 845]

तथा —

[20] कर्तव्यः । कार्यः
[21] स्वातन्त्र्यम् स्वातन्त्र्यं युक्तम्
[22] सर्वस्वं । सर्वं
[23] पूर्वजस्य । पूर्वजस्यैव । पूर्वस्य स्यात्
[24] सहवासश्च । सहवासस्तु
[25] ऽपि । ऽपि वा

रक्ष्यं बालधनमा व्यवहारप्राप्तेः ।। [G 10.48]

इति वचनम्[26] ।

<**18**> अयं च पुत्राणां विभागः पुत्रपौत्रप्रपौत्रपर्यन्तः समानः । नात्रोत्पत्तितः प्रत्त्यासत्तिक्रमेणाधिकारक्रमः । पुत्रादीनां त्रयाणामेव पार्वणे[27] तत्पिण्डतद्भोग्यपिण्डद्वयविधानात्[28] । अत एव **देवलः** —

पिता पितामहश्चैव तथैव प्रपितामहः ।
उपासते सुतं जातं शकुन्ता इव पिप्पलम् ।। [D 1308]
मधुमांसैश्च शाकैश्च पयसा पायसेन च ।
एष नो दास्यति श्राद्धं[29] वर्षासु च मघासु च ।। [D 1309]

तथा **शङ्खलिखित-यमाः** —

पिता पितामहश्चैव तथैव प्रपितामहः ।
जातं पुत्रं प्रशंसन्ति पिप्पलं शकुना इव ।। [ŚL 281]
मधुमांसेन खड्गेन पयसा पायसेन वा[30] ।
एष दास्यति नस्तृप्तिं[31] वर्षासु च मघासु च ।। [ŚL 281]

प्रपितामहग्रहणात्पुत्रपदं प्रपौत्रपर्यन्तपरम् ।

तदनेन प्रपौत्रपर्यन्तस्य श्राद्धदानेन प्रपितामहपर्यन्तोपकारत्वात् प्रपौत्रपर्यन्तस्य तुल्यवद्दायाधिकारः[32] । <**19**> अत एव जीवत्पितृकयोः पौत्रप्रपौत्रयोरनधिकारः पार्वणानधिकारितया पिण्डाप्रदातृत्वात्[33] ।

<**20**> पित्रोरुपरमे च भ्रातॄणां पितृकृतो विशेषः परं निवर्तते । अन्यत्तु सर्वमेव प्रत्येतव्यम् ।

[26] वचनम् । **गोतम**वचनम्
[27] पार्वणे । पार्वण-
[28] -विधानात् । -दानात् । -दानाविशेषात्
[29] नो दास्यति श्राद्धं । दास्यति नस्तृप्तिं
[30] वा । च
[31] दास्यति नस्तृप्तिं । नो दास्यति श्राद्धं
[32] तुल्यवद्दायाधिकारः । तुल्यो दायाधिकारः । तुल्योऽधिकारः
[33] पिण्डाप्रदातृत्वात् । पिण्डादातृत्वात्

<**21**> यदा चैकः पुत्रोऽस्त्यपरस्य पुत्रस्य पुत्राः सन्ति तदा पुत्रस्यैको[34] भागोऽपरश्च बहूनां नप्तॄणां स्वपित्रधीनजन्ममूलत्वाद्धनसबन्धस्य यावत्येव धने तस्य स्वामित्वार्हत्वं तावत्येव तेषामपि[35] ।

<**22**> यच्च —

अनेकपितृकानां तु पितृतो भागकल्पना । [Y 2.120cd = Vi 27.23ab]

इति वचनं[36] तस्य नायं विषयः । पितृव्यपितुरेव तत्सर्वं धनमिति पितृव्यस्यैव सर्वं स्यान्न तु तद्भ्रातृपुत्राणाम्[37] । पितृतो भागकल्पना[38] पितापुत्रविभागवद्भागकल्पने[39] पितुर्भागद्वयसंबन्धात्पितृव्यस्य भागद्वयं भवेत् तद्भ्रातृपुत्राणां[40] त्वेकैको[41] भागः स्यात्तदा च शिष्टाचारविरोधः स्यात् । <**23**> अस्य पुनरेष विषयः यत्रैकस्य भ्रातुरल्पसंख्यकाः पुत्राः सन्ति अपरस्य बहुसंख्यकास्तत्र[42] पितृतो भागकल्पना[43] ।

<**24**> इदानीं सवर्णभ्रातॄणां विभागः । विंशोद्धरादिपूर्वको वा सम एव वेति[44] विकल्पः ।

<**25**> उद्धारमन्तरेणापि समविभागमाह पितरीत्यनुवृत्तौ **हारीतः** —

समानतो मृते रिक्थविभागः ।। [H 4.4]

तथो**शनाः** —

वर्णानामानुलोम्यानां[45] विभागोऽयं प्रकीर्तितः[46] ।

[34] पुत्रस्यैको । तस्यैको
[35] तेषामपि । तेषामिति
[36] वचनं । *om*
[37] तु तद्भ्रातृपुत्राणाम् । तद्भ्रातृपुत्राणाम् । तद्भ्रातुः पुत्राणाम् । भ्रातुः पुत्राणाम्
[38] भागकल्पना । भागकल्पने । भागकल्पनात् । भागकल्पनेति
[39] -कल्पने । -कल्पनेति
[40] तद्भ्रातृपुत्राणं । तद्भ्रातुः पुत्राणां
[41] त्वेकैको । त्वेको
[42] बहुसंख्यकास्तत्र । बहुसंख्यकाः पुत्रास्तत्र
[43] कल्पना । कल्पनेति
[44] सम एव वेति । सम एव वा । समो वेति
[45] वर्णानामानुलोम्यानां । वर्णानामनुलोमानां
[46] प्रकीर्तितः। प्रदर्शितः

समत्वेनैकजातीनां[47] विभागस्तु विधीयते ।। [*Dhko* p. 1238]

तथाच[48] **पैठीनसिः** —

पैतृके विभज्यमाने दायाद्ये समो विभागः ।। [Pai 118]

तथा **याज्ञवल्क्यः** —

विभजेरन् सुताः पित्रोरूर्ध्वं रिक्थमृणं समम् ।। [Y 2.117ab]

अतः सोद्धारानुद्धारविभागयोर्विकल्पः[49] ।

<26> न च केवलसमविभागस्यापि[50] शास्त्रीयत्वान्नित्यवत्तस्यैवानुष्ठानं स्यादिति वाच्यम् । भक्त्यतिशयेन भ्रातृणमुद्धारानुमतेरपि संभवाद्विभागाविभागवद्विकल्पः[51] । **<27>** अत एवाद्यतनानां भक्त्यतिशयाभावात्समभाग[52] एव लोके दृश्यते उद्धारार्हज्येष्ठाभावाच्च[53] ।

<28> यस्तु स्वयोग्यतामात्रपरामर्षात्पितृपितामहादिधनविभागे[54] निस्पृहः स किंचिदेव[55] तण्डुलप्रस्थमपि दत्त्वा तत्पुत्रादेः कालान्तरीयदुरन्ततानिरासार्थं विभजनीयः । तदाह[56] **मनुः** —

भ्रातृणां यस्तु नेहेत धनं शक्तः स्वकर्मणा ।
स निर्भाज्यः स्वकादंशात् किंचिद्दत्त्वोपजीवनम् ।। [Y 9.207]

तथा **याज्ञवल्क्यः** —

शक्तस्यानीहमानस्य किंचिद्दत्त्वा पृथक्क्रिया ।। [Y 2.116ab]

<29> पितरि चोपरते सोदरभ्रातृभिर्विभागे क्रियमाणे मात्रे पुत्रसमांशो[57] दातव्यः समांशहारिणी मातेति [N 13.12c] वचनात् ।

[47] -जातीनां । -जातानां

[48] तथाच । तथा

[49] सोद्धारानुद्धारविभागयोर्विकल्पः । सोद्धारानुद्धारयोर्विकल्पः

[50] -विभाग- । -प्रविभाग-

[51] संभवाद्विभागाविभाग- । संभवाद्विभाग-

[52] समभाग । समविभाग

[53] -भावाच्च । -भावात्

[54] -मात्र- । *om* ।। -विभागे । -विभाग-

[55] किंचिदेव । यत्किंचिदेव

[56] तदाह । यदाह

[57] पुत्रसमांशो । पुत्रसमोंऽशो

<30> मातृपदस्य जननीपरत्वान्न सपत्नीमातृपरत्वमपि । सकृच्छ्रुतस्य मुख्यगौणत्वानुपपत्तेः[58] ।

<31> समांशता च मातुर्भ्रात्रादिभिः स्त्रीधनादाने । दत्ते पुनरर्धम् ।

पित्रा च पुत्रेभ्यः समविभागदाने[59] सर्वपत्नीनामेव पुत्रसमांशता[60] कर्तव्या । तदाह **याज्ञवल्क्यः** —

यदि कुर्यात्समानंशान् पत्न्यः कार्याः[61] समांशिकाः ।
न दत्तं स्त्रीधनं यासां भर्त्रा वा श्वशुरेण वा ।। [Y 2.115]
अधिविन्नस्त्रियै देयमाधिवेदनिकं समम् ।
न दत्तं स्त्रीधनं यासां[62] दत्ते त्वर्धं प्रकल्पयेत् ।। [Y 2.148]

<32> पुत्रहीनाश्च पत्न्यः[63] समानांशा न पुत्रवत्यः । तथा **व्यासः** —

असुतास्तु पितुः पत्न्यः समानांशाः प्रकीर्तिताः ।
पितामह्यश्च सर्वास्ता[64] मातृतुल्याः प्रकीर्तिताः ।। [Vy 250]

तथा **विष्णुः** —

मातरः पुत्रभागानुसारेण[65] भागहारिण्यः । अनूढाश्च दुहितरः[66] ।। [Vi 18.34-35]

<33> पुत्रभागानुसारेण यथा वर्णक्रमेण पुत्राणां[67] चतुस्त्रिद्व्येकभागिता तथा पत्नीनामपीति[68] । **<34>** अनूढानां दुहितॄणां पुत्रभागमनुसृत्य तच्चतुर्थांशः । तदाह **बृहस्पतिः** —

समांशा मातरस्त्वेषां तुरीयांशाश्च कन्यकाः ।। [B 26.22cd]

[58] मुख्यगौण- । मुख्यगौणपर-
[59] -विभाग- । -भाग- । -प्रविभाग-
[60] पुत्र- । *om*
[61] कार्याः । कुर्यात्
[62] यासां । यस्यै
[63] पत्न्यः । पितुः पत्न्यः
[64] सर्वास्ता । ताः सर्वा
[65] पुत्रभागानुसारेण । पुत्रभागानुसार-
[66] अनूढाश्च दुहितरः । अनूढा दुहितरश्च
[67] पुत्राणां । पुत्राणां च
[68] पत्नीमामपीपति । पत्नीमामपि

<**35**> पुत्रस्य भागत्रयं कन्याया[69] एको भागः । यथा[70] **कात्यायनः** —

कन्यकानां त्वदत्तानां चतुर्थो भाग इष्यते ।
पुत्राणां च त्रयो भागाः स्वाम्यं स्वल्पधने[71] स्मृतम् ।। [K 858]

<**36**> अल्पधने पुत्रैः स्वात्स्वादंशादाकृष्य कन्याभ्यश्चतुर्थोंऽशो दातव्यः । तथा[72] **मनुः** —

स्वेभ्योंऽशेभ्यस्तु[73] कन्याभ्यः प्रदद्युर्भ्रातरः पृथक् ।
स्वात्स्वादंशाच्चतुर्भागं पतिताः स्युरदित्सवः ।। [M 9.118]

<**37**> प्रदद्युरिति प्रदानश्रुतेरदाने च पतितत्वश्रुतेर्न कन्याभिरधिकारबुद्ध्या[74] ग्रहीतव्यम् । न ह्यधिकारिणे भ्रात्रेऽपरो भ्राता स्वादंशाद्ददाति ।

<**38**> यथा[75] **याज्ञवल्क्यः** —

असंस्कृरास्तु संस्कार्या भ्रातृभिः पूर्वसंस्कृतैः ।
भगिन्यश्च निजादंशाद्दत्त्वांशं तु तुरीयकम्।। [Y 2.124]

भगिनीनां[76] संस्कार्यतामाह नाधिकारिताम् । <**39**> एवं च बहुतरधने विवाहोचितं[77] धनं दातव्यं न[78] चतुर्थांशनियम इति सिध्यतिः ।

<**40**> एतच्च कन्यापुत्रयोः समसंख्यत्वे[79] ज्ञातव्यम् । विषमसंख्यत्वे[80] च[81] कन्याया एव बहुतरधनं वा स्यात्पुत्रस्य वा निरंशता[82] स्यात् । न चैतदु-

[69] कन्याया । कन्यकाया
[70] यथा । यदाह
[71] स्वल्पधने । त्वल्पधने
[72] तथा । यथा
[73] शेभ्यस्तु : शेभ्यश्च
[74] -धिकार- । -धिकारि-
[75] यथा । तथा
[76] भगिनीनां । इति भगिनीनां
[77] विवाहोचितं । विवाहोचित-
[78] न । न तु
[79] समसंख्यत्वे । समसंख्यात्वे
[80] विषमसंख्यत्वे । विषमसंख्यात्वे । विषमसंख्यायां
[81] च । तु । *om*
[82] निरंशता । निर्धनता

चितं पुत्रस्य प्राधान्यात्[83] ।

<**41**> यच्चेदमत्र बाधकमुक्तम् —

अविद्यमाने पित्रर्थे स्वांशादुद्धृत्य वा पुनः ।
अवश्यकार्याः संस्कारा भ्रातृभिः पूर्वसंस्कृतैः ।। [N 13.34]

अस्मा**न्नारद**वचनादवश्यकर्तव्यत्वाद्भगिनीसंस्कारस्य[84] निरंशतापि न दोषायेति ।

तदयुक्तं भ्रातृसंस्कारार्थत्वादस्य वचनस्य । भ्रातृणां पूर्वसंस्कृतैरिति पाठस्यानाकरत्वाद्भ्रातृसंस्कारस्य प्रकृतत्वात् । इदं हि पूर्वमुक्तम् —

येषां तु न कृताः पित्रा संस्कारविधयः क्रमात् ।
कर्तव्या भ्रातृभिस्तेषां पैतृकादेव तद्धनात् ।। [N 13.33]

येषां तेषामिति पुंलिङ्गनिर्देशात्तदनन्तरमेवाविद्यमान इति वचनारम्भाद्भ्रातृसंस्कारार्थमेवेदं वचनम् ।

<**43**> इति पितृपितामहादिधनविभागः[85] ।

[83] पुत्रस्य प्राधान्यात् । पुत्रस्यैव वित्ते प्राधान्यात् । पुत्रस्य प्रधानत्वात्

[84] अस्मा**न्नारद**- । इत्यस्मा**न्नारद**- ।। -भगिनी- । -भगिनीनां

[85] इति पितृपितामहादिधनविखागः । *om*

<**4.1.1**> अथ स्त्रीधनविभागार्थं प्रथमं स्त्रीधनं[1] निरूप्यते।

तत्र **विष्णुः** —

पितृमातृसुतभ्रातृदत्तमध्यग्न्युपागतं आधिवेदनिकं बन्धुदत्तं
शुल्कान्वाधेयकमिति स्त्रीधनम् ॥ [Vi 17.18]

<**2**> अन्वाधेयकमाह[2] **कात्यायनः** —

विवाहात्परतो यत्तु लब्धं भर्तृकुलात् स्त्रिया ।
अन्वाधेयं तदुक्तं तु लब्धं बन्धुकुलात्तथा ॥ [K 899]
ऊर्ध्वं लब्धं तु यत्किंचित्संस्कारात्प्रीतितः स्त्रिया ।
भर्तुः पित्रोः सकाशाद्वा अन्वाधेयं तु तद्भृगुः ॥ [K 900]

<**3**> बन्धुपदेन मातापित्रोरुपादानम् । तेनायमर्थः — मातापितृद्वारेण संबन्धिनां पित्रोश्च सकाशाद्यत्तु[3] विवाहात्परतो लब्धम् । तथा भर्तुः सकाशाद्भर्तृकुलाच्च श्वशुरादितो यल्लब्धं धनं[4] तदन्वाधेयम् । **विष्णु**वचने च[5] बन्धुपदं मातुलाद्यभिप्रायं पित्रादीनां स्वपदेनैव निर्दिष्टत्वात् । परिणयनसमयलब्धस्य[6] च[7] ब्राह्माद्यासुरादिविशेषेण भर्तुः पित्रोर्वाधिकारात् ।

<**4**> स्त्रीधनमाहतु**र्मनु-कात्यायनौ** —

अध्यग्न्यध्यावाहनिकं दत्तं च प्रीतितः स्त्रियै ।
भ्रातृमातृपितृप्राप्तं षड्विधं स्त्रीधनं स्मृतम् ॥ [M 9.194 = K 894]

तथा **नारदः** —

अध्यग्न्यध्यावाहनिकं भर्तृदायस्तथैव च ।
भ्रातृदत्तं पितृभ्यां च षड्विधं स्त्रीधनं स्मृतम् ॥ [N 13.8]

<**5**> एयद्व्याकुरुते **कात्यायनः** —

विवाहकाले यत्स्त्रीभ्यो दीयते ह्यग्निसंनिधौ ।

[1] स्त्रीधनं । स्त्रीधनमेव
[2] अन्वाधेयकमाह । अन्वाधेयमाह
[3] सकाशाद्यत्तु । सकाशाद्
[4] यल्लब्धं धनं । यद्धनं । यल्लब्धं
[5] च । *om*
[6] परिणयन- । परिणय-
[7] च । *om*

तदध्यग्निकृतं सद्भिः स्त्रीधनं परिकीर्तितम्[8] ।। [K 895]
यत्पुनर्लभते नारी नीयमाना हि पैतृकात् ।
अध्यावाहनिकं नाम तत्स्त्रीधनमुदाहृतम् ।। [K 896]

<6> पैतृकादित्येकशेषेण पितृमातृकुलाद्यल्लभते धनं भर्तृगृहं नीयमाना तदध्यावाहनिकम् ।

<7> भर्तृदायो भर्तृदत्तं[9] धनं भर्तृदायमनभिधाय **मन्वादि**भिर्भर्तृदत्तस्याभिधानात् । **नारदेना**पि भर्तृदत्तमनभिधाय भर्तृदायस्याभिधानात् ।

<8> तथान्यत्रापि भर्तृदत्ते भर्तृदायप्रयोगो[10] दृष्टः । यथा **कात्यायनः** —

भर्तृदायं मृते पत्यौ विन्यसेत्स्त्री यथेष्टतः ।
विद्यमाने तु संरक्षेत् क्षपयेत्तत्कुलेऽन्यथा[11] ।। [K 907]

<9> अस्यार्थः — भर्तृदत्तं[12] धनं भर्तरि मृते यथेष्टं विनियुञ्जीत । जीवति तु तद्रक्षेदमुक्तहस्ततातज्ञापनार्थम्[13] । **<10>** तथा **व्यास**वचनमपि भर्तृदेयपर्यन्तताज्ञापनार्थम्[14] । यथा —

द्विसहस्रः परो[15] दायः स्त्रियै देयो धनस्य तु ।
यच्च भर्त्रा धनं दत्तं सा यथाकाममश्नीयात्[16] ।। [Vy 265]

द्विसहस्रपर्यन्तः स्त्रियै देयो नाधिकः । केनेत्याकाङ्क्षायां भर्त्रेति श्रुतमन्वेति न पुनरश्रुतकल्पना । तथा च देय इति ददातिर्मुख्यः स्यात् । मृतपतिधने[17] तु तावति पत्न्या एव स्वामित्वाद्गौणः । स चान्याय्यः । **<11>** यच्च भर्तृदत्तं[18] धनं तद्यथाकाममश्नीयात् ।

[8] परिकीर्तितम् । तु प्रकीर्तितम्
[9] भर्तृदत्तं । भर्तृदत्त-
[10] भर्तृदाय- । भर्तृदायपद-
[11] क्षपयेत्तत्कुले । क्षेपयेत्तत्कुले
[12] भर्तृदत्तं । भर्तृदत्त-
[13] तद्रक्षेदमुक्तहस्तता- । तद्रक्षेदिदमुक्तहस्तता-
[14] -पर्यन्तता- । -पर्यन्त-
[15] द्विसहस्रः परो । द्विसहस्रपरो । द्विसहस्रपणो
[16] यथाकाममश्नीयात् । यथाकाममश्नुयात्
[17] मृत- । मृतपतित- । मृतप्रव्रजित-
[18] भर्तृदत्तं । भर्तृदत्त-

अतोऽपुत्रस्य मृतस्य[19] पत्युर्धने द्विसहस्रपर्यन्ते[20] पत्न्या अधिकारो[21] न सर्वत्रेति यदुक्तं तद्विद्वद्भिरनादेयम् । <**12**> एतच्च विस्तरेण वक्ष्यते ।

<**13**> आह **याज्ञवल्क्यः** —

पितृमातृपतिभ्रातृदत्तमध्यग्न्युपागतम् ।
आधिवेदनिकं चैव स्त्रीधनं परिकीर्तितम् ।। [Y 2.143]

<**14**> यच्च द्वितीयस्त्रीविवाहार्थिना[22] पूर्वस्त्रियै पारितोषिकं धनं दत्तं तदाधिवेदनिकमधिकस्त्रीलाभार्थत्वात्तस्य ।

<**15**> तथा **देवलः** —

वृत्तिराभरणं शुल्कं लाभश्च स्त्रीधनं भवेत्[23] ।
भोक्त्री तत्स्वयमेवेदं पतिर्नार्हत्यनापदि ।। [D 1604]

<**16**> तथा **व्यासः** —

विवाहकाले यत्किंचिद्वरायोद्दिश्य दीयते ।
कन्यायास्तद्धनं सर्वमविभाज्यं च[24] बन्धुभिः ।। [Vy 266]

<**17**> उद्दिश्येति कन्याया इदं भवत्वित्युद्दिश्य यद्वराय दानं[25] न पुनरेतदभिसंधिं विनापीत्यर्थः । अत एव विवाहकाल इति प्रदर्शनार्थं न पुनरेतदेव प्रयोजकं दात्रभिसंधिनिमित्तत्वात्स्वत्वस्य । तथा[26] प्रामाणिकवचनम्[27] —

यद्दत्तं दुहितुः पत्ये स्त्रियमेव तदन्वियात् ।
मृते जीवति वा पत्यौ[28] तदपत्यमृते स्त्रियाः ।। [*Dhko* p. 1463]

विवाहकाल[29] इति न विशिनष्टि । अभिसंधिस्तु दुहित्रन्वयाभिधानादेव लब्धत्वान्नोक्तः ।

19 मृतस्य । *om*
20 -पर्यन्ते । -पर्यन्त एव
21 पत्न्या अधिकारो । पत्न्यधिकारो
22 -स्त्री- । *om*
23 भवेत् । स्मृतम्
24 च । तु
25 यद्वराय दानं । वराय यद्दानं
26 तथा । तथाच
27 प्रामाणिक- । प्रामाणिकं
28 वा पत्यौ । पत्यौ वा
29 विवाहकाल । विवाह

<**18**> तदेमव्यवस्थितसंख्यस्त्रीधनकीर्तनान्न षट्संख्या[30] विवक्षिता किंतु स्त्रीधनकीर्तनमात्रपराणि[31] मुनिवचनानि । तदेव च स्त्रिया धनं[32] यत्र भर्तृतः[33] स्वातन्त्र्येण दानविक्रयभोगान् कर्तुमधिकरोति ।

<**19**> तदिदं संक्षिप्याह[34] **कात्यायनः** —

प्राप्तं शिल्पैस्तु यद्वित्तं प्रीत्या चैव यदन्यतः ।
भर्तुः स्वाम्यं तदा तत्र शेषं तु स्त्रीधनं स्मृतम् ।। [K 904]

<**20**> अन्यत इति पितृमातृभर्तृकुलव्यतिरिक्ताद्यल्लब्धं शिल्पेन वा यदर्जितं तत्र भर्तुः स्वाम्यं स्वातन्त्र्यम् । अनापद्यपि भर्ता ग्रहीतुमर्हति । तेन स्त्रिया अपि धनं[35] न स्त्रीधनमस्वातन्त्र्यात् ।

<**21**> एतद्द्वयातिरिक्तधनं[36] तु स्त्रिया एव दानविक्रयाधिकारात्[37] । तदाह **कात्यायनः** —

ऊढया कन्यया वापि पत्युः पितृगृहेऽथवा ।
भर्तुः सकाशात्पित्रोर्वा लब्धं सौदायिकं स्मृतम् ।। [K 901]
सौदायिकं धनं प्राप्य स्त्रीणां स्वातन्त्र्यमिष्यते ।
यस्मात्तदानृशंस्यार्थं तैर्दत्तं तत्प्रजीवनम् ।। [K 905]
सौदायिके सदा स्त्रीणां स्वातन्त्र्यं परिकीर्तितम् ।
विक्रये चैव दाने च यथेष्टं स्थावरेष्वपि ।। [K 906]

<**22**> सुदायसंबन्धिभ्यो[38] लब्धं सौदायिकम् ।

<**23**> स्थावरेऽपि भर्तृदत्तमात्रे स्त्रिया न दानाद्यधिकारः[39] । तदाह **नारदः** —

[30] षट्संख्या । षट्त्वसंख्या
[31] -कीर्तन- । *om*
[32] स्त्रिया धनं । स्त्रीधनं
[33] यत्र भर्तृत; । यद्भर्तृतः
[34] संक्षिप्याह । किंचित्संक्षिप्याह
[35] धनं । *om*
[36] -धनं । -धने
[37] -धिकारात् । धिकारः
[38] सुदाय- । सुदायेभ्यः
[39] न दानाद्यधिकारः । दानाद्यनधिकारः

भर्त्रा प्रीतेन यद्दत्तं स्त्रियै तस्मिन्मृतेऽपि तत् ।
सा यथाकाममश्नीयाद्दद्याद्वा स्थावरादृते ।। [N 1.28/24]

भर्तृदत्तविशेषनाद्भर्तृदत्तस्थावरादृतेऽन्यत्स्थावरं देयमेव भवति । अन्यथा यथेष्टं स्थावरेष्वपीति विरुध्येत ।

<**24**> भर्ता तु यदा[40] दुर्भिक्षादौ स्त्रीधनं[41] विना वर्तनाक्षमस्तदापि[42] ग्रहीतुमर्हति नान्यदा । तदाह[43] **याज्ञवल्क्यः** —

दुर्भिक्षे धर्मकार्ये च व्याधौ संप्रतिरोधके ।
गृहीतं स्त्रीधनं भर्ता न स्त्रियै दातुमर्हति ।। [Y 2.147]

अन्यत्र पुनरनधिकारमाह **कात्यायनः** —

न भर्ता नैव च सुतो न पिता भ्रातरो न वा[44] ।
आदाने वा विसर्गे वा स्त्रीधने प्रभविष्णवः ।। [K 911]
यदि ह्येकतरस्त्वेषां स्त्रीधनं भक्षयेद्बलात् ।
सवृद्धिं प्रतिदाप्यः[45] स्याद्दण्डं चैव समाप्नुयात् ।। [K 912]
तदेव यद्यनुज्ञाप्य भक्षयेत्प्रीतिपूर्वकम् ।
मूलमेव स दाप्यः स्यात्[46] यदा स धनवान् भवेत् ।। [K 913]
अथ चेत्स द्विभार्यः स्यान्न च तां भजते पुनः ।
प्रीत्या विसृष्टमपि चेत् प्रतिदाप्यः स तद्बलात् ।। [K 908]
ग्रासाच्छादनवासानामुच्छेदो यत्र योषितः ।
तत्र स्वमाददीत स्त्री विभागं रिक्थिनां तथा ।। [K 909]

<**25**> स्त्रिया धनं गृहीत्वा[47] यद्यपरभार्यया सह वसति तां चावजानीते तदा गृहीतधनं राज्ञा बलाद्दाप्यः[48] ।

[40] यदा । *om*
[41] स्त्रीधनं । यदि स्त्रीधनं
[42] तदापि । तदा । तदपि
[43] तदाह । यदाह । आह
[44] वा । च
[45] प्रतिदाप्यः । स च दाप्यः
[46] स दाप्यः स्यात् । तदा दाप्यो
[47] गृहीत्वा । गृहीत्वा भर्ता
[48] बलाद्दाप्यः । बलाद्दापनीयिः । बलाद्दापयितव्यः

भक्ताच्छादनादिकं यदि भर्ता न ददाति तदा तदपि स्त्रिया आकृष्य ग्राह्यम्[49] ।

<**26**> इति स्त्रीधनलक्षणम् ।

[49] ग्राह्यम् । गृहीतव्यम् । ग्रहीतव्यम्

<**4.2.1**> इदानीं स्त्रीधनविभागोऽभिधीयते[1] ।

तत्र **मनुः** —

जनन्यां संस्थितायां तु समं सर्वे सहोदराः ।
भजेरन्मातृकं रिक्थं भगिन्यश्च सनाभयः ॥ [M 9.192]

<**2**> द्वन्द्वाश्रवणेऽपि तत्तुल्यार्थकचकारेण भ्रातृभगिन्योरितरेतरयुक्तयोर्विभागप्रतिपादनाद्भगिन्यः[2] सोदराश्च विभजेरन्नित्ययमेवास्य वचनस्यार्थः[3] ।

<**3**> **बृहस्पति**रपि चकारात्समुच्चयमाह —

स्त्रीधनं तदपत्यानां दुहिता च तदंशिनी ।
अप्रत्ता चेत्समूढा तु न लभेन्मातृकं धनम् ॥ [B 26.31cdef]

<**4**> अपत्यपदं पुत्रपरम् । तेषामप्रत्ताभिर्दुहितृभिः सह मातृधनविभागः ।

तथाच[4] **शङ्खलिखितौ** —

समं सर्वे सोदर्या द्रव्यमर्हन्ति कुमार्यश्च[5] ॥ [ŚL 297]

<**5**> सर्वत्रैव प्रथमं पुत्रोपादानात्सर्वावस्थस्य पुत्रस्य मातृधनेऽधिकारः । चकारश्रुतिश्च[6] सर्वत्रानुगता समुच्चयवाचिका[7] ।

<**6**> एतावताप्युद्ग्राहमल्लस्य **देवल**वचनं गलहस्तः । यथा —

सामान्यं पुत्रकन्यानां मृतायां स्त्रीधनं स्त्रियाम् ।
अप्रजायां हरेद्भर्ता माता भ्राता पितापि वा ॥ [D 1611]

<**7**> इह पुत्रकन्ययोः साधारणं मातृधनमिति सुव्यक्तम् ।

केवलकुमार्याः[8] सकलमातृधनाधिकारित्वे च यौतकधने विशेषवचनं **मन्वादीनाम**नर्थकं स्यात् सर्वत्राधिकाराविशेषात् ।

[1] स्त्रीधन- । स्त्रीधनस्य
[2] भगिन्यः । भगिन्यश्च
[3] विभजेरन्नित्ययमेवास्य वचनस्यार्थः । विभजेरन्नित्ययमेव तस्यार्थः
[4] तथाच । तथा
[5] कुमार्यश्च । कन्याश्च
[6] चकारश्रुतिश्च । चकारश्च
[7] -चाचिका । -बोधिका
[8] केवल- । केवलं

<**8**> यः पुनरेवं समाधानं ब्रूते — भ्रातृभगिन्योस्तुल्यवज्जननीधनाधिकारित्वे समविभागिताविधानं[9] युक्तम् । केवलभगिनीनां तदभावे च केवलभ्रातृणां धनसंबन्धे समं स्यादश्रुतत्वाद्विशेषस्येति न्यायत एव[10] समत्वप्राप्तेरनर्थकं सममिति । स एवं वाच्यः — भ्रातृभगिन्योरप्यधिकारे समं स्यादिति न्यायात्समत्वप्राप्तेरविशेषादानर्थक्यस्य तदवस्थत्वात् । किंच केवलभ्रात्रधिकारपक्षेऽपि पितृधन इव मतृधनेऽपि विंशोद्धारादिप्रसक्तिनिवर्तकतया समपदस्य सार्थकत्वात्कथमनर्थकता । अतो वचनन्यायानभिज्ञः सर्वैः[11] प्राज्ञैरवज्ञेय एव किंचिज्ज्ञः[12] ।

<**9**> किंतूक्तादेव हेतोः पुत्रकुमारीदुहित्रोस्तुल्यवदधिकारः[13] । एतयोश्चान्यतराभावेऽन्यतरस्य तद्धनम् । द्वयोरप्येतयोरभाव ऊढाया[14] दुहितुः पुत्रवत्याः संभावितपुत्रायाश्च तुल्योऽधिकारः स्वपुत्रद्वारेण पार्वणपिण्डदानसंभवात्[15] । <**10**> अत एव पूर्वोक्तदुहित्रभावे दौहित्रस्यैव[16] धनाधिकारः —

दौहित्रेऽपि ह्यमुत्रैनं संतारयति पौत्रवत् ॥ [M 9.139cd]

इति **मनु**वचनात् । न तु वन्ध्याविधवादुहित्रोः स्वसत्तया स्वजन्यसत्तया च पार्वणपिण्डदानाभावात् । अत एव **नारदः** —

पुत्राभावे तु[17] दुहिता तुल्यसंतानदर्शनात् ॥ [N 13.50ab/47ab]

<**11**> पौत्रदौहित्रयोस्तु सद्भावे पौत्रस्याधिकारः[18] पुत्रेण परिणीतदुहितुर्बाधाद्बाधकपुत्रेण बाध्यदुहितृपुत्रबाधस्य न्याय्यत्वात् ।

[9] समविभागिता- । समभाग-

[10] न्यायत एव । न्यायादेव

[11] सर्वैः । *om*

[12] किंचिज्ज्ञः । किंचिज्ज्ञ इति

[13] -कुमारी- । *om*

[14] -भाव ऊढाया । -भावे त्वूढाया

[15] -दानसंभवात् । -दानात्

[16] दौहित्रस्यैव । दौहित्रस्य

[17] तु । च

[18] पौत्रस्याधिकारः । पौत्रस्यैवाधिकारः

<**12**> उक्तानां तु सर्वेषां[19] दौहित्रपर्यन्तानामभावे वन्ध्याविधवयोरपि मातृधनाधिकारिता तयोरपि तत्प्रजात्वात् प्रजाभावे[20] चान्येषामधिकारात् ।

<**13**> यत्तु दुहितृमात्राधिकारार्थं **गोतम**वचनम्[21] —

स्त्रीधनं दुहितॄणामप्रत्तानामप्रतिष्ठितानां च ।। [G 28.24]

यच्च **नारदस्य** —

मातुर्दुहितरोऽभावे दुहितॄणां तदन्वयः ।। [N 13.2cd]

यच्च **कात्यायन**स्यापि[22] —

दुहितॄणामभावे तु रिक्थं पुत्रेषु[23] तद्भवेत् ।। [K 918ab]

तथा[24] **याज्ञवल्क्यस्य** —

मातुर्दुहितरः शेषमृणात्ताभ्य ऋतेऽन्वयः ।। [Y 2.117cd]

तानि पूर्वोक्त**देवल**वचमविरोधेन[25] यौतकद्रव्यविषयाणि । अत एव **मनुः** —

मातुस्तु[26] यौतकं यत्स्यात्कुमारीभाग एव सः ।। [M 9.131ab]

<**14**> यौतकं परिणयनलब्धम् । यु मिश्रण इति धातोर्युतपदं[27] मिश्रता-वचनम्[28] । मिश्रता च स्त्रीपुरुषयोरेकशरीरता[29] विवाहाच्च तद्भवति —

अस्थिभिरस्थीनि मांसैर्मांसानि त्वचा त्वचम् । [*Pāraskara GṛS* 1.11.5]

इति **श्रुतेः** । अतो विवाहकाले[30] लब्धं यौतकम् ।

<**15**> अत एव **वशिष्ठः** —

[19] तु सर्वेषां। सर्वेषां तु

[20] प्रजाभावे । प्रजाया अभावे

[21] **गोतम-** । **गोतमस्य**

[22] **कात्यायन**स्यापि । **कात्यायनस्य**

[23] पुत्रेषु । पुत्रे तु । पुत्रस्य

[24] तथा । यच्च

[25] -**देवल**- । -**देवलादि**-

[26] मातुस्तु । मातुश्च

[27] पदं । इति पदं

[28] मिश्रतावचनम् । मिश्रतापरम् । मिश्रितापरम्

[29] स्त्रीपुरुषयो- । स्त्रीपुंसयो- ।। -शरीरता । -कता

[30] विवाहकाले । विवाहकाल-

मातुः पारिणाय्यं स्त्रियो विभजेरन् ॥ [Va 17.46]

परिणाय्यं परिणयनलब्धं धनम्[31] ।

<16> यत्तु **मनु**वचनम् —

स्त्रियास्तु यद्भवेद्वित्तं पित्रा दत्तं कथंचन ।

ब्राह्मणी तद्धरेत्कन्या तदपत्यस्य वा भवेत् ॥ [M 9.198]

अत्र[32] पित्रा दत्तमिति विशेषणाद्विवाहसमयादन्यत्रापि[33] यत्पितृदत्तं तत्कन्याया[34] एवेत्येतदर्थम् । ब्राह्मणीपदं चानुवादः[35] । यद्वा ब्राह्मणीपदस्यानर्थक्यभयात्क्षत्रियादिस्त्रीणामनपत्यानां पितृदत्तं धनं[36] सपत्नीदुहिता ब्राह्मणी कन्या हरेत् । न पुनरप्रजास्त्रीधनं भर्तुरिति वचनावकाश इति वचनार्थः । अन्यथा[37] सकलवचनानामसामञ्जस्यं स्यात् ।

<17> न च वाच्यम् — **नारदादि**भिर्दुहितुरभावे दुहितुः पुत्राणामेव धनाधिकारो दर्शितः प्रत्यासन्नदुहितृपदेनैवान्वयपदस्यान्वयादिति ।

यतो दुहितृपदस्यान्वयपदस्य च जन्यविशेषपरत्वेन[38] जनकाकाङ्क्षितत्वान्न[39] जन्यान्तरेणान्वयपदोपात्तेन पुत्रेणान्वयः संभवति समत्वात् । **<18>** न चाधिष्ठानलक्षणयान्वयो वाच्यः मात्रन्वयेनैव सर्वेषां मुख्यत्वसंभवात् । मातृपदान्वये च दुहितृपदस्य मुख्यत्वस्वीकारात्[40] । **<19>** न च तदन्वय इति तच्छब्दोपात्ताया दुहितुरन्वययोग्यता वाच्या तच्छब्दस्यापि प्रकृतवाचितया दुहितृत्वरूपेणैवोपपादकत्वात् ।

<20> किंच **याज्ञवल्क्य**वचने दुहितर इति पदं[41] प्रथमान्तं ताभ्य इति पदं[42] पञ्चम्यन्तमन्वयपदेन षष्ठ्यन्तान्वययोग्येन नान्वीयते। किंतु व्यवहि-

[31] परिणयनलब्धं धनम् । परिणयनलब्धधनम् । परिणयनलब्धम्

[32] अत्र । तत्

[33] विशेषणा- । विशेषवचना-

[34] तत्कन्याया । कन्याया

[35] ब्राह्मणीपदं चानुवादः । ब्राह्मणीपदमत्रानुवादः

[36] धनं । *om*

[37] अन्यथा । *om*

[38] -परत्वेन । -वचनत्वेन

[39] जनकाकाङ्क्षितत्वान्न । जनकाकाङ्क्षित्वान्न

[40] मुख्यत्वस्वीकारात् । मुख्यत्वस्य स्वीकारात् । मुख्यार्थत्वस्य स्वीकारात्

[41] पदं । *om*

तमपि मातुरित्येव पदमन्वयि । तदत्र[43] मातुरन्वये निश्चिते **नारद-कात्यायन**वाक्येऽपि मातुरेवान्वयो न्याय्यः[44] अविरोधात् ।

<21> किंच —

सत्स्वङ्गजेषु तद्गामी ह्यर्थो भवति । [Bau 1.5.11.11]

इति **बौधयन**वचनानुसारेणानन्तर्याच्चाङ्गजपुत्रस्याधिकारो न्याय्यो नानङ्गजव्यवहितदौहित्राधिकारः ।

<22> ततश्च परिणयनलब्धं[45] स्त्रीधनं दुहितुरेव न पुत्राणाम् । तत्रैव च[46] क्रमार्थं **गोतम**वचनम्[47] —

स्त्रीधनं दुहितॄणामप्रत्तानामप्रतिष्ठितानां च ।। [G 28.24]

<23> प्रथममप्रत्तानां तदभावे प्रत्तानां[48] तदभावे च[49] समूढानाम् । स्त्रीधनं दुहितॄणामिति सामान्यतः प्राप्तत्वादप्रत्तानामित्यादेस्तु क्रमार्थत्वेनोपसंहारार्थत्वात्[50] ।

<24> तथा **याज्ञवल्क्यः** —

अप्रजास्त्रीधनं भर्तुर्ब्राह्मादिषु चतुर्ष्वपि ।
दुहितॄणां प्रसूता चेच्छेषेषु पितृगामि तत् ।। [Y 2.145]

<25> ब्राह्मादिविवाहेषु[51] यल्लब्धमध्यग्निधनं स्त्रिया तत्तस्यां मृतायां प्रथमं दुहितॄणामेव । तत्रापि प्रथमं कन्यायास्तदभावे प्रत्तायास्तदभावे परिणीतायाः । सर्वदुहित्रभावे पुत्रस्याधिकारः अप्रजास्त्रीधने भर्तुरधिकारात् ।

[42] पदं । *om*

[43] तदत्र । तत्र

[44] न्याय्यः । वाच्यः । युक्तः

[45] -लब्धं । -लब्ध-

[46] च । *om*

[47] क्रमाथ **गोतम**वचनं । **गोतम**वचनं क्रमार्थम्

[48] तदभावे प्रत्तां । *om*

[49] च । *om*

[50] -संहारार्थत्वात् । -संहारसमर्थत्वात्

[51] ब्राह्मादि- । ब्राह्मादिषु ।। -विवाहेषु । -विवाहे । *om*

<**26**> **बृहस्पतिना** त्वप्रत्तापदेनाप्रत्ताद्यभावे[52] समूढाया अप्यधिकारः सूचितः ।

<**27**> न च यौतकमात्रधनाभिप्रायेण नेदं[53] वचनम् । किंतु ब्राह्मादिविवाहेन विवाहिताया यद्यावद्धनं यौतकमयौतकं वा तदभिप्रायेणेति वाच्यम् । बन्धुदत्तमिति वचनस्य निर्विषयत्वापत्तेः । **मनु**विरोधाच्च । यदाह —

ब्राह्मदैवार्षगान्धर्वप्राजापत्येषु यद्धनम् ।
अतीतायामप्रजायां[54] भर्तुरेव तदिष्यते ।। [M 9.196]
यत्त्वस्याः स्याद्धनं दत्तं विवाहेष्वासुरादिषु ।
अतीतायामप्रजायां मातापित्रोस्तदिष्यते ।। [M 9.197]

अस्याः स्याद्दत्तमिति पराचीनं पूर्वत्रानुषज्यते । तेन विवाहेषु यद्धनं दत्तमिति संबन्धाद्वैवाहिकधनमात्रप्रतीतेर्न[55] यावद्धनविषयत्वम्[56] ।

<**28**> तथा **यमः** —

आसुरादिषु यद्द्रव्यं विवाहेषु प्रदीयते ।। [*Dhko* p. 1462]

विवाहक्रियायां पूर्वापरीभूतायां यद्द्रव्यं प्रदीयत इति यौतकधनमात्रगोचरत्वमेव प्रतीयते ।

<**29**> न च विवाहात्पूर्वं परतो वा स्त्रिया लब्धस्याप्रजास्त्रीधनस्य गतेरश्रूयमाणत्वाद् ब्राह्मादिपदं स्त्रीपरमिति वाच्यम् । पूर्वापरलब्धस्य विस्तरेण गतेर्वक्ष्यमाणत्वात् ।

[52] त्वप्रत्ता- । अप्रत्ता- ।। -पदेनाप्रत्ताद्यभावे । -पदेनापत्यान्तराभावे
[53] न च . . . -प्रायेण नेदं । न च न . . .-प्रायेणेदं
[54] अतीतायामप्रजायां । अप्रजायामतीतायां
[55] -मात्रप्रयीतेर्न । -मात्रं प्रतीयते न
[56] -विषयत्वम् । -विषयम्

<**4.3.1**> संप्रत्यप्रजास्त्रीधने[1]ऽधिकारिणः[2] कथ्यन्ते ।

<**2**> तत्र **याज्ञवल्क्यः** —

अप्रजास्त्रीधनं भर्तुर्ब्राह्मादिषु चतुर्ष्वपि ।। [Y 2.145ab]

<**3**> ब्राह्मादिर्येषां चतुर्णां ते दैवार्षप्राजापत्यगान्धर्वाश्चत्वारो ब्राह्मेण सह पञ्च भवन्ति ब्राह्मदैवार्षगान्धर्वप्राजापत्येष्विति **मनुना** पञ्चानामुक्तत्वात् । तेषु विवाहेषु वर्तमानेषु यद्धनं स्त्रिया लब्धं तदप्रजायामतीतायां भर्तुरेव भवतीति[3] । प्रजा संततिः ।

<**4**> न पुनर्ब्राह्मादिना परिणीताया यद्यावद्धनं विवाहात्पूर्वं परतो वा तया लब्धं तत्सर्वं भर्तुरिति व्याख्यानं युक्तम् । ब्राह्मादिष्विति कालार्थत्वान्निर्देशस्य ब्राह्मादिपदानां स्त्रीपरत्वे एकत्वेन षष्ठ्या च[4] निर्देशः स्यात् । यत्त्वस्याः स्यादिति स्त्रिया एकत्वेन षष्ठ्या च निर्दिष्टत्वात् ।

विवाहकाललक्षणायां[5] च वर्तमानसंबन्धेन लक्षणा स्यात् । स्त्रीपरत्वे त्वातिक्रान्तविवाहक्रियासंबन्धेन[6] लक्षणा जघन्या । सा चायुक्ता ।

न च विवाहितस्त्रीवाचकत्वं[7] ब्राह्मादिपदानां तत्तल्लक्षणविवाहपरत्वेन **मन्वादि**भिर्निर्दिष्टत्वात् । तदाह[8] **मनुः** —

अष्टाविमान्समासेन स्त्रीविवाहान्निबोधत । [M 3.20cd]

इत्युपक्रम्य —

ब्राह्मो दैवस्तथैवार्षः प्राजापत्यस्तथासुर इत्यादि ।। [M 3.21]

तथा **नारदः** —

अष्टौ विवाहा वर्णानां संस्कारार्थं प्रकीर्तिताः ।
ब्राह्मस्तु प्रथमस्तेषामित्यादि । [N 12.38–39]

[1] अप्रजा- । *some mss. consistently* अप्रज-

[2] -स्त्रीधनेऽधिकारिणः । -स्त्रीधनाधिकारिणः

[3] भवतीति । भवति

[4] षष्ठ्या च । च षष्ठ्या

[5] विवाह- । विवाहे

[6] त्वातिक्रान्त- । चातिक्रान्त- ।। -क्रिया- । *om*

[7] -वाचकत्वं । -परत्वं

[8] तेदाह । तथा । तथाच

तथा **विष्णुः** —

अष्टौ विवाहा भवन्ति । ब्राह्मो दैव इत्यादि ।। [Vi 24.17–18]

<5> अतो विवाहकाललब्धस्त्रीधनविषयं ब्राह्मादिवचनमिति **विश्वरूपो-**क्तमादरणीयम् ।

<6> आसुरादिविवाहसमयलब्धं[9] तु स्त्रीधनं जीवत्यपि भर्तरि[10] माता गृह्णीयात्तदभावे पिता । मातापित्रोस्तदिष्यत इत्यत्र[11] क्रमावगतेः । युगपद-धिकारे पित्रोरित्येवाभिदध्यात् । कन्याधने च[12] मातुरभावे पितुरधिकार-श्रवणादत्रापि तथात्वस्यैवोचितत्वात् । <7> तथा **बौधायनः** —

रिक्थं मृतायाः कन्याया गृह्णीयुः सोदराः स्वयम् ।
तदभावे भवेन्मातुस्तदभावे भवेत्पितुः ।। [Bau ? *Dhko* p. 1427]

<8> तदनेन कन्याधनं व्याख्यातम् ।

<9> न च कन्याधन इवात्रापि प्रथमं भ्रात्रधिकारः स्यादिति वाच्यं वचनाभावान्मातापित्रोरेवाधिकारश्रुतेः ।

<10> यत्पुनः परिणयानन्तरं पितृमातृभर्तृकुलात् स्त्रिया लब्धं धनं[13] तद् भ्रातृणामेव । तदाह **याज्ञवल्क्यः** —

बन्धुदत्तं तथा शुल्कमन्वाधेयकमेव च ।
अप्रजायामतीतायां बान्धवास्तदवाप्नुयुः ।। [Y 2.144]

<11> बन्धुदत्तमिति मातापितृभ्यां[14] यद्दत्तम् । तत्पुत्राश्च भ्रातर एव बान्धवाः । <12> तदाह **वृद्धकात्यायनः**[15] —

पितृभ्यां चैव यद्दत्तं दुहितुः स्थावरं धनम् ।
अप्रजायामतीतायां भ्रातृगामि तु सर्वदा ।। [K 919]

[9] -समय- । -विषय-

[10] जीवत्यपि भर्तरि । भर्तरि जीवत्यपि

[11] इत्यत्र । इति

[12] च । *om*

[13] धनं । *om*

[14] मातापितृभ्यां । मातृपितृभ्यां । पितृभ्यां

[15] **वृद्धकात्ययनः** । **कात्यायनः** । **बृहत्कात्यायनः**

<13> अप्रजात्वमात्रनिमित्तत्वेन[16] भ्रातुरधिकारावगतेः सर्वदापदेन ब्राह्मादिपैशाचान्तविवाहिताया[17] अप्रजाया[18] धनं भ्रातृगाम्येव भवतीति **विश्वरूपो**क्तमादरणीयम् । **<14>** स्थावरपदाद्दण्डापूपन्यायादेवापरस्य धनस्य[19] सिद्धिः ।

<15> बन्धुदत्तपदेन कन्यादशायां यत्पितृभ्यां दत्तं तदुच्यते । विवाहात्परतो लब्धधनस्यान्वाधेयपदोपात्तत्वात्[20] । विवाहकालीने च भर्तुः पित्रोर्बाधिकारात् ।

<16> अन्वाधेयमाह[21] **कात्यायनः** —

विवाहात्परतो यत्तु लब्धं भर्तृकुलात् स्त्रिया ।
अन्वाधेयं तदुक्तं तु लब्धं बन्धुकुलात्तथा ।। [K 899]

<17> भर्तृकुलात् श्वशुरादेः । बन्धुकुलात्पितृमातृकुलात् ।

<18> तथापरमाह —

ऊर्ध्वं लब्धं तु यत्किंचित्संस्कारात्प्रीतितः स्त्रिया ।
भर्तुः सकाशात्पित्रोर्वा अन्वाधेयं तु तद्भृगुः ।। [K 900]

<19> शुल्कमाह —

गृहोपस्करवाह्यानां दोह्याभरणकर्मिणाम् ।
मूल्यं लब्धं तु यत्किंचित् शुल्कं तत्परिकीर्तितम् ।। [K 898]

<20> गृहादिकर्मिभिः[22] शिल्पिभिस्तत्कर्मकरणाय[23] भर्त्रादिप्रेरणार्थं स्त्रियै यदुत्कोचदानं तच्छुल्कं । तदेव मूल्यं प्रवृत्त्यर्थत्वात् ।

<21> **व्यासेनो**क्तं वा —

यदानेतुं भर्तृगृहे शुल्कं तत्परिकीर्तितम् ।। [Vy 268]

भर्तृगृहगमनार्थमुत्कोचादि[24] यद्दत्तम् ।

---

[16] निमित्तत्वेन । -निमित्तेन

[17] -पैशाचान्तविवाहिताया । -पैशाचान्तोद्वाहिताया

[18] अप्रजाया । अप्रजा-

[19] धनस्य । *om*

[20] -धन- । *om*

[21] अन्वाधेयमाह । अन्वाधेयकमाह

[22] -कर्मिभिः । -कर्मभिः

[23] -त्कर्म- । -तत्तत्कर्म- ।। -करणाय । -करणार्थं

[24] -गृहगमनार्थ- । -गृहागमनार्थ- ।। -कोचादि यद्दत्तम् । -कोचादिभिर्यद्दत्तम्

<22> तच्च ब्राह्मादिष्वविशिष्टम् । तदेवमादिकमप्रजास्त्रीधनं भ्रातरो गृह्णीयुः । **<23>** न पुनरासुरादिषु विवाहेषु यत्कन्याभ्यः शुल्कदानं तदभिप्रायमासुरमात्रगोचरत्वाच्छुल्कस्य[25] । अत एवोक्तं[26] **मनुना**[27] —

आसुरो द्रविणादानाद्गान्धर्वः समयान्मिथः ।
राक्षसो युद्धहरणात्पैशाचः कन्यकाच्छलात् ॥ [Y 1.63]

<24> अतो राक्षसादौ शुल्काभावात् शुल्कसाहचर्येणासुरादिष्वेव यद्धनं तन्मात्रस्य भ्रातृगामित्वाभिधानं हेयम् । तथा तस्य स्त्रीधनत्वाभावाच्च पित्रादिगृहीतधनस्य च[28] शुल्कत्वेन कीर्तनात् । तथा **मनुः** —

न कन्यायाः पिता विद्वान् गृह्णीयाच्छुल्कमण्वपि ।
गृह्णन् हि शुल्कं लोभेन स्यान्नरोऽपत्यविक्रयी ॥ [M 3.51]

पितेत्युपलक्षणम् । तेन भ्रात्रादिरपि धनं गृह्णन् शुल्कग्राही । तेन पित्रादिगृहीतमेव परं शुल्कं भवतीत्युक्तम्[29] ।

<25> अतो यदुक्तमासुरादिष्वेव[30] शुल्करूपस्त्रीधनसंभवात्तदेकवाक्योपात्तयोर्बन्धुदत्तान्वाधेययोरप्यासुरादिविवाहगोचरयोरेव[31] भ्रातुरधिकार इति निरस्तम्[32] । **<26>** किंतूक्तशुल्कस्त्रीधनस्य सर्वविवाहेष्वेव[33] संभवात् सर्वत्रैव भ्रातुरधिकारो[34] वाक्याद्विशेषानवगमात्[35] ।

<27> तथा **गोयम**वचनं **कात्यायन**वचनसमानार्थम्[36] । यथा —

भगिनीशुल्कं सोदर्याणामूर्ध्वं मातुः । पूर्वं[37] चैके ॥ [G 28.25–26]

[25] -गोचरत्वाच्छुल्कस्य । -गोचरत्वात्तच्छुल्कस्य
[26] अत एवोक्तं । यथोक्तं
[27] **मनुना** । **याज्ञवल्क्येन** । *om*
[28] च । *om*
[29] भवतीत्युक्तम् । भवतीति
[30] यदुक्तमासुरादिष्वेव । यदुक्तमासुर एव
[31] -सुरादिविवाह- । -सुरविवाह-
[32] निरस्तम् । तन्निरस्तम्
[33] सर्वविवाहेष्वेव । सर्वविवाहेषु
[34] भ्रातुरधिकारो । भ्रात्रधिकारो
[35] वाक्याद्विशेषानवगमात् । वाक्याद्विशेषाश्रवणात्
[36] -वचन- । *om*
[37] पूर्वं । पितुश्च पूर्वं

<**28**> अस्यार्थः — प्रथमं सोदर्याणां तेषां पुनरभावे मातुः[38] । पूर्वं चैक इति परमतम् ।

<**29**> अतः प्रथमं सोदराणाम् । तदभावे मातुः । तदभावे[39] पितुः । एषां पुनरभावे तद्धनं भर्तुः । यथा **कात्यायनः** —

बन्धुदत्तं तु[40] बन्धूनामभावे भर्तृगामि तत् ।। [K 918cd]

<**30**> बन्धूनामभाव इत्यनेन भ्रातुरभाव इत्यपि[41] सूचितं भ्रातुरभावे पित्रोर्धनाधिकारित्वाद्दण्डापूपन्यायात्सिद्धेः[42] ।

<**31**> भर्तृपर्यन्तानामभावे पुनरिदमुच्यते । यथा[43] **बृहस्पतिः** —

मातुः[44] स्वसा मातुलानी पितृव्यस्त्री पितृस्वसा ।
श्वश्रूः पूर्वजपत्नी च मातृतुल्याः प्रकीर्तिताः ।। [B 26.32]
यदासामौरसो न स्यात्सुतो दौहित्र एव वा ।
तत्सुतो वा धनं तासां स्वस्रीयाद्याः समाप्नुयुः ।। [B 26.33]

<**32**> औरसपदेन पुत्रकन्ययोरुपादानं तयोः सर्वापवादकत्वात् ।

सुतपदेन च[45] सपत्नीपुत्रस्य —

सर्वासामेकपत्नीनामेका चेत्पुत्रिणी भवेत् ।
सर्वास्तास्तेन पुत्रेण प्राह पुत्रवतीर्मनुः ।। [M 9.183]

इति **स्मृतेः** । न तु सुतपदमौरसविशेषणं वैयर्थ्यात् । सपत्नीपुत्रसद्भावे ऽपि[46] स्वस्रीयाद्यधिकारापत्तेश्च ।

<**33**> औरसपुत्रकन्ययोः[47] सपत्नीपुत्रस्य[48] चाभावे दौहित्राधिकारः[49] ।

[38] मातुः । मातुः तदभावे पितुः । मातुरभावे पितुः

[39] तदभावे । मातुरभावे

[40] तु । हि

[41] इत्यपि । इति च

[42] -धिकारित्वा- । -धिकारा- ।। -दण्डापूपन्यायात्सिद्धेः । -दण्डापूपन्यायात्सिद्धिः

[43] यथा । यदाह

[44] मातुः । मातृ-

[45] च । *om*

[46] ऽपि । *om*

[47] औरसपुत्रकन्ययोः । औरसपुत्रकन्ययोः पौत्रस्य

[48] सपत्नीपुत्रस्य । सपत्नीपुत्रस्य पौत्रस्य

[49] दौहित्राधिकारः । दौहित्रस्याधिकारः ।। -धिकारः । -धिकारिता

<**34**> तत्सुत इति तच्छब्देन स्वपुत्रसपत्नीपुत्रयोरुपादानम् । तेन तत्पुत्रयोरधिकारो न तु दौहित्रपुत्रस्यापि तस्य पिण्डदानबहिर्भावात्[50] ।

<**35**> तदेषां पुत्रादीनां भ्रात्रादिभर्तृपर्यन्तानां चाभावे सत्स्वपि श्वशुर-भ्रातृश्वशुरादिषु सपिण्डेषु भगिनीपुत्रादीनामधिकारिता अनन्यगतेर्वचनात् । स्त्रीणां मातृतुल्यत्वप्रतिपादनेनामीषां पुत्रतुल्यत्वज्ञापनेन[51] पिण्डदातृत्व-सूचनस्य[52] दायप्रकरणे धनाधिकारज्ञापनैकप्रयोजनत्वत् ।

<**36**> तत्र स्वस्रीयाद्या इति वचनाद्भगिनीसुतस्वभर्तृभागिनेयदेवरपुत्र-भ्रातृश्वशुरपुत्रभ्रातृपुत्रजामातृदेवराणां[53] पूर्वपूर्वस्याभावे[54] परपरस्याधिकारे[55] देवरस्यैव सर्वशेषेऽधिकारापत्तेर्महाजनविरोध इति वस्तुबलमालम्ब्य वचनं वर्ण्यते ।

तत्र **मनुना** —

त्रयाणामुदकं कार्यं त्रिषु पिण्डः प्रवर्तते । [M 9.186ab]

इति दायभागप्रकरणे कीर्तनात् ।

याज्ञवल्क्येनापि —

पिण्डदोंऽशहरश्चैषाम् । [Y 2.132c]

इति पिण्डदानेनाधिकारदर्शनात् ।

पुत्रस्यापि सातिशयपिण्डदानेन नरकत्राणकारणतया मुख्यभावेनाधि-कारावगतेः ।

मातुलो भागिनेयस्य स्वस्रीयो मातुलस्य च ।
श्वशुरस्य गुरोश्चैव सख्युर्मातामहस्य च ॥ [?]
एतेषां चैव भार्याभ्यः स्वसुर्मातुः पितुस्तथा ।
श्राद्धदानं तु कर्तव्यमिति वेदविदां स्थितिः ॥ [?]

इति **वृद्धशातातप**वचनात् ।

<**37**> अमीषां पिण्डदत्वप्रतिपादनादयं पिण्डदानविशेषादधिकारक्रमः ।

[50] पिण्डदान- । पिण्डदाने
[51] -तुल्यत्व- । -तुल्य-
[52] -दातृत्व- । -दत्व-
[53] -स्वभर्तृ- । -भर्तृ- ॥ -देवरपुत्र- । -देवर- ॥ -भ्रातृपुत्र- । -भ्रातृसुत-
[54] पूर्वपूर्वस्याभावे । पूर्वस्य पूर्वस्याभावे
[55] परपरस्याधिकारे । परस्याधिकारे । ऽपरस्याधिकारे

प्रथमं[56] देवरः तत्पिण्डतद्भर्तृपिण्डतद्भर्तृदेयपूर्वपुरुषत्रयपिण्डदातृत्वात्सपिण्डत्वाच्च तद्धनेऽधिक्रियते ।

तदभावे भ्रातृश्वशुरदेवरयोः सुतः तत्पिण्डतद्भर्तृपिण्डतद्भर्तृदेयपूर्वपुरुषद्वयपिण्डदातृत्वात्सपिण्डत्वाच्च[57] पितृव्यस्त्रीधनेऽधिकारी ।

तदभावेऽसपिण्डोऽपि[58] भगिनीपुत्रः तत्पिण्डतत्पुत्रदेयतत्पित्रादिपिण्डत्रयदानान्मातृस्वसृधनेऽधिकारी[59] ।

तदभावे स्वभर्तृभागिनेयः पुत्राद्भर्तृदुर्बलत्वात्तत्स्थानपातिनोरपि तथैव बलाबलस्य न्याय्यत्वात् । तद्भर्तृदेयपूर्वपुरुषत्रयपिण्डदानात्तत्पिण्डदानात्तद्भर्तृपिण्डदानाच्च मातुलानीधनेऽधिकारी ।

तदभावे भ्रातृसुतः तत्पितृपितामहयोस्तस्यांश्च पिण्डदानात्पितृस्वसृधनेऽधिकारी ।

तस्याप्यभावे श्वशुरयोः पिण्डदानाज्जामाता श्वश्रूधनेऽधिकारी[60] ।

<**38**> अयं क्रमो ग्राह्यः । स्वस्रीयाद्या इति[61] न क्रमार्थं किंत्वधिकारमात्रपरम्[62] ।

<**39**> षण्णां पुनरेतेषामभावे श्वशुरभ्रातृश्वशुरादेः सपिण्डानन्तर्यकृतो धनाधिकारो बोद्धव्यः । <**40**> न च सपिण्डाभावे सतीदं वचनमिति[63] वाच्यम् । अस्यामधिकारशृङ्खलायां देवरदेवरसुतयोर्भ्रातृश्वशुरसुतस्य चाधिकारज्ञापनात् । आसन्नतरश्वशुरभ्रातृश्वशुरादेः परित्यागात् । <**41**> अतो वचनतदर्थापरिज्ञानकृतो[64] व्यवहारः प्रमाणपरतन्त्रैरतन्त्रीकर्तव्यः ।

<**42**> इत्यतिगहनमुक्तमप्रजास्त्रीधनम्[65] ।

[56] प्रथमं । तत्र प्रथमं

[57] -तद्भर्तृपिण्ड- । -तदीयभर्तृपिण्ड-

[58] ऽसपिण्डोऽपि । त्वसपिण्डोऽपि

[59] -त्रयपिण्ड- । -पिण्डत्रय-

[60] श्वश्रूधनेऽधिकारी । श्वश्रूधने भवत्यधिकारः

[61] इति । इति तु

[62] -परम् । -ज्ञापनार्थपरम्

[63] सतीदं वचनमिति । सतीदमिति

[64] वचनतदार्था- । वचनार्था-

[65] -प्रजा- । -प्रज-

<**5.1**> संप्रति विभागानधिकारिणः कथ्यन्ते । तत्पर्युदासेनाधिकारिज्ञापनार्थम् ।

तत्र**आपस्तम्बः** —

सर्वे हि धर्मयुक्ता धनभागिनो द्रव्यमर्हन्ति । यस्त्वधर्मेण द्रव्याणि प्रतिपादयति ज्येष्ठोऽपि तमभागं कुर्वीत ॥ [Āp 2.6.14.14–15]

<**2**> इदं **बालेना**कुलीकृत्य[1] पठितम् —

यस्तु धर्मेण द्रव्याणि प्रतिपादयति ज्येष्ठस्तं पितृसमभागं कुर्वीतेति ।

तदनाकरम् ।

<**3**> तथा —

अपपात्रितस्य रिक्थपिण्डोदकानि निवर्तन्ते ॥ [ŚL 299]

अपपात्रितो भिन्नोदकीकृतः[2] ।

<**4**> तथा[3] **बृहस्पतिः** —

सवर्णाजोऽप्यगुणवान्नार्हः स्यात्पैतृके धने ।
तत्पिण्डदाः श्रोत्रिया ये तेषां तदभिधीयते ॥ [B 26.34]
उत्तमर्णाधमर्णेभ्यः पितरं त्रायते सुतः ।
अतस्तद्विपरीतेन नास्ति तेन प्रयोजनम् ॥ [B 26.35]
तया गवा किं क्रियते या न धेनुर्न गर्भिणी ।
कोऽर्थः पुत्रेण जातेन यो न विद्वान्न धार्मिकः ॥ [B 26.36]
शास्त्रशौर्यार्थरहितस्तपोविज्ञानवर्जितः[4] ।
आचारहीनः पुत्रस्तु मूत्रोच्चारसमस्तु सः ॥ [B 26.37]

[1] **बालेन- । बालोकेन- । बालकेन**

[2] भिन्नोदकीकृतः । बन्धुभिर्भिन्नोदकीकृतः

[3] तथा । तथाच

[4] -शौर्यार्थ- । शौर्यादि-

<5> अयमर्थः[5] — पित्रादेरौर्ध्वदेहिकस्य[6] कर्मणोऽसंस्कृतः सुतः श्रेष्ठो नापरो वेदपारग इति ।

<6> पुन्नाम्नो नरकाद्यस्मात्[7] त्रायत[8] । [B 26.38ab = Vi 15.44]

इत्यादिवचनेन पुत्रकर्तृकतया महाफलश्रुतेस्तत्कर्मवेतनं धनसंबन्धित्वम् । अतस्तदकुर्वतः कुतो वेतनम् । अत एवाह[9] **मनुः** —

सर्व एव विकर्मस्था नार्हन्ति भ्रातरो धनम् ।। [M 9.214ab]

<7> तथा —

अनंशौ क्लीबपतितौ जात्यन्धबधिरौ तथा ।
उन्मत्तजडमूकाश्च ये च केचिन्निरिद्रियाः ।। [M 9.201]

<8> क्लीबः[10] **कात्यायनेन** दर्शितः —

न मूत्रं फेनिलं यस्य विष्ठा चाप्सु निमज्जति ।
मेढ्रं चोन्मादशुक्राभ्यां हीनं[11] क्लीबः स उच्यते ।। [K 861]

<9> जातिपदमन्धबधिराभ्यां संबध्यते । वर्णानुच्चारको मूकः । जडः वेद-ग्रहणासमर्थः[12] ।

<10> आह[13] **याज्ञवल्क्यः** —

पतितस्तत्सुतः क्लीबः पङ्गुरुन्मत्तको जडः ।
अन्धोऽचिकित्स्यरोगार्तो[14] भर्तव्यास्ते निरंशकाः ।। [Y 2.140]

पदा[15] न गच्छतीति पङ्गुः । **<11>** निरंशकत्वेऽपि पतिततत्सुतव्यतिरिक्ता भर्तव्याः । तदाह **देवलः** —

मृते पितरि न क्लीबकुष्ठ्युन्मत्तजडान्धकाः ।

[5] अयमर्थः । **आपस्तम्बः** । **आपस्तम्ब**स्यायमर्थः

[6] -देहिकस्य । -देहिक-

[7] नरकाद्यस्मात् । नरकात्

[8] त्रायत । त्रायते पितरं सुतः

[9] अत एवाह । अत एव । अत आह

[10] क्लीबः । क्लीबश्च

[11] हीनं । हीनः

[12] जडो वेदग्रहणासमर्थः । वेदग्रहणासमर्थो जडः ।। -समर्थो । -शक्तो

[13] आह । तदाह

[14] -चिकित्स्य- । -चिकित्स-

[15] पदा । पदाभ्यां

पतितः पतितापत्यं लिङ्गी दायांशभागिनः ॥ [D 1573]
तेषां पतितवर्जेभ्यो भक्तवस्त्रं प्रदीयते ।
तत्सुताः पितृदायांशं लभेरन् दोषवर्जिताः ॥ [D 1574]

लिङ्गी प्रव्रजितादिः । <12> पतितपदेन तत्सुतस्याप्युपादानं पतितोत्पन्नत्वेन पतितत्वात् । तदाह **बौधायनः** —

अतीतव्यवहारान् ग्रासाच्छादनैर्बिभृयुः । अन्धजडक्लीबव्यस-निव्याधितादींश्चाकर्मिणः[16] । पतिततज्जातवर्जम् ॥ [Bau 2.2.3.37–40]

<13> तत्र **नारदः** —

पितृद्विट् पतितः पण्डो यश्च स्यादौपपातिकः ।
औरसा अपि नैतेंऽशं लभेरन् क्षेत्रजा कुतः ॥ [N 13.21/20]

<14> आह **कात्यायनः** —

अक्रमोढासुतश्चैव सगोत्राद्यस्तु जायते ।
प्रव्रज्यावसितश्चैव न रिक्थं तेषु चार्हति ॥ [K 862]

<15> हीनवर्णस्त्रीपरिणयनानन्तरमुत्तमवर्णस्त्रीपरिणयने[17] द्वयोरप्यक्रमोढा-त्वम् । तयोः सगोत्रान्नियुक्तादुत्पन्नः[18] क्षेत्रजः पुत्रो नार्हति धनम् ।

अक्रमोढायामपि सवर्णेन परिणेत्रोत्पादितः पुत्रो धनाधिकारी क्रमो-ढायामसवर्णजातोऽपि[19] । <16> तदाह **कात्यायनः** —

अक्रमोढासुतस्त्वृक्थी सवर्णश्च यदा पितुः ।
असवर्णप्रसूतश्च क्रमोढायां तु[20] यो भवेत् ॥ [K 863]
प्रतिलोमप्रसूतायास्तस्याः[21] पुत्रो न रिक्थभाक् ।
ग्रासाच्छादनमात्रं तु देयं यद्बन्धुभिर्मतम् ॥ [K 864]
बन्धूनामप्यभावे तु पित्र्यं द्रव्यं तदाप्नुयात्[22] ।

[16] -जडक्लीब- । -क्लीबजड- । -जडमूकक्लीब-
[17] हीनवर्णस्त्री- । हीनस्त्री- ॥ -त्तमवर्णस्त्री-। -त्तमस्त्री-
[18] सगोत्रान्नियुक्तादुत्पन्नः । सगोत्रान्नियुक्तोत्पन्नः
[19] क्रमो- । क्रमेण
[20] क्रमोढायां तु । क्रमोढायां च । क्रमोढायस्तु
[21] -प्रसूतायास्तस्याः । -प्रसूतो यस्तस्याः
[22] द्रव्यं तदाप्नुयात् । द्रव्यमवाप्नुयात्

स्वपित्र्यं तद्धनं प्राप्तं दापनीया न बान्धवाः ।। [K 865]

<**17**> अस्ति च क्लीबादीनां दारपरिग्रहः[23] —

यद्यर्थिता तु दारैः स्यात् क्लीबादीनां कथंचन ।
तेषामुत्पन्नतन्तूनामपत्यं दायमर्हति ।। [M 9.203]

तन्तुरपत्यम् ।

<**18**> न चापुंस्त्वात् क्लीबस्य जननासामर्थ्यात् अध्ययनाभावान्मूकादेरुपनयनाभावेन[24] पतितत्वात्कथं दारसंबन्ध इति वाच्यम् । क्लीबस्य पत्न्यामन्येन पुत्रोत्पादसंभवात्[25] । उपनयनानर्हस्यानुपनीतत्वे शूद्रवदपतितत्वात् । <**19**> तेनैषां यथासंभवमौरसक्षेत्रजाः क्लीबत्वादिशून्याः स्वपित्रनुसारेण भागहारिणः । दुहितरश्च परिणयनं यावद्भर्तव्याः । अपुत्राश्च स्त्रियो यावज्जीवम् । यदाह[26] **याज्ञवल्क्यः** —

औरसाः[27] क्षेत्रजास्त्वेषां निर्दोषा भागहारिणः ।
सुताश्चैषां प्रभर्तव्या यावन्न[28] भर्तृसात्कृताः ।। [Y 2.141]
अपुत्रा योषितश्चैषां भर्तव्याः साधुवृत्तयः ।
निर्वास्या व्यभिचारिण्यः प्रतिकूलास्तथैव च ।। [Y 2.143]

[23] -परिग्रहः । -परिग्रहः यथा **मनुः**

[24] अध्ययनाभावान्मूका- । अध्ययनासामर्थ्यान्मूका-

[25] क्लीबस्य ... -संभवात् । *om*

[26] यदाह । तदाह

[27] औरसा । औरस-

[28] यावन्न । यावन्नो

<**6.1.1**> संप्रति विभाज्यमविभाज्यं चोच्यते ।

तत्र **कात्यायनः** —

पैतामहं च पित्र्यं च यच्चान्यत्स्वयमर्जितम् ।
दायादानां विभागे तु[1] सर्वमेतद्विभज्यते ।। [K 840]

<**2**> यच्चान्यदिति चकारः स्वयमित्यनेन संबध्यते स्वयं चार्जितमिति । चकारादन्यस्यापि तदर्जनं साधारणधनद्वारेणेत्यर्थः ।

<**3**> अनुपघात्तोपात्तमविभाज्यमाहतु**र्मनु-विष्णू**[2] —

अनुपघ्नन् पितृद्रव्यं श्रमेण यदुपार्जयेत्[3] ।
स्वयमीहितलब्धं तन्नाकामो दातुमर्हति ।। [M 9.208 = Vi 18.42]

<**4**> पितृद्रव्योपघाताभावेन[4] द्रव्यद्वारेण नेतरेषां व्यापारः स्वचेष्टालब्धत्वेन शारीरोऽपि व्यापारो नेतरेषामित्यर्जकस्यैव[5] तदसाधारणं स्वयमीहितलब्धं तदिति हेतुत्वेनोपन्यासात् ।

<**5**> तथा **व्यासः** —

अनाश्रित्य पितृद्रव्यं स्वशक्त्याप्नोति यद्धनम् ।
दायादेभ्यो न तद्दद्याद्विद्यालब्धं तु[6] यद्भवेत् ।। [Vy 256]

<**6**> स्वशक्तिमात्रेण यत्प्राप्तमिति[7] सामान्येनाभिधानात्सर्वमेवंविधमसाधारणं द्रव्यम्[8] । स्वशक्तिप्राप्तस्यापि विद्याधनस्य समानाधिकविद्यैः[9] साधारणत्वान्न्यूनविद्याविद्यनिराकरणार्थं विद्यालब्धपदम् ।

<**7**> तथा **याज्ञवल्क्यः** —

[1] विभागे तु । विभागेषु
[2] अनुपघातोपात्त- । अनुपघात्यादित-
[3] यदुपार्जयेत । यदुपार्जितम्
[4] -घाताभावेन । -घाताभावे
[5] नेतरेषामित्य- । नापरेषामित्य-
[6] तु । च
[7] यत्प्राप्तमिति । यदर्जितमिति
[8] सर्वमेवंविध- । सर्वमेव स्वकीय- । सर्वमेवंविधं स्वकीय-
[9] समानाधिक- । समाधिक-

पितृद्रव्याविरोधेन[10] यदन्यत्स्वयमर्जितम्[11] ।
मैत्रमौद्वाहिकं चैव दायादानां न तद्भवेत् ।। [Y 2.118]

<**8**> मैत्रादिग्रहणं[12] प्रदर्शनार्थमेवमादिषु प्रायेणानुपघातसंभवात् ।

<**9**> तथा **मनुः** —

विद्याधनं तु यद्यस्य तत्तस्यैव धनं भवेत् ।
मैत्रमौद्वाहिकं चैव माधुपार्किकमेव च ।। [M 9.206]

<**10**> तथाच[13] **व्यासः** —

विद्याप्राप्तं शौर्यधनं[14] यच्च सौदायिकं भवेत् ।
विभागकाले तत्तस्य नान्वेष्टव्यं स्वरिक्थिभिः ।। [Vy 257]

<**11**> पितृपितृव्यादिभ्यः सुदायसंबन्धिभ्यः प्रसादादिना लब्धं सौदायिकम् ।

<**12**> तथा **नारदः** —

शौर्यभार्याधने हित्वा यच्च विद्याधनं भवेत् ।
त्रीण्येतान्यविभाज्यानि प्रसादो यश्च पैतृकः ।। [N 13.6]

<**13**> भार्याप्राप्तिकाले लब्धं[15] भार्याधनमौद्वाहिकमित्यर्थः । एतानि वर्जयित्वा अन्यत् । विभजेदित्यनुवर्तते वाक्यान्तरीयम् ।

<**14**> तदेवमादिभिः शौर्यादिधनत्वमविभाज्यत्वे कारणं नोच्यते । शौर्याद्यर्जितस्यापि विभागश्रुतेः ।

तदाह **व्यासः** —

साधारणं समाश्रित्य यत्किंचिद्वाहनायुधम् ।
शौर्यादिनाप्नोति धनं भ्रातरस्तत्र भागिनः ।। [Vy 259]
तस्य भागद्वयं देयं शेषास्तु समभागिनः ।। [Vy 260]

साधारणद्रव्येणार्जितस्य[16] धनस्य विभागं वदति ।

[10] -विरोधेन । -विनाशेन
[11] यदन्य- । यत्किंचि- ।। -स्वयमर्जितं । -स्वयमर्जयेत्
[12] -ग्रहणं । -पदं
[13] तथाच । तथा
[14] शौर्यधनं । शौर्यलब्धं
[15] लब्धं । लब्धं धनं
[16] -द्रव्येणार्जितस्य । -द्रव्याश्रितेनार्जितस्य

तथा **नारदः** —

कुटुम्बं बिभृयाद् भ्रातुर्यो विद्यामधिगच्छतः ।
भागं विद्याधनात्तस्मात्स लभेताश्रुतोऽपि सन् ।। [N 13.10]

<15> बिभृयादित्येकवचननिर्देशाद्यदि विद्यामभ्यस्यतो[17] भ्रातुः कुटुम्बमपरो भ्राता स्वधनव्ययशरीरायासाभ्यां संवर्धयति तदा तद्विद्योपार्जितधने तस्याप्यधिकारः[18] ।

<16> तथा —

वैद्योऽविद्याय[19] नाकामो दद्यादंशं स्वतो धनात् ।
पित्र्यं द्रव्यं समाश्रित्य न चेत्तेन तदर्जितम् ।। [N 13.11]

<17> पित्र्यपदं साधारणपरम् । तदनाश्रित्यार्जितं वैद्योऽविद्यायानिच्छन्न[20] दद्यात् । वैद्याय विदुषे पुनः साधारणधनमन्तरेणाप्यर्जितं[21] दद्यादेव ।

तथा **गोतमः** —

स्वयमर्जितमवैद्येभ्यो वैद्योऽकामं[22] न दद्यात् ।। [G 28.30]

<18> असाधारणधनशरीरव्यपाारार्जितं स्वयमर्जितमविद्वद्भ्यो दातुमनिच्छन्न दद्याद्विद्वद्भ्यः पुनर्दद्यादेव ।

<19> एतच्च विद्याधनमात्रविषयम् । तदाह **कात्यायनः** —

नाविद्यानां[23] तु वैद्येन देयं विद्याधनात्क्वचित्[24] ।
समविद्याधिकानां तु देयं वैद्येन तद्धनम् ।। [K 875]

<20> तन्त्रोच्चरितविद्यापदमुभाभ्यां[25] समाधिकपदाभ्यां[26] संबध्यते । तेन समविद्याधिकविद्यानां दातव्यम् । न्यूनविद्याविद्ययोः पुनरनधिकारः[27] ।

[17] विद्यागभ्यस्यतो । विद्यामधिगच्छतो
[18] तस्याप्यधिकारः । तस्याधिकारः
[19] ऽविद्याय । ऽवैद्याय
[20] ऽविद्याया- । ऽवैद्याया-
[21] -धन- । *om*
[22] वैद्योऽकामं । वैद्योऽकामो
[23] नाविद्यानां । नावैद्यानां
[24] विद्याधनात्क्वचित् । विद्याधनं क्वचित्
[25] -पदमुभाभ्यां । पदमुभयाभ्यां
[26] समाधिकपदाभ्यां । *om*
[27] पुनरनधिकारः । परमनधिकारः

<**21**> तदेवमादिवचनैर्विद्याशौर्यादिधनेष्वपि साधारणधनोपघातानुपघाताभ्यां विभागाविभागयोरवगमात्तस्यैव प्रयोजकत्वात्तत्पदवत्येव श्रुतिः कल्पनीया उपघातार्जितं विभजेदिति । न पुनः शौर्यादिपदवत्यपि अवश्यकल्पनीयसामान्यश्रुतिकल्पनयैवोपपत्तेः[28] । <**22**> होलाकाधिकरणस्यायमेव[29] विषयः ।

<**23**> यद्वा न्यायप्राप्त एवायमर्थः — यद्येनार्जितं तत्तस्मिन् जीवति तस्यैवासति विशेषवचने । यत्र पुनः साधारणधनमात्रेणैकस्य[30] व्यापारोऽपरस्य धनशरीराभ्यां[31] तत्रैकस्यैको[32] भागोऽपरस्य भागद्वयं न्यायावगतमेव[33] निबद्धम्[34] । एतेन चैतदपि[35] सिध्यति यत्साधारणधनोपघाते यस्य[36] यावतोंऽशस्याल्पस्य[37] महतो वोपघातस्तस्य तदनुसारेण भागकल्पना कार्या ।

<**24**> किंच **कात्यायन**वचनम् —

विभक्ताः पितृवित्ताच्चेदेकत्र प्रतिवासिनः ।
विभजेयुः पुनर्द्व्यंशं स लभेतोदयो यतः ।। [K 892]

<**25**> इदं संसृष्टस्य साधारणधनोपघातेनार्जकस्य भागद्वयमितरेषामेकैको भाग इति **श्रीकरेण** व्याख्यातम् । <**26**> तेनानुपघातार्जितमर्जकस्यैव[38] । संसृष्टत्वेऽपि न पुनस्तद्धनं साधारणमित्यभिप्रायो मुनेर्व्याख्यातुश्च लक्ष्यते अनुपघातार्जिते भागविशेषानभिधानात् ।

<**27**> एवं चेत्संसृष्टवदविभक्तस्यापि तथात्वमेव युक्तम् । विभागप्रागभावे तत्प्रध्वंसेऽप्येकत्र[39] प्रतिवासस्य हेतोरविशेषात् । साधारणधनोपघाता-

[28] अवश्य- । अवश्यं
[29] होलाकाधिकरण- । होलाकाधिकरणन्याय-
[30] -धन- । *om*
[31] -शरीराभ्यां । -शरीरायासाभ्यां
[32] तत्रैकस्यैको । तत्र पूर्वस्यैको
[33] न्यायावगतमेव । न्यायागतमेव । न्यायगतमेव
[34] निबद्धम् । सिद्धम्
[35] एतेन चैतदपि । एतेनैतदपि
[36] यस्य । सति यस्य
[37] -शस्याल्पस्य । -शस्य स्वल्पस्य
[38] -कस्यैव । -कस्यैव धनम्
[39] ऽप्येकत्र । चैकत्र

र्जितेऽर्जकस्य[40] भागद्वयमिति ज्ञापनार्थत्वेन वचनस्याप्युपपत्तेः । न केवलं संसृष्टविषयत्वं युक्तं होलाकाधिकरणस्यात्रैव[41] जागरूकत्वात्[42] ।

<28> किंचोपघातार्जिते तावदर्जकस्य[43] भागद्वयमिति निर्विवादम्[44] —

साधारणं समाश्रित्य यत्किंचिद्वाहनायुधम् ।
शौर्यादिनाप्नोति धनं भ्रातरस्तत्र भागिनः ।। [Vy 259]
तस्य भागद्वयं देयं शेषास्तु समभागिनः ।। [Vy 260]

इत्यनेनोपघात एव भागद्वयविधानात्[45] । असाधारणधनशरीरव्यापारमात्रार्जिते[46] तु न भागद्वयं न्याय्यम् । किंत्वधिकं सर्वमेव वा किंचिदूनं[47] वा । तत्र किंचिदूनस्य मुनिभिर्निबन्धृभिश्चानुक्तत्वात् साधारणधनव्यापारणे[48] भ्रात्रन्तरभागनिर्गमात्[49] तदभावे भागाभाव एव युक्तः ।

<29> द्विरर्जयितुरित्येतस्य च[50] न्यायमूलत्वमेव युक्तम् । अन्यथा श्रुतिकल्पनेऽर्जकत्वानुप्रवेशो वा पृथग्वाधिकारी कल्पनीयः स्यात् ।

<30> तस्मादनुपघातार्जितमर्जकस्यैव नेतरेषामिति सिद्धम् ।

<31> किंचाविभक्तार्जितं सर्वे विभजेयुरिति न तावत्[51] सामान्येन वचनं कल्पनीयं शौर्यादिधनपर्युदासदर्शनात् ।

तथा **मनुः** —

विद्याधनं तु यद्यस्य तत्तस्यैव धनं भवेत् ।
मैत्रमौद्वाहिकं चैव माधुपर्किकमेव च ।। [M 9.206]

तथा **मनु-विष्णू** —

[40] ऽर्जकस्य । चार्जकस्य । त्वर्जकस्य । ऽर्जकस्यापि
[41] होलाकाधिकरण- । होलाकाधिकरणन्याय-
[42] जागरूकत्वात् । जागरणात्
[43] तावदर्जकस्य । अर्जकस्य
[44] निर्विवादम् । तावन्निर्विवादम्
[45] भागद्वय- । भागद्वयस्य
[46] -व्यापारमात्रार्जिते । -व्यापारार्जिते
[47] किंचिदूनं । किंचिन्न्यूनं
[48] -धन- । *om* ।। -व्यापारेण । व्यापारे
[49] भ्रात्रन्तर- । भ्रात्रन्तरस्य ।। -निर्गमात् । -दर्शनात् । -निर्णयात्
[50] च । *om*
[51] न तावत् । तावन्न

अनुपघ्नन् पितृद्रव्यं श्रमेण यदुपार्जयेत्[52] ।
स्वयमीहितलब्धं तन्नाकामो दातुमर्हति ।। [M 9.208 = Vi 18.42]

<**32**> अनुपघ्नन्निति विद्याधनेऽपि संबध्यते[53] सत्युपघाते[54] विभागवचनदर्शनात् ।

<**33**> तथा **याज्ञवल्क्यः** —

पितृद्रव्याविनाशेन[55] यदन्यत्स्वयमर्जितम्[56] ।
मैत्रमौद्वाकिकं चैव दायादानां न तद्भवेत् ।। [Y 2.118]
क्रमादभ्यागतं द्रव्यं हृतमभ्युद्धरेत्तु यः ।
दायादेभ्यो न तद्दद्याद्विद्यया लब्धमेव च ।। [Y 2.119]

तथा **नारदः** —

शौर्यभार्याधने हित्वा यच्च विद्याधनं भवेत् ।
त्रीण्येतान्यविभाज्यानि प्रसादो यश्च पैतृकः ।। [N 13.6]

तथा **व्यासः** —

विद्याप्राप्तं शौर्यधनं यच्च सौदायिकं भवेत् ।
विभागकाले तत्तस्य नान्वेष्टव्यं स्वरिक्थिभिः ।। [Vy 257]

<**34**> सौदायिकं सुदायसंबन्धिभ्यो यल्लब्धम् ।

<**35**> पितामहेन यद्दत्तं पित्रा वा प्रीतिपूर्वकम् ।
तस्य तन्नापहर्तव्यं मात्रा दत्तं च यद्भवेत् ।। [Vy 261]
अनाश्रित्य पितृद्रव्यं स्वशक्त्याप्नोति यद्धनम् ।
दायादेभ्यो न तद्दद्याद्विद्यालब्धं च यद्भवेत् ।। [Vy 256]

<**36**> तदेवमादिवचनैर्यावद्वर्णवर्णान्तरालानां संकीर्णजातानां सकलविद्यानिमित्तस्य सौदायिकस्य च स्वजनदत्तस्य[57] तथा मैत्रविवाहमधुपर्कप्राप्तस्य शौर्येण च युद्धादिना प्राप्तस्य[58] कृषिसेवावाणिज्यादिना च श्रमेणार्जि-

[52] यदुपार्जयेत् । यदुपार्जितम्
[53] विद्याधने । विद्यादिधने ।। ऽपि संबध्यते । ऽप्यनुषज्यते
[54] सत्युपघाते । सत्युपघातेऽपि
[55] -विनाशेन । -विरोधेन
[56] यदन्य- । यत्किंचि- ।। -स्वयमर्जितम् । -स्वयमर्जयेत्
[57] स्वजनदत्तस्य । स्वजनदत्तस्य च
[58] प्राप्तस्य । लब्धस्य

तस्यानुपघातेन[59] च स्वशक्तिमात्रार्जितस्य पर्युदासात्सर्वमेव पर्युदस्तमिति तदितराभावान्निर्विषयो विधिः ।

<37> अथ यथाकथंचिदेको द्विको वा विषयो लभ्यते तदा तदेव स्वपदेन निर्देष्टुमुचितं मुनीनाम् । अविभक्तार्जितममुकधनं विभजेदिति लाघवात् । स्वपदाच्च शीघ्रप्रतीतेः[60] । न तु शौर्यादिधनेतरतया बहुतर-पदप्रयोगापत्त्या गौरवात् ।

पर्युदासत्वे च सर्वमुनिभिरेव[61] सकलपर्युदासनीयपदानुकीर्तनं[62] कर्तव्यं तद्विना तदितरज्ञानानुपपत्तेः[63] । मुनीनां पर्युदासवचनं बालप्रलपितमिव[64] स्यात् । प्रदर्शनार्थत्वे त्वनास्थया केनचित् किंचित्कीर्तनं[65] केनचिच्च किंचिदिति युक्तं सर्वस्याकीर्तनम् ।

<38> तस्मात्साधारणधनोपघातार्जितं धनं विभजेदिति विधिः । शौर्या-दिपदं च वाक्येषु प्रदर्शनार्थम् । **<39>** अतोऽविभक्तार्जितत्वमात्रेण धनस्य साधारणत्वाभिधानमप्रामाणिकम् ।

<40> किंच —

क्रमादभ्यागतं[66] द्रव्यं हृतमभ्युद्धरेत्तु यः ।
दायादेभ्यो न तद्दद्याद्विद्यया लब्धमेव च ।। [Y 2.119]

अत्र **याज्ञवल्क्य**वचने[67] पितृपितामहादिधनमपि केनचिदपहृतं योऽभ्युद्ध-रेत्तस्यैव तन्नान्येषामिति भवतोऽपि संमतम् । तेन पूर्वसंबन्धलेशे सत्यप्य-विभक्तानामप्यभ्युद्धारकत्वेन तत्र[68] संबन्धं निराकुर्वन्न पूर्वत्वेन स्वार्जिते सुदूरमेवान्येषां संबन्धं निरस्यति ।

[59] श्रमेणार्जितस्यानुपघातेन । श्रमेणोपार्जितस्यानुपघातेन
[60] स्वपदाच्च शीघ्रप्रतीतेः । स्वपदात् शीघ्रप्रतीतेश्च
[61] सर्व- । सकल-
[62] सकल- । सर्व- ।। -पदानुकीर्तनं । -पदार्थकीर्तनं
[63] -ज्ञानानुपपत्तेः । -ज्ञापनानुपपत्तेः
[64] -प्रलपितमिव । -प्रलपितमेव । -प्रलपितं
[65] -कीर्तनं । -कीर्तितं
[66] -गतं । -गत-
[67] -वचने । -वचनेऽपि
[68] -विभक्तानामभ्युद्धारकत्वेन तत्र । -विभक्तानामपि

<**41**> यच्चोक्तं **श्रीकरेण** — यदि पितृद्रव्यानुपघातार्जितमर्जकस्यैव तदा[69] प्रतिग्रहोपात्तं[70] धनं न कदाचिद् भ्रात्रन्तरस्य भवेत् । न हि प्रतिग्रहः पितृद्रव्यविनाशेन[71] संभवति[72] । द्रव्यं हि दातुरानतिद्वारा[73] प्रतिग्रह उपयुज्यते । एकहायन्यादिकमिव सोमक्रये कर्तृशरीरधारणेन वा पयोव्रतादिकमिव ज्योतिष्टोमे । तत्र तावददृष्टार्थदाने[74] द्रव्यान्तरग्रहणेन न दातुरानतिरपेक्षितेति न दात्रानत्या द्रव्यमुपयुज्यते । प्रतिग्रहस्य चाल्पकालीनत्वान्न[75] तत्कर्तुर्भोजनमपेक्षितम् । दीर्घकालीनज्योतिष्टोमेनेव स्वर्गकर्तुतिति ।

<**42**> तन्मन्दम् । दापकानत्यर्थमुपहारप्रदानादिना[76] धनोपघातस्य लोके बहुलमुपलम्भात् । कलौ च प्रतिग्रहधनस्य सेवाधनसमानत्वात् । अत एव कलौ त्वनुगमान्वित इति स्मरन्ति ।

<**43**> यच्च — चिरावस्थितेर्व्यभिचारान्न प्रतिग्रहकारणत्वमानतेरत आनतिद्वारा न प्रतिग्रहार्थत्वं द्रव्यस्येत्युक्तम् ।

तन्मन्दतरम् । आनतिद्वारेण चिराश्रयणादीनां प्रतिग्रहकारणत्वात् पुरुषाशयवैचित्र्येण[77] कस्यचिद्धनदानेन कस्यचिच्चिराश्रयणादिना कस्यचित्तत्तद्गुणानुसंधानमात्रेण[78] दर्शनात् । सहकार्यभावेन कार्यानुत्पत्तेर्नाकारणता । अत एवोक्तम् — आनतेरनियतोपायपरिणामत्वात् ।

<**44**> यदप्युक्तम् — अथ तत्संनिधिमन्तरेण प्रतिग्रहस्यासंभवाद्भोजनमन्तरेण च[79] तदयोगात् तस्यां स्थितौ व्याप्रियमाणं[80] धनं प्रणाल्या प्रतिग्रहं

[69] तदा । तत्तदा
[70] प्रतिग्रहोपात्तं । प्रतिग्रहार्जितं
[71] -द्रव्य- । -द्रव्यस्य
[72] संभवति । भवति
[73] दातुरानतिद्वारा । तावद्दातुरानतिमुखेन । दातुरानमनमुखेन । दातुरानमनेन
[74] तावददृष्टार्थदाने । तावददृष्टार्थे दाने
[75] प्रतिग्रहस्य चाल्प- । प्रतिग्रहस्याल्प-
[76] -पहारप्रदानादिना । -पदादानादिना
[77] पुरुषाशय- । पुरुषस्याशय-
[78] कस्यचित्तत्तद्गुणा- । कस्यचिद्गुणा-
[79] च । *om*
[80] व्याप्रियमाणं । व्याप्रियमाण-

निष्पादयतीति[81] । तदा ज्योतिष्टोमादिकर्मणः प्राचीनमपि भोजनं शरीरस्थितौ व्याप्रियमाणं प्राचीनशरीरस्थितिमन्तरेण ज्योतिष्टोमानिष्पत्तेः[82] प्रणाल्या ज्योतिष्टोमार्थमिति सर्वमेव भोजनं क्रत्वर्थं स्यान्न पुरुषार्थम् । तथाच तत्साधनमपि यद्द्रव्यं तत्क्रत्वर्थं[83] स्यात् । तदर्जनोपायोऽपि क्रत्वर्थः[84] स्यादिति पुरुषार्थत्वं द्रव्यार्जनस्य द्रव्यस्य भोजनस्य च हीयेतेति[85] ।

<**45**> तन्मन्दतमम् । प्रणाल्या ज्योतिष्टोमोपकारकत्वेऽपि भोजनस्य साक्षात्तृप्त्यर्थत्वात् । पुरुषार्थस्यैव सतः क्रतूपकारकत्वात्तत्रैदमर्थे[86] प्रमाणाभावात् । उपकारकत्वस्य तादर्थ्यव्यभिचारात् । अतः कथं द्रव्यार्जनस्य द्रव्यस्य भोजनस्य च क्रत्वर्थत्वमापद्येत[87] ।

<**46**> अत एवास्यापि पर्यनुयोगस्यानवकाशः । यदि द्रव्यस्य प्रतिग्रहे[88] प्राचीनभोजनद्वारा प्रतिग्रहोपकारकत्वमिष्यते तदा जन्मत आरभ्य भोजनं विना शरीरावस्थितेरभावान्नार्जनं[89] संभवतीति सर्व एव धनोपायः पितृद्रव्यविनाशेन स्यात् । अतोऽनुपघ्नन् पितृद्रव्यमिति विशेषणं न स्यादिति । यतो[90] विशेषणानर्थक्यादेव भक्षणाद्युपभोगोपयुक्तधनोपघातादन्यस्यैवोपघातादिरूपस्य[91] वचनार्थत्वात् ।

<**47**> किंच भक्षणाद्युपभोगार्थं[92] धनोपघातस्य गृहगतेनाप्यवश्यकर्तव्यत्वान्न[93] धनार्जनार्थत्वमुपघातस्य । तादर्थ्यमरेव च प्रयोजकमिति नातिप्रसक्तिः ।

[81] निष्पादयतीति । निष्पादयतीति चेत्
[82] ज्योतिष्टमानिष्पत्तेः । ज्योतिष्टोमाद्यनिष्पत्तेः
[83] यद्द्रव्यं तत्क्रत्वर्थं । द्रव्यं क्रत्वर्थं
[84] क्रत्वर्थः । क्रत्वर्थं
[85] हीयेतेति । हीयत इति
[86] -त्वात्तत्रैदमर्थे । -त्वात्तत्रैदमार्थ्ये । -त्वात्तदैदमर्थे
[87] क्रत्वर्थत्वमापद्येत । क्रत्यवर्थत्वमापद्येत इति
[88] प्रतिग्रहे । *om* । प्रतिग्रह- । प्रतिग्राहक-
[89] -भावान्नार्जनं । -भावाद्धनार्जनं
[90] यतो । ततो
[91] -वोपघातादि- । -वोपचारादि-
[92] -पभोगार्थं । -पाभोगार्थ-
[93] -वश्य- । -वश्यं

<**48**> अत एवोक्तं **विश्वरूपेण** — पितृद्रव्यं दत्त्वा यदि नोपार्जितं धनं[94] तदा तस्यैवासाधारणं वैवाहिकवदेवोक्तम् । न तु भक्षणाद्युपभोगमात्रेण तस्य स्तन्यपानादितुल्यत्वादित्यनेन ।

<**49**> अत एव पुत्रोपनयनविवाहयोः सोत्सुकसव्ययपितृकृतबहुतरधन-व्ययेऽपि[95] न व्रतभिक्षादिलब्धस्य वैवाहिकस्य वा साधारण्यं धनप्रेप्सया धनव्ययस्याकृतत्वात् ।

<**50**> तस्माद्धनोद्देशेनैव साधारणधनोपघातेनार्जितं[96] साधारणं नान्यदि-ति सिद्धम् ।

<**51**> **जितेन्द्रियेण**ापि बहुप्रकारं विमृश्योक्तम् — तदस्य यावदुक्तप्र-पञ्चस्य संक्षेपेणायमर्थः प्रत्येतव्यः । यत्किंचिद्धनमसाधारणधनोपाघाता-र्जितं[97] तदसाधारणम् । यत्किंचिद्धनं साधारणोपर्जितं तत्साधारणम्[98] । विस्पष्टार्थं तु विद्याधनं तु यद्यस्येत्यादिनोदाहरणप्रपञ्चेनोपन्यस्तम् । असाधारणत्वादेवाविभाज्यमेवंविधं[99] धनं साधारणमपि साधारणहेतुसमु-त्थमेवंविधमेव । तदपि सुखावबोधार्थम् । क्वचिदर्थसाधारण्येन क्वचिच्च व्यापारतथात्वेन[100] संबन्धसाधारण्येन च प्रदर्शितमित्यन्तेन ।

<**52**> **बालकेन**ाप्युक्तम् — न ह्येकेन भ्रात्रा विद्यादिना लब्धेऽपरेषाम-धिकारसंभवः प्रमाणाभावादित्यन्तेन[101] ।

<**53**> यश्चानुपघातप्रतिग्रहार्जितधनस्य विभागः शिष्टानां दृश्यते स भ्रातृस्नेहेन वा[102] पौरुषबुद्ध्या वा नानुपपन्नः ।

[94] धनं । *om*

[95] सोत्सुकसव्यय- । सोत्सुकतया

[96] -धनोपघातेनार्जितं । -धनोपघातार्जितं

[97] यत्किंचिद्धनमसाधरणधनोपघातार्जितं । यत्किंचिद्धनमसाधारणोपायार्जितं

[98] यत्किंचिद्धनं . . . तत्साधारणम् । *om*

[99] -विभाज्यमेवंविधं । -विभाज्यमप्येवंविधं

[100] -तथात्वेन । -वत्त्वेन । -साधारण्येन

[101] -त्यन्तेन । -त्यन्तम्

[102] वा । *om*

यद्वा प्रतिग्रहधनस्य विद्याधनत्वाद्विद्याधने च साधारणधनानुपघातार्जिते ऽपि समविद्याधिकविद्यानां विभागस्य[103] वाचनिकत्वात्तद्विभागं पश्यन्तो विद्याधनस्य[104] विद्याविशेषकृतोऽयं विभाग इत्यजानन्तोऽविभक्तार्जितत्वे-नायं विभाग इति भ्रान्ताः । स्वयमपि तथैव व्यवहृतवन्तः[105] । तन्मूलश्चापरापरव्यवहार इति न किंचिदनुचितम् ।

<**54**> यत्पुनर्**मनु**वचनम् —

> यत्किंचित्पितरि प्रेते धनं ज्येष्ठोऽधिगच्छति ।
> भागो यवीयसां तत्र यदि विद्यानुपालिनः ।। [M 9.204]

तस्यायमर्थः[106] —

> पितेव पालयेत्पुत्रान् ज्येष्ठो भ्रातॄन्[107] यवीयसः ।
> पुत्रवच्चानुवर्तेरन्[108] ज्येष्ठे भ्रातरि धर्मतः ।। [M 9.108]

एतस्माद्वचनात्पितापुत्रवदवस्थानात्पित्रर्जित इवानुपताघार्जितेऽपि ज्येष्ठधने कनिष्ठानामधिकारः । एतावान् परं विशेषः । पित्रर्जितेऽविदुषामप्यधि-कारो ज्येष्ठार्जिते[109] पुनर्विदुषामेव ।

<**55**> एतच्च पितरि प्रेत इति ज्येष्ठ इति यवीयसामिति विद्यानुपालिन इत्यादिपदप्रयोगस्यानर्थकयात्सिध्यति[110] ।

<**56**> तस्मादविभक्तार्जितत्वमात्रेणाविभक्तभ्रात्रन्तरस्य भवतीत्यसंगतं वचनम् ।

[103] विभागस्य । भागस्य
[104] विद्याधनस्य । विद्याधनस्य च
[105] व्यवहृतवन्तः । कृतवन्तः
[106] तस्यायमर्थः । अस्यायमर्थः
[107] भ्रातॄन् । भ्राता
[108] पुत्रवच्चानुवतm् । पुत्रवच्चापि वतm्
[109] ज्येष्ठार्जिते । ज्येष्ठधने । ज्येष्ठार्जितधने
[110] इत्यादि- । इति

<**6.2.1**> तत्र[1] विद्याधनं तावदभिधीयते ।

तत्र **कात्यायनः** —

उपन्यस्ते तु यल्लब्धं विद्यया पणपूर्वकम् ।
विद्याधनं तु तद्विद्याद्विभागे न[2] नियोजयेत्[3] ।। [K 868]
शिष्यादार्त्विज्यतः प्रश्नात्संदिग्धप्रश्ननिर्णयात् ।
स्वज्ञानशंसनाद्वादाल्लब्धं प्राध्ययनाच्च यत् ।। [K 869abcd]
विद्याधनं तु तत्प्रहुर्विभागे न विभज्यते[4] । [K 869ef]
शिल्पेष्वपि हि धर्मोऽयं मूल्याद्यच्चाधिकं भवेत् ।। [K 870]
परं निरस्य यल्लब्धं विद्यया द्यूतपूर्वकम् ।
विद्याधनं तु तद्विद्यान्न विभाज्यं बृहस्पतिः ।। [K 871]

<**2**> यदि भवान् भद्रकमुन्यस्यति तदा भवते मया एतावद्देयमिति[5] पणितम् । यत्रोपन्यासं[6] निस्तीर्य लभते तन्न विभाज्यम् ।

<**3**> शिष्यादध्यापितात् ।

<**4**> आर्त्विज्यतः यजमानाद्दक्षिणादिना लब्धम्[7] । <**5**> दक्षिणा च न प्रतिग्रहो वेतनरूपत्वात्तस्याः ।

<**6**> तथा यत्किंचिद्विद्यायां प्रश्ने निस्तीर्णेऽपणितमेव यदि कश्चित्परितोषाद्ददाति ।

<**7**> तथा यो ह्यस्मिन् शास्त्रार्थे मम संशयमपनयति तस्मै सुवर्णमिदं ददानीत्युपस्थितस्य[8] संशयमपनीय यल्लब्धं वादिनोर्वा[9] संदेहे न्यायकरणार्थमागतयोः सम्यङ्निरूपणेन यल्लब्धं[10] षष्ठांशादिकम् ।

[1] तत्र । अत्र
[2] तद्विद्याद्विभागे न । तद्विद्यान्न विभागे
[3] नियोजयेत् । नियुज्यते । विभाज्यते
[4] विभज्यते । प्रयुज्यते
[5] एतावद्देयमिति । एतद्देयमिति
[6] यत्रोपन्यासं । तत्रोपन्यासं
[7] लब्धम् । यल्लब्धम्
[8] ददानी- । ददामी-
[9] वादिनोर्वा । वादिनोर्वाद-
[10] यल्लब्धं । लब्धं

<8> तथा शास्त्रादिषु प्रकृष्टज्ञानं[11] विभाव्य यत्प्रतिग्रहादिना[12] लब्धम् ।

<9> तथा द्वयोः शास्त्रज्ञानविवादेऽन्यत्रापि[13] यत्र कुत्रचिदन्योन्यज्ञान-विवादे निर्जित्य यल्लब्धम् ।

<10> तथैकस्मिन् देये बहूनामुपप्लवे येन प्रकृष्टमधीत्य यल्लब्धम् ।

<11> तथा शिल्पादिविद्यया चित्रकारसुवर्णकारादिभिर्यल्लब्धम्[14] ।

<12> द्युतेनापि[15] परं निर्जित्य यल्लब्धम् ।

<13> तत्सर्वमविभाज्यमितरैः । तदयमर्थो यया कयाचिद्विद्यया यल्लब्ध-मर्जकस्यैव तन्नेतरेषाम्[16] । प्रदर्शनार्थं तु **कात्यायनेन** विस्तरेणोक्तं **श्रीकरा-दि**भ्रमनिरासार्थम् ।

<14> अतः स्वज्ञानख्यापनादिना यत्प्रतिग्रहलब्धं तदपि विद्याधनमेव विद्ययैव[17] विदुषे प्रतिग्रहदानात् । **<15>** तथा **यमः** —

विद्यायुक्तो धर्मशीलः[18] प्रशान्तः
क्षान्तो दान्तः सत्यवादी कृतज्ञः ।
वृत्तिग्लानो गोहितो गोशरण्यो
दाता यज्वा ब्राह्मणः पात्रमाहुः ॥
अव्रतानाममन्त्राणां जातिमात्रोपजीविनाम् ।
नैषां प्रतिग्रहो देयो न शिला तारयेच्छिलाम् ॥

<16> विद्वत्तयैव पात्रत्वादविदुषां चापात्रत्वात् ।

[11] प्रकृष्टज्ञानं । स्वप्रकृष्टज्ञानं । स्वज्ञानं । ज्ञानं

[12] यत्प्रतिग्रहादिना । प्रतिग्रहादिना

[13] -ज्ञान- । -विज्ञान-

[14] चित्रकारसुर्वणकारादि- । चित्रकरसुवर्णकरादि- ॥ -यल्लब्धम् । -लब्धम्

[15] द्युतेनापि । तथा द्यूतेनापि

[16] यल्लब्धमर्जकस्यैव तन्नेतरेषाम् । यल्लब्धं तदर्जकस्यैव नेतरेषाम्

[17] विद्ययैव । विद्वत्तयैव

[18] -शीलः । -युक्तः

<17> अतो यत्केनचिदुक्तम् — विद्याधनं तु विद्याध्यापननिमित्तं यत्तदुच्यत इति तदुक्तवचनादर्शनेनेति हेयमेव[19] विद्याशब्दस्य[20] विद ज्ञान इत्यस्माद्धातोर्निष्पत्तेर्ज्ञानमात्रवचनत्वात्[21] ।

<18> यच्च प्रतिग्रहधनस्यापि विद्याधनत्वेन याजनाध्यापनप्रतिग्रहाणां संकीर्णत्वमापादितं **श्रीकरेण** तदतिमन्दम् । विद्याधनत्वसामान्यस्य याजनाध्यापनप्रतिग्रहादिनानाव्यक्तिसंबन्धेऽपि व्यक्तीनामसंकीर्णत्वात्तदापि याजनाध्यापनस्याप्रतिग्रत्वात् । गोत्वसमवायेऽपि नीलकपिलकापोतिकादिव्यक्तीनामसंकीर्णत्वस्याविवादात्[22] । **<19>** अत एव शिष्यादार्त्विज्यतः प्राप्तयोर्विद्याधनत्वं स्मरन्मुनिर्याजनाध्यापनयोः संकारात्कथं न बिभेति ।

अतः पक्षग्रहणमात्रेण तदभिधानमिति हेयम् ।

<20> शौर्यादिधनमाह[23] **कात्यायनः** —

आरुह्य संशयं यत्र प्रसभं कर्म कुर्वते ।
तस्मिन् कर्मणि तुष्टेन प्रसादः स्वामिना कृतः ।
तत्र लब्धं तु यत्किंचिद्धनं शौर्येण तद्भवेत् ।। [K 876]
ध्वजाहृतं भवेद्यत्तु विभाज्यं नैव तत्स्मृतम् ।
संग्रामादाहृतं यत्तु विजित्य[24] द्विषतां बलम्[25] ।
स्वाम्यर्थं[26] जीवितं त्यक्त्वा तद् ध्वजाहृतमुच्यते ।। [K 878]
<21> वैवाहिकं तु तद्विद्याद्भार्यया यत्सहागतम् ।। [K 880ab]

<22> भार्याप्राप्तिकाले[27] लब्धमित्यर्थः ।

<23> तथा अपरमप्यविभाज्यमाहतु**र्मनु-विष्णू**[28] —

[19] हेयमेव । हेयमेव तत्
[20] दिद्याशब्दस्य । तच्छब्दस्य
[21] -मात्र- । *om* ।। -वचनत्वात् । -वचनात्
[22] -कापोतिकादि- । -कपोतकादि- ।। -विवादात् । -विवादसिद्धत्वात्
[23] शौर्यादिधनमाह । शौर्यधनमाह
[24] विजित्य । विच्छिद्य । विभाव्य । विद्राव्य
[25] बलम् । कुलम्
[26] स्वाम्यर्थं । स्वाम्यर्थे
[27] -प्राप्ति- । -लाभ- । *om*
[28] तथा अपरमप्यविभाज्य- । तथापरमविभाज्य-

वस्त्रं पत्रमलंकारो[29] कृतान्नमुदकं स्त्रियः ।
योगक्षेमप्रचारं च न विभाज्यं प्रचक्षते ।। [M 9.219 = Vi 18.44]

<24> वस्त्रमङ्गयोजितं पङ्क्तिपरिच्छदार्थं च । पत्रं वाहनमश्वादि । अलंकारोऽङ्गुलीयकादि[30] । कृतान्नं लड्डुकादि । उदकं कूपवापीगतं[31] प्रचारोपयुक्तम् । स्त्रियो दासीव्यतिरिक्ताः । योगक्षेमप्रचारं च शय्याभोजनाचमनाद्युपयुक्तभाजनादीनि[32] ।

<25> तथा **व्यासः** —

अविभाज्यं सगोत्राणामा सहस्रकुलादपि ।
याज्यं क्षेत्रं च पत्रं च कृतान्नमुदकं स्त्रियः ।। [Vy 262]

<26> याज्यं यागस्थानं देवता वा । न तु याजनलब्धं धनं तस्य विद्याधनत्वेनैव गतार्थत्वात् ।

<27> तथा **कात्यायनः** —

गोप्रचारश्च रथ्या च वस्त्रं यच्चाङ्गयोजितम् ।
प्रायोज्यं न विभज्येत[33] शिल्पार्थं च[34] बृहस्पतिः ।। [K 884]

<28> प्रायोज्यं यद्यस्य प्रयोजनार्हम् । यथा श्रुतादौ पुस्तकादि । न तन्मूर्खैर्विभजनीयम्[35] । शिल्पोपयुक्तं च शिल्पिनामेव नातद्विदाम् ।

<29> तथा **शङ्खलिखितौ** —

न वास्तुविभागो नोदकपात्रालंकारानुपयुक्तस्त्रीवाससामपां[36]
प्रचारार्थानां विभागश्चेति प्रजापतिः ।। [ŚL 278]

[29] पत्रमलंकारो । पत्रमलंकारं
[30] अलंकारोऽ । अलंकारम-
[31] कूपवापीगतं । कूपवापीतडागगतं
[32] शय्या- । शय्यासन- ।। -भोजनाचमना- । -भोजना-
[33] विभज्यते । विभाज्यं तु
[34] च । तु
[35] न तन्मूर्खैर्विभजनीयम् । तन्मूर्खैर्न विभजनीयम्
[36] नोदक- । नोद-

<**30**> पितरि जीवति यस्मिन् वास्तौ येन गृहोद्यानादिकं[37] कृतं तत्तस्य न विभाज्यं[38] पितुरप्रतिषेधेन तदनुमतत्वात्[39] ।

<**31**> तथा पैतामहमपि[40] द्रव्यं यच्चिरं नष्टमक्षमत्वादथवा प्रतीकार-पराङ्मुखतया[41] इतरैरप्रतिकृतं पित्रा च[42] स्वधनशरीरायासाभ्यां प्रतिकृतं तत्पितुरेव न साधारणम् ।

<**32**> यथा **मनुः** —

पैतृकं तु पिता द्रव्यमनवाप्तं यदाप्नुयात् ।
न तत्पुत्रैर्भजेत्सार्धमकामः स्वयमर्जितम् ।। [M 9.209]

<**33**> पैतृकं द्रव्यं पुत्रैरनवाप्तमप्रतिकृतम् । अनवाप्यमित्यनवाप्येति च[43] पाठावनाकरौ ।

<**34**> आह **बृहस्पतिः** —

पैतामहं हृतं पित्रा स्वशक्त्या यदुपार्जितम् ।
विद्याशौर्यादिना प्राप्तं तत्र स्वाम्यं पितुः स्मृतम् ।। [B 26.58]
प्रदानं स्वेच्छया कुर्याद्भोगं चैव ततो धनात् ।
तदभावे तु तनयाः समांशाः परिकीर्तिताः ।। [B 26.59]

<**35**> स्वशक्त्येत्यसाधारणधनशरीरव्यापारं दर्शयति ।

<**36**> वचनद्वयेऽपि[44] पितृपदमुपलक्षणं स्वयमर्जितमिति हेतोरभिधा-नात्[45] । <**37**> एवं च स्वार्जिताक्रमागतद्रव्यवदेव क्रमागतेऽप्येवंरूपे भूमि-व्यतिरिक्ते व्यवस्था बोद्धव्या । <**38**> भूमौ तु विशेषमाह **शङ्खः** —

पूर्वनष्टां तु[46] यो भूमिमेक एवोद्धरेच्छ्रमात् ।

[37] गृहोद्यानादिकं । गृहोद्यानादि
[38] तत्तस्य न विभाज्यं । तत्तस्याविभाज्यं । न तत्तस्य विभाज्यं
[39] पितुरप्रतिषेधेन तदनुमतत्वात् । पितुरप्रतिषेधेनानुमतत्वात्
[40] पैतामहमपि । पैतामहं
[41] -प्रतीकार- । -प्रतिकार-
[42] च । *om*
[43] च । *om*
[44] वचनद्वयेऽपि । वचनद्वये
[45] हेतोरभिधानात् । हेतोरविशेषात्
[46] तु । च

यथाभागं भजन्त्यन्ये[47] दत्त्वा भागं[48] तुरीयकम् ॥ [ŚL 273]

<**39**> यद्यप्यसाधारणधनशरीरव्यापारमेवकारेण दर्शयति तथाप्युद्धर्तुर्नासाधारण्यम् । किंतु प्रतिकृतभूमेश्चतुर्थांशोऽधिकस्तस्मै दातव्यः । भूमिपदसामर्थ्यात्तदविवक्षाकारणाभावात् ।

<**40**> इति विभाज्याविभाज्यनिरूपणम् ।

[47] भजन्त्यन्ये । लभन्तेऽन्ये

[48] दत्त्वा भागं । दत्त्वांशं तु

<**7.1**> संप्रति विभागानन्तरजातस्य विभागः कथ्यते ।

तत्र **मनु-नारदौ** —

ऊर्ध्वं विभागाज्जातस्तु पित्र्यमेव हरेद्धनम् ।
संसृष्टास्तेन वा ये स्युर्विभजेत स तैः सह ।। [M 9.216 = N 13.44/42n]

<**2**> यदि पिता पुत्रान् विभज्य स्वयं च यथाशास्त्रं भागं[1] गृहीत्वा पुत्रैरसंसृष्ट एव मृतस्तदा विभागानन्तरजातः[2] पितृधनमेव[3] गृह्णीयात् । स एव तस्य भागः। अथ कैश्चित्पुत्रैः सह[4] संसृष्टः पिता मृतस्तदा संसृष्टेभ्यो भागं गृह्णीयात् ।

<**3**> तथा **गोतमः** —

विभक्तजः पित्र्यमेव ।। [G 28.29]

<**4**> विभागानन्तरं यस्य गर्भाधानं स विभक्तजः विभक्तेन जनितो गर्भाधानादृते जनकस्य जननव्यापाराभावात् । अतो यद्यज्ञातगर्भायामेव स्त्रियां विभक्ताः पुत्रास्तदनन्तरजातो[5] भ्रातृभ्य एव भागं[6] गृह्णीयात् ।

<**5**> न केवलमेक एव किंतु बहवोऽपि विभक्तजाः[7] पित्र्यमेव धनं गृह्णीयुः । यदाह[8] **बृहस्पतिः** —

पित्रा सह विभक्ता ये सापत्ना वा सहोदराः ।
जघन्यजाश्च ये तेषां पितृभागहरास्तु ते । [B 26.54]
अनीशः पूर्वजः पित्र्ये भ्रातृभागे विभक्तजः ।। [B 26.55]

<**6**> विभागात्पूर्वं जातः[9] पित्र्ये धनेऽनधिकारी विभक्तजश्च भ्रातृधने ।

तथा —

1 भागं । विभागं
2 विभागानन्तर- । विभागानन्तरं
3 पितृधनमेव । पित्र्यमेव धनं
4 सह । *om*
5 तदनन्तर- । तदनन्तरं
6 भागं । विभागं
7 विभक्तजाः । विभक्तजाताः
8 यदाह । यथा
9 बिभागात्पूर्वं जातः । विभागात्पूर्वजातः । विभागात्पूर्वजः

पुत्रैः सह विभक्तेन पित्रा यत्स्वयमर्जितम् ।
विभक्तजस्य तत्सर्वमनीशाः पूर्वजाः स्मृताः । [B 26.56]
यथा धने तथर्णेऽपि दानाधानक्रयेषु च ॥ [B 26.57ab]

<7> सर्वशब्दाद्बहुतरमपि[10] धनं पित्रार्जितं[11] विभक्तजस्यैव ।

<8> परस्परमनीशास्ते मुक्त्वाशौचोदकक्रियाः[12] ॥ [B 26.57cd]

<9> अशौचोदकक्रियामात्रप्रदर्शनेन सुदूरं धनाधिकारं निरस्यति ।

<10> इदं च पित्रुपात्तधनमात्रविषयम् । यदि तु[13] पैतामहमपि[14] भूम्यादिकं विभक्तं तदा तद्धनविभागं भ्रातृभ्यो गृह्णीयात् । मातुर्निवृत्ते रजसि तद्विभागविधानात् ।

<11> तदाह **विष्णुः** —

पितृविभक्ता विभागानन्तरोत्पन्नस्य[15] विभागं[16] दद्युः ॥ [Vi 17.3]

<12> तथा **याज्ञवल्क्यः** —

विभक्तेषु सुतो जातः सवर्णायां विभागभाक् ।
दृश्याद्वा तद्विभागः स्यादायव्ययविशोधितात् ॥ [Y 2.122]

<13> पित्र्यमेव हरेदिति[17] विरोधादुक्तयुक्तेश्च क्रमागतधनविषयमिदम् ।

10 सर्वशब्दाद्बहुतरमपि । सर्वशब्दाद्बहुतरं
11 पित्रार्जितं । पित्रर्जितं
12 मुक्त्वा- । त्यक्त्वा-
13 तु । च
14 पैतामहमपि । पैतामहधनमपि
15 विभागा- । विभक्ता-
16 विभागं । भागं
17 हरेदिति । हरेद्धनमिति

<**8.1**> अथ विभागानन्तरागतविभागः ।

तत्र **बृहस्पतिः** –

कृतेऽकृते विभागे वा रिक्थी यत्र प्रवर्तते[1] ।
सामान्यं चेद्भवेद्यत्तु[2] तत्र भागहरस्तु सः ।। [B 26.63]
ऋणं लेख्यं गृहं क्षेत्रं[3] यस्य पैतामहं भवेत् ।
चिरकालप्रोषितोऽपि भागभागागतस्तु सः ।। [B 26.64]
<**2**> गोत्रसाधारणं त्यक्त्वा योऽन्यदेशं समाश्रितः ।
तद्वंशस्यागतस्यांशः प्रदातव्यो न संशयः ।। [B 26.65]
तृतीयः पञ्चमश्चैव सप्तमो वापि यो भवेत् ।
जन्मनामपरिज्ञाने लभेतांशं क्रमागतम् ।। [B 26.66]
<**3**> यं परम्परया मौलाः सामन्ताः स्वामिनं विदुः ।
तदन्वयस्यागतस्य दातव्या गोत्रजैर्मही ।। [B 26.67]

<**4**> तदनेन चिरप्रोषितवंशेन[4] समन्ताद्वासिभिर्मौलैरात्मज्ञापनपूर्वकं भागग्रहणं कार्यम्[5]।

<**5**> इति विभक्तागतविभागः[6] ।

[1] प्रवर्तते । प्रदृश्यते
[2] चेद्भवेद्यत्तु । च भवेद्यत्तु
[3] लेख्यं गृहं क्षेत्रं । क्षेत्रं गृहं लेख्यं
[4] -वंशेन । -वंश्येन
[5] कार्यम् । *om*
[6] विभक्तागतविभागः । विभागानन्तरागतविभागः । *om*

<**9.1**> संप्रत्येकपितृकाणां सवर्णानुलोमपरिणीतस्त्रीजातानां पुत्राणां विभागः कथ्यते ।

<**2**> अस्ति च सवर्णानुलोस्त्रीपरिणयनम् । तथाच[1] **मनुः** —

सवर्णाग्रे द्विजातीनां प्रशस्ता दारकर्मणि ।
कामतस्तु प्रवृत्तानामिमाः स्युः क्रमशोऽवराः[2] ॥ [M 3.12]
शूद्रैव भार्या शूद्रस्य सा च स्वा च विशः स्मृते ।
ते च स्वा चैव राज्ञस्तु ताश्च[3] स्वा चाग्रजन्मनः ॥ [M 3.13]

<**3**> शूद्रैवेत्येवकारः सर्वत्र संबध्यते । सा ते ता इत्यनन्तरपूर्वोक्तपरामर्शात्[4] । प्रतिलोमपरिणयनं सर्वथैव[5] न कार्यमित्यर्थः ।

<**4**> कामतस्तु प्रवृत्तानामिमाः स्युरिति[6] दोषाल्पत्वख्यापनार्थं न तु दोषाभाव एव[7] । <**5**> तदाहतुः **शङ्खलिखितौ** —

भार्याः कार्याः[8] सजातीयाः[9] । सर्वेषां श्रेयसः[10] स्युरिति पूर्वः[11]
कल्पः । ततोऽनुकल्पश्च[12] । चतस्रो ब्राह्मणस्यानुपूर्वेण
तिस्रो राजन्यस्य द्वे वैश्यस्य एका शूद्रस्य ॥ [ŚL 64]

<**6**> जात्यवच्छेदेन चतुरादिसंख्या संबध्यते ।

<**7**> एताश्च[13] परिणीता एव भार्या भवन्ति । तदाह[14] **पैठीनसिः** —

[1] तथाच । तथा
[2] ऽवराः । वराः
[3] राज्ञस्तु ताश्च । राज्ञः स्युस्ताश्च
[4] इत्यनन्तर- । इत्यनन्तर ॥ -परामर्शात् । -परामर्षात्
[5] सर्वथैव । सर्वथा । सर्वत्रैव । *om*
[6] प्रवृत्तानामिमाः स्युरिति । प्रवृत्तानामिति
[7] दोषाभाव एव । दोषाभावः
[8] कार्याः । *om*
[9] सजातीयाः । स्वजातीयाः
[10] सर्वेषां श्रेयसः । श्रेयसः सर्वेषां
[11] पूर्वः । पूर्व-
[12] ऽनुकल्पश्च । ऽनुकल्पः
[13] एताश्च । एताः
[14] तदाह । तथाह

चतस्रो ब्रह्मणस्य विवाहितास्तिस्रो[15] द्वे चैका चेतरेषाम्[16]
|| [Pai ?]

<**8**> इतरेषां[17] राजन्यादीनां यथाक्रमं तिस्रो द्वे चैका चेति ।

<**9**> आनुलोम्येऽपि द्विजातेः शूद्रायां बहुदोषमाहतुर्**मनु-विष्णू** —

हीनजातिस्त्रियं[18] मोहादुद्वहन्तो द्विजातयः ।
कुलान्येव नयन्त्याशु ससंतानानि शूद्रताम् ॥ [M 3.15 = Vi 26.6]
शूद्रावेदी पतत्यत्रेरुतथ्यतनयस्य च ।
शौनकस्य सुतोत्पत्त्या तदपत्यतया भृगोः ॥ [M 3.16]
शूद्रां शयनमारोप्य ब्राह्मणो यात्यधोगतिम् ।
जनयित्वा सुतं तस्यां ब्राह्मण्यादेव हीयते ॥ [M 3.17]

<**10**> तदनेन क्रमोढाविषयत्वं वचनानाम् । **हारीत**वचनमपि **मन्वाद्ये**क-वाक्यतया परिणीताविषयम् । यथा —

ब्रह्महा न भवत्यन्यो ब्रह्महा वृषलीपतिः ।
यस्तस्यामाहितो गर्भः स तेन ब्राह्मणो हतः ॥ [H ?]

अत एव शूद्रावर्जं द्विजातिभार्यामाह **शङ्खः** —

ब्राह्मणी क्षत्रिया वैश्या ब्राह्मणस्य प्रकीर्तिताः[19] ।
क्षत्रिया चैव वैश्या च क्षत्रियस्य प्रकीर्तिते[20] ।
वैश्यैव भार्या वैश्यस्य शूद्रा शूद्रस्य कीर्तिता ॥ [ŚL 65]

<**11**> अतः स्वयमनूढायां शूद्रायामपत्यजनने नैते दोषाः[21] । किंत्वल्प-दोषः[22] प्रायश्चित्तं चाल्पमिति वक्ष्यति ।

<**12**> अत्र[23] चातुर्वर्ण्यपुत्राणां विभागमाह **मनुः** —

[15] विवाहिता- । परिणीता-
[16] चेतरेषाम् । चेतीतरेषाम्
[17] इतरेषां । *om*
[18] हीनजाति- । हीनजातिं
[19] प्रकीर्तिताः । प्रकीर्तिता
[20] प्रकीर्तिते । प्रकीर्तिता
[21] -जनने नैते दोषाः । -जननेऽपि नैष दोषः
[22] किंत्वल्पदोषः । किंतु स्वल्पदोषः
[23] अत्र । तत्र

त्र्यंशं दायाद्धरेद्विप्रो द्वावंशौ क्षत्रियासुतः ।
वैश्याजोऽध्यर्धमेकांशमंशं शूद्रासुतो हरेत् ॥ [M 9.151]
सर्वं वा रिक्थजातं तु दशधा परिकल्प्य तत्[24] ।
धर्म्यं विभागं कुर्वीत विधिनानेन धर्मवित् ॥ [M 9.152]
चतुरोंऽशान् हरेद्विप्रस्त्रीनंशान् क्षत्रियासुतः ।
वैश्यापुत्रो हरेद् द्व्यंशमंशं शूद्रासुतो हरेत् ॥ [M 9.153]

<13> किंचिद्गुणवत्त्वेन विभागप्रकारद्वयम् ।

<14> तत्र **विष्णुः** ब्राह्मणस्य चतसृषु चेत्पुत्रा[25] भवेयुरित्यादि [Vi 18.1] अनेन क्रमेणांशकल्पनान्यत्रापि भवतीत्यन्तम् [Vi 18.40] ।

<15> ब्राह्मणजातो राजन्यापुत्र एव यदि जन्मना ज्येष्ठो[26] गुणवांश्च[27] तदा ब्राह्मणेन सह तुल्यभागी कार्यः । ब्राह्मणेन क्षत्रियेण वा जातो वैश्यश्चेत्तद्रूपस्तदा क्षत्रियपुत्रेण सह[28] तुल्यांशी[29] ।

यदाह[30] **बृहस्पतिः** —

विप्रेण क्षत्रियाजातो जन्मज्येष्ठो गुणान्वितः ।
भवेत्समांशः क्षत्रेण वैश्याजातस्तथैव च ॥ [B 26.20]

तथा **बौधायनः** —

सवर्णापुत्रानन्तरापुत्रयोरनन्तरापत्रुश्चेद्गुणवान् स[31] ज्येष्ठांशं हरेत्[32] । गुणवान् हि शेषाणां भर्ता भवतीति ॥ [Bau 2.2..3.12–13]

<16> अनेन[33] शूद्रस्याप्येवंविधस्य वैश्येन सह समांशिता दर्शिता ।

[24] तत् । तु
[25] चतसृषु चेत्पुत्रा । चेत् चतसृषु पुत्रा
[26] ज्येष्ठो । सर्वज्येष्ठो
[27] गुणवांश्च । गुणवांश्च भवति
[28] सह । *om*
[29] तुल्यांशी । तुल्याधिकारी
[30] यदाह । यथाह
[31] स । *om*
[32] ज्येष्ठांशं हरेत् । ज्येष्ठभागं गृह्णीयात्
[33] अनेन । अनेनैव

<**17**> या तु प्रतिग्रहेण पित्रार्जिता[34] भूमिः सा ब्राह्मणीपुत्रस्यैव न क्षत्रियादेः । गृहं क्रमागतं[35] क्षेत्रं च द्विजातिपुत्राणां[36] न शूद्रस्य । तदाह **बृहन्मनुः** —

ब्रह्मदायागतां भूमिं हरेयुर्ब्राह्मणीसुताः ।
गृहं द्विजातयः सर्वे तथा क्षेत्रं क्रमागतम् ।। [*Dhko* p. 1252]

<**18**> क्रमागतायाः[37] पितामहप्रपितामहादिगृहीतायाः[38] सकलद्विजातिसंबन्धः क्रमागतमित्यविशेषेणाभिधानात् । प्रतिग्रहभूमौ च[39] क्षत्रियादिसुतानामेवाधिकारनिषेधेन नप्त्रादीनामप्यननुज्ञानम् । <**19**> तदाह **बृहस्पतिः** —

न प्रतिग्रहभूर्देया क्षत्रियादिसुताय वै ।
यद्यप्यस्य पिता दद्यान्मृते विप्रासुतो हरेत् ।। [B 26.121]

एवं च प्रतिग्रहभूरेव[40] ब्रह्मदायागतेत्युक्तम् । ब्रह्म वेदस्तदध्ययनतदर्थज्ञानवत्तया प्रतिग्रहविधानात् ।<**20**> न पुन**र्मनू**क्तार्चनलब्धा । यथा —

आवृत्तानां गुरुकुलाद्विप्राणां पूजको भवेत् ।
नृपाणामक्षयो ह्येष विधिर्ब्राह्मो विधीयते[41]।। [M 7.82]

अर्चनरूपत्वादस्य ।

<**21**> अथवा इयमेकेन निषिद्धान्या चापरेण[42] ।

<**22**> न तु ब्राह्मणस्य भूमिर्ब्रह्मदायः । द्विजातीनां क्रमागतक्षेत्रसंबन्धस्य वाचनिकत्वात्केवलशूद्रस्यैव निषिद्धत्वाच्च[43] । यथा **बृहस्पतिः**[44] —

शूद्र्यां द्विजातिभिर्जातो न भूमेर्भागमर्हति ।

[34] पित्रार्जिता । पित्रर्जिता
[35] क्रमागतं । क्रमागत-
[36] द्विजातिपुत्राणां । द्विजातिपुत्राणामेव
[37] क्रमागतायाः । क्रमागतयोः
[38] पितामह- । *om* ॥ -गृहीतायाः । -गृहीतयोः
[39] च । *om*
[40] प्रतिग्रहभूरेव । प्रतिग्रहभूमिरेव
[41] विधीयते । ऽभिधीयते
[42] चापरेण । चापरेण मुनिना । परेण
[43] निषिद्धत्वाच्च । निषेधाच्च
[44] **बृहस्पतिः** । **स्मृतिः**

सजातावाप्नुयात्सर्वमिति धर्मो व्यवस्थितः ।। [B 26.122]

<23> भूमिमात्रोपादानात्क्रयप्रसादादिनापि[45] द्विजातिलब्धभूमौ शूद्रस्यानधिकारः सिध्यति ।

<24> यस्तु शूद्र एवैकः पुत्रो ब्राह्मणस्य स तृतीयभागाधिकारी । भागद्वयं सपिण्डानाम् । तदभावे सकुल्यानाम् । तदभावे श्राद्धकर्तुः । यथा **देवलः** —

निषाद एकपुत्रस्तु[46] विप्रस्य स[47] तृतीयभाक् ।
द्वौ सपिण्डः सकुल्यो वा स्वधादाताथवा[48] हरेत् ।। [D 1594]

<25> ब्राह्मणेन शूद्रायां[49] जातो निषाद उच्यते[50] । सपिण्डसकुल्ययोस्तु भेदं वक्ष्यति ।

<26> क्षत्रियवैश्ययोस्तु यदि शूद्र एवैकः पुत्रस्तदा तद्धनस्यार्धहरः । अपरमर्धं वक्ष्यमाणापुत्रधनाधिकारक्रमेण गृह्णीयुः । तथा **विष्णुः** —

द्विजातीनां शूद्रस्त्वेकपुत्रोऽर्धहरः[51] । अपुत्ररिक्थस्य या गतिः
सार्धस्य द्वितीयस्य ।। [Vi 18.32-33]

<27> इदं च तृतीयभागाधिकारित्वमर्धहरत्वं[52] च विद्याविनयधर्मसंपन्नस्येति[53] वेदितव्यम् ।

यदाह[54] **मनुः** —

यद्यपि स्यात्तु सत्पुत्रो यद्यपुत्रोऽपि वा भवेत् ।
नाधिकं दशमाद्दद्यात् शूद्रापुत्राय धर्मतः ।। [M 9.154]

45 -प्रसादादिनापि । -प्रसादादिना
46 एकपुत्रस्तु । एकः पुत्रस्तु
47 विप्रस्य स । विप्रस्वस्य
48 स्वधादाताथवा हरेत् । स्वधादाता च संहरेत्
49 शूद्रायां । शूद्यां
50 निषाद उच्यते । निषादः
51 शूद्रस्त्वेकपुत्रो । शूद्रस्त्वेकः पुत्रो
52 -भागाधिकारित्व- । -भागहरत्व-
53 -धर्म- । *om*
54 यदाह । यस्मादाह

अनेन द्विजातिपुत्राभावेऽपि[55] दशमांशाधिकदाननिषेधात्[56] पूर्वस्योत्तमैक-शूद्रापुत्रगोचरत्वमेव ज्ञायते ।

यच्च **मनुना**[57] —

ब्राह्मणक्षत्रियविशां शूद्रापुत्रो न रिक्थभाक् ।
यदेवास्य पिता दद्यात्तदेवास्य धनं भवेत् ।। [M 9.155]

अनेन[58] रिक्थभागित्वमेव निषिद्धम् । तत्पितृप्रसादलब्धधनदशमांशत्वे सतीति विज्ञेयम् ।

<**28**> यच्चाह[59] **बृहस्पतिः** —

अनपत्यस्य शुश्रूषुर्गुणवान् शूद्रयोनिजः ।
लभेताजीवनं शेषं सपिण्डाः समवाप्नुयुः ।। [B 26.125]

वर्तनोचितकृष्याद्यर्थं किंचिद्दातव्यमित्यर्थः । निर्गुणस्यान्तेवासिविधिना वृत्तिमूलं भक्तादिकं पादशुश्रूषया देयम् ।

यच्चाह **मनुः** —

यं ब्राह्मणस्तु शूद्रायां कामादुत्पादयेत्सुतम् ।
स पारयन्नेव शवस्तस्मात्पारशवः स्मृतः ।। [M 9.178]

तदपरिणीतशूद्रासुताभिप्रायं परिणीतायाः सकृदृतावुपगमनस्य वैधत्वात् । तत्रैव च[60] गर्भस्थितेर्न द्वितीयादिसंपर्केष्वपि ।

यथा[61] **याज्ञवल्क्यः** —

अपुत्रे भ्रातरि मृते तां तु गच्छेदृतौ सकृत् ।। [Y ?]

तथा **मनुः** —

यथाविध्युपगम्यैनां शुक्लवस्त्रां शुचिव्रताम् ।
मिथो भजेदा प्रसवात् सकृत्सकृदृतावृतौ ।। [M 9.70]

[55] ऽपि । *om*
[56] -दान- । *om*
[57] यच्च **मनुना** । यन्**मनुना**
[58] अनेन । इत्यनेन । इति
[59] यच्चाह । यदाह
[60] च । *om*
[61] यथा । तथा

प्रथमोपगमनमात्रस्य गर्भहेतुत्वे सकृद्वचनं दृष्टार्थं स्यात् । अन्यथादृष्टार्थत्वमस्य कल्पनीयम् ।

अत एव लोकेऽपि प्रथमसंपर्कदिवसमादाय मङ्गलाचारार्थं नियतमासविहितपुंसवनसीमन्तोन्नयनाद्यार्थं मासगणना दृश्यते ।

अतः कामादुत्पादयेत्सुतमित्यपरिणीतशूद्राभिप्रायमेव[62] ।

<**29**> शूद्रस्य पुनरपरिणीतदास्यादिसूद्रापुत्रः पितुरनुमत्या पुत्रान्तरतुल्यांशहरः[63] । यथा[64] **मनुः** —

दास्यां वा दासदास्यां वा यः शूद्रस्य सुतो भवेत् ।
सोऽनुज्ञातो हरेदंशमिति धर्मो व्यवस्थितः ॥ [M 9.179]

<**30**> अनुमतिमन्तरेण त्वर्धांशहरः[65] । तदाह **याज्ञवल्क्यः** —

जातोऽपि दास्यां शूद्रेण कामतोंऽशहरो भवेत् । [Y 2.133cd]
मृते पितरि कुर्युस्तं भ्रातरस्त्वर्धभागिनम् ॥ [Y 2.134ab]

<**31**> परिणीतस्त्रीजातभ्रातृशून्यस्तु[66] सर्वमेव धनं गृह्णीयाद्यदि दौहित्रो नास्ति । तदाह **याज्ञवल्क्यः** —

अभ्रातृको हरेत्सर्वं दुहितॄणां सुतादृते ॥ [Y 2.134cd]

सति[67] दौहित्रे समं विभज्य गृह्णीयाद्विशेषाश्रवणात् । तथा ह्यपरिणीताजातत्वेऽप्यस्य पुत्रत्वादपरस्य तु[68] परिणीतासंतानत्वेऽपि[69] दौहित्रत्वात्तुल्यांशस्यैव युक्तत्वात् ।

[62] -परिणीत- । -नूढ-
[63] पुत्रान्तर- । भात्रन्तर-
[64] यथा । तदाह
[65] त्वर्धांशहरः । त्वर्धांशहरत्वम्
[66] परिणीतस्त्रीजातभ्रातृशून्यस्तु । अपरिणीतस्त्रीजातो भ्रातृशून्यस्तु
[67] सति । सति तु
[68] तु । *om*
[69] परिणीता- । परिणीत-

<**10.1**> संप्रति पुत्रिकाकरणानन्तरमौरसपुत्रे जाते तयोर्विभागः प्रतिपद्यते ।

<**2**> तत्र पुत्रिकौरसयोस्तुल्यांशित्वम् । न पुनः पुत्रिकाया ज्येष्ठत्वेन विंशोद्धारार्हता । तदाह **मनुः** —

पुत्रिकायां कृतायां तु यदि पुत्रोऽनुजायते ।
समस्तत्र विभागः स्याज्ज्येष्ठता नास्ति हि स्त्रियाः ।। [M 9.134]

स्वतो ज्येष्ठपुत्रकार्याकरणात्स्वपुत्रद्वारेण[1] पुत्रिकायाः पिण्डदातृत्वात् । तदाह **मनुः** —

अपुत्रोऽनेन विधिना सुतां कुर्वीत पुत्रिकाम् ।
यदपत्यं भवेदस्यां[2] तन्मम स्यात्स्वधाकरम् ।। [M 9.127]

<**3**> न च पुत्रिकायामेव प्रथमं पुत्रे जाते तदनन्तरमौरसपुत्रोत्पत्तौ पुत्रिकापुत्रस्य ज्येष्ठांशता भवेदिति[3] वाच्यं तस्य पौत्रत्वात् । तदाह **मनुः** —

अकृता वा कृता वापि यं विन्देत्सदृशात्सुतम् ।
पौत्री मातामहस्तेन दद्यात्पिण्डं[4] हरेद्धनम् ।। [M 9.136]

पुत्रिका हि पुत्रस्तस्याः[5] पुत्रः पौत्र एव भवति । तद्वांश्च पौत्री भवति । न च ज्येष्ठत्वेन पौत्रस्यांशातिरेकः श्रुतोऽस्ति ।

<**4**> यत्तु[6] **वशिष्ठ**वचनम् —

अभ्रातृकां प्रदास्यामि तुभ्यं कन्यामलंकृताम् ।
अस्यां यो जायते पुत्रः स मे पुत्रो भविष्यति[7] ।। [Va 17.17]

पुत्रिकापुत्रस्यैव पुत्रत्वं वदति । तेन पुत्रिकायास्तत्पुत्रस्य च पुत्रत्वम् ।

तन्न[8] **मनु**विरोधात् । पिण्डदानमात्रयोगात्पुत्रत्वमस्य गौणम् । तद्द्वारेणैव पुत्रिकायाः पिण्डदातृत्वादेकस्य स्वतोऽन्यस्य तद्योगात् ।

[1] -स्वपुत्रद्वारेण । -स्वपुत्रद्वारेण हि

[2] भवेदस्यां । भवेत्तस्यां

[3] भवेदिति । भवत्विति

[4] दद्यात्पिण्डं । पिण्डं दद्याद्

[5] पुत्रस्तस्याः । सुतस्तस्याः

[6] यत्तु । यच्च

[7] भविष्यति । भवेदिति

[8] तन्न **मनु**विरोधत् । तन्**मनु**विरोधात्

<**5**> पुत्रिकौरसयोश्च[9] सवर्णत्वे सति पूर्वोक्तविभागो बोद्धव्यः । असवर्णत्वे तु तयोरसवर्णैरौसपुत्रवदेव विभागः कार्यः[10] । पुत्रिकौरसयोः समानत्वात् ।

<**6**> यदि च[11] कृतापि पुत्रिका पुत्रमनुत्पाद्यैव विधवा भूता वन्ध्यात्वेन वावधृता तदा तस्याः पितृधनेऽनधिकारः । स्वधाकरपुत्रार्थं पुत्रिकायाः कृतत्वात् । तदभावे दुहित्रन्तरतुल्यत्वात् ।

<**7**> औरसेन तु[12] क्षेत्रजादीनां विभागे ये पितृसवर्णा औरसपुत्राच्चोत्तमवर्णाः[13] पुत्रिकापुत्रक्षेत्रजकानीनगूढजापविद्धसहोढपौनर्भवदत्तकस्वयमुपागतकतृकक्रीताः[14] पुत्रास्ते औरसपुत्रभागस्य तृतीयांशाधिकारिणः[15] । तदाह द्वादशपुत्रानभिधाय **देवलः** —

एते द्वादशपुत्रास्तु संतत्यर्थमुदाहृताः ।
आत्मजाः परजाश्चैव लब्धा यादृच्छिकास्तथा ।। [D 1582]
तेषां षड् बन्धुदायादाः पूव□न्ये पितुरेव षट् ।
विशेषश्चापि पुत्राणमानुपूर्व्या विशिष्यते[16] ।। [D 1583]
सव□ह्यनौरसस्यैते पुत्रा दायहराः स्मृताः ।
औरसे पुनरुत्पन्ने तेषां ज्यैष्ठ्यं न विद्यते[17] ।। [D 1584]
तेषां सवर्णा ये पुत्रास्ते तृतीयांशभागिनः ।
हीनास्तमुपजीवेयुर्ग्रासाच्छादनसंभृताः ।। [D 1585]

[9] पुत्रिकौरसयोश्च । पुत्रिकौरसयोस्तु । पुत्रिकौरसयोः
[10] कार्यः । *om*
[11] च । *om*
[12] तु । *om*
[13] औरसपुत्राच्चोत्तमवर्णाः । औरसपुत्राच्चोत्तमसमवर्णाः
[14] -दत्तक- । -दत्त-
[15] तृतीयांशाधिकारिणः । तृतीयांशभागिनः
[16] -नुपूर्व्या विशिष्यते । -नुपूर्वाद्विशिष्यते
[17] विद्यते । सिध्यति

<**8**> औरसादयः षट् न केवलं पितृदायहराः किंतु बन्धूनां सपिण्डादीनामपि[18] दायहराः । अपरे[19] परभूताः पितुरेव परं[20] दायहराः न सपिण्डादीनाम् ।

<**9**> औरसपुत्रशून्यस्य पितुः सर्वहराः । औरसे तु सति[21] तृतीयांशहराः[22] । <**10**> पुत्रिकाया अप्यौरसतुल्यत्वादयमेव भागक्रमः ।

<**11**> ये तु पितुर्हीनवर्णा औरसपुत्राच्चोत्तमवर्णास्ते औरसस्य पञ्चमं षष्ठं वांशं गुणवदगुणापेक्षया[23] गृह्णीयुः । यथा[24] **मनुः** —

षष्ठं तु क्षेत्रजस्यांशं प्रदद्यात्पैतृकाद्धनात् ।
औरसो विभजन् दायं पित्र्यं पञ्चममेव वा ।। [M 9.164]

<**12**> **देवल**वचने सर्वेषां क्षेत्रजतुल्यत्वाभिधानात्[25] **मनु**वचने क्षेत्रजपदमुपलक्षणम् ।

<**13**> ये तु पितुरौरसाच्च[26] भ्रातुर्हीनवर्णास्ते ग्रासाच्छादनमात्राधिकारिणः । तदाह **मनुः** —

एक एवौरसः पुत्रः पित्र्यस्य वसुनः प्रभुः ।
शेषाणामानृशंस्यार्थं प्रदद्यात्तु प्रजीवनम् ।। [M 9.163]

तथा **कात्यायनः** —

उत्पन्ने त्वौरसे पुत्रे तृतीयांशहराः स्मृताः ।
सवर्णा असवर्णास्तु[27] ग्रासाच्छादनभागिनः ।। [K 857]

<**14**> **मनु**वचने शेषपदं **कात्यायन**वचने चासवर्णपदं[28] हीनवर्णपरं **देवलेनै**कवाक्यत्वात्[29] ।

[18] बन्धूनां सपिण्डादीनामपि । बन्धूनामपि सपिण्डादीनां
[19] अपरे । अन्ये
[20] परं। *om*
[21] तु सति । सति तु
[22] तृतीयांशहराः । ये पितृसवर्णास्ते तृतीयांशहराः
[23] गुणवदगुणापेक्षया । गुणवदगुणतया
[24] यथा । तथा
[25] -तुल्यत्वाभिधानात् । -तुल्यत्वात्
[26] पितुरौरसाच्च । पितुरौरसपुत्राच्च
[27] सवर्णा असवर्णास्तु । सवर्णास्त्वसवर्णास्तु
[28] चासवर्णपदं । असवर्णपदं
[29] **देवलेनै**कवाक्यात् । **देवल**वचनेनैकवाक्यात्

<**15**> अनियोगोत्पन्नक्षेत्रजस्यौरसेन सह विभागमाह **मनुः** —

यद्येकरिक्थिनौ स्यातामौरसक्षेत्रजौ सुतौ ।
यद्यस्य पैतृकं रिक्थं तत्स गृह्णीत[30] नेतरः ॥ [M 9.162]

<**16**> यस्य बीजाद्यो जातः स तस्य धनं गृह्णीयात् । इतरोऽन्यबीजजो न गृह्णीयादित्यर्थः । अत एव **नारदः** —

द्वौ सुतौ विवदेयातां द्वाभ्यां जातौ स्त्रिया धने ।
तयोर्यद्यस्य पित्र्यं स्यात्तत्स गृह्णीत[31] नेतरः ॥ [N ? = M 9.191]

<**17**> यत्पितृदत्तं यद्धनं[32] स्त्रियास्तत्पुत्रस्तद्बीजजस्तद्धनं गृह्णीयान्नान्य इत्यस्तु किं विस्तरेण ।

[30] तत्स गृह्णीत । स तद् गृह्णीत
[31] स्यात्तत्स गृह्णीत । स्यात्स तद् गृह्णीत
[32] यद्धनं । धनं

<**11.1.1**> अथापुत्रस्य मृतस्य[1] धने परस्परविरुद्धवचनदर्शनाद्व्याख्यातारो[2] विवदन्ते ।

<**2**> तथा[3] **बृहस्पतिः** —

आम्नाये स्मृतितन्त्रे च लोकाचारे च सूरिभिः ।
शरीरार्धं स्मृता जाया पुण्यापुण्यफले समा ॥ [B 26.92]
यस्य नोपरता भार्या देहार्धं तस्य जीवति ।
जीवत्यर्धशरीरेऽर्थं कथमन्यः समाप्नुयात् ॥ [B 26.93]
सकुल्यैर्विद्यमानैस्तु पितृमातृसनाभिभिः ।
अपुत्रस्य[4] प्रमीतस्य पत्नी तद्भागहारिणी ॥ [B 26.94]
पूर्वप्रमीताग्निहोत्रं[5] मृते भर्तरि तद्धनम् ।
विन्देत्पतिव्रता नारी[6] धर्म एष सनातनः ॥ [B 26.95]
जङ्गमं स्थावरं हेम कुप्यं धान्यं रसाम्बरम्[7] ।
आदाय दापयेच्छ्राद्धं मासषान्मासिकादिकम् ॥ [B 26.96]
पितृव्यगुरुदौहित्रान् भर्तुः स्वस्रीयमातुलान् ।
पूजयेत्कव्यपूर्ताभ्यां वृद्धानथातिथीन् स्त्रियः ॥ [B 26.98]
तत्सपिण्डा बान्धवा वा ये तस्याः परिपन्थिनः ।
हिंस्युर्धनानि तान् राजा चौरदण्डेन शासयेत् ॥ [B 26.105]

<**3**> तदेतैः सप्तवचनैरपुत्रस्य[8] मृतस्य यद्यावद्धनं स्थावरजङ्गमहेमादिकं भर्तुस्तत्सर्वं सोदरभ्रातृपितृव्यदौहित्रादिषु सत्स्वपि[9] पत्न्या एवेति[10] । ये तु[11]

[1] मृतस्य । *om*
[2] -परस्पर- । परस्परं ॥ -दर्शनाद्व्याख्यातारो । -दर्शनेन व्याख्यातारो
[3] तथा । तथाच । तदाह
[4] अपुत्रस्य । असुतस्य
[5] पूर्व- । पूर्वं ॥ -प्रमीता- । प्रणीता-
[6] नारी । साध्वी
[7] रसाम्बरम् । रसादिकम्
[8] सप्तवचनैरपुत्रस्य । सप्तभिर्वचनैरपुत्रस्य
[9] -दौहित्रादिषु सत्स्वपि । दौहित्रादिसत्त्वेऽपि
[10] एवेति । एव
[11] तु । *om*

तद्धनग्रहणे प्रतिपक्षाः स्वयमेव वा गृह्णन्ति ते चौरवद्दण्डनीया इति ब्रुवाणो[12] **बृहस्पतिः** पत्नीसद्भावे पितृभ्रातृप्रभृतीनां धनाधिकारं सुदूरं निरस्यति ।

<**4**> तथाच[13] **याज्ञवल्क्यः** —

पत्नी दुहितरश्चैव पितरौ भ्रातरस्तथा ।
तत्सुतो गोत्रजो बन्धुः शिष्यः सब्रह्मचारिणः ॥ [Y 2.135]
एषामभावे पूर्वस्य धनभागुत्तरोत्तरः ।
स्वर्यातस्य ह्यपुत्रस्य सर्ववर्णेष्वयं विधिः ॥ [Y2.136]

अनेन पूर्वपूर्वस्याभावे परपरस्याधिकारं वदन् सर्वेभ्यः पूर्वं पत्न्या एव धनाधिकारमभिधत्ते ।

<**5**> तथा **विष्णुः** —

अपुत्रधनं[14] पत्न्यभिगामि । तदभावे दुहितृगामि । तदभावे पितृगामि । तदभावे मातृगामि । तदभावे भ्रातृगामि । तदभावे भ्रातृपुत्रगामि । तदभावे सकुल्यगामि । तदभावे बन्धुगामि । तदभावे शिष्यगामि । तदभावे सहाध्यायिगामि । तदभावे ब्राह्मणधनवर्जं राजगामि[15] ॥ [Vi 17. 4–13]

<**6**> अनेनापि क्रमपरेण[16] प्रथमं पत्न्या एव धनाधिकारो निरूपितः ।

न च वर्तनोपयुक्तधनमात्राधिकारार्थं पत्नीवचनं[17] वाच्यम् । सकृच्छ्रुतधनपदस्य[18] पत्न्यपेक्षमकृत्स्नपरत्वं कृत्स्नपरत्वं च भ्रात्राद्यपेक्षमिति तात्पर्यभेस्यान्याय्यत्वात् । अतः कृत्स्नधनगोचर एव पत्न्यधिकारो[19] वाच्यः ।

<**7**> तथा **वृद्धमनुः**[20] —

[12] ब्रुवाणो । वदन्
[13] तथाच । तथा
[14] अपुत्र- । अपुत्रस्य
[15] राजगामि । राजगामीति । राजा स्वामी
[16] क्रमपरेण । क्रमेण
[17] पत्नीवचनं । पत्नीवचनमिति
[18] सकृच्छ्रुत- । सकृच्छ्रुतस्य
[19] पत्न्यधिकारो । पत्न्या अधिकारो
[20] **वृद्धमनुः** । **बृहन्मनुः**

अपुत्रा शयनं भर्तुः पालयन्ती व्रते स्थिता ।
पत्न्येव दद्यात्तत्पिण्डं कृत्स्नमंशं लभेत च ।। [vM 92]

<**8**> तत्पिण्डमित्यतस्तदित्यनुषज्यते । तच्छब्देन भर्तुः परामर्शाद्भर्तुः[21] कृत्स्नमंशं पत्नी लभेत न तु स्वांशं[22] कृत्स्नमित्यर्थः । कृत्स्नस्वांशोद्देशेन लभेतेति विधानानुपपत्तेः स्वामिभावज्ञापनार्थत्वादस्य[23] । न च स्वांशे स्वामिभावज्ञापनमर्हति स्वांशज्ञापनेनैव ज्ञातत्वात् ।

<**9**> न च ग्रहणविधानार्थं तदिति वाच्यम् । स्वधनग्रहणस्य रागादेव प्राप्तत्वात् ।

<**10**> न च नियमार्थं वचनमिति[24] वाच्यम् । अदृष्टार्थत्वापत्तेः । नियमे च नियोज्यादिकल्पनमपि[25] स्यात् ।

<**11**> यच्चोक्तम् — न ह्यनन्धादिः पुत्रोंऽशं कृत्स्नं[26] लभेतेत्युक्ते पित्र्यं कृत्स्नमंशमिति किं तर्हि कृत्स्नं स्वांशमिति । तथात्रापि कृत्स्नं स्वांशापेक्षमिति ।

तन्न । अनन्धादिः पुत्रोंऽशं कृत्स्नं लभेतेति वचनाभावाद्दृष्टान्तानुपपत्तेः । भवतु वा । तथापि पूर्वोक्तहेतुना स्वांशं लभेतेति विध्यनुपपत्तेः पित्रंशापेक्षमेव वर्णनं युक्तम्[27] । <**12**> अत एव सर्वत्रान्यधन एवान्यसंबन्धज्ञापनं मुनयः कुर्वन्ति । यथा पितृधने पुत्राणामपुत्रधने पत्न्यादीनामित्यादि । न पुनः स्वांशग्रहणे प्रेरयन्ति ।

<**13**> यच्च संबन्धिशब्दत्वेन स्वसंबन्ध्युपस्थापकत्वम् । यथा मातेति न परमातावगम्यत[28] इत्युक्तम् ।

[21] परामर्शाद्भर्तुः । परामर्षाद्भर्तुः
[22] स्वांशं । स्वांश-
[23] -ज्ञापनार्थत्वादस्य । -ज्ञापनार्थत्वादस्य चवनस्य
[24] वचनमिति । वचनं
[25] -कल्पनमपि । -कल्पनमेव । कल्पनं
[26] पुत्रोंऽशं कृत्स्नं । पुत्रः कृत्स्नमंशं
[27] युक्तम् । कार्यम्
[28] परमातावगम्यत । परमातेत्यवगम्यत

तदप्ययुक्तम् । अनुपात्तसंबन्धिविषयत्वात्तस्य । न हि डित्थस्य मातरमानयेत्युक्ते प्रयोज्यस्य मातावगम्यते[29] प्रयोजकस्य वा । तद्वदत्रापि तत्पिण्डमिति तत्पदोपात्तत्वात्संबन्धिनः कथं पत्न्यपेक्षिता । विधानानुपपत्तिश्च पूर्वमुक्तैच ।

<14> तस्मात्कृत्स्नं[30] तदंशग्रहणमेव पत्न्या **वृद्धमनु**र्बोधयति ।

<15> तथा पत्न्यधिकारविपरीतानि[31] वचनानि । यथा **शङ्खलिखित-पैठीनसि-यमाः** —

> अपुत्रस्य स्वर्यातस्य भ्रातृगामि द्रव्यम् । तदभावे पितरौ लभेतां[32] पत्नी वा ज्येष्ठा सगोत्रशिष्यसब्रह्मचारिणः ।। [ŚL 293 = Pai 119]

<16> अत्र भ्रातुरभावे पित्रोस्तयोरभावे पत्न्यधिकार इति विरोधः ।

<17> तथा **देवलः** —

> ततो दायमपुत्रस्य विभजेरन्[33] सहोदराः ।
> तुल्या दुहितरो वापि ध्रियमाणः पितापि वा ।। [D 1570]
> सवर्णा भ्रातरो माता भार्या चेति यथाक्रमम् ।
> तेषामभावे[34] गृह्णीयुः कुल्यानां सहवासिनः ।। [D 1571]

<18> अत्र सर्वादौ भ्रातुरधिकारः सर्वशेषे च भार्याया इति विरोधः ।

<19> अत्र **केचिद**विभक्तसंसृष्टगोचरो भ्रात्रधिकारः प्रथमं विभक्तासंसृष्टगोचरश्च पत्न्यधिकार इति समादधति ।

<20> तद् **बृहस्पति**विरुद्धम् । यदाह —

> विभक्ता भ्रातरो ये च संप्रीत्यैकत्र संस्थिताः ।
> पुनर्विभागकरणे तेषां ज्यैष्ठ्यं न विद्यते ।। [B 26.106cdef]
> यदा कश्चित्प्रमीयेत प्रव्रजेद्वा कथंचन ।

[29] मातावगम्यते । माता प्रतीयते
[30] तस्मात्कृत्स्नं । तस्मात्कृत्स्न-
[31] -विपरीतानि । विपरीतबोधकानि
[32] लभेतां । हरेतां
[33] विभजेरन् । विभजेयुः
[34] तेषामभावे । एषामभावे

न लुप्यते तस्य भागः सोदरस्य[35] विधीयते ।। [B 26.107]
या तस्य भगिनी सा तु ततोऽशं लब्धुमर्हति ।
अनपत्यस्य धर्मोऽयमभार्यापितृकस्य च ।। [B 26.108]
संसृष्टानां तु यः कश्चिद्विद्याशौर्यादिना धनम् ।
प्राप्नोति तस्य दातव्यो द्व्यंशः शेषाः समांशिनः ।। [B 26.112]

<**21**> अत्रोप्रक्रमोपसंहारयोः संसृष्टत्वकीर्तनात्तत्संदंशपठितम् —

न लुप्यते तस्य भागः सोदरस्य विधीयते । [B 26.107cd]

इति वचनं संसृष्टविषयं वाच्यम् । तत्र[36] —

अनपत्यस्य धर्मोऽयमभार्यापितृकस्य च । [B 26.108cd]

इति पुत्रदुहितृपत्नीपितृणामभावे संसृष्टस्य[37] सोदरभ्रातुरधिकारं[38] बोधयतीति[39] कथं तस्य पत्नीबाधकत्वम् ।

<**22**> किंच न लुप्यत इति । अविभक्तत्वे संसृष्टत्वे च भ्रात्रन्तरीयद्रव्यमिश्रीभूतस्य[40] पृथगप्रतीतौ लोपाशङ्कायां न लुप्यत इति वचनमुपपद्यते। विभक्तस्यासंसृष्टस्य तु धने विभक्तत्वप्रतीतौ[41] का लोपाशङ्का ।

तस्मात्संसृष्टविषयत्वमेवामीषां वचनानाम् ।

<**23**> किंच पत्न्यादेः पूर्वं भ्रात्रधिकारज्ञापक**शङ्खादि**वचनानां संसृष्टभ्रातृविषयत्वं वचनाद्वा न्यायाद्वा । तत्र न तावद्वचनाद्विशेषवचनाभावात् । संसृष्टिनस्तु संसृष्टीत्यादिवचनानां तु भ्रात्रधिकारावसरे विशेषज्ञापनपरत्वेन भ्रात्रधिकारमात्रपरत्वानुपपत्तेः । <**24**> अनन्तरोपन्यस्त**बृहस्पति**वचनानां च[42] संसृष्टविषयत्वे[43] पुत्रदुहितृपत्नीपितृपर्यन्तराभावे सोदरभ्रात्रधिकारज्ञापकत्वात्तद्विरुद्धत्वादसंसृष्टविषयत्वमेव तावद्युक्तं न तु संसृष्टविषयत्वम् ।

[35] सोदरस्य । सोदर्यस्य
[36] तत्र । अत्र च
[37] संसृष्टस्य । संसृष्ट-
[38] सोदर- । सोदरस्य
[39] बोधयतीति । बोधयति
[40] -मिश्रीभूतस्य । -मिश्रीभूतस्य द्रव्यस्य
[41] विभक्तत्व- । विभक्त-
[42] च । तु
[43] -विषयत्वे । -विषये

<**25**> अथ न्यायादिदमभिधीयते । तथा हि संसृष्टत्वे यदेकस्य भ्रातुर्धनं तदपरस्यापि । तत्रैकस्य मरणेन स्वत्वनाशेऽपि जीवतस्तत्र स्वामित्वानपायात्तस्यैव तद्भवति न तु पत्न्या भर्तृमरणेन पत्नीस्वत्वस्यापि नाशात् । यथा सत्सु पुत्रादिषु न तद्धनं पत्न्या इति ।

<**26**> तन्मन्दम् । न हि संसृष्टत्वेऽपि यदेवैकस्य तदपरस्यापि । किंत्वविज्ञातैकदेशविषयम् । तद् द्वयोर्न तु समग्रमेव । समग्रस्वत्वकल्पनाप्रमाणाभावादित्युक्तमादावेव[44] । परिणयनोत्पन्नं भर्तृधने पत्न्याः स्वामित्वम् । भर्तृमरणान्नश्यतीत्यत्र च[45] प्रमाणाभावात् । सति तु पुत्रे तदधिकारशास्त्रादेव पत्नीस्वत्वनाशोऽवगम्यते ।

<**27**> अत्रापि संसृष्टभ्रात्रधिकारशास्त्रात्तद्विनाशोऽवगम्यत इति चेन्न[46] संसृष्टभ्रातृगोचरत्वस्याद्याप्यसिद्धेः[47] । सिद्धे हि भ्रातृसंसृष्टभर्तृमरणेन पत्नीस्वामित्वनाशे भ्रात्रधिकारशास्त्रस्य संसृष्टविषयत्वम् । सति च[48] तद्विषयत्वे शास्त्रस्य पत्नीस्वामित्वनाश इतीतरेतराश्रयत्वम्।

<**28**> किंच **शङ्खलिखितादि**वचनानामविभक्तसंसृष्टगोचरत्वेऽविभक्तस्य संसृष्टस्य च[49] धनं तद्विधभ्रातृगामि । तस्य तु तथाविधस्याभावे पितरौ हरेतामित्यन्वयो[50] वाच्यः ।

तदा च[51] विकल्पनीयम्। किं विभक्तासंसृष्टौ पितरौ गृह्णीयाताम् । उताविभक्तसंसृष्टौ ।

न तत्र[52] प्रथमः[53] कल्पः । पत्नी दुहितरश्चेत्यादिना विभक्तासंसृष्टयोः पित्रोः पत्नीबाध्यत्वात् कथं पत्नीतः पूर्वं तयोरधिकारः ।

[44] -स्वत्व- । -स्वामत्वि- ।। -कल्पना- । -कल्पनायां

[45] च । *om*

[46] चेन्न । चेत्तन्न

[47] -गोचरत्वस्याद्याप्यसिद्धेः । -गोचरत्वस्याप्यसिद्धेः

[48] च । तु । *om*

[49] च । *om*

[50] हरेताम- । लभेताम-

[51] तदा च । तथाच

[52] न तत्र । तत्र न

[53] प्रथमः । प्रथम-

नापि द्वितीयः । अविभक्तसंसृष्टभ्रातृसद्भावेऽप्यविभक्तसंसृष्टपितृग्राह्यत्वस्य सर्वेषामविवादात् ।

<**29**> किंच यथा पित्रा भ्रात्रा च विभक्तासंसृष्टधने शरीरदातृतया आत्मा वै जायते पुत्र इत्येकत्वश्रुतेर्धनशरीरयोश्च[54] प्रभुत्वात् तत्पितृदेयपितामहप्रपितामहपिण्डद्वये च सपिण्डनेन मृतस्य भोक्तृत्वाज्जीवति च पितरि पुत्राणां पार्वणपिण्डदानाभावात्[55] भ्रातृभ्यः पूर्वं पितुरधिकारः तथेतरत्रापि युक्तः ।

अविभागसंसर्गयोर्वाविशेषात्[56] पितृभ्रात्रोस्तुल्यवदधिकारो युक्तः । न तु भ्रातुरभावे पितुरिति युक्तम् ।

<**30**> किंचाविभक्तसंसृष्टौ[57] पितरौ गृह्णीयातामिति द्विवचनमनुपपन्नम् । मात्रा सह विभागाविभागयोरभावात् । अत एव संसर्गाभावोऽपि[58] । यदाह **बृहस्पतिः** —

विभक्तो यः पुनः पित्रा भ्रात्रा चैकत्र संस्थितः ।
पितृव्येणाथवा प्रीत्या स तु संसृष्ट उच्यते ।। [B 26.113]

अनेनैतद्दर्शयति — येषामेव हि पितृभ्रातृपितृव्यादीनां पितृपितामहार्जितद्रव्येणाविभक्तत्वमुत्पत्तितः संभवति त एव विभक्ताः सन्तः परस्परप्रीत्या यदि[59] पूर्वकृतविभागध्वंसेन यत्तव धनं तन्मम[60] यन्मम धनं तत्तवेति[61] एकगृह[62] एकगृहिरूपतया संस्थिताः संसृज्यन्ते ।

न पुनरनेवंरूपाणां द्रव्यसंसर्गमात्रेण संभूय[63] वणिजामपि संसर्गित्वम् । नापि विभक्तानां द्रव्यसंसर्गमात्रेण पूर्वोक्तप्रीतिपूर्वकाभिसंधानं विना ।

54 -श्रुतेर्धन- । -स्मृतेश्च धन-
55 -पिण्ड- । *om*
56 अविभागसंसर्गयोर्वाविशेषात् । अविभक्तसंसृष्टयोर्वाविशेषात्
57 -संसृष्टौ । -संसृष्ट-
58 संसर्गाभावो । धनसंसर्गाभावो
59 यदि । *om*
60 तन्मम । तन्मम धनं
61 तत्तवेति । तत्तवापीति
62 एकगृह । एकत्र गृह
63 संभूय । संभूयकारिणां

अतः संसर्गित्वाविभक्तत्वयोर्मात्रा सहासंभवात्[64] कथं मातृगतो भ्रातृसद्भावाधिकारविरोधः समाधेयः ।

<**31**> संप्रति[65] धीमद्भिः समाधीयते ।

तत्र **विष्ण्वादि**वचनेभ्यः पुत्राद्यभावमात्रेण पत्न्यधिकारः[66] स्पष्टमवगम्यते[67] । युक्तं चैतद्यन्मृतधनं पुत्रपौत्रप्रपौत्राणामेव प्रथमं[68] भवति ।

तथा हि **मनु-विष्णू** —

पुन्नाम्नो नरकाद्यस्मात्पितरं त्रायते सुतः ।
तस्मात्पुत्र इति प्रोक्तः स्वयमेव स्वयंभुवा ।। [M 9.138 = Vi 15.44]

तथा **हारीतः** —

पुन्नामा निरयः प्रोक्तश्छिन्नतन्तुश्च नैरयः ।
तत्र वै त्रायते यस्मात्तस्मात्पुत्र इति स्मृतः ।। [H 4.10]

तथा **शङ्खलिखितौ** —

पितॄणामनृणो जीवन् दृष्ट्वा पुत्रमुखं पिता ।
स्वर्गी स तेन जातेन[69] तस्मिन्संन्यस्य तदृणम् ।। [ŚL 285]
अग्निहोत्रं त्रयो वेदा यज्ञाश्च शतदक्षिणाः[70] ।
ज्येष्ठपुत्रप्रसूतस्य कलां नार्हन्ति षोडशीम् ।। [ŚL 284]

अत्र[71] **मनु-शङ्ख-विष्णु-वशिष्ठ-हारीताः**[72] —

पुत्रेण लोकान् जयति पौत्रेणानन्त्यमश्नुते ।
अथ पुत्रस्य पौत्रेण ब्रध्नस्याप्नोति पिष्टपम् ।। [M 9.137 = ŚL 283 = Vi 15.46 - Va 17.5 = H 4.14]

तथा **याज्ञवल्क्यः** —

64 सहासंभवात् । सहाभावात्
65 संप्रति । अत्र
66 पत्न्यधिकारः । पत्न्या अधिकारः
67 स्पष्टमवगम्यते । स्पष्टमेव गम्यते
68 प्रथमं । *om*
69 जातेन । पुत्रेण
70 यज्ञाश्च शतदक्षिणाः । यज्ञाश्चैव सदक्षिणाः
71 अत्र । अथ । तथा
72 **-शङ्ख-विष्णु-** । **-शङ्खलिखित-**

लोकानन्त्यं दिवः प्राप्तिः पुत्रपौत्रप्रपौत्रकैः ।। [Y 1.78ab]

<32> तदेवं पुत्रादिभिर्जन्मतः प्रभृति पितुः परलोकोचितमहोपकारनिष्पादनात् मृतस्य तस्य[73] पार्वणविधिना पिण्डदानात् पुत्राद्यर्थं तद्धनं मृतमेवोपकरोतीति न्यायप्राप्तं पुत्रादीनां स्वामित्वं श्रुतम् ।

तथोपकारकत्वेनैव[74] धनसंबन्धं **मनु**रप्याह[75] —

ज्येष्ठेन जातमात्रेण पुत्री भवति मानवः ।
पितॄणामनृणश्चैव स तस्माल्लब्धुमर्हति ।। [M 9.106]

<33> तस्मादिति हेतूपन्यासाद्दायभागप्रकरणे च पुत्रादीनां नानाविधपित्राद्युपकारकत्वकीर्तनस्यानन्यप्रयोजकत्वादुपकारत्वादेव[76] धनसंबन्धो **मनोर**नुमत इति गम्यते । **<34>** अत एव पुत्रपदं प्रपौत्रपर्यन्तपरं तत्पर्यन्तानामेव पार्वणविधिना पिण्डदानोपकारकत्वस्याविशेषात्[77] । **<35>** अन्यथा पुत्रपदस्य स्वार्थत्यागानुपपत्तेः पौत्राधिकारज्ञापकं[78] वचनं कथंचिद्यदि लभ्येतापि प्रपौत्रस्य न तु पृथग्वचनमस्ति । **<36>** तस्मादुपकारकत्वादेव प्रपौत्रस्याप्यधिकार[79] इति पुत्रपदमुपलक्षणम् ।

<37> अत एव **बौधायनः** —

प्रपितामहः पितामहः पिता स्वयं सोदर्या भ्रातरः सवर्णायाः पुत्रः पौत्रः प्रपौत्र एतानविभक्तदायादान् सपिण्डानाचक्षते । विभक्तदायादान् सकुल्यानाचक्षते । सत्स्वङ्गजेषु तद्गामी ह्यर्थो भवति । सपिण्डाभावे सकुल्यः । तदभावे चाचार्यो ऽन्तेवास्यृत्विग्वा हरेत् । तदभावे राजा ।। [Bau 1.5.11.9–14]

[73] तस्य । *om*
[74] -कारकत्वेनैव । -कारकत्वेन
[75] **मनु**रप्याह । **मनु**राह
[76] -पकारकत्वादेव । -पकारादेव
[77] -पकारकत्वस्या- । -पकारस्या-
[78] -ज्ञापकं । -ज्ञापनार्थं
[79] प्रपौत्रस्याप्यधिकार । प्रपौत्रस्याधिकार

<**38**> अस्यायमर्थः[80] — पित्रादित्रयपिण्डेषु[81] सपिण्डनेन भोक्तृत्वात् पुत्रादिभिस्त्रिभिस्तत्पिण्डस्यैव[82] दानात् यश्च जीवन् यत्पिण्डदाता स मृतः सन् सपिण्डनात्तत्पिण्डभोक्ता ।

एवं च[83] सति मध्यस्थितः पुरुषः पूर्वेषां जीवन् पिण्डदाता[84] मृतस्तत्पिण्डभोक्ता च[85] परेषां जीवतां पिण्डसंप्रदानभूत आसीत् । मृतैश्च तैः सह दौहित्रादिदेयपिण्डभोक्ता ।

अतो येषामयं पिण्डदाता ये वा तत्पिण्डदातारस्तेऽविभक्तं[86] पिण्डरूपं दायमश्नन्तीत्यविभक्तदायादाः[87] सपिण्डाः ।

पञ्चमस्य तु[88] पूर्वस्य मध्यमः पञ्चमो न पिण्डदाता । न च तत्पिण्डभोक्ता । एवमधस्तनोऽपि पञ्चमो न मध्यमस्य[89] पिण्डदाता नापि[90] तत्पिण्डभोक्ता । तेन[91] वृद्धप्रपितामहात्प्रभृति त्रयः[92] पूर्वपुरुषाः प्रतिप्रणप्तुश्च प्रभृत्यधस्तनास्त्रयः पुरुषा एकपिण्डभोक्तृत्वाभावाद्विभक्तदायादाः सकुल्या इत्याचक्षते ।

<**39**> इदं च[93] सपिण्डत्वं सकुल्यत्वं च दायग्रहणार्थमुक्तम् । <**40**> अत एव **मनुना**पि —

न भ्रातरो न पितरः पुत्रा रिक्थहराः पितुः । [M 9.185ab]

इत्यभिधाय कुत इत्यपेक्षायाम् —

[80] अस्यायमर्थः । अस्यार्थः
[81] पित्रादित्रयपिण्डेषु । पित्रादिपिण्डत्रयेषु
[82] पुत्रादिभिस्त्रि- । पुत्रादिभिश्च त्रि- ॥ -तत्पिण्डस्यैव । -तत्पिण्डस्य
[83] च । *om*
[84] पिण्डदाता । पिण्डदाता स
[85] च । *om*
[86] तत्पिण्ड- । तस्य पिण्ड- ॥ ऽविभक्तं । ऽविभक्त-
[87] दायमश्नन्ती- । दायमदन्ती-
[88] तु । *om*
[89] मध्यमस्य । मध्यमस्य पञ्चमस्य
[90] नापि । न च
[91] तेन । एतेन
[92] -प्रभृति त्रयः । -प्रभृतयः
[93] च । *om*

त्रयाणामुदकं कार्यं त्रिषु पिण्डः प्रवर्तते ।
चतुर्थः संप्रदातैषां पञ्चमो नोपपद्यते[94] ।। [M 9.186]

इत्युक्तम् ।

<**41**> अशौचाद्यर्थं तु पिण्डलेपभुजामपि तद्दत्तपिण्डलेपभोक्तृत्वेन सपिण्डत्वं ***मार्कण्डेयपुराणे*** निर्दिष्टम् । यथा —

पिण्डलेपभुजश्चान्ये पितामहपितामहात् ।
प्रभृत्युक्तास्त्रयस्तेषां यजमानश्च सप्तमः।
इत्यवं मुनिभिः प्रोक्तः संबन्धः साप्तपौरुषः ।। [Mpu 31.4–5ab]

अशौचकर इत्यर्थः । <**42**> अत एव **मनुना**प्युक्तमशौचप्रकरणे —

सपिण्डता तु पुरुषे सप्तमे विनिवर्तते ।
समानोदकभावस्तु जन्मनाम्नोरवेदने ।। [M 5.60]

अन्यथा त्रयाणामित्यनेन विरोधः स्यात्[95] ।

<**43**> प्रपौत्रपर्यन्ताभावे तु[96] वैधव्यात्प्रभृति व्रतादिना भर्तुः परलोक-हिताचरणेन पुत्रादिभ्यो जघन्येति तेषामभावे धनाधिकारिणी[97] पत्नी । तदाह **व्यासः** —

मृते भर्तरि साध्वी स्त्री ब्रह्मचर्यव्रते स्थिता[98] ।
स्नाता प्रतिदिनं दद्यात्स्वभर्त्रे सलिलाञ्जलीन्[99] ।। [Vy 241]
कुर्याच्चानुदिनं भक्त्या देवतानां च पूजनम् ।
विष्णोराराधनं चैव कुर्यान्नित्यमुपोषिता[100] ।। [Vy 242]
दानानि विप्रमुख्येभ्यो दद्यात्पुण्यविवृद्धये ।
उपवासांश्च विविधान् कुर्याच्छास्त्रोदितान् शुभे ।। [Vy 243]
लोकान्तरस्थं भर्तारमात्मानं च वरानने ।

[94] त्रिषु . . . नोपपद्यते । *om*
[95] विरोधः स्यात् । विरोधात्
[96] तु । *om*
[97] धनाधिकारिणी । धनहारिणी
[98] ब्रह्मचर्यव्रते स्थिता । ब्रह्मचर्ये व्यवस्थिता
[99] सलिलाञ्जलीन् । सतिलाञ्जलीन्
[100] -पोषिता । -पोषणम्

तारयत्युभयं नारी नित्यं[101] धर्मपरायणा ॥ [Vy 244]

<**44**> तदेवमादिभिर्वचनैः[102] पत्न्या अपि नरकनिस्तारकत्वश्रुतेः धनहीनतया वाकार्यं कुर्वती पुण्यापुण्यफलसमत्वेन[103] भर्तारमपि पातयतीति तदर्थं तद्धनं पूर्वस्वाम्यर्थमेव भवतीति युक्तं पत्न्याः स्वाम्यम्[104] ।

<**45**> अतः **शङ्खादि**वचनेषु व्यवहितयोजना[105] कार्या[106] । अपुत्रस्य स्वर्यातस्य धनं ज्येष्ठा पत्नी हरेत्[107] । तदभावे पितरौ हरेताम्[108]। तदभावे भ्रातृगामीति । तदभाव इति मध्यपठितं पूर्वेण भ्रातृगामीत्यनेन परेण च पितरौ हरेतामित्यनेन[109] संबध्यते अविरोधान्न्यायस्य चोक्तत्वात्[110] ।

<**46**> न त्वश्रुताविभक्तसंसृष्टगोचरत्वकल्पना । अतोऽविशेषेणैव विभक्तत्वाद्यनपेक्षयैवापुत्रस्य[111] भर्तुः कृत्स्नधने पत्न्यधिकारो **जितेन्द्रिय**निगदित[112] आदरणीयः ।

<**47**> पत्नीत्वं च प्रथममुत्तमवर्णायाः । ज्येष्ठा पत्नीत्यभिधानाद्वर्णक्रमेण[113] ज्येष्ठत्वात् । तदाह **मनुः** —

यदि स्वाश्च पराश्चैव विन्देरन् योषितो द्विजाः ।
तासां वर्णक्रमेणैव ज्यैष्ठ्यं पूजा च वेश्म च ॥ [M 9.85]

[101] नित्यं । नित्य-
[102] तदेव- । एव- ॥ -दिभिर्ववनैः । -दिवचनैः
[103] -समत्वेन । -संबन्धेन
[104] स्वाम्यम् । स्वत्वम्
[105] व्यवहित- । विपरीत-
[106] कार्या । कार्या यथा
[107] हरेत् । लभेत
[108] हरेताम् । लभेताम्
[109] हरेता- । लभेता-
[110] न्यायस्य चोक्तत्वात् । न्यायस्योक्तत्वात्
[111] -पेक्षयैवा- । -पेक्षमेवा-
[112] **जितेन्द्रिय**निगदित । **जितेन्द्रियो**क्त
[113] -क्रमेण । -क्रमेण च

अतः परिणयनकनिष्ठापि सवर्णा ज्येष्ठैव । तस्या एव[114] यज्ञादिषु व्यापाराधिकारात्पत्नीत्वम् । तथाच[115] **मनुः** —

भर्तुः शरीरशुश्रूषां धर्मकार्यं च नैत्यकम् ।
स्वा चैव[116] कुर्यात्सर्वेषां नान्यजातिः कथंचन ।। [M 9.86]
यस्तु तत्कारयेन्मोहात्स्वजात्या स्थितयान्यया ।
यथा ब्राह्मणचाण्डालः पूर्वदृष्टस्तथैव सः ।। [M 9.87]

सवर्णायाः पुनरभावेऽनन्तरवर्णा पत्नी । यथा[117] **विष्णुः** —

सवर्णाया अभावे[118] त्वनन्तरयैवापदि । न त्वेव[119] द्विजः शूद्रया ।। [Vi 26.3–4]

धर्मकार्यं कुर्यादित्यनुवर्तते ।

तेन ब्राह्मणस्य ब्राह्मणी पत्नी[120] तदभावे क्षत्रियाप्यापदि न तु परिणीतेऽपि वैश्याशूद्रे । क्षत्रियस्य क्षत्रिया पत्नी तदभावे वैश्याप्यनन्तरवर्णत्वान्न तु[121] शूद्रा । वैश्यस्य वैश्यैवैका[122] न त्वेव[123] द्विजः शूद्रयेति द्विजमात्रस्य[124] शूद्रानिषेधात् ।

<**48**> अननैव पत्नीभावक्रमेणैव[125] धनाधिकारिता बोद्धव्या । अतः परिणीतस्त्रीणामप्यपत्नीत्वात्तदभिप्रायेण[126] **नारद**वचनम् —

भ्रातृणामप्रजः प्रेयात् कश्चिच्चेत्प्रव्रजेद्यदि[127] ।

114 एव । एव च
115 तथाच । तथा
116 चैव । स्वैव
117 यथा । तथा । तथाच
118 सवर्णाया अभावे । सवर्णाभावे
119 त्वेव । त्वेवं
120 ब्राह्मणस्य पत्नी । पत्नी ब्राह्मणस्य
121 तु । *om*
122 वैश्यैवैका । वैश्या चैका
123 त्वेव । त्वेवं
124 द्विजमात्रस्य । द्विजमात्रस्यैव
125 -क्रमेणैव । -क्रमेण
126 -भिप्रायेण । -भिप्रायकमेव । -भिप्रायमेव
127 -प्रव्रजेद्यदि । -प्रव्रजेत वा

विभजेरन् धनं तस्य शेषास्ते स्त्रीधनं विना ।। [N 13.25/24]
भरणं चास्य कुर्वीरन् स्त्रीणामा जीवितक्षयात्[128] ।
रक्षन्ति शय्यां भर्तुश्चेदाच्छिन्द्युरितरासु च ।। [N 13.26/25]

तथा तस्यैव —

अन्यत्र ब्राह्मणात् किंतु राजा धर्मपरायणः ।
तत्स्त्रीणां जविनं दद्यादेष दायविधिः स्मृतः ।। [N 13.52/49]

तदीयस्त्रीणामपत्नीनां वर्तनधनदानं[129] पत्नीनां पुनः कृत्स्नधनाधिकारितेत्यविरोधः[130] । <49> अत एव **बृहस्पतिः** —

येऽपुत्राः क्षत्रविट्शूद्राः पत्नीभ्रातृविवर्जिताः ।
तेषां धनं हरेद्राजा सर्वस्याधिपतिर्हि सः ।। [B 26.119]

पत्न्यभावे राज्ञो धनसंबन्धं दर्शयति । **नारदस्**तु तत्स्त्रीणां जीवनं दद्यादिति वर्तनधनं दत्त्वा राज्ञा सर्वधनं ग्रहीतव्यमिति यो विरोधः स पत्नीस्त्रियोर्भेदेन समाधेयः ।

अत एव पत्न्यधिकारवचनेषु पत्नीपदानुस्मृतिः । वर्तनवचनेषु च[131] स्त्रीनारीभार्यादिशब्दप्रयोगः ।

<50> यदपि **देवल**वचनम् —

ततो दायमपुत्रस्य विभजेरन् सहोदराः ।
तुल्या दुहितरो वापि ध्रियमानः पितापि वा ।। [D 1570]
सवर्णा भ्रातरो माता भार्या चेति यथाक्रमम् ।
तेषामभावे[132] गृह्णीयुः कुल्यानां सहवासिनः ।। [D 1571]

तुल्याः सवर्णा दुहितरः । सवर्णा भ्रातरः सापत्न्या[133] अभिमताः। सहोदराणां[134] स्वपदोपात्तत्वाद्विशेषणानुपपत्तेः[135] ।

[128] जीवित- । -जीवन-
[129] वर्तनधनदानं । वर्तनदानं । वर्तनाय देयं धनं
[130] कृत्स्नधनाधिकारि- । कृत्स्नधनेऽधिकारि-
[131] च । *om*
[132] तेषामभावे । एषामभावे
[133] सपत्न्या । सापत्ना
[134] सहोदराणां । सोदरभ्रातॄणां
[135] स्वपदोपात्त- । स्वपदेनैव निर्दिष्ट-

तत्रापि सहोदरादिभार्यान्तस्य लिखनक्रमो नाधिकारक्रमार्थः **विष्ण्वादि-विरोधात्** । किंतु **विष्ण्वाद्युक्त**क्रमेण गृह्णीयुरित्येतदर्थः । लिखनक्रमेऽनास्थाव्यञ्जनार्थमेव[136] दुहितरो वापि पितापि वेत्यपि वाशब्दमुभयत्र प्रयुक्तवान् । तच्चान्यत्राप्यनुषज्यते । तेन सहोदरा वा दुहितरो वा पिता वेत्यनास्था कीर्तनक्रमस्य **देवलेन**[137] दर्शिता ।

<51> यच्च **बालोकेनो**क्तम्[138] — असवर्णाविषयं वा युवत्यभिप्रायं वाविभक्तसंसृष्टविषयं वा **शङ्खादि**वचनमिति तेनाव्यवस्थितशास्त्रार्थकथने-नात्मनो बालरूपत्वमेव[139] प्रकटीकृतम्[140] । संदेहादेकतरानुष्ठानानुपपत्तेः ।

<52> यदप्यनूढावारुद्धाभिप्रायं वर्तनवचनं वर्णितं तदपि धर्मपत्नी-नामनुग्रहार्थमिति हेयमेव । वर्तनविधानविषयस्य[141] स्त्रीणां पूर्वमेव दर्शित-त्वात् ।

<53> किंच सवर्णत्वासवर्णत्वाभ्यां[142] पत्नीगतविशेषेऽपि[143] पित्रोर्भ्रातॄणां चाधिकारे विरोधः कथं[144] समाधेयः । संसर्गासंसर्गाभ्यां चेत्स एव विशेषः सर्वव्यापी भवतु । किं पत्नीगोचरसवर्णादिविशेषपरिकल्पनेनायमपि[145] विशेषो दूषितोऽस्माभिः पूर्वप्रपञ्चेन ।

<54> सोदरासोदरकृतश्च विशेषो **बृहस्पतिना**[146] पराहतः । तदाह —

सकुल्यैर्विद्यमानैस्तु पितृमातृसनाभिभिः ।
अपुत्रस्य[147] प्रमीतस्य पत्नी तद्भागहारिणी ।। [B 26.94]

[136] -क्रमेऽनास्था- । -क्रमानास्था-

[137] **देवलेन** । **देवल**वचनेन

[138] **बालोकेन**- । **बालकेन**- ।। -**नो**क्ततम् । -**ना**भिहितम्

[139] बालरूपत्वमेव । बालत्वमेव

[140] प्रकटीृतम् । प्रकटिकृतम्

[141] -विषयस्य । -विषय-

[142] सवर्णत्वासवर्णत्वाभ्यां । सवर्णासवर्णत्वाभ्यां

[143] -गत- । -कृत-

[144] विरोधः कथं । कथं विरोधः

[145] -परिकल्पनेना- । -कल्पनेना-

[146] **बृहस्पतिना** । **बृहस्पति**-

[147] अपुत्रस्य । असुतस्य

सनाभयः सोदराः[148] । तेषु सत्स्वपि पत्न्या धनसंबन्धं बोधयति । तद्भाग-शब्दाच्च कृत्स्न एव भर्तृभागोऽवगम्यते न पुनस्तदेकदेशः ।

<**55**> तस्मादस्मद्दर्शितैव व्यवस्था शास्त्रार्थः[149] ।

<**56**> पत्नी च भर्तृधनं भुञ्जीतैव परं न तु तस्य दानाधानविक्रयान् कर्तुमर्हति ।

तदाह **कात्यायनः** —

अपुत्रा शयनं भर्तुः पालयन्ती गुरौ स्थिता ।
भुञ्जीता मरणात् क्षान्ता दायादा ऊर्ध्वमाप्नुयुः ।। [K 921]

<**57**> गुरौ श्वशुरादौ भर्तृकुले[150] स्थिता यावज्जीवं भर्तृधनं[151] भुञ्जीत[152] । न तु स्त्रीधवत्स्वच्छन्दं दानाधानविक्रयानपि कुर्वीत ।

तस्यां तु मृतायां पत्नयभावे ये[153] दुहित्रादयो दायाधिकारिणस्ते[154] गृह्णीयुः ।

न पुनर्ज्ञातयः । तेषां दुहित्रादिभ्यो जघन्यत्वात्तद्बाधकत्वानुपपत्तेः । पत्नी हि तेषां बाधिका । तदधिकारस्य प्रागभावे प्रध्वंसे च बाधका-भावस्याविशेषाद्बाधानुपपत्तेः ।

<**58**> नापि स्त्रीधनाधिकारिणो गृह्णीयुः । तेषां स्त्रीधनविषयत्वात् । **कात्यायनेनै**व च स्त्रीधनाधिकारिणां वचनान्तरैरुक्तत्वात्पुनरुक्तत्वापत्तेः[155] ।

<**59**> अतः पत्नी दुहितरश्चेत्यादिना ये पूर्वपूर्वस्याभावे[156] परभूता-धिकारिणो निर्दिष्टास्ते यथा पत्न्यधिकारप्रागभावे गृह्णीयुस्तथा जाताधिका-रायाः पत्न्या[157] अधिकारप्रध्वंसेऽपि भोगावशिष्टं[158] गृह्णीयुः ।

[148] सोदराः । सहोदराः
[149] शास्त्रार्थः । शास्त्रार्थस्य
[150] -कुले । -गृहे
[151] भर्तृधनं । *om*
[152] भुञ्जीत । भुञ्जीतैव
[153] ये । *om*
[154] दायाधि- । ऽधि-
[155] -पत्तेः । -पत्तेश्च
[156] पूर्वपूर्व- । पूर्व-
[157] जाताधिकारायाः पत्न्या । पत्न्या जाताधिकाराया
[158] भोगावशिष्टं । भोगावशिष्टं धनं

तदानी दुहित्रादीनामेवान्यपेक्षया मृतोपकारकत्वाद्युक्तो धनाधिकारः[159] ।

<**60**> तथा ***दानधर्मे***[160] —

स्त्रीनां स्वपतिदायस्तु[161] उपभोगफलः स्मृतः ।
नापहारं स्त्रियः कुर्युः पतिदायात्कथंचन[162] ।। [Mbh 13.47.24]

<**61**> उपभोगेऽपि[163] न सूक्ष्मवस्त्रपरिधानादिना किंतु स्वशरीरधारणेन पत्युरुपकारकत्वाद्देहधारणोचितोपभोगानुज्ञानम्[164] । एवं च पत्युरौर्ध्वदेहिकक्रियाद्यर्थं[165] दानादिकमप्यनुमतम् । अत एव नापहारं स्त्रियः कुर्युरित्याह[166] । अपहारश्च धनस्वाम्यनुपयोगे भवति । <**62**> अत एव वर्तनाशक्तावाधानमप्यनुमतम् । तत्राप्यशक्तौ विक्रयणमपि न्यायस्याविशेषात् ।

<**63**> भर्तुरौर्ध्वदेहिकक्रियार्थमर्थानुरूपं भर्तृपितृव्यादिभ्यो दद्यात् । तदाह **बृहस्पतिः** —

पितृव्यगुरुदौहित्रान् भर्तुः स्वस्रीयमातुलान् ।
पूजयेत्कव्यपूर्ताभ्यां वृद्धानथातिथीन् स्त्रियः ।। [B 26.98}

पितृव्यपदं भर्तृसपिण्डपरम्[167] । दौहित्रपदं भर्तृदुहितृसंतानपरम्[168] । स्वस्रीयपदं भर्तुः स्वस्रीयसंतानपरम्[169] । मातुलपदं च भर्तृमातृकुलपरम् । तदेवमादिभ्यो दद्यात् । न पुनरेतेषु सत्स्वेव स्वपितृकुलेभ्यो दद्यात्[170] पितृव्यादिवचनानर्थक्यात् । <**64**> तदनुमत्या तु स्वपितृमातृकुलेभ्योऽपि[171] दद्यात् । तदाह **नारदः** —

[159] -कारकत्वाद्युक्तो धनाधिकारः । -कारकत्वाद्धनाधिकारो युक्तः
[160] ***दानधर्मे*** । ***महाभारते दानधर्मे***
[161] -दायस्तु । -दायश्च
[162] -दायात्कथंचन । -वित्तात्कथंचन
[163] ऽपि । *om*
[164] -भोगानुज्ञनम् । -भोगाभ्यनुज्ञानम्
[165] पत्युरौर्ध्वदेहिक- । भर्तुरौर्ध्वदेहिक-
[166] कुर्युरित्याह । कुर्युरित्युक्तम् । कुर्युरित्यपहारवचनम्
[167] भर्तृ- । भर्तुः
[168] भर्तृदुहितृ- । भर्तुर्दुहितृ-
[169] स्वस्रीय- । स्वसृ-
[170] स्वपितृकुलेभ्यो दद्यात् । स्वपितृकुलेभ्यः प्रदद्यात्
[171] ऽपि । *om*

मृते भर्तर्यपुत्रायाः पतिपक्षः प्रभुः स्त्रियाः ।
विनियोगार्थरक्षासु भरणे च स ईश्वरः ॥ [N 13.28/27]
परिक्षीणे पतिकुले निर्मनुष्ये निराश्रये ।
तत्सपिण्डेषु चासत्सु पितृपक्षः प्रभुः स्त्रियाः ॥ [N 13.29/28]

विनियोगे दानादौ । पतिपुत्राभावे भर्तृकुलपरतन्त्रता तस्याः ।

<65> एवं च दुहितुरप्यधिकारे जाते तस्यां मृतायां तदभावोक्ताः पितृधनाधिकारिणो गृह्णीयुः । न तु दुहितृधनाधिकारिणः ।

<66> पत्न्या च भर्तृधनात्कन्यायै विवाहार्थं तुरीयांशो देयः । पुत्राणामेव तद्दानप्रतिपादनाद्दण्डापूपायितं पत्न्यादीनां दानम् ।

<67> इति पत्न्यधिकारः ।

<**11.2.1**> पत्न्यभावे दुहितुरधिकारः ।

तत्र **मनु-नारदौ** —

यथैवात्मा तथा पुत्रः पुत्रेण दुहिता समा ।
तस्यामात्मनि जीवन्त्यां कथमन्यो हरेद्धनम् ॥ [M 9.130 = N ?]

दुहितरं विशिनष्टि **नारदः** —

पुत्राभावे तु[1] दुहिता तुल्यसंतानदर्शनात् ।
पुत्रश्च दुहिता चोभे पितुः[2] संतानकारिके ॥ [N 13.50/47]

दुहितुरधिकारे संतानदर्शनं[3] हेतुतया निगदितम्[4] । संतानश्च[5] पिण्डदोऽभिमतः । अपिण्डदस्यानुपकारकत्वेनान्यसंतानादसंतानाच्चाविशेषात् ।

<**2**> दौहित्रश्च तत्पिण्डदाता न च[6] तत्पुत्रो नापि दौहित्री । तत्पर्यन्तेन पिण्डविच्छेदात् । <**3**> अतः पुत्रवती संभावितपुत्रा चाधिकारिणी । विधवात्ववन्ध्यात्वदुहितृप्रसूत्वादिना[7] विपर्यस्तपुत्रा पुनरनधिकारिण्येवेति **दीक्षित**मतमादरणीयम् ।

<**4**> तत्र प्रथमं कन्यैवैका पितृधनहारिणी[8] ।

यथा[9] **पराशरः** —

अपुत्रस्य मृतस्य कुमारी रिक्थं गृह्णीयात्तदभावे चोढा ॥
Dhko p. 1527]

ऊढापदं पूर्वोक्तविशेषपरम् ।

<**5**> तथा **देवलः** —

[1] तु । च
[2] पितुः । तुल्य-
[3] -दर्शनं । -कारकत्वं
[4] निगदितम् । निर्दिशति
[5] समानश्च । समानः
[6] च । *om*
[7] विधवात्व- । वैधव्य- ॥ विधवात्ववन्ध्यात्वदुहितृप्रसूत्वादिना । विधवावन्ध्यादुहितृप्रसूत्यादिना
[8] -धनहारिणी । -धनाधिकारिणी
[9] यथा । तथा

कन्याभ्यश्च पितृद्रव्याद्देयं[10] वैवाहिकं वसु ।
अपुत्रिकस्य कन्या स्वा धर्मजा पुत्रवद्धरेत्[11] ।। [D 1598]

पुत्रिकापदं पुत्रोपलक्षणम् । स्वा सवर्णा[12] । धर्मजा औरसी ।

<**6**> युक्तं चैतत् । धनमन्तरेणापरिणीतायाः कन्याया ऋतुदर्शने पित्रादीनां नरकपातश्रुतेः[13] ।

तदाह **वशिष्ठः**[14] —

यावत्तु कन्यामृतवः स्पृशन्ति
तुल्यैः सकामामपि याच्यमानाम् ।
तावन्ति भूतानि हतानि ताभ्यां
मातापितृभ्यामिति धर्मवादः ।। [Va 17.71]

तथा **पैठीनसिः** —

यावन्नोद्भिद्येते स्तनौ तावदेव देया । अथर्तुमती भवति तदा दाता प्रतिग्रहीता च नरकमाप्नोति[15] । पितृपितामहप्रपितामहाश्च विष्ठायां जायन्ते । तस्मान्नग्निका दातव्या ।। [Pai 11]

<**7**> तस्माद्विवाहोपयुक्तत्वेन[16] पित्रादीनां नरकनिस्तारात्[17] परिणीतायाश्च पुत्रद्वारेणाप्युपकारकत्वात् तदर्थं धनं स्वाम्यर्थमेव भवतीति पत्न्यभावे न्याय्यं कन्यास्वत्वम् ।

<**8**> कन्यायास्त्वभावे[18] संभावितपुत्रायाः पुत्रवत्याश्चाधिकारः । तदाह **बृहस्पतिः** —

सदृशी सदृशेनोढा साध्वी[19] शुश्रूषणे रता ।

[10] पितृद्रव्याद्देयं । पितुर्द्रव्याद्देयं
[11] पुत्रवद्धरेत् । पुत्रवद्भवेत्
[12] सवर्णा । सवर्णजा
[13] -पात- । -पतन-
[14] **वशिष्ठः** । **विष्णुः**
[15] नरकमाप्नोति । नरकं प्राप्नोति
[16] तस्माद्विवाहो- । अतस्तद्विवाहो-
[17] -निस्तारात् । -निस्तारकत्वात्
[18] कन्यायास्त्वभावे । कन्यायास्त्वसंभवे
[19] साध्वी । भर्तृ-

कृताकृता वापुत्रस्य पितुर्धनहरी तु सा ।। [B 26.132]

<9> सदृशी पितृसवर्णा । सदृशेनोढेत्युत्तमाधमवर्णपरिणयननिरासार्थम् । उत्तमाधमपरिणीतदुहितृजातस्याधमोत्तमवर्णमातामहादिश्राद्धनिषेधात्[20] । सवर्णेनोढायास्तु पुत्रद्वारेण पित्रुपकारकत्वात् ।

<10> पुत्रिकापुत्रस्य तु पुत्रवदेवोपकारकत्वातिशयात्तद्द्वारेण[21] पुत्रिकायाः पुत्रतुल्यत्वात् पुत्रिकौरसयोः समो धनाधिकारः । अपुत्रिकायास्तूढायाः पुत्रादिन्यूनोपकारकस्वपुत्रद्वारेणोपकारकत्वमिति कन्यापर्यन्तानामभाव एव धनाधिकारिता युक्ता ।

<11> न च वाच्यम् — एवं तर्हि पुत्रवत्या एव प्रथमाधिकारोऽस्तु[22] । तदभावे तु संभावितपुत्राया इति ।

यतस्तस्याः पश्चादुत्पन्नस्य दौहित्रस्यानधिकारापत्तेः । न च तद्युक्तं दौहित्रतया द्वयोरप्युपकाराविशेषात्[23] । **<12>** भर्तृशुश्रूषापरत्वेनावैधव्यं प्रदर्शयन्[24] संभावितपुत्रतां दर्शयति[25] ।

<13> सेति च पूर्ववचनोपात्ता दुहिता परामृश्यते । तदेवं सदृशी सदृशेनोढा इत्यादिविशेषणान्न दुहितृमात्रतया पितृधनाधिकारितेति[26] दर्शयति । **<14>** अन्यथा[27] —

अङ्गादङ्गात्संभवति पुत्रवद्दुहिता नृणाम् ।
तस्याः पितधनं त्वन्यः कथं गृह्णीत मानवः ।। [B 26.127]

इत्यनेन[28] दुहित्रधिकारे कथिते सदृशी सदृशेनोढेत्यादिना तस्यैवाभिधानं पुनरुक्तं स्यात् । सामान्यप्राप्तेस्तु विशेषकथनमपुनरुक्तमेव ।

[20] उत्तमाधमपरिणीत- । उत्तमाधमवर्णपरिणीत-
[21] -तिशयात्तद्द्वारेण । -तिशयेन
[22] प्रथमाधिकारो । प्रथममधिकारो
[23] द्वयोरप्युपकाराविशेषात् । द्वयोरप्युपकारत्वाविशेषात् । द्वयोरप्युपकारकत्वाविशेषात्
[24] प्रदर्शयन् । दर्शयन्
[25] दर्शयति । प्रदर्शयति
[26] -कारितेति । -कार इति
[27] अन्यथा । *om*
[28] इत्यनेन । इत्यनेनैव

<**15**> यत एव स्वपुत्रद्वारेण पिण्डदातृतया दुहितुः पितृधनाधिकारोऽत एव पुत्रिकाया अपि पित्रुपरमजातधनसंबन्धायाः[29] पश्चाद्वन्ध्यात्वेन तद्भर्तुर्वा[30] प्रसवासामर्थ्येन विपर्यस्तपुत्राया मरणे तद्धनं न भर्तुः ।

यथा **शङ्खलिखितौ** —

प्रेतायाः पुत्रिकायास्तु[31] न भर्ता द्रव्यमर्हत्यपुत्रायाः ॥ [ŚL 295]

तथा **पैठीनसिः** —

प्रेतायां पुत्रिकायां तु न भर्ता द्रव्यमर्हति[32] ।
अपुत्रायां कुमार्यां वा स्वस्रा ग्राह्यं तदन्यया ॥ [Pai 120]

ततः कुमार्या स्वस्रान्यया[33] वा पुत्रवत्या[34] संभावितपुत्रया स्वस्रा तद्धनं ग्राह्यम् । अतः स्त्र्यधिकारे व्यावृत्तिरन्याधिकारस्य ।

<**16**> यत्तु **मनु**वचनम् —

अपुत्रायां मृतायां तु पुत्रिकायां कथंचन ।
धनं तत्पुत्रिकाभर्ता हरेतैवाविचारयन् ॥ [M 9.135]

तदविपर्यस्तपुत्राया उत्पन्नमृतपुत्रायाः पुत्रिकाया[35] मरणे वेदितव्यम् ।

<**17**> पिण्डदानमेव च द्वयोरेकं[36] निमित्तमनुवदति[37] **बृहस्पतिः** —

यथा पितृधने स्वाम्यं तस्याः सत्स्वपि बन्धुषु ।
तथैव तत्सुतोऽपीष्टे मातृमातामहे धने ॥ [B 26.133]

यथा येन दौहित्रदेयपिण्डेन दुहिता पितृधनाधिकारिणी तथैव तेनैव पिण्डदानेन दुहितृसुतोऽपि मातामहधने स्वामी[38] सत्स्वपि पित्रादिषु ।

<**18**> न च पुत्रिकापुत्राभिप्रायेणेदं वचनम् ।

[29] -धनसंबन्धायाः । -धनाधिकारायाः
[30] तद्भर्तुर्वा । भर्तुर्वा
[31] पुत्रिकायास्तु । पुत्रिकाया
[32] द्रव्यमर्हति । धनमर्हति
[33] कुमार्या स्वस्रान्यया । कुमार्यान्यया
[34] स्वस्रान्यया वा पुत्रवत्या । अन्यया वा
[35] -पुत्रायाः पुत्रिकाया । -पुत्राया
[36] द्वयोरेकं । द्वयोरेक-
[37] निमित्तमनुवदति । निमित्तं वदति
[38] स्वामी । ऽधिकारी

कृताकृता वापुत्रस्य पितुर्धनहरी तु सा ।। [B 26.132cd]

एतद्वचनोपात्तकृताकृतदुहित्रोरेव[39] तस्या इति तत्सुत इति च[40] तत्पदेन परामर्शात्[41] । प्रत्यासत्त्यतिरेकाद्वा अकृतापरामर्श[42] एव युक्तो न तु[43] तत्परित्यागः ।

<**19**> अत एव **मनुः** —

दौहित्रो ह्यखिलं रिक्थमपुत्रस्य पितुर्हरेत्[44]।
स एव दद्याद् द्वौ पिण्डौ पित्रे मातामहाय च ।। [M 9.132]
पौत्रदौहित्रयोर्लोके विशेषो नास्ति धर्मतः ।
तयोर्हि मातापितरौ संभूतौ तस्य देहतः ।। [M 9.133]

मातामहदेहाद्दुहितुः संभवं दौहित्रस्य धनाधिकारे हेतुत्वेन निर्दिशति । न तु[45] पुत्रिकाकरणम् । इतरथा तदेव निर्दिशेत् ।

<**20**> तथा व्यक्तमाह स एव —

अकृता वा कृता वापि यं विन्देत्सदृशात्सुतम् ।
पौत्री मातामहस्तेन दद्यात्पिण्डं हरेद्धनम् ।। [M 9.136]

अकृताजातस्यापि दौहित्रस्याधिकारमभिदधाति[46] ।

<**21**> किंच स्मृतिषु दौहित्रपदमकृतपुत्रिकाजातपरं नियतम् । तथा[47] **बौधायनः** —

अभ्युपगम्य दुहितरि जातं पुत्रिकापुत्रमन्यं दौहित्रम् ।। [Bau 2.2.3.15]

विद्यादित्यनुवर्तते ।

<**22**> अत एव **भोजदेवे**नापि कृताकृतदुहित्रधिकारे **बृहस्पति**रित्यभिधाय यथा पितृधने स्वाम्यमिति वचनं लिखितम् ।

[39] -कृताकृत- । -कृताकृता-
[40] च । *om*
[41] परामर्शात् । परामर्षात्
[42] -परामर्श । -परामर्ष
[43] तु । *om*
[44] पितुर्हरेत् । हरेतपितुः
[45] तु । *om*
[46] -धिकारमभिदधाति । -धिकारं निर्दिशति । -धिकारं वदति
[47] तथा । यथा

<23> तथा[48] **गोविन्दराजेना**पि ***मनुटीकायाम्*** —

अपुत्रपौत्रे संसारे दौहित्रा धनमाप्नुयुः ।
पूर्वेषां हि[49] स्वधाकारे पौत्रदौहित्रका: समाः ।। [*Dhko* p. 1471]

एत**द्विष्णु**वचनबलेन[50] ऊढातः प्रागेव दौहित्रस्याधिकारो दर्शितः ।

<24> स चास्मभ्यं न रोचते सदृशी सदृशेनोढेत्यादिविरोधात्[51] । **<25>** किंतूढायाः पूर्वोक्तरूपाया[52] अभाव एव सत्स्वपि पित्रादिषु दौहित्रस्याधिकारः । तथैवेति दुहितृवद्भावविधानात् । तत्सुतोऽपीत्यप्यर्थतया च निर्देशात् । दौहित्रस्य जघन्यतावगतेः ।

अतो दुहित्रनन्तरं दौहित्रस्याधिकार[53] इति सिद्धम्[54] ।

<26> सत्स्वपि बन्धुष्वित्यनेन पित्रोरधिकारः पत्न्यभावे न्याय्योऽपि दुहितृदौहित्राभ्यां बाधित इति । बाधकाभावे पित्रोरधिकारः सूचितः[55] । अत एवानन्तरं **बृहस्पतिः** —

तदभावे भ्रातरस्तु भ्रातृपुत्राः सनाभयः ।
सकुल्या बान्धवाः शिष्याः श्रोत्रियाश्च धनार्हकाः[56] ।। [B 26.134]

तच्छब्देन दौहित्रस्य पित्रोश्च[57] सूचितयोः परामर्शः[58] । तेनामीषामभावे[59] भ्रात्रादीनामधिकारः ।

<27> यत्तु[60] **बालक**वचनम् —

पत्नी दुहितरश्चैव पितरौ भ्रातरस्तथा ।। [Y 2.185ab]

[48] तथा । *om*
[49] हि । तु
[50] -वचनबलेन । -वचनेन
[51] सदृशेनोढे- । सदृशेने-
[52] पूर्वोक्त- । प्रागुक्त-
[53] दौहित्रस्याधिकारः । दैहित्राधिकारः
[54] सिद्धम् । युक्तम्
[55] सूचितः । स्मृतः
[56] श्रोत्रियाश्च धनार्हकाः । श्रोत्रिया धनहारकाः
[57] पित्रोश्च । पित्रोः
[58] परामर्शः । परामर्षः
[59] तेनामीषामभावे । तेनामीषामभाव एव
[60] यत्तु । यद्

इत्यादिनियतक्रमादधस्तन[61] एव दौहित्रस्याधिकार इति तद् **बृहस्पति-** विरोधाद्बालवचनमेव[62] । बहुवचनान्तदुहितृपदेनैव कन्योढादौहित्राणां निर्दिष्टत्वात्क्रमविरोधाभावात् ।

यथा स्वर्यातस्य ह्यपुत्रस्येति पुत्रपदं प्रपौत्रपर्यन्तपरं पिण्डदत्वाविशेषात्[63] तथा दौहित्रस्यापि पिण्डदत्वात्तत्पर्यन्तं[64] दुहितृपदम् ।

यथा वा —

पुत्राभावे तु दुहिता तुल्यसंतानदर्शनात्[65] । [N 13.50ab/47ab]

इत्यत्र पुत्रपदं पत्नीपर्यन्तपरम् ।

अन्यथा दुहितर इति बहुवचनमनर्थकं स्यात् । पत्नी तत्सुत इत्यादिवदेकवचनमेव कुर्यात् । भ्रातर इत्यस्यापि बहुवचनस्यार्थवत्तां[66] वक्ष्यामः ।

<28> किंच पित्रादीनां राजपर्यन्तानां क्रमनियमाद्राज्ञोऽभावे दौहित्रस्याधिकारो वाच्यः । न च[67] कदाचिद्राज्ञोऽभावे दौहित्रस्यानधिकार[68] एवाभिहितो भवेत् ।

<29> तस्मा**द्विश्वरूप-जितेन्द्रिय-भोजदेव-गोविन्दराजै**र्दुहित्रभावे दौहित्रस्याधिकारो निरूपित आदरणीयः ।

<30> यदा च कन्या जाताधिकारा पश्चात्परिणीता सती म्रियते तदा तद्धनं कन्याया अनुत्पन्नाधिकाराया अभावे येषामूढादीनां प्रतिपादितमुत्पन्नाधिकाराया अप्यभावे तेषामेव तद्धनम् । न तु तद्भर्त्रादीनां तद्भवति[69] तस्य स्त्रीधनविषयत्वात् ।

भुञ्जीता मरणात् क्षान्तेति वचनेन जाताधिकारायाः पत्न्या अभावेऽनुत्पन्नाधिकारपत्न्यभावोक्तानां पूर्वधनस्वामिदायग्राहिणां दुहित्रादीनामधि-

[61] -नियतक्रमादधस्तन । -नियतक्रमाणामन्त

[62] **बृहस्पति**- । **बृहपति**वचन-

[63] -दत्वा- । -दातृत्वा-

[64] -दत्वा- -दातृत्वा-

[65] तुल्यसंतानदर्शनात् । *om*

[66] बहुवचनस्यार्थवत्तां । बहुवचनार्थवत्तां

[67] च । *om*

[68] कदाचिद्राज्ञोऽभावे दौहित्रस्यानधिकार । कदाचिदपि राज्ञोऽभावोऽस्तीत्यनधिकार

[69] तद्भवति । भवति

कारस्य[70] दर्शितत्वात् पत्नीतो जघन्यदुहितृदौहित्रयोरधिकारे दण्डापूप-न्यायसिद्धोऽयमर्थः । **<31>** यद्वा पत्नीत्युपलक्षणम् । स्त्रीमात्राधिकारेऽयमर्थो बोद्धव्य इति तात्पर्यम् ।

<32> इति दुहितृदौहित्रयोरधिकारः ।

[70] दुहित्रादीनामधिकारस्य । दुहित्रादीनां धनाधिकारस्य

<**11.3.1**> दौहित्रस्याभावे पितुरधिकारो न मातुः[1] नापि युगपन्मातापित्रोः ।

तदभावे पितृगामि । तदभावे मातृगामि ।। [Vi 17.6–7]

इति **विष्णु**वचनविरोधात्[2] ।

<**2**> यत्तु **मनु**वचनम् —

अनपत्यस्य पुत्रस्य माता दायमवाप्नुयात् ।
मातर्यपि च वृत्तायां पितुर्माता हरेद्धनम् ।। [M 9.217]

यच्च **बृहस्पति**वचनम् —

भार्यासुतविहीनस्य तनयस्य मृतस्य च[3] ।
माता रिक्थहरी ज्ञेया भ्राता वा तदनुज्ञया ।। [B 26.135cdef]

तत्पितृपर्यन्ताभावे बोद्धव्यम् ।

<**3**> न्यायगतं चैतत् । दौहित्रात्परतो मातृतश्च[4] पूर्वं पितुरधिकार इति मृतपिण्डमृतभोग्यान्यपिण्डद्वयदातुर्दौहित्रान् मृतभोग्यान्यपिण्डद्वदमात्रदातृतया पितुर्जघन्यत्वात् । मात्रादिभ्यस्तु मृतभोग्यान्यपिण्डद्वयदातृतया ।

बीजस्य चैव[5] योन्याश्च बीजमुत्कृष्टमुच्यते । [M 9.35ab]

इति **मनु**वचनावगतोत्कर्षेण च बलवत्त्वात् ।

<**4**> पितरावित्यत्र च[6] पितृक्रम एवावगम्यते । तथा हि पितृपदात्प्रातिपदिकात्प्रथमं पितुरवगतेः पश्चाद्[7] द्विवचनबलेनैकशेषकल्पनया मातुरवगमात् ।

<**5**> अतः क्रमज्ञानं क्रमाभिधानव्याप्तम् । तन्निवर्तमानं क्रमज्ञानं निवर्तयतीत्यनुमानं तदप्रमाणम् । व्यापकनिवृत्तेरसिद्धत्वाद्**विष्णु**वचनविरोधाच्च हेयम् ।

<**6**> इति पितुरधिकारः ।

[1] पितुरधिकारो न मातुः । पितुर्न मातुः
[2] -वचन- । *om*
[3] च । तु
[4] मातृतश्च । मातृतः । मातुः
[5] चैव । चैवं
[6] पितरावित्यत्र च । पितरावित्यत्रापि
[7] पश्चाद् । पश्चात्तु

<**11.4.1**> पितुरभावे मातुरधिकारः[1] ।

पितुरधिकारानन्तरम् —

तदभावे मातृगामि ॥ [Vi 17.7]

इति **विष्णु**श्रुतेः[2] ।

<**2**> युक्तं चैतत् । गर्भधारणपोषणाभ्यां[3] कृतोपकारकतया तन्निष्क्रयस्यावश्यकर्तव्यत्वात् । पुत्रभोग्यान्यपिण्डदजननेनाप्युपकारकत्वाच्च[4] भ्रात्रादिभ्यः पूर्वमधिकारस्य न्याय्यत्वात् ।

<**3**> अतः पितृतो गौरवातिरेकश्रुतेर्मातुरधिकारः पितृतः[5] पूर्वमिति हेयम् । गौरवातिरेकस्य धनसंबन्धहेतुत्वे[6] —

उत्पादकब्रह्मदात्रोर्गरीयान् ब्रह्मदः पिता ॥ [M 9.146ab]

इति पितृतः पूर्वमाचार्यस्याधिकारापत्तेः । कनिष्ठे च भ्रातरि भ्रातृसुते वा सत्यपि पितृव्यादीनामधिकारापत्तेश्च[7] ।

अतः पितृतः परत एव मातुरधिकारः[8] ।

<**4**> एवं च मृतस्य पितृसंतानात्पूर्वं पितुश्च परतो मातुरधिकार इति वदता पितामहसंतानात्पूर्वं पितामहाच्च परतः पितामह्या धनाधिकारः सूचितः । अन्यथा पितरौ भ्रातरस्तथेति क्रमविरोधात्[9] ।

अत एव **मनुः** —

मातर्यपि च वृत्तायां पितुर्माता हरेद्धनम् ॥ [M 9.217cd]

ससंतानायां वृत्तायामित्यर्थः । <**5**> अपिशब्दचकारयोश्चोभयत्रान्वय कार्यः । तेन मातरि व वृत्तायां पितामह्यपि गृह्णीयात् । किं पुनर्भ्रात्रादयः ।

[1] मातुरधिकारः । मातुः

[2] **विष्णु**श्रुतेः । श्रुतेः

[3] -पोषणाभ्यां । -पालनाभ्यां । -पोषणात् । -पालनात्

[4] -कारकत्वाच्च । -कारकत्वात्

[5] पितृतः । पितुः

[6] धनसंबन्धहेतुत्वे । धनं प्रत्यहेतुत्वात् तथात्वे सति

[7] -पत्तेश्च । -पत्तेः

[8] मातुरधिकारः । मातुरधिकार इति ।

[9] -विरोधात् । -विरोधः स्यात्

पितामहपर्यन्ता इत्यपिशब्दसूचिता[10] भ्रात्रादयः । <**6**> तदयं वचनार्थः — दौहित्रान्तान्मृतसंतानात्परतः स्वसंतानाच्च पूर्वमुक्तक्रमेण पित्रोरधिकारः । अतः स्वसंतानात्पूर्वं पितामहपितामह्योरधिकारोऽनेनैव[11] दर्शितः[12] ।

अत एव **याज्ञवल्क्येन** मातुरधिकारप्रदर्शनेनैव पितृव्यादिभ्यः पूर्वं पितामहपितामह्योरधिकारस्याप्यनुक्तत्वान्न पृथगुक्तः ।

<**7**> इति मातुरधिकारः ।

[10] -सूचिता । समुच्चिता

[11] ऽनेनैव । ऽनेन

[12] दर्शितः । सूचितः

<**11.5.1**> मातुरभावे भ्रातुर्धनम् ।

मातृगामीत्यभिधाय —

तदभावे भ्रातृगामि ॥ [Vi 17.8]

इति **विष्णु**वचनात्[1] । तदिति[2] मातुः परामर्शः[3] ।

पितरौ भ्रातरस्तथा ॥ [Y 2.135b]

इत्यत्रापि पित्रोरभावे भ्रातुरधिकारावगतेः ।

<**2**> न च भ्रातरस्तथा तत्सुत इति यथा भ्रातरोऽधिकृतास्तथा भ्रातृपुत्रोऽपि मातुरनन्तरमधिकारी स्यादिति[4] वाच्यम् ।

भ्रातृगामीत्यभिधाय तदभावे भ्रातपुत्रगामीति **विष्णु**विरोधात्[5] । तदिति भ्रातुः परामर्शः[6] ।

<**3**> न्याय्यं चैतत् । मृतधनिभोग्यपित्रादित्रयपिण्डदानेन भ्रातुरुपकारकत्वात् । तथा तद्देयमातामहादिपिण्डत्रयदानेन तत्स्थानपाताच्च । अनेवंरूपाद् भ्रातृपुत्राद्बलवत्त्वान्मातृमूलत्वाच्च भ्रातुरेवंरूपस्य मातृतो जघन्यतेति मातृतः परत एवाधिकारो युक्तः ।

<**4**> किंच तथापदं भ्रात्रैव कुतो न संबध्यते । तेन यथा पितरौ भ्रातरोऽपि तथेति पित्रोर्भ्रातॄणां च तुल्योऽधिकारः[7] स्यात् ।

<**5**> तस्माद्**विष्णु**चवनविरोधेनैवायं पर्यनुयोगः परिहर्तव्यः । स चान्यत्रापि समानः ।

तथा[8] **मनुः** —

पिता हरेदपुत्रस्य रिक्थं भ्रातर एव वा ॥ [M 9.185cd]

[1] -वचनात् । -वचनम्

[2] तदिति । तदित्यनेन

[3] परामर्शः । परामर्षः

[4] -धिकारी स्यादिति । -धिकारीति

[5] **विष्णु**- । **विष्णु**वचन-

[6] परामर्शः । परमर्षः

[7] तुल्योऽधिकारः । तुल्याधिकारः

[8] तथा । तथाच

भ्रातर एव हरेयुर्न तु भ्रातृपुत्रोऽधिकारीत्याह[9] ।

<**6**> किंच[10] जीवत्पितृकस्यापि भ्रातृपुत्रस्य किमधिकारो[11] नेष्यते । नात्रान्यो[12] हेतुर्जीवत्पितृकस्य पिण्डदत्वाभावेनानुपकारकत्वादित्यतः । एवं चेन्मृतपितृकस्यापि भ्रातृतुल्योपकारकत्वाभावात् कथं तुल्यवदधिकारिता । अत एव **देवलेन** —

ततो दायमपुत्रस्य विभजेरन् सहोदराः ।
तुल्या दुहितरो वापि ध्रियमाणः पितापि वा । [D 1570]
सवर्णा भ्रातरो माता भार्या चेति यथाक्रमम् ।। [D 1571ab]

इत्यनेन[13] भार्यासवर्णदुहितृपितृमातृसहोदरभ्रातृसापत्नभ्रातृपर्यन्ताधिकारिशृङ्खलायां[14] भ्रातृपुत्रस्याकीर्तनात्सापत्नभ्रातृपर्यन्ताभाव एव[15] भ्रातृपुत्राणामधिकारः[16] कथितः ।

<**7**> यच्च —

सर्वे ते तेन पुत्रेण । [M 9.182c]

इति पुत्रत्वस्मरणं[17] तत्पिण्डदानार्थम् । भ्रात्रभावे च धनाधिकारार्थं पूर्वोक्तवचनविरोधात् । अन्यथा भ्रातृभ्यः[18] पूर्वमेव कुतो न स्यात् ।

<**8**> तस्माद् भ्रातुरेव प्रथममधिकारः ।

<**9**> तत्रापि प्रथमं सोदरस्यैव । तदुक्तम् —

सोदरस्य तु सोदरः[19] । [Y 2.138b]

[9] भ्रातृपुत्रोऽधिकारीत्याह । भ्रातृपुत्रा अपीत्याह
[10] किंच । किंतु
[11] किमधिकारो । किमित्यधिकारो
[12] नात्रान्यो । न चात्रान्यो
[13] इत्यनेन । अनेन
[14] -सवर्णदुहितृ- । -सवर्णादुहितृ- ।। -सापत्न- । -सापत्न्य-
[15] -सापत्न- । -सापत्न्य- ।। -पर्यन्ताभाव एव । -पर्यन्ताभावे
[16] भ्रातृपुत्राणामधिकारः । भ्रातृपुत्रादीनामधिकारः
[17] पुत्रत्वस्मरणं । तत्पुत्रत्वस्मरणं
[18] भ्रातृभ्यः । भ्रातृतः
[19] सोदरः । सोदर इति

भ्रातरस्तथेत्युक्ते भ्रातुरधिकारावसरे प्रथमं सोदरो गृह्णीयादित्यर्थः । तस्य त्वभावे सापत्नो भ्राता[20] । एकप्रभवत्वेन तस्यापि भ्रातृशब्दार्थत्वात् । **<10>** तथाच —

संसृष्टिनस्तु संसृष्टी सोदरस्य तु सोदरः ।
दद्याच्चापहरेदंशं जातस्य च मृतस्य च ॥ [Y 2.138]

इदमपि **याज्ञवल्क्य**वचनं सोदरासोदरयोर्भ्रातृशब्दार्थत्वं दर्शयति । अन्यथा सोदरमात्रस्य तदर्थत्वे सोदरस्य तु सोदर इति न पुनर्विशेषणीयमिति[21] । भ्रातृशब्दादेव सोदरावगतेः ।

<11> तस्मात्पितरौ भ्रातर इत्यनेन सोदरासोदरयोरेवाधिकारो दर्शितः । सोदरवचनेन तु सोदरस्य प्रथममधिकारः ।

<12> सापत्नस्य[22] च[23] सोदरान् मृतदेयषाट्पौरुषिकपिण्डदातुर्मृतभोग्यमात्रपित्रादिपिण्डत्रयदातृतया[24] जघन्यत्वाद् भ्रातृपुत्राच्च मृतभोग्यपिण्डद्वयदातुर्मृतभोग्यपिण्डत्रयदातृतया उपकारकत्वातिरेकेण बलवत्त्वान्मध्य एवाधिकारः **श्रीकर-विश्वरूपो**क्त एवादरणीयः[25] ।

<13> तत्र किं संसृष्टिनोऽप्यसोदरस्य सोदराज्जघन्यत्वं न वेत्यपेक्षायामाह **याज्ञवल्क्यः** —

अन्योदर्यस्तु संसृष्टी नान्योदर्यो धनं हरेत् ।
असंसृष्ट्यपि चादद्यात् संसृष्टो नान्यमातृजः ॥ [Y 2.139]

<14> अस्यार्थः — संसृष्टी पुनरन्योदर्यः प्रथमं हरेत् । न पुनरन्योदर्यमात्रः । प्रथमं च[26] हरन् सोदरं बाधित्वैव वा तेन सह वेत्यपक्षायामुत्तरार्धम् — असंसृष्ट्यपि सोदरो गृह्णीयात् । सोदरपदमनुवर्तते । नान्यमातृज एव संसृष्टी[27] गृह्णीयात् ।

[20] सापत्नो भ्राता । सापत्न्यभ्राता
[21] न पुनर्विशेषणीयमिति । पुनर्न विशेषणीयम्
[22] सापत्नस्य । सापत्न्यस्य
[23] च । तु । *om*
[24] -मात्र- । *om*
[25] एवादरणीयः । आदरणीयः
[26] च । *om*
[27] संसृष्टी । संसृष्टो

संसृष्टपदमेव वा सोदरमभिधत्ते । अत एव **बृहद्याज्ञवल्क्य**वचनं[28] सोदरो नान्यमातृज इति **जितेन्द्रियेण** लिखितम् । तदा च[29] पूर्वार्धस्य संसृष्टीत्यनुवर्तते ।

<15> तेन न केवलमन्योदर्य एव संसृष्टी गृह्णीयात् किंत्वसंसृष्ट्यपि सोदर इत्यर्थः[30] । तेनासंसृष्टिना सोदरेण संसृष्टिना चासोदरेण विभज्य ग्रहीतव्यम्[31] । अत एवापिशब्दं प्रयुक्तवान् ।

<16> यच्च[32] **श्रीकरमिश्रै**रुक्तम् — संसृष्टिनस्तु संसृष्टीत्यस्यासोदरसंसृष्टिमात्रविषयत्वेऽन्यानपेक्षत्वात् । सोदरस्य तु सोदर इत्यस्याप्यसंसृष्टसोदरमात्रविषयत्वे नैरपेक्षात्[33] । असोदरे संसृष्टिनि सोदरे चासंसृष्टिन्युभयोः प्राप्तौ यदि द्वयमेव[34] प्रवर्तेते तदान्योन्यसापेक्षमुभयोर्विधायकत्वं भवेत् । न चैकस्य सापेक्षं निरपेक्षं च विधायकत्वमुचितं विधिवैषम्यप्रसङ्गात् ।

यथा दर्शितं द्वयोः प्रणयन्तीत्यधिकरणे पर्वचतुष्टयविहिताया वेदेर्न[35] पर्वद्वये प्रतिषेध उपपद्यते । तत्र पर्वद्वये विकल्पसापेक्षं विधानं पर्वद्वये तु[36] निरपेक्षमित्युत्तरवेदिविधिवैषम्यापत्तेः ।

तथा चात्र[37] यत्रैव निरपेक्षविधायकत्वं[38] तत्रैव संसृष्टिनस्तु संसृष्टीत्यस्य सोदरस्य तु सोदर इत्यस्य च प्रवृत्तिः स्यात् । तत्रासोदरे संसृष्टिनि सोदरे चासंसृष्टिनि सत्युभयोरप्रवृत्तेस्तद्धनं न कश्चिदपि गृह्णीयादित्यापतति ।

[28] **बृहद्याज्ञवल्क्य- । वृद्धयाज्ञवल्क्य-**
[29] तदा च । तथाच
[30] सोदर इत्यर्थः । सोदरो गृह्णीयादित्यर्थः
[31] ग्रहीतव्यम् । गृहीतव्यम्
[32] यच्च । यत्तु
[33] नैरपेक्षात् । नैरपेक्ष्यात् । निरपेक्षत्वात्
[34] द्वयमेव । द्वयमपि
[35] वेदेर्न । उत्तरवेदेर्न
[36] तु । च
[37] चात्र । च
[38] निरपेक्ष- । निरपेक्षं

तस्मात्संसृष्टिनस्तु संसृष्टीति संसृष्टधने[39] सामान्यतः संसृष्टिनो[40] भागप्राप्तौ तदपवादार्थं सोदरस्य तु सोदर इति वचनम्[41] । एवं च संसृष्टिनोऽप्यसोदरस्य सोदरे सति न प्राप्तिः । किं तर्हि विभागसंसृष्टस्यासंसृष्टस्य वा[42] सोदरस्यैव विभाग[43] इत्यन्तम् ।

<**17**> तदसंगतम् । न हि द्वयोरुभयत्रैकैकशः प्रवृत्तयोर्युगपदेकत्र प्रवृत्तिमात्रेण विधिवैरूप्यम् ।

<**18**> केवलोद्गातृप्रतिहर्त्रपच्छेदेन[44] निरपेक्षप्रवृत्तयोः सर्वस्वदाक्षिण्यादाक्षिण्यशास्त्रयोर्युगदुभयापच्छेदे सति नैकमपि शास्त्रं प्रवर्तेत विधिवैरूप्यात् ।

<**19**> तथा चातुर्होत्रां पौर्णमासीमभिमृषेत् पञ्चहोत्राममावास्यामिति शास्त्रयोरुपांशुयागाग्नीषोमीययोरैन्द्रदध्यैन्द्रपयसोरेकैकशः प्रवृत्तयोर्द्वयोराग्नेये प्रवृत्तौ विधिवैषम्यापत्तेर्नैकमपि प्रवर्तेत ।

<**20**> तस्माद्बाधनिरपेक्षं नित्यवद्विधानं क्वचित्क्वचिद्विध्यन्तरबाधसापेक्षमिति[45] वैरूप्यलक्षणम् ।

तथाहि उपात्र वपन्तीति वेदिविधिसापेक्षो निषेधस्तद्बाधं विना विधिरेव न स्यादिति वेदिविधिबाधसापेक्षं[46] विधानम् । न च नित्यवदेव तस्य बाधः। तथाच[47] सति निषेधो विफलः । निषेधं विनापि वेद्यकरणस्य प्राप्तेः । ततश्च वेदिविधिरपि निषेधविधिबाधसापेक्षविधिभावः । पर्वद्वये तु निरपेक्ष इति भवति । विधिवैरूप्यं[48] विकल्पश्च स्यात् । रागप्राप्ते[49] तु नित्यवद्बाधः कादाचित्कस्याकरणस्य निषेधमन्तरेण प्राप्तेः ।

39 संसृष्ट- । संसृष्टि-

40 सामान्यतः संसृष्टिनो । संसृष्टिनः सामान्यतो

41 वचनम् । वाच्यम्

42 वा । च

43 विभाग । *om*

44 -प्रतिहर्त्रपच्छेदेन । -प्रतिस्तोत्रपच्छेदेन

45 क्वचित्क्वचिद्विध्यन्तर- । क्वचित्क्वचिच्च विध्यन्तर-

46 -बाध- । *om*

47 तथाच । तथा

48 -वैरूप्यं । वैषम्यं

49 रागप्राप्ते । रागतः प्राप्ते

<**21**> अत एव षोडशिग्रहणाग्रहणयोर्विकल्पः[50] ।

<**22**> ये तु ब्रुवते — प्राप्तिपूर्वकत्वान्निषेधस्य न निमित्तं विधिरपबाधत इति न्यायेन विकल्प इति । तेषां मते न तौ पाशौ करोतीत्यादौ राग-प्राप्तनिषेधे[51] च विकल्पः स्यात् ।

<**23**> किंचैवं निमित्तिनः स्वनिमित्तबाधाक्षमत्वात् कथं पक्षेऽपि बाधो ऽतुल्यबलत्वात्[52] । अथ निषेधस्यैवायं स्वभावो यत्स्वनिमित्तमुन्मूलयतीति तदा सर्वदैवोन्मूलयेत्प्राप्तेरेव दुर्बलत्वात् ।

<**24**> ये तु ब्रुवते — यादृच्छिकग्रहणप्राप्तिनिषेधोऽयं न तु विधितः प्राप्तस्येति । तदतीवाज्ञवचनम्[53] । वैधग्रहणस्यावैधग्रहणनिषेधस्य च युगप-दुपसंहारासंभवाद्विकल्पाभावप्रसक्तेः । क्रत्वर्थतया च यादृच्छिकग्रहण-प्रसक्त्यभावान्निषेधो न क्रत्वर्थः स्यात्।

<**25**> तस्मादस्मदुक्तन्यायादेव विकल्पः । तदस्तु । किं विस्तरेण ।

<**26**> यच्च स्वयमेव[54] वर्णितम् — असोदरे संसृष्टिनि सोदरे चास-सृष्टिनि संसृष्टिनस्तु संसृष्टीत्यनेनासोदरस्य[55] धनसंबन्धप्राप्तौ[56] तदपवादार्थं सोदरस्य तु सोदर इति वचनं तदप्ययुक्तम् । अस्मिन्नेव विषये सोदरस्य तु सोदर इति सोदरस्य धनसंबन्धप्रसक्तौ तदपवादार्थं संसृष्टिवचनस्यापि संभवाद्विनिगमनाकारणाभावात् ।

<**27**> यच्च संसृष्टिनस्तु संसृष्टीत्येतद्विवरणार्थत्वेनान्योदर्य इति[57] वचनं व्याख्यातम् । तदप्यतीवायुक्तम्[58] । अन्योदर्यवचनादेव विवक्षितार्थलाभात्सं-सृष्टिन इत्यस्यानर्थक्यापत्तेः[59] ।

[50] -ग्रहणाग्रहणयोर्विकल्पः । -ग्रहणाग्रहणशास्त्रयोर्विकल्पः

[51] रागप्राप्त- । रागप्राप्ते

[52] -ऽतुल्यबलत्वात् । -ऽतुल्यत्वात्

[53] तदतीवाज्ञवचनम् । तदतीवासंगतम्

[54] स्वयमेव । स्वयं

[55] संसृष्टीत्यनेनासोदरस्य । संसृष्टीत्यसोदरस्य

[56] -प्राप्तौ । -प्रसक्तौ

[57] इति । *om*

[58] तदप्यतीवायुक्तम् । तदतीवायुक्तम्

[59] -संसृष्टिन इत्यस्या- । -संसृष्टिनस् त्वित्यस्या-

<28> किंचान्योदर्यस्तु संसृष्टीत्यस्यायमर्थः — अन्योदर्यस्तु[60] संसृष्टी यः स नान्योदर्यधनं हरेत् । किंत्वसंसृष्ट्यपि सोदरपदानुषङ्गात्सोदर एव गृह्णीयात् । संसृष्टोऽपि नान्यमातृजो गृह्णीयादिति व्याख्यातम् । तदपि न । पूर्वार्ध एकस्यान्योदर्यपदस्य पुनरुक्तत्वात् । तथोत्तरार्धेऽपि नान्यमातृज इत्यस्यानर्थक्यापत्तेः । अपिशब्दस्य चैवकारार्थेऽवर्णनात् ।

<29> किंच सोदरे चासंसृष्टिनि[61] असोदरस्य संसृष्टिनोऽपवादार्थं सोदरवचनस्य वर्णितत्वात् । सोदरासोदरयोरसंसृष्टिनोरप्रवृत्तत्वात्तुल्यवदेवाधिकारः[62] स्यान्न वा कस्यचिदपि स्यात् । <30> अथात्रापि सोदरवचनमेव प्रवर्तते तदैकत्र संसृष्टिवचनबाधसापेक्षमन्यत्र तु बाधानापेक्षमिति भवतामेव विधिवैरूप्यम् । यथा सोमे विधीयमाना वेदिर्दीक्षणीयादिष्वतिदेशप्राप्तवेदिबाधेनान्यत्र[63] बाधं विनैवेति वैरूप्यादवेदिमतां तद्द्रष्टव्यमित्युक्तम् ।

<31> अस्मन्मते तु **श्रीकर**संमतमपि विधिवैरूप्यं नास्ति । संसृष्टिसोदरवचनयोरेकैकविषयत्वादन्योदर्यवचनस्य च[64] सोदरस्यासंसृष्टिनः संसृष्टिनश्चासोदरस्य तुल्यवदधिकारज्ञापनार्थत्वात् । तथाहि अन्योदर्यस्तु संसृष्टी सन् सत्यपि सोदरेऽसंसृष्टिनि धनं हरेत् । नान्योदर्योऽसंसृष्ट्यपि गृह्णीयादिति पूर्वार्धस्यार्थः । तत्र किं सोदरस्तदानीं न गृह्णीयादेवेत्यपेक्षायामुत्तरार्धेनोत्तरम्[65] । असंसृष्ट्यपि चादद्यात् । सोदर इत्यनुषज्यते । संसृष्टोऽन्यमातृज एव न केवलः किंतूभाभ्यां विभज्य ग्रहीतव्यमित्यर्थः[66] । अतो[67] विधिवैरूप्यमपि[68] परिहृतम् ।

<32> तथा **मनु**रप्येतदेव दर्शयति —

[60] अन्योदर्यस्तु । अन्योदर्यः

[61] चासंसृष्टिनि । -ऽसंसृष्टिनि

[62] -प्रवृत्तत्वात्तुल्यवदेवाधिकार । -प्रवृत्तत्वात्तुल्यवदधिकारः

[63] -वेदिबाधेना- । -वेदिविधिबाधेना-

[64] च । *om*

[65] गृह्णीयादेवेत्यपेक्षा- । गृह्णीयादित्यपेक्षा-

[66] ग्रहीयव्य- । गृहीतव्य-

[67] ग्रहीतव्यमित्यर्थः अतो । ग्रहीतव्यमित्यतो

[68] विधिवैरूप्यमपि । विधिवैषम्यमपि

सोदर्या विभजेयुस्तं समेत्य सहिताः समम् ।
भ्रातरो ये च संसृष्टा भगिन्यश्च सनाभयः ।। [M 9.212]

<**33**> सोदर्यमात्राणां सोदर्या इत्यसोदराणां च संसृष्टानां संसृष्टा इति बहुवचनान्तस्वपदादेवेतरेतरयोगावगतेः समेत्य[69] सहिता इतिपदमुभयसाहित्यार्थमेव युक्तम् अन्यथानर्थक्यात् । अत[70] उभयोरितरेतरयोगस्याश्रवणादित्यहृदयव्याहृतम्[71] । किंच ये चेति चकारश्रुतेश्चाथ□द्वन्द्वसमासस्यापि[72] श्रवणादितरेतरयोगस्याश्रवणाभिधानं द्वन्द्वस्याप्यतदर्थतामापादयति ।

<**34**> तस्मात्सोदरासोदरमात्रसद्भावे सोदराणामेव[73] । अत एव **बृहन्मनुः**[74] —

एकोदरे जीवति तु सापत्नो[75] न लभेद्धनम् ।
स्थावरेऽप्येवमेव स्यात्तदभावे लभेत वै ।। [bM 93]

<**35**> स्थावरेऽप्येवमेव स्यादिति[76] विभक्तस्थावराभिप्रायेण । यस्मादनन्तरमेवाह **यमः** —

अविभक्तं स्थावरं यत्सर्वेषामेव तद्भवेत् ।
विभक्तं स्थावरं ग्राह्यं नान्योदर्यैः कथंचन ।। [*Dhko* p. 1561]

<**36**> सर्वेषां सोदरासोदराणामित्यर्थः ।

सोदराणामेव[77] मध्य एकस्य संसृष्टत्वे तस्यैव ।
असंसृष्टिसोदरासोदरसंसृष्टिसद्भावे च द्वयोरेव ।

[69] समेत्य । *om*
[70] अत । अत एव
[71] -व्याहृतम् । -व्याख्यातम्
[72] द्वन्द्वसमासस्यापि । द्वन्द्वस्यापि
[73] सोदराणामेव । सोदराणामेव स्यादिति
[74] **बृहन्मनुः** । **वृद्धमुनः**
[75] सापत्नो । सापत्न्यो
[76] -प्येवमेव स्यादिति । -प्येवमेवेति
[77] सोदराणामेव । सोदराणां

सापत्नमात्रसद्भावेऽपि[78] प्रथमं संसृष्टिनस्तदभावे चासंसृष्टिनोऽसोदरस्य[79] मृतधनं प्रत्येतव्यम्[80] ।

<**37**> अत एवोक्तक्रमेण[81] बहूनामधिकारप्रतिपत्त्यर्थं भ्रातर इति बहुवचनमुक्तम् । अन्यथानर्थकं भवेत्[82] । <**38**> संसृष्टिनस्तु संसृष्टीत्येतच्च तुल्यरूपसंबन्धिसमवाये[83] संसर्गकृतविशेषप्रतिपत्त्यर्थम् । <**39**> तेन सोदराणां सापत्नानां[84] वा[85] तथा भ्रातृपुत्राणां पितृव्यादीनां वा तुल्यानां सद्भावे संसर्गी गृह्णीयात् । वाक्यादविशेषश्रुतेः । पूर्ववचनेन[86] सर्वेषामेव प्रकृतत्वात्सर्वेष्वेव[87] चापेक्षासद्भावात् । अतो भ्रातृमात्रविषयं वचनमित्यनादरणीयम् ।

<**40**> इति भ्रात्रधिकारः ।

[78] सापत्न- । सापत्न्य-
[79] -ऽसोदरस्य । -प्यसोदरस्य
[80] प्रत्येतव्यम् । अवगन्तव्यम् । वेदितव्यम्
[81] अत एवोक्त- । अत एव चोक्त-
[82] भवेत् । स्यात्
[83] -समवाये । -सद्भावे
[84] सापत्नानां । सापत्न्यानां
[85] वा । *om*
[86] पूर्ववचनेन । पूर्ववचनेन च
[87] -सर्वेष्वेव । सर्वेषु

<**11.6.1**> तदभावे भ्रातृपुत्रस्य ।

भ्रातृगामीत्यभिधाय —

तदभावे भ्रातृपुत्रगामि ॥ [Vi 17.9]

अति **विष्णु**वचनात् ।

<**2**> तत्र प्रथमं सोदरभ्रातृपुत्रस्य तस्य चाभावेऽसोदरभ्रातृपुत्रस्याधिकारः[1] । सोदरस्य तु सोदर इति वचनात्[2] । असोदरभ्रातृपुत्रो हि धनिनो मृतस्य[3] मातरं विहाय स्वपितामहीविशिष्टस्य धनिपितुः पिण्डदातेति सोदरभ्रातृपुत्राज्जघन्यस्तदनन्तरं धनमधिकरोति ।

<**3**> न च सापत्नीकत्वेन[4] सपत्नीमातुः[5] सपत्नीपितामह्याः[6] सपत्नीप्रपितामह्याश्च[7] श्राद्धेऽनुप्रवेशः । मात्रादिशब्दानां स्वजननीपितृजननीपितामहजननीष्वेव मुख्यत्वात् । तैरेव च पदैः श्राद्धेऽनुप्रवेशात् । यथा[8] —

स्वेन भर्त्रा सह श्राद्धं माता भुङ्क्ते स्वधामयम् ।
पितामही च स्वेनैव स्वेनैव प्रपितामही ॥ [B *Śrāddha* 75]

सपत्नीमात्रादीनां[9] च पार्वणश्राद्धानुप्रवेशो[10] निषिद्ध एव । यथा[11] पठन्ति —

अपुत्रा ये मृताः केचित् स्त्रियो वा पुरुषाश्च ये[12] ।
तेषामपि च देयं स्यादेकोद्दिष्टं न पार्वणम् ॥

[1] तस्य चाभावे । तस्याभावे
[2] सोदरस्य तु सोदर इति वचनात् । *om*
[3] मृतस्या । *om*
[4] सापत्नीकत्वेन । सापत्नीकत्वमात्रेण
[5] सापत्नी- । सापत्न्य-
[6] सापत्नी- । सापत्न्य-
[7] सापत्नी- । सापत्न्य-
[8] यथा । तथा
[9] सपत्नी- । सापत्न्य-
[10] -श्राद्ध- । *om*
[11] यथा । यथा च । तथा
[12] स्त्रियो वा पुरुषाश्च ये । पुमांसो योषितोऽपि वा

<**4**> किंच सपत्नीकश्राद्धविधानस्य नित्यत्वं सर्वजनगामित्वात्[13] । सपत्नी-मात्रादीनां[14] चानित्यत्वात् । नित्यानित्यसंयोगविरोधेन मात्राद्यपेक्षमेव सपत्नीकश्राद्धविधानं[15] युक्तम् ।

<**5**> ननु सोदरभ्रातृपुत्रवत्सोदरपितृव्यस्य[16] धनिदेयसपत्नीकपूर्वपुरुषद्वय-पिण्डदातृत्वाद्धनिपितृव्यभ्रातृपुत्रयोः समानोऽधिकारः स्यात् ।

उच्यते[17] — पितृव्यो हि धनिनः पितामहप्रपितामहयोः पिण्डदः[18] । भ्रातृपुत्रस्तु[19] धनिनः प्रधानं पितरमेवादाय पुरुषद्वयस्य पिण्डदातेति[20] स एव बलवानिति पितृव्यात्पूर्वमधिक्रियते ।

<**6**> अत एव भ्रातृनप्तापि[21] पितृव्यस्य बाधकः । मृतधनिकपितुः[22] प्रधानस्यैव पिण्डदातृत्वात् ।

<**7**> भ्रातुः[23] प्रतिनप्ता धनिनः पितृसंततिरपि पितृव्येण बाध्यते । पञ्च-मत्वेन पिण्डबहिर्भावात्[24] । तथा च **मनुः**[25] —

त्रयाणामुदकं कार्यं त्रिषु पिण्डः प्रवर्तते ।
चतुर्थः संप्रदातैषां पञ्चमो नोपपद्यते ।। [M 9.186]

इत्यनेन पञ्चमो निषिद्धः ।

[13] -गामित्वात् । -सिद्धत्वात्
[14] सपत्नी- । सापत्न्य-
[15] -श्राद्ध- । *om*
[16] -पितृव्यस्य । -पितृव्यस्यापि
[17] उच्यते । मैवम्
[18] पिण्डदः । पिण्डप्रदः
[19] भ्रातृ- । भ्रातुः
[20] पिण्डदातेति । पिण्डद्वयदातेति
[21] -नप्तापि । -नप्ता
[22] मृतधनिक- । मृतधनिकस्य
[23] भ्रातुः । भ्रातुस्तु । भ्रातृ-
[24] -बहिर्भावात् । -दातृत्वाभावात्
[25] **मनुः** । **मनुना**

<8> किंतु पितुरपि प्रपौत्रपर्यन्ताभावे पितृदौहित्रस्याधिकारो बोद्धव्यो धनिदौहित्रिस्येव । **<9>** एवं पितामहप्रपितामहसंततेरपि दौहित्रान्तायाः पिण्डप्रत्यासत्तिक्रमेणाधिकारो बोद्धव्यः[26] ।

दौहित्रोऽपि ह्यमुत्रैनं संतारयति पौत्रवत् ।। [M 9.139cd]

इति हेतोरविशेषात् स्वदौहित्रवत्पित्रादिदौहित्रस्यापि तद्भोग्यपिण्डदानेन संतारकत्वात् ।

<10> अत एव **मनुना** पृथगमीषामधिकारो न दर्शितः[27] । त्रयाणामित्यनन्तर इति वचनद्वयेनैव संगृहीतत्वात् । **याज्ञवल्क्येन** च पित्रादिदौहित्रस्यापि तद्गोत्रजातस्य पिण्डदानानन्तर्यक्रमेणाधिकारप्रतिपत्त्यर्थं गोत्रजपदं कृतम् । सपिण्डस्त्रीणां च व्युदासार्थं तासामतद्गोत्रजत्वात्[28] । **<11>** अत एव अर्हति स्त्रीत्यनुवृत्तौ **बौधायनः** —

न दायं निरिन्द्रिया ह्यदायाश्च स्त्रियो मता[29] इति श्रुतेः ।।
[Bau 2.2.3.46]

न दायमर्हति स्त्रीत्यन्वयः[30] । पत्न्यादीनां त्वधिकारो विशेषवचनादविरुद्धः।

<12> प्रपितामहसंतानस्य तु[31] दौहित्रान्तस्य मृतभोग्यपिण्डदातुरभावे मृतदेयमातामहादिपिण्डदानेन पिण्डानन्तर्यान्मातुलादिग्रहणार्थं[32] बन्धुपदं प्रयुक्तवान् **याज्ञवल्क्यः** । **मनुना** तु पिण्डदानानन्तर्यवचनेनैव दर्शितम् ।

<13> मृतदेयमातामहादिपिण्डत्रयस्य मातुलादिभिर्दीयमानत्वान्मातुलाद्यर्थत्वं धनस्य धनद्वारेण तस्यापि तत्पिण्डदातृत्वात् ।

धनार्जनस्य हि प्रयोजनद्वयम् । भोगार्थं दानाद्यदृष्टार्थं वा[33] । तत्रार्जकस्य[34] मृतत्वाद्धने भोग्यत्वाभावेनादृष्टार्थत्वमेव[35] युक्तम् ।

[26] बोद्धव्यः । वेदितव्यः
[27] न दर्शितः । नाभिहितः
[28] तासामतद्गोत्र- । अतद्गोत्र- ।। -जत्वात् । -जातत्वात्
[29] स्त्रियो मता । स्त्रिय
[30] दायमर्हति स्त्रीत्यन्वयः । दायमर्हन्ति स्त्रिय इत्यन्वयः
[31] तु । *om*
[32] पिण्डानन्तर्या- । पिण्डदानानन्तर्या-
[33] वा । च
[34] तत्रार्जकस्य । तत्रार्जकस्य तु
[35] -भावेनादृष्टा- । -भावेन दानादृष्टा-

अत एव **बृहस्पतिः** —

समुत्पन्नाद्धनादर्धं तदर्थे स्थापयेत्पृथक् ।
मासषाण्मासिके श्राद्धे वार्षिके च प्रयत्नतः[36] ॥ [B 26.137]

तथा**पस्तम्बः** —

अन्तेवासी वार्थान् तदर्थेषु धर्मकृत्येषु प्रयोजयेत् । दुहिता वा ॥ [Āp 2.6.14.3–4]

मासिकादिना तद्भोगार्थं धर्मकृत्येष्वित्यदृष्टार्थत्वे[37] हेतुः । अत एव दत्त-भुक्तफलं धनमिति पठन्ति[38] ।

तस्मात्तद्भोग्यपिण्डदातुरभावे तद्देयपिण्डदातुर्मातुलादेरधिकारो न्याय्यः[39] ।

<**14**> अत एव त्रयाणामित्यनन्तर इति वचनद्वयेनैवायमर्थो दर्शित इति मत्वानन्तरं[40] **मनुनो**क्तम् —

अत ऊर्ध्वं सकुल्यः स्यादाचार्यः शिष्य एव वा ॥ [M 9.187cd]

<**15**> सकुल्यो वृद्धप्रपितामहादिसंततिः । समानोदकाश्च भण्यन्ते[41] । तेषा-मुपन्यासक्रमेणाधिकारः । तदभाव आर्चायशिष्यादीनाम्[42] ।

<**16**> अन्यथा कथं मातुलादीनां **मनु**विरुद्धोऽन्तर्भावः शक्यते । तस्मान्**मनुना** पूर्ववचनद्वयप्रतिपादितोऽयमर्थ इत्यविरोधः[43] ।

<**17**> अत एव दायभागप्रकरणे —

त्रयाणामुदकं कार्यं त्रिषु पिण्डः प्रवर्तते ।
चतुर्थः संप्रदातैषां पञ्चमो नोपपद्यते ॥ [M 9.186]

इत्युक्त्वा[44] —

अनन्तरः सपिण्डाद्यस्तस्य तस्य धनं भवेद् ॥ [M 9.187ab]

[36] प्रयत्नतः । विशेषतः
[37] -दृष्टार्थत्वे । -दृष्टार्थत्वं च
[38] पठन्ति । स्मरन्ति
[39] न्याय्यः । न्याय्य एव
[40] मत्वनन्तरं । मत्वा तदनन्तरं
[41] समानोदकाश्च भण्यन्ते । समानोदकश्च भण्यते
[42] आचार्य- । चाचार्य-
[43] इत्यविरोधः । इति न विरोधः
[44] इत्युक्त्वा । *om*

इति लिखितम् । पञ्चमस्यैकपिण्डसंबन्धहीनस्य पितृमातृकुलजातैकपिण्डसंबन्धिसद्भावेऽनधिकारार्थम् । अन्यथा —

सपिण्डता तु पुरुषे सप्तमे विनिवर्तते ।। [M 5.60ab]

इति सपिण्डत्वस्योक्तत्वादनन्तरः[45] सपिण्डाद्य इत्यनेन चानन्तर्यस्य धनग्रहणकारणत्वेनाभिहितत्वात् त्रयाणामित्यनर्थकं स्यात् ।

न च त्रैपुरुषिकश्राद्धविधानार्थमिति वच्याम् । दायभागसंदंशमध्यपाठात्[46] । श्राद्धस्य च[47] वचनान्तरविहितत्वात् । तथाच **मनुः** —

स्वाध्यायेनार्चयेदृषीन् होमैर्देवान् यथाविधि ।
पितॄन् श्राद्धेन नृनन्नैर्भूतानि बलिकर्मणा ।। [M 3.81]

<18> न च जननक्रमेणानन्तर्यग्रहणार्थं वचनम् । न तु प्रदातृत्वेनानन्तर्यार्थमिति[48] वाच्यम् । जननक्रमस्य वचनादनवगतेः । किंतूदकवत् त्रिभ्यः पिण्डदानं चतुर्थोऽधस्तनः पिण्डदाता पञ्चमस्तु पूर्वतनो न संप्रदानं नाप्यधस्तनः पञ्चमः पिण्डदातेत्यभिधायानन्तर्यमभिदधानो **मनुः** प्रदातृत्वातिशयेनैवानन्तर्यं ज्ञापयति ।

<19> तस्माद्यो यस्तत्कुलोत्पन्नोऽतद्गोत्रोऽपि[49] स्वदौहित्रपितृदौहित्रादिरतत्कुलोत्पन्नो वा मातुलादिर्धनिनो मृतस्य पितृमातृकुलगतत्रैपुरुषिकपिण्डदातृतया एकपिण्डसंबन्धेन सपिण्डस्तस्य[50] तस्याप्यधिकारार्थं त्रयाणामिति वचनम् । आनन्तर्येण च विशेषार्थमनन्तर इति वचनं वर्णनीयम् ।

<20> तेन मृतभोग्यमृतदेयपित्रादित्रयपिण्डदातुः[51] पितृदौहित्रादेरभावे मृतदेयमातामहादिपिण्डदातॄणां मातुलादीनामानन्तर्यक्रमेणाधिकारो[52] बोद्धव्यः ।

<21> एतत्पर्यन्ताभावे तु सकुल्यः । तदाह **मनुः** —

[45] सपिण्डत्व- । सपिण्ड-

[46] -मध्य- । -मध्ये ।। -पाठात् । -पाठानुपपत्तेः

[47] च । *om*

[48] प्रदातृत्वेनानन्तर्यार्थमिति । प्रदातृत्वानन्तर्यार्थमिति

[49] तस्माद्यो यस्तत्कुलो- । तस्माद्यो यत्कुलो-

[50] सपिण्डस्तस्य । सपिण्डस्-

[51] मृतभोग्यमृतदेय- । मृतदेयमृतभोग्य-

[52] -धिकारो । -धिकारक्रमो

तदभावे सकुल्यः स्यादाचार्यः शिष्य एव वा ॥ [M 9.187cd]

सकुल्यो विभक्तपिण्डः प्रतिप्रणप्तृतः प्रभृति पुरुषत्रयमधस्तनं वृद्धप्रपितामहादिसंततिश्च ।

<22> तत्रापि प्रतिप्रणप्त्रादेरानन्तर्यं पिण्डलेपद्वारेण तेषामुपकारकत्वात् । तदभावे च[53] वृद्धप्रपिमहादिसंततिः । मृतदेयपिण्डलेपभुग्भ्यो[54] वृद्धप्रपितामहादिभ्यः पिण्डदातृत्वात् ।

<23> एवंविधसकुल्याभावे च समानोदकाः । सकुल्यपदेनैवोपात्ता मन्तव्याः ।

<24> तेषमभाव आचार्यः[55] । तस्याप्यभावे शिष्यः । आचार्यः शिष्य एव वेति **मनु**वचनात् ।

तदभावे सब्रह्मचारी । शिष्यः सब्रह्मचारिण इति निर्देशात्[56] ।

<25> तदभावे चैकगोत्राः । तदभावे चैकप्रवराः —

पिण्डगोत्रर्षिसंबन्धा रिक्थं भजेरन् ॥ [G 28.21]

इति **गोतम**वचनात् ।

<26> उक्तपर्यन्तानां तु[57] सर्वेषामभावे[58] ब्राह्मणास्तद्धनं गृह्णीयुः । यदाह[59] **मनुः** —

सर्वेषामप्यभावे तु ब्राह्मणा रिक्थभागिनः[60] ।
त्रैविद्याः शुचयो दान्ता एवं धर्मो न हीयते ॥ [M 9.188]

भोगेन क्षीयमाणोऽपि धर्मस्तदीयधनस्य ब्राह्मणगामित्वेनापरधर्मप्राप्त्या पूर्यमाणो[61] न हीयत इत्यत्रापि धनस्य तादर्थ्यमेव पुरस्करोति ।

[53] च । *om*

[54] -भुग्भ्यो । -भोगिभ्यो

[55] तेषामभाव आचार्यः । तेषामभावे चाचार्यः

[56] निर्देषात्। वचनात्

[57] तु । *om*

[58] सर्वेषामभावे । सर्वसंबन्धिनामभावे । सर्वेषामेवंविधानामभावे

[59] यदाह । तदाह

[60] -भागिनः । -हारिणः

[61] पूर्यमाणो । आपूर्यमाणो

<**27**> तदभावे[62] ब्राह्मणधनवर्जं राजा गृह्णीयात् ।

गोत्रर्षिसंबन्धानां ब्राह्मणानां चाभावस्तद्ग्रामे बोद्धव्यः । अन्यथा राजाधिकारस्य निर्विषयत्वापत्तेः[63] ।

<**28**> तत्र यदि त्रयाणामित्यादिना पितृदौहित्रमातुलादीनामधिकारो नोक्तः स्यात्तदा सकुल्यादीनां नियतक्रमाणां मध्येऽनुप्रवेशाभावादधिकार एव न स्यात् ।

न च मा भूदिति वाच्यम् । **याज्ञवल्क्येन** तेषां[64] गोत्रजबन्धुपदाभ्यां दर्शितत्वात् । तस्मान्**मनुना**पि त्रयाणामित्यनेनैव[65] दर्शितमिति[66] वाच्यम् ।

तस्माद्यथा यथा मृतधनस्य तदुपकारकत्वं भवति तथा तथाधिकारक्रमोऽनुसरणीयः ।

<**29**> अत एव पुत्रपौत्रप्रपौत्राणां तुल्यवदधिकार सिध्यति[67] । पुत्रेण लोकान् जयतीत्यादिवाक्येभ्यस्तुल्यवदुपकारश्रुतेः[68] तत्पिण्डदानाविशेषात् ।

अत एव जीवत्पितृकयोः पौत्रप्रपौत्रयोरनधिकारः सिध्यति । न जीवन्तमतिदद्यादिति श्रुत्या जीवन्तं पितरमतिक्रम्य तयोः पार्वणनिषेधादनुपकारकत्वात् । अन्यथा मृतपितृकयोरिव तयोरपि स्यात् । जननक्रमेण वा[69] सपिण्डानन्तर्यात्पुत्रस्यैव स्यान्न पौत्रप्रपौत्रयोः । न च पुत्रादीनां त्रयाणां युगपगधिकारप्रतिपादकं वचनमस्ति ।

तस्मादुपकाराविशेषादेव तुल्यवद्धनसंबन्धोऽभिधेयः । <**30**> एवं पूर्वोक्तरीत्या[70] मृतधनस्य मृतार्थत्वमनुसंधेयमुक्तक्रमेण ।

<**31**> स चायमर्थो दायभागप्रकरणे पुत्रादीनामुपकारकत्वातिशयाभिधानस्यानन्यप्रयोजनकत्वात् ।

[62] तदभावे । तदभावे तु

[63] राजाधिकारस्य निर्विषयत्वापत्तेः । राजाधिकारो न स्यादेव

[64] तेषां । च तेषां

[65] त्रयाणामित्यनेनैव । त्रयाणामित्यादिनैव

[66] दर्शितमिति । दर्शितोऽयमर्थ इति

[67] सिध्यति । *om*

[68] -तुल्यवदुपकार- । -तुल्योपकार-

[69] वा । च

[70] पूर्वोक्त- । सर्वत्रोक्त-

पितॄणामनृणश्चैव स तस्माल्लब्धुमर्हति ॥ [M 9.106cd]

इत्यानृण्यकरणस्य धनलाभहेतुत्वेन कीर्तनात् ।

दौहित्रेऽपि ह्यमुत्रैनं संतारयति पौत्रवत् ॥ [M 9.139cd]

इत्यनेनापि संतारणस्य धनसंबन्धहेतुत्वेन निर्देशात् ।

पुत्रादीनां च[71] त्रयाणां संतारणादन्यस्य[72] तुल्यवद्धनसंबन्धकारणस्याभावात् त्रयाणामुदकमित्यादेश्चानर्थक्यापत्तेः ।

क्लीबपतितजात्यन्धादीनां चानुपकारकत्वादेवानंशित्वाभिधानस्योपपत्तेः[73]।

प्रतिसंबन्धिनां चाधिकारार्थं वचनकल्पनागौरवात् ।[74]

तदर्जितधनस्य च तदुपकारतारतम्येन तादर्थ्यसंपादनस्य न्याय्यत्वात् ।

उपकारकत्वेनैव धनसंबन्धो[75] न्यायप्राप्तो **मन्वादीनाम**भिमत इति गम्यते[76] ।

<**32**> इति[77] निरवद्य**विद्योद्योतेन** द्योतितोऽयमर्थो[78] विद्वद्भिरादरणीयः ।

<**33**> अथात्रापरितोषो विदुषां वाचनिक एवायमर्थस्तथापि यथोक्त एव वचनयोरर्थो[79] ग्राह्य इत्यस्तु । किं विस्तरेण ।

<**34**> ब्राह्मणधनवर्जं राजा गृह्णीयात् । तदाह **मनुः** —

अहार्यं ब्राह्मणद्रव्यं राज्ञा नित्यमिति स्थितिः ।
इतरेषां तु वर्णानां सर्वाभावे हरेन्नृपः ॥ [M 9.189]

सर्वशब्देन ब्राह्मणपर्यन्तस्योपादानम् ।

<**35**> वानप्रस्थयतिब्रह्मचारिनां धनं धर्मभ्रातृसच्छिष्याचार्या गृह्णीयुः । तदभाव एकतीर्थ्येकाश्रमी गृह्णीयात् । तदाह **याज्ञवल्क्यः** —

वानप्रस्थयतिब्रह्मचारिणां रिक्थभागिनः ।

[71] च । *om*
[72] संतारणादन्यस्य । संतारकत्वादन्यस्य
[73] -वनांशित्वाभिधान- । -वनांशाभिधान-
[74] वचन- । श्रुति-
[75] धन- । धनस्य
[76] गम्यते । मन्यते । लक्ष्यते
[77] इति । *om*
[78] द्योतितोऽयम- । द्योतितत्वेनायम-
[79] वचनयोरर्थो । वचनार्थो

क्रमेणाचार्यसच्छिष्यधर्मभ्रात्रेकतीर्थिनः ॥ [Y 2.137]

<**36**> प्रतिलोमक्रमेण यथासंभवं[80] धनं ज्ञेयम् ।

ब्रह्मचारी च नैष्ठिकोऽभिमतः । पित्रादिपरित्यागेन यावज्जीवमाचार्यकुलनिवासपरिचर्यानिष्ठायास्तेन कृतत्वात् । उपकुर्वाणस्य तु[81] धनं पित्रादिभिरेव[82] ग्राह्यम् ।

<**37**> इत्यपुत्रादिधनाधिकारः ।

[80] यथासंभवं । यथासंभवं च

[81] तु । *om*

[82] पित्रादिभिरेव ग्राह्यम् । पित्रादिभिर्ग्राह्यम् ॥ ग्राह्यम् । ग्राह्यमिति

<**12.1**> अथ संसृष्टधनविभागः[1] ।

तत्र **मनु-विष्णू** —

विभक्ताः सह जीवन्तो विभजेरन् पुनर्यदि[2] ।
समस्तत्र विभागः स्याज्जयैष्ट्यं तत्र न विद्यते ।।[M 9.210 = Vi 18.41]

<**2**> समस्तत्रेति सवर्णभ्रातृसंसर्गाभिप्रायेण । ब्राह्मणक्षत्रिययोस्तु संसर्गे पूर्वक्लृप्तभागानुसारेणैव भागव्यवस्था बोद्धव्या[3] । पूर्वक्लृप्तज्येष्ठांशनिषेधमात्रपरं हि समवचनम्[4] । अत एव **बृहस्पतिः** —

विभक्ता भ्रातरो ये तु संप्रीत्यैकत्र संस्थिताः[5] ।
पुनर्विभागकरणे तेषां ज्यैष्ठ्यं न विद्यते ।। [B 26.106cdef]

इति[6] ज्येष्ठांशमात्रं[7] निषेधयति न तु भागसाम्यमपि[8] बोधयति ।

<**3**> संसर्गिनश्च **बृहस्पत्यु**क्ताः[9] —

विभक्तो यः पुनः पित्रा भ्रात्रा चैकत्र संस्थितः ।
पितृव्येणाथवा प्रीत्या स तु संसृष्ट उच्यते ।। [B 26.113]

<**4**> इति[10] परिगणितव्यतिरिक्तेषु संसर्गकृतो[11] विशेषो नादरणीयः परिगणनानर्थक्यात् । <**5**> अपरे तु[12] विशेषा भ्रात्रधिकारनिरूपणप्रकरणोक्ता[13] अनु-

[1] -धन- । *om*
[2] पुनर्यदि । पुनर्यदा
[3] भागव्यवस्था बोद्धव्या । भागो बोद्धव्यः
[4] -मात्रपरं हि समवचनम् । -मात्रपरं वचनम् । -मात्रपरत्वाद्वचनस्य
[5] संस्थिताः । वासिनः
[6] इति । *om*
[7] -मात्रं । -मात्रमेव
[8] -साम्यमपि । -साम्यमेव
[9] **बृहस्पत्यु**क्ताः । **बृहस्पतिना** दर्शिताः
[10] इति । *om*
[11] -कृतो । -कृत-
[12] तु । च
[13] -निरूपण- । *om*

सरणीयाः[14] ।

<**6**> इति संसृष्टविभागः[15] ।

[14] अनुसरणीयाः । अनुसंधेयाः । आदरणीयाः

[15] इति संसृष्टविभागः । *om* । इति संसृष्टाधिकारः

<**13.1**> अथ विभागकाले निह्नुतस्य पश्चादवगतस्य विभागः ।

तत्र **मनुः** —

ऋणे धने च सर्वस्मिन् प्रविभक्ते यथाविधि ।
पश्चाद्दृश्येत यत्किंचित्तत्सर्वं समतां नयेत् ।। [M 9.218]

<**2**> पूर्वं यथा यस्य भागकल्पना[1] कृता तत्समानैव कार्या । न पुनरपहर्तुरपहर्तृतयाल्पभागो दातव्यो न दातव्य एव[2] वेति समतां नयेदिति शब्दस्यार्थः । न पुनस्तत्र द्रव्ये सर्वेषां समभागार्थं वचनम्[3] विंशोद्धारादिबाधे हेत्वभावात् । ब्राह्मणक्षत्रियादीनां च समभागतापत्तेः[4] ।

<**3**> तथा[5] **याज्ञवल्क्यः** —

अन्योन्यापहृतं द्रव्यं विभक्तैर्यत्र दृश्यते ।
तत्पुनस्ते समैरंशैर्विभजेरन्निति स्थितिः ।। [Y 2.126]

<**4**> तथा **कात्यायनः** —

प्रच्छादितं तु यद्येन पुनरागत्य तत्समम् ।
भजेरन् भ्रातृभिः सार्धमभावेऽपि पितुः सुताः[6] ।। [K 885]
अन्योन्यापहृतं द्रव्यं दुर्विभक्तं च यद्भवेत् ।
पश्चात्प्राप्तं विभज्येत समभागेन तद् भृगुः ।। [K 886]

<**5**> असम्यग्विभक्तस्यापि[7] पुनर्विभागं दर्शयति । सकृदंशो निपततीति सम्यग्विभागविषयम्[8] । <**6**> पश्चात्प्राप्तमिति न[9] पूर्वविभक्तमपि विभजनीयमित्यर्थः ।

<**7**> तथा **कात्यायनः** —

बन्धुनापहृतं द्रव्यं बलान्नैव प्रदापयेत् ।

[1] भाग- । विभाग-
[2] एव । *om*
[3] वचनम् । वचनमिदम्
[4] समभागतापत्तेः । समभागापत्तेः
[5] तथा । तथाच । तथाह
[6] पितुः सुताः । हि तत्सुताः
[7] -भक्तस्यापि । -भागस्यापि
[8] निपततीति सम्यग्विभागविषयम् । निपततीत्यस्य सम्यग्विभागविषयत्वम्
[9] न । न पुनः

बन्धूनामविभक्तानां भोगं नैव प्रदापयेत[10] ।। [K 888]

सामादिना[11] दाप्यो न[12] बलात् । अविभक्तेन च[13] यदधिकं[14] भुक्तं तदसौ न दाप्यः ।

<**8**> अत्र च साधारणधने परधनमप्यस्तीति तन्निह्नवे स्तेन एव भवति किल्बिषी चेति ये[15] मन्यन्ते तान् प्रत्युच्यते — य एव हि परस्येदमिति विशेषेण[16] जानानः परस्वे स्वत्वहेतुमन्तरेणैव स्वत्वमारोपयति स स्तेन इति लोकप्रसिद्धोऽर्थः । न चात्रेदं परकीयमिदं वा ममेति विवेक्तुं शक्नोति द्रव्य-स्याविभक्तत्वात् ।

यथा[17] यदेव हि ममेदमिति विशेषेण[18] जानानः परस्वत्वापत्तये स्वामी त्यजति परश्च विशेषेणेदं ममेति स्वत्वं प्रत्येति तत्रैव दाननिष्पत्तिः । न च साधारणधने तथा संभवतीति साधारणधनमदेयमुक्तम्[19] । तथा स्तेयमपि नैतन्मम धनं परस्येदमिति जानत एव भवतीति न साधारणधनस्यापहारे[20] स्तेयनिष्पत्तिः ।

<**9**> अपहारपदं तु संगोपनाभिप्रायम् । न च संगोपनमेव स्तेयम्[21] । असंगुप्तहरणेऽपि स्तेयप्रयोगदर्शनात्[22] । तथा **कात्यायनः** —

प्रच्छन्नं वा प्रकाशं वा निशायामथवा दिवा ।
यत्परद्रव्यहरणं स्तेयं तत्परिकीर्तितम् ।। [K 810]

अत एव राज्ञा बलान्न दाप्य इति पूर्वमुक्तम् । चौरत्वे तु —

[10] प्रदापयेत् । प्रवर्तयेत्
[11] सामादिना । सामदानादिना
[12] न । न तु
[13] च । तु
[14] यदधिकं । यद्यदधिकं
[15] ये । ये तु
[16] विशेषेण । विशेषं
[17] यथा । तद्यथा
[18] विशेषेण । विशेषं
[19] साधारणधन- । साधारण-
[20] -धनस्यापहारे । -धनापहारे
[21] संगोपनमेव स्तेयम् । संगोपनं स्तेयमुक्तम्
[22] स्तेयप्रयोगदर्शनात् । स्तेयदर्शनात् । स्तेयपददर्शनात्

चौरं प्रदाप्यापाहृतं घातयेद्विविधैर्वधैः ॥ [Y 2.270ab]

इति वचनादास्तां सामादिना दापनं घातनमपि कार्यम् ।

<10> एतच्च मुनिभिरपहर्तुरपि विभागदानप्रतिपादनादुन्नीयते । <11> तदुक्तं[23] **विश्वरूपेणा**पि — अतस्तस्करदोषो[24] नास्ति[25] वचनारम्भसामर्थ्यत् । स्तेयधात्वर्थानिष्पत्तेरित्यभिप्रायः ।

<12> अत एव ***प्रायश्चित्तकाण्डे*** **जितेन्द्रियेण** भणितम् — यदि सुवर्णमेव[26] परकीयं लौहादिबुद्ध्या गृह्णात्यसुवर्णमेव[27] सुवर्णबुद्ध्या आत्मीयसदृशं वा परकीयमेवात्मीयबुद्ध्या गृह्णाति सर्वत्र नापहारनिष्पत्तिः । सर्वत्र यथावस्तु परकीयबुद्धेरभावात्[28] ।

तद्वदत्रापि समानम् । विभागात्पूर्वं तद्धंन्यैकदेशविशेषगतस्वत्वस्यापरिज्ञानात् । अतो नात्र स्तेयनिष्पत्तिः ।

<13> सत्यपि वा स्तेयेऽपहर्तुरपि विभागवचनदर्शनान्न स्तेयदोषः । अन्यथा सुवर्णादिनिह्नवे पतितस्य भागो न स्यात् ।

<14> अथ पातकहेतुसुवर्णापहारेऽपि[29] स्तेनस्य भाग इति विशेषवचनाभावाद्[30] द्रव्यान्तरस्तेयविषयो भागविधिर्वर्ण्यते[31] । एवं तर्हि सुवर्णादिस्तेयनिषेध एव किमित्यसाधारणपरकीयमात्रद्रव्यगोचरो[32] न व्यवस्थाप्यते । तथापि किं विनिगमनाप्रमाणमिति चेत् ।

उच्यते — परद्रव्यहरणं[33] स्तेयमिति परशब्दादात्मीयत्वव्यवच्छेदेनैव परकीयत्वस्यावगमात्साधारणासाधारणयोश्चासाधारणस्यैव शीघ्रप्रतीतेः । यथेष्टिपूर्वकमेवादः पौर्णमासं हविरित्यग्नीषोमीयपुरोडाशस्यैवोत्कर्षो नोपांशुयाजी । याज्यस्या-

[23] तदुक्तं । अत एवोक्तं
[24] अतस्तस्करदोषो । तस्करदोषो । अत्र तस्करदोषो
[25] नास्ति । नास्तीति
[26] सुवर्णमेव । स्वर्णमेव
[27] -सुवर्णमेव । सुवर्णं
[28] -बुद्धेरभावात् । -बुद्ध्यभावात्
[29] -पहारेऽपि । -पहारे
[30] -वचनाभावाद् । -वचनासंभवात्
[31] भाग- । विभाग-
[32] किमित्यसाधारण- । किमर्थमसाधारण-
[33] -हरणं । -ग्रहणं

ग्नीषोमीयानग्नीषोमीयस्य साधारणत्वात् । <**15**> अत एव लोकेऽपि नैवंविध-विषये क्वचिद्विनिगमनादिकं दृश्यते ।

<**16**> अतो यद् **बालक**वचनम् — यथा मुद्गापचारे माषप्रतिनिधौ मुद्गानां माषाणां च यज्ञसंबन्धेऽयज्ञिया वै माषा इति माषा निषिद्धास्तथात्मीयानात्मीयहरणेऽप्यनात्मीयापहारो[34] निषिद्ध इति[35] ।

तद्बालकवचनमेव । पूर्वव्याहृतस्य स्तेयपदार्थस्यैवाभावात्[36] । माषगतमुद्गावयवोपादाने तु[37] माषाणां यज्ञसंबन्धो नास्तीति न शक्यते वक्तुम् । माषामिश्रितानामेव यज्ञसंबन्धप्रतीतेः ।

<**17**> इत्यन्योन्यापहृतविभागः ।

[34] -त्मीयहरणे- । -त्मीयापहारे-

[35] निषिद्ध इति । निषिद्धः

[36] -पदार्थस्यैवाभावात् । -पदार्थस्याभावात्

[37] तु । ऽपि

<14.1> अथ वृत्तविभागसंदेहनिर्णयः[1] ।

तत्र **नारदः** —

विभागधर्मसंदेहे दायादानां विनिर्णयः ।
ज्ञातिभिर्भागलेख्येन पृथक्कार्यप्रवर्तनात् ।। [N 13.36]

<2> ज्ञातीनां कीर्तनं तेषे सत्सु नान्यसाक्षिग्रहणमित्येतदर्थम् ।

अत एव **याज्ञवल्क्यः** —

विभागनिह्नवे ज्ञातिबन्धुसाक्ष्यभिलेखितैः ।
विभागभावना ज्ञेया गृहक्षेत्रैश्च यौतकैः[2] ।। [Y 2.149]

<3> प्रथमं ज्ञातयः सपिण्डाः[3] साक्षिणः । तदभावे बन्धुपदोपनीताः[4] संबन्धिनः। तदभावे उदासीना अपि साक्षिणः । तुल्यवद्भावे साक्षिपदेनैवोपात्तत्वात् । ज्ञातिबन्धुपदानर्थकतापत्तेः[5] ।

<4> अत एव **शङ्खः** —

गोत्रभागविभागार्थसंदेहे समुपस्थिते ।
गोत्रजैश्चापरिज्ञाते कुलं साक्षित्वमर्हति ।। [ŚL 280]

गोत्रजैर्ज्ञातिभिरित्यर्थः । तैरज्ञाते कुलं बन्धुः साक्षित्वमर्हति । न पुनरसंबन्धी । तेनाप्यपरिज्ञातेऽन्यः साक्षीत्यर्थः ।

<5> अत एव मुख्यभूता ज्ञातय एव **नारदेन** निर्दिष्टाः । ज्ञातृभिरिति पाठोऽनाकरः ।

<6> तथा लिखितेन वा निर्णयः । लिखितं तु[6] साक्षिभ्यो बलवदेवेत्युक्तम्[7] ।

<7> तथा पृथक्कार्यप्रवर्तनादपि निर्णयः ।

[1] -संदेह- । -संदेहे

[2] यौतकैः । यौतुकैः

[3] सपिण्डाः । *om*

[4] -पदोपनीताः । -पदोपात्ताः

[5] -पदानर्थकतापत्तेः । -पदानर्थक्यात्

[6] तु । च

[7] बलवदेवेत्युक्तम् । बलवदित्युक्तम्

यथोक्तं[8] **नारदेन** —

दानग्रहणपश्वन्नगृहक्षेत्रपरिग्रहाः ।
विभक्तानां पृथग्ज्ञेयाः पाकधर्मागमव्ययाः ।। [N 13.38]
साक्षित्वं प्रातिभाव्यं च दानं ग्रहणमेव च ।
विभक्ता भ्रातरः कुर्युर्नाविभक्ताः परस्परम् ।। [N 13.39]
येषामेताः क्रिया लोके प्रवर्तन्ते स्वरिक्थतः ।
विभक्तानवगच्छेयुर्लेख्यमप्यन्तरेण तान् ।। [N 13.40]

<8> तथा **बृहस्पतिः** —

साहसं स्थावरं न्यासः प्राग्विभागश्च रिक्थिनाम् ।
अनुमानेन विज्ञेयं न स्यातां पत्रसाक्षिणौ ।। [B 26.143]
बलानुबन्धव्याघातं होढं साहसभावकम् ।
स्वस्य भोगः स्थावरस्य विभागस्य पृथग्धनम् ।। [B 26.146]
पृथगायव्ययधनाः कुसीदं[9] च परस्परम् ।
वणिक्पथं च ये कुर्युर्विभक्तास्ते न संशयः ।। [B 26.147]

<9> एको भ्राता ददात्यपरश्च गृह्णाति[10] । गृहादिकमायव्ययस्थितिश्च पृथक् पृथक् । एकेन[11] ऋणादिषु क्रियमानेष्वपरः[12] साक्षी प्रतिभूर्वा क्रियते । परस्परं वा ऋणादिव्यवहारः[13] । एको यत्किंचिद्द्रव्यमन्यतः क्रीत्वा वाणिज्यार्थं भ्रातरि विक्रीणीते । एवमादिका एकैकापि क्रिया परस्परविभक्तानामेव[14] संभवति । तया विभागानुमानं विद्वद्भिरनुसंधयम्[15] ।

[8] यथोक्तं । तथा चोक्तं
[9] कुसीदं । कुषीदं
[10] गृह्णाति । तद् गृह्णाति
[11] एकेन च
[12] -परः । -परश्च
[13] ऋणादि- । ऋणादिक- ।। -व्यवहारः । -व्यवहारः क्रियते
[14] परस्पर- । परस्परं
[15] विद्वद्भिर- । धीमद्भिर- ।। -नुसंधेयम् । -नुसंधेयमिति

<**10**> न च[16] येषामेताः क्रिया इत्येतच्छब्देन बह्वीनामुपादानान्मिलितानामेव[17] गमकत्वं वाच्यम् । न्यायमूलत्वाद्वचनानाम्[18] । एकैकत्रापि च न्यायस्याविशेषात् ।

<**11**> न स्यातां पत्रसाक्षिणावित्यनेन पत्रसाक्षिणोरभावेऽनुमानमनुसरणीयमित्युक्तम् ।

[16] च । तु

[17] बह्वीनामुपादाना- । बहुवचनोपादाना-

[18] -मूल- । -मूलक-

<**15.1**> नाचार्यगौरवपराहतदायभाग-
तत्त्वप्रबोधजनरञ्जनमत्र शक्यम् ।
किंतु प्रमाणपरतन्त्रधियां मुनीनां[1]
संवादमात्रकृतये कृतिनः प्रयत्नः ॥
<**2**> बहुविधपूर्वनिबन्धृव्याख्यासंजातसंशयस्यैतत्[2] ।
जीमूतवाहनकृतं[3] प्रकरणमपनुत्तये ध्येयम् ॥[4]

<**3**> इति पारिभद्रीयमहामहोपाध्यायश्रीजीमूतवाहनकृते[5] धर्मरत्ने दायभागः समाप्तः ।

[1] -धियां मुनीनां । -धियाममीषां
[2] -निबन्धृ- । -निबन्ध-
[3] -कृतं । -कृत-
[4] *add* पारिभद्रकुलोद्भूतः श्रीमान् जीमूतवाहनः ।
दायभागं चकारेमं विदुषां संशयच्छिदे ॥
[5] -श्री- । -श्रील- । -श्रीयुक्त- । श्रीयुत- ॥ -कृते । -कृतौ

BIBLIOGRAPHY

Acharyya, Bijay Kisor. 1914. *Codification in British India*. *TLL* 1912. Calcutta: S.K. Banerji.

Agni-purāṇa. Ed. *ĀnSS* 41. 2d ed. 1957. Tr. N. Gangadharan. Ancient Indian Tradition and Mythology 27–29. Delhi: Motilal Banarsidass, 1984–86.

Aitareya-brāhmaṇa. Ed. Theodor Aufrecht. Bonn: Marcus, 1879. Tr. A. Berriedale Keith. *HOS* 25. 1929.

Alexandrowicz, C.. B. 1958. *A Bibliography of Indian Law*. Madras: Oxford University Press.

Aparārka or Aparāditya, comm. on Yājñavalkya. Ed. *ĀnSS* 46. 1903. Tr. (section on inheritance) S. Srinivasa Aiyar. Madras: Ananda Press, 1911.

Āpastamba (*Āpastamba-dharmasūtra*). Ed. Georg Bühler. *BSS* 44, 50. 3d ed. 1932. Tr. Bühler. *SBE* 2. 1879; see Olivelle 1999, 2000.

Āpastamba-śrautasūtra. Ed. Richard Garbe. *BI* 92. 3 vols. 1882–1902. Tr. Willem Caland. Vol. 1, Göttingen: Vandenhoeck and Ruprecht, 1921. Vols. 2–3, Verhandelingen der Koninklijke Akademie van Wetenschappen, Amsterdam. Afd. Letterkunde, n.r. 24.2. 1924; 26.4. 1928.

Arthasaṃgraha, by Laugākṣi Bhāskara. Ed. tr. D.V. Gokhale. Poona: Oriental Book Agency.

Aṣṭādhyāyī, by Pāṇini. Ed. tr. Otto Böhtlingk. Leipzig: Haessel, 1887. Repr. Hildesheim: Olms, 1964. Includes the *Dhātupāṭha*. See also *Kāśikā* and *Mahābhāṣya*.

Āśvalāyana-gṛhyasūtra. Ed. tr. Adolf F. Stenzler. *AKM* 3.4. 1864–65. Tr. Hermann Oldenberg. *SBE* 29. 1886.

Bālakrīḍā, by Viśvarūpa, comm. on Yājñavalkya. Ed. T. Gaṇapati Śāstrī. *TSS* 74, 81. 1922, 1924. Ed. tr. (section on inheritance) S. Sivarama Sastri. Madras: Lawrence Asylum Steam Press, 1900.

Bālambhaṭṭī, by Vaidyanātha Pāyaguṇḍa, comm. on the *Mitākṣarā*. Ed. Nityānanda Panta Pārvatīya. *ChSS* 41. 1914.

Banerjea, Tara Prosonno. 1893. *A Manual of Hindu Law of Succession*. 3 vols. Vol. 1: *The Bengal School*. Calcutta: Calcutta Central Press.

Banerjee, Gooroodas. 1984. *The Hindu Law of Marriage and Stridhana*. *TLL* 1878. Calcutta: Thacker, Spink. 4th ed. 1915. Repr. Delhi: Mittal Publications.

Banerji, Suresh Chandra. 1942–43a. "The Dīpakalikā of Śūlapāṇi with Special Reference to the Vyavahāra Section." *NIA* 5: 31–35.

______. 1942–43b. "Śūlapāṇi, the Sāhuḍiyān." *NIA* 5: 145–56, 170–76.

______. 1943–44. "Jīmūtavāhana, Śūlapāṇi and Raghunandana on Certain Laws of Inheritance." *NIA* 6: 197–205.

______. 1949. "Smṛti-nibandha Literature and Bengal's Contribution." *IHQ* 25: 38–51.

______. 1962a. *Smṛtiśāstre Bāṅgālī (Contributions of Bengalee Scholars to Smṛti Śastra)*. Calcutta: A. Mukherji.

______. 1962b. *Dharma-sūtras. A Study in Their Origin and Development*. Calcutta: Punthi Pustak.

Baudhāyana (*Baudhāyana-dharmasūtra*). Ed. Eugen Hultzsch. *AKM* 8.4. 1884; with comm. of Govindasvāmi. *KSS* 104. 1934. Tr. Georg Bühler. *SBE* 14. 1882; see Olivelle 1999, 2000.

Bhandarkar, Ramakrishna Gopala. 1983. *Early History of the Deccan*. Repr. Poona: Bhandarkar Oriental Research Institute. Repr. of *Collected Works*, vol. 3. 1927.

Bhāruci, comm. on Manu. Ed. tr. J. D. M. Derrett. 2 vols. Schriftenreihe des Südasien-Instituts der Universität Heidelberg 18. Wiesbaden: Steiner, 1975.

Bhattacharya, Bhabatosh. 1935. "Pre-Raghunandana Digests of Bengal and Bihar." 7 *AIOC* (Baroda 1933). Baroda: Oriental Institute, pp. 31–35.

______. 1950. "A Few Remarks on S. C. Banerjee's 'Smṛti-nibandha Literature and Bengal's Contribution.'" *ABORI* 31: 298–303.

Bhattacharya, Jogendra Nath. 1885. *A Commentary on the Hindu Law of Inheritance, Succession, Partition, Adoption, Marriage, and Stridhan*. Calcutta: Thacker, Spink.

______. 1893. *Commentaries on the Hindu Law of Inheritance, Succession, Partition, Wills, Adoption, Marriage, Maintenance, Stridhan, Endowments, Castes, and Priests*. 2d ed. Calcutta: Thacker, Spink.

______. 1909. *Commentaries on Hindu Law*. 3d ed., revised and enlarged by Nares Chandra Sen-Gupta and Rajendra Nath Bhattacharyya. Vol. 1. Calcutta: S.K. Lahiri.

Böhtlingk, Otto. 1870–73. *Indische Sprüche*. 2d ed. 3 vols. St. Petersburg: Kaiserliche Akademie der Wissenschaften. Leipzig: Voss. Repr. Osnabrück: Zeller; Wiesbaden: Harrassowitz, 1966.

______. 1887. See *Aṣṭādhyāyī*.

Böhtlingk, Otto and Rudolph Roth. 1855–75. *Sanskrit-Wörterbuch*. St. Petersburg: Kaiserliche Akademie der Wissenschaften. Repr. Osnabrück: Zeller; Wiesbaden: Harrassowitz, 1966.

Bose, B. C. 1880. *Hindu Matrimony*. Calcutta: J.N. Ghose.

Bṛhan-Manu. See Vṛddha-Manu.

Bṛhaspati (*Bṛhaspati-smṛti*). Ed. (reconstr.) K. V. Rangaswami Aiyangar. *GOS* 85. 1941. Tr. Julius Jolly. *SBE* 33. 1889. [Unless otherwise specified, the verses are numbered according to the 1941 ed.]

Brinkhaus, Horst. 1978. *Die altindischen Mischkastensysteme*. Alt- und Neu-Indische Studien 19. Wiesbaden: Steiner.

Brough, John. 1946–47. "The Early History of the Gotras." *JRAS* 1946: 32–45; 1947: 76–90.

______. 1953. *The Early Brahmanical System of Gotra and Pravara*. Cambridge University Press.

Brown, W. Norman. 1968. "Agni, Sun, Sacrifice and Vāc: A Sacerdotal Ode to Dīrghatamas (Rig Veda 1.164)." *JAOS* 88: 199–218. Repr. "Dīrghatamas's Vision of Creation." *India and Indology: Selected Articles by W. Norman Brown*. Ed. Rosane Rocher. Delhi: Motilal Banarsidass. 1978, pp. 53–74.

Bühler, Georg. 1879. See Āpastamba and Gautama.

______. 1882. See Baudhāyana and Vasiṣṭha.

______. 1886. See Manu.

Caland, Willem. 1888. *Über Totenverehrung bei einigen der indogermanischen Völker*. Verhandelingen der Koninklijke Akademie van Wetenschappen, Amsterdam. Afd. Letterkunde 17.

______. 1893. *Altindischer Ahnencult. Das Śrāddha nach den verschiedenen Schulen mit Benützung handschriftlicher Quellen dargestellt*. Leiden: Brill.

______. 1896. *Die altindischen Todten- und Bestattungsgebräuche. Mit Benützung handschriftlicher Quellen dargestellt.* Verhandelingen der Koninklijke Akademie van Wetenschappen, Amsterdam. Afd. Letterkunde n.r. 1.6.

Cannon, Garland (ed.). 1970. *The Letters of Sir William Jones.* 2 vols. Oxford: Clarendon.

Carnac, John 1788. "*An* Indian Grant *of* Land *in Y.C.* 1018, *literally translated from the* Sanscrit, *as explained by* Rámalóchan Pandit, *communicated by General* Carnac." *AsRes* 1: 357–67.

Chakravarti, Monmohan. 1907. "Sanskrit Literature in Bengal during the Sena Rule." *JASB* n.s. 2: 157–76.

______. 1912. "Bhaṭṭa Bhavadeva of Bengal." *JASB* n.s. 8: 333–48.

______. 1915. "Contributions to the History of Smṛti in Bengal and Mithilā." *JASB* n.s. 11: 311–406.

Chakravorty, Bani. 1965. "The Date of Raghunandana." *Calcutta Review* 176, no. 3: 177–82.

______. 1970. *Samājasaṃskāraka Raghunandana. Raghunandana. A Social Reformer.* 2d ed. Calcutta: Nava Granthanā.

Chatterjee (Śāstrī), Heramba. 1958. "An Incomplete Commentary on Dāyabhāga by Rāmabhadra." *OH* 6.1: 43–54.

______. 1959–. See *Vivādatāṇḍava.*

______. 1972–74. *Studies in the Social Background of the Forms of Marriage in Ancient India.* 2 vols. Calcutta: Sanskrit Pustak Bhandar.

______. 1978. See *Dāyabhāga.* Editions.

Chatterjee, Nirmal Chandra. 1923. "Patria Potestas in Ancient India." 2 *AIOC* (Calcutta 1922). Calcutta: University, pp. 365–77.

Chunder, Bholanauth. 1869. *The Travels of a Hindoo to Various Parts of Bengal and Upper India.* 2 vols. London: Trübner.

Cochrane, John. 1872. *Hindoo Law. Defence of the Daya Bhaga.* London: Wm. A. Allen.

Colebrooke, Henry Thomas. 1798. *A Digest of Hindu Law on Contracts and Successions, with a Commentary.* 4 vols. Calcutta: Honourable Company's Press. 1874. 4th ed. 2 vols. Madras: Higginbotham.

______. 1801. "The Religious Ceremonies of the Hindus, and of the Brahmans Especially. Essay II." *AsRes* 7: 232–85. Repr. Colebrooke 1873: 2.166–216

______ . 1810. *Two Treatises on the Hindu Law of Inheritance.* See *Dāyabhāga.* Translation.

______. 1825. "Account by H. T. Colebrooke, Esq. of the Hindu Schools of Law." In T. A. L. Strange 1825: 1.313–18.

______. 1827. "On the Philosophy of the Hindus, Part 3." *Proceedings of the Royal Asiatic Society* 1: 439–61. Repr. Colebrooke 1873: 2.319–99.

______. 1873. *Miscellaneous Essays. With the Life of the Author by His Son* (Thomas Edward Colebrooke). New ed. by E. B. Cowell. 3 vols. London: Trübner.

Cowell, Edward Byles. 1867. "Report on the Tolls of Nudea." *Proceedings of the Asiatic Society of Bengal*, pp. 86–102.

Cowell, Herbert. 1870–71. *The Hindu Law: Being a Treatise on the Law Administered Exclusively to Hindus by the British Courts in India. TLL* 1870, 1871. Calcutta: Thacker, Spink.

Crooke, William. 1908. "Ancestor-Worship and Cult of the Dead (Indian)." *ERE* 1: 450a–54b.

Dānakāṇḍa. See *Kṛtyakalpataru*.
Dānakriyākaumudī, by Govindānanda Kavikaṅkaṇācārya. Ed. Kamala Kṛṣṇa Smṛtibhūṣaṇa. *BI* 155. 1903.
Dānasāgara, by Ballālasena/Vallālasena. Ed. Bhabatosh Bhattacharya. *BI* 274. 1953–56.
Dattakacandrikā, by Kubera Upādhyāya. Ed. Bharata Candra Śiromaṇi. Calcutta: Girīśa Vidyāratna Press, 1867. Tr. J. C. C. Sutherland (see *Dattakamīmāṃsā*).
Dattakamīmāṃsā, by Nandapaṇḍita. Ed. Bharata Candra Śiromaṇi. Calcutta: Girīśa Vidyāratna Press, 1867. Tr. J. C. C. Sutherland. 2d ed. Calcutta: Baptist Mission Press, 1834. In Setlur 1911, 1: 355–422.

- - - - - - - - - -

Dāyabhāga, by Jīmūtavāhana.[1]

Editions

1813. 104 oblong folios. With Śrīkṛṣṇa's comm.
1829. Ed. Lakṣmī Nārāyaṇa Śarmā. With Śrīkṛṣṇa's comm. Calcutta: Education Press.
1850. Ed. Bharata Candra Śiromaṇi. With Śrīkṛṣṇa's comm. Calcutta: Saṃskṛta Press.
1863. Ed. Bharata Candra Śiromaṇi. With the comm. of Śrīnātha Ācāryacūḍāmaṇi, Rāmabhadra Nyāyālaṅkāra, Acyutānanda Cakravartin, Maheśvara Bhaṭṭācārya, Raghunandana Bhaṭṭācārya, and Śrīkṛṣṇa Tarkālaṅkāra. Calcutta: Vidyāratna Press.
1866. Kṛṣṇakānta Vidyāvāgīśa Bhaṭṭācārya's *Dāyabhāga-ṭīkā*. Ed. Bharata Candra Śiromaṇi. Calcutta: Girīśa Vidyāratna Press. (pp. 361–458, continued from 1863 ed.)
1867/68. Ed. Caṇḍīcaraṇa Smṛtibhūṣaṇa. With Śrīkṛṣṇa's comm. and Bengali tr. Calcutta.
1870a. Ed. Candramohana Siddhāntavāgīśa. With Śrīkṛṣṇa's comm. and Bengali tr. Calcutta: Prākṛta Press.
1870b. Ed. Mathurānātha Tarkaratna. With Śrīkṛṣṇa's comm. and Bengali tr. Calcutta.
1877/78. Ed. Caṇḍīcaraṇa Smṛtibhūṣaṇa. With Śrīkṛṣṇa's comm. and Bengali tr. Calcutta.
1883. 2d ed. of 1870a.
1893. Ed. Jīvānanda Vidyāsāgara. With Śrīkṛṣṇa's comm. 2d ed. Calcutta: Siddheswar Press.
1897/98. Ed. Nīlakamala Vidyānidhi. With Śrīkṛṣṇa's comm. and Bengali tr. Calcutta: Dākṣayaṇī Press.
1909/10. 2d ed. of 1867/68.
1929/30. 2d ed. of 1897/98.
1973. Ed. A. Subrahmanya Sastri. With Hindi intro. 3d ed. Mimansa Dharmashastra Text Society 5. Pañcagaṅgā-Vārāṇasī: Parvatīya Mudraṇālaya.
1978. Ed. tr. Heramba Chatterjee. Part 1. Howrah: Howrah Saṃskṛta Sāhitya Samāja.

Translation

1810. H. T. Colebrooke: *Two Treatises on the Hindu Law of Inheritance*. Calcutta: Hindoostani Press, pp. 1–240.

Reprints

1822. Madras. Repr. of 1810.

[1] As far as the *Dāyabhāga* is concerned I have made an effort to compile as complete a list as possible of its editions and of the several reprints of Colebrooke's translation. Some items in this list I have not been able to consult personally.

1864. Madras: Graves, Cookson and Co.
1865. Whitley Stokes: *Hindú Law Books. Edited, with Notes and an Index.* Madras: Higginbotham, pp. 181–363 (= 1864).
1867. Repr. of 1822 (called 3d ed.). With Preface by William Sloane, and an index.
1868. Ed. Girish Chundra Turkalankar. (Containing a collection of precedents bearing upon the subjects treated by the author). Calcutta: S. Banerjee.
1870. New and improved 2d ed. of 1868. Calcutta: Tomohur Press, Serampore.
1883. *Two Treatises on the Hindu Law of Inheritance.* Ed. Golap Chandra Sarkar Śastri and Sris Chandra Chaudhuri. Calcutta: B. Banerjee.
1895. *Three Treatises on the Hindu Law of Inheritance.* Madras: Higginbotham (called repr. of 1867; also includes tr. of *Dāyādhikārakramasaṃgraha*).
1911. In Setlur 2:1–108.
1984. Repr. of 1867. Parimal Sanskrit Series 13. Delhi: Parimal.

- - - - - - - - - -

Dāyādhikārakramasaṃgraha, by Śrīkṛṣṇa Tarkālaṅkāra. Ed. Lakṣmī Nārāyaṇa Śarmā. Calcutta: Education Press, 1828. Tr. (+ text) Paul Marrist Wynch. 2d ed., revised, corrected, and enlarged by Giris Chandra Tarkalankara. Bhowanipore: Sreenath Chatterjee, 1878. In *Three Treatises on the Hindu Law of Inheritance* (see *Dāyabhāga* tr. 1895). In Setlur 1911, 2: 109–58.
Dāyakaumudī, by Rāmajaya Tarkālaṅkāra. Calcutta: Church Mission Press, 1827.
Dāyatattva, by Raghunandana. Ed. Jīvānanda Vidyāsāgara. *Smṛtitattva*. Calcutta: Siddhesvar Press. 2d ed., 1885, vol. 2, pp. 161–97. Tr. (+ text) Golap Chandra Sarkar. 2d ed. Calcutta: Cambray, 1904. In Setlur 1911, 2: 469–514.
Derrett, J. Duncan M. 1952a. "The Relative Antiquity of the Mitākṣarā and the Dāyabhāga." M.L.J. 2, Journal 9–14 (= *Essays* 1.198–206).
______. 1952b. "A New Light on the Mitaksara as a Legal Authority." *JIH* 30: 35–55.
______. 1956. "An Indian Contribution to the Study of Property." *BSOAS* 18: 475–98 (= *Essays* 1.333–57).
______. 1957a. "Prohibition and Nullity: Indian Struggles with a Jurisprudential Lacuna." *BSOAS* 20: 203–15 (= *Essays* 1.266–79).
______. 1957b. *Hindu Law Past and Present.* Calcutta: A. Mukherjee.
______. 1957c. "Adoption in Hindu Law." *ZVR* 60: 34–90 (= *Essays* 3.25 83).
______. 1958a. "Factum Valet: The Adventures of a Maxim." *The International and Comparative Law Quarterly* 7: 280–302 (= *Essays* 3.1–24).
______. 1958b. "A Strange Rule of Smṛti, and a Suggested Solution." *JRAS* 17–25 (= *Essays* 1.217–26).
______. 1962. "The Development of the Concept of Property in India c. A.D. 800-1800." *ZVR* 64: 15–130 (= *Essays* 2.8–130).
______. 1963. *Introduction to Modern Hindu Law.* Bombay: Oxford UP.
______. 1965a. "The Father's Share: A Forgotten Chapter of Dayabhaga Law." 69 C.W.N.: xxxvii–xxxix.
______. 1965b. "A Juridical Fabrication of Early British India: The Mahānirvāṇa-tantra." *ZVR* 67: 203–36 (= *Essays* 2.197–242).
______. 1968. *Religion, Law and the State in India.* London: Faber and Faber.
______. 1969. "The Indian Subcontinent under European Influence." John Gilissen (ed.): *Bibliographical Introduction to Legal History and Ethnology* E/8. Brussels: Institut de Sociologie.

______. 1971. "A Want of Legal History in the Supreme Court." M.L.J. 1, Journal 39–45 (= *Essays* 4.1–7).

______. 1973a. *Dharmaśāstra and Juridical Literature.* A History of Indian Literature, ed. J. Gonda. Part of vol. 4. Wiesbaden: Harrassowitz.

______. 1973b. *History of Indian Law (Dharmaśāstra).* Handbuch der Orientalistik., ed. B. Spuler et al. II.3.1. Leiden: Brill.

______. 1975. See Bhāruci.

______. 1976–78. *Essays in Classical and Modern Hindu Law.* 4 vols. Leiden: Brill.

______. 1977a. "The Relation of a Married Woman to Her Husband's Adopted Son in Hindu Theory and Practice: A Correction." Addendum to 1957c (= *Essays* 3.84–88).

______. 1977b. "'Must' and 'Ought': Problems of Translation in Sanskritic Hindu Law." *Language and Thought. Anthropological Issues.* Ed. William C. McCormack and Stephen A. Wurm. The Hague: Mouton, pp. 251–59 (= *Essays* 4.415–23).

______. 1978. Foreword to Chatterjee's 1978 *Dāyabhāga* ed.

Deshpande, V. V. 1943. *Dharma-sastra and the Proposed Hindu Code.* Kashi: S.M. Parande.

Devala (*Devala-smṛti*). Mukund Lalji Wadekar: *Reconstruction and Critical Study.* 2 vols. Delhi: Koshal Book Depot, 1996–97.

Devasthali, G. V. 1991. *Mimamsa: The Ancient Indian Science of Sentence Interpretation.* 2d ed. Delhi: Satguru.

Dharmakośa, Vyavahārakāṇḍa. Ed. Laxmanshastri Joshi. Wai: Prajñā Pāṭhaśālā Maṇḍala, 1941. (For the section on inheritance, see part 2, pp. 1120–1589.)

Dhātupāṭha. See *Aṣṭādhyāyī*, ed. Böhtlingk.

Dīpakalikā, by Śūlapāṇi, comm. on Yājñavalkya. Ed. Jagannātha Raghunātha Gharpure. The Collection of Hindu Law Texts 26. Bombay: Office of The Collection of Hindu Law Texts, 1939.

Donner, Otto. 1870. *Das Piṇḍapitṛyajña, oder Manenopfer mit Klössen bei den Indern.* Berlin: S. Calvary.

Durgotsavaviveka, by Śūlapāṇi. Sanskrit Sāhitya Parishad Series 1. Calcutta: Siddheshvara Press, 1924.

Eggeling, Julius. 1891. *Catalogue of the Sanscrit Manuscripts in the Library of the India Office.* Part I.3. London: Gilbert, Rivington.

Elberling, Frederik Emil. 1844. *A Treatise on Inheritance, Gift, Will, Sale and Mortgage; with an Introduction on the Laws of the Bengal Presidency.* Serampore: Mission Press.

Gajendragadkar, P. B. 1963. "The Historical Background and Theoretic Basis of Hindu Law." A.I.R. 50, Journal 18–26. [Also in *The Cultural Heritage of India.* Calcutta: Ramakrishna Mission Insitute of Culture. 2d ed. 1962. 2.414–33.]

Ganapathi Iyer, P. R. 1915. *Hindu Law: A Treatise.* Book I: General Principles and Marriage. Madras: Minerva Press.

Gautama (*Gautama-dharmasūtra*). Ed. A. F. Stenzler. London: Trübner, 1876. Ed. with Haradatta's comm. *Mitākṣarā. ĀnSS* 61. 1910. Tr. Bühler. *SBE* 2. 1879; see Olivelle 1999, 2000.

Gerow, Edwin. 1977. *Indian Poetics.* A History of Indian Literature, ed. J. Gonda. Vol. 5.3. Wiesbaden: Harrassowitz.

Gharpure, Jagannātha Raghunātha. 1931. *Hindu Law.* 4th ed. Bombay: Office of The Collection of Hindu Laws Texts.

______. 1943. *Sāpiṇḍya or the Law of Sapiṇḍa Relationship.* Bombay: Office of The Collection of Hindu Law Texts.

Ghose, Jogendra Chunder. 1903. *The Principles of Hindu Law*. Calcutta: B.C. Audrey. 3d ed. 3 vols. 1917–19. Calcutta: S.C. Auddy.

Ghose, Panchanan. 1917. "Jimutavahana." 26 C.L.J., Journal 17–31.

Goldstücker, Theodor. 1871. *On the Deficiencies in the Present Administration of Hindu Law*. London: Trübner.

Grady, Standish Grove. 1868. *A Treatise on the Hindoo Law of Inheritance*. London: Wildy; Madras: Gantz.

Gupte, S. V. 1947. *Hindu Law in British India*. 2d ed. Bombay: N.M. Tripathi.

______. 1963. *Hindu Law of Succession*. Bombay: N.M. Tripathi.

[Hamilton, Alexander]. 1811. Review of Mark Wilks' s *Historical Sketches of the South of India*. *Edinburgh Review* vol. 18, no. 36: 343–70.

Hārīta (*Hārīta-smṛti*). Ed. (reconstr.). tr. J. Jolly. *Abhandlungen der philosophisch-philologischen Classe der Königlich Bayerischen Akademie der Wissenschaften* 18, 1890, 505–24.

Harṣacarita, by Bāṇa. Ed. P. V. Kane. 2d ed. Delhi: Motilal Banarsidass, 1965.

Hastings, James (ed.). 1910–27. *Encyclopaedia of Religion and Ethics*. Edinburgh: T. & T. Clark; New York: Scribner. Repr. New York: Scribner, 1951.

Hazra, Rajendra Chandra. 1950a. "A Note on Smārta Raghunandana's Works and Time." *BhV* 11: 178–82.

______. 1950b. "Śrīnātha Ācārya-cūḍāmaṇi (His Works and History)." *IHQ* 26: 277–92.

______. 1951. "Śrīnātha Ācārya-cūḍāmaṇi, a Smṛti Writer of Bengal." *ABORI* 32: 34–52.

Herberich, Gustav. See Vṛddha-Manu.

Hillebrandt, Alfred. 1879. *Das altindische Neu- und Vollmondsopfer in seiner einfachsten Form*. Jena: Gustav Fischer. Repr. Gratz: Akademische Druck- und Verlagsanstalt, 1977.

Hunter, William Wilson. 1875–77. *A Statistical Account of Bengal*. 20 vols. London: Trübner.

Inden, Ronald B. 1976. *Marriage and Rank in Bengali Culture. A History of Caste and Class in Middle Period Bengal*. Berkeley: University of California Press.

Jain, H. C. 1970. *Indian Legal Materials. A Bibliographic Guide*. Bombay: N.M. Tripathi.

Jha, Ganganatha. 1911. *The Prabhākara School of Pūrva Mīmāmsā*. Allahabad: The Manager "Indian Thought."

______. 1920–29. *Manu-smṛti. The Laws of Manu with the Bhāṣya of Medhātithi*. 5 vols. Calcutta: University. Repr. Delhi: Motilal Banarsidass, 1999.

______. 1930–33. *Hindu Law in Its Sources*. 2 vols. Allahabad: The Indian Press.

______. 1942a. *Pūrva-mīmāṃsā in Its Sources*. Benares: Benares Hindu University.

______. 1942b. See *Vivādacintāmaṇi*.

Jolly, Julius. 1885. *Outlines of an History of the Hindu Law of Partition, Inheritance and Adoption, as Contained in the Original Sanskrit Treatises*. *TLL* 1883. Calcutta: Thacker, Spink.

______. 1887. See Manu.

______. 1889. See Bṛhaspati and Nārada.

______. 1890. See Hārīta.

______. 1896. *Recht und Sitte (inschlieslich der einheimischen Litteratur)*. Grundriss der Indo-Arischen Philologie und Altertumskunde II.8. Strassburg: Trübner. Tr. (authorized) Batakrishna Ghosh: *Hindu Law and Custom*. Calcutta: Greater India Society, 1928.

______. 1924. "Viśvarūpa." *JIH* 3: 1–27.

Jones, Sir William. See Cannon.

Kālaviveka, by Jīmūtavāhana. Ed. Pramathanātha Tarkabhūṣaṇa. *BI* 136. 1905.

Kane, Pandurang Vaman. 1921–23. "Vedic Basis of Hindu Law." *JBBRAS* 26: 57–82.

______. 1925. "The Predecessors of Vijñāneśvara." *JBBRAS* n.s. 1: 193–224.

______. 1930–. *History of Dharmaśāstra (Ancient and Mediaeval Religious and Civil Law*). Vol. 1, 1930; 2d ed. in 2 parts, 1968, 1975. Vol. 2, in 2 parts, 1941; 2d ed. 1974. Vol. 3, 1946; repr. 1973. Vol. 4, 1953; repr. 1973. Vol. 5, in 2 parts, 1958, 1962; repr. 1974, 1977. Poona: Bhandarkar Oriental Research Institute.

______. 1933. See Kātyāyana.

______. 1965. See *Harṣacarita*.

Kāśikā, by Vāmana and Jayāditya, comm. on Pāṇini's *Aṣṭādhyāyī*. Ed. tr. Śrīśa Chandra Vasu. Allahabad: Indian Press/Panini Office, 1891–98. Repr. Delhi: Motilal Banarsidass, 1962.

Kāṭhaka-saṃhitā. Ed. Leopold von Schroeder. 3 vols. Leipzig: Deutsche Morgenländische Gesellschaft, 1900, 1909, 1910.

Kātyāyana (*Kātyāyana-dharmaśāstra*). Ed. tr. (reconstr.). P. V. Kane. Poona: Oriental Book Agency, 1933.

Kātyāyana-śrautasūtra. Ed. A. Weber. *ChSS* 19. 1908. Repr. *ChSS* 104. 1972.

Keith, A. Berriedale. 1921. *The Karma-mīmāṃsā*. The Heritage of India Series. London: Oxford University Press.

Knipe, David. 1977. "*Sapiṇḍīkaraṇa*: The Hindu Rite of Entry into Heaven." Frank E. Reynolds and Earle H. Waugh (ed.): *Religious Encounters with Death*. University Park: Pennsylvania State University Press, pp. 111–24.

Kohler, Josef. 1888. "Ueber die Gewohnheitsrechte von Bengalen." *ZVR* 9: 321–60.

______. 1910. "Das älteste Lehrbuch der juristischen Auslegungs- und Methodenlehre. Jaiminis Mimansa-Regeln." *Archiv für Rechts- und Wirtschaftsphilosophie* 4: 235–43.

Kṛtyakalpataru, by Lakṣmīdhara. Ed. K. V. Rangaswami Aiyangar.

______. *Dānakāṇḍa*. *GOS* 92. 1941.

______. *Śrāddhakāṇḍa*. *GOS* 110. 1950.

______. *Vyavahārakāṇḍa*. *GOS* 119. 1953.

______. Introduction to *Vyavahārakāṇḍa*. *GOS* 127. 1958.

Lingat, Robert. 1967. *Les sources du droit dans le système traditionnel de l'Inde*. Paris: Mouton. Tr. (with additions) J. D. M. Derrett: *The Classical Law of India*. Berkeley: University of California Press, 1973.

Long, James. 1868. *Adam's Reports on Vernacular Education in Bengal and Bihar*. Submitted to Government in 1835, 1936, and 1838. Calcutta: Home Secretariat.

Macdonell, Arthur Anthony. 1921. "Vedic Religion." *ERE* 12: 601a-18b.

Macnaghten, Francis Workman. 1824. *Considerations on the Hindu Law as It Is Current in Bengal*. Serampore: Mission Press. See Wilson 1825.

Macnaghten, William Hay. 1829, 1828. *Principles and Precedents of Hindu Law*. 2 vols. Calcutta: Baptist Mission Press.

Mahābhārata. Ed. Vishnu S. Sukthankar et al. Poona: Bhandarkar Oriental Research Institute, 1927–72.

Mahābhāṣya, by Patañjali. Ed. Franz Kielhorn. *BSS* 18–20, 28–30, 1880–85. Repr. Osnabrück: Zeller, 1970.

Maitrāyaṇīya-saṃhitā. Ed. Leopold von Schroeder. 4 vols. Leipzig: Deutsche Morgenländische Gesellschaft, 1881.

Majumdar, Ramesh Chandra (ed.) 1966. *The Struggle for Empire.* 2d ed. Bombay: Bharatiya Vidya Bhavan.

______. 1971. *History of Ancient Bengal.* Calcutta: G. Bharadwaj.

Mandlik, Vishvanath Narayan. 1880. See *Vyavahāramayūkha.*

______. 1886. See Manu.

Manu (*Manu-smṛti, Mānava-dharmaśāstra*). Ed. J. Jolly. London: Trübner, 1887. Ed. Visvanath Narayan Mandlik, with comm. of Medhātithi, Sarvajñanārāyaṇa, Kullūkabhaṭṭa, Rāghavānanda, Nandana, and Rāmacandra. Bombay: Ganpat Krishnaji's Press, 1886. Tr. G. Bühler. *SBE* 25. 1886. See also Bhāruci.

Manunāradīyasaṃhitā, with Bhavasvāmin's comm. Ed. Sāmbaśiva Śastrī. *TSS* 97. 1929.

Mārkaṇḍeya-purāṇa. Ed. K. M. Banerjea. *BI* 29. 1862. Tr. F. Eden Pargiter. *BI* 125. 1904.

Mayne, John Dawson. 1878. *A Treatise on Hindu Law and Usage.* Madras: Higginbotham; London: Stevens and Haynes.

______. 1950. 11th ed. by N. Chandrasekhara Aiyar. Madras: Higginbotham.

______. 1986. 12th ed. by Alladi Kuppuswami. New Delhi: Bharat Law House.

Mayr, Aurel. 1873. *Das indische Erbrecht.* Vienna: Beck'sche Universitäts-Buchhandlung.

Mayrhofer, Manfred. 1956–. *Kurzgefasstes etymologisches Wörterbuch des Altindischen.* Heidelberg: Winter.

Mīmāṃsānyāyaprakāśa, by Āpadeva. Ed. tr. Franklin Edgerton. New Haven: Yale University Press, 1929. Repr. Delhi: Satguru, 1986.

Mīmāṃsāsūtras, attributed to Jaimini. Ed. with comm. 3 vols. *ĀnSS* 97. 1929–33. Tr. Ganganatha Jha, with Śabara's comm. 3 vols. *GOS* 66. 1933–36.

Mitākṣarā, comm. on Yājñavalkya, by Vijñāneśvara. Ed. Vāsudeva Lakṣmaṇa Paṇaśīkara. 4th ed. Bombay: Nirnaya Sagara Press, 1936. Tr. (section on inheritance) H. T. Colebrooke. Cf. *Dāyabhāga* tr. 1810, pp. 241–377. In Setlur 1911, 1:1–61. See also *Bālambhaṭṭī* and *Subodhinī*.

Mitra, Sarada Charan. 1905-1906. "Origin and Development of the Bengal School of Hindu Law." *LQR* 21: 380–92; 22: 50–63. See Setlur 1907.

Mitra, Trailokyanath. 1881. *The Law Relating to the Hindu Widow. TLL* 1879. Calcutta: Thacker, Spink.

Mitter, Dwarkanath. 1870. *Guru Gobind Shaha Mandal* v. *Anand Lal Ghose Mazumdar* 5 Beng. (F.B.) 15, 34–46. See Sanyal.

Mitter, Dwarka Nath. 1913. *The Position of Women in Hindu Law.* Calcutta: University.

Monier-Williams, Monier. 1899. *A Sanskrit-English Dictionary.* New ed. Oxford: Clarendon.

Mookerjee, Asutosh. See *Vyavahāramātṛkā.*

Morley, William Hook. 1858. *The Administration of Justice in British India; Its Past History and Present State: Comprising an Account of the Laws Peculiar to India.* London: Williams and Norgate.

Mulla, Dinshah Fardunji. 1912. *Principles of Hindu Law.* Bombay: N.M. Tripathi.

______. 1952. 11th ed. by Bijan Kumar Mukherjea. Calcutta: Eastern Law House.

______. 1959. 12th ed. by Sunderlal T. Desai. Bombay: N.M. Tripathi.

______. 1966. 13th ed. by Sunderlal T. Desai. Bombay: N.M. Tripathi. Repr. 1970.

______. 1982. 15th ed. by Sunderlal T. Desai. Bombay: N.M. Tripathi.

Müller, Klaus-Werner. 1992. *Das brahmanische Totenritual nach der Antyeṣṭipaddhati des Nārāyaṇabhaṭṭa.* Beiträge zur Südasienforschung. Südasien-Institut Universität Heidelberg 151. Stuttgart: Steiner.

Nārada (*Nārada-smṛti*). Ed. J. Jolly. *BI* 102. 1885. Tr. J. Jolly. *SBE* 33. 1889. Ed. tr. Richard. W. Lariviere. University of Pennsylvania Studies in South Asia 4–5. Philadelphia: Benjamins, 1989. [When Jolly's and Lariviere's numberings differ, I include them both, separated by a virgule.]

Nataraja Aiyyar, A. S. 1952. *Mīmāmsā Jurisprudence (The Sources of Hindu Law).* Allahabad: Ganganatha Jha Research Institute.

Nath, Vijay. 1987. *Dāna: Gift System in Ancient India (c. 600 B.C. - c. A.D. 300).* Delhi: Munshiram Manoharlal.

New Catalogus Catalogorum. 1949–. Ed. C. Kunhan Raja et al. Madras: University

Nyāya-sūtras, attributed to Gautama. Ed. tr., with Vātsyāyana's comm., Ganganatha Jha. Poona Oriental Series 58–59. Poona: Oriental Book Agency, 1939.

Olivelle, Patrick. 1999. *Dharmasūtras. The Law Codes of Āpastamba, Gautama, Baudhāyana, and Vasiṣṭha. Translated from the Original Sanskrit and Edited.* Oxford University Press.

______. 2000. *Dharmasūtras. The Law Codes of Āpastamba, Gautama, Baudhāyana, and Vasiṣtha. Annotated Text and Translation.* Delhi: Motilal Banarsidass.

Paiṭhīnasi (*Paiṭhīnasi-smṛti*). T. R. Chintamani: "Fragments of Paiṭhīnasi Dharmasūtra." *Annals of Oriental Research, Madras* 4, 1939–40, Sanskrit 1–40.

Pal, Radhabinod. 1929. *The History of the Law of Primogeniture, with Special Reference to India, Ancient and Modern. TLL* 1925. Calcutta: University.

Pandey, Raj Bali. 1969. *Hindu Saṃskāras (Socio-religious Study of the Hindu Sacraments).* 2d ed. Delhi: Motilal Banarsidass.

Pāṇini. See *Aṣṭādhyāyī.*

Pāraskara-gṛhyasūtra. Ed. tr. A. F. Stenzler. 2 vols. *AKM* 6.2, 4. 1876, 1878. Tr. H. Oldenberg. *SBE* 29. 1886.

Paul, Pramode Lal. 1939–40. *The Early History of Bengal (from the Earliest Times to the Muslim Conquest).* Indian Research Institute Publications. Indian History Series 2. 2 vols. Calcutta: Indian Research Institute.

Pawate, Iṣṭalingappa S. 1975. *Dāya-vibhāga: Or the Individualization of Communal Property and the Communalization of Individual Property in the Mitakshara Law.* 2d ed. Dharwar: Karnatak University.

Pitāmaha (*Pitāmaha-smṛti*). Ed. tr. (reconstr.) Karl Scriba. Leipzig: Drugulin, 1902.

Pramathanātha Tarkabhūṣaṇa. See *Kālaviveka.*

Prasad, R. C. 1995. *The Śrāddha. The Hindu Book of the Dead.* Delhi: Motilal Banarsidass.

Raghunandana Bhaṭṭācārya. See *Smṛtitattva.*

Rankin, George Claus. 1946. *Background to Indian Law.* Cambridge University Press.

Risley, Herbert Hope. 1891. *The Tribes and Castes of Bengal.* 2 vols. Calcutta: Bengal Secretariat Press. Repr. Calcutta: K.L. Mukhopadhyay, 1981.

Rocher, Ludo. 1953–54. "Quotations in Jīmūtavāhana's Vyavahāramātṛkā." *JOIB* 3: 134–46.

______. 1954. "Het positieve recht in het Oude Indië; zijn plaats in de Dharma en zijn vertakkingen." *Indonesië* 7: 296–319.

______. 1965. "Droit hindou ancien." John Gilissen (ed.): *Introduction bibliographique à l'histoire du droit et à l'ethnologie juridique* E/6. Brussels: Institut de Sociologie.

______. 1971. "*Janmasvatvavāda* and *Uparamasvatvavāda*: The First Chapters on Inheritance in the *Mitākṣarā* and *Dāyabhāga*." *OH* 19.1: 1–13.

______. 1972. "Schools of Hindu Law." J. Ensink and P. Gaeffke (ed.): *India Maior. Congratulatory Volume Presented to J. Gonda*. Leiden: Brill, pp. 167–76.

______. 1975. "Caste and Occupation in Classical India: The Normative Texts." *Contributions to Indian Sociology* n.s. 9.1: 139–51.

______. 1976. "In Defense of Jīmūtavāhana." *JAOS* 96: 107–9.

______. 1979. "The Sūtras and Śāstras on the Eight Types of Marriage." *Ludwik Sternbach Felicitation Volume*. Lucknow: Akhila Bharatiya Sanskrit Parishad, pp. 207–14.

______. 1980-81. "Notes on Mixed Castes in Classical India." *ALB* 44–45: 132–46.

______. 1984. "Henry Thomas Colebrooke (1765–1837): The Fourth President of the Asiatic Society." *South Asian Review* 8.5: 90–94.

______. 1992. "Inheritance and *Śrāddha*: The Principle of Spiritual Benefit." A. D. van den Hoek et al. (ed.): *Ritual, State and History in South Asia. Essays in Honour of J.C. Heesterman*. Leiden: Brill, pp. 637–49.

______. 1993. "Law Books in an Oral Culture: The Indian *Dharmaśāstras*." *Proceedings of the American Philosophical Society* 137: 254–67.

______. 1995. "Jīmūtavāhana's *Dāyabhāga* and the Maxim *Factum Valet*." *ALB* 59: 83–96.

______. 1997. "Quandoque bonus dormitat Jīmūtavāhanas?" Siegfried Lienhard and Irma Piovano (ed.): *Lex et litterae. Studies in Honour of Professor Oscar Botto*. Turin: Edizioni dell'Orso, pp. 425–31.

______. 1999. "The Aurasa Son." M. A. Dhaky and J. B. Shah (ed.): *Makaranda (Madhukar Anant Mehendale Festschrift)*. Ahnedabad: S. C. Research Centre, pp. 127-38.

______. Forthcoming. "*Dāsadāsī*." *JAOS*.

______. With Rosane Rocher, forthcoming. " Ownership by Birth: The *Mitākṣarā* Stand." *Journal of Indian Philosophy*.

Rocher, Rosane. 1983–84. "A Ghost-Author on Dharma: Sūta." *JOIB* 33: 245–46.

Roy, Rammohun. 1830. *Essay on the Rights of Hindoos over Ancestral Property, According to the Law of Bengal*. Baptist Mission Press. 2d ed. *With an Appendix, Containing Letters on the Hindoo Law of Inheritance*. London: Smith, Elder, 1832.

Saindon, Marcelle. 1998. *Le* Pitrikalpa *du* Harivamsha. *Traduction, analyse, interprétation*. Saint-Nicolas (Québec): Les Presses de l'Université Laval.

Sankararama Sastri, C. 1926. *Fictions in the Development of the Hindu Law Texts*. Adyar: Vasanta Press.

Śaṅkha-Likhita (*Śaṅkha-Likhita-smṛti*). Ed. (reconstr.) P. V. Kane. *ABORI* 7, 1926–27, 101–28; 8, 1927–28, 93–132.

Sanyal, Dinabandhu. 1883. *Life of the Honb'le Justice Dwarkanath Mitter: One of the Judges of Her Majesty's High Court of Calcutta*. Calcutta: Author.

Sarasvatīvilāsa, by Pratāparudradeva. Ed. (*Vyavahārakāṇḍa*) R. Shama Sastry. *BS* 71. 1927. Tr. (+ text) (section on inheritance) Thomas Foulkes. London: Trübner, 1881. In Setlur 1911, 1:119–211.

Sarkar, Golap Chandra. 1879. Repr. 1986. See *Vyavahāraprakāśa*.

______. 1897. *Hindu Law with an Appendix of Mahomedan Law on Inheritance* Calcutta: B. Banerjee. 4th ed. *Treatise on Hindu Law*. Calcutta: B. Banerjee, 1910. 6th ed. by Rishindra Nath Sarkar. Calcutta: Eastern Law House, 1927.

______. 1899. See *Vivādaratnākara*.

______. 1904. See *Dāyatattva*.

Sarkar, Kisori Lal. 1909. *The Mimamsa Rules of Interpretation as Applied to Hindu Law*. *TLL* 1905. Calcutta: Thacker, Spink.

Sarkar, S.C. (Shyámácharan; also S. C. Sircar). 1883. *Vyavasthá Darpana. A Digest of the Hindu Law as Current in Bengal*. 3d. ed. Calcutta: Stanhope.

Sarvadhikari, Rajkumar. 1882. *The Principles of the Hindu Law of Inheritance*. *TLL* 1880. Calcutta: Thacker, Spink. 2d ed. by Jyoti Prasad Sarvadhikari. Madras: The Law Book Depot, 1922.

Śatapatha-brāhmaṇa. Ed. Albrecht Weber. Berlin: Dümmler; London: Williams and Norgate, 1855. Repr. Leipzig: Harrassowitz, 1924. Tr. Julius Eggeling. *SBE* 12, 26, 41, 43. 44. 1882–1900. Repr. Delhi: Motilal Banarsidass, 1963.

Scharfe, Hartmut. 1993. *Investigations in Kauṭalya's Manual of Political Science*. Wiesbaden: Harrassowitz.

Schrader, Otto. 1909. "Aryan Religion." *ERE* 2: 11-57.

Sen, Priyanath. 1918. *The General Principles of Hindu Jurisprudence*. *TLL* 1909. Calcutta: University. Vol. 1 ed. annot. Heramba Chatterji. Calcutta: Saraswat Library, 1980.

Setlur, S. Śrīnivāsa. 1907. "Bengal School of Hindu Law." *LQR* 23: 202–19. [A response to S. C. Mitra 1905–1906.]

______. 1911. *A Complete Collection of Hindu Law Books on Inheritance*. Madras: V. Kalyanaram Iyer.

Sharma, Brij Kishore. 1959. "Sapindaship and Religious Efficacy." 61 Bom., Journal 177–83.

Shastri, Dakshina Ranjan. 1963. *Origin and Development of the Rituals of Ancestor Worship in India*. Calcutta: Bookland.

Siddhāntakaumudī, by Bhaṭṭojī Dīkṣita. Ed. tr. Srisa Chandra Vasu. 5 vols., 1904–7. Repr. 2 vols. Delhi: Motilal Banarsidass, 1962.

Smṛticandrikā, by Devaṇṇa Bhaṭṭa. Ed. L. Srinivasacharya. *Vyavahārakāṇḍa*. 2 vols. *BS* 45, 48. 1914, 1916. Tr. (section on inheritance) T. Kristnasawmy Iyer. Madras: Gantz, 1867. In Setlur 1911, 1:212–316.

Smṛtitattva, by Raghunandana Bhaṭṭācārya. Ed. Jīvānanda Vidyāsāgara. 2 vols. Calcutta: Siddheśvara Press, 1895.

Sontheimer, Günther-Dietz. 1977. *The Joint Hindu Family. Its Evolution as a Legal Institution*. Delhi: Munshiram Manoharlal.

Śrāddhakāṇḍa, by Lakṣmīdhara. See *Kṛtyakalpataru*.

Śrāddhakriyākaumudī, by Govindānanda Kavikaṅkanācārya. Ed. Kamalakṛṣṇa Smṛtibhūṣaṇa. *BI* 157. 1904.

Śrāddhasāgara, by Kullūkabhaṭṭa. Ed. S. G. Moghe. New Delhi: Printworld, 1994.

Sternbach, Ludwik. 1973. *Bibliography on* Dharma *and* Artha *in Ancient and Mediaeval India*. Wiesbaden: Harrassowitz.

Strange, Thomas Andrew Lumisden. 1825. *Elements of Hindu Law; Referable to British Judicature*. 2 vols. London: Payne and Foss.

Subodhinī, by Viśveśvara Bhaṭṭa, comm. on the *Mitākṣarā*. Ed. S. S. Setlur. Madras: Brahmavadin Press, 1912. Tr. (section on inheritance) J. R. Gharpure. *The Collection of Hindu Law Texts* 4. Bombay: Office of The Collection of Hindu Law Texts, 1930.

Sutherland, James Charles Colebrooke. See *Dattakamīmāṃsā*.

Tagore, Prosonno Coomar. 1880. *Table of Succession According to the Hindu Law as Prevalent in Bengal*. 2d ed. Calcutta: Sarodainee Press.

Taittirīya-saṃhitā. Ed. Albrecht Weber. Leipzig: Brockhaus. 2 vols 1871, 1872. Tr. A. Berriedale Keith. *HOS* 18,19. 1914.

Tope, Trimbak Krishna and H. S. Ursekar. 1950. *Why Hindu Code? A Historical, Analytical and Critical Exposition of the Hindu Code Bill.* Lonavla: Dharma Nirnaya Mandal.

Vasiṣṭha (*Vāsiṣṭha-dharmaśāstra).* Ed. Alois Anton Führer. *BSS* 23. 3d ed. 1930. Tr. G. Bühler. *SBE* 14. 1882; see Olivelle 1999, 2000.

Verpoorten, Jean-Marie. 1987. *Mīmāṃsā Literature.* A History of Indian Literature, ed. J. Gonda. Part of vol. 4. Wiesbaden: Harrassowitz.

Viṣṇu (*Viṣṇu-smṛti*). Ed. J. Jolly. *BI* 91. 1881. Repr. *ChSS* 95. 1962. Tr. J. Jolly. *SBE* 7. 1880.

Viśvarūpa. See *Bālakrīḍā.*

Vivādacintāmaṇi, by Vācaspatimiśra. Ed. Lakshmīkānta Jhā. Patna: United Press, 1937. Tr. Ganganatha Jha. *GOS* 99. 1942.

Vivādaratnākara, by Caṇḍeśvara. Ed. Kamalakṛṣṇa Smṛtitīrtha. *BI* 103. 1931. Tr. (+ text) (section on inheritance) Golápchandra Sarkár and Digamvar Chattopádhyáya. Calcutta: Bose Brothers, 1899. Repr. Delhi: Gian Publishing House, 1986. In Setlur 1911, 2:159–242.

Vivādārṇavasetu. Ed. Bombay: Veṅkaṭeśvara Press, 1888.

Vivādatāṇḍava, by Kamalākara Bhaṭṭa. Ed. tr (Gujarati) Maṇilāla Nabhubhāī Dvivedī. Baroda: Lakṣmīvilāsa Press, 1901. Ed. Heramba Chatterjee. *OH* 7.2, 1959, 1–23; 8.2, 1960, 25–37; 11.1, 1963, 39–50; 13.1, 1965, 51–58.

Vṛddha-Manu (+ Bṛhan-manu). Ed. tr. (reconstr.) G. Herberich. Würzburg: Universitätsdruckerei, 1893.

Vyāsa (*Vyāsa-smṛti*). Ed. (reconstr.) B. K. Ghosh: "Vyāsa's Verses on Vyavahāra." *Indian Culture* 9, 1942, 65–98.

Vyavahāramātṛkā, by Jīmūtavāhana. Ed. Asutosh Mookerjee. Memoirs of the Asiatic Society of Bengal 3.5, 1912, 277–353.

Vyavahāramayūkha, by Nīlakaṇṭha Bhaṭṭa. 2 vols. Bombay: Education Society's Press, 1880. Ed. P. V. Kane. *BSS* 80. Poona: Bhandarkar Oriental Research Institute, 1926.

Vyavahāraprakāśa, by Mitramiśra. Ed. Viṣṇuprasāda Bhaṇḍārī. *ChSS* 30.7. 1932. Tr. (+ text) G. C. Sarkar: *The Law of Inheritance as in the Viramitrodaya of Mitra Misra.* Calcutta: Thacker, Spink, 1879. Repr. Delhi: Gian Publishing House, 1986. In Setlur 1911, 2:275-468.

Whitney, William Dwight. 1889. *Sanskrit Grammar.* 2d ed. Cambridge: Harvard University Press.

Wilson, Horace Hayman. 1825. Rev. of Macnaghten 1824. *Quarterly Oriental Magazine* 3: 171–240. Repr. *Works*, ed. Reinhold Ross. London: Trübner, 1865. Vol. 5, pp. 1–98.

______. 1855. *A Glossary of Judicial and Revenue Terms.* London: Allen. Repr. Delhi: Munshiram Manoharlal, 1968.

Winternitz, Moriz. 1890. "Notes on Śrāddhas and Ancestral Worship among the Indo-European Nations." *WZKM* 4: 199–212.

Yājñavalkya (*Yājñavalkya-smṛti*). Ed. tr. Adolf F. Stenzler. Berlin: Dümmler, 1849. See also Aparārka, *Bālakrīḍā*, *Dīpakalikā*, and *Mitākṣarā.*

QUOTATIONS FROM ANCIENT TEXTS

INDEX